Arbitration

Arbitration
Law, Policy, and Practice

Maureen A. Weston
PROFESSOR OF LAW
PEPPERDINE UNIVERSITY SCHOOL OF LAW

Kristen M. Blankley
ASSOCIATE PROFESSOR OF LAW
UNIVERSITY OF NEBRASKA

Jill I. Gross
PROFESSOR OF LAW
ELISABETH HAUB SCHOOL OF LAW
PACE UNIVERSITY

Stephen Huber
EMERITUS PROFESSOR OF LAW
UNIVERSITY OF HOUSTON LAW CENTER

CAROLINA ACADEMIC PRESS
Durham, North Carolina

ISBN 978-1-5310-0888-8
eISBN 978-1-53100-889-5
LCCN 2018933302

Carolina Academic Press, LLC
700 Kent Street
Durham, North Carolina 27701
Telephone (919) 489-7486
Fax (919) 493-5668
www.cap-press.com

Printed in the United States of America

For Francine, Kathy, Christine, Joe, Cindy, and Cedric — M.A.W.

For Mike, James, Billie, Corrinne, and Camden — K.M.B.

For Robert and Bonny Israeloff — J.I.G.

Contents

Table of Principal Cases

Preface

Arbitration has become a standard method of private dispute resolution designated in commercial contracts in the United States. Almost every American business and individual with the legal capacity to contract has entered into an agreement that specifies arbitration as the forum for resolving most or all disputes that might arise between the parties. The importance of arbitration as the preferred mode of dispute resolution has grown dramatically during the last twenty-five years, and this trend has not yet run its course. Since 1983, the U.S. Supreme Court has been the leader in promoting the enforcement of arbitration terms. This favorable legal environment has prompted business organizations to dramatically expand the use of arbitration provisions in their contracts with both individuals and other firms.

A few examples of contexts in which arbitration is commonly used should suffice to prove its importance in the domestic economy. Arbitration has long been the norm for multinational transactions because businesses do not relish the prospect of litigation in the courts of another country. At the most sophisticated end of the business spectrum, reinsurance contracts between insurance companies mandate arbitration, as do maritime bills of lading. Numerous trade associations have long mandated arbitration of all disputes among members. Collective bargaining agreements have called for arbitration of grievances at least since World War II and now many contracts with individual employees do so as well. Franchise agreements call for arbitration, at least where favorable to the franchisor. Sellers of computers and many other consumer products require arbitration. Virtually all contracts between securities brokers and their customers mandate arbitration. Most contracts used by banks, providers of medical services, and online retailers specify arbitration for the resolution of disputes.

Another reflection of the importance of arbitration is the vast amount of litigation it has generated, a rather ironic standard because a central purpose of arbitration is to avoid the courts. Hotly litigated issues relate to whether to enforce a written arbitration term in an apparently binding arbitration agreement. The court's (and arbitrator's) answer is generally yes.

That there has been more litigation about arbitration in recent years is not an understatement. At both the state and federal levels, courts issued hundreds of arbitration decisions per year. Since 1983, the U.S. Supreme Court has decided more than fifty arbitration cases, including twenty-five since the turn of the century. During the 2002–2003 Term alone, the Supreme Court handed down four arbitration decisions. From 2006 to 2010, the Court issued eight decisions, and another ten between 2011 and 2017. The U.S. Supreme Court under Justice Roberts has evidenced a continued pro-arbitration stance. These caseload numbers bespeak considerable disputation about arbitration, as well as the central importance of arbitration as an ever more important form of binding dispute resolution. Congress and state legislatures, as well as federal and state courts, the business community, and consumer rights groups, undoubtedly continue to be concerned with arbitration law issues.

Throughout *Arbitration: Law, Policy, and Practice,* we focus on many of the recent cases decided by the United States Supreme Court, the federal courts, and state supreme courts. Although the courts, led by the United States Supreme Court, are leaders in promoting the growing use and finality of arbitration, the explosive growth in the use of arbitration is not regarded as entirely beneficial by all commentators. Critiques of the important recent developments are found throughout these materials. Chapter 1(B) provides an historical perspective on arbitration in America, but our focus is on the many recent developments in arbitration law and practice.

These materials have two central objectives: to provide an introduction to the law of arbitration, and to show how arbitration works in a variety of contexts. The chapters are structured to take the reader chronologically through the primary issues that may arise in an arbitration setting. The introductory chapter provides an overview on the nature and scope of arbitration, while Chapter 2 presents the legal framework governing arbitration, principally examining the federal and state arbitration law, including how these laws interact and issues of preemption. Chapters 3 and 4 address "gateway" issues of arbitrability and defenses to arbitration. Chapters 5 through 8 focus on the arbitration process itself, including arbitrator selection and ethical standards, an arbitrator's vast remedial powers, and issues relating to judicial review of arbitration awards. Chapters 10 and 11 examine arbitration in the context of multiple forums, including arbitral class actions. The final chapter considers international arbitration. The Appendices contain the text of the Federal Arbitration Act, the Uniform Arbitration Act (1955), and the [Revised] Uniform Arbitration Act (2000), as well as an Arbitration Case File, and a chronology of U.S. Supreme Court arbitration decisions.

Most footnotes from articles and cases, and citations within the text of cases, are omitted without specific notation. Some of the retained footnote or endnote materials have been incorporated into the texts. Where notes are reproduced, the original numbering is retained. Omissions from text are indicated by ellipses.

The authors gratefully acknowledge and thank Elisabeth R. Ebben and Susan Trimble at Carolina Academic Press. We are also grateful to those of you who have chosen to use our book. We welcome any and all comments on these materials.

> Maureen A. Weston
> Malibu, CA
>
> Kristen M. Blankley
> Lincoln, NE
>
> Jill I. Gross
> White Plains, NY
>
> Stephen K. Huber
> Houston, TX

Arbitration

Chapter 1

The Nature and Scope of Arbitration

A. Introduction and Overview

Arbitration is a private, quasi-judicial system of adjudication for resolving disputes. Arbitration is a form of Alternative Dispute Resolution (ADR) in which legal disputes are resolved outside the court system. Arbitration is also a consensual process in that the parties have agreed to have their existing or future disputes heard before, and decided by, an arbitrator or arbitral tribunal (as private judges) to render a final and legally binding decision (the "award"). Arbitration affords parties the opportunity to select their own decision-makers, as well as the ability to control the procedural rules governing the process. Depending upon your perspective, benefits of arbitration also include limited discovery, procedural flexibility, privacy, and a final and binding decision that the law respects and enforces. Depending upon your perspective, these attributes might also be drawbacks of the process.

The foundation for arbitration is contract. By agreeing to arbitration, parties relinquish the right to their "day in court" through the public judicial system. Although arbitration is typically a private process, federal, state, and even international legislation provide the regulatory framework in which arbitration operates. Enacted in 1925, the Federal Arbitration Act (FAA), 9 U.S.C. §§ 1 *et seq.*, is the primary law governing commercial arbitration in the United States and will be a central focus of our study of arbitration law, policy, and practice. As an example of how the public law supports private arbitration, consider that the FAA calls for courts to enforce written agreements to resolve disputes by arbitration, to compel arbitration and stay litigation pending arbitration, and to appoint arbitrators when needed, as well as to confirm, modify, and, under certain conditions, vacate (overturn) arbitration awards. Chapters Two and Three of the FAA codify the commitment of courts in the United States to enforce eligible international arbitration awards. Overall, the process of arbitration is accorded considerable deference. According to the U.S. Supreme Court, the FAA evinces a "national policy favoring arbitration." *Southland Corp. v. Keating*, 465 U.S. 1, 10 (1984); *see also Rent-A-Ctr., W., Inc. v. Jackson*, 561 U.S. 63 (2010).

1. Arbitration in the U.S. and Global Economy

Arbitration has a long history of use in specialized business, commercial, and labor-management industries. Arbitration has been the preferred method of dispute resolution where parties have a continuing relationship, relatively equal bargaining power, and consider that their business relationships, and other interests, are best served by agreeing to a binding dispute resolution process that can be (but is not always) faster and less expensive than litigation. Franchise agreements commonly call for arbitration of most disputes. *See, e.g., Southland; Doctor's Assocs. v. Casarotto*, 517 U.S. 681 (1996). At the most sophisticated end of the business spectrum, arbitration terms are standard features of reinsurance contracts (i.e., sharing of risk agreements between insurance companies), as well as in maritime bills of lading (shipping contracts). Arbitration also is the leading method for resolution of international and cross-border commercial disputes. Businesses want to avoid the prospect of litigation in the courts of another country, with concerns about dealing with unfamiliar legal systems, potential bias in the courts of the opponent's country, language barriers, and even cultural differences. Arbitration provides parties operating in the global commercial context the autonomy and certainty to designate how and where their disputes will be heard, under the protection of international arbitration laws.

While arbitration has been used for centuries in industries involving merchants and businesses, over the past few decades, arbitration has increasingly become the norm for adjudicating disputes arising from consumer transactions and employment agreements. In fact, you are most likely a party to an arbitration contract. How? Identify the scenarios in which you are a party to an arbitration agreement. Did you "choose" arbitration? How would you proceed in a dispute with the other party?

Arbitration has become a central feature for the binding resolution of disputes in the modern U.S. and global economy. Today, arbitration provisions are a standard feature in contracts that touch the daily lives of everyone. Virtually every business or individual with the legal capacity to contract (and some who lack such capacity) has entered into multiple agreements that specify arbitration as the forum for resolving most or all disputes that might arise between the parties. Credit/debit card issuers and banking organizations commonly require arbitration in their customer agreements. Virtually everyone with a trading account with a broker-dealer has agreed to arbitrate any and all disputes arising out of or related to that relationship. *See* Jill I. Gross, *The End of Mandatory Securities Arbitration?*, 30 PACE L. REV. 1174, 1179 (2010). Consumer purchase contracts regularly require arbitration, so consider that your cell phone, Internet, and "online" shopping and activities (including Snapchat, AirBnb, and Uber) are likely subject to arbitration. *See e.g.,* Thomas H. Koenig & Michael L. Rustad, *Fundamentally Unfair: An Empirical Analysis of Social Media Arbitration Clauses,* 65 WESTERN L. REV. 341 (2014) (finding that more than 42 percent of social media contracts in the United States require arbitration). Agreements related to medical services, which include paying the employers and insurers as well as the actual providers, commonly require arbitration. Contracts for car rentals, apartment leases, and nursing home placement may designate arbitration. Even entering a Whataburger restaurant in Liberty, Texas, or a contest sponsored by McDonald's might call for arbitration of all disputes. *See, e.g., James v. McDonald's Corp.*, 417 F.3d 672 (7th Cir. 2005). None of these consumer transactions was subject to arbitration prior to the U.S. Supreme Court's 1985 decision in *Southland. See* **Chapter 2.**

Arbitration also has become a common feature of employment contacts since the Supreme Court in *Gilmer v. Interstate/Johnson Lane Corp.*, 500 U.S. 20 (1991), ruled that employers may require individual employees to arbitrate statutory rights claims. This outcome was reinforced after *Circuit City Stores, Inc. v. Adams*, 532 U.S. 105 (2001), which held that the exception in § 1 of the FAA, exempting "contracts of employment of seamen, railroad employees or any other class of workers engaged in foreign or interstate commerce" from the FAA's application, applied only to transportation workers and not to employment contracts generally. Thus, employees may be required to arbitrate all employment disputes as a condition of employment. Mandatory arbitration clauses are not limited to contracts with rank-and-file employees, but also are included in many executive and professional employment contracts.

The importance of arbitration as the preferred mode of binding dispute resolution has grown dramatically during the last several decades, and this trend has yet to run its course. Federal legislation, specifically the FAA, is cited as the legal basis for supporting the judicial enforcement of arbitration contracts and awards. Although initially reluctant to interpret the FAA expansively, the U.S. Supreme Court now regularly relies on the statute as the basis to preempt conflicting state laws regulating arbitration and to uphold the enforcement of arbitration contracts in a variety of contexts, including resolution of statutory and common law claims in employment and consumer transactions. This favorable legal environment has, in turn, prompted business organizations to dramatically expand the use of arbitration provisions in their contracts with both individuals and other businesses. Thus, arbitration continues to be a growth industry.

2. Policy and Fairness Considerations

Arbitration law and practice continues to develop, and ironically, to be the subject of substantial litigation and legislative discussion at both the state and federal levels. The Supreme Court has decided more than 50 commercial arbitration cases since expressing an initial "judicial hostility" to arbitration in *Wilko v. Swan*, 346 U.S. (1953). *See* **Appendix III.** Many of these cases involve constitutional questions examining the interaction between state and federal law; in particular, the FAA's preemptive effect on state laws that seek to ensure judicial or administrative access in certain situations.

The expanded use of arbitration, particularly pre-dispute arbitration contracts in the consumer and employment settings, has also generated considerable litigation and scholarly, legislative, and public criticism. In arbitration, the arbitrators are generally directly paid by the parties. Some have argued that this creates monetary incentives for arbitrators to favor "repeat players," usually corporations, who more frequently use arbitration. *See* Carrie Menkel-Meadow, *Do the Haves Come Out Ahead in Alternative Judicial Systems? Repeat Players in ADR*, 15 Ohio St. L. J. on Disp. Res. 16 (1999); Maureen A. Weston, *Reexamining Arbitral Immunity in an Age of Mandatory and Professional Arbitration*, 88 Minn. L. Rev. 449 (2004). In 2016, the New York Times published a multipart series entitled *"Beware the Fine Print," "Privatized Justice System,"* and *"In Religious Arbitration Scripture is the Rule of Law,"* reporting on actual and potential abuses of arbitration when that process is "mandatory" or "forced," private, and in some cases, expensive.

These concerns have prompted numerous calls for congressional and executive branch action and exemptions from the FAA for certain industries or types of cases. Congress has enacted bans on pre-dispute arbitration contracts in certain situations, such as in government contracts with employers regarding employee civil rights and sexual assault claims; in motor vehicle manufacturer franchise agreements; and in consumer credit disputes involving military personnel. The Dodd-Frank Wall Street Reform and Consumer Protection Act of 2010, 12 U.S.C. § 5301, directed the Consumer Financial Protection Bureau (CFPB) to investigate uses of arbitration resulting from consumer financial contracts. In its *Arbitration Study: Report to Congress 2015*, the CFPB reported that "[t]ens of millions" of consumers are covered by arbitration (most of which prohibit class actions) and that consumers generally do not know they are subject to an arbitration clause. In 2017, the CFPB promulgated a rule prohibiting class action waivers in pre-dispute arbitration provisions in certain consumer financial agreements. The rule was to be effective September 2017 but was challenged by the business community as unconstitutional and arbitrary and struck down in a 51–50 Senate vote (Vice President Pence broke the tie) in October 2017. Is the CFPB rule viable or necessary? This proposal is discussed in more detail in **Chapter 10**.

Keep in mind that Congress *could* amend the FAA to address the fairness concerns leveled against mandatory arbitration of consumer and employment disputes. Such changes are sought in the proposed Arbitration Fairness Act, *infra* **Chapter 1.C.1.c**. The future of arbitration law, policy, and practice also depends on you, as a future advocate, scholar, neutral, judge, or party. As you embark upon your study of arbitration, consider how you can impact arbitration.

3. Overview of the Course and This Book

Given the prevalence of arbitration, a study of the law, the policy, and the practice of arbitration is increasingly vital to a lawyer's practice. This casebook provides an examination of the legal framework for arbitration, the evolving policy relating to the legitimacy and uses of arbitration, and the practical aspects of how the arbitration process works.

These teaching materials focus predominantly on binding commercial arbitration, based on an agreement by the parties to arbitrate the dispute. For these purposes, "commercial" includes the study of arbitration between two or more business entities, businesses and their customers, and employers and non-unionized employees, whose arbitrations are generally governed by the FAA and related state arbitration laws. The growing importance of international commercial arbitration is treated in **Chapter 12**.

Labor arbitration—grievance arbitration pursuant to a collective bargaining agreement (CBA)—is given only limited attention. In the labor context, the contracting parties are a company and a labor union—not the employees that the union represents. Labor and commercial arbitration have different histories, traditions, and governing statutes.

The basis for arbitration is contract—an agreement that the law will enforce. The general plan of the book is to follow arbitration from contract drafting through final judicial review and then to cover several additional arbitration topics. The structure of the course is laid out in the table of contents, which you should promptly read from beginning to end. (We recommend that you do so again before the final examination to remind you of the major topics covered in the course.)

4. Subject Matter of This Chapter

This chapter provides a historical overview of arbitration in America (and its English antecedents), introduces the statutes (both federal and state) that govern arbitration, and examines the outer limits of what constitutes arbitration (and what turns on the answer to that inquiry).

Section B provides a historical overview of arbitration law and practice in earlier America (and England). Arbitration law is statutory law, and section C introduces that legislation: the Federal Arbitration Act (FAA), the model acts for state arbitration law, the Uniform Arbitration Acts (UAA) and (RUAA), adopted in nearly all the states. Section D seeks to define and to map the outer limits of arbitration by considering what is, and *is not*, arbitration, comparing other types of processes, such as nonbinding "arbitration," expert determination, valuation, and appraisal. Section E illustrates the use of arbitration in specialized industries. As you read this chapter, consider whether the process designated for resolving disputes is "arbitration." What are the essential features of an arbitration? Why might that matter?

B. Historical Background of Commercial Arbitration

Disputes inevitably arise in a society in which people live and engage in trade and commerce. Court systems are not always accessible, desired, or necessary to resolve such disputes. The submission of disputes to an independent third party has been a form of ordering society throughout history. Arbitration has deep historical roots as a method for settling disputes. Historical accounts of arbitration use date back to ancient Greece, Icelandic, Roman, and medieval times. Since at least the thirteenth century, mercantile and trade industry disputes have been decided by arbitration, with volunteer merchants serving as arbitrators. *See* Peter Sayre, *Development of Commercial Arbitration Law*, 34 YALE L. J. 595 (1928).

The history of arbitration in the United States' economy can be traced to use among merchants, medieval guilds, and maritime practitioners in England and to English arbitration law. The securities industry has used arbitration to resolve intra-industry disputes since the formation of the earliest stock exchanges in the late 1700s. In the nineteenth and early twentieth centuries, contracts used by merchants and commercial trade associations often provided for arbitration to resolve potential disputes.

Early American law was hostile toward arbitration, treating it as a creature outside the law. Prior to 1920, for example, courts were reluctant to enforce executory arbitration agreements. Executory (pre-dispute) arbitration agreements are those in which the parties agree to arbitrate a future dispute. If one party to an arbitration agreement asked for specific performance of the arbitration agreement (i.e., to order the parties to arbitrate), the court would reject that request on the basis that the parties were attempting to "oust" the courts of supervision or jurisdiction over legal disputes. When a dispute arose, if a party to an arbitration contract refused to arbitrate, the other party was powerless to compel arbitration or stay litigation. Courts would refuse to enforce arbitration agreements?even if the arbitration had already begun. Courts, however, could enforce an actual arbitration award for an arbitration that was completed, but local practice varied widely from state to state. *See* Soia Mentschikoff, *Commercial Arbitration*, 61 COLUM. L. REV. 846 (1961).

At that time, merchants could not predictably rely on arbitration, because it required post-dispute consent by both parties. In the 1920s, the state of New York enacted a statute to require courts to enforce agreements to arbitrate, irrespective of whether the dispute was existing or prospective. In 1925, the U.S. Congress passed the United States Arbitration Act, which was modeled largely on the New York law. Codified at 9 U.S.C. §§ 1–16 and more commonly known as the Federal Arbitration Act (FAA), the Act's purpose was to reverse the common law hostility toward arbitration and direct courts to enforce agreements to arbitrate, whether entered into pre- or post-dispute.

The following two cases provide a brief introduction to arbitration in earlier America, and to its English arbitration law antecedents. As you read *Tobey v. Bristol*, consider the rationale for the anti-arbitration animus that prevailed in America before the FAA's enactment in 1925. Compare the judicial interpretation of arbitration after the FAA's enactment in *Kulukundis Shipping*, which also provides a historical account of arbitration in America often cited in judicial opinions, including at least three times by the Supreme Court. *See Southland Corp. v. Keating*, 465 U.S. 1 (1984); *Mitsubishi Motors Corp. v. Soler Chrysler-Plymouth, Inc.*, 473 U.S. 614 (1984); *Rodriguez de Quijas v. Shearson/American Express, Inc.*, 490 U.S. 477 (1989).

Tobey v. County of Bristol

23 Fed. Cas. 1313 (D. Mass. 1845)

STORY, CIRCUIT JUSTICE.

[C]ourts of equity do not refuse to interfere to compel a party specifically to perform an agreement to refer to arbitration, because they wish to discourage arbitrations, as against public policy. On the contrary, they have and can have no just objection to these domestic forums, and will enforce, and promptly interfere to enforce their awards when fairly and lawfully made, without hesitation or question. But when they are asked to proceed farther and to compel the parties to appoint arbitrators whose award shall be final, they necessarily pause to consider, whether such tribunals possess adequate means of giving redress, and whether they have a right to compel a reluctant party to submit to such a tribunal, and to close against him the doors of the common courts of justice, provided by the government to protect rights and to redress wrongs. One of the established principles of courts of equity is, not to entertain a bill for the specific performance of any agreement, where it is doubtful whether it may not thereby become the instrument of injustice, or to deprive parties of rights which they are otherwise fairly entitled to have protected....

It is certainly the policy of the common law not to compel men to submit their rights and interests to arbitration, or to enforce agreements for such a purpose. Nay, the common law goes much farther, and even if a submission has been made to arbitrators ... with an express stipulation that the submission shall be irrevocable, it still is revocable and countermandable by either party before the award is actually made, although not afterwards.

Kulukundis Shipping Co., S/A v. Amtorg Trading Corp.

126 F.2d 978 (2d Cir. 1942)

[*Ed*: Kulunkundis Shipping Company sued Armtorg Trading Corporation for its alleged breach of contract to charter a ship with Kulukundis Shipping. Armtorg's answer denied that anyone authorized to act on its behalf had so agreed and thus pled that no contract had been made. Two months before trial, Armtorg sought to amend its answer to include as a separate defense that the alleged charter contract contained an arbitration clause, no arbitration demand was made, and thus the suit was prematurely brought. The district court denied the motion to amend and, after a trial finding Armtorg liable for breach of contract, Armtorg appealed.]

FRANK, CIRCUIT JUDGE.

The arbitration clause reads as follows: '24. [O]wners and Charterers agree, in case of any dispute or claim, to settle same by arbitration in New York. Also, in case of a dispute of any nature whatsoever, same is to be settled by arbitration in New York. In both cases arbitrators are to be commercial men.'

In 1925 Congress enacted the Arbitration Act, U.S.C.A., Title 9. [Quoting sections 2, 3, and 4 of the FAA, which provide for judicial enforcement of written agreements to arbitrate, a judicial stay of litigation, and power for a federal court to compel contracting parties to arbitrate]....

Appellant admits, as it must, that the district court had jurisdiction to determine whether the parties had made an agreement to arbitrate. Appellant contends, however, that, once the court determined in this suit that there was such an arbitration agreement, the court lost all power over the suit beyond that of staying further proceedings until there had been an arbitration as agreed to; in that arbitration, argues appellant, the arbitrators will have jurisdiction to determine all issues except the existence of the arbitration clause. This jurisdiction, it is urged, is broad enough to permit an independent determination, by the arbitrator, that the contract itself is not valid or binding. Appellee asserts that the defendant had repudiated the charter-party, and that, therefore, the arbitration clause must be wholly disregarded.

In considering these contentions in the light of the precedents, it is necessary to take into account the history of the judicial attitude towards arbitration: The English courts, while giving full effect to agreements to submit controversies to arbitration after they had ripened into arbitrators' awards, would — over a long period beginning at the end of the 17th century — do little or nothing to prevent or make irksome the breach of such agreements when they were still executory.... The ordinary executory arbitration agreement thus lost all real efficacy since it was not specifically enforceable in equity, and was held not to constitute the basis of a plea in bar in, or a stay of, a suit on the original cause of action. In admiralty, the rulings were much the same....

It has been well said that the legal mind must assign some reason in order to decide anything with spiritual quiet. And so, by way of rationalization, it became fashionable in the middle of the 18th century to say that such agreements were against public policy because they "oust the jurisdiction" of the courts. But that was a quaint explanation, inasmuch as an award, under an arbitration agreement, enforced both at law and in equity, was no less an ouster; and the same was true of releases and covenants not to sue, which were given full effect. Moreover, the agreement to arbitrate was not illegal, since suit could be maintained for its breach. Here was a clear instance of what Holmes called a "right" to break a contract and to substitute payment of damages for non-performance; as, in this type of case, the damages were only nominal, that "right" was indeed meaningful. Holmes, *The Path of The Law*, 10 Harv. L. Rev. 457 (1897).

An effort has been made to justify this judicial hostility to the executory arbitration agreement on the ground that arbitrations, if unsupervised by the courts, are undesirable, and that legislation was needed to make possible such supervision. But if that was the reason for unfriendliness to such executory agreements, then the courts should also have refused to aid arbitrations when they ripened into awards. And what the English courts, especially the equity courts, did in other contexts, shows that, if they had had the will, they could have devised means of protecting parties to arbitrations. Instead, they restrictively interpreted successive statutes intended to give effect to executory arbitrations.

Lord Campbell explained the English attitude as due to the desire of the judges, at a time when their salaries came largely from fees, to avoid loss of income. There was no disguising the fact that, as formerly, the emoluments of the Judges depended mainly, or almost entirely, upon fees, and as they had no fixed salaries, there was great competition to get as much as possible of litigation into Westminster Hall for the division of the spoil. And they had great jealousy of arbitrations whereby Westminster Hall was robbed of those cases.... Therefore they said that the courts ought not to be ousted of their jurisdiction, and that it was contrary to the policy of the law to do so. Indignation has been voiced at this suggestion; perhaps it is unjustified. Perhaps the true explanation is the hypnotic power of the phrase, "oust the jurisdiction." Give a bad dogma a good name and its bite may become as bad as its bark....

[T]he hostility of the English courts to executory arbitrations ... was largely taken over in the 19th century by most courts in this country ... and continued to use the "ouster of jurisdiction" concept: An executory agreement to arbitrate would not be given specific performance or furnish the basis of a stay of proceedings on the original cause of action.... In the case of broader executory agreements, no more than nominal damages would be given for a breach.

Generally speaking, then, the courts of this country were unfriendly to executory arbitration agreements. The lower federal courts, feeling bound to comply with the precedents, nevertheless became critical of this judicial hostility. There were intimations in the Supreme Court that perhaps the old view might be abandoned, but in the cases hinting at that newer attitude the issue was not raised.

Effective state arbitration statutes were enacted beginning with the New York Statute of 1920. The United States [Federal] Arbitration Act of 1925 was sustained as constitutional, in its application to cases arising in admiralty. The purpose of the Act ... was deliberately to alter the judicial atmosphere previously existing. The report of the House Committee stated, in part,

> Arbitration agreements are purely matters of contract, and the effect of the bill is simply to make the contracting party live up to his agreement. He can no longer refuse to perform his contract when it becomes disadvantageous to him. An arbitration agreement is placed upon the same footing as other contracts, where it belongs. The need for the law arises from an anachronism of our American law. Some centuries ago, because of the jealousy of the English courts for their own jurisdiction, they refused to enforce specific agreements to arbitrate upon the ground that the courts were thereby ousted from their jurisdiction. This jealousy survived for so long a period that the principle became firmly embedded in the English common law and was adopted with it by the American courts. The courts have felt that the precedent was too strongly fixed to be overturned without legislative enactment, although they have frequently criticized the rule and recognized its illogical nature and the injustice which results from it.... [S]uch agreements for arbitration shall be enforced, and provides a procedure in the Federal courts for their enforcement. It is particularly appropriate that the action should be taken at this

> time when there is so much agitation against the costliness and delays of lit-
> igation. These matters can be largely eliminated by agreements for arbitration,
> if arbitration agreements are made valid and enforceable.

In the light of the clear intention of Congress, it is our obligation to shake off the old judicial hostility to arbitration. Accordingly, in a case like this, involving the federal Act, we should not follow English or other decisions which have narrowly construed the terms of arbitration agreements or arbitration statutes. With this new orientation, we approach the problems here presented.

1. Comments and Questions

a. *Early Judicial Hostility to Arbitration.* Judges, as public officials, have a central role in ensuring fairness and due process in the public justice system. What were the justifications for applying the revocability doctrine to arbitration contracts, as expressed in *Tobey*? What policy concerns underlie the "ouster of jurisdiction" rationale? Do these concerns still exist today?

b. *Tobey* referenced a court's need to ensure that arbitration is fair and equitable. Historically, do you think the courts were concerned more about the fairness and equity of the arbitration process or the substance of the award? Does the FAA remedy the concerns expressed by the "ouster" doctrine? How does arbitration affect the ability to establish judicial precedent in the American legal system?

c. *Kulukundis* suggests English judges historically refused to enforce arbitration agreements because they lost fees (and thus income) by sending cases to arbitration. The court announced a reversal of judicial hostility to arbitration. Judges, now salaried, readily enforce such agreements. Although arbitrators historically were volunteers from the industry, many private arbitrators are now full-time, professional neutrals. A number of public judges have opted to leave the bench and embark on a career as a private neutral and to associate with one of the many private dispute resolution provider companies or organizations, notably JAMS or the American Arbitration Association (AAA), or simply to self-administer a case as an arbitrator or neutral. *See* Maureen Weston, *Retired to Greener Pastures: The Public Costs of Private Judging*, in B. Bornstein & R. Wiener (eds.), JUSTICE, CONFLICT AND WELLBEING (Springer 2014). Could the popularity of arbitration affect the impartiality of arbitrators who may depend on large corporations for their work on deciding cases?

d. Blackstone, writing in the eighteenth century, noted the widespread use of arbitration for commercial disputes, praising "the great use of these peaceable and domestic tribunals, especially in settling matters of account and other mercantile transactions, which are difficult and almost impossible to be adjusted on a trial at law." WILLIAM BLACKSTONE, 3 COMMENTARIES 17 (1765). Professor Stipanowich, writing in 2010, asserted that arbitration is increasingly more "judicialized," formal, costly, and subject to extensive discovery and motion practice, as well as hardball advocacy. Thomas Stipanowich, *Arbitration: The New "Litigation,"* 2010 U. ILL. L. REV. 1. What might be the impact of this trend?

e. The law school focus on legal rules can cause us to overlook the significance of common practices that are not sanctioned by the formal legal order. Despite the absence of legislative or judicial backing, arbitration was in common use for many centuries, particularly by merchants and trade associations. Without any court intervention, members followed association rules and complied with arbitration awards because expulsion from the association was a highly effective sanction. *See, e.g.*, Lisa Bernstein, *Opting Out of the Legal System: Extralegal Contractual Relations in the Diamond Industry*, 21 J. LEGAL STUD. 115 (1992).

C. Modern U.S. Commercial Arbitration Law and Practice

The regulatory framework for commercial arbitration is governed by public legislation as well as the parties' private contractual agreements to arbitrate and the designation of arbitration procedural rules. The following describes these components in more detail.

1. Arbitration Legislation

Modern arbitration law in the United States is governed by statutes at the federal, state, and international levels. These laws governing the arbitral process are covered extensively throughout this book. **Chapter 2** specially examines the interaction between federal and state commercial arbitration, as well as select state arbitration statutes. The following, however, provides a brief overview of arbitration legislation.

a. *Federal Arbitration Act.* The Federal Arbitration Act (FAA), codified at 9 U.S.C. §§ 1–16 (2016), remains the primary legislation governing commercial arbitration in the United States. Originally known as the United States Arbitration Act of 1925, the FAA was enacted due to the active leadership and support of commercial interests to ensure enforceability of arbitration agreements. The modern usage of FAA is employed throughout these materials.

The FAA regulates the interface between private arbitration and the courts and is a fairly short, essentially procedural statute comprised of 16 sections. The full text of the FAA is located in **Appendix I.** You will need to read the statute in detail; however, the basic provisions and operation of the FAA are (seemingly) straightforward.

Section 1 of the Act sets out definitions for "maritime transactions," and "commerce," and also lists some exceptions to the Act's coverage. The heart of the statute lies in section 2, which provides for the validity and enforcement of written agreements to arbitrate, "save upon such grounds as exist at law or in equity for the revocation of any contract." Section 3 provides for a stay of any lawsuit brought "in any of the courts of the United States" if any issue in the lawsuit is referable to arbitration. Section 4 permits a party to an arbitration agreement to petition U.S. district courts, otherwise having jurisdiction, to compel arbitration. Section 5 provides for the judicial appointment of an arbitrator or arbitrators where needed. Section 6 provides that applications and motions pertaining to arbitration are heard in the same manner as court motions. Under section 7, arbitrators are granted subpoena powers equivalent to a court of law. Section 8 addresses maritime litigation. Section 9 authorizes a party, within one year of entering the arbitral award, to seek judicial confirmation of the award, upon which a court can enter a judgment. Section 10 specifies grounds upon which a federal court may vacate an arbitral award. Section 11 permits courts to correct or modify awards containing evident formalistic or technical errors. Sections 12 provides for notice of motions to vacate or modify awards. Section 13 sets forth requirements for filing papers with motions seeking relief under the Act. Section 14 clarifies that the Act was not retroactive prior to 1926. Section 15 speaks to the inapplicability of the Act of State doctrine (which generally applies in the transborder context and limits a federal court from reviewing the acts of a sovereign state or nation taken within foreign borders). Finally, section 16 provides for a right of interlocutory appeal that may be taken from orders essentially denying arbitration. *See* Maureen A. Weston, *Preserving the Federal Arbitration Act by Reining in Judicial Expansion and Mandatory Use*, 7 Nev. L.J. 385 (2007).

Although the text of the (domestic) FAA has not changed materially since its inception, the Supreme Court has interpreted it expansively in recent decades, and the scope and significance of arbitration has grown dramatically. In a series of decisions starting with *Prima Paint Corp. v. Flood & Conklin Mfg. Co.*, 388 U.S. 395 (1967), the Supreme Court has expanded the ambit of disputes subject to arbitration by upholding arbitration agreements and subsequent arbitration awards against (almost) all challenges. Since 1983, the Supreme Court has decided an average of more than one arbitration decision per year. These decisions, many of which are reprinted in these materials, form the backbone of current arbitration law. In many of these cases, the Court has read the FAA to largely preempt state law limitations on arbitration. The interaction of federal and state law is examined in Chapter 2.

The response to the expansive judicial reading of the FAA has been just what one would expect: a dramatic rise in the use of arbitration and a concomitant increase in the number of judicial proceedings that raise arbitration issues. During the last two decades, the federal courts of appeals have decided hundreds of arbitration cases per year. This figure is particularly impressive because most cases arising under the FAA are heard by state, rather than federal courts. In "something of an anomaly in the field of federal-court jurisdiction," the FAA created substantive federal law but not an independent basis for federal jurisdiction. *Moses H. Cone Memorial Hosp. v. Mercury Constr. Corp.*, 460 U.S. 1 (1983).

b. *Uniform State Arbitration Acts.* Concerned that the FAA applied only in federal courts, each state adopted legislation to ensure similar enforcement in state courts. In 1955, the National Conference of Commissioners on Uniform State Laws (NC-CUSL) promulgated a model state arbitration statute, the Uniform Arbitration Act (UAA). The provisions of the UAA are virtually identical to those in the FAA, intended to ensure enforcement of arbitration agreements and confirmation of arbitration awards in state courts. More than 35 states enacted the UAA, with other states having adopted similar arbitration statutes.

After a comprehensive five-year review of the UAA and developments in arbitration law and practice, the NCCUSL promulgated a Revised Uniform Arbitration Act (RUAA) in August 2000. Unlike the UAA, the RUAA includes extensive explanatory comments. The RUAA does not depart from the basic provisions of the UAA (or the FAA), but it covers a considerable number of topics not covered by the other statutes. These topics address matters such as (1) whether a court or arbitrator determines whether a dispute can be arbitrated (arbitrability), and by what criteria; (2) provisional remedies; (3) initiation of arbitration proceedings; (4) consolidation of arbitration proceedings; (5) arbitrator disclosures; (6) immunity from suit of arbitrators and arbitral organizations; (7) testimony of arbitrators in other proceedings; (8) arbitrator power to manage the arbitration process, including discovery, summary disposition motions, and protective orders; (9) judicial enforcement of pre-award rulings by arbitrators; (10) arbitral remedial authority; (11) award of fees and costs by courts to prevailing party and/or arbitrators; and (12) specification of which RUAA provisions are waivable by contract. *See* Bruce Meyerson, *The Revised Uniform Arbitration Act: Fifteen Years Later*, 71 Disp. Resol. L. J. 1 (2016).

As of 2017, the RUAA had been enacted in 18 states (Alaska, Arizona, Arkansas, Colorado, Florida, Hawaii, Michigan, Minnesota, Nevada, New Jersey, New Mexico, North Carolina, North Dakota, Oklahoma, Oregon, Utah, Washington, and West Virginia) and in the District of Columbia. Massachusetts, Pennsylvania, Kansas, and Connecticut have introduced bills to adopt the RUAA in 2017. Major commercial states, such as California and New York, have developed their own arbitration statutes. For an update on RUAA enactments, see Uniform Law Commission, Arbitration Act (2000), http://www.uniformlaws.org.

c. *Proposed Federal Arbitration Fairness Legislation.* In response to concerns that arbitration may be forced on individuals in disparate bargaining situations, legislators in both houses of Congress have proposed the Arbitration Fairness Act of 2017 (AFA), Sen. 537 (introduced by Sen. Franken); H.R. 1374, 115th Cong. (2017), versions of which have been introduced in Congress nearly annually since 2007. The AFA seeks to prohibit enforcement of pre-dispute arbitration agreements in employment, consumer, antitrust, or civil rights matters. The findings of the proposed AFA state that:

(1) The Federal Arbitration Act ... was intended to apply to disputes between commercial entities of generally similar sophistication and bargaining power; (2) A series of decisions by the Supreme Court of the United States have interpreted the Act so that it now extends to consumer disputes and employment disputes, contrary to the intent of Congress; (3) [m]ost consumers and employees have *little or no meaningful choice* whether to submit their claims to arbitration. Often, consumers and employees are not even aware that they have given up their rights; (4) [m]andatory arbitration undermines the development of public law because there is inadequate transparency and inadequate judicial review of arbitrators' decisions; and (5) [a]rbitration can be

an acceptable alternative when consent to the arbitration is truly voluntary, and occurs after the dispute arises.

By recent count, the bill has only a small chance of passing. Does the proposed legislation revive the traditional "ouster of jurisdiction" and judicial hostility concerns the FAA was intended to reverse? Should the FAA apply to these types of transactions? States may also seek to enact protective legislation. **Chapter 2** examines the application of the federal preemption doctrine on the viability of state law that may be more restrictive than the FAA.

d. *International Arbitration Conventions.* In 1970, the United States ratified the Convention on the Recognition and Enforcement of Foreign Arbitral Awards, also known as the New York Convention, which provides for the enforcement of foreign arbitral awards. Chapter 2 of the FAA implements the New York Convention in the United States, while FAA Chapter 3 similarly provides for the enforcement of the 1975 Inter-American Convention on International Commercial Arbitration (the "Panama Convention") governing the enforceability of arbitration agreements and awards in Latin American countries. International arbitration is addressed more specifically in **Chapter 12**.

2. Arbitration Contractual Standards

While state, national, and international laws provide the legal framework for arbitration, the basis for the law to enforce arbitration is the parties' agreement to choose arbitration instead of litigation to resolve a dispute. A valid arbitration agreement triggers operation of arbitration legislation. Step one in the analysis is thus to determine that a valid arbitration agreement exists and that the concerned parties are bound by that agreement. *See* **Chapters 3 and 4**. In arbitration, parties can be empowered to design and choose the procedures and rules for how disputes will be resolved. An arbitration agreement thus can designate where the arbitration will be conducted, who will administer the arbitration, the procedural rules governing the process, and how the substantive law is applicable to the merits of the arbitrated dispute. *See* **Chapter 6**. Consider why these matters would be set forth in a pre-dispute arbitration clause, as opposed to the parties deciding these matters later.

a. *Private Institutional Administration and Procedural Rules.* A number of domestic and international organizations have developed procedural rules that provide a framework for conducting an arbitration and also provide services to administer it. While these rules are not public legislation, parties may contract to abide by these procedural rules. Arbitration clauses frequently specify an administering institution and application of a particular institution's procedural rules. Organizations that have published institutional rules and provided arbitration administrative functions, including assisting with arbitrator appointment and case management, include the American Arbitration Association (AAA), JAMS, the Financial Industry Regulatory Authority (FINRA), the International Court of Arbitration (ICC), the London Court of Arbitration, as well as the Court of Arbitration for Sports (CAS). Parties may choose to have their arbitration administered by an arbitral institution or proceed in a self-administered *ad hoc* arbitration. What might be the advantages or disadvantages of these options?

b. *Choice of Law Governing Merits of the Case.* Parties are free to contract under the laws of a particular state. Thus, an arbitration agreement may also contain a choice-of-law clause specifying the substantive law to be applied in determining the merits of the underlying dispute. For example, a clause may state, "This agreement is governed and shall be construed in accordance with the laws of [State A]." This may be particularly important for transactions involving parties from different states or countries. The impact of choice-of-law clauses in arbitration agreements is explored in **Chapter 2**.

D. What Is and *Is Not* Arbitration?

1. Defining Arbitration

What is arbitration? What are the defining features of "arbitration" that distinguish it from other forms of review or determination? When is a process "arbitration," as opposed to something else that may be labeled or look like arbitration, within the meaning of the law? Most important, why does it matter? Surprisingly, neither the federal nor uniform arbitration acts define arbitration.

Arbitration is customarily defined as "a simple proceeding voluntarily chosen by parties who want a dispute determined by an impartial judge of their own mutual selection, whose decision, based on the merits of the case, they agree in advance to accept as final and binding." ELKOURI & ELKOURI, HOW ARBITRATION WORKS 2 (Kenneth May, ed., 8th ed. 2016). Arbitration is also defined as "[u]sually (but not always) a private process of adjudication in which the parties in dispute with each other choose decision-makers (sometimes one, often a panel of three) and the rules of procedure, evidence, and decision by which their disputes will be settled." Carrie J. Menkel-Meadow, *Ethics Issues in Arbitration and Related Dispute Resolution Processes: What's Happening and What's Not*, 56 U. MIAMI L. REV. 949 (2002). In the classic sense, arbitration occurs when "parties in dispute choose a judge to render a final binding decision on the merits of the controversy and on the basis of the proofs presented by the parties." *Rush Prudential HMO, Inc. v. Moran*, 536 U.S. 355 (2002). In the modern conception of arbitration, "(1) the parties must agree or consent to arbitrate the dispute between them; (2) the parties select a method of dispute resolution intended to obtain a fair decision by a neutral third party in less time and at less cost than would be expected in court; and (3) the decision or award of the arbitrator is, with limited exceptions, final." IAN R. MACNEIL ET AL., FEDERAL ARBITRATION LAW § 2.1.1 (1994).

The arbitration process is often touted as an inexpensive, speedy, informal, and private alternative to the judicial system. *See Allied-Bruce Terminix Cos. v. Dobson*, 513 U.S. 265, 280 (1995) ("The advantages of arbitration are many: it is usually cheaper and faster than litigation; it can have simpler procedural and evidentiary rules; it normally minimizes hostility and is less disruptive of ongoing and future business dealings among the parties...."). Consider whether these traditional characterizations of arbitration have continued vitality in modern commercial arbitration practice. *See* Jill I. Gross, *Justice Scalia's Hat Trick and the Supreme Court's Flawed Understanding of Twenty-First Century Arbitration*, 81 BROOKLYN L. REV. 111 (2015) (examining the Supreme Court's description of arbitration in its recent decision and concluding that these decisions are built on a narrative of an arbitration process that no longer exists, although it may have existed in the twentieth century when Congress passed the FAA). But, as Professor Davis has noted:

> [t]he core of arbitration is not simplicity, though most who choose that forum escape from the convolutions of the courtroom. Nor is reduced expense the essence of arbitration, though few would quarrel with trimming counsel fees. The central element of arbitration is the intention of the parties as expressed in the arbitration agreement. The agreement determines the process.

Kenneth R. Davis, *When Ignorance of the Law Is No Excuse: Judicial Review of Arbitration Awards*, 45 BUFF. L. REV. 49 (1997). Arbitration, as a mechanism for private dispute resolution, and increasingly a complex social institution, largely depends upon party intent and the central terms of the arbitration agreement.

2. The Outer Limits of Arbitration

Although the classic definition of arbitration appears straightforward, consider that a variety of extrajudicial processes exist that parties may employ to resolve issues in dispute. The spectrum of ADR approaches includes consensual processes, such as mediation, in which a third-party neutral (the mediator) assists the parties to resolve their dispute, but lacks power to impose a decision. It seems rather obvious that mediation is *not* arbitration. *Advanced Bodycare Solutions, LLC v. Thione International, Inc.*, 524 F.3d 1235 (11th Cir. 2008) (holding that the dispute resolution clause requiring mediation did not qualify as arbitration because the clause was not "an agreement to settle by arbitration a controversy" and was thus not enforceable under the FAA). But how a process is labeled is not always accurate or dispositive. The contract in *Ditto v. RE/MAX Preferred Properties*, 861 P.2d 1000 (Okla. 1993), provided for "mediation" of the dispute before a committee whose decision, after a hearing, would be "final and binding" on all parties. This looked and sounded liked arbitration in all but name, and the court accordingly treated the decision as "arbitration" under the state arbitration act.

Contracting parties may incorporate multistep dispute resolution clauses in their contracts, requiring parties to attempt negotiation, mediation, non-binding arbitration, or other processes before resorting to arbitration or litigation. A contract may provide that arbitration is binding in some circumstances but not others. For example, standard physician-patient arbitration clauses provide that medical malpractice awards below a certain dollar threshold (commonly, $25,000) are binding on the parties, while higher awards are subject to *de novo* judicial trial at the behest of either party. This provision is not entirely a one-way street favoring physicians; one can imagine cases where a patient with large damages claims would opt for a *de novo* trial rather than accepting a $40,000 arbitration award. Is this "arbitration"?

Commercial contracts may provide for a third party or panel/committee to decide a particular issue in dispute or designate a process calling for expert determination, or appraisal.

A company or association's grievance or disciplinary process may call for a manda-tory internal review and hearing procedure. Is this an exhaustion of remedies pro-cedure or arbitration? Member institutions of the National Collegiate Athletic Association (NCAA), which regulates intercollegiate athletics, agree to submit to a typically three-to-five-person panel of the NCAA's Infractions Committee, with the right to appeal before the five-member NCAA Infractions Appeals Committee for final determination of whether the member has violated NCAA bylaws. Is this arbi-tration? A contract may call for an appraiser to assess valuation of an asset, or for an accountant to fix the buyout price for a departing partner. A marital divorce agreement may incorporate an agreement to bring disputes over spousal support or custody before a church or a rabbinical tribunal. Similarly, "parenting coordinators" have au-thority to determine day-to-day custody disputes arising under an existing parenting plan. A medical insurance plan may delegate evaluation of a "disability" diagnosis to a doctor for a "final and binding" determination. *Bakoss v. Certain Underwriters at Lloyds of London Issuing Certificate No.,* 707 F.3d 140 (2d Cir. 2013) (holding the doc-tor's "final and binding" evaluation of a disability diagnosis met the definition of ar-bitration). Consider your own law school's honor code procedure. Is that arbitration? Is it surprising that whether these processes are "arbitration" depends, not on label, but upon parties' intent and whether the procedure provides the essential attributes of arbitration?

If these processes are "arbitration" within the meaning of the FAA, for example, the statute's panoply of protections for judicial enforcement, stay of litigation, and limited review of the third party's decision would apply. That result may not only *not* reflect the parties' intention, but also can unintentionally give substantial powers to the third party decision-maker and import a wide array of other processes into the arbitration system. If the third party's decision is not arbitration, the prospect of litigation is available, or, at most, failure to accept the decision would be a con-tractual breach.

The following sections examine whether and when a particular private dispute resolution process qualifies as "arbitration" under the FAA (or similar state statutes). Consider precisely what factor(s) define characterizing an activity as "arbitration," or something else. Attention is focused on two borderline situations: non-binding ar-bitration-type proceedings, and appraisal or similar valuation processes. Again, con-sider whether the process designated for resolving disputes is "arbitration." Why might that matter (and does it)?

3. Non-Binding Arbitration

A contract may provide for arbitration that is (a) final and binding, in which case an award can be entered as a judgement of the court; or (b) non-binding, in which the parties are free to accept or reject the award. Is "non-binding" arbitration "arbitration" under the FAA?

Wolsey, Ltd. v. Foodmaker, Inc.

144 F.3d 1205 (9th Cir. 1998)

O'SCANNLAIN, CIRCUIT JUDGE:

In February of 1991, Foodmaker, a franchiser of Jack in the Box fast food restaurants, entered into a Development Agreement with Wolsey, a Hong Kong corporation, which gave Wolsey the right to develop Jack in the Box restaurants in Hong Kong and Macau for five years. The Development Agreement established a three-step dispute resolution process to be used for all disputes between Foodmaker and Wolsey: (1) a senior executive officer meeting; (2) non-binding arbitration under the rules of the AAA; (3) litigation in federal court.

In March of 1994, Wolsey invoked the dispute resolution procedure in the Development Agreement. Wolsey alleged that it had been fraudulently induced to enter into the Development Agreement by the express and implied misrepresentations of various Foodmaker executives....

After an unsuccessful meeting of the companies' senior executives in May 1994, Wolsey submitted the dispute to the AAA. Wolsey asserted [a broad array of contract-based claims]. After limited discovery and two weeks of arbitration, a Final Award of Arbitrators was issued in December of 1995. The panel determined Wolsey to be the prevailing party and rendered an award providing for various forms of relief, including an extension of Wolsey's development term for seven years and $200,000 for attorneys' fees. Foodmaker declined to comply with the arbitration award. In April of 1996, Wolsey filed a complaint in federal court. In the complaint, Wolsey asserted claims for violations of the Lanham Act [and other claims], ... none of which was asserted in the arbitration.

Arguing that Wolsey's complaint asserted claims not advanced in the arbitration, Foodmaker moved to compel arbitration of the Lanham Act claims.... The district court denied the motion, and Foodmaker filed a timely appeal. We have jurisdiction over an appeal from an order denying a motion to compel arbitration under 9 U.S.C. § 16(a)(1)(C).

Section 19.3 of the Development Agreement between Wolsey and Foodmaker provides that [with an exception not applicable here] ... "all controversies, disputes or claims ... shall be submitted for non-binding arbitration." Foodmaker seeks to compel such arbitration pursuant to section 4 of the FAA, which allows a party to an arbitration agreement to "petition any United States district court ... for an order directing that ... arbitration proceed in the manner provided for in [an arbitration] agreement."

As a threshold matter, Wolsey maintains that the FAA does not apply to non-binding arbitration such as that provided for in the Development Agreement. The FAA does not specifically define the term "arbitration." In arguing that the FAA does not apply to non-binding arbitration, Wolsey relies on section 2 of the Act.... Wolsey maintains that a provision ... to submit a controversy to non-binding arbitration is not a provision to "settle" a controversy. However, Wolsey's reliance on the use of the word "settle" in Section 2 of the FAA does not get it far. Black's Law Dictionary 1230 (1979) defines "settle" as:

> A word of equivocal meaning; meaning different things in different connections, and the particular sense in which it is used may be explained by the context or surrounding circumstances. Accordingly, the term may be employed as meaning to agree, to approve, to arrange, to ascertain, to liquidate, to come to or reach an agreement, to determine, to establish, to fix, to free from uncertainty, to place, or to regulate.

Although the Ninth Circuit has never addressed whether the FAA applies to non-binding arbitration, other courts have. In *AMF Inc. v. Brunswick Corp.*, 621 F. Supp. 456 (E.D.N.Y. 1985), Judge Weinstein examined whether a contract containing a non-binding agreement to arbitrate was covered by the Act. Judge Weinstein observed:

> Case law following the passage of the FAA reflects unequivocal support of agreements to have third parties decide disputes — the essence of arbitration. No magic words such as "arbitrate" or "binding arbitration" or "final dispute resolution" are needed to obtain the benefits of the Act. Arbitration is a creature of contract, a device of the parties rather than the judicial process. If the parties have agreed to submit a dispute for a decision by a third party, they have agreed to arbitration....

According to Judge Weinstein's analysis, parties agree to submit to arbitration under the FAA when they "agree to submit a dispute for a decision by a third party." In addition ... the parties must not only agree to submit the dispute to a third party, but also agree not to pursue litigation "until the process is completed."

We are persuaded that, under the reasoning adopted by these courts, the dispute resolution procedures established by section 19 of the Development Agreement between Wolsey and Foodmaker qualify as "arbitration" for purposes of the FAA.... Section 19.3 clearly provides for the submission of claims to "a third party." [T[he Development Agreement does not explicitly permit one of the parties to "seek recourse to the courts" after submitting claims for non-binding arbitration but before the "process is completed and the arbitrator makes a decision."

In light of the strong presumption in favor of arbitrability ... we hold that arbitration need not be binding in order to fall within the scope of the FAA.

4. Comments and Questions

a. Identifying a circuit split on the definition of arbitration, the Eleventh Circuit set forth a four-factor test to help determine whether a dispute resolution procedure is "classic arbitration": (i) an independent adjudicator, (ii) who applies substantive legal standards (i.e., the parties' agreement and background contract law), (iii) considers evidence and argument (however formally or informally) from each party, and (iv) renders a decision that purports to resolve the rights and duties of the parties, typically by awarding damages or equitable relief." *Advanced Bodycare Solutions, LLC v. Thione Int'l, Inc.*, 524 F.3d 1235, 1239 (11th Cir. 2008); *see also Fit Tech Inc. v. Bally Total Fitness Holding Corp.*, 374 F.3d 1 (1st Cir. 2004) (holding that "common incidents" of classic arbitration include a final, binding remedy by a third party, "an independent adjudicator, substantive standards, ... and an opportunity for each side to present its case"); *Harrison v. Nissan Motor Corp.*, 111 F.3d 343 (3d Cir. 1997) ("the essence of arbitration" is that parties "agreed to arbitrate [their] disputes through to completion, i.e. to an award made by a third-party arbitrator."). Which law should provide the definition of "arbitration"? Federal law or state law? *See Bakoss v. Certain Underwriters at Lloyds of London Issuing Certificate 0510135*, 707 F.3d 140 (2d Cir. 2013) ("We hold that the meaning of 'arbitration' under the Federal Arbitration Act is governed by federal common law—not state law.").

b. Although parties generally have freedom to structure their own systems for dispute resolution, including flexibility in designing their arbitration process, it remains important that such a process retains key elements of arbitration (a third-party neutral, finality, and a binding decision) for statutory protections to apply. If the procedure is not "arbitration," FAA provisions to compel participation or to enforce awards are unavailable.

c. *Label Not Dispositive.* While not common, instances where the parties mislabeled a dispute resolution process are easily found. *See, e.g., Cheng-Canindin v. Renaissance Hotel Assocs.*, 50 Cal. App. 4th 676 (1996) (process for committee review of employee termination lacked attributes of arbitration, including mechanism ensuring impartiality of arbitrator, and was not arbitration); *Society of Am. Foresters v. Renewable Natural Resources Found.*, 689 A.2d 662 (Md. Ct. App. 1997) (process called for by contract was arbitration although not so named). Neither state arbitration nor mediation confidentiality statutory protections were available in *Saeta v. Superior Court.*, 11 Cal. Rptr. 3d 610 (2004), because the procedure for a hearing before a three-member review board whose decision was reviewable by the employer was not arbitration or mediation.

d. *Accountants as Arbitrators?* In determining whether contractual provisions calling for independent accountant process constituted "arbitration," courts have applied the *Fit Tech* standards. *See* Martin & Jones v. Olson, 2017 NCBC 85 (2017) (holding that the independent accounting process resembles "classic arbitration" if it is binding and conclusive on the parties, allows parties to present evidence, and requires the independent accountant to provide substantive standards; but not where those protections are absent and where a party may unilaterally select and engage the independent accountant).

e. *Internet Domain Name Dispute Resolution Process.* As a condition of registering a domain name, the Internet Corporation for Assigned Names and Numbers (ICCAN) requires registrants to agree to use the Uniform Domain Name Dispute Resolution Policy ("UDRP"), a mandatory administrative procedure in which a panel is convened to resolve complaints concerning registered domain names. The World Intellectual Property Organization (WIPO) administers the UDRP proceedings. *See* http:// www.wipo.int/amc/en/domains/guide/. In *Dluhos v. Strasberg*, 321 F.3d 365 (3d Cir. 2003), the Estate of Lee Strasberg invoked the UDRP process, which ordered cancellation of the "leestrasberg.com" trademark registered by alleged cybersquatter Dluhos. The Third Circuit held that the UDRP process did *not* fall under the FAA because no provision of the policy prevented a party from filing suit before, after, or during the administrative proceedings, and the dispute was [not necessarily] settled by those proceedings. It noted that the UDRP procedure did not permit discovery, the presentation of live testimony, or any remedy other than the transfer or cancellation of the domain name in question, and thus did not constitute arbitration under the FAA. The Third Circuit noted:

> Federal courts primarily invoke the FAA to give effect to contracting parties' expectations for resolving disputes. Accordingly, the FAA revolves around contract interpretation.... [T]he essence of arbitration ... is that, when the parties agree to submit their disputes to it, they have agreed to arbitrate these disputes through to completion, i.e. to an award made by a third-party arbitrator. Arbitration does not occur until the process is completed and the arbitrator makes a decision.

Although the UDRP dispute resolution process is not "arbitration" for FAA purposes, the process is similar to arbitration and in fact nearly always produces a rapid, expert, and final resolution of domain-name disputes. In an ever more technological world, where time really is of the essence, more parties resorting to near-arbitration processes to settle disputes is to be expected. Will our views of what constitutes "arbitration" have to adjust to these new realities in the ensuing decades?

5. Appraisal, Valuation, and Similar Processes

Commercial contracts may contain a dispute resolution procedure that calls for an assessment by an accountant or appraisal in order to establish the value of an asset. Parties may also call for expert determination by an independent third party. Is this process "arbitration" under the FAA or UAA? Suppose the contract also contains a general arbitration provision for the settlement of all disputes "arising out of or relating to" the contract between the parties? Suppose the contract used the word "arbitration" in lieu of "appraisal" or that it provides for a "binding appraisal"?

Salt Lake Tribune Publishing Co., LLC v.
Management Planning, Inc.

390 F.3d 684 (10th Cir. 2004)

Lucero, Circuit Judge.

At issue is whether a certain appraisal constituted an arbitration under the FAA. Finding that the appraisal was an arbitration, the district court granted the considerable deference owed to arbitrators' decisions.... Because we conclude that the appraisal did not constitute an arbitration, we.... Reverse.

Shareholders of the Kearns-Tribune Corporation, which owned *The Salt Lake Tribune* newspaper, sold their company ... to MediaNews. Kearns-Tribune shareholders formed a new company, SLTPC, and, at the time of the sale, acquired an option to purchase the newspaper from MediaNews after five years ("Option Agreement"). Under the Option Agreement, the exercise price of the option equaled the "Fair Market Value" of the newspaper's assets. If the parties could not agree on an exercise price, each side was to appoint an appraiser ("party appraisers") to assess the newspaper's Fair Market Value.... The Option Agreement included detailed provisions regarding the definition and determination of Fair Market Value.] If the party appraisers differed from each other by more than ten percent in their estimation of the newspaper's value, they would jointly select a third appraiser and the exercise price would equal the average of the two closest appraisal values reported by the three appraisers.

In August 2002, SLTPC began negotiations with MediaNews to establish the exercise price. Unable to agree on a price, the parties each retained appraisers. MediaNews's appraiser issued a report appraising the Fair Market Value of the newspaper's assets at $380 million, which exceeded SLTPC's appraiser's evaluation of $218 million. Because the party appraisers differed by more than ten percent, they [selected MPI as the] third appraiser.... Pursuant to the Appraisal Agreement, and after conducting the necessary investigation and receiving comments from both parties, MPI issued its final report valuing the newspaper's assets at $331 million.

Claiming that MPI failed to produce its appraisal under the standards required by the Option Agreement, SLTPC sued MediaNews and MPI in district court seeking, inter alia, (1) a declaration that MPIs' appraisal may not be used to calculate the exercise price; (2) a ruling imposing a new appraisal process using all new appraisals, a new valuation date, and a new selection of a third appraiser; (3) compensatory damages from MPI based on its alleged breach of contract; (4) compensatory and punitive damages based on MPI's alleged breach of fiduciary duty; and (5) if MPI's appraisal were deemed an "arbitration award," an order vacating such award....

We begin by analyzing whether MPI's appraisal constituted an arbitration within the meaning of the FAA. Because Congress did not define "arbitration" in the FAA, we must first decide which source of law provides that definition. Relying on the Option Agreement's choice-of-law provision electing Delaware law, the district court turned to Delaware law to define "arbitration." Our review of the authorities leads us to conclude that ... federal law supplies the standard by which we must determine whether MPI's appraisal was an arbitration.

In the absence of clear evidence that Congress intended state law to define "arbitration," we must assume that federal law provides the definition. The meaning that the law attaches to the term arbitration establishes the scope and force of the FAA. Unless Congress plainly intended the various states' laws to define "arbitration," and to therefore regulate the FAA's application within their borders, we will look to federal law for the definition. ...

[A]pplying federal law is the only way to ensure national uniformity. ... "It should not be necessary, but it definitely is, to stress that whether a given dispute resolution procedure is *arbitration* within the meaning of the FAA is a question of federal, not state, law." Ian R. MacNeil, *Federal Arbitration Law* § 2.1.2A (1999).

Under federal law, we must determine if the process at issue sufficiently resembles classic arbitration to fall within the purview of the FAA. *See, e.g., Fit Tech, Inc. v. Bally Total Fitness Holding Corp.*, 374 F.3d 1 (1st Cir. 2004) ("the question is how closely the specified procedure resembles classic arbitration"). Central to any conception of classic arbitration is that the disputants empowered a third party to render a decision settling their dispute. Under this test, MPI's appraisal did not constitute an arbitration. ...

Parties need not establish quasi-judicial proceedings resolving their disputes to gain the protections of the FAA, but may choose from a broad range of procedures and tailor arbitration to suit their peculiar circumstances. However, one feature that must necessarily appertain to a process to render it an arbitration is that the third party's decision will settle the dispute. Furthermore, the language employed by the parties in their contract has little probative weight. If the contract states that the third party's decision is final and binding, courts must nonetheless scrutinize the process created by the parties to ascertain whether the third party's decision does in fact resolve the dispute. ... Here, MPI's appraisal would by no means definitively settle the dispute between SLTPC and MediaNews. At most, MPI supplied a data point that the parties could use in establishing the exercise price.

MPI was not asked to decide between two values established by SLTPC and MediaNews, nor were they asked to assign independently a single value binding on the parties. Indeed the parties did not even agree to average MPI's figure with one or both of their own. The parties merely asked MPI to prepare a report evaluating the newspaper and establishing the Fair Market Value of the newspaper's assets, a value which the parties may, under certain circumstances, have used to fix the exercise price under the Option Agreement. MPI's report would not necessarily settle a dispute between SLTPC and MediaNews.

Perhaps recognizing that MPI's appraisal, standing alone, does not constitute an arbitration, MediaNews stated at oral argument that the entire process, including the party appraisals, was an arbitration. MediaNews suggests that the appraisers respectively hand-picked by the two parties, whose qualifications, abilities, and methods have been thoroughly impugned by the opposing party in the briefs, were somehow co-equal arbitrators with MPI. The appraisers selected by the individual parties functioned more like dueling experts than arbitrators. Also belying the suggestion that the process constituted arbitration is the express language of the Appraisal Agreement that provides in the event the Option Agreement "preclude[s] an appraisal in accordance with ... industry standards and principles, ... the parties agree to then seek guidance from the Court to resolve that conflict." This hardly sounds like arbitration to us. Because the three-appraisal process does not resemble classic arbitration, we reject MediaNews's suggestion that the entire process constituted an arbitration....

We merely hold that MPI's appraisal did not constitute an arbitration within the meaning of the FAA.

6. Notes and Comments

a. *Arbitration versus Appraisal?* Arbitration and appraisal are distinct methods of dispute resolution. The FAA, however, only applies to "arbitration." What is the difference between the two processes? Arbitrators decide disputes between the parties and determine liability, generally through the adversarial hearing process. Thomas H. Oehmke, COMMERCIAL ARBITRATION, § 1:3 (2004) ("Appraisal agreements, on the other hand, are typically limited to ministerial determinations (e.g., the ascertainment of the quality or quantity of items, the ascertainment of loss or damage to property, or the ascertainment of the value of property")).

b. *Valuations of assets or purchase prices. Salt Lake Tribune* held that the agreement to accept a third-party appraisal to determine "fair market value" in a repurchase agreement was not an agreement to arbitrate where the appraisal at issue would only fix the purchase price under certain circumstances, and therefore would "not necessarily settle a dispute" between the parties. Compare *Salt Lake* with *Evanston Ins. Co. v. Cogswell Properties, LLC*, 683 F.3d 684 (6th Cir. 2012). In *Evanston*, the Sixth Circuit examined whether the appraisal provision in the case was "arbitration" under the FAA based upon "how closely it resembles classic arbitration." Noting that a central feature of classic arbitration is that the disputants empowered a third party to render a decision settling the dispute between parties to completion, the court held that the appraisal provision did not constitute arbitration for purposes of the FAA where the appraisal provision stated that "[a] decision agreed to by any two [umpire and appraisers] will be binding," and "[i]f there is an appraisal, we [Evanston Insurance] will still retain our right to deny the claim." The Policy did not provide for a final and binding remedy by a neutral third party.

c. Key differences between appraisals and arbitration are that "[a]ppraisals are informal. Appraisers typically conduct independent investigations and base their decisions on their own knowledge, without holding formal hearings." *Hartford Lloyd's Ins. Co. v. Teachworth*, 898 F.2d 1058, 1062 (5th Cir. 1990); *see also McDonnell v. State Farm Mut. Auto. Ins. Co.*, 299 P.3d 715, 722 (Alaska 2013) ("Appraisal follows an expedited timeline and is resolved by a panel of independent appraisers, while arbitration is a quasi-judicial proceeding that is governed by a much more detailed statutory scheme and includes formal evidentiary hearings with depositions and witness testimony."); *Montview Blvd. Presbyterian Church v. Church Mut. Ins. Co.*, 2016 U.S. Dist. LEXIS 6531 (D. Colo. Jan. 20, 2016) (concluding that the appraisal process is *not* arbitration).

d. *Expert determinations.* Parties may agree to appoint a person who is an expert to decide a particular question, usually highly technical or involving valuation. This determination may be based upon the expert's personal knowledge or expertise, as opposed to arbitration, where the decision is based upon party submissions.

While the parties may contractually agree to accept the expert's determination, the binding effect is based upon contract, as opposed to arbitration, upon which the law confers considerable judicial support and deference.

E. Specialized Uses and Forms of Arbitration

Arbitration is used as the preferred and, in some cases, exclusive method of dispute resolution in a variety of specialized industries. Even within the commercial arbitration context, providers may offer specialized rules, procedures, and rosters tailed for specific industries, such as construction, energy, healthcare, financial services, biotech, insurance, government, technology, as well as sports and entertainment. The following provides a brief overview of the various types of uses of arbitration in specific industries.

1. Labor-Management Arbitration

Labor arbitration in the unionized context is also a prominent feature of U.S. arbitration law and is separately regulated under Section 301(a) of the 1947 Taft-Hartley Act amendments to the Labor Management Relations Act (LMRA), 29 U.S.C. § 185(a). Section 301, the statutory basis for labor arbitration, provides that: "Suits for violation of contracts between an employer and a labor organization representing employees in an industry affecting commerce ... may be brought in any United States district court ... having jurisdiction of the parties, without respect to the amount in controversy or ... the citizenship of the parties." Although this short and simple provision does not even mention arbitration, section 301 is the statutory basis for labor arbitration because it authorizes federal courts to enforce the terms of collective bargaining agreements (CBAs) and provides a basis for the creation of substantive federal law, despite contrary state law. In *Textile Workers Union v. Lincoln Mills of Alabama*, 353 U.S. 448 (1957), the Supreme Court ruled that a CBA provision calling for arbitration of grievances was, like other contract provisions, enforceable by the federal courts.

Labor arbitration refers mainly to grievance arbitration pursuant to a collective bargaining agreement (CBA). Upon rare occasions, the parties agree to authorize an arbitrator to determine the substantive terms and conditions of employment, which is known as "interest arbitration." Interest arbitration is almost exclusively utilized in the public sector. In contrast, arbitration of disputes between employers and employees outside the CBA context is "employment arbitration" and is governed by the FAA.

It is national policy to promote industrial self-government and industrial peace. Much of our present system grew out of the World War II experience, when industrial strife was an unacceptable threat to the success of the war effort. Congress established a War Labor Board (WLB) with power to "finally determine" any labor dispute that might interfere with the war effort. The WLB encouraged resort to arbitration and recognized the awards of arbitral tribunals. Since World War II, express provision for arbitration of labor grievances has been a standard feature of almost every CBA.

In 1960, the Supreme Court decided three cases that conclusively validated CBA grievance arbitration and adopted an extremely deferential posture toward such awards that left little place for judicial review. *See United Steelworkers of America v. American Mfg. Co.*, 363 U.S. 564 (1960); *United Steelworkers of America v. Warrior & Gulf Navigation Co.*, 363 U.S. 574 (1960); and *United Steelworkers of America v. Enterprise Wheel & Car Corp.*, 363 U.S. 593 (1960). These decisions, all authored by Justice Douglas and appearing on consecutive pages of the United States Reports, are universally known as "the Steelworkers Trilogy." Simply stated, in these cases the Supreme Court adopted the following principles:

> 1. The courts will enforce contractual promises to arbitrate and will presume that the parties want the arbitrators to determine whether the parties agreed to arbitrate a type or class of disputes;

> 2. The courts should order arbitration without enquiring into the merits of the underlying grievance; and

> 3. The courts should enforce an arbitration award so long as it can be said to have "drawn its essence" (the "essence" test) from the CBA.

The limited judicial review given to labor arbitration awards was reaffirmed in the high-profile sport cases, *Major League Baseball Players' Ass'n v. Garvey*, 532 U.S. 504 (2001), and *Brady v. Nat'l Football League*, 640 F.3d 785 (2d Cir. 2016).

The Supreme Court also has affirmed the ability of unions to negotiate arbitration clauses that require unionized employees to arbitrate their statutory, in addition to contractual, claims. *See 14 Penn Plaza LLC v. Pyett*, 556 U.S. 247 (2009); *see also Granite Rock v. Int'l Teamsters*, 561 U.S. 287, 289 (2012) (noting presumption of federal policy favoring arbitration of labor disputes applies, provided the court ensures the parties intended to arbitrate and that their agreement was validly formed and encompasses the dispute); *Wright v. Universal Maritime Serv. Corp.*, 525 U.S. 70 (1998) (holding that waiver of an employee's right to pursue statutory claims in court must be clearly and unmistakably stated in the collective bargaining agreement).

Labor arbitration will receive limited consideration in this course because it is fundamentally different from commercial arbitration. Labor and commercial arbitration have different histories, traditions, procedures, and statutes upon which they are based. Even the alternatives to arbitration are fundamentally different: for commercial arbitration it is a lawsuit, while for grievance arbitration it is industrial strife. One is a substitute forum for judicial proceedings, while the other is an alternative to a strike or a lockout. Commercial arbitration represents a breakdown of the relationship between the parties, while grievance arbitration is just another skirmish within the framework of an ongoing relationship.

2. Arbitration of Investor-Broker Disputes

Since the very beginnings of stock and bond trading in the United States, the securities industry has used arbitration to resolve disputes among industry participants. In fact, the very first constitution of the New York Stock and Exchange Board (predecessor to the modern New York Stock Exchange) in 1817 required disputes to be arbitrated before the full Board. *See* Jill I. Gross, *The Historical Basis of Securities Arbitration as an Investor Protection Mechanism*, 2016 J. Disp. Resol. 171 (2016) (detailing the history of arbitration in the securities industry).

Despite securities arbitration's deep roots in American history, most descriptions of its background and use begin with the Supreme Court's 1987 watershed decision in *Shearson/American Express, Inc. v. McMahon*, 482 U.S. 220 (1987), in which the Court held that claims arising under the Securities and Exchange Act of 1934 were arbitrable. Two years later, in *Rodriguez de Quijas v. Shearson/American Express, Inc.*, 490 U.S. 477 (1989), the Court held that claims arising under the Securities Act of 1933 also were arbitrable. The Court's comfort level with securities arbitration in both cases was enhanced by the substantial oversight of securities arbitration exercised by the Securities and Exchange Commission (SEC).

Since *McMahon* and *Rodriguez*, because virtually all broker-dealers include a pre-dispute arbitration clause in their customer agreements, arbitration in forums sponsored by the securities industry has been the primary mechanism for the resolution of disputes among investors, brokerage firms, and brokers. Due to a consolidation of several forums, today, virtually all securities arbitrations are heard in the Office of Dispute Resolution of the Financial Industry Regulatory Authority (FINRA), a securities self-regulatory organization supervised by the SEC. Brokerage customers who allege, for example, that their broker recommended unsuitable investments or strategies, placed unauthorized trades or committed fraud must, because of the arbitration clause in their customer agreements, arbitrate those claims in the FINRA arbitration forum. Moreover, even if the customer agreement does not contain a pre-dispute arbitration clause, FINRA Code of Arbitration Procedure for Customer Disputes Rule 12200 requires broker-dealers and their associated persons to submit to arbitration upon the demand of a customer.

While fundamentally, the FINRA arbitration process is similar to other forms of commercial arbitration, it also includes many features that protect investors. In addition to subsidizing fees for customer claimants, FINRA provides customers with the right to select a panel consisting of no arbitrators with ties to the securities industry and the right to presumptively discoverable documents from respondents. Forum rules sharply restrict respondents from filing pre-hearing dispositive motions. These features collectively ensure that a customer claimant has an opportunity for a full hearing before a panel of unbiased arbitrators. Also, the forum enforces its policy of not accepting class arbitrations, instead preserving by rule an investor's right to bring any aggregable claims as a class or collective action in court. To enhance transparency, the forum now requires arbitrators to issue an explained award if all parties jointly request one. And, most significantly, a member firm and/or an associated person's failure to pay an arbitration award to an investor results in membership suspension or revocation. Collectively, these features have somewhat protected the FINRA arbitration process from challenges to the fairness of adhesive arbitration in other industries. *See* Jill I. Gross, *The End of Mandatory Securities Arbitration?*, 30 PACE L. REV. 1174, 1179 (2010).

3. Sports Arbitration

Arbitration is the primary, often exclusive, method for dispute resolution in the major professional sports in the United States. Professional athletes in all major sports in the United States are unionized and represented by a players' association. The collective bargaining agreements between the player association and league, which represents the team owners, generally require arbitration of grievances, salary disputes, and injury determinations. Thus, much of this is governed by labor arbitration statutes. But the commercial aspects of sports contracts often provide for arbitration. And techniques used in sport arbitration can have application in commercial arbitration. You might have heard of "baseball arbitration," which is a method designated in the collective bargaining agreement with Major League Baseball for adjudicating salary disputes. Also known as "final offer" or "either/or" arbitration, each party presents a proposed monetary award (or salary) to the arbitrator, who selects one without modification. This approach may be used in commercial arbitration cases as well. What might be the reason for choosing such an approach?

In Olympic and international sports, arbitration is the exclusive means of adjudicating disputes involving claims of athletes, coaches, or parties regarding participation. At the domestic level, the Ted Stevens Amateur Sports Act, 36 U.S.C. § 220501, requires arbitration for any claims involving the opportunity to participate in the Olympics in the United States. In 1984, the International Olympic Committee created the Court of Arbitration for Sport (CAS) to provide a single forum where parties submit to arbitration to resolve Olympic sport-related disputes. Since 1995, the Olympic Charter has provided that "[A]ny dispute arising on the occasion of or in connection with the Olympic Games shall be submitted exclusively to the [CAS]." Thus, as a condition of participating in the Olympics or sanctioned international sports competitions, both commercial parties and athletes around the world must consent to CAS arbitration and thereby waive rights to national courts. Headquartered (and seated) in Lausanne, Switzerland, CAS also operates an *ad hoc* division with a roster of CAS arbitrators on site during the Olympic Games to render decisions within 24 hours.

4. Arbitration in the Entertainment Industry

Arbitration is also widely used in the entertainment industry, either through a collectively bargained provision or by party contract. For example, controversies between writers over who is entitled to credit for writing a screenplay or motion picture must be submitted to credit arbitration in accordance with Credit Determination Procedures of the Writer's Guilds of America (WGA), pursuant to the WGA Theatrical and Television Basic Agreement. *See* WGA (West), SCREEN CREDITS, http://www.wga.org/contracts/credits/manuals/screen-credits-manual. Challenges to the WGA arbitration procedures were analyzed in *Marino v. Writers Guild of America, East, Inc.*, 992 F.2d 1480 (9th Cir. 1993). Collective bargaining agreements with the Screen Actors Guild, the Directors Guild of America, and the Producers Guild of America also provide for arbitration within industry parameters. Even parties not part of a guild or union may stipulate to arbitration. For example, film distributor agreements with parties in foreign countries may contract to use the arbitration services and rules of the International Film and Television Alliance (IFTA). Consider that even the parties who go before "Judge Judy" on court television are in arbitration if the contract so provides. *See Kabia v. Koch*, 713 N.Y.S.2d 250 (N.Y. Civ. Ct. 2000) (holding that "People's Court" television show qualified as an arbitration and its judge was entitled to arbitral immunity).

5. Arbitration in ...

Where arbitration is designed by contract or agreed to by the parties, it may be used in almost any context. Although the focus of this book is commercial arbitration, note that arbitration is sometimes used to adjudicate disputes in religious communities, domestic cases, and can range from a two-party proceeding to a multiparty, complex proceeding. Consider whether the particular dispute is suitable for arbitration. Are there contexts in which courts should refuse to enforce these arbitration agreements or awards?

F. A Roadmap for Studying Arbitration

Your study thus far should have given you an introduction to the prevalence and uses of arbitration in the modern economy, fairness considerations, arbitration's historical roots in the United States, the legislation governing arbitration, the defining elements of arbitration, the outer limits of arbitration, and specialized industry uses of arbitration. The following chapters cover the many legal and practical questions that may arise before, during, and after an arbitration. Keep in mind that arbitration *mostly* works! That is, parties who have elected to use arbitration, either before or after a dispute arises (pre- or post-dispute), typically use the process in the manner envisioned to accomplish an expedited and binding resolution of a dispute.

The following chapters begin our study of arbitration. **Chapter 2** examines in detail the federal and state arbitration laws and how these laws interact or preempt the ability of state law to regulate arbitration. **Chapters 3 and 4** address the initial determinative questions of whether a valid arbitration agreement exists, whether the parties and dispute in issue are covered by the agreement, and whether the particular dispute is covered by the arbitration contract. These seemingly simple questions can be technical and complicated, particularly in the wake of claims that one party never truly consented to the arbitration clause that was part of an adhesion contract, or that the contract or arbitration process contemplated in the contract is unconscionable. Perhaps surprisingly, rather than answering these questions, much of the case law in this area focuses on *who decides* these questions and the allocation of authority between arbitrators and courts.

Chapters 5 through 9 focus on the arbitration process itself, including the arbitration agreement, drafting considerations, arbitrator selection and ethical standards, advocacy and the hearing process, and judicial review of arbitration awards. When a dispute arises between (or among) parties to a contract containing an arbitration provision, the complaining party serves notice of arbitration upon the respondent. This can be initiated through the services of an arbitration provider organization that may be designated in the contract to administer the arbitration. The parties select an arbitrator or panel of arbitrators, who are to be neutral and otherwise have vast authority over the proceedings. The parties are afforded an opportunity to present evidence, although the formality of extensive discovery, motions, and evidentiary rules are expected to be relaxed. The arbitral award is final and binding on the parties, and arbitrators have significant remedial authority. *See* **Chapters 5–7**. Parties dissatisfied with the award, arbitrator, or process, however, may seek to challenge the arbitral award. **Chapter 9** surveys the various grounds for judicial review of arbitral awards, including whether the parties may contractually expand the scope of review. Disputes in commercial dealings among businesses, with consumers, or with employees often involve multiple parties or common issues where consolidation of the proceedings or a class action proceeding is sought. **Chapter 10** covers the somewhat controversial topic of class actions in arbitration, while **Chapter 11** addresses questions when arbitration involves multiple forums, procedures, and parties. Business entities increasingly conduct business on a global scale. **Chapter 12** addresses the use and growing importance arbitration of international disputes.

Each Chapter also contains a number of "Problems" to set a context for how the arbitration issues arise in a practical setting and to provide a concrete set of facts to analyze and apply the legal principles and case materials. The Notes and Comments also contain supplemental questions, illustrations, and practice questions. The Appendices contain the major arbitration statutes, a chronology of U.S. Supreme Court commercial arbitration decisions, and an arbitration case file.

Chapter 2

Arbitration Preemption, Jurisdiction, and Choice of Law

A. Introduction

Before delving into the specifics of the arbitration process, this Chapter seeks to give an overview of the legal landscape governing arbitration, focusing on the intersection of federal and state arbitration laws. In most cases, parties voluntarily submit their disputes to arbitration and comply with arbitration awards, and the information contained in this chapter is merely background. However, when the parties do not agree on how to proceed, they often seek judicial assistance. Courts are asked to intervene on matters such as:

- Enforcing an agreement to arbitrate
- Declaring an agreement to arbitrate unenforceable
- Appointing an arbitrator
- Enforcing an arbitration award
- Vacating or modifying an arbitration award

Laws governing arbitration provide remedies when the parties cannot agree. Over time, legislatures and courts have created legal rules to ensure that parties arbitrate when they have agreed to arbitrate and enforce awards when those awards were the product of a process meeting certain minimum standards.

This Chapter begins with an overview of the laws explicitly governing arbitration. Notably, Section B outlines the reach of the United States Arbitration Act of 1925, more commonly known as the Federal Arbitration Act (FAA) and builds on the history of arbitration and the FAA from **Chapter 1**. Having a thorough understanding of the FAA and its underlying policies is a fundamental first step in understanding the law governing arbitration. Section B also discusses state arbitration laws, notably the Uniform Arbitration Act of 1955 (UAA) and the Revised Uniform Arbitration Act of 2000 (RUAA).

Section C then turns to the important question of the interplay between federal and state laws regarding arbitration. Technically, arbitration is a dual regulatory system with both federal and state laws governing the process. What, then, happens if a state attempts to regulate arbitration in a way that conflicts with the FAA? In the early to mid-twentieth century, courts understood the FAA to apply only in federal courts while state arbitration laws applied in state courts. This understanding, however, changed in 1986 when the Supreme Court decided *Southland Corporation v. Keating*. The *Southland* Court held that, under the Supremacy Clause of the U.S. Constitution, the FAA preempts conflicting state law. Over time, the Supreme Court has considerably expanded its interpretation of the FAA's preemptive power. Preemption remains one of the most controversial topics in arbitration law, and Section C will delve into the policy and practical effects of broad FAA preemption.

Section D explores jurisdictional issues under the FAA. Recall from Civil Procedure that courts must have both subject matter and personal jurisdiction to hear a case and that federal courts are courts of limited subject matter jurisdiction, while state courts generally have common jurisdiction to hear both federal and state law matters. The two most common grounds for federal court subject matter jurisdiction are federal question and diversity of citizenship. The FAA is often described as an "anomaly" among federal statutes because the statute has substantive provisions, but it does not provide subject matter jurisdiction in federal courts. In other words, parties who would like a federal court to hear their arbitration cases must have independent grounds for jurisdiction. Despite the relatively simple pronouncement that parties must have an independent basis to access the federal courts, determining whether those grounds are met can be extraordinarily complicated. Section D lays out many of these issues and gives practical guidance for working with these issues in practice.

Finally, Section E briefly considers the enforceability of choice of law and choice of forum clauses in agreements to arbitrate. Arbitration is a creature of contract, and parties have significant control over the process. To the extent that governing arbitration law serves as a default position, parties should have the opportunity to change the default legal rules.

Problem

The State of Dover has serious concerns with the increased use of arbitration in consumer contracts, particularly cellular telephone contracts. A majority of legislators in Dover are interested in passing consumer protection legislation that would prohibit all pre-dispute arbitration provisions in contracts between cellular telephone companies and consumers. Specifically, the language of the bill they propose to states:

> Pre-dispute arbitration agreements between cellular telephone companies and consumers are unenforceable.

The legislators seek your counsel on whether such a law would withstand a legal challenge on the basis of the FAA. If this law is problematic, the legislators would be willing to consider two variations:

> Pre-dispute arbitration agreements in contracts for cellular telephone service between cellular telephone companies and consumers are unenforceable unless the language is underlined and specifically initialed by the consumer.

-or-

Any class-action waiver in such cellular telephone service agreements is strictly unenforceable.

Advise the legislators on each of the proposed state statutes.

B. The Federal Arbitration Act and State Arbitration Laws

1. The Federal Arbitration Act

The study of arbitration law begins in earnest with a comprehensive look at the Federal Arbitration Act. The FAA is a relatively short statute, with only 16 provisions. Please take the time now to read the statute in its entirety, which is found in Appendix A. Many arbitration legal questions involve an interpretation or application of the FAA. Although FAA provisions will be discussed in greater depth in other parts of this book, this Section aims to give readers an understanding of the structure of the Act, and to gain a sense of what is and is not covered in the FAA.

2. Comments and Questions

a. Consider the breadth of the FAA. What is covered by the Act? What is left out? Scholars often discuss the coverage of the FAA to include "front end" and "back end" issues. Stated another way, the FAA covers how parties can enforce agreements to arbitrate (front-end issues) and challenge or enforce arbitration awards (back-end issues). Should the FAA also cover other issues, such as how arbitration hearings should be administered and other procedural matters?

b. Section 2 is considered to be the most important provision of the FAA, and it will be discussed in greater depth in the next section. Based on the text, what does Section 2 instruct courts to do?

c. The FAA is unquestionably written in a way that is pro-arbitration. How does the FAA create a preference for the arbitration forum over the litigation forum in contested cases? In particular, consider sections 3, 4, 9, and 16.

d. The FAA is also pro-arbitration in the procedures that it invokes. Consider the language in Section 6. What do these procedural mechanisms say about arbitration practice?

e. What does the FAA say about the jurisdiction of the federal courts to hear arbitration-related motions? Consider the jurisdictional language of Section 4, for instance. The issue of jurisdiction is discussed in greater depth later in this Chapter.

f. Ensuring finality is an important aspect of the FAA. How do the grounds for vacatur and modification of arbitration awards promote finality?

g. Section 13 has the ability to turn an arbitration award into a court judgment. Why is that important and what does this Section suggest about arbitration?

3. Uniform and Select State Arbitration Acts

In addition to the FAA, each state has its own arbitration laws. Although the interplay between these two sets of laws is explored in Section C of this Chapter, this Section explains the variation of arbitration regulation from the FAA and among state statutes.

In 1955, the National Conference of Commissioners on Uniform State Laws (NCCUSL) promulgated the Uniform Arbitration Act (UAA). At the time, the general understanding of the law was that the FAA applied in federal courts and that states also had the ability to regulate arbitration within their borders. Roughly half of the states adopted the UAA.

In many ways, the UAA mirrors the FAA. Like the FAA, the UAA ensures that: (1) arbitration agreements are specifically enforced, UAA §§ 1–2, (2) courts can appoint arbitrators if necessary, UAA § 3, (3) arbitrators can issue subpoenas, UAA § 7, and (4) state courts can confirm or vacate awards, UAA §§ 11–14. The UAA also contains procedural mechanisms similar to those in the FAA for arbitration practice in state courts. Under the UAA, the parties can engage in motion practice, UAA § 16, and interlocutory appeals are only available for anti-arbitration rulings. UAA § 19.

The UAA also includes a limited number of provisions on issues that the FAA does not address at all. Those provisions include additional guidance on how arbitrators should conduct hearings, UAA § 5, the availability of pre-hearing depositions, § 7, the form of the award, § 9, and the division of forum fees. § 10. In addition, the UAA makes explicit that parties have the right to be represented by counsel in arbitration. § 6. Yet overall, the UAA has a limited reach in many of the same ways that the reach of the FAA is limited. As with the FAA, the UAA is silent on much of how arbitrations should be conducted and the ethical standards that govern arbitrators and arbitration participants.

Arbitration practice has become much more complex since the 1950s, and the NCCUSL convened in 2000 to reexamine arbitration law in considering the Revised Uniform Arbitration Act of 2000 (RUAA). Since then, 18 states and the District of Columbia have adopted the RUAA, and the legislation has been introduced in four other states in 2017. Consider the Prefatory Note to the RUAA and various state statutes on possible state regulation of arbitration. The entire text of the RUAA is located at Appendix B.

Revised Uniform Arbitration Act
Commentary (2000)

Prefatory Note

A primary purpose of the 1955 Act was to insure the enforceability of agreements to arbitrate in the face of oftentimes hostile state law. That goal has been accomplished. Today arbitration is a primary mechanism favored by courts and parties to resolve disputes in many areas of the law. This growth in arbitration caused the Conference to appoint a Drafting Committee to consider revising the Act in light of the increasing use of arbitration, the greater complexity of many disputes resolved by arbitration, and the developments of the law in this area.

The UAA did not address many issues which arise in modern arbitration cases. The statute provided no guidance as to (1) who decides the arbitrability of a dispute and by what criteria; (2) whether a court or arbitrators may issue provisional remedies; (3) how a party can initiate an arbitration proceeding; (4) whether arbitration proceedings may be consolidated; (5) whether arbitrators are required to disclose facts reasonably likely to affect impartiality; (6) what extent arbitrators or an arbitration organization are immune from civil actions; (7) whether arbitrators or representatives of arbitration organizations may be required to testify in another proceeding; (8) whether arbitrators have the discretion to order discovery, issue protective orders, decide motions for summary dispositions, hold prehearing conferences and otherwise manage the arbitration process; (9) when a court may enforce a preaward ruling by an arbitrator; (10) what remedies an arbitrator may award, especially in regard to attorneys' fees, punitive damages or other exemplary relief; (11) when a court can award attorney's fees and costs to arbitrators and arbitration organizations; (12) when a court can award attorney's fees and costs to a prevailing party in an appeal of an arbitrator's award; and (13) which sections of the UAA would not be waivable, an important matter to insure fundamental fairness to the parties will be preserved, particularly in those instances where one party may have significantly less bargaining power than another; and (14) the use of electronic information and other modern means of technology in the arbitration process. The Revised Uniform Arbitration Act (RUAA) examines all of these issues and provides state legislatures with a more up-to-date statute to resolve disputes through arbitration.

In light of a number of decisions by the United States Supreme Court concerning the Federal Arbitration Act (FAA), any revision of the UAA must take into account the doctrine of preemption. The rule of preemption, whereby FAA standards and the emphatically pro-arbitration perspective of the FAA control, applies in both the federal courts and the state courts. To date, the preemption-related opinions of the Supreme Court have centered in large part on the two key issues that arise at the front end of the arbitration process — enforcement of the agreement to arbitrate and issues of substantive arbitrability. *Prima Paint Corp. v. Flood & Conklin Mfg. Co.*, 388 U.S. 35 (1967); *Moses H. Cone Mem'l Hosp. v. Mercury Constr. Corp.*, 460 U.S. 1 (1983); *Southland Corp. v. Keating*, 465 U.S. 2 (1984); *Perry v. Thomas*, 482 U.S. 483 (1987); *Allied-Bruce Terminix Cos. v. Dobson*, 513 U.S. 265 (1995); *Doctor's Assocs. v. Cassarotto*, 517 U.S. 681 (1996). That body of case law establishes that state law of any ilk, including adaptations of the RUAA, mooting or limiting contractual agreements to arbitrate must yield to the pro-arbitration public policy voiced in sections 2, 3, and 4 of the FAA....

[T]here are other areas of arbitration law where the FAA does not preempt state law, in the absence of definitive federal law set out in the FAA or determined by the federal courts. First, the Supreme Court has made clear its belief that ascertaining when a particular contractual agreement to arbitrate is enforceable is a matter to be decided under the general contract law principles of each State. The sole limitation on state law in that regard is the Court's assertion that the enforceability of arbitration agreements must be determined by the same standards as are used for all other contracts. *Terminix*, 513 U.S. at 281 (1995); and *Cassarotto*, 517 U.S. at 688. Arbitration agreements may not be invalidated under state laws applicable only to arbitration provisions. The FAA will preempt state law that does not place arbitration agreements on an "equal footing" with other contracts....

It is likely that matters not addressed in the FAA are also open to regulation by the States. State law provisions regulating purely procedural dimensions of the arbitration process (e.g., discovery [RUAA § 17], consolidation of claims [RUAA § 10], and arbitrator immunity [RUAA § 14]) likely will not be subject to preemption. Less certain is the effect of FAA preemption with regard to substantive issues like the authority of arbitrators to award punitive damages (RUAA § 21) and the standards for arbitrator disclosure of potential conflicts of interest (RUAA § 12) that have a significant impact on the integrity and/or the adequacy of the arbitration process. These "borderline" issues are not purely procedural in nature but unlike the "front end" and "back end" issues they do not go to the essence of the agreement to arbitrate or effectuation of the arbitral result. Although there is no concrete guidance in the case law, preemption of state law dealing with such matters seems unlikely as long as it cannot be characterized as anti-arbitration or as intended to limit the enforceability or viability of agreements to arbitrate.

a. Select State Arbitration Laws

As a point of comparison to the FAA, consider the following state laws dealing with arbitration procedure. How are these laws similar to or different from the FAA? Before you started this class, what did you think arbitration laws would cover? Does the FAA cover those items? Do these sample state laws cover those items?

California Code of Civil Procedure § 1282.2

Unless the arbitration agreement otherwise provides, or unless the parties to the arbitration otherwise provide by an agreement which is not contrary to the arbitration agreement as made or as modified by all the parties thereto:

(a)(1) The neutral arbitrator shall appoint a time and place for the hearing and cause notice thereof to be served personally or by registered or certified mail on the parties to the arbitration and on the other arbitrators not less than seven days before the hearing. Appearance at the hearing waives the right to notice.

(2) ... [I]n the event the aggregate amount in controversy exceeds fifty thousand dollars ($50,000) and the arbitrator is informed thereof by any party in writing by personal service, registered or certified mail, prior to designating a time and place of hearing pursuant to paragraph (1), the neutral arbitrator by the means prescribed in paragraph (1) shall appoint a time and place for hearing not less than 60 days before the hearing, and the following provisions shall apply:

(A) Either party shall within 15 days of receipt of the notice of hearing have the right to demand in writing, served personally or by registered or certified mail, that the other party provide a list of witnesses it intends to call designating which witnesses will be called as expert witnesses and a list of documents it intends to introduce at the hearing provided that the demanding party provides such lists at the time of its demand. A copy of such demand and the demanding party's lists shall be served on the arbitrator.

(B) Such lists shall be served personally or by registered or certified mail on the requesting party 15 days thereafter. Copies thereof shall be served on the arbitrator.

(C) Listed documents shall be made available for inspection and copying at reasonable times prior to the hearing.

(D) Time limits provided herein may be waived by mutual agreement of the parties if approved by the arbitrator.

(E) The failure to list a witness or a document shall not bar the testimony of an unlisted witness or the introduction of an undesignated document at the hearing, provided that good cause for omission from the requirements of subparagraph (A) is shown, as determined by the arbitrator.

(F) The authority of the arbitrator to administer and enforce this paragraph shall be as provided in subdivisions (b) to (e), inclusive, of Section 1283.05.

(b) The neutral arbitrator may adjourn the hearing from time to time as necessary....

(c) The neutral arbitrator shall preside at the hearing, shall rule on the admission and exclusion of evidence and on questions of hearing procedure and shall exercise all powers relating to the conduct of the hearing.

(d) The parties to the arbitration are entitled to be heard, to present evidence and to cross-examine witnesses appearing at the hearing, but rules of evidence and rules of judicial procedure need not be observed. On request of any party to the arbitration, the testimony of witnesses shall be given under oath.

(e) If a court has ordered a person to arbitrate a controversy, the arbitrators may hear and determine the controversy upon the evidence produced notwithstanding the failure of a party ordered to arbitrate, who has been duly notified, to appear.

(f) If an arbitrator, who has been duly notified, for any reason fails to participate in the arbitration, the arbitration shall continue but only the remaining neutral arbitrator or neutral arbitrators may make the award.

(g) If a neutral arbitrator intends to base an award upon information not obtained at the hearing, he shall disclose the information to all parties to the arbitration and give the parties an opportunity to meet it.

Montana Code Annotated 27-5-213

Unless otherwise provided by the agreement, the following apply:

(1) The arbitrators shall appoint a time and place for the hearing and cause notification to the parties to be served personally or by certified mail not less than 5 days

before the hearing. Appearance at the hearing waives such notice. The arbitrators may adjourn the hearing from time to time as necessary and, on request of a party and for good cause or upon their own motion, may postpone the hearing to a time not later than the date fixed by the agreement for making the award unless the parties consent to a later date. The arbitrators may hear and determine the controversy upon the evidence produced, notwithstanding the failure of a party duly notified to appear. The district court on application may direct the arbitrators to proceed promptly with the hearing and determination of the controversy.

(2) The parties are entitled to be heard, present evidence material to the controversy, and cross-examine witnesses appearing at the hearing.

(3) The hearing must be conducted by all the arbitrators, but a majority may determine any question and render a final award. If during the course of the hearing an arbitrator for any reason ceases to act, the remaining arbitrator or arbitrators appointed to act as neutrals may continue with the hearing and determination of the controversy.

Vernon's Texas Statutes and Codes Annotated § 171.047

Unless otherwise provided by the agreement to arbitrate, a party at the hearing is entitled to:

(1) be heard;

(2) present evidence material to the controversy; and

(3) cross-examine any witness.

Wisconsin Statutes Annotated, 788.07

Upon petition, approved by the arbitrators or by a majority of them, any court of record in and for the county in which such arbitrators, or a majority of them, are sitting may direct the taking of depositions to be used as evidence before the arbitrators, in the same manner and for the same reasons as provided by law for the taking of depositions in suits or proceedings pending in the courts of record in this state.

4. Comments and Questions

a. Compare the range of subjects covered by the FAA and those covered by the RUAA or other state law. What role *should* the states have in regulating arbitration? Is there room for both the state and the federal government to regulate arbitration?

b. How much *should* any government regulate arbitration? Alternatively, how much of arbitration practice should be regulated by parties' own agreements to arbitrate?

c. The laws governing arbitration are generally considered default rules if the parties do not contract otherwise. How often do you think that parties actually negotiate the arbitration clauses in contracts? Do you think that the likelihood of a negotiated agreement to arbitrate is more likely in a business-to-business dispute or a business-to-consumer dispute?

d. Given the FAA's preemptive effect (which is discussed in detail in the next section), does state arbitration law matter? *See* Kristen M. Blankley, *Impact Preemption: A New Theory of Federal Arbitration Act Preemption*, 67 FLA. L. REV. 711 (2015) (arguing that post-*Concepcion*, the United States Supreme Court has created a unique type of preemption for the FAA that goes beyond the conflict-style preemption it claims it is applying); Stephen K. Huber, *State Regulation of Arbitration Proceedings: Judicial Review of Arbitration Awards by State Courts*, 10 CARDOZO J. CONFLICT RESOL. 509 (2009); Maureen A. Weston, *The Other Avenues of Hall Street*, 7 LEWIS & CLARK L.J. 930, 943–47 (2010) (arguing that state law becomes more relevant after *Hall Street*'s ruling that private parties may not contract to expand judicial review beyond the grounds set forth in the FAA, in that expanded review may be available under state arbitration law).

C. FAA Preemption of State Law

Under the Supremacy Clause of the U.S. Constitution, federal law preempts, and thus invalidates, conflicting state law. Preemption generally falls within three categories: (1) express preemption, when a statute explicitly states that the statute has preemptive power, (2) field preemption, when Congress so pervasively regulates a field, and (3) conflict preemption, when a federal law and state law conflict. The FAA does not contain express preemption language, and the short statute would not occupy the field of arbitration. Only conflict preemption can apply to the FAA.

FAA § 2 provides that "[a] written provision in any maritime transaction or a contract evidencing a transaction *involving commerce* to settle by arbitration ... shall be valid, irrevocable, and enforceable, save upon such grounds as exist at law or in equity for the revocation of any contract." (emphasis added). The following cases interpret this statutory language in considering the FAA's scope and preemptive effect on state laws. As you read these cases, consider the policies underlying the FAA, such as enforcement of arbitration agreements and efficiency, and whether those policies are being served. You should also consider the competing policies underlying state regulation, such as consumer protection, and which policies should prevail.

Southland Corporation v. Keating

465 U.S. 1 (1984)

CHIEF JUSTICE BURGER delivered the opinion of the Court.

We noted probable jurisdiction to consider (a) whether the California Franchise Investment Law, which invalidates certain arbitration agreements covered by the FAA violates the Supremacy Clause and (b) whether arbitration under the Federal Act is impaired when a class action structure is imposed on the process by the state courts. Southland Corporation is the owner and franchisor of 7-Eleven convenience stores.... Appellees are 7-Eleven franchisees. [Their contracts called for arbitration of all claims or controversies.] ...

The California Franchise Investment Law provides: "Any condition, stipulation or provision purporting to bind any person acquiring any franchise to waive compliance with any provision of this law or any rule or order hereunder is void." The California Supreme Court interpreted this statute to require judicial consideration of claims brought under the State statute and accordingly refused to enforce the parties' contract to arbitrate such claims. So interpreted the California Franchise Investment Law directly conflicts with section 2 of the FAA and violates the Supremacy Clause.

In enacting section 2 of the federal Act, Congress declared a national policy favoring arbitration and withdrew the power of the states to require a judicial forum for the resolution of claims which the contracting parties agreed to resolve by arbitration....

The FAA rests on the authority of Congress to enact substantive rules under the Commerce Clause. In *Prima Paint Corp. v. Flood & Conklin Mfg. Corp.*, 388 U.S. 395 (1967), the Court examined the legislative history of the Act and concluded that the statute "is based upon ... the incontestable federal foundations of control over interstate commerce and over admiralty." The contract in *Prima Paint*, as here, contained an arbitration clause. One party in that case alleged that the other had committed fraud in the inducement of the contract, although not of the arbitration clause in particular, and sought to have the claim of fraud adjudicated in federal court. The Court held that, notwithstanding a contrary state rule, consideration of a claim of fraud in the inducement of a contract "is for the arbitrators and not for the courts." The Court relied for this holding on Congress' broad power to fashion substantive rules under the Commerce Clause.

At least since 1824 Congress' authority under the Commerce Clause has been held plenary. *Gibbons v. Ogden*, 22 U.S. 1 (1824). The statements of the Court in *Prima Paint* that the FAA was an exercise of the Commerce Clause power clearly implied that the substantive rules of the Act were to apply in state as well as federal courts.... In *Moses H. Cone Memorial Hospital* ... we reaffirmed our view that the FAA "creates a body of federal substantive law" and expressly stated what was implicit in *Prima Paint*, i.e., the substantive law the Act created was applicable in state and federal court.

Although the legislative history is not without ambiguities, there are strong indications that Congress had in mind something more than making arbitration agreements enforceable only in the federal courts. The House Report plainly suggests the more comprehensive objectives: "The purpose of this bill is to make valid and enforceable agreements for arbitration contained in contracts involving interstate commerce or within the jurisdiction of admiralty, or which may be the subject of litigation in the Federal courts."

This broader purpose can also be inferred from the reality that Congress would be less likely to address a problem whose impact was confined to federal courts than a problem of large significance in the field of commerce. The Arbitration Act sought to "overcome the rule of equity, that equity will not specifically enforce any arbitration agreement." The House Report accompanying the bill stated: "[t]he need for the law arises from ... the jealousy of the English courts for their own jurisdiction.... This jealousy survived for so lon[g] a period that the principle became firmly embedded in the English common law and was adopted with it by the American courts. The courts have felt that the precedent was too strongly fixed to be overturned without legislative enactment...." Surely this makes clear that the House Report contemplated a broad reach of the Act, unencumbered by state law constraints....

Justice O'CONNOR argues that Congress viewed the Arbitration Act "as a procedural statute, applicable only in federal courts." If it is correct that Congress sought only to create a procedural remedy in the federal courts, there can be no explanation for the express limitation in the Arbitration Act to contracts "involving commerce." For example, when Congress has authorized this Court to prescribe the rules of procedure in the federal Courts of Appeals, District Courts, and bankruptcy courts, it has not limited the power of the Court to prescribe rules applicable only to causes of action involving commerce. We would expect that if Congress, in enacting the Arbitration Act, was creating what it thought to be a procedural rule applicable only in federal courts, it would not so limit the Act to transactions involving commerce.

On the other hand, Congress would need to call on the Commerce Clause if it intended the Act to apply in state courts. Yet at the same time, its reach would be limited to transactions involving interstate commerce. We therefore view the "involving commerce" requirement in section 2, not as an inexplicable limitation on the power of the federal courts, but as a necessary qualification on a statute intended to apply in state and federal courts.

Under the interpretation of the Arbitration Act urged by Justice O'Connor, claims brought under the California Franchise Investment Law are not arbitrable when they are raised in state court. Yet it is clear beyond question that if this suit had been brought as a diversity action in a federal district court, the arbitration clause would have been enforceable. The interpretation given to the Arbitration Act by the California Supreme Court would therefore encourage and reward forum shopping. We are unwilling to attribute to Congress the intent, in drawing on the comprehensive powers of the Commerce Clause, to create a right to enforce an arbitration contract and yet make the right dependent for its enforcement on the particular forum in which it is asserted. And since the overwhelming proportion of all civil litigation in this country is in the state courts, we cannot believe Congress intended to limit the Arbitration Act to disputes subject only to federal court jurisdiction. Such an interpretation would frustrate Congressional intent to place "[a]n arbitration agreement ... upon the same footing as other contracts, where it belongs."

In creating a substantive rule applicable in state as well as federal courts, Congress intended to foreclose state legislative attempts to undercut the enforceability of arbitration agreements. We hold that section 31512 of the California Franchise Investment Law violates the Supremacy Clause. The judgment of the California Supreme Court denying enforcement of the arbitration agreement is reversed....

JUSTICE STEVENS, concurring in part and dissenting in part.

The Court holds that an arbitration clause that is enforceable in an action in a federal court is equally enforceable if the action is brought in a state court. I agree with that conclusion. Although Justice O'Connor's review of the legislative history of the FAA demonstrates that the 1925 Congress that enacted the statute viewed the statute as essentially procedural in nature, I am persuaded that the intervening developments in the law compel the conclusion that the Court has reached....

I am nevertheless troubled by one aspect of the case that seems to trouble none of my colleagues. For me it is not "clear beyond question that if this suit had been brought as a diversity action in a Federal District Court, the arbitration clause would have been enforceable." The general rule prescribed by section 2 of the FAA is that arbitration clauses in contracts involving interstate transactions are enforceable as a matter of federal law. That general rule, however, is subject to an exception based on "such grounds as exist at law or in equity for the revocation of any contract." I believe that exception leaves room for the implementation of certain substantive state policies that would be undermined by enforcing certain categories of arbitration clauses.

The exercise of State authority in a field traditionally occupied by State law will not be deemed preempted by a federal statute unless that was the clear and manifest purpose of Congress. Moreover, even where a federal statute does displace State authority, it "rarely occupies a legal field completely, totally excluding all participation by the legal systems of the states.... Federal legislation, on the whole, has been conceived and drafted on an ad hoc basis to accomplish limited objectives. It builds upon legal relationships established by the states, altering or supplanting them only so far as necessary for the special purpose."

The limited objective of the FAA was to abrogate the general common law rule against specific enforcement of arbitration agreements, and a state statute which merely codified the general common law rule — either directly by employing the prior doctrine of revocability or indirectly by declaring all such agreements void — would be preempted by the Act. However, beyond this conclusion, which seems compelled by the language of section 2 and case law concerning the Act, it is by no means clear that Congress intended entirely to displace State authority in this field. Indeed, while it is an understatement to say that "the legislative history of the ... Act ... reveals little awareness on the part of Congress that state law might be affected," it must surely be true that given the lack of a "clear mandate from Congress as to the extent to which state statutes and decisions are to be superseded, we must be cautious in construing the act lest we excessively encroach on the powers which Congressional policy, if not the Constitution, would reserve to the states."

The textual basis in the Act for avoiding such encroachment is the provision of section 2 which provides that arbitration agreements are subject to revocation on such grounds as exist at law or in equity for the revocation of any contract. The Act, however, does not define what grounds for revocation may be permissible, and hence it would appear that the judiciary must fashion the limitations as a matter of federal common law. *Cf. Textile Workers v. Lincoln Mills*, 353 U.S. 448 (1957). In doing so, we must first recognize that as the "saving clause in section 2 indicates, the purpose of Congress in 1925 was to make arbitration agreements as enforceable as other contracts, but not more so." The existence of a federal statute enunciating a substantive federal policy does not necessarily require the inexorable application of a uniform federal rule of decision notwithstanding the differing conditions which may exist in the several States and regardless of the decisions of the States to exert police powers as they deem best for the welfare of their citizens....

A contract which is deemed void is surely revocable at law or in equity, and the California legislature has declared all conditions purporting to waive compliance with the protections of the Franchise Disclosure Act, including but not limited to arbitration provisions, void as a matter of public policy. Given the importance to the State of franchise relationships, the relative disparity in the bargaining positions between the franchisor and the franchisee, and the remedial purposes of the California Act, I believe this declaration of State policy is entitled to respect....

A state policy excluding wage claims from arbitration, *cf. Merrill Lynch, Pierce, Fenner & Smith v. Ware*, 414 U.S. 117 (1973), or a state policy of providing special protection for franchisees, such as that expressed in California's Franchise Investment Law, can be recognized without impairing the basic purposes of the federal statute. Like the majority of the California Supreme Court, I am not persuaded that Congress intended the pre-emptive effect of this statute to be "so unyielding as to require enforcement of an agreement to arbitrate a dispute over the application of a regulatory statute which a state legislature, in conformity with analogous federal policy, has decided should be left to judicial enforcement."

Thus, although I agree with most of the Court's reasoning and specifically with its jurisdictional holdings, I respectfully dissent from its conclusion concerning the enforceability of the arbitration agreement. On that issue, I would affirm the judgment of the California Supreme Court.

Justice O'Connor with whom Justice Rehnquist joins, dissenting.

Section 2 of the FAA provides that a written arbitration agreement "shall be valid, irrevocable, and enforceable, save upon such grounds as exist at law or in equity for the revocation of any contract." Section 2 does not, on its face, identify which judicial forums are bound by its requirements or what procedures govern its enforcement. The FAA deals with these matters in sections 3 and 4. Section 9, which addresses the enforcement of arbitration awards, is also relevant....

Today, the Court takes the facial silence of section 2 as a license to declare that state as well as federal courts must apply section 2. In addition, though this is not spelled out in the opinion, the Court holds that in enforcing this newly-discovered federal right state courts must follow procedures specified in section 3. The Court's decision is impelled by an understandable desire to encourage the use of arbitration, but it utterly fails to recognize the clear congressional intent underlying the FAA. Congress intended to require federal, not state, courts to respect arbitration agreements.

The FAA was enacted in 1925. As demonstrated below, Congress thought it was exercising its power to dictate either procedure or "general federal law" in federal courts. The issue presented here is the result of three subsequent decisions of this Court.

In 1938 this Court decided *Erie Railroad Co. v. Tompkins*, 304 U.S. 64. *Erie* denied the federal government the power to create substantive law solely by virtue of the Article III power to control federal court jurisdiction. Eighteen years later the Court decided *Bernhardt v. Polygraphic Co.*, 350 U.S. 198 (1956). *Bernhardt* held that the duty to arbitrate a contract dispute is outcome-determinative—i.e., "substantive"— and therefore a matter normally governed by state law in federal diversity cases.

Bernhardt gave rise to concern that the FAA could thereafter constitutionally be applied only in federal court cases arising under federal law, not in diversity cases. In *Prima Paint v. Flood & Conklin*, 388 U.S. 395 (1967), we addressed that concern, and held that the FAA may constitutionally be applied to proceedings in a federal diversity court. The FAA covers only contracts involving interstate commerce or maritime affairs, and Congress "plainly has the power to legislate" in that area.

Nevertheless, the *Prima Paint* decision "carefully avoided any explicit endorsement of the view that the Arbitration Act embodied substantive policies that were to be applied to all contracts within its scope, whether sued on in state or federal courts." Today's case is the first in which this Court has had occasion to determine whether the FAA applies to state court proceedings....

The majority opinion decides three issues. First, it holds that section 2 creates federal substantive rights that must be enforced by the state courts. Second, though the issue is not raised in this case, the Court states, that section 2 substantive rights may not be the basis for invoking federal court jurisdiction under 28 U.S.C. § 1331. Third, the Court reads section 2 to require state courts to enforce § 2 rights using procedures that mimic those specified for federal courts by FAA sections 3 and 4. The first of these conclusions is unquestionably wrong as a matter of statutory construction; the second appears to be an attempt to limit the damage done by the first; the third is unnecessary and unwise.

One rarely finds a legislative history as unambiguous as the FAA's. That history establishes conclusively that the 1925 Congress viewed the FAA as a procedural statute, applicable only in federal courts, derived, Congress believed, largely from the federal power to control the jurisdiction of the federal courts.

In 1925 Congress emphatically believed arbitration to be a matter of "procedure." At hearings on the Act congressional subcommittees were told: "The theory on which you do this is that you have the right to tell the Federal courts how to proceed." The House Report on the FAA stated: "Whether an agreement for arbitration shall be enforced or not is a question of procedure." ... If characterizing the FAA as procedural was not enough, the draftsmen of the Act, the House Report, and the early commentators all flatly stated that the Act was intended to affect only federal court proceedings....

Since *Bernhardt*, a right to arbitration has been characterized as "substantive," and that holding is not challenged here. But Congress in 1925 did not characterize the FAA as this Court did in 1956. Congress believed that the FAA established nothing more than a rule of procedure, a rule therefore applicable only in the federal courts....

Yet another indication that Congress did not intend the FAA to govern state court proceedings is found in the powers Congress relied on in passing the Act. The FAA might have been grounded on Congress's powers to regulate interstate and maritime affairs, since the Act extends only to contracts in those areas. There are, indeed, references in the legislative history to the corresponding federal powers. More numerous, however, are the references to Congress's pre-Erie power to prescribe "general law" applicable in all federal courts. At the congressional hearings, for example: "Congress rests solely upon its power to prescribe the jurisdiction and duties of the Federal courts."...

The structure of the FAA itself runs directly contrary to the reading the Court today gives to section 2. Sections 3 and 4 are the implementing provisions of the Act, and they expressly apply only to federal courts. Section 4 refers to the "United States district court[s]," and provides that it can be invoked only in a court that has jurisdiction under Title 28 of the United States Code. As originally enacted, section 3 referred, in the same terms as section 4, to "courts [or court] of the United States." There has since been a minor amendment in section 4's phrasing, but no substantive change in either section's limitation to federal courts....

Section 2, like the rest of the FAA, should have no application whatsoever in state courts. Assuming, to the contrary, that section 2 does create a federal right that the state courts must enforce, state courts should nonetheless be allowed, at least in the first instance, to fashion their own procedures for enforcing the right. Unfortunately, the Court seems to direct that the arbitration clause at issue here must be specifically enforced; apparently no other means of enforcement is permissible.

If my understanding of the Court's opinion is correct, the Court has made section 3 of the FAA binding on the state courts. But as we have noted, section 3 by its own terms governs only federal court proceedings. Moreover, if section 2, standing alone, creates a federal right to specific enforcement of arbitration agreements sections 3 and 4 are, of course, largely superfluous. And if section 2 implicitly incorporates sections 3 and 4 procedures for making arbitration agreements enforceable before arbitration begins, why not also section 9 procedures concerning venue, personal jurisdiction, and notice for enforcing an arbitrator's award after arbitration ends? One set of procedures is of little use without the other.

It is settled that a state court must honor federally created rights and that it may not unreasonably undermine them by invoking contrary local procedure.... But absent specific direction from Congress the state courts have always been permitted to apply their own reasonable procedures when enforcing federal rights.

Before we undertake to read a set of complex and mandatory procedures into section 2's brief and general language, we should at a minimum allow state courts and legislatures a chance to develop their own methods for enforcing the new federal rights. Some might choose to award compensatory or punitive damages for the violation of an arbitration agreement; some might award litigation costs to the party who remained willing to arbitrate; some might affirm the "validity and enforceability" of arbitration agreements in other ways. Any of these approaches could vindicate section 2 rights in a manner fully consonant with the language and background of that provision.

The unelaborated terms of section 2 certainly invite flexible enforcement. At common law many jurisdictions were hostile to arbitration agreements. That hostility was reflected in two different doctrines: "revocability," which allowed parties to repudiate arbitration agreements at any time before the arbitrator's award was made, and "invalidity" or "unenforceability," equivalent rules that flatly denied any remedy for the failure to honor an arbitration agreement. In contrast, common law jurisdictions that enforced arbitration agreements did so in at least three different ways— through actions for damages, actions for specific enforcement, or by enforcing sanctions imposed by trade and commercial associations on members who violated arbitration agreements. In 1925 a forum allowing any one of these remedies would have been thought to recognize the "validity" and "enforceability" of arbitration clauses....

In summary, even were I to accept the majority's reading of section 2, I would disagree with the Court's disposition of this case. After articulating the nature and scope of the federal right it discerns in section 2, the Court should remand to the state court, which has acted, heretofore, under a misapprehension of federal law. The state court should determine, at least in the first instance, what procedures it will follow to vindicate the newly articulated federal rights.

The Court rejects the idea of requiring the FAA to be applied only in federal courts partly out of concern with the problem of forum shopping. The concern is unfounded. Because the FAA makes the federal courts equally accessible to both parties to a dispute, no forum shopping would be possible even if we gave the FAA a construction faithful to the congressional intent. In controversies involving incomplete diversity of citizenship there is simply no access to federal court and therefore no possibility of forum shopping. In controversies with complete diversity of citizenship the FAA grants federal court access equally to both parties; no party can gain any advantage by forum shopping. Even when the party resisting arbitration initiates an action in state court, the opposing party can invoke FAA section 4 and promptly secure a federal court order to compel arbitration.

Ironically, the FAA was passed specifically to rectify forum shopping problems created by this Court's decision in *Swift v. Tyson*, 41 U.S. 1 (1842). By 1925 several major commercial states had passed state arbitration laws, but the federal courts refused to enforce those laws in diversity cases. The drafters of the FAA might have anticipated *Bernhardt* by legislation and required federal diversity courts to adopt the arbitration law of the state in which they sat. But they deliberately chose a different approach. As was pointed out at congressional hearings, an additional goal of the Act was to make arbitration agreements enforceable even in federal courts located in states that had no arbitration law. The drafters' plan for maintaining reasonable harmony between state and federal practices was not to bludgeon states into compliance, but rather to adopt a uniform federal law, patterned after New York's path-breaking state statute, and simultaneously to press for passage of coordinated state legislation....

Today's decision adds yet another chapter to the FAA's already colorful history. In 1842 this Court's ruling in *Swift v. Tyson* (1842) set up a major obstacle to the enforcement of state arbitration laws in federal diversity courts. In 1925 Congress sought to rectify the problem by enacting the FAA; the intent was to create uniform law binding only in the federal courts. In Erie (1938), and then in *Bernhardt* (1956), this Court significantly curtailed federal power. In 1967 our decision in *Prima Paint* upheld the application of the FAA in a federal court proceeding as a valid exercise of Congress's Commerce Clause and Admiralty powers. Today the Court discovers a federal right in FAA section 2 that the state courts must enforce. Apparently confident that state courts are not competent to devise their own procedures for protecting the newly discovered federal right, the Court summarily prescribes a specific procedure, found nowhere in section 2 or its common law origins, that the state courts are to follow.

Today's decision is unfaithful to congressional intent, unnecessary, and, in light of the FAA's antecedents and the intervening contraction of federal power, inexplicable. Although arbitration is a worthy alternative to litigation, today's exercise in judicial revisionism goes too far. I respectfully dissent.

1. Questions and Comments

a. What is the basis for the Court's holding in *Southland*, reversing the California Supreme Court, that the FAA preempted the antiwaiver provision in the California Franchise Investment Law?

b. Was *Southland v. Keating* wrongly decided? *See, e.g.,* David S. Schwartz, *Correcting Federalism Mistakes in Statutory Interpretation: The Supreme Court and the Federal Arbitration Act*, 67 LAW & CONTEMP. PROBS. 5 (2004) (noting that "no member of the *Southland* majority remained on the Court as of 1994, and five current members of the Court have at one time or another dissented from *Southland*...."); David S. Schwartz, *The Federal Arbitration Act and the Power of Congress over State Courts*, 83 OR. L. REV. 541 (2004) (asserting that "[t]he Federal Arbitration Act is unconstitutional as applied to the states—and no one has noticed ... FAA preemption is nothing more or less than procedural regulation of state courts, and ... Congress lacks the power to regulate procedures in state courts."); Paul D. Carrington & Paul H. Haagen, *Contract and Jurisdiction*, 1996 S. CT. REV. 331, 380 (1996) ("[T]the opinion of the Court was an extraordinarily disingenuous manipulation of the history of the 1925 Act"). *But see* Christopher R. Drahozal, *In Defense of*

Southland: Reexamining the Legislative History of the Federal Arbitration Act, 78 NOTRE DAME L. REV. 101 (2002) (arguing that the Supreme Court was correct in deciding *Southland*). If *Southland* were overruled, would the mixture of federal and state statutes be workable? How would you recommend Congress amend the FAA, if at all?

c. Despite the scholarly criticisms, perhaps *Southland* can be better understood in a historical context. *Southland* was not the first instance in which courts and scholars considered the powers under which Congress passed the FAA. Simply stated, if Congress passed the FAA under Congress' power to regulate interstate commerce (the "Commerce Power"), then the FAA would be "substantive" law with preemptive power over state laws. If Congress passed the FAA under the court's ability to regulate the courts, then the FAA would apply only in federal courts.

Congress passed the FAA prior to the Supreme Court's decision in *Erie Railroad Co. v. Tompkins*, 304 U.S. 64 (1938). The resulting "Erie doctrine" requires that federal courts apply substantive state law in diversity cases. Is arbitration a substantive law or a procedural law? This is a more difficult question to answer than it appears. If arbitration law is "substantive" under *Erie*, then state arbitration law would apply in federal court cases filed under diversity jurisdiction, and the FAA would apply only in federal cases filed under federal question jurisdiction.

This question appeared before the Court first in *Bernhardt v. Polygraphic Company of America, Inc.*, 350 U.S. 198 (1956). The *Bernhardt* Court suggested that arbitration law is "substantive" and that state law should apply in diversity cases *unless* Congress passed the FAA under its Commerce Power. The Court re-visited the issue in *Prima Paint v. Flood & Conklin Mfg. Co.*, 388 U.S. 395 (1967) (which is discussed in greater detail in **Chapter 3**). The *Prima Paint* Court specifically held that Congress passed the FAA under its Commerce Power. Unlike *Southland*, which originated in state court, the *Prima Paint* case originated in federal court under diversity jurisdiction. The *Prima Paint* Court was trying to determine if the FAA should apply in federal court in diversity cases — *not* whether the FAA would displace state arbitration law.

Does this history change your reaction to the Court's decision in *Southland*?

d. Consider how different approaches to interpreting a statute can influence the outcome of a case. Judges often use canons of construction to help guide their interpretation and application of a statute. These tools of construction can yield quite different outcomes. A helpful way to organize these rules of construction is in order of how "abstract" they are on a continuum or a "funnel of abstraction." *See* William N. Eskridge, Jr. et al., LEGISLATION: STATUTES AND THE CREATION OF PUBLIC POLICY (5th ed. 2014). The following is a simplified funnel with the lowest "rung" being most concrete to the highest "rung" being most abstract.

Policy — Considers how modern policies are implicated by different readings of the language?

History — Determines what Congress meant when it enacted the statute, taking into consideration the major issues of the day? This look at history is different and significantly broader than looking at the legislative history of a statute.

Canons of Statutory Interpretation — Sets forth basic rules and maxims that courts apply in interpreting statute. Common canons of statutory interpretation include the "Plain Meaning Rule," which states that if the words to a statute are clear and unambiguous, a court need not inquire further into the meaning or intent of the statute. The "Rule to Avoid Surplusage," assumes that each word used in a statute has meaning and thus an interpretation that would render a term redundant or meaningless should be rejected. "Ejusdem Generis" (of the same kind, class, nature) is interpreting a word in a statute consistent with similar words in a list around it, and "Expressio Unius is the statement of one thing excludes other things.

Legislative History — Examines the official legislative history of the Act. In contrast with textualism, an *intentionalism* approach tends to focus on legislative intent and history.

Consistency Among Acts — Considers how the court can read the language together with the language of similar types of legislation.

Whole Act Analysis — Assumes that legislatures draft statutes in an internally consistent manner and asks how terms and language used multiple times in a statute can be read together.

Textual Analysis/Plain Meaning — Focuses on the exact text or plain meaning of the words used in the statute to interpret meaning.

In *Southland v. Keating*, which tools of statutory interpretation did the different Justices use? legislative history

e. Because the *Southland* Court determined that Congress enacted the FAA under the Commerce Power, when does an agreement to arbitrate "evidence" a transaction "involving commerce"? The Court answered this question in *Allied-Bruce Terminix, Inc. v. Dobson*, 513 U.S. 265 (1995). Homeowners Mr. and Mrs. Dobson bought a house that had a Terminix termite protection plan. That plan included an arbitration agreement. The sellers transferred the termite plan to the Dobsons. Shortly after buying the house, the Dobsons discovered that the home had a termite infestation. Following an unsuccessful remediation, the Dobsons sued Terminix and the sellers in Alabama state court. Terminix moved to compel arbitration under the arbitration agreement in the termite protection plan.

At the time, Alabama state law invalidated any pre-dispute arbitration agreement in consumer contracts. The Alabama Supreme Court held that the arbitration clause was unenforceable under state law, and Terminix appealed to the U.S. Supreme Court. The question for the Supreme Court essentially asked: which contracts did Congress intend to cover under the FAA? Must the contracts involve "only persons or activities within the flow of interstate commerce," or something broader, such as conduct that is "affecting" interstate commerce?

What could be more local than a contract to remove termites from real property? How does this contract "involve" interstate commerce? The Supreme Court held that Congress intended to have the FAA apply to the fullest extent of the Commerce Power, and that the test for "involving commerce" and "evidencing a transaction" is broad. Under the facts of this case, the fact that Terminix is a national company and that pest control supplies crossed state lines to fulfill the contract was sufficient to show that the contract evidenced a transaction involving commerce under the FAA. Given the breadth of the FAA, the Court held that Alabama's law prohibiting pre-dispute arbitration agreements in consumer contracts was preempted.

Interestingly, in *Allied-Bruce*, Justices Scalia and Thomas issued separate dissents stating that they would support overruling *Southland v. Keating*. In later cases, such as *AT&T Mobility v. Concepcion*, Justice Scalia broadened the scope of the preemptive power of the FAA, and Justice Thomas was the deciding vote on the preemption issue.

Almost 20 years after *Southland*, in a case involving debt restructuring agreements, the Supreme Court reaffirmed its broad reading of the language "involving commerce." *See Citizens Bank v. Alafabco*, 539 U.S. 52 (2003).

If Congress passed the FAA under its Commerce Power, does it make sense for the Court to find that Congress intended the FAA to apply to nearly every type of contract? Can you imagine any contract in which parties might agree to arbitrate and the arbitration does not involve interstate commerce? What does this ruling mean about a state's ability to regulate arbitration for its own citizens? Should it matter that Congress enacted the FAA before the Supreme Court expanded the scope of the Commerce Power?

Doctor's Associates, Inc. v. Casarotto

517 U.S. 681 (1996)

JUSTICE GINSBURG delivered the opinion of the Court.

This case concerns a standard form franchise agreement for the operation of a Subway sandwich shop in Montana. When a dispute arose between parties to the agreement, franchisee Paul Casarotto sued franchisor Doctor's Associates, Inc. (DAI) and DAI's Montana development agent, Nick Lombardi, in a Montana state court. DAI and Lombardi sought to stop the litigation pending arbitration pursuant to the arbitration clause set out on page nine of the franchise agreement.

The FAA declares written provisions for arbitration "valid, irrevocable, and enforceable, save upon such grounds as exist at law or in equity for the revocation of any contract." 9 U.S.C. §2. Montana law, however, declares an arbitration clause unenforceable unless "[n]otice that [the] contract is subject to arbitration" is "typed in underlined capital letters on the first page of the contract." Mont. Code Ann. §27-5-114(4) (1995). The question here presented is whether Montana's law is compatible with the federal Act. We hold that Montana's first-page notice requirement, which governs not "any contract," but specifically and solely contracts "subject to arbitration," conflicts with the FA A and is therefore displaced by the federal measure.

Petitioner DAI is the national franchisor of Subway sandwich shops. In April 1988, DAI entered a franchise agreement with respondent Paul Casarotto, which permitted Casarotto to open a Subway shop in Great Falls, Montana. The franchise agreement stated, on page nine and in ordinary type: "Any controversy or claim arising out of or relating to this contract or the breach thereof shall be settled by Arbitration...."

In October 1992, Casarotto sued DAI and Lombardi, in Montana state court, alleging state-law contract and tort claims relating to the franchise agreement. DAI demanded arbitration of those claims, and successfully moved in the Montana trial court to stay the lawsuit pending arbitration.

The Montana Supreme Court reversed. *Casarotto v. Lombardi*, 886 P.2d 931 (1994). That court left undisturbed the trial court's findings that the franchise agreement fell within the scope of the FAA and covered the claims Casarotto stated against DAI and Lombardi. The Montana Supreme Court held, however, that Mont. Code Ann. §27-5-114(4) rendered the agreement's arbitration clause unenforceable. The Montana statute provides: "Notice that a contract is subject to arbitration ... shall be typed in underlined capital letters on the first page of the contract; and unless such notice is displayed thereon, the contract may not be subject to arbitration."

Notice of the arbitration clause in the franchise agreement did not appear on the first page of the contract. Nor was anything relating to the clause typed in underlined capital letters. Because the State's statutory notice requirement had not been met, the Montana Supreme Court declared the parties' dispute "not subject to arbitration."

DAI and Lombardi unsuccessfully argued before the Montana Supreme Court that §27-5-114(4) was preempted by §2 of the FAA. DAI and Lombardi dominantly relied on our decisions in *Southland* and *Perry v. Thomas*, 482 U.S. 483 (1987). In *Southland*, we held that §2 of the FAA applies in state as well as federal courts, and "withdr[aws] the power of the states to require a judicial forum for the resolution of claims which the contracting parties agreed to resolve by arbitration." We noted in the pathmarking *Southland* decision that the FAA established a "broad principle of enforceability," and that section 2 of the federal Act provided for revocation of arbitration agreements only upon "grounds as exist at law or in equity for the revocation of any contract." In *Perry*, we reiterated: "[S]tate law, whether of legislative or judicial origin, is applicable if that law arose to govern issues concerning the validity, revocability, and enforceability of contracts generally. A state-law principle that takes its meaning precisely from the fact that a contract to arbitrate is at issue does not comport with [section 2]."

The Montana Supreme Court, however, read our decision in *Volt Information Sciences, Inc. v. Board of Trustees*, 489 U.S. 468, (1989), as limiting the preemptive force of section 2 and correspondingly qualifying *Southland* and *Perry*. As the Montana Supreme Court comprehended *Volt*, the proper inquiry here should focus not on the bare words of section 2, but on this question: Would the application of Montana's notice requirement, contained in §27-5-114(4), "undermine the goals and policies of the FAA." Section 27-5-114(4), in the Montana court's judgment, did not undermine the goals and policies of the FAA, for the notice requirement did not preclude arbitration agreements altogether; it simply prescribed "that before arbitration agreements are enforceable, they be entered knowingly." DAI and Lombardi petitioned for certiorari. Last Term, we granted their petition, vacated the judgment of the Montana Supreme Court, and remanded for further consideration in light of *Allied-Bruce*. In *Allied-Bruce*, we restated what our decisions in *Southland* and *Perry* had established: "States may regulate contracts, including arbitration clauses, under general contract law principles and they may invalidate an arbitration clause 'upon such grounds as exist at law or in equity for the revocation of any contract.' What States may not do is decide that a contract is fair enough to enforce all its basic terms (price, service, credit), but not fair enough to enforce its arbitration clause. The Act makes any such state policy unlawful, for that kind of policy would place arbitration clauses on an unequal footing, directly contrary to the Act's language and Congress's intent."

On remand, without inviting or permitting further briefing or oral argument, the Montana Supreme Court adhered to its original ruling. [Dissenting Justice Gray thought it "cavalier" of her colleagues to ignore the defendants' request for an "opportunity to brief the issues raised by the ... remand and to present oral argument."] The court stated: "After careful review, we can find nothing in the [*Allied-Bruce*] decision which relates to the issues presented to this Court in this case." Elaborating, the Montana court said it found "no suggestion in [*Allied-Bruce*] that the principles from *Volt* on which we relied have been modified in any way." We again granted certiorari, and now reverse.

Section 2 of the FAA provides that written arbitration agreements "shall be valid, irrevocable, and enforceable, save upon such grounds as exist at law or in equity for the revocation of any contract." Repeating our observation in *Perry*, the text of section 2 declares that state law may be applied "if that law arose to govern issues concerning the validity, revocability, and enforceability of contracts generally." Thus, generally applicable contract defenses, such as fraud, duress or unconscionability, may be applied to invalidate arbitration agreements without contravening section 2.

Courts may not, however, invalidate arbitration agreements under state laws applicable only to arbitration provisions. By enacting section 2, we have several times said, Congress precluded States from singling out arbitration provisions for suspect status, requiring instead that such provisions be placed "upon the same footing as other contracts." Montana's section 27-5-114(4) directly conflicts with section 2 of the FAA because the State's law conditions the enforceability of arbitration agreements on compliance with a special notice requirement not applicable to contracts generally.

The FAA thus displaces the Montana statute with respect to arbitration agreements covered by the Act.

At oral argument, counsel for Casarotto urged a broader view, under which § 27-5-114(4) might be regarded as harmless surplus. Montana could have invalidated the arbitration clause in the franchise agreement under general, informed consent principles, counsel suggested. She asked us to regard § 27-5-114(4) as but one illustration of a cross-the-board rule: unexpected provisions in adhesion contracts must be conspicuous. But the Montana Supreme Court announced no such sweeping rule. The court did not assert as a basis for its decision a generally applicable principle of "reasonable expectations" governing any standard form contract term. Montana's decision trains on and upholds a particular statute, one setting out a precise, arbitration-specific limitation. We review that disposition, and no other. It bears reiteration, however, that a court may not "rely on the uniqueness of an agreement to arbitrate as a basis for a state-law holding that enforcement would be unconscionable, for this would enable the court to effect what ... the state legislature cannot."

The Montana Supreme Court misread our *Volt* decision and therefore reached a conclusion in this case at odds with our rulings. *Volt* involved an arbitration agreement that incorporated state procedural rules, one of which, on the facts of that case, called for arbitration to be stayed pending the resolution of a related judicial proceeding. The state rule examined in *Volt* determined only the efficient order of proceedings; it did not affect the enforceability of the arbitration agreement itself. We held that applying the state rule would not "undermine the goals and policies of the FAA," because the very purpose of the Act was to "ensur[e] that private agreements to arbitrate are enforced according to their terms."

Applying § 27-5-114(4) here, in contrast, would not enforce the arbitration clause in the contract between DAI and Casarotto; instead, Montana's first-page notice requirement would invalidate the clause. The "goals and policies" of the FAA, this Court's precedent indicates, are antithetical to threshold limitations placed specifically and solely on arbitration provisions....

Section 27-5-114(4) of Montana's law places arbitration agreements in a class apart from "any contract," and singularly limits their validity. The State's prescription is thus inconsonant with, and is therefore preempted by, the federal law.... [R]eversed....

AT&T Mobility LLC v. Concepcion

536 U.S. 333 (2010)

Justice Scalia delivered the opinion of the Court.

I

[The Concepcions entered into contracts with AT&T (then Cingular) for wireless cellular phone service. When they entered into the contract, they were offered a "free" telephone, but AT&T charged the Concepcions $30.22 in sales taxes on the "free" phone. The Concepcions filed suit, despite the presence of an arbitration clause in their contract. They argued that the arbitration clause was unconscionable because it included a class action waiver.

The district court denied AT&T's motion to compel arbitration, applying the California Supreme Court's test in *Discover Bank v. Superior Court*, 113 P.3d 1100 (Cal. 2005). Under *Discover Bank*, a class action waiver can be invalidated if the consumer meets the following test: (1) the waiver is found in a contract of adhesion, (2) disputes between the parties predictably involve small amounts of damages, and (3) the party challenging the agreement alleges that the party with more bargaining power alleges a scheme to deliberately cheat a large number of people out of a small amount of money. The U.S. Supreme Court grated certiorari to determine whether the *Discovery Bank* test is preempted by the FAA.]

III

B

The "principal purpose" of the FAA is to "ensur[e] that private arbitration agreements are enforced according to their terms." This purpose is readily apparent from the FAA's text. Section 2 makes arbitration agreements "valid, irrevocable, and enforceable" as written (subject, of course, to the saving clause); § 3 requires courts to stay litigation of arbitral claims pending arbitration of those claims "in accordance with the terms of the agreement"; and § 4 requires courts to compel arbitration "in accordance with the terms of the agreement" upon the motion of either party to the agreement (assuming that the "making of the arbitration agreement or the failure ... to perform the same" is not at issue).

The point of affording parties discretion in designing arbitration processes is to allow for efficient, streamlined procedures tailored to the type of dispute. It can be specified, for example, that the decisionmaker be a specialist in the relevant field, or that proceedings be kept confidential to protect trade secrets. And the informality of arbitral proceedings is itself desirable, reducing the cost and increasing the speed of dispute resolution....

Contrary to the dissent's view, our cases place it beyond dispute that the FAA was designed to promote arbitration. They have repeatedly described the Act as "embod[ying a] national policy favoring arbitration," and "a liberal federal policy favoring arbitration agreements, notwithstanding any state substantive or procedural policies to the contrary." Thus, in *Preston v. Ferrer*, holding preempted a state-law rule requiring exhaustion of administrative remedies before arbitration, we said: "A prime objective of an agreement to arbitrate is to achieve 'streamlined proceedings and expeditious results,'" which objective would be "frustrated" by requiring a dispute to be heard by an agency first. 552 U.S., at 357–358. That rule, we said, would "at the least, hinder speedy resolution of the controversy."

California's *Discover Bank* rule similarly interferes with arbitration. Although the rule does not *require* classwide arbitration, it allows any party to a consumer contract to demand it *ex post*. The rule is limited to adhesion contracts, but the times in which consumer contracts were anything other than adhesive are long past.

The rule also requires that damages be predictably small, and that the consumer allege a scheme to cheat consumers. The former requirement, however, is toothless and malleable (the Ninth Circuit has held that damages of $4,000 are sufficiently small, and the latter has no limiting effect, as all that is required is an allegation). Consumers remain free to bring and resolve their disputes on a bilateral basis under *Discover Bank,* and some may well do so; but there is little incentive for lawyers to arbitrate on behalf of individuals when they may do so for a class and reap far higher fees in the process. And faced with inevitable class arbitration, companies would have less incentive to continue resolving potentially duplicative claims on an individual basis.

Although we have had little occasion to examine classwide arbitration, our decision in *Stolt-Nielsen* is instructive. In that case we held that an arbitration panel exceeded its power under § 10(a)(4) of the FAA by imposing class procedures based on policy judgments rather than the arbitration agreement itself or some background principle of contract law that would affect its interpretation. We then held that the agreement at issue, which was silent on the question of class procedures, could not be interpreted to allow them because the "changes brought about by the shift from bilateral arbitration to class-action arbitration" are "fundamental." This is obvious as a structural matter: Classwide arbitration includes absent parties, necessitating additional and different procedures and involving higher stakes. Confidentiality becomes more difficult. And while it is theoretically possible to select an arbitrator with some expertise relevant to the class-certification question, arbitrators are not generally knowledgeable in the often-dominant procedural aspects of certification, such as the protection of absent parties. The conclusion follows that class arbitration, to the extent it is manufactured by *Discover Bank* rather than consensual, is inconsistent with the FAA.

First, the switch from bilateral to class arbitration sacrifices the principal advantage of arbitration—its informality—and makes the process slower, more costly, and more likely to generate procedural morass than final judgment. "In bilateral arbitration, parties forgo the procedural rigor and appellate review of the courts in order to realize the benefits of private dispute resolution: lower costs, greater efficiency and speed, and the ability to choose expert adjudicators to resolve specialized disputes."

Second, class arbitration *requires* procedural formality. The AAA's rules governing class arbitrations mimic the Federal Rules of Civil Procedure for class litigation. Compare AAA, Supplementary Rules for Class Arbitrations (effective Oct. 8, 2003), with Fed. Rule Civ. Proc. 23. And while parties can alter those procedures by contract, an alternative is not obvious. If procedures are too informal, absent class members would not be bound by the arbitration. For a class-action money judgment to bind absentees in litigation, class representatives must at all times adequately represent absent class members, and absent members must be afforded notice, an opportunity to be heard, and a right to opt out of the class. At least this amount of process would presumably be required for absent parties to be bound by the results of arbitration.

We find it unlikely that in passing the FAA Congress meant to leave the disposition of these procedural requirements to an arbitrator. Indeed, class arbitration was not even envisioned by Congress when it passed the FAA in 1925; as the California Supreme Court admitted in *Discover Bank,* class arbitration is a "relatively recent development." And it is at the very least odd to think that an arbitrator would be entrusted with ensuring that third parties' due process rights are satisfied.

Third, class arbitration greatly increases risks to defendants. Informal procedures do of course have a cost: The absence of multilayered review makes it more likely that errors will go uncorrected. Defendants are willing to accept the costs of these errors in arbitration, since their impact is limited to the size of individual disputes, and presumably outweighed by savings from avoiding the courts. But when damages allegedly owed to tens of thousands of potential claimants are aggregated and decided at once, the risk of an error will often become unacceptable. Faced with even a small chance of a devastating loss, defendants will be pressured into settling questionable claims.... Arbitration is poorly suited to the higher stakes of class litigation....

The Concepcions contend that because parties may and sometimes do agree to aggregation, class procedures are not necessarily incompatible with arbitration. But the same could be said about procedures that the Concepcions admit States may not superimpose on arbitration: Parties *could* agree to arbitrate pursuant to the Federal Rules of Civil Procedure, or pursuant to a discovery process rivaling that in litigation. Arbitration is a matter of contract, and the FAA requires courts to honor parties' expectations. But what the parties in the aforementioned examples would have agreed to is not arbitration as envisioned by the FAA, lacks its benefits, and therefore may not be required by state law.

* * *

Because it "stands as an obstacle to the accomplishment and execution of the full purposes and objectives of Congress," California's *Discover Bank* rule is preempted by the FAA....

It is so ordered.

Justice THOMAS, concurring.

* * *

To clarify the meaning of § 2, it would be natural to look to other portions of the FAA. Statutory interpretation focuses on "the language itself, the specific context in which that language is used, and the broader context of the statute as a whole." "A provision that may seem ambiguous in isolation is often clarified by the remainder of the statutory scheme ... because only one of the permissible meanings produces a substantive effect that is compatible with the rest of the law." ...

Reading §§ 2 and 4 harmoniously, the "grounds ... for the revocation" preserved in § 2 would mean grounds related to the making of the agreement. This would require enforcement of an agreement to arbitrate unless a party successfully asserts a defense concerning the formation of the agreement to arbitrate, such as fraud, duress, or mutual mistake. Contract defenses unrelated to the making of the agreement — such as public policy — could not be the basis for declining to enforce an arbitration clause....

[The] *Discover Bank* rule is not a "groun[d] ... for the revocation of any contract" as I would read § 2 of the FAA in light of § 4. Under this reading, the FAA dictates that the arbitration agreement here be enforced and the *Discover Bank* rule is pre-empted.

Justice BREYER, with whom Justice GINSBURG, Justice SOTOMAYOR, and Justice KAGAN join, dissenting.

The *Discover Bank* rule does not create a "blanket policy in California against class action waivers in the consumer context." Instead, it represents the "application of a more general [unconscionability] principle." Courts applying California law have enforced class-action waivers where they satisfy general unconscionability standards. And even when they fail, the parties remain free to devise other dispute mechanisms, including informal mechanisms, that, in context, will not prove unconscionable.

II

A

The *Discover Bank* rule is consistent with the federal Act's language. It "applies equally to class action litigation waivers in contracts without arbitration agreements as it does to class arbitration waivers in contracts with such agreements." Linguistically speaking, it falls directly within the scope of the Act's exception permitting courts to refuse to enforce arbitration agreements on grounds that exist "for the revocation of *any* contract." The majority agrees.

B

The *Discover Bank* rule is also consistent with the basic "purpose behind" the Act.... Congress was fully aware that arbitration could provide procedural and cost advantages. The House Report emphasized the "appropriate[ness]" of making arbitration agreements enforceable "at this time when there is so much agitation against the costliness and delays of litigation." And this Court has acknowledged that parties may enter into arbitration agreements in order to expedite the resolution of disputes.

But we have also cautioned against thinking that Congress' primary objective was to guarantee these particular procedural advantages. Rather, that primary objective was to secure the "enforcement" of agreements to arbitrate.... The relevant Senate Report points to the Act's basic purpose when it says that "[t]he purpose of the [Act] is *clearly set forth in section 2*," S.Rep. No. 536, at 2 (emphasis added), namely, the section that says that an arbitration agreement "shall be valid, irrevocable, and enforceable, save upon such grounds as exist at law or in equity for the revocation of any contract."

Thus, insofar as we seek to implement Congress' intent, we should think more than twice before invalidating a state law that does just what § 2 requires, namely, puts agreements to arbitrate and agreements to litigate "upon the same footing."

2. Comments and Questions

a. If the Supreme Court is still applying conflict preemption analysis, what is the conflict between the *Discover Bank* rule and the FAA? FAA Section 2 ensures that agreements to arbitrate are enforceable. The *Discover Bank* rule invalidates a class action waiver in a consumer contract. Is there a conflict?

b. Was the *Discover Bank* rule one of general applicability or one that was aimed at arbitration agreements? What if courts applied the *Discover Bank* rule more often in situations involving waivers of class action *litigation*? How might these factors affect the preemption analysis?

c. What tools of statutory interpretation did the majority use in holding that the FAA preempted the California Supreme Court's decision in *Discover Bank* ? Did the Supreme Court apply the same analysis and reasoning in *Southland* as in *Concepcion*?

d. *Concepcion* did not have to deal with the question of whether the mobile telephone agreements are contracts "involving commerce." AT&T Mobility had a national presence, and the telephones may or may not have crossed state lines to get to the ultimate consumers. What about a contract between a nursing home and its residents? What if such a nursing home contract were signed by a person with a power of attorney, and not the resident him- or herself? Can a state create a rule that an attorney-in-fact has the power to enter into an arbitration agreement only if the power of attorney specifically grants such right? *See Kindred Nursing Centers Ltd. v. Clark*, 137 S. Ct. 1421 (2017) (holding Kentucky's "clear statement" rule "requiring power of attorney to have specific authorization to enter arbitration in nursing home arbitration contracted violated the FAA by singling out arbitration agreements for disfavored treatment violated the FAA).

e. Consider whether the following state laws would be subject to FAA preemption if enacted by State X. Also consider why a state might choose to enact a law it knows would be preempted if challenged.

1. All agreements to arbitrate shall be valid, irrevocable, and enforceable, save upon such grounds as exist at law or in equity for the revocation of any contract.

2. Pre-dispute arbitration agreements in consumer cases are invalid.

3. Agreements to arbitrate must be in red ink. Agreements to arbitrate that are not in red ink are invalid.

4. Agreements to arbitrate must be in red ink. If the drafting party does not put the arbitration clause in red ink, the drafting party will be responsible for the non-drafting party's attorney's fees in arbitration.

5. Arbitrators must disclose the names of the parties and the amount of their last five arbitration awards.

f. The preemption rules apply only at the intersection of federal law and state law. When might the FAA preemption implicate the Tenth Amendment federalism concerns and infringe upon state rights to regulate traditional areas of state police powers? Are laws and enforcement relating to worker and consumer protection "within the state's historic police powers"?

g. *Arbitration and Administrative Agency Access.* Do mandatory pre-dispute arbitration agreements displace a party's right to access state and federal administrative agency procedures, or laws authorizing representative actions? As a result of its broad preemptive scope, the FAA preempts most state laws that delay or disfavor the enforcement of arbitration agreements. The U.S. Supreme Court addressed the interaction of federal and state administrative law in *Preston v. Ferrer*, 552 U.S. 346 (2008), holding that "[w]hen parties agree to arbitrate all questions arising under a contract, the FAA supersedes state laws lodging primary jurisdiction in another forum, whether judicial or administrative." Read together, *Southland*, *Preston*, and *Concepcion* make clear that the source of state law (statute, agency rule, or judge-made common law) does not matter for the purposes of preemption analysis. *See also Sonic-Calabasas A, Inc. v. Moreno* (Sonic II), 311 P.3d 184, 191–92 (Cal. 2013) (holding, reluctantly, that the FAA preempts state law entitling wage and hour claimants to administrative hearings before Labor Commissioner but remanding for unconscionability analysis), *cert. denied*, 134 S. Ct. 2724 (2014). Do you agree that a private arbitration agreement protected by the FAA should deny access to state administrative agency relief? Maureen A. Weston, *The Clash: Squaring Mandatory Arbitration with Administrative Agency and Representative Recourse*, 89 So. Cal. L. Rev. 103 (2015).

h. *Private Attorney General Claims.* A possible "carve out" or "end run" around FAA preemption is to bring a lawsuit in a representative capacity on behalf of the government in a federal *qui tam* or private attorney general action (PAGA). *Iskanian v. CLS Transportation Los Angeles*, 327 P.3d 129, 133 (Cal. 2014), *cert. denied.*, 135 S. Ct. 1155 (2015) (holding that although individual claims remain subject to arbitration, the FAA does not preempt state PAGA law that "deputizes" employees in giving them the right to sue in a representative capacity for labor code violations). In *EEOC v. Waffle House, Inc.*, 534 U.S. 279 (2002), the federal agency was not a party to the employee's arbitration contract and thus not precluded from suing to obtain victim-specific relief. Although California courts have since considered PAGA claims nonwaivable, the Ninth Circuit has held that even PAGA claims may heard in arbitration where the arbitration clause explicitly covers representative claims. *Valdez v. Terminez Int'l Co. Ltd.*, 681 Fed. Appx. 592 (9th Cir. 2017) (stating that "*Iskanian* does not require a PAGA claim be pursued in a judicial forum; it holds only that a complete waiver of the right to bring a PAGA claim is invalid.").

D. Federal Court Jurisdiction for Arbitration Matters

The FAA does not provide an independent basis of federal subject matter jurisdiction, which has been described as an "anomaly" among federal laws. How do courts determine federal subject matter jurisdiction for FAA-related motions? When can a party ask a federal court to enforce an arbitration agreement or award under the FAA? Should the availability of federal court jurisdiction depend on whether a party is seeking to enforce an agreement to arbitrate or an arbitrator's award?

Vaden v. Discover Bank

129 S. Ct. 1262 (2009)

JUSTICE GINSBURG delivered the opinion of the Court.

Section 4 of the FAA authorizes a U.S. district court to entertain a petition to compel arbitration if the court would have jurisdiction, "save for [the arbitration] agreement," over "a suit arising out of the controversy between the parties." We consider in this opinion two questions concerning a district court's subject-matter jurisdiction over a §4 petition: Should a district court, if asked to compel arbitration pursuant to §4, "look through" the petition and grant the requested relief if the court would have federal-question jurisdiction over the underlying controversy? And if the answer to that question is yes, may a district court exercise jurisdiction over a §4 petition when the petitioner's complaint rests on state law but an actual or potential counterclaim rests on federal law?

The litigation giving rise to these questions began when Discover Bank's servicing affiliate filed a complaint in Maryland state court. Presenting a claim arising solely under state law, Discover sought to recover past-due charges from one of its credit cardholders, Betty Vaden. Vaden answered and counterclaimed, alleging that Discover's finance charges, interest, and late fees violated state law. Invoking an arbitration clause in its cardholder agreement with Vaden, Discover then filed a §4 petition in the U.S. District Court for the District of Maryland to compel arbitration of Vaden's counterclaims. The District Court had subject-matter jurisdiction over its petition, Discover maintained, because Vaden's state-law counterclaims were completely preempted by federal banking law. The District Court agreed and ordered arbitration. Reasoning that a federal court has jurisdiction over a §4 petition if the parties' underlying dispute presents a federal question, the Fourth Circuit eventually affirmed.

We agree with the Fourth Circuit in part. A federal court may "look through" a §4 petition and order arbitration if, "save for [the arbitration] agreement," the court would have jurisdiction over "the [substantive] controversy between the parties." We hold, however, that the Court of Appeals misidentified the dimensions of "the controversy between the parties." ...

This case originated as a garden-variety, state-law-based contract action: Discover sued its cardholder, Vaden, in a Maryland state court to recover arrearages amounting to $10,610, plus interest and counsel fees. Vaden's answer asserted usury as an affirmative defense. Vaden also filed several counterclaims, styled as class actions. Like Discover's complaint, Vaden's pleadings invoked only state law: Vaden asserted that Discover's demands for finance charges, interest, and late fees violated Maryland's credit laws. Neither party invoked—by notice to the other nor petition to the state court—the clause in the credit card agreement providing for arbitration....

Faced with Vaden's counterclaims, Discover sought federal-court aid. It petitioned the United States District Court for the District of Maryland for an order, pursuant to §4 of the FAA compelling arbitration of Vaden's counterclaims. Although those counterclaims were framed under state law, Discover urged that they were governed entirely by federal law, specifically, §27(a) of the Federal Deposit Insurance Act (FDIA), 12 U.S.C. §1831d(a). Section 27(a) prescribes the interest rates state-chartered, federally insured banks like Discover can charge, "notwithstanding any State constitution or statute which is hereby preempted." This provision, Discover maintained, was completely preemptive, i.e., it superseded otherwise applicable Maryland law, and placed Vaden's counterclaims under the exclusive governance of the FDIA. On that basis, Discover asserted, the District Court had authority to entertain the §4 petition pursuant to 28 U.S.C. §1331, which gives federal courts jurisdiction over cases "arising under" federal law.

Vaden "concede[d] that the FDIA completely preempts any state claims against a federally insured bank." Accepting this concession, the District Court expressly held that it had federal-question jurisdiction over Discover's §4 petition and ordered arbitration. Recognizing that "a party may not create jurisdiction by concession," the Fourth Circuit majority conducted its own analysis of FDIA §27(a), ultimately concluding that the provision completely preempted state law and therefore governed. (Our disposition of this case makes it unnecessary to take up the question of §27(a)'s preemptive force generally or in the particular context of Discover's finance charges. We therefore express no opinion on those issues.) The Fourth Circuit affirmed, dividing 2 to 1....

We granted certiorari in view of the conflict among lower federal courts on whether district courts, petitioned to order arbitration pursuant to §4 of the FAA, may "look through" the petition and examine the parties' underlying dispute to determine whether federal question jurisdiction exists over the §4 petition. As this case shows, if the underlying dispute is the proper focus of a §4 petition, a further question may arise. The dispute brought to state court by Discover concerned Vaden's failure to pay over $10,000 in past-due credit card charges. In support of that complaint, Discover invoked no federal law. When Vaden answered and counterclaimed, however, Discover asserted that federal law, specifically §27(a) of the FDIA, displaced the state laws on which Vaden relied. What counts as the underlying dispute in a case so postured? May Discover invoke §4, not on the basis of its own complaint, which had no federal element, but on the basis of counterclaims asserted by Vaden? To answer these questions, we first review relevant provisions of the FAA, and controlling tenets of federal jurisdiction....

The relevant "controversy between the parties," Vaden insists, is simply and only the parties' discrete dispute over the arbitrability of their claims. She relies, quite reasonably, on the fact that a §4 petition to compel arbitration seeks no adjudication on the merits of the underlying controversy. Indeed, its very purpose is to have an arbitrator, rather than a court, resolve the merits. A §4 petition, Vaden observes, is essentially a plea for specific performance of an agreement to arbitrate, and it thus presents principally contractual questions: Did the parties validly agree to arbitrate? What issues does their agreement encompass? Has one party dishonored the agreement? Vaden's argument, though reasonable, is difficult to square with the statutory language. Section 4 directs courts to determine whether they would have jurisdiction "save for [the arbitration] agreement." How, then, can a dispute over the existence or applicability of an arbitration agreement be the controversy that counts?

The "save for" clause, courts espousing the view embraced by Vaden respond, means only that the "antiquated and arcane" ouster notion no longer holds sway. Adherents to this "ouster" explanation of §4's language recall that courts traditionally viewed arbitration clauses as unworthy attempts to "oust" them of jurisdiction; accordingly, to guard against encroachment on their domain, they refused to order specific enforcement of agreements to arbitrate. The "save for" clause, as comprehended by proponents of the "ouster" explanation, was designed to ensure that courts would no longer consider themselves ousted of jurisdiction and would therefore specifically enforce arbitration agreements.

We are not persuaded that the "ouster" explanation of §4's "save for" clause carries the day. To the extent that the ancient "ouster" doctrine continued to impede specific enforcement of arbitration agreements, §2 of the FAA directly attended to the problem.... Having commanded that an arbitration agreement is enforceable just as any other contract, Congress had no cause to repeat the point. The effort to connect the "save for" language to the ancient problem of "ouster of jurisdiction" is imaginative, but utterly unfounded and historically inaccurate. Because the ouster problem was just as great under state law as it was under federal, the absence of "save for" language in contemporaneous state arbitration acts bolsters our conclusion that §4 was not devised to dislodge the common-law ouster doctrine.

In addition to its textual implausibility, the approach Vaden advocates has curious practical consequences. It would permit a federal court to entertain a §4 petition only when a federal-question suit is already before the court, when the parties satisfy the requirements for diversity of citizenship jurisdiction, or when the dispute over arbitrability involves a maritime contract. Vaden's approach would not accommodate a §4 petitioner who *could* file a federal-question suit in (or remove such a suit to) federal court, but who has not done so. In contrast, when the parties' underlying dispute arises under federal law, the "look through" approach permits a §4 petitioner to ask a federal court to compel arbitration without first taking the formal step of initiating or removing a federal-question suit—that is, without seeking federal adjudication of the very questions it wants to arbitrate rather than litigate. The approach Vaden advocates creates a totally artificial distinction based on whether a dispute is subject to pending federal litigation....

Having determined that a district court should "look through" a §4 petition, we now consider whether the court "would have [federal-question] jurisdiction" over "a suit arising out of the controversy" between Discover and Vaden. As explained above,

§ 4 of the FAA does not enlarge federal court jurisdiction; rather, it confines federal courts to the jurisdiction they would have "save for [the arbitration] agreement." Mindful of that limitation, we read § 4 to convey that a party seeking to compel arbitration may gain a federal court's assistance only if, "save for" the agreement, the entire, actual "controversy between the parties," as they have framed it, could be litigated in federal court. We conclude that the parties' actual controversy, here precipitated by Discover's state-court suit for the balance due on Vaden's account, is not amenable to federal court adjudication. Consequently, the § 4 petition Discover filed in the U.S. District Court must be dismissed. ...

Neither Discover nor THE CHIEF JUSTICE defends the Fourth Circuit's reasoning. Instead, the dissent insists that a federal court "would have" jurisdiction over the controversy Discover seeks to arbitrate — namely, whether Discover Bank charged illegal finance charges, interest and late fees. The dissent hypothesizes two federal suits that might arise from this purported controversy: "an action by Vaden asserting that the charges violate the FDIA, or one by Discover seeking a declaratory judgment that they do not." There is a fundamental flaw in the dissent's analysis: In lieu of focusing on the whole controversy as framed by the parties, the dissent hypothesizes discrete controversies of its own design. As the parties' state-court filings reflect, the originating controversy here concerns Vaden's alleged debt to Discover. Vaden's responsive counterclaims challenging the legality of Discover's charges are a discrete aspect of the whole controversy Discover and Vaden brought to state court. Whether one might imagine a federal-question suit involving the parties' disagreement over Discover's charges is beside the point. The relevant question is whether the whole controversy between the parties — not just a piece broken off from that controversy — is one over which the federal courts would have jurisdiction....

In sum, § 4 of the FAA instructs district courts asked to compel arbitration to inquire whether the court would have jurisdiction, "save for [the arbitration] agreement," over "a suit arising out of the controversy between the parties." We read that prescription in light of the well-pleaded complaint rule and the corollary rule that federal jurisdiction cannot be invoked on the basis of a defense or counterclaim. Parties may not circumvent those rules by asking a federal court to order arbitration of the portion of a controversy that implicates federal law when the court would not have federal-question jurisdiction over the controversy as a whole. It does not suffice to show that a federal question lurks somewhere inside the parties' controversy, or that a defense or counterclaim would arise under federal law. Because the controversy between Discover and Vaden, properly perceived, is not one qualifying for federal-court adjudication, § 4 of the FAA does not empower a federal court to order arbitration of that controversy, in whole or in part.

Discover, we note, is not left without recourse. Under the FAA, state courts as well as federal courts are obliged to honor and enforce agreements to arbitrate. Discover may therefore petition a Maryland court for aid in enforcing the arbitration clause of its contracts with Maryland cardholders. True, Maryland's high court has held that §§ 3 and 4 of the FAA prescribe federal-court procedures and, therefore, do not bind the state courts. (This Court has not decided whether §§ 3 and 4 apply to proceedings in state courts, and we do not do so here.) But Discover scarcely lacks an available state remedy. Section 2 of the FAA, which does bind the state courts, renders agreements to arbitrate "valid, irrevocable, and *enforceable.*" This provision "carries with it duties to credit and enforce arbitration agreements] indistinguishable from those imposed on federal courts by FAA §§ 3 and 4. Notably, Maryland, like many other States, provides a statutory remedy nearly identical to § 4. Even before it filed its debt-recovery action in a Maryland state court, Discover could have sought from that court an order compelling arbitration of any agreement-related dispute between itself and cardholder Vaden. At no time was federal-court intervention needed to place the controversy between the parties before an arbitrator.

CHIEF JUSTICE ROBERTS, with whom JUSTICE STEVENS, JUSTICE BREYER, and JUSTICE ALITO join, concurring in part and dissenting in part.

I agree with the Court that a federal court asked to compel arbitration pursuant to § 4 of the FAA should "look through" the dispute over arbitrability in determining whether it has jurisdiction to grant the requested relief. But look through to what? The statute provides a clear and sensible answer: The court may consider the § 4 petition if the court would have jurisdiction over the subject matter of a suit arising out of the controversy between the parties.... Vaden agrees that the legality of Discover's charges and fees is governed by the FDIA. A federal court therefore would have jurisdiction ... of the subject matter of a suit arising out of the controversy Discover seeks to arbitrate....

The majority's approach will allow federal jurisdiction to compel arbitration of *entirely* state-law claims. Under that approach the "controversy" is not the one the § 4 petitioner seeks to arbitrate, but a broader one encompassing the "whole controversy" between the parties. If that broader dispute involves both federal and state-law claims, and the "originating" dispute is federal, a party could seek arbitration of just the state-law claims. The "controversy" under the majority's view would qualify as federal, giving rise to § 4 jurisdiction to compel arbitration of a purely state-law claim....

By focusing on the sequence in which state-court litigation has unfolded, the majority crafts a rule that produces inconsistent results. Because Discover's debt-collection claim was filed before Vaden's counterclaims, the majority treats the debt-collection dispute as the "originating controversy." But nothing would have prevented the same disagreements between the parties from producing a different sequence of events. Vaden could have filed a complaint raising her FDIA claims before Discover sought to collect on any amounts Vaden owes. Because the "originating controversy" in that complaint would be whether Discover has charged fees illegal under federal law, in that situation Discover presumably *could* bring a § 4 petition to compel arbitration of the FDIA dispute. The majority's rule thus makes § 4 jurisdiction over the same controversy entirely dependent upon the happenstance of how state-court litigation has unfolded. Nothing in § 4 suggests such a result.

The majority glosses over another problem inherent in its approach: In many if not most cases under § 4, no complaint will have been filed. Normally, § 4 motions are brought in independent proceedings. What to "look through" to then? The majority instructs courts to look to the "full-bodied controversy." But as this case illustrates, that would lead to a different result had the state-court complaint not been filed. Discover does not seek to arbitrate whether an outstanding debt exists; indeed, Discover's § 4 petition does not even allege any dispute on that point. A district court would therefore not understand the § 4 "controversy" to include the debt-collection claim in the absence of the state-court suit. Under the majority's rule, the FDIA dispute would be treated as a "controversy" qualifying under § 4 before the state suit and counterclaims had been filed, but not after. The far more concrete and administrable approach would be to apply the same rule in all instances: Look to the controversy the § 4 petitioner seeks to arbitrate — as set forth in the § 4 petition — and assess whether a federal court would have jurisdiction over the subject matter of a suit arising out of that controversy. The controversy the moving party seeks to arbitrate and the other party will not would be the same controversy used to assess jurisdiction to compel arbitration. . . .

That is why the majority's recital of the basic rules of federal-court jurisdiction is beside the point: No one disputes what those rules are, and no one disputes that they must be followed under § 4 in deciding whether a federal court "would have jurisdiction . . . of the subject matter of a suit arising out of the controversy between the parties." The issue is instead *what* suit should be scrutinized for compliance with those rules. In defining "controversy" by reference to existing litigation, the majority artificially limits the reach of § 4 to the particular suit filed. The correct approach is to accord § 4 the scope mandated by its language and look to "a suit," arising out of the "subject matter" of the "controversy" the § 4 petitioner seeks to arbitrate, and determine whether a federal court would have jurisdiction over such a suit. * * *

Dorscher v. Sea Port Group Securities, LLC

832 F.3d 372 (2d Cir. 2016)

WESLEY, CIRCUIT JUDGE.

This [employment] case arises from the dismissal of a petition to vacate an arbitral award pursuant to section 10 of the Federal Arbitration Act (the "FAA" or the "Act"), 9 U.S.C. § 10. It requires us to reconsider the continuing viability of our Court's precedent in *Greenberg v. Bear, Stearns & Co.*, 220 F.3d 22 (2d Cir. 2000), in which we held that a district court may exercise federal-question jurisdiction over a § 10 petition only if the petition states a substantial federal question on its face — i.e., a district court may not "look through" the petition to determine if the underlying dispute that was subject to arbitration involved substantial questions of federal law. *Greenberg* premised its conclusion on a now-overruled decision of this Court that rejected a look-through approach as applied to section 4 of the Act. . . . We conclude that *Greenberg* cannot survive *Vaden*'s later-established precedent; accordingly, we vacate the order and the judgment of the District Court.

B.

… *Vaden* provides us with three critical pieces of guidance. First, it reiterated the longstanding rule that the Act's provisions do not bestow or enlarge subject matter jurisdiction. Second, it relied heavily upon the text of, and interaction between, the relevant provisions of the Act. Third, it identified the practical consequences resulting from the interpretive choices. The application of these three guideposts, however, is significantly more complicated.

Beginning with the most obvious point, § 10 lacks the textual "save for" clause contained in § 4. This distinction is not to be taken lightly, particularly in the face of the Supreme Court's statement that "[t]he text of § 4 drives our conclusion" adopting the look-through approach. *Vaden*, 556 U.S. at 62. In construing § 10, however, we must also keep in mind "the cardinal rule that a statute is to be read as a whole, since the meaning of statutory language, plain or not, depends on context." We think *Vaden*'s other two guiding principles counsel against a too-hasty reliance on the absence of the "save for" clause. Perhaps in an ordinary case, this absence would end our inquiry — but the Act's anomalous characteristics warrant, we think, a more careful examination. We focus first on the jurisdictional context of *Vaden* and this case and second on the practical consequences of both interpretations.

Vaden repeated the Supreme Court's longstanding conclusion that the Act "bestows no federal jurisdiction but rather requires for access to a federal forum an independent jurisdictional basis over the parties' dispute." The "independent jurisdictional basis" in *Vaden*, like this case, was federal-question jurisdiction deriving from § 1331. After laying out the contours of federal-question jurisdiction, the Court concluded that the "dispute" giving rise to § 1331 jurisdiction was the "substantive conflict between the parties." Although the Court was unanimous on these points — and on the applicability of the look-through approach — it was divided on how to define the substantive controversy. Despite this disagreement over the scope of the dispute, all nine Justices agreed that "the basic rules of federal-court jurisdiction … must be followed under § 4."

The only reasonable reading of *Vaden*'s jurisdictional analysis thus makes clear two conclusions. First, the district court possessed jurisdiction only by operation of § 1331. Second, the federal question required by § 1331 arose from the underlying dispute, not the face of the petition. These conclusions, however, pose a challenge to the proposition that no look-through approach is appropriate in § 10 petitions, based solely on the statutory text.

Pre-*Vaden*, rejecting the look-through approach with respect to all of the Act's provisions made sense, because a federal court simply compared its jurisdictional statutes to the face of the petition. Under such a construction, for example, whether an action under the Act presented a substantial federal question sufficient to confer jurisdiction under § 1331 always depended on whether the face of the petition met the standards of federal-question jurisdiction. In essence, the "well-pleaded complaint" for our jurisdictional inquiries was the petition, regardless of which particular remedy under the Act the petitioner sought. Post-*Vaden*, however, that consistency has been called into question. If we assume that § 4's unique textual clause is dispositive regarding jurisdiction, then, for most of the Act's provisions, federal-question jurisdiction under § 1331 lies (or not) on the face of the petition. In other words, the "ordinary" § 1331 inquiry—i.e., the one conducted absent any special textual clause—requires examining the face of the petition. For § 4 petitions, however, a court's federal-question jurisdiction lies (or not) on the basis of the underlying substantive dispute.

The inconsistency here is evident: if "§ 4 of the FAA does not enlarge federal-court jurisdiction," e.g., *Vaden*, 556 U.S. at 66, how can a federal court's jurisdiction under the same jurisdictional statute differ between § 4 and all other remedies under the Act? Post-*Vaden*, there is no question that a federal court's § 1331 jurisdiction extends to § 4 petitions that it would have been unable to entertain applying a face-of-the-petition approach. A district court's jurisdiction over disputes in which a party seeks a § 4 remedy is, therefore, broader than its jurisdiction over disputes in which a party seeks one of the other remedies provided by the Act. Put differently, the necessary result of limiting the look-through approach solely to § 4 petitions is to conclude that the same dispute between the parties would be sufficient to confer § 1331 jurisdiction for the purposes of § 4 petitions but insufficient to confer § 1331 jurisdiction for the purposes of any of the Act's other remedies. That is simply not logically possible without construing § 4 to expand federal jurisdiction—a conclusion the Supreme Court has expressly forbidden us to draw.

Thus, there is some tension between two controlling principles in *Vaden*: the first emphasizing § 4's text in concluding that a court has federal-question jurisdiction over § 4 petitions based on the underlying substantive dispute, and the second emphasizing that the provisions of the Act do not affect a federal court's jurisdiction. If we apply the first principle to conclude that the absence of the "save for" clause in § 10 requires us to maintain the rule of *Greenberg*, we have, in essence, converted § 4's "save for" clause into an expansion of jurisdiction—which violates the second principle. The only way to avoid this contradictory result is to reject the premise that produced it—i.e., to conclude that the "ordinary" jurisdictional inquiry under § 1331 looks to the underlying substantive dispute with respect to all remedies under the Act, not just § 4.

This tension is further resolved when we examine the nature and function of the "save for" clause in § 4 and the language of the Act's other remedies. To some degree, each of the Act's sections contains some language identifying which courts are authorized to issue which remedies. The most consistent statutory interpretation is to read the "save for" clause as defining the availability of the remedy, rather than a court's jurisdiction. Because Congress intended to ensure the broadest availability possible for compulsion of arbitration, § 4 authorizes it in the context of every dispute over which Title 28 confers jurisdiction. The lack of the "save for" clause and the presence of other text narrowing the availability of the remedies in the Act's other sections similarly authorize particular remedies to issue in particular courts to serve important congressional interests. Specifically, the Act's other sections largely ground their authorizing language by reference to geography, not the jurisdiction of the issuing court.

For example, the remedy permitting a federal court to compel the attendance of witnesses limits its authorization to "the United States district court for the district in which such arbitrators, or a majority of them, are sitting." 9 U.S.C. § 7. Section 9 uses the same geographical hook, only linked to the district "within which such award was made" and also expressly establishes personal jurisdiction over the parties; §§ 10–11 are similarly geographically connected to the location of the arbitration. The identification of district courts by geography in §§ 7 and 9–11 performs functions more analogous to venue or personal jurisdiction than to subject matter jurisdiction. These sections signal nothing about jurisdiction, suggesting—consistent with *Vaden*—that they do not affect the ordinary jurisdictional inquiry, which is focused on the underlying dispute. There is thus no reason to construe the "save for" clause—or its absence from the other remedies—as governing the predicate question of whether a federal court possesses jurisdiction over the dispute at all. Construing the language of these sections as authorizing the availability of the remedies, rather than controlling jurisdiction over the dispute, is therefore a more consistent interpretation of the statute as a whole—not to mention being in full accordance with the Supreme Court's characterization of the Act as having a "nonjurisdictional cast." ...

A construction of the Act's provisions as lacking jurisdictional impact is not only consistent with but also well suited to these congressional purposes. Under this approach, if a federal court would possess federal-question jurisdiction over the dispute when pleaded in a complaint, the federal courts are also able to enforce Congress's narrow and defined remedies in the same controversy. The Act thus favors arbitration by constraining the role of the federal courts where arbitration agreements exist, without displacing their ability to enforce the remedies Congress created in disputes in which they would otherwise be the determinative forum. The authorizing language of the Act with respect to particular remedies maps onto congressional interests well: the remedy of compulsion may be obtained in "any United States district court" possessing subject matter jurisdiction, § 4, but where the federal courts must engage with an ongoing or concluded arbitration, a geographical nexus is required, see §§ 7, 9–11.

Finally, we note that applying a look-through approach to the entire Act also prevents absurd and illogical discrepancies, the final animating principle we identified in *Vaden*. As detailed above, absurd or bizarre inconsistencies in jurisdiction among the Act's provisions were a central concern in both our prior decisions. *Vaden*'s discussion of the practical consequences confirms that our desire to achieve consistent results was not misplaced, even if the Court disagreed with our interpretation of § 4. The *Vaden* Court identified a principal "curious practical consequence[ ]": that a face-of-the-petition "approach would not accommodate a § 4 petitioner who could file a federal-question suit in (or remove such a suit to) federal court, but who has not done so." 556 U.S. at 65. Yet the same kind of absurd result would occur here if we reject a look-through approach for § 10....

[T]here is a certain absurdity to an interpretation that permits parties to file motions to compel arbitration in any case where the underlying dispute raises a federal question but precludes them from seeking the same federal court's aid under the Act's other remedial provisions related to the same dispute. Our sister circuit has posited an argument why there may be a disparity between congressional interests in §4 and in §10—specifically, that "[t]he central federal interest was enforcement of agreements to arbitrate, not review of arbitration decisions" and therefore "once the arbitration agreement is enforced, there exists no compelling need for the federal courts to be involved."

If enforcement were Congress's only goal, however, it would have had no need to pass §§10 or 11 at all. Merely enacting §§2 and 3—declaring arbitration agreements enforceable and providing for a stay and referral to arbitration of disputes in federal court governed by such an agreement—would suffice to ensure that federal courts did not sidestep arbitration agreements. The fact that Congress decided to enact substantive rules governing vacatur and modification makes as clear as one can imagine that Congress intended a substantive—albeit limited—review of certain arbitration awards. Considering that Congress did authorize freestanding petitions to compel arbitration, compel witness attendance, and confirm, vacate, or modify awards, neither Minor nor the parties give us any reason why Congress would create a set of remedies yet make some more enforceable than others.

The bizarre jurisdictional tangle resulting from a look-through approach to §4 and a face-of-the-petition approach to the other remedies will produce the exact opposite of the Act's goals. Intelligent practitioners who wish to preserve access to federal courts for later disputes over arbitrators, subpoenas, or final awards will attempt to "lock in" jurisdiction by filing a federal suit first, followed by motions to compel and a stay of proceedings. In other words, it will increase the number of parties "seeking federal adjudication of the very questions [they] want[ ] to arbitrate rather than litigate"—again, the same perverse incentive and procedural incongruity identified by the *Vaden* Court. Construing the Act in a way that encourages the protective filing of federal suits would be the height of absurdity in light of Congress's desire to cabin federal involvement in disputes subject to arbitration—before, during, and after the proceeding.

Finally, we note that, in a twist of irony, a post-*Vaden* conclusion that §10 requires a federal question on the face of the petition seems oddly to mimic the kind of "ouster" that concerned the *Westmoreland* and *Greenberg* panels and, to a lesser degree, the *Vaden* Court. In other words, if the substantive dispute between the parties is otherwise cognizable before a federal district court, the limitation to the face of the petition seems to restrict the federal courts not on the basis of principles like res judicata or enforceability of arbitration agreements—which are rules of decision—but on the basis of a lack of jurisdiction. Thus, federal courts have been "ousted" of jurisdiction over a substantive dispute between the parties that they would otherwise be empowered under §1331 to hear, merely because of the presence of an arbitration agreement. By contrast, if we conclude that federal-question jurisdiction arises from the underlying dispute, the arbitration agreement limits the remedies a federal court may employ but does not affect the court's jurisdiction. This result seems to us the more internally consistent approach, given the current state of Supreme Court precedent.

Returning to where we began, we have confronted the difficult task of reconciling the guiding principles that the Supreme Court has handed down—principles which are admittedly in some tension. To read *Vaden's* text-driven analysis as a jurisdictional inquiry would, on the surface, lead us to reject the look-through approach. But that result would require us, as a matter of internal consistency, to conclude that § 4 did exactly what the Supreme Court says it does not do: enlarge a federal court's jurisdiction. Further, it would produce anomalous discrepancies in the administration of the Act that both we and the Supreme Court have consistently rejected as impermissible results. We think the only way to reconcile this tension is to adopt the following principles:

First, the existence of federal-question jurisdiction over an FAA petition turns on whether the district court would possess jurisdiction over the underlying dispute under the standards of § 1331;

Second, the "save for" clause in § 4 evinces congressional authorization for the remedy of compulsion of arbitration in any district court with jurisdiction; and

Third, the Act's other sections similarly authorize particular courts with jurisdiction to issue particular remedies but do not affect the jurisdictional inquiry.

Having conducted this analysis, we must now conclude that *Vaden*, as an intervening Supreme Court decision, has rendered *Greenberg's* result fundamentally inconsistent with the Act's statutory context and judicial interpretations. We are therefore obliged to overrule it and adopt the rule that a federal district court faced with a § 10 petition may "look through" the petition to the underlying dispute, applying to it the ordinary rules of federal-question jurisdiction and the principles laid out by the majority in *Vaden*. Because the District Court concluded below that a look-through approach was foreclosed by Greenberg, it did not conduct an analysis of the underlying dispute. We think the proper disposition is therefore to vacate the order and the judgment and remand for consideration of that question in the first instance.

1. Comments and Questions

a. The *Vaden* decision is quite limited. Factually, the case deals with: (1) federal question jurisdiction and (2) a motion to compel in a case that (3) originated in state court. The following factors can greatly change the analysis:

- Is the application to the court for an order compelling arbitration or an order confirming or vacating an award?
- Did the parties initiate the application in state court or federal court?
- If federal court, is subject matter jurisdiction premised on a federal question or diversity?
- Is the current application connected to a larger underlying litigation, or is this a "free-standing" motion for consideration by the court?

b. *Diversity of Citizenship Jurisdiction.* In *Northport Health Servs. of Ark., LLC v. Rutherford*, 605 F.3d 483 (8th Cir. 2010), the Eighth Circuit held a federal court has diversity jurisdiction over a §4 petition to compel arbitration of claims that are part of a pending state court action, so long as the parties to the petition to compel the proceeding are diverse, even if the pending state court action also includes one or more non-diverse parties that are not named in the §4 petition. Thus, diversity jurisdiction for petitions to compel arbitration under §4 of the FAA is determined by looking to the citizenship of the parties in the petition not the citizenship of all the parties in the underlying state case. Does *Northport*, in refusing to "look through" the petition to compel arbitration based on diversity, follow the U.S. Supreme Court's approach in *Vaden*? Would you change your opinion if you knew that the Supreme Court had previously heard an arbitration case on the merits where the parties to the petition were diverse but the parties to the underlying state court action were not?

c. The following chart attempts to summarize the variety of tests in the area of federal court jurisdiction in arbitration matters. A nearly identical version of this chart was originally published in Kristen M. Blankley, *A Uniform Theory of Federal Court Jurisdiction Under the Federal Arbitration Act*, 23 GEO. MASON L. REV. 525 (2016):

Legal Tests for Determining Federal Court Jurisdiction in Arbitration Cases

	Federal Question Jurisdiction	Diversity Jurisdiction	
		Diversity	Amount in Controversy
Motions to Compel §4	• "Look through" to state court complaint in non-freestanding cases • "Look through" to the entire controversy in free-standing cases	• Only consider the parties to the petition	• "Look through" to state court complaint in non-freestanding case • "Look through" to entire controversy in free-standing cases • Consider only the petition
Motions to Confirm or Vacate §10, 11	• Jurisdiction in open federal cases • Questionable jurisdiction if a court is reviewing for manifest disregard of a federal law • "Look through" to the award or subject of arbitration • No jurisdiction?	• Only consider the parties to the petition	• "Demand approach," a "look through" to the arbitration • "Award approach," a "look through" to the award • "Mixed approach"

For cases in which a petitioner moving to compel arbitration bases federal subject matter jurisdiction on a federal question, courts take two approaches. If there is a state court complaint, then *Vaden* instructs the courts to look through to the state court complaint to determine if federal court jurisdiction would exist. If there is no state court complaint [i.e., a "free-standing" motion], *Vaden* instructs the courts to look through to the entire controversy to determine if a federal court would have jurisdiction.

For cases in which a petitioner moving to confirm or vacate an arbitration award bases federal subject matter jurisdiction on a federal question, courts take a variety of approaches to determine if jurisdiction exists. If the parties previously accessed the court on a motion to compel, the earlier action can be reopened on a motion to confirm or vacate. In addition, some jurisdictions will consider whether the arbitrators manifestly disregarded federal law and find jurisdiction in those instances. *See Sharlands Terrace, LLC v. 1930 Wright St., LLC,* 2011 WL 3566816 (N.D. Cal. Aug. 11, 2011). Some jurisdictions, such as the Second Circuit, will apply a look-through approach to determine if the arbitration involved a federal question. *Dorscher v. Sea Port Group Securities, LLC,* 832 F.3d 372 (2d Cir. 2016). In other jurisdictions, courts refuse to find any federal question jurisdiction, even if the underlying arbitration involved a clear federal question, if the case was not previously filed in federal court on a motion to compel. *Crews v. S&S Service Center,* 848 F. Supp.2d 595 (E.D. Va. 2012).

For cases involving diversity, no matter the posture, courts uniformly look only to the parties to the petition to determine whether the parties are diverse. *Northport Health Servs. of Ark, LLC v. Rutherford,* 605 F.3d 483 (8th Cir. 2010). On a motion to compel, courts use various tests to determine the amount in controversy. In cases involving a state court complaint, some jurisdictions will look through to the state court complaint to determine if that amount is met. *CMH Homes, Inc. v. Goodner,* 729 F.3d 832 (8th Cir. 2013). Others will not. *Geographic Expeditions, Inc. v. Estate of Lhota,* 599 F.3d 1102 (9th Cir. 2010). In cases involving a "free-standing" motion, courts sometimes consider the entire arbitration controversy to determine the amount, *Greystone, Nev., LLC v. Anthem Highlands Community Ass'n,* 549 Fed. Appx. 621 (9th 2013), and sometimes consider only the amount noted on the federal court filing.

On a motion to confirm or vacate, courts have created three approaches to determine the amount in controversy. Some courts will consider the amount sought in the arbitration, i.e., the "demand approach." *Smith v. Tele-Town Hall, LLC.,* 798 F. Supp. 2d 748 (E.D. Va. 2011). Other courts consider only the amount awarded, i.e., the "award approach." *Baltin v. Alaron Trading Co.,* 128 F.3d 1466 (11th Cir. 1997). The award approach is problematic when the claimant loses, and the "award" is $0.00. Some courts employ an approach that mixes the demand and the award approaches. Under the mixed approach, if the parties seek to reopen the arbitration, the court considers the demand; if the parties do not seek to reopen the arbitration, the court considers the award. *Sirotzky v. N.Y. Stock Exchange,* 347 F.3d 985, 989 (7th Cir. 2003).

d. Practice Problem.

Consider the following scenarios:

1. Carrie Consumer sues Production, Inc., in state court on a claim of products liability and breach of warranty. Carrie alleges that she purchased a Production, Inc. blender that exploded and caused her injury. Inside of the blender box are a series of terms and conditions, such as warranties, limitations on damages, and an arbitration agreement. Carrie lives in Delaware, and Production, Inc.,

is incorporated in Delaware. In the state court action, Carrie alleges that the exploding blender caused her $500,000 in damages. Production, Inc., files a petition in the U.S District Court for the District of Delaware asking for a stay and an order to compel the parties to arbitration. Does the district court have jurisdiction?

2. Same facts as problem 1, only Carrie Consumer is a citizen of Delaware, and Production, Inc., is a citizen of California. Does the district court in Delaware have jurisdiction in this instance?

3. Same facts as problem 2, only Carrie's demand in state court alleges damages "in excess of $25,000." Does the district court in Delaware have jurisdiction in this instance?

4. Barry's Business files a demand in arbitration against Consuela's Company for breach of a licensing agreement. The legal issues all pertain to federal intellectual property law. The parties arbitrate the case, and Barry's Business ultimately wins an arbitration award in the amount of $2.5 million. Barry's Business wants to confirm the award, and Consuela's Company wants to vacate it. The parties are both citizens of New Mexico, and the arbitration took place in New Mexico. Do New Mexico federal courts have jurisdiction to hear the motions?

5. Same facts as problem 4, only Barry's Business previously filed a motion to compel in the federal courts prior to the arbitration. Does this fact make a difference?

E. Choice of Law Provisions in Arbitration Agreements

Volt Information Sciences, Inc. v. Leland Stanford University

489 U.S. 468 (1989)

CHIEF JUSTICE REHNQUIST delivered the opinion of the Court.

Unlike its federal counterpart, the California Arbitration Act, contains a provision allowing a court to stay arbitration pending resolution of related litigation. We hold that application of the California statute is not pre-empted by the Federal Arbitration Act, in a case where the parties have agreed that their arbitration agreement will be governed by the law of California. Appellant Volt Information Sciences, Inc. (Volt), and appellee Board of Trustees of Leland Stanford Junior University (Stanford) entered into a construction contract under which Volt was to install a system of electrical conduits on the Stanford campus. The contract contained an agreement to arbitrate all disputes between the parties "arising out of or relating to this contract or the breach thereof." The contract also contained a choice-of-law clause providing that "[t]he Contract shall be governed by the law of the place where the Project is located."

During the course of the project, a dispute developed regarding compensation for extra work, and Volt made a formal demand for arbitration. Stanford responded by filing an action against Volt in California Superior Court, alleging fraud and breach of contract; in the same action, Stanford also sought indemnity from two other companies involved in the construction project, with whom it did not have arbitration agreements. Volt petitioned the Superior Court to compel arbitration of the dispute. Stanford in turn moved to stay arbitration pursuant to Cal. Civ. Proc. Code Ann. § 1281.2(c) (West 1982), which permits a court to stay arbitration pending resolution of related litigation between a party to the arbitration agreement and third parties not bound by it, where "there is a possibility of conflicting rulings on a common issue of law or fact." The Superior Court denied Volt's motion to compel arbitration and stayed the arbitration proceedings pending the outcome of the litigation on the authority of § 1281.2(c).

The California Court of Appeal affirmed. The court acknowledged that the parties' contract involved interstate commerce, that the FAA governs contracts in interstate commerce, and that the FAA contains no provision permitting a court to stay arbitration pending resolution of related litigation involving third parties not bound by the arbitration agreement. However, the court held that ... the parties had incorporated the California rules of arbitration, including § 1281.2(c), into their arbitration agreement. Finally, the court rejected Volt's contention that, even if the parties had agreed to arbitrate under the California rules, application of § 1281.2(c) here was nonetheless pre-empted by the FAA because the contract involved interstate commerce.

The court reasoned that the purpose of the FAA was not to mandate the arbitration of all claims, but merely the enforcement of privately negotiated arbitration agreements. While the FAA pre-empts application of state laws which render arbitration agreements unenforceable, "[i]t does not follow, however, that the federal law has preclusive effect in a case where the parties have chosen in their [arbitration] agreement to abide by state rules." To the contrary, because "[t]he thrust of the federal law is that arbitration is strictly a matter of contract," the parties to an arbitration agreement should be "at liberty to choose the terms under which they will arbitrate." Where, as here, the parties have chosen in their agreement to abide by the state rules of arbitration, application of the FAA to prevent enforcement of those rules would actually be "inimical to the policies underlying state and federal arbitration law," because it would "force the parties to arbitrate in a manner contrary to their agreement".

The California Supreme Court denied Volt's petition for discretionary review.

Appellant acknowledges, as it must, that the interpretation of private contracts is ordinarily a question of state law, which this Court does not sit to review. But appellant nonetheless maintains that we should set aside the Court of Appeal's interpretation of this particular contractual provision for two principal reasons.

Appellant first suggests that the Court of Appeal's construction of the choice-of-law clause was in effect a finding that appellant had "waived" its "federally guaranteed right to compel arbitration of the parties' dispute," a waiver whose validity must be judged by reference to federal rather than state law. This argument fundamentally misconceives the nature of the rights created by the FAA. The Act was designed "to overrule the judiciary's longstanding refusal to enforce agreements to arbitrate," and place such agreements "upon the same footing as other contracts." ... [Section] 4 of the FAA ... confers only the right to obtain an order directing that "arbitration proceed in the manner provided for in [the parties'] agreement." Here the Court of Appeal found that, by incorporating the California rules of arbitration into their agreement, the parties had agreed that arbitration would not proceed in situations which fell within the scope of § 1281.2(c). This was not a finding that appellant had "waived" an FAA-guar-anteed right to compel arbitration of this dispute, but a finding that it had no such right in the first place, because the parties' agreement did not require arbitration to proceed in this situation. Accordingly, appellant's contention that the contract interpretation issue presented here involves the "waiver" of a federal right is without merit. Second, appellant argues that we should set aside the Court of Appeal's construction of the choice-of-law clause because it violates the settled federal rule that questions of arbitrability in contracts subject to the FAA must be resolved with a healthy regard for the federal policy favoring arbitration.

... [W]e do not think the Court of Appeal offended [this] principle by interpreting the choice-of-law provision to mean that the parties intended the California rules of arbitration, including the § 1281.2(c) stay provision, to apply to their arbitration agreement. There is no federal policy favoring arbitration under a certain set of procedural rules; the federal policy is simply to ensure the enforceability, according to their terms, of private agreements to arbitrate. Interpreting a choice-of-law clause to make applicable state rules governing the conduct of arbitration—rules which are manifestly designed to encourage resort to the arbitral process—simply does not offend ... any policy embodied in the FAA.

The question remains whether ... application of § 1281.2(c) is nonetheless preempted by the FAA to the extent it is used to stay arbitration under this contract involving interstate commerce. It is undisputed that this contract falls within the coverage of the FAA, since it involves interstate commerce, and that the FAA contains no provision authorizing a stay of arbitration in this situation....

Unlike the dissent, we think the California arbitration rules ... generally foster the federal policy favoring arbitration.... [T]he FAA itself contains no provision designed to deal with the special practical problems that arise in multiparty contractual disputes when some or all of the contracts at issue include agreements to arbitrate. California has taken the lead in fashioning a legislative response to this problem, by giving courts authority to consolidate or stay arbitration proceedings in these situations in order to minimize the potential for contradictory judgments.

The FAA contains no express pre-emptive provision, nor does it reflect a congressional intent to occupy the entire field of arbitration. But even when Congress has not completely displaced state regulation in an area, state law may nonetheless be pre-empted to the extent that it actually conflicts with federal law—that is, to the extent that it "stands as an obstacle to the accomplishment and execution of the full purposes and objectives of Congress." The question before us, therefore, is whether application of § 1281.2(c) to stay arbitration under this contract in interstate commerce, in accordance with the terms of the arbitration agreement itself, would undermine the goals and policies of the FAA. We conclude that it would not....

[T]he FAA does not require parties to arbitrate when they have not agreed to do so, nor does it prevent parties who do agree to arbitrate from excluding certain claims from the scope of their arbitration agreement. It simply requires courts to enforce privately negotiated agreements to arbitrate, like other contracts, in accordance with their terms. In recognition of Congress' principal purpose of ensuring that private arbitration agreements are enforced according to their terms, we have held that the FAA pre-empts state laws which "require a judicial forum for the resolution of claims which the contracting parties agreed to resolve by arbitration." *Southland Corp. v. Keating*, 465 U.S. 1 (1984) (finding pre-empted a state statute which rendered agreements to arbitrate certain franchise claims unenforceable); *Perry v. Thomas* (finding pre-empted a state statute which rendered unenforceable private agreements to arbitrate certain wage collection claims). But it does not follow that the FAA prevents the enforcement of agreements to arbitrate under different rules than those set forth in the Act itself. Indeed, such a result would be quite inimical to the FAA's primary purpose of ensuring that private agreements to arbitrate are enforced according to their terms....

Where, as here, the parties have agreed to abide by state rules of arbitration, enforcing those rules according to the terms of the agreement is fully consistent with the goals of the FAA, even if the result is that arbitration is stayed where the Act would otherwise permit it to go forward. [In so doing], we give effect to the contractual rights and expectations of the parties, without doing violence to the policies behind by the FAA.

JUSTICE BRENNAN, with whom JUSTICE MARSHALL joins, dissenting.

The litigants in this case were parties to a construction contract which contained a clause obligating them to arbitrate disputes and making that obligation specifically enforceable. The contract also incorporated provisions of a standard form contract prepared by the American Institute of Architects and endorsed by the Associated General Contractors of America; among these general provisions was § 7.1.1: "The Contract shall be governed by the law of the place where the Project is located." When a dispute arose between the parties, Volt invoked the arbitration clause, while Stanford attempted to avoid it (apparently because the dispute also involved two other contractors with whom Stanford had no arbitration agreements).

The Federal Arbitration Act (FAA) requires courts to enforce arbitration agreements in contracts involving interstate commerce. The California courts nonetheless rejected Volt's petition to compel arbitration in reliance on a provision of state law that, in the circumstances presented, permitted a court to stay arbitration pending the conclusion of related litigation. Volt, not surprisingly, suggested that the Supremacy Clause compelled a different result. The California Court of Appeal found, however, that the parties had agreed that their contract would be governed solely by the law of the State of California, to the exclusion of federal law.

In reaching this conclusion the court relied on no extrinsic evidence of the parties' intent, but solely on the language of the form contract.... I have no quarrel with the general proposition that the interpretation of contracts is a matter of state law. By ending its analysis at that level of generality, however, the Court overlooks well-established precedent to the effect that, in order to guard against arbitrary denials of federal claims, a state court's construction of a contract in such a way as to preclude enforcement of a federal right is not immune from review in this Court as to its "adequacy." ... Where "the existence or the application of a federal right turns on a logically antecedent finding on a matter of state law, it is essential to the Court's performance of its function that it exercise an ancillary jurisdiction to consider the state question. Federal rights could otherwise be nullified by the manipulation of state law." I agree with the Court that "the FAA does not require parties to arbitrate when they have not agreed to do so." ...

The substantive question in this case is whether or not they have done so. And that question, we have made clear in the past, is a matter of federal law.... Not only does the FAA require the enforcement of arbitration agreements, but we have held that it also establishes substantive federal law that must be consulted in determining whether (or to what extent) a given contract provides for arbitration.... I agree fully with the Court that "the federal policy is simply to ensure the enforceability, according to their terms, of private agreements to arbitrate," but I disagree emphatically with its conclusion that that policy is not frustrated here. Applying the California procedural rule, which stays arbitration while litigation of the same issue goes forward, means simply that the parties' dispute will be litigated rather than arbitrated.

Construction of a contractual provision is, of course, a matter of discerning the parties' intent. It is important to recall, in the first place, that in this case there is no extrinsic evidence of their intent. We must therefore rely on the contract itself. But the provision of the contract at issue here was not one that these parties drafted themselves. Rather, they incorporated portions of a standard form contract commonly used in the construction industry. That makes it most unlikely that their intent was in any way at variance with the purposes for which choice-of-law clauses are commonly written and the manner in which they are generally interpreted. It seems to me beyond dispute that the normal purpose of such choice-of-law clauses is to determine that the law of one State rather than that of another State will be applicable; they simply do not speak to any interaction between state and federal law. A cursory glance at standard conflicts texts confirms this observation: they contain no reference at all to the relation between federal and state law in their discussions of contractual choice-of-law clauses. The same is true of standard codifications. *See* Uniform Commercial Code § 1-105(1); Restatement (Second) of Conflict of Laws § 187. Indeed the Restatement of Conflicts notes expressly that it does not deal with "the ever-present problem of determining the respective spheres of authority of the law and courts of the nation and of the member States." *Id.*, § 2. Decisions of this Court fully bear out the impression that choice-of-law clauses do not speak to any state-federal issue....

Moreover, the literal language of the contract—"the law of the place"—gives no indication of any intention to apply only state law and exclude other law that would normally be applicable to something taking place at that location. By settled principles of federal supremacy, the law of any place in the United States includes federal law. As the dissenting judge below noted, "under California law, federal law governs matters cognizable in California courts upon which the United States has definitively spoken." Thus, "the mere choice of California law is not a selection of California law over federal law...." In the absence of any evidence to the contrary it must be assumed that this is what the parties meant by "the law of the place where the Project is located."

Most commercial contracts written in this country contain choice-of-law clauses, similar to the one in the Stanford-Volt contract, specifying which State's law is to govern the interpretation of the contract. Were every state court to construe such clauses as an expression of the parties' intent to exclude the application of federal law, as has the California Court of Appeal in this case, the result would be to render the Federal Arbitration Act a virtual nullity as to presently existing contracts. I cannot believe that the parties to contracts intend such consequences to flow from their insertion of a standard choice-of-law clause. Even less can I agree that we are powerless to review decisions of state courts that effectively nullify a vital piece of federal legislation. I respectfully dissent.

DirecTV, Inc. v. Imburgia

136 S. Ct. 463 (2015)

Breyer, J., delivered the opinion of the Court

The Federal Arbitration Act states that a "written provision" in a contract providing for "settle[ment] by arbitration" of "a controversy ... arising out of" that "contract ... shall be valid, irrevocable, and enforceable, save upon such grounds as exist at law or in equity for the revocation of any contract." 9 U. S. C. §2. We here consider a California court's refusal to enforce an arbitration provision in a contract. In our view, that decision does not rest "upon such grounds as exist ... for the revocation of any contract," and we consequently set that judgment aside.

I

DIRECTV, Inc., the petitioner, entered into a service agreement with its customers, including respondents Amy Imburgia and Kathy Greiner. Section 9 of that contract provides that "any Claim either of us asserts will be resolved only by binding arbitration." It then sets forth a waiver of class arbitration, stating that "[n]either you nor we shall be entitled to join or consolidate claims in arbitration." It adds that if the "law of your state" makes the waiver of class arbitration unenforceable, then the entire arbitration provision "is unenforceable." Section 10 of the contract states that §9, the arbitration provision, "shall be governed by the Federal Arbitration Act."

In 2008, the two respondents brought this lawsuit against DIRECTV in a California state court. They seek damages for early termination fees that they believe violate California law. After various proceedings not here relevant, DIRECTV, pointing to the arbitration provision, asked the court to send the matter to arbitration. The state trial court denied that request, and DIRECTV appealed.

The California Court of Appeal thought that the critical legal question concerned the meaning of the contractual phrase "law of your state," in this case the law of California. Does the law of California make the contract's class-arbitration waiver unenforceable? If so, as the contract provides, the entire arbitration provision is unenforceable. Or does California law permit the parties to agree to waive the right to proceed as a class in arbitration? If so, the arbitration provision is enforceable.

At one point, the law of California would have made the contract's class-arbitration waiver unenforceable. In 2005, the California Supreme Court held in *Discover Bank v. Superior Court*, that a "waiver" of class arbitration in a "consumer contract of adhesion" that "predictably involve[s] small amounts of damages" and meets certain other criteria not contested here is "unconscionable under California law and should not be enforced." But in 2011, this Court held that California's *Discover Bank* rule "'stands as an obstacle to the accomplishment and execution of the full purposes and objectives of Congress'" embodied in the Federal Arbitration Act. *AT & T Mobility LLC v. Concepcion*, 563 U.S. 333, 352 (2011). [The California Court of Appeals recognized that *Discover Bank* had been preempted by *Concepcion*; however, the court distinguished *Concepcion* due to the choice-of-law clause in the parties' contract. The court reasoned that the parties agreed to California law, including the *Discover Bank* rule. The California Supreme Court denied discretionary review.]

… While all accept this elementary point of law, that point does not resolve the issue in this case. As the Court of Appeal noted, the Federal Arbitration Act allows parties to an arbitration contract considerable latitude to choose what law governs some or all of its provisions, including the law governing enforceability of a class-arbitration waiver. In principle, they might choose to have portions of their contract governed by the law of Tibet, the law of pre-revolutionary Russia, or (as is relevant here) the law of California including the *Discover Bank* rule and irrespective of that rule's invalidation in *Concepcion*. The Court of Appeal decided that, as a matter of contract law, the parties did mean the phrase "law of your state" to refer to this last possibility. Since the interpretation of a contract is ordinarily a matter of state law to which we defer, *Volt Information Sciences, Inc. v. Board of Trustees of Leland Stanford Junior Univ.*, 489 U.S. 468 (1989), we must decide not whether its decision is a correct statement of California law but whether (assuming it is) that state law is consistent with the Federal Arbitration Act. ***

We recognize, as the dissent points out, that when DIRECTV drafted the contract, the parties likely believed that the words "law of your state" included California law that then made class-arbitration waivers unenforceable. But that does not answer the legal question before us. That is because this Court subsequently held in *Concepcion* that the *Discover Bank* rule was invalid. Thus the underlying question of contract law at the time the Court of Appeal made its decision was whether the "law of your state" included invalid California law. We must now decide whether answering that question in the affirmative is consistent with the Federal Arbitration Act. After examining the grounds upon which the Court of Appeal rested its decision, we conclude that California courts would not interpret contracts other than arbitration contracts the same way. Rather, several considerations lead us to conclude that the court's interpretation of this arbitration contract is unique, restricted to that field.

First, we do not believe that the relevant contract language is ambiguous. The contract says that "[i]f ... the law of your state would find this agreement to dispense with class arbitration procedures unenforceable, then this entire Section 9 [the arbitration section] is unenforceable." App. 129. Absent any indication in the contract that this language is meant to refer to invalid state law, it presumably takes its ordinary meaning: valid state law. Indeed, neither the parties nor the dissent refer us to any contract case from California or from any other State that interprets similar language to refer to state laws authoritatively held to be invalid. While we recognize that the dissent believes this phrase to be "ambiguous," or "anomalous," we cannot agree with that characterization.

Second, California case law itself clarifies any doubt about how to interpret the language. The California Supreme Court has held that under "general contract principles," references to California law incorporate the California Legislature's power to change the law retroactively. As far as we are aware, the principle of California law announced in Harris, not the Court of Appeal's decision here, would ordinarily govern the scope of phrases such as "law of your state."

Third, nothing in the Court of Appeal's reasoning suggests that a California court would reach the same interpretation of "law of your state" in any context other than arbitration. The Court of Appeal did not explain why parties might generally intend the words "law of your state" to encompass "invalid law of your state." To the contrary, the contract refers to "state law" that makes the waiver of class arbitration "unenforceable," while an invalid state law would not make a contractual provision unenforceable. Assuming—as we must—that the court's reasoning is a correct statement as to the meaning of "law of your state" in this arbitration provision, we can find nothing in that opinion (nor in any other California case) suggesting that California would generally interpret words such as "law of your state" to include state laws held invalid because they conflict with, say, federal labor statutes, federal pension statutes, federal antidiscrimination laws, the Equal Protection Clause, or the like. Even given our assumption that the Court of Appeal's conclusion is correct, its conclusion appears to reflect the subject matter at issue here (arbitration), rather than a general principle that would apply to contracts using similar language but involving state statutes invalidated by other federal law.

Fourth, the language used by the Court of Appeal focused only on arbitration. The court asked whether "law of your state" "mean[s] 'the law of your state to the extent it is not preempted by the [Federal Arbitration Act],' or 'the law of your state without considering the preemptive effect, if any of the [Federal Arbitration Act].' " Framing the question in such terms, rather than in generally applicable terms, suggests that the Court of Appeal could well have meant that its holding was limited to the specific subject matter of this contract—arbitration.

Fifth, the Court of Appeal reasoned that invalid state arbitration law, namely the Discover Bank rule, maintained legal force despite this Court's holding in *Concepcion.*

The court stated that "[i]f we apply state law alone ... to the class action waiver, then the waiver is unenforceable." And at the end of its opinion it reiterated that "[t]he class action waiver is unenforceable under California law, so the entire arbitration agreement is unenforceable." But those statements do not describe California law ... The view that state law retains independent force even after it has been authoritatively invalidated by this Court is one courts are unlikely to accept as a general matter and to apply in other contexts.

Sixth, there is no other principle invoked by the Court of Appeal that suggests that California courts would reach the same interpretation of the words "law of your state" in other contexts. The court said that the phrase "law of your state" constitutes "'a specific exception'" to the agreement's "'general adoption of the [Federal Arbitration Act].' But that tells us nothing about how to interpret the words "law of your state" elsewhere. It does not answer the relevant question: whether those words encompass laws that have been authoritatively held invalid...."

Taking these considerations together, we reach a conclusion that, in our view, falls well within the confines of (and goes no further than) present well-established law. California's interpretation of the phrase "law of your state" does not place arbitration contracts "on equal footing with all other contracts." For that reason, it does not give "due regard ... to the federal policy favoring arbitration." Thus, the Court of Appeal's interpretation is pre-empted by the Federal Arbitration Act. Hence, the California Court of Appeal must "enforc[e]" the arbitration agreement. 9 U.S.C. §2.

The judgment of the California Court of Appeal is reversed, and the case is remanded for further proceedings not inconsistent with this opinion.

It is so ordered.

Justice GINSBURG, with whom Justice SOTOMAYOR joins, dissenting.

The Court today holds that the California Court of Appeal interpreted the language in DIRECTV's service agreement so unreasonably as to suggest discrimination against arbitration in violation of the FAA. As I see it, the California court's interpretation of the "law of your state" provision is not only reasonable, it is entirely right.

Arbitration is a matter of "consent, not coercion." The FAA "requires courts to enforce privately negotiated agreements to arbitrate, like other contracts, in accordance with their terms." "[T]he interpretation of private contracts is ordinarily a question of state law, which this Court does not sit to review." Historically, this Court has respected state-court interpretations of arbitration agreements. Indeed, in the more than 25 years between *Volt Information Sciences* and this case, not once has this Court reversed a state-court decision on the ground that the state court misapplied state contract law when it determined the meaning of a term in a particular arbitration agreement. Today's decision is a dangerous first....

1. Comments and Questions

a. In *Volt*, what is the California law at issue? Under *Concepcion*, would that California law be preempted? If so, can it still be incorporated into parties' arbitration agreements? To what extent do the parties still have freedom to contract around the FAA?

b. Does *Imburgia* overrule *Volt* directly or indirectly? Can these decisions be read together? The *Imburgia* majority cites *Volt* in its opinion. Does that make a difference?

c. Between *Volt* and *Imburgia*, the Supreme Court decided another case involving a choice-of-law clause. In 1995, the Court decided *Mastrobuono v. Shearson Lehman Hutton, Inc.*, 514 U.S. 52 (1995), another case that called into question *Volt's* continuing applicability. The *Mastrobuono* case arose from a securities industry arbitration between a customer and a broker. The arbitration agreement contained two potential choice-of-law provisions. First, the arbitration agreement contained a provision designating New York law as the applicable law. Second, the arbitration agreement specified that the arbitration would proceed in accordance with the rules of the National Association of Securities Dealers (NASD) (a predecessor to FINRA).

The question in *Mastrobuono* was whether the arbitration award should be overturned after the arbitrator awarded punitive damages. New York law did not permit arbitrators to award punitive damages. The NASD arbitration rules, on the other hand, gave arbitrators broad remedial powers. The Supreme Court upheld the award, finding that the New York choice-of-law clause did not apply with respect to the award of punitive damages and that the NASD rules applied with respect to the types of available remedies. Justice Thomas dissented on the ground that a straightforward application of *Volt* would mean that New York's prohibition on arbitrators awarding punitive damages would apply. Given *Mastrobuono*, does the Court's decision in *Imburgia* surprise you?

2. Choice of Forum Provisions: Comments and Questions

a. The Supreme Court has long upheld forum-selection clauses as part of parties' freedom to contract. *See Carnival Cruise Lines, Inc. v. Shute*, 499 U.S. 585 (1991). The *Shute* case involved a forum-selection clause in a consumer contract for a cruise. As the Eleventh Circuit noted, "After *Shute*, it is clear that some contractual forum-selection clauses, even if not freely negotiated, are prima facie enforceable.... Such a clause avoids litigation in multiple fora; it determines beforehand where disputes can be brought and therefore reduces the time and expense of litigation and promotes ease of judicial administration. All of these factors result in a lowering of overall consumer costs." *Estate of Myhra v. Royal Caribbean Cruises, Ltd.*, 695 F.3d 1233 (11th Cir. 2012).

b. Because arbitration is a creature of contract, can the parties choose the forum, or location, of the arbitration? Theoretically, the answer is yes. One of arbitration's many benefits is the ability to have an arbitration at a location that makes sense for the parties. In business-to-business disputes, the parties may choose to arbitrate in a location convenient to one or both of the parties. In some circumstances, parties may choose an inconvenient—but neutral—locale for the hearing. For instance, if one party is located in the state of New York and the other party is located in California, the parties could easily decide to arbitrate all disputes in Chicago. Choosing a location like Chicago would put both parties on neutral ground, and the inconvenient location might serve as a financial incentive to settle disputes prior to the hearing. Parties to international arbitration agreements often choose a neutral location to avoid any perceived benefits for a party arbitrating on "home turf."

c. What about consumers and employees? Can and should businesses use a choice-of-forum clause in arbitration agreements? On the one hand, a business that arbitrates many cases might find it convenient to arbitrate all of the cases in one location. On the other hand, can companies force consumers and employees to travel a great distance in order to arbitrate a case? Should the value of the case matter? Business entities should determine whether requiring consumers and employees to arbitrate far from their home would render an arbitration agreement unconscionable. *Compare* Tompkins v. 23andMe, Inc., 840 F.3d 1016 (9th Cir. 2016) (upholding a forum-selection clause requiring arbitration in San Francisco, California, in a contract to provide genetic testing services) *with* Aral v. Earthlink, 134 Cal. App. 4th 544 (Cal. Ct. App. 2005) (finding unconscionable an arbitration agreement requiring customers to travel to Georgia to arbitrate claims that were predictably valued under $50).

d. A discussion of "choice of forum" can also refer to the choice of an arbitration services provider, as opposed to a choice of the physical location of the hearing. What should happen if the provider designated in the arbitration agreement is unavailable? *See, e.g.,* Jackson v. Payday Financial, LLC, 764 F.3d 765 (7th Cir. 2014) (court held an agreement to arbitrate was illusory when the arbitration forum designated in the contract—the Cheyenne River Sioux Tribe—did not have a procedure to arbitrate cases); Flagg v. First Premier Bank, 644 Fed. Appx. 893 11th Cir. 2016) (invalidating arbitration agreement when the agreement designated the National Arbitration Forum, a now-defunct arbitration provider, as the provider organization).

Chapter 3

Allocation of Authority between Courts and Arbitrators

A. Introduction

The Federal Arbitration Act (FAA) provides that a written agreement to arbitrate existing or future disputes is "valid, enforceable and irrevocable, save upon such grounds as exist at law or in equity for the revocation of any contract." FAA § 2. This section applies in both federal court and state court to arbitration agreements "in any maritime transaction or a contract evidencing a transaction involving commerce." FAA § 2. Thus, private arbitration of commercial disputes depends on some form of written agreement by the parties (contractual arbitration).

Parties whose disputes are subject to contractual arbitration generally proceed voluntarily before an arbitrator for final and binding adjudication. However, when parties do not agree about their obligation to arbitrate, courts can become involved in a variety of ways. For example, one party—either unaware of its contractual obligation to arbitrate or unwilling to arbitrate—may simply file a lawsuit in court. If so, the party wanting to arbitrate may seek an order from the court compelling the "reluctant" party to arbitrate and staying the litigation. Alternatively, a party desiring arbitration may initiate the arbitration process by giving appropriate notice to the reluctant party or to an arbitration services provider to effect notice, and moving in a court of competent jurisdiction for an order compelling arbitration. The reluctant party may, in turn, seek an order staying the arbitration. In either situation, a court might need to determine "gateway" legal issues regarding the validity and scope of the arbitration agreement before it can stay litigation or compel arbitration. *See* FAA § 3 (empowering court to stay litigation "upon being satisfied that the issue involved in such suit or proceeding is referable to arbitration under [an agreement in writing]"); FAA § 4 (empowering court to compel arbitration "upon being satisfied that the making of the agreement for arbitration or the failure to comply therewith is not in issue").

The legal question as to whether a dispute is subject to a valid arbitration clause is known as "arbitrability." The Supreme Court has developed important principles governing this "arbitrability" inquiry. First, a court may order arbitration of a particular dispute only where the court is satisfied that the parties agreed to arbitrate *that dispute*. Even if plaintiff's complaint contains both arbitrable and non-arbitrable claims, a court must order arbitrable disputes to arbitration. *See KPMG LLP v. Cocchi*, 565

U.S. 18 (2011). Second, when deciding whether the parties agreed to arbitrate a certain matter, courts should apply ordinary state-law principles that govern the formation of contracts. *See First Options of Chicago, Inc. v. Kaplan*, 514 U.S. 938, 944 (1995). Third, and perhaps most significantly, under what is now known as the presumption of arbitrability, "[a]ny doubts concerning the scope of arbitrable issues should be resolved in favor of arbitration." *Moses H. Cone Mem'l Hosp. v. Mercury Constr. Corp.*, 460 U.S. 1, 24–25 (1983).

Despite this "presumption of arbitrability," many of these arbitrability inquiries question the competency of arbitrators — as opposed to judges — to decide certain types of claims. This Chapter explores the Supreme Court decisions that impact the allocation of decisional authority between courts and arbitrators. Section B addresses the threshold question of **who decides** the question of arbitrability; that is, does a court or an arbitrator decide whether a dispute is arbitrable or not?

Section C addresses another issue implicating the allocation of authority between courts and arbitrators: the "**separability**" **doctrine.** Set forth originally in *Prima Paint Corp. v. Flood & Conklin Mfg. Co.*, 388 U.S. 395 (1967), and reaffirmed in *Buckeye Check Cashing, Inc. v. Cardegna*, 546 U.S. 440 (2006), and *Rent-A-Center, W., Inc. v. Jackson*, 561 U.S. 63 (2010), this doctrine addresses the situation where a party challenges the validity of an overall contract containing an arbitration agreement on a ground that is not directed at the arbitration clause specifically, such as fraud of the underlying contract. If the entire contract is illegal or the product of fraud, then isn't the arbitration agreement invalidated, too? As you will read, under the "separability" doctrine, a court is to consider claims opposing arbitration only where a claim of unenforceability is directed to the arbitration clause itself.

Section D focuses on the **arbitrability of federal statutory claims.** Since the passage of the FAA, reluctant parties have argued that claims arising under federal or state statutes (e.g., claims arising under federal anti-discrimination, securities, or antitrust laws or even state consumer protection laws) should not be subject to arbitration at all, on the grounds that arbitrators are not qualified to rule on such claims or that the arbitration process does not permit claimants to effectively prove statutory claims. The Supreme Court's view on this issue has evolved over time, but in modern times the Court has rejected these arguments, instead ruling that statutory claims are arbitrable absent a "contrary Congressional command." *See CompuCredit Corp. v. Greenwood*, 565 U.S. 95, 100–01 (2012).

Section E addresses the interaction of the FAA and state insurance regulation. The normal rule that federal law supersedes state law is inapplicable in the insurance context because Congress has expressly granted the states authority to regulate insurance in the McCarran-Ferguson Act. The extent to which state insurance law effects a "**reverse preemption**" of the FAA is a complex and interesting topic. It also raises questions as to the competence of arbitrators, as several states' insurance laws purport to strip arbitrators of the authority to decide insurance disputes.

B. Who Decides Arbitrability?

This section explores the seemingly arcane and technical, but extremely significant, question of who decides—the court or arbitrator—the question of arbitrability. The first case in this section, *First Options v. Kaplan*, 514 U.S. 938 (1995), sets forth a basic allocation of authority between the court and the arbitrator in accord with parties' presumed expectations. Unless the parties have explicitly agreed otherwise, courts determine whether the parties have entered into a valid arbitration agreement and whether the dispute is within the scope of such agreement. Once a court has made this determination, the arbitrator decides all other issues. As subsequent cases demonstrate, however, many other issues permeate determining the validity of an arbitral agreement. Who, for example, addresses claims, unrelated to the merits of the underlying case, but which contend that arbitration may not be ordered because certain procedural aspects were either not satisfied or unconscionable in themselves? In reading these cases, consider whether the proposed analytical distinction between substantive and procedural arbitrability in allocating decisional authority is helpful.

1. Substantive Arbitrability

First Options of Chicago, Inc. v. Kaplan

514 U.S. 938 (1995)

Justice Breyer delivered the opinion of the Court.

In this case we consider ... how a district court should review an arbitrator's decision that the parties agreed to arbitrate a dispute ... The case concerns several related disputes between, on one side, First Options of Chicago, Inc., a firm that clears stock trades on the Philadelphia Stock Exchange, and, on the other side, three parties: Manuel Kaplan; his wife, Carol Kaplan; and his wholly owned investment company, MK Investments, Inc. (MKI), whose trading account First Options cleared. The disputes center around a "workout" agreement, embodied in four separate documents, which governs the "working out" of debts to First Options that MKI and the Kaplans incurred as a result of the October 1987 stock market crash ... [Subsequent losses led First Options to make further financial demands.] When its demands went unsatisfied, First Options sought arbitration by a panel of the Philadelphia Stock Exchange.

MKI, having signed the only workout document (out of four) that contained an arbitration clause, accepted arbitration. The Kaplans, however, who had not personally signed that document, denied that their disagreement with First Options was arbitrable and filed written objections to that effect with the arbitration panel. The arbitrators decided that they had the power to rule on the merits of the parties' dispute, and did so in favor of First Options. [A federal district court confirmed the award, but the Court of Appeals reversed.] ...

We granted certiorari to consider ... the standard[] that the Court of Appeals used to review the determination that the Kaplans' dispute with First Options was arbitrable. First, the Court of Appeals said that courts "should independently decide whether an arbitration panel has jurisdiction over the merits of any particular dispute." First Options asked us to decide whether this is so (i.e., whether courts, in "reviewing the arbitrators' decision on arbitrability," should "apply a de novo standard of review or the more deferential standard applied to arbitrators' decisions on the merits") when the objecting party "submitted the issue to the arbitrators for decision." ...

The first question — the standard of review applied to an arbitrator's decision about arbitrability — is a narrow one. To understand just how narrow, consider three types of disagreement present in this case. First, the Kaplans and First Options disagree about whether the Kaplans are personally liable for MKI's debt to First Options. That disagreement makes up the merits of the dispute. Second, they disagree about whether they agreed to arbitrate the merits. That disagreement is about the arbitrability of the dispute. Third, they disagree about who should have the primary power to decide the second matter. Does that power belong primarily to the arbitrators (because the court reviews their arbitrability decision deferentially) or to the court (because the court makes up its mind about arbitrability independently)? We consider here only this third question.

Although the question is a narrow one, it has a certain practical importance. That is because a party who has not agreed to arbitrate will normally have a right to a court's decision about the merits of its dispute (say, as here, its obligation under a contract). But, where the party has agreed to arbitrate, he or she, in effect, has relinquished much of that right's practical value. The party still can ask a court to review the arbitrator's decision, but the court will set that decision aside only in very unusual circumstances. Hence, who — court or arbitrator — has the primary authority to decide whether a party has agreed to arbitrate can make a critical difference to a party resisting arbitration.

We believe the answer to the "who" question (i.e., the standard-of-review question) is fairly simple. Just as the arbitrability of the merits of a dispute depends upon whether the parties agreed to arbitrate that dispute, so the question "who has the primary power to decide arbitrability" turns upon what the parties agreed about that matter. Did the parties agree to submit the arbitrability question itself to arbitration? If so, then the court's standard for reviewing the arbitrator's decision about that matter should not differ from the standard courts apply when they review any other matter that parties have agreed to arbitrate. That is to say, the court should give considerable leeway to the arbitrator, setting aside his or her decision only in certain narrow circumstances. If, on the other hand, the parties did not agree to submit the arbitrability question itself to arbitration, then the court should decide that question just as it would decide any other question that the parties did not submit to arbitration, namely independently. These two answers flow inexorably from the fact that arbitration is simply a matter of contract between the parties; it is a way to resolve those disputes — but only those disputes — that the parties have agreed to submit to arbitration.

We agree with First Options, therefore, that a court must defer to an arbitrator's arbitrability decision when the parties submitted that matter to arbitration. Nevertheless, that conclusion does not help First Options win this case. That is because a fair and complete answer to the standard-of-review question requires a word about how a court should decide whether the parties have agreed to submit the arbitrability issue to arbitration. And, that word makes clear that the Kaplans did not agree to arbitrate arbitrability here.

When deciding whether the parties agreed to arbitrate a certain matter (including arbitrability), courts generally (though with a qualification we discuss below) should apply ordinary state-law principles that govern the formation of contracts. The relevant state law here, for example, would require the court to see whether the parties objectively revealed an intent to submit the arbitrability issue to arbitration.

... [H]owever ... [c]ourts should not assume that the parties agreed to arbitrate arbitrability unless there is "clea[r] and unmistakabl[e]" evidence that they did so. In this manner the law treats silence or ambiguity about the question "who (primarily) should decide arbitrability" differently from the way it treats silence or ambiguity about the question "*whether* a particular merits-related dispute is arbitrable because it is within the scope of a valid arbitration agreement" — for in respect to this latter question the law reverses the presumption.

But, this difference in treatment is understandable. The latter question arises when the parties have a contract that provides for arbitration of some issues. In such circumstances, the parties likely gave at least some thought to the scope of arbitration. And, given the law's permissive policies in respect to arbitration, one can understand why the law would insist upon clarity before concluding that the parties did not want to arbitrate a related matter. On the other hand, the former question — the "who (primarily) should decide arbitrability" question — is rather arcane. A party often might not focus upon that question or upon the significance of having arbitrators decide the scope of their own powers. And, given the principle that a party can be forced to arbitrate only those issues it specifically has agreed to submit to arbitration, one can understand why courts might hesitate to interpret silence or ambiguity on the "who should decide arbitrability" point as giving the arbitrators that power, for doing so might too often force unwilling parties to arbitrate a matter they reasonably would have thought a judge, not an arbitrator, would decide.

On the record before us, First Options cannot show that the Kaplans clearly agreed to have the arbitrators decide (i.e., to arbitrate) the question of arbitrability. First Options relies on the Kaplans' filing with the arbitrators a written memorandum objecting to the arbitrators' jurisdiction. But merely arguing the arbitrability issue to an arbitrator does not indicate a clear willingness to arbitrate that issue, i.e., a willingness to be effectively bound by the arbitrator's decision on that point. To the contrary, insofar as the Kaplans were forcefully objecting to the arbitrators deciding their dispute with First Options, one naturally would think that they did not want the arbitrators to have binding authority over them....

We conclude that, because the Kaplans did not clearly agree to submit the question of arbitrability to arbitration, the Court of Appeals was correct in finding that the arbitrability of the Kaplan/First Options dispute was subject to independent review by the courts. ...

The judgment of the Court of Appeals is affirmed.

2. Procedural Arbitrability

Howsam v. Dean Witter Reynolds, Inc.

537 U.S. 79 (2002)

JUSTICE BREYER delivered the opinion of the Court.

This case focuses upon an arbitration rule of the National Association of Securities Dealers (NASD). The rule states that no dispute "shall be eligible for submission to arbitration ... where six (6) years have elapsed from the occurrence or event giving rise to the ... dispute." NASD Code of Arbitration Procedure § 10304 (1984) (NASD Code). We must decide whether a court or an NASD arbitrator should apply the rule to the underlying controversy. We conclude that the matter is for the arbitrator.

The underlying controversy arises out of investment advice that Dean Witter Reynolds, Inc. (Dean Witter), provided its client, Karen Howsam, when, some time between 1986 and 1994, it recommended that she buy and hold interests in four limited partnerships. Howsam says that Dean Witter misrepresented the virtues of the partnerships. The resulting controversy falls within their standard Client Service Agreement's arbitration clause.... The agreement also provides that Howsam can select the arbitration forum. And Howsam chose arbitration before the NASD.

To obtain NASD arbitration, Howsam signed the NASD's Uniform Submission Agreement. That agreement specified that the "present matter in controversy" was submitted for arbitration "in accordance with" the NASD's "Code of Arbitration Procedure." And that Code contains the provision at issue here, a provision stating that no dispute "shall be eligible for submission ... where six (6) years have elapsed from the occurrence or event giving rise to the ... dispute."

After the Uniform Submission Agreement was executed, Dean Witter filed this lawsuit in Federal District Court. It asked the court to declare that the dispute was "ineligible for arbitration" because it was more than six years old. And it sought an injunction that would prohibit Howsam from proceeding in arbitration. The District Court dismissed the action on the ground that the NASD arbitrator, not the court, should interpret and apply the NASD rule. The Court of Appeals for the Tenth Circuit, however, reversed. In its view, application of the NASD rule presented a question of the underlying dispute's "arbitrability"; and the presumption is that a court, not an arbitrator, will ordinarily decide an "arbitrability" question.

The Courts of Appeals have reached different conclusions about whether a court or an arbitrator primarily should interpret and apply this particular NASD rule. We granted Howsam's petition for certiorari to resolve this disagreement. And we now hold that the matter is for the arbitrator.

II

This Court has determined that "arbitration is a matter of contract and a party cannot be required to submit to arbitration any dispute which he has not agreed so to submit." Although the Court has also long recognized and enforced a "liberal federal policy favoring arbitration agreements," *Moses H. Cone Memorial Hospital v. Mercury Constr. Corp.*, 460 U.S. 1 (1983), it has made clear that there is an exception to this policy: The question whether the parties have submitted a particular dispute to arbitration, i.e., the "*question of arbitrability*," is "an issue for judicial determination unless the parties clearly and unmistakably provide otherwise." *AT&T Technologies, Inc. v. Communications Workers*, 475 U.S. 643 (1986). We must decide here whether application of the NASD time limit provision falls into the scope of this last-mentioned interpretive rule.

Linguistically speaking, one might call any potentially dispositive gateway question a "question of arbitrability," for its answer will determine whether the underlying controversy will proceed to arbitration on the merits. The Court's case law, however, makes clear that, for purposes of applying the interpretive rule, the phrase "question of arbitrability" has a far more limited scope. The Court has found the phrase applicable in the kind of narrow circumstance where contracting parties would likely have expected a court to have decided the gateway matter, where they are not likely to have thought that they had agreed that an arbitrator would do so, and, consequently, where reference of the gateway dispute to the court avoids the risk of forcing parties to arbitrate a matter that they may well not have agreed to arbitrate.

Thus, a gateway dispute about whether the parties are bound by a given arbitration clause raises a "question of arbitrability" for a court to decide. *See* [*First Options*] (holding that a court should decide whether the arbitration contract bound parties who did not sign the agreement); *John Wiley & Sons, Inc. v. Livingston*, 376 U.S. 543 (1964) (holding that a court should decide whether an arbitration agreement survived a corporate merger and bound the resulting corporation). Similarly, a disagreement about whether an arbitration clause in a concededly binding contract applies to a particular type of controversy is for the court. *See, e.g., AT&T Technologies* (holding that a court should decide whether a labor-management layoff controversy falls within the arbitration clause of a collective-bargaining agreement); *Atkinson v. Sinclair Refining Co.*, 370 U.S. 238 (1962) (holding that a court should decide whether a clause providing for arbitration of various "grievances" covers claims for damages for breach of a no-strike agreement).

At the same time the Court has found the phrase "question of arbitrability" *not* applicable in other kinds of general circumstance where parties would likely expect that an arbitrator would decide the gateway matter. Thus " 'procedural' questions which grow out of the dispute and bear on its final disposition" are presumptively *not* for the judge, but for an arbitrator, to decide. *John Wiley, supra* (holding that an arbitrator should decide whether the first two steps of a grievance procedure were completed, where these steps are prerequisites to arbitration). So, too, the presumption is that the arbitrator should decide "allegations of waiver, delay, or a like defense to arbitrability." Indeed, the Revised Uniform Arbitration Act of 2000 (RUAA), seeking to "incorporate the holdings of the vast majority of state courts and the law that has developed under the [Federal Arbitration Act]," states that an "arbitrator shall decide whether a condition precedent to arbitrability has been fulfilled." RUAA § 6(c). And the comments add that "in the absence of an agreement to the contrary, issues of substantive arbitrability ... are for a court to decide and issues of procedural arbitrability, i.e., whether prerequisites such as *time limits*, notice, laches, estoppel, and other conditions precedent to an obligation to arbitrate have been met, are for the arbitrators to decide." *Id.*, § 6, cmt 2.

Following this precedent, we find that the applicability of the NASD time limit rule is a matter presumptively for the arbitrator, not for the judge. The time limit rule closely resembles the gateway questions that this Court has found not to be "questions of arbitrability." *E.g., Moses H. Cone Memorial Hospital* (referring to "waiver, delay, or a like defense"). Such a dispute seems an "aspect of the [controversy] which called the grievance procedures into play."

Moreover, the NASD arbitrators, comparatively more expert about the meaning of their own rule, are comparatively better able to interpret and to apply it. In the absence of any statement to the contrary in the arbitration agreement, it is reasonable to infer that the parties intended the agreement to reflect that understanding. And for the law to assume an expectation that aligns (1) decisionmaker with (2) comparative expertise will help better to secure a fair and expeditious resolution of the underlying controversy — a goal of arbitration systems and judicial systems alike.

We consequently conclude that the NASD's time limit rule falls within the class of gateway procedural disputes that do not present what our cases have called "questions of arbitrability." And the strong pro-court presumption as to the parties' likely intent does not apply.

III

Dean Witter argues that, in any event, i.e., even without an anti-arbitration presumption, we should interpret the contracts between the parties here as calling for judicial determination of the time limit matter. Howsam's execution of a Uniform Submission Agreement with the NASD in 1997 effectively incorporated the NASD Code into the parties' agreement. Dean Witter notes the Code's time limit rule uses the word "eligible." That word, in Dean Witter's view, indicates the parties' intent for the time limit rule to be resolved by the court prior to arbitration.

We do not see how that is so. For the reasons stated in Part II, parties to an arbitration contract would normally expect a forum-based decisionmaker to decide forum-specific procedural gateway matters. And any temptation here to place special antiarbitration weight on the appearance of the word "eligible" in the NASD Code rule is counterbalanced by a different NASD rule; that rule states that "arbitrators shall be empowered to interpret and determine the applicability of all provisions under this Code." NASD Code § 10324.

Consequently, without the help of a special arbitration-disfavoring presumption, we cannot conclude that the parties intended to have a court, rather than an arbitrator, interpret and apply the NASD time limit rule. And as we held in Part II, that presumption does not apply.... For these reasons, the judgment of the Tenth Circuit is *Reversed*.

3. Comments and Questions

a. Questions of arbitrability are potentially dispositive, "for [their] answer will determine whether the underlying controversy will proceed to arbitration on the merits." *Howsam*, 537 U.S. at 83. Indeed, in both *First Options* and *Howsam*, the respective challenges to arbitration — that the Kaplans were not parties to the arbitration agreement and that Howsam's claim was time-barred under forum rules — were dispositive of whether either party would be required to arbitrate the underlying controversy. Why did the court decide that question in *First Options*, yet the arbitrator decided in *Howsam*?

b. What happened to the *Moses H. Cone* (*see supra*) presumption of arbitrability in *First Options*?

c. Recall that, in *First Options*, the Kaplans had filed written objections with the arbitration panel, which ruled that the claims against the Kaplans (although nonsignatories) could go forward in the arbitration. In affirming reversal of the award, the Supreme Court ruled that a district court should apply a *de novo* standard of review of the arbitrator's decision on arbitrability. As a procedural matter, how would you advise clients, such as the Kaplans, to raise their arbitrability objection? Must a party raise the arbitrability objection at the outset of the case, whether in arbitration or in court? Is there a risk in not doing so?

d. Note that, in *Howsam*, the Supreme Court construes the term "arbitrability" narrowly, stating that "questions of arbitrability are for the court." 537 U.S. at 85. In practice, the term "arbitrability" is more broadly used to refer to many threshold determinations, and subsequent Supreme Court cases have clarified that "arbitrability" issues that are reserved for a court to decide are those challenging the *making* of the arbitration agreement; i.e., did *these parties* agree to arbitrate *this dispute*?

e. The Supreme Court has applied the same *First Options/Howsam* analytical framework for the "who decides" question in labor arbitration. *See Granite Rock Co. v. Int'l Brotherhood of Teamsters*, 561 U.S. 287, 296–97 (2010); *AT&T Technologies, Inc. v. Communications Workers*, 475 U.S. 643 (1986). For that rare arbitration not subject to the FAA, the RUAA adopts that same framework. *See* RUAA, § 2(b). In international arbitration, the standard expression for the arbitrability question is "competence about competence" (also called *kompetenz-kompetenz*). *See* William W. Park, *The Arbitrability Dicta in* First Options v. Kaplan: *What Sort of Kompetenz-Kompetenz Has Crossed the Atlantic*, 12 ARB. INT'L 137 (1996).

f. In 2014, in *BG Group, PLC v. Republic of Argentina*, 134 S. Ct. 1198 (2014), an investor-state arbitration held in Washington, D.C., that arose out of an investment treaty, the Supreme Court ruled that arbitrators, not a court, decide whether the parties met a condition precedent to arbitration. In *BG Group*, the condition precedent at issue was the treaty's provision that disputes arising out of the treaty should be submitted to a local court first, and then, if 18 months passed without a final decision from that court, the dispute could be arbitrated. The arbitrators had decided that compliance with the litigation requirement was excused because of a series of Argentinian laws that would block any lawsuit by the investor. The Supreme Court, applying the *First Options/Howsam* framework, held that courts should presume that "parties intend arbitrators, not courts, to decide disputes about the meaning and application of particular procedural preconditions for the use of arbitration." Do you think the result in *BG Group* is consistent with the *First Options/Howsam* framework?

g. If parties agree to arbitrate pursuant to a forum's rules, and those forum rules provide that its arbitrators have the authority to decide questions of arbitrability (the rules of the American Arbitration Association [AAA] provide this), does that forum rule constitute "clear and unmistakable evidence" under *First Options* that the parties have delegated arbitrability to the arbitrator? Most federal courts hold that it does. *See, e.g., Eckert/Wordell Architects, Inc. v. FJM Properties of Willmar LLC*, 756 F.3d 1098, 1100 (8th Cir. 2014) (AAA rules); *Brennan v. Opus Bank*, 796 F.3d 1125, 1131 (9th Cir. 2015) (same). *But see Chesapeake Appalachia, LLC v. Scout Petroleum, LLC*, 809 F.3d 746 (3d Cir. 2016) (incorporation of AAA rules is not "clear and unmistakable" evidence parties intended to delegate issue of class arbitrability to arbitrators).

4. Problem

Many issues do not fit neatly within the substantive/procedural arbitrability distinction. Under the *First Options/Howsam* framework, who decides the following questions—the arbitrator or court? Would it make a difference if the contract assigned this decision to the arbitrator?

(a) The applicability of a relevant statute of limitations.

(b) Whether the parties agreed to a one- or three-arbitrator panel.

(c) Whether provisions in the contract may be illegal and thus divest the arbitrator of authority.

(d) Whether the parties agreed to class arbitration if the arbitration clause is silent.

(e) Whether the arbitration agreement forbids consolidated arbitration.

(f) The venue/location of the arbitration merits hearing.

(g) Whether a class action waiver provision in an arbitration clause is unconscionable.

C. The Separability Doctrine and Delegation Clauses: *Prima Paint* and Its Progeny

Most contract issues discussed in this Chapter should be familiar to law students from their first-year Contracts course, even if the arbitration context is initially unfamiliar. The separability doctrine, by contrast, is unique to arbitration agreements. The following materials examine what is separability and how this doctrine operates in arbitration. Discussions of separability begin with the Supreme Court's *Prima Paint* decision and continue with *Buckeye* and *Rent-A-Center*. Questions regarding the outer limits of the separability doctrine continue to be raised in recent cases.

Prima Paint Corp. v. Flood & Conklin Mfg. Co.
388 U.S. 395 (1967)

JUSTICE FORTAS delivered the opinion of the Court.

This case presents the question whether the federal court or an arbitrator is to resolve a claim of "fraud in the inducement," under a contract governed by the FAA, where there is no evidence that the contracting parties intended to withhold that issue from arbitration.

The agreement involved here is a consulting agreement in which Flood & Conklin agreed to perform certain services for and not to compete with Prima Paint. The agreement contained a broad arbitration clause providing that: "Any controversy or claim arising out of or relating to this Agreement shall be settled by arbitration in the City of New York." F & C, contending that Prima had failed to make a payment under the contract, sent Prima a Notice of Intention to Arbitrate pursuant to the [Federal] Arbitration Act. Invoking diversity jurisdiction, Prima brought this action in federal district court to rescind the entire consulting agreement on the ground of fraud. The fraud allegedly consisted of F & C's misrepresentation at the time the contract was made, that it was solvent and able to perform the agreement, while in fact it was completely insolvent. Prima alleged that it would not have made any contract at all with F & C but for this misrepresentation. Prima simply contended that there was never a meeting of minds between the parties. F & C moved to stay Prima's lawsuit for rescission pending arbitration of the fraud issue raised by Prima. [This paragraph is taken from Justice Black's dissent.]

Having determined that the contract in question is within the coverage of the Arbitration Act [because the underlying transaction involved interstate commerce], we turn to the central issue in this case: whether a claim of fraud in the inducement of the entire contract is to be resolved by the federal court, or whether the matter is to be referred to the arbitrators.

With respect to cases brought in federal court involving maritime contracts or those evidencing transactions in commerce, we think that Congress has provided an explicit answer. That answer is to be found in section 4 of the Act, which provides a remedy to a party seeking to compel compliance with an arbitration agreement. Under section 4, with respect to a matter within the jurisdiction of the federal courts save for the existence of an arbitration clause, the federal court is instructed to order arbitration to proceed once it is satisfied that "the making of the agreement for arbitration or the failure to comply (with the arbitration agreement) is not in issue." Accordingly, if the claim is fraud in the inducement of the arbitration clause itself—

an issue which goes to the making of the agreement to arbitrate — the federal court may proceed to adjudicate it. But the statutory language does not permit the federal court to consider claims of fraud in the inducement of the contract generally. Section 4 does not expressly relate to situations like the present in which a stay is sought of a federal action in order that arbitration may proceed. But it is inconceivable that Congress intended the rule to differ depending upon which party to the arbitration agreement first invokes the assistance of a federal court. We hold, therefore, that in passing upon a section 3 application for a stay while the parties arbitrate, a federal court may consider only issues relating to the making and performance of the agreement to arbitrate. In so concluding, we not only honor the plain meaning of the statute but also the unmistakably clear congressional purpose that the arbitration procedure, when selected by the parties, be speedy and not subject to delay and obstruction in the courts. * * *

In the present case no claim has been advanced by Prima Paint that F & C fraudulently induced it to enter into the agreement to arbitrate "(a)ny controversy or claim arising out of or relating to this Agreement, or the breach thereof." This contractual language is easily broad enough to encompass Prima Paint's claim that both execution and acceleration of the consulting agreement itself were procured by fraud. Indeed, no claim is made that Prima Paint ever intended that "legal" issues relating to the contract be excluded from arbitration, or that it was not entirely free so to contract. Federal courts are bound to apply rules enacted by Congress with respect to matters — here, a contract involving commerce — over which it has legislative power. The question which Prima Paint requested the District Court to adjudicate preliminarily to allowing arbitration to proceed is one not intended by Congress to delay the granting of a section 3 stay. Accordingly, the decision below dismissing Prima Paint's appeal is affirmed.

Mr. Justice Black, with whom Mr. Justice Douglas and Mr. Justice Stewart join, dissenting.

The Court here holds that the FAA as a matter of federal substantive law, compels a party to a contract containing a written arbitration provision to carry out his "arbitration agreement" even though a court might, after a fair trial, hold the entire contract — including the arbitration agreement — void because of fraud in the inducement. The Court holds, what is to me fantastic, that the legal issue of a contract's voidness because of fraud is to be decided by persons designated to arbitrate factual controversies arising out of a valid contract between the parties. And the arbitrators who the Court holds are to adjudicate the legal validity of the contract need not even be lawyers, and in all probability will be nonlawyers, wholly unqualified to decide legal issues, and even if qualified to apply the law, not bound to do so. I am by no means sure that thus forcing a person to forgo his opportunity to try his legal issues in the courts where, unlike the situation in arbitration, he may have a jury trial and right to appeal, is not a denial of due process of law. I am satisfied, however, that Congress did not impose any such procedures in the [FAA]. And I am fully satisfied that a reasonable and fair reading of that Act's language and history shows that both Congress and the framers of the Act were at great pains to emphasize that nonlawyers designated to adjust and arbitrate factual controversies arising out of valid contracts would not trespass upon the courts' prerogative to decide the legal question of whether any legal contract exists upon which to base an arbitration. * * *

... [T]he Court holds that the language of section 4 of the Act provides an "explicit answer" to the question of whether the arbitration clause is "separable" from the rest of the contract in which it is contained. Section 4 merely provides that the court must order arbitration if it is satisfied that the making of the agreement for arbitration is not in issue. That language, considered alone, far from providing an explicit answer, merely poses the further question of what kind of allegations put the making of the arbitration agreement in issue. * * *

[I]t is clear to me from the bill's sponsors' understanding of the function of arbitration that they never intended that the issue of fraud in the inducement be resolved by arbitration. They recognized two special values of arbitration: (1) the expertise of an arbitrator to decide factual questions in regard to the day-to-day performance of contractual obligations, and (2) the speed with which arbitration, as contrasted to litigation, could resolve disputes over performance of contracts and thus mitigate the damages and allow the parties to continue performance under the contracts. Arbitration serves neither of these functions where a contract is sought to be rescinded on the ground of fraud....

* * *

[T]he plain purpose of the Act as written by Congress was this and no more: Congress wanted federal courts to enforce contracts to arbitrate and plainly said so in the Act. But Congress also plainly said that whether a contract containing an arbitration clause can be rescinded on the ground of fraud is to be decided by the courts and not by the arbitrators. Prima here challenged in the courts the validity of its alleged contract with F & C as a whole, not in fragments. If there has never been any valid contract, then there is not now and never has been anything to arbitrate. If Prima's allegations are true, the sum total of what the Court does here is to force Prima to arbitrate a contract which is void and unenforceable before arbitrators who are given the power to make final legal determinations of their own jurisdiction, not even subject to effective review by the highest court in the land.... I would reverse.

Buckeye Check Cashing, Inc. v. Cardegna

546 U.S. 440 (2006)

JUSTICE SCALIA delivered the opinion of the Court.

We decide whether a court or an arbitrator should consider the claim that a contract containing an arbitration provision is void for illegality. Respondents John Cardegna and Donna Reuter entered into various deferred-payment transactions with petitioner Buckeye, in which they received cash in exchange for a personal check in the amount of the cash plus a finance charge. For each separate transaction they signed a "Deferred Deposit and Disclosure Agreement" (Agreement), which included ... arbitration provisions....

Respondents brought this putative class action in Florida state court, alleging that Buckeye charged usurious interest rates and that the Agreement violated various Florida lending and consumer protection laws, rendering it criminal on its face. Buck-eye moved to compel arbitration. The trial court denied the motion, holding that a court rather than an arbitrator should resolve a claim that a contract is illegal and void *ab initio*. The District Court of Appeal of Florida for the Fourth District reversed, holding that because respondents did not challenge the arbitration provision itself, but instead claimed that the entire contract was void, the agreement to arbitrate was enforceable, and the question of the contract's legality should go to the arbitrator. The Florida Supreme Court reversed, reasoning that to enforce an agreement to arbitrate in a contract challenged as unlawful "could breathe life into a contract that not only violates state law, but also is criminal in nature...."

To overcome judicial resistance to arbitration, Congress enacted the FAA. Section 2 embodies the national policy favoring arbitration and places arbitration agreements on equal footing with all other contracts.... Challenges to the validity of arbitration agreements "upon such grounds as exist at law or in equity for the revocation of any contract" can be divided into two types. One type challenges specifically the validity of the agreement to arbitrate. The other challenges the contract as a whole, either on a ground that directly affects the entire agreement (e.g., the agreement was fraudulently induced), or on the ground that the illegality of one of the contract's provisions renders the whole contract invalid. Respondents' claim is of this second type. The crux of the complaint is that the contract as a whole (including its arbitration provision) is rendered invalid by the usurious finance charge....

In *Prima Paint Corp. v. Flood & Conklin Mfg. Co.*, we addressed the question of who—court or arbitrator—decides these two types of challenges. The issue in the case was "whether a claim of fraud in the inducement of the entire contract is to be resolved by the federal court, or whether the matter is to be referred to the arbitrators." Guided by §4 of the FAA, we held that "if the claim is fraud in the inducement of the arbitration clause itself—an issue which goes to the making of the agreement to arbitrate—the federal court may proceed to adjudicate it. But the statutory language does not permit the federal court to consider claims of fraud in the inducement of the contract generally." We rejected the view that the question of "severability" was one of state law, so that if state law held the arbitration provision not to be severable a challenge to the contract as a whole would be decided by the court.

Subsequently, in *Southland Corp.*, we held that the FAA "create[d] a body of federal substantive law," which was "applicable in state and federal court." We rejected the view that state law could bar enforcement of §2, even in the context of state-law claims brought in state court.

Prima Paint and *Southland* answer the question presented here by establishing three propositions. First, as a matter of substantive federal arbitration law, an arbitration provision is severable from the remainder of the contract. Second, unless the challenge is to the arbitration clause itself, the issue of the contract's validity is considered by the arbitrator in the first instance. Third, this arbitration law applies in state as well as federal courts. The parties have not requested, and we do not undertake, reconsideration of those holdings. Applying them to this case, we conclude that because respondents challenge the Agreement, but not specifically its arbitration provisions, those provisions are enforceable apart from the remainder of the contract. The challenge should therefore be considered by an arbitrator, not a court.

In declining to apply *Prima Paint's* rule of severability, the Florida Supreme Court relied on the distinction between void and voidable contracts. "Florida public policy and contract law," it concluded, permit "no severable, or salvageable, parts of a contract found illegal and void under Florida law." ... We simply rejected the proposition that the enforceability of the arbitration agreement turned on the state legislature's judgment concerning the forum for enforcement of the state-law cause of action. So also here, we cannot accept the Florida Supreme Court's conclusion that enforceability of the arbitration agreement should turn on "Florida public policy and contract law."

Respondents assert that *Prima Paint's* rule of severability does not apply in state court. They argue that *Prima Paint* interpreted only §§ 3 and 4 — two of the FAA's procedural provisions, which appear to apply by their terms only in federal court — but not § 2, the only provision that we have applied in state court. This does not accurately describe *Prima Paint*. Although § 4, in particular, had much to do with *Prima Paint's* understanding of the rule of severability, this rule ultimately arises out of § 2, the FAA's substantive command that arbitration agreements be treated like all other contracts. The rule of severability establishes how this equal-footing guarantee for "a written [arbitration] provision" is to be implemented. Respondents' reading of *Prima Paint* as establishing nothing more than a federal-court rule of procedure also runs contrary to *Southland's* understanding of that case....

Respondents point to the language of § 2, which renders "valid, irrevocable, and enforceable" "a written provision in" or "an agreement in writing to submit to arbitration an existing controversy arising out of" a "contract." Since, respondents argue, the only arbitration agreements to which § 2 applies are those involving a "contract," and since an agreement void *ab initio* under state law is not a "contract," there is no "written provision" in or "controversy arising out of" a "contract," to which § 2 can apply. This argument echoes Justice Black's dissent in *Prima Paint*: "Sections 2 and 3 of the Act assume the existence of a valid contract. They merely provide for enforcement where such a valid contract exists." We do not read "contract" so narrowly.... We note that neither *Prima Paint* nor *Southland* lends support to respondents' reading; as we have discussed, neither case turned on whether the challenge at issue would render the contract voidable or void....

We reaffirm today that, regardless of whether the challenge is brought in federal or state court, a challenge to the validity of the contract as a whole, and not specifically to the arbitration clause, must go to the arbitrator.

The judgment of the Florida Supreme Court is reversed, and the case is remanded for further proceedings not inconsistent with this opinion.

JUSTICE THOMAS, dissenting.

I remain of the view that the FAA does not apply to proceedings in state courts. Thus, in state court proceedings, the FAA cannot be the basis for displacing a state law that prohibits enforcement of an arbitration clause contained in a contract that is unenforceable under state law. Accordingly, I would leave undisturbed the judgment of the Florida Supreme Court.

Rent-A-Center, West, Inc. v. Jackson

561 U.S. 63 (2010)

JUSTICE SCALIA delivered the opinion of the Court.

We consider whether, under the FAA, a district court may decide a claim that an arbitration agreement is unconscionable, where the agreement explicitly assigns that decision to the arbitrator. [Answer: No.]

Antonio Jackson filed suit for employment discrimination against his former employer, Rent-A-Center (RAC).] RAC sought to enforce the written arbitration. Jackson responded that the agreement was unconscionable, and therefore unenforceable. The contract specified that the arbitrator "shall have exclusive authority to resolve" all contract-related issues.

The FAA reflects the fundamental principle that arbitration is a matter of contract. The FAA places arbitration agreements on an equal footing with other contracts, and requires courts to enforce them according to their terms, like other contracts, however, they may be invalidated by generally applicable contract defenses, such as fraud, duress, or unconscionability. The Act also establishes procedures by which federal courts implement § 2's substantive rule.... The Agreement here contains multiple written provisions to settle by arbitration a controversy. Two are relevant to our discussion. The first, titled "Claims Covered By The Agreement" provides for arbitration of all "past, present or future" disputes arising out of Jackson's employment with Rent-A-Center. Second, the section titled "Arbitration Procedures" provides that "the Arbitrator ... shall have exclusive authority to resolve any dispute relating to the ... enforceability ... of this Agreement including, but not limited to any claim that all or any part of this Agreement is void or voidable." The current "controversy" between the parties is whether the Agreement is unconscionable. It is the second provision, which delegates resolution of that controversy to the arbitrator that Rent-A-Center seeks to enforce.... We will refer to it as the delegation provision.

The delegation provision is an agreement to arbitrate threshold issues concerning the arbitration agreement. We have recognized that parties can agree to arbitrate "gateway" questions of "arbitrability," such as whether the parties have agreed to arbitrate or whether their agreement covers a particular controversy. This line of cases merely reflects the principle that arbitration is a matter of contract. There is one caveat. *First Options of Chicago, Inc. v. Kaplan*, 514 U.S. 938 (1995), held that courts should not assume that the parties agreed to arbitrate arbitrability unless there is clear and unmistakable evidence that they did so. The parties agree the heightened standard applies here.... Jackson does not dispute that the text of the Agreement was clear and unmistakable on this point. What he argues now, however, is that it is not "clear and unmistakable" that his *agreement* to that text was valid, because of the unconscionability claims he raises.

This mistakes the subject of the *First Options* "clear and unmistakable" requirement. It pertains to the parties' *manifestation of intent*, not the agreement's *validity*. It is an "interpretive rule," based on an assumption about the parties' expectations. In circumstances where contracting parties would likely have expected a court to have decided the gateway matter, we assume that is what they agreed to. Thus, unless the parties clearly and unmistakably provide otherwise, the question of whether the parties agreed to arbitrate is to be decided by the court, not the arbitrator.

The *validity* of a written agreement to arbitrate (whether it is legally binding, as opposed to whether it was in fact agreed to—including, of course, whether it was void for unconscionability) is governed by §2's provision that it shall be valid "save upon such grounds as exist at law or equity for the revocation of any contract." Those grounds do not include, of course, any requirement that its lack of unconscionability must be "clear and unmistakable."

There are two types of validity challenges under §2: One type challenges specifically the validity of the agreement to arbitrate, and the other challenges the contract as a whole, either on a ground that directly affects the entire agreement (*e.g.,* the agreement was fraudulently induced), or on the ground that the illegality of one of the contract's provisions renders the whole contract invalid. Only the first type of challenge is relevant to a court's determination whether the arbitration agreement at issue is enforceable. The issue of the agreement's "validity" is different from the issue whether any agreement between the parties was ever concluded, and, we address only the former. That is because §2 states that a written provision to settle by arbitration a controversy is valid, irrevocable, and enforceable" *without mention* of the validity of the contract in which it is contained. Thus, a party's challenge to another provision of the contract, or to the contract as a whole, does not prevent a court from enforcing a specific agreement to arbitrate. As a matter of substantive federal arbitration law, an arbitration provision is severable from the remainder of the contract. * * *

Here, the written provision to settle by arbitration a controversy that Rent-A-Center asks us to enforce is the delegation provision—the provision that gave the arbitrator exclusive authority to resolve any dispute relating to the enforceability of this Agreement. The remainder of the contract is the rest of the agreement to arbitrate claims arising out of Jackson's employment with Rent-A-Center. To be sure this case differs from *Prima Paint, Buckeye,* and *Preston,* in that the arbitration provisions sought to be enforced in those cases were contained in contracts unrelated to arbitration—contracts for consulting services, check-cashing services, and "personal management" or "talent agent" services. In this case, the underlying contract is itself an arbitration agreement. But that makes no difference. The dissent calls this a "breezy assertion," but it seems to us self-evident. When the dissent comes to discussing the point, it gives no logical reason why an agreement to arbitrate one controversy (an employment-discrimination claim) is not severable from an agreement to arbitrate a different controversy (enforceability). There is none. Since the dissent accepts that the invalidity of one provision *within an arbitration agreement* does not necessarily invalidate its other provisions, it cannot believe in some sort of magic bond between arbitration provisions that prevents them from being severed from each other. According to the dissent, it is fine to sever an invalid provision within an arbitration agreement when severability is a matter of state law, but severability is not allowed when it comes to applying *Prima Paint*.

Application of the severability rule does not depend on the substance of the remainder of the contract. Section 2 operates on the specific written provision to settle by arbitration a controversy that the party seeks to enforce. Accordingly, unless Jackson challenged the delegation provision specifically, we must treat it as valid under § 2, and must enforce it under §§ 3 and 4, leaving any challenge to the validity of the Agreement as a whole for the arbitrator.

Jackson challenged only the validity of the contract as a whole.... Jackson stated that "the *entire agreement* seems drawn to provide Rent-A-Center with undue advantages should an employment-related dispute arise." At one point, he argued that the limitations on discovery "further support his contention that the *arbitration agreement as a whole* is substantively unconscionable." And before this Court, Jackson describes his challenge in the District Court as follows: He "opposed the motion to compel on the ground that the *entire arbitration agreement*, including the delegation clause, was unconscionable."

As required to make out a claim of unconscionability under Nevada law, he contended that the Agreement was both procedurally and substantively unconscionable. But we need not consider that claim because none of Jackson's substantive unconscionability challenges was specific to the delegation provision. First, he argued that the Agreement's coverage was one sided in that it required arbitration of claims an employee was likely to bring — contract, tort, discrimination, and statutory claims — but did not require arbitration of claims Rent-A-Center was likely to bring — intellectual property, unfair competition, and trade secrets claims. This one-sided-coverage argument clearly did not go to the validity of the delegation provision.

Jackson's other two substantive unconscionability arguments assailed arbitration procedures called for by the contract — the fee-splitting arrangement and the limitations on discovery — procedures that were to be used during arbitration under *both* the agreement to arbitrate employment-related disputes *and* the delegation provision. It may be that had Jackson challenged the delegation provision by arguing that these common procedures *as applied* to the delegation provision rendered *that provision* unconscionable, the challenge should have been considered by the court. To make such a claim based on the discovery procedures, Jackson would have had to argue that the limitation upon the number of depositions causes the arbitration of his claim that the Agreement is unenforceable to be unconscionable. That would be, of course, a much more difficult argument to sustain than the argument that the same limitation

renders arbitration of his fact-bound employment discrimination claim unconscionable. Likewise, the unfairness of the fee-splitting arrangement may be more difficult to establish for the arbitration of enforceability than for arbitration of more
complex and fact-related aspects of the alleged employment discrimination. Jackson,
however, did not make any arguments specific to the delegation provision; he argued
that the fee-sharing and discovery procedures rendered the *entire* Agreement invalid.

In his brief to this Court, Jackson made the contention, not mentioned below,
that the delegation provision itself is substantively unconscionable because the *quid
pro quo* he was supposed to receive for it—that "in exchange for initially allowing
an arbitrator to decide certain gateway questions," he would receive "plenary post-
arbitration judicial review"—was eliminated by the Court's subsequent holding in
Hall Street Associates, L.L.C. v. Mattel, Inc., 552 U.S. 576 (2008), that the nonplenary
grounds for judicial review in § 10 of the FAA are exclusive. He brought this challenge
to the delegation provision too late, and we will not consider it.

We reverse the judgment of the Court of Appeals for the Ninth Circuit.

JUSTICE STEVENS, with whom JUSTICES GINSBURG, BREYER, and SOTOMAYOR join,
dissenting.

Neither petitioner nor respondent has urged us to adopt the rule the Court does
today: Even when a litigant has specifically challenged the validity of an agreement
to arbitrate he must submit that challenge *to the arbitrator* unless he has lodged an
objection to the particular line in the agreement that purports to assign such challenges
to the arbitrator—the so-called "delegation clause."

The Court's decision today goes beyond *Prima Paint*. Its breezy assertion that the
subject matter of the contract at issue—in this case, an arbitration agreement and
nothing more—"makes no difference," is simply wrong. This written arbitration
agreement is but one part of a broader employment agreement between the parties,
just as the arbitration clause in *Prima Paint* was but one part of a broader contract
for services between those parties. Thus, that the subject matter of the agreement is
exclusively arbitration makes *all* the difference in the *Prima Paint* analysis. . . .

We might have resolved this case by simply applying the *First Options* rule: Does
the arbitration agreement at issue "clearly and unmistakably" evince petitioner's and
respondent's intent to submit questions of arbitrability to the arbitrator? The answer
to that question is no. Respondent's claim that the arbitration agreement is unconscionable undermines any suggestion that he "clearly" and "unmistakably" assented
to submit questions of arbitrability to the arbitrator. The fact that the agreement's
"delegation" provision suggests assent is beside the point, because the gravamen of
respondent's claim is that he never consented to the terms in his agreement. In other
words, when a party raises a good-faith validity challenge to the arbitration agreement
itself, that issue must be resolved before a court can say that he clearly and unmistakably intended to *arbitrate* that very validity question. . . .

Prima Paint and its progeny allow a court to pluck from a potentially invalid *contract*
a potentially valid *arbitration agreement*. Today the Court adds a new layer of sever-

ability—something akin to Russian nesting dolls—into the mix: Courts may now pluck from a potentially invalid *arbitration agreement* even narrower provisions that refer particular arbitrability disputes to an arbitrator. I do not think an agreement to arbitrate can ever manifest a clear and unmistakable intent to arbitrate its own validity. In my view, a general revocation challenge to a stand-alone arbitration agreement is, invariably, a challenge to the "making" of the arbitration agreement itself, and therefore, under *Prima Paint*, must be decided by the court.... Because we are dealing in this case with a challenge to an independently executed arbitration agreement—rather than a clause contained in a contract related to another subject matter—any challenge to the contract itself is also, necessarily, a challenge to the arbitration agreement. They are one and the same.

1. Comments and Questions

a. Consider the range of defenses, such as fraud in the inducement (alleged in *Prima Paint*), unconscionability, duress, lack of consideration, mutual mistake, frustration of purpose, or lack of mutuality, that a party may assert to render a contract voidable. Under the separability doctrine, which is applicable in state and federal court, only where the defense is directed at the arbitration provision itself is judicial intervention at the "gateway" permitted; otherwise, the issue of the contract's validity is for the arbitrator.

What is the practical significance of this doctrine? Does it result in the seeming paradox of an arbitrator ruling that the contract that gave rise to his own jurisdiction was the product of fraud, and therefore invalid? Why should a person be required to arbitrate a claim based on an (apparent) agreement that is voidable because induced by material representation? Does this give arbitrators too much power to police fraud and provide companies with a mechanism to avoid the courthouse? *See* Thomas J. Stipanowich, *Revelation and Reaction: The Struggle to Shape American Arbitration, in* Contemporary Issues in International Arbitration and Mediation: The Fordham Papers 2010 (Martinus Nijhoff Publishers 2011).

In some ways, the same issue has application in litigation, too. If a court determines that a contract is invalid, then the court loses jurisdiction to hear the merits of the underlying claim. Does this distinction matter more in arbitration, a system under which arbitrators are paid by the parties on a per-case basis, as opposed to judges, who are paid by taxpayers on a salary basis?

b. The *Buckeye* Court expressly carved out of its holding defenses as to whether an agreement was ever concluded:

> The issue of the contract's validity is different from the issue whether any agreement between the alleged obligor and obligee was ever concluded. Our opinion today addresses only the former, and does not speak to the issue decided in the cases cited by respondents (and by the Florida Supreme Court), which hold that it is for courts to decide whether the alleged obligor ever signed the contract, *Chastain v. Robinson-Humphrey Co.*, 957 F.2d 851 (C.A.11

1992), whether the signor lacked authority to commit the alleged principal, *Sandvik AB v. Advent Int'l Corp.*, 220 F.3d 99 (C.A.3 2000); *Sphere Drake Ins. Ltd. v. All American Ins. Co.*, 256 F.3d 587 (C.A.7 2001), and whether the signor lacked the mental capacity to assent, *Spahr v. Secco*, 330 F.3d 1266 (C.A.10 2003).

Buckeye Check Cashing, 546 U.S. at 444, n.1. Before *Buckeye*, lower courts were divided on this issue. *Compare Spahr v. Secco*, 330 F.3d 1266 (10th Cir. 2003) (holding that a court is to decide mental capacity challenges), *with Primerica Life Ins. Co. v. Brown*, 304 F.3d 469 (5th Cir. 2002) (holding *Prima Paint* applicable and that mental capacity challenge was a defense to the entire contract, not to the making of the arbitration clause itself, therefore to be heard by the arbitrator). How does *Buckeye* impact these holdings, if at all?

c. As we learned earlier in this section from *First Options*, parties can include a "clear and unmistakable" waiver in their arbitration agreement to place arbitrability questions in the hands of the arbitrator. In the context of the separability doctrine, this provision is known as a "delegation clause." *Rent-A-Center* reaffirmed the separability doctrine when addressing the precise issue of "whether a district court or an arbitrator should decide claims that an arbitration agreement under the Federal Arbitration Act is unconscionable when the parties to the agreement have clearly and unmistakably assigned this 'gateway' issue to the arbitrator for resolution." Under *Rent-A-Center*, unconscionability challenges to the arbitration provision can be contractually "delegated" to the arbitrator.

If an arbitrator decides a gateway question of arbitrability, and then decides the parties never entered into an arbitration agreement to cover the underlying dispute, does that mean the arbitrators never had the power to decide the gateway question in the first place?

d. In *Rent-A-Center*, Jackson also challenged the delegation provision itself as unconscionable, but the Court did not consider that argument because he did not raise it in the lower courts. If he had raised it on time, under *Rent-A-Center*, should a court or an arbitrator consider that challenge?

e. Considerable literature discusses the separability doctrine and related matters. *See, e.g.*, Karen Halverson Cross, *Letting the Arbitrator Decide Unconscionability Challenges*, 26 OHIO ST. J. ON DISP. RESOL. (2011); Alan Scott Rau, *Everything You Really Need to Know About "Separability" in Seventeen Simple Propositions*, 14 AM. REV. INT'L ARB. 1 (2003); Stephen J. Ware, *Arbitration Law's Separability Doctrine after* Buckeye Check Cashing, Inc. v. Cardegna, 8 NEV. L. J. 107 (2007).

2. Problem

Emily Smith has retained you to represent her on her claim that she was denied a promotion because of her race. Smith's former employer, We-Haul, is a national company that rents storage and moving equipment. On her behalf, you filed an employment discrimination suit under Title VII of the U.S. Code against We-Haul in federal court. Shortly thereafter, We-Haul filed a motion under the FAA to stay the case and compel arbitration, claiming that Smith had signed an arbitration agreement which required all "past, present, or future disputes" arising out of Smith's employment be submitted to arbitration. The arbitration agreement also states that the "arbitrator, and not any federal, state, or local court, shall have exclusive authority to resolve any dispute relating to the interpretation of this agreement." Smith claims that she was not aware of the impact of signing the arbitration agreement because it was included with a number of other employment documents and was non-negotiable. Smith strongly opposes arbitration because she believes that We-Haul has a culture of discrimination and wants her case to be decided in a public forum, not in a private arbitration proceeding.

Your initial reaction is to file a motion on the ground that the arbitration agreement is unconscionable and therefore unenforceable, but you are unsure of the impact of the clause in the agreement that gives an arbitrator "exclusive authority" to resolve issues relating to the interpretation of the agreement.

1. Who should decide whether the arbitration agreement is unconscionable — the court or an arbitrator? Would it make a difference if you argue the entire agreement is unconscionable, or just the section giving an arbitrator exclusive authority to decide issues related to interpretation?

2. What if Emily instead claimed she lacked the capacity to contract? Who decides?

3. What if she claimed the signature on the contract was a forgery?

D. Arbitrability of Statutory Claims

When Congress enacted the FAA in 1925, few private rights of action existed under federal or state statutes. Fast-forward almost 100 years and consider the vast range of laws that Congress and state legislatures have since enacted. Among these new laws are securities and antitrust laws, as well as civil rights laws against discrimination on the basis of race, gender, national origin, age, disability, or sexual orientation.

If the FAA evinces a national policy favoring arbitration, should parties to a broad arbitration agreement be bound to arbitrate these federal and state statutory claims, in addition to contractual and common law claims? Are these claims capable of arbitration (arbitrable)? Are arbitrators — often selected precisely because of their industry-specific expertise and not necessarily legally trained — qualified to issue awards based on complex or protective statutory laws, state or federal? Are there particular legal claims or situations that are uniquely within the province of the public judiciary to resolve? May states or Congress enact such legislation requiring a judicial forum for certain types of legal claims? What are the policy implications of a securities or international arbitrator adjudicating claims arising under federal or state statutes? What are the alternatives?

Consider these policy questions as you read this section.

1. Federal Securities Laws

The evolving debate over the arbitrability of federal statutory claims is illustrated by the Supreme Court's decisions regarding claims arising under the federal securities laws, in particular the Securities Act of 1933 (Securities Act) and the Securities Exchange Act of 1934 (Exchange Act). In a series of cases, the Court considered whether the rights and duties arising under those statutes are subject to pre-dispute arbitration agreements (PDAAs), or whether the intended beneficiaries of those laws are entitled to have their claims heard in a judicial forum.

In an early case interpreting the FAA, the Supreme Court ruled that claims arising under the Securities Act could be raised in a judicial forum despite a PDAA in the account agreement between the parties. *Wilko v. Swan*, 346 U.S. 427 (1953). Wilko, a customer of a securities brokerage firm, sued principals in the firm alleging they committed fraud by recommending he purchase stock in a company on the basis of a pending merger, when a director of the firm was selling the same stock, including the stock Wilko purchased. Wilko sold his stock at a loss two weeks later.

When the defendants sought arbitration on the basis of the arbitration clause, Wilko argued it was void under the Securities Act's anti-waiver section, which provided that "[a]ny condition, stipulation, or provision binding any person acquiring any security to waive compliance with any provision of this subchapter or of the rules and regulations of the Commission shall be void." (Securities Act, § 14) The district court denied defendants' request for a stay of litigation, and a divided Second Circuit reversed.

The Supreme Court reversed again, ruling the Securities Act claims were not arbitrable. Justice Reed's majority opinion reflects a strong distrust of arbitrators and the arbitration process, as well as the Court's judgment that arbitration was inadequate to enforce the substantive rights created by the statute. The *Wilko* Court specifically noted aspects of the arbitration process that may lessen the Act's substantive protections: arbitration proceedings were not suited for cases requiring "subjective findings on the purpose and knowledge of an alleged violator"; arbitrators must make legal determinations "without judicial instruction on the law"; an arbitration award "may be made without explanation of [the arbitrator's] reasons and without a complete record of their proceedings"; the "power to vacate an [arbitration] award is limited," and "interpretations of the law by the arbitrators in contrast to manifest disregard are not subject, in the federal courts, to judicial review for error in interpretation." *Id.* at 435–37.

After a series of opinions in the interim that chipped away at some of the distrustful assumptions about arbitration in *Wilko* (including *Mitsubishi Motors Corp. v. Soler Chrysler-Plymouth, Inc.,* 473 U.S. 614 (1985), which held that antitrust claims arising under the Sherman Act were arbitrable in international arbitration), in the late 1980s, the Court looked at the current securities arbitration process and concluded that it now provided an adequate means of enforcing rights arising under both the Securities Act (*Rodriguez*) and the Exchange Act (*McMahon*). The majority opinion in *McMahon* reflects a dramatic shift in the attitude of the Supreme Court toward arbitration.

Shearson/American Express, Inc. v. McMahon

482 U.S. 220 (1987)

JUSTICE O'CONNOR delivered the opinion of the Court [5–4 decision].

[The McMahons brought suit alleging that Shearson, and one of its brokers]....
had violated section 10(b) of the Securities Exchange Act of 1934 and Rule 10b-5,
by engaging in fraudulent, excessive trading on respondents' accounts and by making
false statements and omitting material facts from the advice given to respondents.
Relying on the customer agreements, petitioners moved to compel arbitration of the
McMahons' claims pursuant to section 3 of the FAA....

The FAA provides the starting point for answering the questions raised in this
case.... The FAA establishes a "federal policy favoring arbitration," *Moses H. Cone
Memorial Hospital*, 460 U.S. 1, 24 (1983), requiring that "we rigorously enforce agreements to arbitrate." *Dean Witter Reynolds Inc. v. Byrd*, 470 U.S. at 221. This duty to
enforce arbitration agreements is not diminished when a party bound by an agreement
raises a claim founded on statutory rights.... The FAA provides no basis for disfavoring
agreements to arbitrate statutory claims by skewing the otherwise hospitable inquiry
into arbitrability.

The FAA, standing alone, therefore mandates enforcement of agreements to arbitrate statutory claims. Like any statutory directive, the FAA mandate may be overridden by a contrary congressional command. The burden is on the party opposing
arbitration, however, to show that Congress intended to preclude a waiver of judicial
remedies for the statutory rights at issue.... To defeat application of the FAA in this
case, therefore, the McMahons must demonstrate that Congress intended to make
an exception to the FAA for claims arising under the Exchange Act, an intention discernible from the text, history, or purposes of the statute....

When Congress enacted the Exchange Act in 1934, it did not specifically address
the question of the arbitrability of section 10(b) claims. The McMahons contend,
however, that congressional intent to require a judicial forum for the resolution of
section 10(b) claims can be deduced from section 29(a) of the Exchange Act, 15
U.S.C. § 78cc(a), which declares void "any condition, stipulation, or provision binding
any person to waive compliance with any provision of [the Act]." We reject the McMahons' argument that section 29(a) forbids waiver of section 27 of the Exchange Act.
Section 27 provides:

> The district courts of the United States ... shall have exclusive jurisdiction
> of violations of this title or the rules and regulations thereunder, and of all
> suits in equity and actions at law brought to enforce any liability or duty cre-
> ated by this title or the rules and regulations thereunder.

The McMahons contend that an agreement to waive this jurisdictional provision
is unenforceable because section 29(a) voids the waiver of "any provision" of the Exchange Act. The language of section 29(a), however, does not reach so far. What the
antiwaiver provision of section 29(a) forbids is enforcement of agreements to waive

"compliance" with the provisions of the statute. But section 27 itself does not impose any duty with which persons trading in securities must "comply." By its terms, section 29(a) only prohibits waiver of the substantive obligations imposed by the Exchange Act. Because section 27 does not impose any statutory duties, its waiver does not constitute a waiver of "compliance with any provision" of the Exchange Act under section 29(a).

We do not read *Wilko v. Swan* as compelling a different result. In *Wilko*, the Court held that a predispute agreement could not be enforced to compel arbitration of a claim arising under section 12(2) of the Securities Act.... The conclusion in *Wilko* was expressly based on the Court's belief that a judicial forum was needed to protect the substantive rights created by the Securities Act: "As the protective provisions of the Securities Act require the exercise of judicial direction to fairly assure their effectiveness, it seems to us that Congress must have intended section 14 ... to apply to waiver of judicial trial and review." *Wilko* must be understood, therefore, as holding that the plaintiff's waiver of the "right to select the judicial forum," was unenforceable only because arbitration was judged inadequate to enforce the statutory rights created by section 12(2).

The second argument offered by the McMahons is that the arbitration agreement effects an impermissible waiver of the substantive protections of the Exchange Act. Ordinarily, "by agreeing to arbitrate a statutory claim, a party does not forgo the substantive rights afforded by the statute; it only submits to their resolution in an arbitral, rather than a judicial, forum." *Mitsubishi*. The McMahons argue, however, that section 29(a) compels a different conclusion. Initially, they contend that predispute agreements are void under section 29(a) because they tend to result from broker overreaching. They reason, as do some commentators, that *Wilko* is premised on the belief "that arbitration clauses in securities sales agreements generally are not freely negotiated." According to this view, *Wilko* barred enforcement of predispute agreements because of this frequent inequality of bargaining power, reasoning that Congress intended for section 14 generally to ensure that sellers did not "maneuver buyers into a position that might weaken their ability to recover under the Securities Act." The McMahons urge that we should interpret section 29(a) in the same fashion.

We decline to give *Wilko* a reading so far at odds with the plain language of section 14, or to adopt such an unlikely interpretation of section 29(a).... The voluntariness of the agreement is irrelevant to this inquiry: if a stipulation waives compliance with a statutory duty, it is void under section 29(a), whether voluntary or not. Thus, a customer cannot negotiate a reduction in commissions in exchange for a waiver of compliance with the requirements of the Exchange Act, even if the customer knowingly and voluntarily agreed to the bargain. Section 29(a) is concerned, not with whether brokers "maneuver customer into" an agreement, but with whether the agreement "weaken[s] their ability to recover under the [Exchange] Act." The former is grounds for revoking the contract under ordinary principles of contract law; the latter is grounds for voiding the agreement under section 29(a).

The other reason advanced by the McMahons for finding a waiver of their section 10(b) rights is that arbitration does "weaken their ability to recover under the [Exchange] Act." That is the heart of the Court's decision in *Wilko*, and respondents urge that we should follow its reasoning. *Wilko* listed several grounds why, in the Court's view, the "effectiveness [of the Act's provisions] in application is lessened in arbitration." First, the *Wilko* Court believed that arbitration proceedings were not suited to cases requiring "subjective findings on the purpose and knowledge of an alleged violator." *Wilko* also was concerned that arbitrators must make legal determinations "without judicial instruction on the law," and that an arbitration award "may be made without explanation of [the arbitrator's] reasons and without a complete record of their proceedings." Finally, *Wilko* noted that the "[p]ower to vacate an award is limited," and that "interpretations of the law by the arbitrators in contrast to manifest disregard are not subject, in the federal courts, to judicial review for error in interpretation." *Wilko* concluded that in view of these drawbacks to arbitration, section 12(2) claims "require[d] the exercise of judicial direction to fairly assure their effectiveness." ...

Indeed, most of the reasons given in *Wilko* have been rejected subsequently by the Court as a basis for holding claims to be nonarbitrable.... The suitability of arbitration as a means of enforcing Exchange Act rights is evident from our decision in *Scherk* [*v. Alberto-Culver Co.*, 417 U.S. 506 (1974)]. Although the holding in that case was limited to international agreements, the competence of arbitral tribunals to resolve section 10(b) claims is the same in both settings....

[T]he mistrust of arbitration that formed the basis for the *Wilko* opinion in 1953 is difficult to square with the assessment of arbitration that has prevailed since that time. This is especially so in light of the intervening changes in the regulatory structure of the securities laws. Even if *Wilko*'s assumptions regarding arbitration were valid at the time *Wilko* was decided, most certainly they do not hold true today for arbitration procedures subject to the SEC's oversight authority. In 1953, when *Wilko* was decided, the Commission had only limited authority over the rules governing self-regulatory organizations (SROs) — the national securities exchanges and registered securities associations — and this authority appears not to have included any authority at all over their arbitration rules. See Brief for SEC as *Amicus Curiae* 14–15. Since the 1975 amendments to section 19 of the Exchange Act, however, the Commission has had expansive power to ensure the adequacy of the arbitration procedures employed by the SROs. No proposed rule change may take effect unless the SEC finds that the proposed rule is consistent with the requirements of the Exchange Act, and the Commission has the power, on its own initiative, to "abrogate, add to, and delete from" any SRO rule if it finds such changes necessary or appropriate to further the objectives of the Act. In short, the SEC has broad authority to oversee and to regulate the rules adopted by the SROs relating to customer disputes, including the power to mandate the adoption of any rules it deems necessary to ensure that arbitration procedures adequately protect statutory rights.

In the exercise of its regulatory authority, the SEC has specifically approved the arbitration procedures of the New York Stock Exchange, the American Stock Exchange, and the NASD, the organizations mentioned in the arbitration agreement at issue in this case. We conclude that where, as in this case, the prescribed procedures are subject to the Commission's section 19 authority, an arbitration agreement does not effect a waiver of the protections of the Act. While *stare decisis* concerns may counsel against upsetting *Wilko's* contrary conclusion under the Securities Act, we refuse to extend *Wilko's* reasoning to the Exchange Act in light of these intervening regulatory developments....

JUSTICE BLACKMUN, concurring in part and dissenting in part.

.... I disagree, however, with the Court's conclusion that respondents' section 10(b) claims are subject to arbitration. Both the Securities Act of 1933 and the Securities Exchange Act of 1934 were enacted to protect investors from predatory behavior of securities industry personnel. In *Wilko*, the Court recognized this basic purpose when it declined to enforce a predispute agreement to compel arbitration of claims under the Securities Act. Following that decision, lower courts extended *Wilko's* reasoning to claims brought under § 10(b) of the 1934 Act, and Congress approved of this extension. In today's decision, however, the Court effectively overrules *Wilko* by accepting the SEC's newly adopted position that arbitration procedures in the securities industry and the SEC's oversight of the self-regulatory organizations (SROs) have improved greatly since *Wilko* was decided. The Court thus approves the abandonment of the judiciary's role in the resolution of claims under the Exchange Act and leaves such claims to the arbitral forum of the securities industry at a time when the industry's abuses towards investors are more apparent than ever....

There are essentially two problems with the Court's conclusion that predispute agreements to arbitrate section 10(b) claims may be enforced. First, the Court gives *Wilko* an overly narrow reading so that it can fit into the syllogism offered by the SEC and accepted by the Court, namely, (1) *Wilko* was really a case concerning whether arbitration was adequate for the enforcement of the substantive provisions of the securities laws; (2) all of the *Wilko* Court's doubts as to arbitration's adequacy are outdated; (3) thus *Wilko* is no longer good law. Second, the Court accepts uncritically petitioners' and the SEC's argument that the problems with arbitration, highlighted by the *Wilko* Court, either no longer exist or are not now viewed as problems by the Court. This acceptance primarily is based upon the Court's belief in the Commission's representations that its oversight of the SROs ensures the adequacy of arbitration.

I agree with the Court's observation that, in order to establish an exception to the FAA for a class of statutory claims, there must be "an intention discernible from the text, history, or purposes of the statute." Where the Court first goes wrong, however, is in its failure to acknowledge that the Exchange Act, like the Securities Act, constitutes such an exception. This failure is made possible only by the unduly narrow reading of *Wilko* that ignores the Court's determination there that the Securities Act *was* an exception to the FAA....

In light of a proper reading of *Wilko*, the pertinent question then becomes whether the language, legislative history, and purposes of the Exchange Act call for an exception to the FAA for section 10(b) claims. The Exchange Act waiver provision is virtually identical to that of the Securities Act. More importantly, the same concern with investor protection that motivated the Securities Act is evident in the Exchange Act, although the latter, in contrast to the former, is aimed at trading in the secondary securities market. We have recognized that both Acts were designed with this common purpose in mind. *Ernst & Ernst v. Hochfelder*, 425 U.S. 185 (1976) ("The 1933 and 1934 Acts constitute interrelated components of the federal regulatory scheme governing transactions in securities"). Indeed, the application of both Acts to the same conduct suggests that they have the same basic goal. And we have approved a cumulative construction of remedies under the securities Acts to promote the maximum possible protection of investors. In sum, the same reasons that led the Court to find an exception to the Arbitration Act for section 12(2) claims exist for section 10(b) claims as well. It is clear that *Wilko*, when properly read, governs the instant case and mandates that a predispute arbitration agreement should not be enforced as to section 10(b) claims. . . .

Even if I were to accept the Court's narrow reading of *Wilko*, as a case dealing only with the inadequacies of arbitration in 1953, I do not think that this case should be resolved differently today so long as the policy of investor protection is given proper consideration in the analysis. Despite improvements in the process of arbitration and changes in the judicial attitude towards it, several aspects of arbitration that were seen by the *Wilko* court to be inimical to the policy of investor protection still remain. Moreover, I have serious reservations about the Commission's contention that its oversight of the SROs' arbitration procedures will ensure that the process is adequate to protect an investor's rights under the securities Acts. * * *

The Court's "mistrust" of arbitration may have given way recently to an acceptance of this process, not only because of the improvements in arbitration, but also because of the Court's present assumption that the distinctive features of arbitration, its more quick and economical resolution of claims, do not render it inherently inadequate for the resolution of statutory claims. Such reasoning, however, should prevail only in the absence of the congressional policy that places the statutory claimant in a special position with respect to possible violators of his statutory rights. As even the most ardent supporter of arbitration would recognize, the arbitral process *at best* places the investor on an equal footing with the securities industry personnel against whom the claims are brought.

Furthermore, there remains the danger that, *at worst*, compelling an investor to arbitrate securities claims puts him in a forum controlled by the securities industry. This result directly contradicts the goal of both securities Acts to free the investor from the control of the market professional. The Uniform Code provides some safeguards but despite them, and indeed because of the background of the arbitrators, the investor has the impression, frequently justified, that his claims are being judged by a forum composed of individuals sympathetic to the securities industry and not drawn from the public. It is generally recognized that the codes do not define who falls into the category "not from the securities industry." Accordingly, it is often possible for the "public" arbitrators to be attorneys or consultants whose clients have been exchange members or SROs. The uniform opposition of investors to compelled arbitration and the overwhelming support of the securities industry for the process suggest that there must be *some* truth to the investors' belief that the securities industry has an advantage in a forum under its own control. *See N.Y. Times*, Mar. 29, 1987, p. 8 (statement of Sheldon H. Elsen, Chairman, American Bar Association Task Force on Securities Arbitration: "The houses basically like the present system because they own the stacked deck").

More surprising than the Court's acceptance of the present adequacy of arbitration for the resolution of securities claims is its confidence in the Commission's oversight of the arbitration procedures of the SROs to ensure this adequacy. Such confidence amounts to a wholesale acceptance of the Commission's *present* position that this oversight undermines the force of *Wilko* and that arbitration therefore should be compelled because the Commission has supervisory authority over the SROs' arbitration procedures. The Court, however, fails to acknowledge that, until it filed an *amicus* brief in this case, the Commission consistently took the position that section 10(b) claims, like those under section 12(2), should not be sent to arbitration, that predispute arbitration agreements, where the investor was not advised of his right to a judicial forum, were misleading, and that the very regulatory oversight upon which the Commission now relies could not alone make securities industry arbitration adequate. It is most questionable, then, whether the Commission's recently adopted position is entitled to the deference that the Court accords it....

Moreover, the Commission's own description of its enforcement capabilities contradicts its position that its general overview of SRO rules and procedures can make arbitration adequate for resolving securities claims. The Commission does not pretend that its oversight consists of anything other than a general review of SRO rules and the ability to require that an SRO adopt or delete a particular rule. It does not contend that its "sweeping authority" includes a review of specific arbitration proceedings. It neither polices nor monitors the results of these arbitrations for possible misapplications of securities laws or for indications of how investors fare in these proceedings.

JUSTICE STEVENS, concurring in part and dissenting in part.

Gaps in the law must, of course, be filled by judicial construction. But after a statute has been construed, either by this Court or by a consistent course of decision by other federal judges and agencies, it acquires a meaning that should be as clear as if the judicial gloss had been drafted by the Congress itself. This position reflects both respect for Congress' role, and the compelling need to preserve the courts' limited resources. During the 32 years immediately following this Court's decision in *Wilko v. Swan*, each of the eight Circuits that addressed the issue concluded that the holding of *Wilko* was fully applicable to claims arising under the Securities Exchange Act of 1934. This longstanding interpretation creates a strong presumption, in my view, that any mistake the courts may have made in interpreting the statute is best remedied by the Legislative, not the Judicial, Branch.

a. Comments and Questions

i. Notice the shift in the Supreme Court's attitude toward arbitration, from "mistrust" in *Wilko* to a near-full endorsement of securities arbitration in *McMahon*. However, *McMahon* did not need to expressly overrule *Wilko*, as the former involved the Exchange Act and the latter the Securities Act. The Court seized on the opportunity to expressly overrule *Wilko* just two years later. *See Rodriguez de Quijas v. Shearson/ American Express, Inc.*, 490 U.S. 477 (1989) (enforcing predispute agreement to arbitrate claims under the Securities Act).

Justice Kennedy's majority opinion in *Rodriguez* stated that:

> The Court's characterization of the arbitration process in *Wilko* is pervaded by what Judge Jerome Frank called "the old judicial hostility to arbitration." *Kulukundis Shipping Co. v. Amtorg Trading Corp.*, 126 F.2d 978 (2d Cir. 1942). That view has been steadily eroded over the years. The erosion intensified in our most recent decisions upholding agreements to arbitrate federal claims raised under the Securities Exchange Act of 1934.... The shift in the Court's views on arbitration away from those adopted in *Wilko* is shown by the flat statement in *Mitsubishi*: **"By agreeing to arbitrate a statutory claim, a party does not forgo the substantive rights afforded by the statute; it only submits to their resolution in an arbitral, rather than a judicial, forum."** To the extent that *Wilko* rested on suspicion of arbitration as a method of weakening the protections afforded in the substantive law to would-be complainants, it has fallen far out of step with our current strong endorsement of the federal statutes favoring this method of resolving disputes.
>
> ... We now conclude that *Wilko* was incorrectly decided and is inconsistent with the prevailing uniform construction of other federal statutes governing arbitration agreements in the setting of business transactions....

490 U.S. at 481 (emphasis added). Note that the Court now has quoted the "flat statement" in *Mitsubishi* a total of seven times, including in *Rodriguez*. That "flat statement" reflects the Court's ironclad view today that arbitrators are just as capable as judges of resolving disputes involving statutory claims. Do you agree with the Court? Does it impact your opinion to know that significantly more arbitrations involve attorney arbitrators today than in the 1950s?

ii. The impact of *McMahon* and *Rodriguez* on the securities industry was immediate and comprehensive, as virtually all disputes arising between customers and their brokerage firms and individual brokers are now arbitrated in a forum sponsored by the Financial Industry Regulatory Authority (FINRA).

Note these observations of subsequent developments in securities arbitration:

> The Court's views on arbitration had changed from distrust to acceptance of the process. Moreover, in the specific area of securities arbitration, the Court pointed to changes in the SEC's regulatory authority since *Wilko* to ensure the adequacy of the SROs' arbitration procedures. One explanation

is that the Justices believed that the characteristics (principally, speed and informality) that previously made arbitration deficient because it was not the functional equivalent of a judicial proceeding had become virtues that made arbitrate on an attractive alternative. If this explanation is true, we would expect subsequent regulatory developments to focus on enhancing the virtues of the process yet ensuring that arbitrators apply the law. In fact, this is not what has happened. Instead, the regulatory approach has been to make the arbitration process more closely resemble a judicial proceeding and to ignore the issue of the application of the substantive law.

See Barbara Black & Jill I. Gross, *Making It Up as They Go Along: The Role of Law in Securities Arbitration*, 23 CARDOZO L. REV. 991 (2002); *see also* Jill I. Gross, *McMahon Turns Twenty: The Regulation of Fairness in Securities Arbitration*, 76 U. CIN. L. REV. 493 (2008)(arguing that the SEC adequately polices fairness of securities arbitration).

iii. The *McMahon* plaintiffs also claimed a civil RICO violation, and argued that this claim was not subject to arbitration. All nine Justices rejected this argument, though four Justices dissented from the holding that Exchange Act claims were arbitrable. Since *McMahon*, each time the Court has had an occasion to address the issue, it has found claims arising under other federal statutes to be subject to arbitration. The next subsections discuss some of these cases.

2. Employment Discrimination Claims

Gilmer v. Interstate/Johnson

500 U.S. 20 (1991)

JUSTICE WHITE delivered the opinion of the Court.

The question presented in this case is whether a claim under the Age Discrimination in Employment Act of 1967 (ADEA), as amended, can be subjected to compulsory arbitration pursuant to an arbitration agreement in a securities registration application. The Court of Appeals held that it could, 895 F.2d 195 (CA4 1990), and we affirm.

I

Respondent Interstate/Johnson Lane Corporation (Interstate) hired petitioner Robert Gilmer as a Manager of Financial Services in May 1981. As required by his employment, Gilmer registered as a securities representative with several stock exchanges, including the New York Stock Exchange (NYSE). His registration Application, entitled "Uniform Application for Securities Industry Registration or Transfer," provided, among other things, that Gilmer "agreed to arbitrate any dispute, claim or controversy" arising between him and Interstate "that is required to be arbitrated under the rules, constitutions or by-laws of the organizations with which I register." Of relevance to this case, NYSE Rule 347 provides for arbitration of "any controversy between a registered representative and any member or member organization arising out of the employment or termination of employment of such registered representative."

Interstate terminated Gilmer's employment in 1987, at which time Gilmer was 62 years of age. After first filing an age discrimination charge with the Equal Employment Opportunity Commission (EEOC), Gilmer subsequently brought suit in the United States District Court for the Western District of North Carolina, alleging that Interstate had discharged him because of his age, in violation of the ADEA. In response to Gilmer's complaint, Interstate filed in the District Court a motion to compel arbitration of the ADEA claim. In its motion, Interstate relied upon the arbitration agreement in Gilmer's registration application, as well as the Federal Arbitration Act (FAA). The District Court denied Interstate's motion, based on this Court's decision in *Alexander v. Gardner-Denver Co.*, 415 U.S. 36 (1974), and because it concluded that "Congress intended to protect ADEA claimants from the waiver of a judicial forum." The United States Court of Appeals for the Fourth Circuit reversed, finding "nothing in the text, legislative history, or underlying purposes of the ADEA indicating a congressional intent to preclude enforcement of arbitration agreements." We granted certiorari to resolve a conflict among the Courts of Appeals regarding the arbitrability of ADEA claims.

II

* * *

It is by now clear that statutory claims may be the subject of an arbitration agreement, enforceable pursuant to the FAA. . . .

Although all statutory claims may not be appropriate for arbitration, "having made the bargain to arbitrate, the party should be held to it unless Congress itself has evinced an intention to preclude a waiver of judicial remedies for the statutory rights at issue." In this regard, we note that the burden is on Gilmer to show that Congress intended to preclude a waiver of a judicial forum for ADEA claims. If such an intention exists, it will be discoverable in the text of the ADEA, its legislative history, or an "inherent conflict" between arbitration and the ADEA's underlying purposes. Throughout such an inquiry, it should be kept in mind that "questions of arbitrability must be addressed with a healthy regard for the federal policy favoring arbitration."

III

Gilmer concedes that nothing in the text of the ADEA or its legislative history explicitly precludes arbitration. He argues, however, that compulsory arbitration of ADEA claims pursuant to arbitration agreements would be inconsistent with the statutory framework and purposes of the ADEA. Like the Court of Appeals, we disagree.

Congress enacted the ADEA in 1967 "to promote employment of older persons based on their ability rather than age; to prohibit arbitrary age discrimination in employment; [and] to help employers and workers find ways of meeting problems arising from the impact of age on employment." To achieve those goals, the ADEA, among other things, makes it unlawful for an employer "to fail or refuse to hire or to discharge any individual or otherwise discriminate against any individual with respect to his compensation, terms, conditions, or privileges of employment, because of such individual's age." This proscription is enforced both by private suits and by the EEOC.

* * *

As Gilmer contends, the ADEA is designed not only to address individual grievances, but also to further important social policies. We do not perceive any inherent inconsistency between those policies, however, and enforcing agreements to arbitrate age discrimination claims. It is true that arbitration focuses on specific disputes between the parties involved. The same can be said, however, of judicial resolution of claims. Both of these dispute resolution mechanisms nevertheless also can further broader social purposes....

We also are unpersuaded by the argument that arbitration will undermine the role of the EEOC in enforcing the ADEA. An individual ADEA claimant subject to an arbitration agreement will still be free to file a charge with the EEOC, even though the claimant is not able to institute a private judicial action. Indeed, Gilmer filed a charge with the EEOC in this case. In any event, the EEOC's role in combating age discrimination is not dependent on the filing of a charge; the agency may receive information concerning alleged violations of the ADEA "from any source," and it has independent authority to investigate age discrimination. Moreover, nothing in the ADEA indicates that Congress intended that the EEOC be involved in all employment disputes. Such disputes can be settled, for example, without any EEOC involvement. Finally, the mere involvement of an administrative agency in the enforcement of a statute is not sufficient to preclude arbitration. For example, the Securities Exchange Commission is heavily involved in the enforcement of the Securities Exchange Act of 1934 and the Securities Act of 1933, but we have held that claims under both of those statutes may be subject to compulsory arbitration.

Gilmer also argues that compulsory arbitration is improper because it deprives claimants of the judicial forum provided for by the ADEA. Congress, however, did not explicitly preclude arbitration or other nonjudicial resolution of claims, even in its recent amendments to the ADEA. "If Congress intended the substantive protection afforded [by the ADEA] to include protection against waiver of the right to a judicial forum, that intention will be deducible from text or legislative history." Moreover, Gilmer's argument ignores the ADEA's flexible approach to resolution of claims. The EEOC, for example, is directed to pursue "informal methods of conciliation, conference, and persuasion," which suggests that out-of-court dispute resolution, such as arbitration, is consistent with the statutory scheme established by Congress. In addition, arbitration is consistent with Congress' grant of concurrent jurisdiction over ADEA claims to state and federal courts, because arbitration agreements, "like the provision for concurrent jurisdiction, serve to advance the objective of allowing [claimants] a broader right to select the forum for resolving disputes, whether it be judicial or otherwise."

In arguing that arbitration is inconsistent with the ADEA, Gilmer also raises a host of challenges to the adequacy of arbitration procedures. Initially, we note that in our recent arbitration cases we have already rejected most of these arguments as insufficient to preclude arbitration of statutory claims. Such generalized attacks on arbitration "rest on suspicion of arbitration as a method of weakening the protections afforded in the substantive law to would-be complainants," and as such, they are "far out of step with our current strong endorsement of the federal statutes favoring this method of resolving disputes." Consequently, we address these arguments only briefly.

Gilmer first speculates that arbitration panels will be biased. However, "[w]e decline to indulge the presumption that the parties and arbitral body conducting a proceeding will be unable or unwilling to retain competent, conscientious and impartial arbitrators." In any event, we note that the NYSE arbitration rules, which are applicable to the dispute in this case, provide protections against biased panels. The rules require, for example, that the parties be informed of the employment histories of the arbitrators, and that they be allowed to make further inquiries into the arbitrators' backgrounds. In addition, each party is allowed one peremptory challenge and unlimited challenges for cause. Moreover, the arbitrators are required to disclose "any circumstances which might preclude [them] from rendering an objective and impartial determination." The FAA also protects against bias, by providing that courts may overturn arbitration decisions "[w]here there was evident partiality or corruption in the arbitrators." There has been no showing in this case that those provisions are inadequate to guard against potential bias.

Gilmer also complains that the discovery allowed in arbitration is more limited than in the federal courts, which he contends will make it difficult to prove discrimination. It is unlikely, however, that age discrimination claims require more extensive discovery than other claims that we have found to be arbitrable, such as RICO and antitrust claims. Moreover, there has been no showing in this case that the NYSE discovery provisions, which allow for document production, information requests, depositions, and subpoenas will prove insufficient to allow ADEA claimants such as Gilmer a fair opportunity to present their claims. Although those procedures might not be as extensive as in the federal courts, by agreeing to arbitrate, a party "trades the procedures and opportunity for review of the courtroom for the simplicity, informality, and expedition of arbitration." Indeed, an important counterweight to the reduced discovery in NYSE arbitration is that arbitrators are not bound by the rules of evidence.

A further alleged deficiency of arbitration is that arbitrators often will not issue written opinions, resulting, Gilmer contends, in a lack of public knowledge of employers' discriminatory policies, an inability to obtain effective appellate review, and a stifling of the development of the law. The NYSE rules, however, do require that all arbitration awards be in writing, and that the awards contain the names of the parties, a summary of the issues in controversy, and a description of the award issued. In addition, the award decisions are made available to the public. Furthermore, judicial decisions addressing ADEA claims will continue to be issued because it is unlikely that all or even most ADEA claimants will be subject to arbitration agreements.

Finally, Gilmer's concerns apply equally to settlements of ADEA claims, which, as noted above, are clearly allowed.

It is also argued that arbitration procedures cannot adequately further the purposes of the ADEA because they do not provide for broad equitable relief and class actions. As the court below noted, however, arbitrators do have the power to fashion equitable relief. Indeed, the NYSE rules applicable here do not restrict the types of relief an arbitrator may award, but merely refer to "damages and/or other relief." The NYSE rules also provide for collective proceedings. But "even if the arbitration could not go forward as a class action or class relief could not be granted by the arbitrator, the fact that the [ADEA] provides for the possibility of bringing a collective action does not mean that individual attempts at conciliation were intended to be barred." Finally, it should be remembered that arbitration agreements will not preclude the EEOC from bringing actions seeking class-wide and equitable relief.

An additional reason advanced by Gilmer for refusing to enforce arbitration agreements relating to ADEA claims is his contention that there often will be unequal bargaining power between employers and employees. Mere inequality in bargaining power, however, is not a sufficient reason to hold that arbitration agreements are never enforceable in the employment context. Relationships between securities dealers and investors, for example, may involve unequal bargaining power, but we nevertheless held in *Rodriguez de Quijas* and *McMahon* that agreements to arbitrate in that context are enforceable.... There is no indication in this case, however, that Gilmer, an experienced businessman, was coerced or defrauded into agreeing to the arbitration clause in his registration application. As with the claimed procedural inadequacies discussed above, this claim of unequal bargaining power is best left for resolution in specific cases.

* * *

We conclude that Gilmer has not met his burden of showing that Congress, in enacting the ADEA, intended to preclude arbitration of claims under that Act. Accordingly, the judgment of the Court of Appeals is *Affirmed*.

JUSTICE STEVENS, with whom JUSTICE MARSHALL joins, dissenting.

The Court today, in holding that the FAA compels enforcement of arbitration clauses even when claims of age discrimination are at issue, skirts the antecedent question whether the coverage of the Act even extends to arbitration clauses contained in employment contracts, regardless of the subject matter of the claim at issue. In my opinion, arbitration clauses contained in employment agreements are specifically exempt from coverage of the FAA, and for that reason respondent Interstate/Johnson Lane Corporation cannot, pursuant to the FAA, compel petitioner to submit his claims arising under the ADEA to binding arbitration....

Not only would I find that the FAA does not apply to employment-related disputes between employers and employees in general, but also I would hold that compulsory arbitration conflicts with the congressional purpose animating the ADEA, in particular. As this Court previously has noted, authorizing the courts to issue broad injunctive relief is the cornerstone to eliminating discrimination in society. The ADEA, like Title VII of the Civil Rights Act of 1964, authorizes courts to award broad, class-based injunctive relief to achieve the purposes of the Act. Because commercial arbitration is typically limited to a specific dispute between the particular parties and because the available remedies in arbitral forums generally do not provide for class-wide injunctive relief, I would conclude that an essential purpose of the ADEA is frustrated by compulsory arbitration of employment discrimination claims. Moreover, as Chief Justice Burger explained:

> "Plainly, it would not comport with the congressional objectives behind a statute seeking to enforce civil rights protected by Title VII to allow the very forces that had practiced discrimination to contract away the right to enforce civil rights in the courts. For federal courts to defer to arbitral decisions reached by the same combination of forces that had long perpetuated invidious discrimination would have made the foxes guardians of the chickens."

In my opinion the same concerns expressed by Chief Justice Burger with regard to compulsory arbitration of Title VII claims may be said of claims arising under the ADEA. The Court's holding today clearly eviscerates the important role played by an independent judiciary in eradicating employment discrimination.

a. Comments and Questions

i. Gilmer set forth several arguments against arbitration of his statutory age discrimination claim, such that arbitration is inconsistent with the statutory framework, that arbitration will undermine the role of the EEOC in enforcing the statute, and that compulsory arbitration deprives claimants of a judicial forum provided in the ADEA. He also asserted that arbitration panels will be biased, limit discovery and restrict access to evidence, and result in unequal bargaining power, ineffective appellate review, and stifle the development of law. The majority rejected these arguments. Why? Do you agree? Note that the arbitration institution in *Gilmer* is the New York Stock Exchange, which at the time was regulated by the SEC similar to the regulation of the NASD forum at issue in *McMahon*. In 2007, both of those arbitration forums merged to form FINRA Dispute Resolution.

ii. FAA § 1 states that "nothing herein contained shall apply to contracts of employment of seamen, railroad employees, or any other class of workers engaged in foreign or interstate commerce." Despite the argument that a plain reading of the statute exempts employment contracts, the Supreme Court, in a 5–4 decision, held that the exemption applied only to workers involved in transportation in interstate commerce and does not exclude all employment contracts. *Circuit City Stores, Inc. v. Adams*, 532 U.S. 105 (2001). Do you have any concerns regarding mandatory arbitration of employment claims?

iii. *EEOC v. Waffle House, Inc.*, 534 U.S. 279 (2002), upheld the EEOC's right to judicial enforcement on behalf of workers otherwise bound to arbitrate. Recognizing that the arbitration clause in an employee's contract does not bind anyone other than parties to the clause, EEOC was free to pursue victim-specific remedies for discrimination such as "backpay, reinstatement, and damages," on behalf of the employee, in an Americans with Disabilities Act enforcement action.

3. Other Statutory Claims

a. *Antitrust Law.* In *Mitsubishi Motors Corp. v. Soler Chrysler-Plymouth, Inc.*, 473 U.S. 614 (1985), the issue was whether a standard arbitration clause referring to claims arising out of a contract should be construed to cover statutory claims that have only an indirect relationship to the contract. Holding yes, the Court ruled that federal antitrust claims were arbitrable, although the arbitration would take place in Japan and before a panel of international arbitrators. What concerns might the claimant have raised to this result?

b. *Fair Labor Standards Act.* Federal courts have interpreted the FAA as not conflicting with employee rights under the FLSA, holding that such claims can be vindicated in arbitration. *See Sutherland v. Ernst & Young*, 726 F.3d 290 (2d Cir. 2013) (ruling that an employee's ability to proceed collectively under the FLSA can be waived in an arbitration agreement and was not rendered invalid even though her claim—potential recovery of $1,900—was not economically worth pursuing individually where her attorneys' fees and expert costs would likely reach $200,000); *see also Walthour v. Chipio Windshield Repair, LLC*, 745 F.3d 1326 (11th Cir. 2014) (noting that the Second, Fourth, Fifth, and Eighth Circuits have upheld class waivers of FLSA claims on the grounds that the FLSA contains no contrary congressional command to override the FAA).

c. *Consumer Protection Laws.* The Supreme Court has emphasized that courts are to presume that a federal statutory claim is arbitrable, absent an explicit "contrary Congressional command." *See CompuCredit Corp. v. Greenwood*, 565 U.S. 95, 100–01 (2012). The *CompuCredit* plaintiffs filed a class action lawsuit against a credit card marketing company and issuing bank alleging deceptive practices by a "credit repair organization" under the Credit Repair Organizations Act (CROA), 15 U.S.C. §1679, a consumer-protection statute. After the district court denied defendants' motion to compel arbitration and the Ninth Circuit affirmed, the Supreme Court ruled that CROA claims are arbitrable.

Justice Scalia's 6–3 majority opinion concluded that the CROA's disclosure provision requiring credit repair organizations to notify consumers that they "have a right to sue a credit repair organization that violates the Credit Repair Organization Act" does not reflect congressional intent to preclude arbitration of claims arising under the Act. The Court similarly concluded that the Act's nonwaiver provision, which voids enforcement of a consumer's waiver of protections and rights under the CROA, did not render unenforceable an arbitration agreement that waives the right to bring CROA claims in court. These two provisions—disclosure and nonwaiver—did not create a consumer's right to bring a CROA claim in court; they created only a consumer's right to receive the statutory notice. Thus, the provisions did not constitute a "contrary congressional command" sufficient to overcome the default rule that federal statutory claims are arbitrable. Such a command must be far more explicit. What language in a statute is sufficient to constitute a "contrary Congressional command"?

d. *Contrary Congressional Command.* In *CompuCredit*, the Court cited examples of congressional language more explicit than that in the CROA, including: "No pre-dispute arbitration agreement shall be valid or enforceable, if the agreement requires arbitration of a dispute arising under this section," 7 U.S.C. § 26(n)(2), which applies to whistleblower claims under the Commodities Exchange Act. Other examples where Congress has expressly banned pre-dispute arbitration agreements include provisions in the Military Lending Act of 2007 (in consumer credit contracts with military personnel), and the Dodd-Frank Wall Street Reform and Protection Act of 2010 (for whistleblower claims arising under the Sarbanes-Oxley Act of 2002 as well as residential mortgage loans).

What if Congress delegated to an administrative agency the power to regulate arbitration of disputes relating to its field of regulation, and the agency adopted a rule banning PDAAs for those disputes? Is that a sufficient command?

In *CompuCredit*, the Court also cited as an example of a contrary Congressional command a section of the Dodd-Frank Wall Street Reform and Consumer Protection Act, 12 U.S.C. § 5518(b), which "granted authority to the newly created Consumer Financial Protection Bureau to regulate predispute arbitration agreements in contracts for consumer financial products or services." In July 2017, pursuant to this power, the CFPB issued its Final Rule on Arbitration Agreements, 12 C.F.R. 1040. The Final Rule, which applied to banks and other financial services companies, (1) prohibited class action waivers in pre-dispute arbitration provisions in certain consumer financial product and service contracts, and (2) required providers involved in consumer financial contractual arbitration to submit arbitral and court records. *See* https://www.consumerfinance.gov/policy-compliance/rulemaking/final-rules/arbitration-agreements/. The Rule was supposed to be effective in September 2017, but, after challenges by the business community and the 2016 election, Congress passed legislation to repeal the rule, which President Trump signed into law. Stay tuned for developments. Is the CFPB rule necessary?

e. Statutory laws are intended to further important social policies. Does arbitration enable claimants to vindicate these social policies? Is the Supreme Court delegating interpretations of public law to private arbitrators? How can the law develop if private arbitrators are the only ones interpreting these statutes? For a recent argument that the law is no longer developing, see Myriam Gilles, *The Day Doctrine Died, Private Arbitration and the End of Law*, 2016 U. ILL. L. REV. 371.

E. Insurance: Reverse Preemption of the FAA

Insurance is a highly regulated activity, and only state-licensed entities are permitted to engage in the business of insurance. Although insurance clearly involves interstate commerce, Congress has nevertheless ceded authority to regulate insurance to the states, under the McCann-Ferguson Act. Pursuant to that power, some states have passed laws barring arbitration of insurance disputes, voiding pre-dispute arbitration clauses in insurance contracts or providing courts with exclusive jurisdiction to resolve certain insurance disputes. These laws reflect that state's policy choice that courts, not arbitrators, should resolve insurance disputes arising under that state's law.

The interaction of state insurance laws and the FAA has resulted in important litigation because the stakes are high. Both insurance companies and state insurance agencies are able to fund litigation regarding arbitration issues. When reading the cases below, consider why a state might not want the underlying dispute to be arbitrated.

Davister Corp. v. United Republic Life Ins. Co.
152 F.3d 1277 (10th Cir. 1998)

JOHN C. PORFILIO, CIRCUIT JUDGE.

This case considers whether the district court erred by abstaining from enforcing arbitration of a dispute between Davister Corporation and the Liquidator of United Republic Life Insurance Company (United), an insurance company domiciled in Utah and currently under liquidation in insolvency proceedings in Utah state court. We believe this question must be resolved under the McCarran-Ferguson Act, not under other doctrines of abstention. So focused, we hold the district court correctly refused to compel arbitration. We therefore affirm its judgment.

The facts of this matter are relatively simple. Prior to insolvency, United had entered into a transaction with Davister in which it agreed to transfer some of its stock to Davister in exchange for 100% of the stock of R.G. Acquisition Corporation (RGA). As part of that agreement, United was to obtain certain real property interests in Waco, Texas, that were the principal assets of RGA. Subsequently, the Commissioner of the Utah Insurance Department notified United this and other similar transactions were improper and must cease. Moreover, the Commissioner advised United the transaction involving the stock of RGA "must be reversed" because United had not obtained required authorization from the commission to exchange its stock for the stock of RGA.

Before the reversal was accomplished, however, the Commissioner filed an action in Utah state court to seize control of the company. He also filed an action in Texas state court to gain control of the Waco real property interests. Davister intervened in the Texas action seeking rescission of its transaction with United, claiming the Utah Commissioner's order to reverse caused a failure of consideration in its agreement with United. Davister also sought a judgment establishing its right to the Texas property interests.

Meanwhile, in the Utah state court action, the Commissioner obtained an order liquidating United and appointing him the Liquidator. Contemporaneously, the state court issued an order staying all claims against United. *See* Utah Code Ann. § 31A-27-317 ("The filing of a petition for liquidation of a domestic insurer or of an alien insurer domiciled in this state stays all actions and all proceedings against the insurer. . . ."). That stay was honored by the Texas court which also stayed all of Davister's claims pending in that forum, although the court permitted the continuation of the balance of the Texas action.

Davister then filed this case against United and the Commissioner (Defendants) in the United States District Court for the District of Utah to compel arbitration of the dispute over the Texas real property interests in accordance with the agreements between Davister and United. In addition, Davister sought a stay of the entire Texas action and the Utah liquidation. After a hearing on the merits, the federal district court abstained from compelling arbitration and refused to grant the stay requested by Davister. Davister then brought this appeal.

On appeal, Davister argues clear national policy and the FAA mandate arbitration in place of state litigation when the parties have contracted to submit disputes to arbitration. Davister contends once a federal court determines a dispute exists between the parties which they have agreed to arbitrate, it must stay all other proceedings and compel arbitration. Defendants respond that abstention was proper on grounds of comity, but if not on that basis, certainly under the McCarran-Ferguson Act. Defendants rely upon 15 U.S.C. § 1012 which states: "No Act of Congress shall be construed to invalidate, impair, or supersede any law enacted by any State for the purpose of regulating the business of insurance," contending it trumps the federal policy favoring arbitration. Defendants also urge their position is supported by *United States v. Fabe*, 508 U.S. 491 (1993).

In *Fabe*, the Court was called upon to determine whether in an Ohio statutory procedure for the liquidation of an insolvent insurance company the United States was entitled to assert a priority claim granted it under a federal statute. "In order to resolve this case, we must decide whether a state statute establishing the priority of creditors' claims in a proceeding to liquidate an insolvent insurance company is a law enacted 'for the purpose of regulating the business of insurance,' within the meaning of § 2(b) of the McCarran-Ferguson Act, 15 U.S.C. § 1012(b)." The Court's analysis produced what we have come to call a three-part test for the determination of whether the Mc-Carran-Ferguson Act should be applied: (1) does the federal statute at issue "specifically relate to the business of insurance"; (2) was the state statute enacted "for the purpose of regulating the business of insurance"; (3) would application of the federal statute "impair, interfere, or supersede" the state statute? Part (1) of the test is not an issue in this case because the FAA does not specifically relate to the business of insurance.

The United States maintained the Ohio liquidation act could not have been enacted for the purpose of regulating the business of insurance because it merely determined the order in which claims of creditors would be paid. It also contended the statute did not deal with the insurer-insured relationship because it pertained only to resolution of conflicts between policyholders and other creditors of the insolvent insurance company. . . . Although the government maintained the Ohio liquidation statute was a bankruptcy law and not an insurance statute, the Court disagreed. "The primary purpose of a statute that distributes the insolvent insurer's assets to policyholders in preference to other creditors is identical to the primary purpose of the insurance company itself: the payment of claims made against policies."

Contrary to the position advanced in the dissent, we do not view *Fabe* to permit *all* actions arising under a state insurance liquidation statute to "automatically fall under the purview of the McCarran-Ferguson Act." As we have noted, a carefully constructed three-part test must be satisfied before the Act can apply. This examination must be implemented on a case-by-case basis, and the result will be dictated by the precise statutes involved in each case. Because Fabe dealt only with competing claims for priority of distribution in a liquidation setting, it does not completely inform our decision. We are called upon to go beyond that point to decide whether rights created under the FAA must give way to a state court blanket stay in the liquidation setting.

Our quest leads us to *Munich American Reinsurance Co. v. Crawford*, 141 F.3d 585 (5th Cir. 1998). In that case, the Fifth Circuit was called upon to decide "whether state laws governing insurance company delinquency proceedings reverse preempt the FAA under the McCarran-Ferguson Act." The court held they did. At issue in Munich was whether claims asserted by two reinsurers to certain policy proceeds arising out of reinsurance agreements between an insolvent Oklahoma insurance company and the claimants must be resolved by arbitration. The Oklahoma Insurance Commissioner, who was the liquidator of the insolvent company and holder of the proceeds, refused to submit to arbitration. The claimants filed an action in federal district court to compel arbitration under the FAA, and the district court granted relief. The Fifth Circuit reversed the judgment, stating:

> [T]he specific provisions of the statute at issue here—vesting exclusive original jurisdiction of delinquency proceedings in the Oklahoma state court *and authorizing the court to enjoin any action interfering with the delinquency proceedings* are laws enacted clearly for the purpose of regulating the business of insurance. These provisions give the state court the power to decide all issues relating to disposition of an insolvent insurance company's assets, including whether any given property is part of the insolvent estate in the first place.

The court continued, "Oklahoma has not only adopted a comprehensive scheme to oversee liquidation of insolvent insurers, it has provided a particular court ... to oversee liquidation proceedings." This, the Fifth Circuit noted, is "a special relationship [which] contributes markedly to the orderly liquidation or rehabilitation of the insurance company and the adjudication of claims against it." Moreover, giving the state court ultimate control over all issues relating to the insolvent insurance company is "aimed at protecting the relationship between the insurance company and its policyholders."

Dispatching the reinsurers' argument that the state law which consolidated disposition of all claims, including those of creditors other than policyholders, was not a law enacted for the purpose of regulating the business of insurance, the court turned to *Fabe*. The Fifth Circuit reminded that *Fabe* decided the Ohio law dealing with insolvency preferences for administrative expenses was "reasonably necessary" to the goal of protecting policyholders, hence, that law was enacted for the purpose of regulating the business of insurance. The court applied the same reasoning to the Oklahoma liquidation proceedings in state court, holding that although some of the benefits from the liquidation could devolve upon non-policy holding creditors, none of those which inure to the benefit of policyholders "are insignificant or attenuated," and are "indistinguishable from the Ohio provision giving a preference to administrative expenses in *Fabe*." Thus, the court concluded, "these provisions were enacted for the purpose of regulating the business of insurance."

The dissent overreads *Munich*. The court did not in any way adopt a "per se rule of reverse preemption of federal enforcement of all arbitration agreements against an insurance company in insolvency proceedings." To the contrary, the Fifth Circuit carefully conducted the three-part *Fabe* test and concluded the Oklahoma law vesting exclusive jurisdiction in the state court and providing for a blanket stay of all other proceedings was "clearly for the purpose of regulating the business of insurance." Nothing contained within the court's reasoning or inferable therefrom suggests the adoption of a per se test. More importantly, we purpose no such result ourselves.

We hold the same result applies here. The Utah statute consolidating all claims against a liquidating insurer, by its nature and express terms, was enacted to protect policyholders. By offering benefits to other creditors, that ultimate purpose is neither diminished nor denigrated. Adding to the stated statutory purpose is the statutory blanket stay against all proceedings against the insolvent insurance company. The stay makes clear it is the policy of the State of Utah to consolidate in one forum all matters attendant to the liquidation of a domiciled insurance company. That policy guarantees that the entire process is more than a simple liquidation of debt. Indeed, all decisions in Utah affecting the ultimate benefits to be accorded policyholders of a liquidated insurance company are circumscribed in one proceeding. Because the stay prevents conflicting rulings on claims, the unequal treatment of claimants, and the unnecessary and wasteful dissipation of the remaining funds of the insolvent insurer, the stay manifests a purpose of protecting policyholders. We think it evident the Utah statute meets the test of having been enacted for the purpose of regulating the business of insurance.

The dissent takes the position that the "facts before us are not related to the business of insurance as defined in *Fabe*," citing in support *Garcia v. Island Program Designer, Inc.*, 4 F.3d 57 (1st Cir. 1993). *Garcia*, in fact makes the point we adopt. The federal statute in *Garcia* gave the United States a priority in the state liquidation proceeding. The law under which the liquidation was conducted would have deprived the federal government from participating in the proceeds of liquidation until after all other claims had been satisfied. Clearly, the Commonwealth statute prescribing the order in which claims were to be liquidated had nothing to do with the regulation of the business of insurance. Indeed, that statute would have applicability in any form of debt liquidation proceeding and it is not in any way peculiar to the business of insurance. In contrast, application of the federal statute here (having nothing to do with regulating the insurance business) would remove a dispute over a potentially significant piece of the liquidation proceeding (having by definition everything to do

with regulating the insurance business) from the state court whose jurisdiction is exclusive and submit it for resolution by a non-judicial forum. That process would
thoroughly denigrate Utah Code Ann. § 31A-27-101(2), the state law enacted for the
protection of policyholders. *Garcia* is simply inapposite.

That decision leaves us with only the third part of the *Fabe* test, that is, whether,
under the McCarran-Ferguson Act, the FAA "invalidate[s], impair[s], or supersede[s]."
Again, we believe the answer is obvious. Allowing a putative creditor to pluck from
the entire liquidation proceeding one discrete issue and force arbitration contrary to
the blanket stay entered by the Utah state court would certainly impair the progress
of the orderly resolution of all matters involving the insolvent company. Unquestionably, that result would directly impact the policyholders because it deals with a purported asset of the insurance company that could be apportioned to them. Recognition
of that consequence makes apparent the conflict between the terms of the FAA and
the Utah law. Neither *Fabe* nor any other authority holds that the applicability of the
McCarran-Ferguson Act is dependent upon the existence of a Utah law "mandating
against arbitration" as the dissent contends. With all due respect, that approach turns
the *Fabe* test inside out. The issue is not whether Utah prohibits arbitration, but
whether enforcing arbitration invalidates, impairs, or supersedes the enforcement of
the state process designed to protect the interests of policyholders. We agree whole-
heartedly with the Fifth Circuit that "[r]egardless of the nature of the reinsurers'
action, ordering it resolved in a forum other than the receivership court nevertheless
conflicts with [state] law giving the state court the power to enjoin any action inter-
fering with the delinquency proceedings."

Our resolution does not leave Davister without a remedy. Indeed, it can bring this
matter before the liquidation court, and if arbitration is the best way to resolve the conflict, it can be ordered by that court under its own aegis. Moreover, if the stay is unfairly
limiting Davister's pursuit of its rights in Texas, the Utah court can certainly grant relief
from that stay as well. A federal court need not interfere in the process. AFFIRMED.

LUCERO, CIRCUIT JUDGE, dissenting.

Because I believe that the issue presented before us is governed by *United States v.
Fabe*, 508 U.S. 491 (1993), and because my reading of that carefully limited opinion
delivered by a divided Supreme Court precludes both the approach and result reached
by the majority opinion, I respectfully dissent. Unlike the majority, I do not understand *Fabe* to permit a conclusion that all actions arising under a state insurance liquidation statute automatically fall under the purview of the McCarran-Ferguson Act
merely because of the operation of the state statute. *Fabe*'s holding is much more nu-
anced—requiring a close inquiry into whether the operation of each provision of
the statute implicates the "business of insurance."

In *Fabe*, after reviewing relevant precedent, the Court concluded that a state
statute "regulate[s] the business of insurance only to the extent that it protect[s]
policyholders." I recognize that the interests of policyholders are indirectly implicated
by any claims on the assets of insolvent insurers by potential creditors. Emphasizing

the "narrowness of our actual holding," however, the *Fabe* Court cautioned against defining all such indirect connections as pertaining to the "business of insurance" under McCarran-Ferguson.

The facts before us are not related to the business of insurance as defined in *Fabe*. I disagree with the majority's adoption of *Munich Amer. Reins. Co. v. Crawford*, 141 F.3d 585 (5th Cir. 1998), to the extent that *Munich* imposes a per se rule of reverse preemption of federal enforcement of all arbitration agreements against an insurance company in insolvency proceedings. *Fabe* requires the examination of individual provisions of an insurance liquidation statute to determine which of those provisions specifically protect policyholders. *See Fabe*, 508 U.S. at 508–10 (finding reverse preemption of federal priority statute with respect to policyholders, but not with respect to other creditors); *see also Garcia v. Island Program Designer* 4 F.3d 57, 62 (1st Cir. 1993) (BREYER, C.J.) (finding no reverse-preemption of filing deadline provision of Puerto Rico insurance insolvency statute because provision "cannot be said to directly 'regulate policyholders,' for it is neither directed at, nor necessary for, the protection of policyholders, as the *Fabe* Court required. The provision helps policyholders only to the extent that (and in the same way as) it helps all creditors."). Like the provision at issue in *Garcia*, a blanket stay of all arbitration proceedings is of general benefit to all creditors and not specifically for the benefit of policyholders.

Nor is *Munich* clearly apposite on its facts to the situation before us. The *Munich* court considered the enforceability of arbitration clauses in reinsurance contracts which covered losses on claims paid under an insurance policy by the insolvent insurer, contracts which arguably relate with some directness to protecting policyholders. The precise question before the district court below, however, was whether to compel specific performance of the arbitration clause in a stock purchase agreement forming part of a real estate deal. Davister is neither a policyholder of United Republic nor an insurer of United Republic's policies. The contract to be interpreted is a real estate contract. Though an insurance company, albeit now insolvent, is a party, the contract has no connection to policyholders or their policies. The deliberately narrow holding of *Fabe* forecloses a scope of reverse preemption so broad that it could encompass the arbitration of such a contract.

Furthermore, this is not a case where the enforcement of the federal right would conflict with a specific provision of a state law precluding arbitration in insurance cases or insurance liquidation proceedings. *Cf. Stephens v. American Int'l Ins. Co.*, 66 F.3d 41 (2d Cir. 1995) (concluding that specific antiarbitration provision in Kentucky insurance liquidation law precludes compelling arbitration under federal law); *Mutual Reins. Bureau v. Great Plains Mut. Ins. Co.*, 969 F.2d 931 (10th Cir. 1992) (holding that Kansas arbitration statute specifically exempting "contracts of insurance" was protected from FAA preemption by McCarran-Ferguson Act). Utah has no state law, either within or outside of its insurance liquidation scheme, mandating against arbitration in the insurance context. Thus, it is by no means clear that enforcement of the FAA would "invalidate, impair, or supersede" the Utah liquidation statute.

I am mindful that "the statutory question the majority considers with care is difficult." To bring this dispute within the reach of McCarran-Ferguson reverse preemption would swallow the very fine distinction set forth by *Fabe*'s majority, potentially precluding federal jurisdiction over any dispute involving an insolvent insurance company. Because I believe that the majority's result is neither contemplated by nor consistent with *Fabe*, nor required by McCarran-Ferguson, I would conclude that the federal court has jurisdiction over this dispute and would reach the question of whether the district court below properly abstained from exercising that jurisdiction.

Kremer v. Rural Community Ins. Co.

788 N.W.2d 538 (Neb. 2010)

CONNOLLY, J.

Robert Kremer and Gary Moody, two insureds, appeal from the district court's decisions in their actions to enforce compromise and settlement agreements with their crop insurer, Rural Community Insurance Company (RCIC). In each case, the insured alleged that RCIC's adjuster agreed to pay specified amounts to the insureds. In both cases, RCIC moved to dismiss the action or, alternatively, to compel arbitration and stay the proceedings. In both cases, the court compelled arbitration and stayed judicial proceedings.

We are asked to decide two issues: Whether this court has jurisdiction to review an order that stays judicial proceedings and compels arbitration; and whether federal law preempts Neb.Rev.Stat. § 25-2602.01(f)(4), which precludes arbitration agreements for future controversies relating to insurance policies. We conclude that the orders are final and that we have jurisdiction. We also conclude that federal regulations under the Federal Crop Insurance Act (FCIA), preempt § 25-2602.01(f)(4). Thus, the district court did not err in compelling the insureds to arbitrate their disputes with RCIC....

The court found that RCIC issued the MPCI [Multiple Peril Crop Insurance] policies under the FCIA and that all MPCI policies contain a provision requiring arbitration. But the parties fail to recognize that the arbitration provision in each policy is invalid under Nebraska law because it required arbitration of future controversies related to an insurance policy.... Under § 25-2602.01(f)(4), agreements to arbitrate future controversies concerning an insurance policy are invalid, with certain exceptions that are not applicable here. So unless federal law preempts § 25-2602.01, the arbitration provisions in these insurance policies were invalid.

The FAA governs whether an arbitration provision in a contract touching on interstate commerce is enforceable. But under the federal McCarran-Ferguson Act, state law regulating the business of insurance preempts federal law that does not specifically govern insurance. Section 1012(b) sets out the state law exemptions:

> No Act of Congress shall be construed to invalidate, impair, or supersede any law enacted by any State for the purpose of regulating the business of insurance, or which imposes a fee or tax upon such business, unless such Act specifically relates to the business of insurance: Provided, That [the federal antitrust statutes] shall be applicable to the business of insurance to the extent that such business is not regulated by State Law.

Congress passed the McCarran-Ferguson Act to overturn a U.S. Supreme Court decision under the Commerce Clause that threatened the continued supremacy of states to regulate "the activities of insurance companies in dealing with their policyholders." *SEC v. National Securities, Inc.*, 393 U.S. 453 (1969). The U.S. Supreme Court has interpreted the second clause of § 1012(b) to provide an exemption to an insurer from antitrust scrutiny if its challenged practices constitute the "business of insurance" and are regulated by state law. The first clause, which is at issue here, shields state regulation of the insurance business from federal preemption under Congress' Commerce Clause authority, whether dormant or exercised, unless the federal statute specifically relates to the business of insurance.

Under the McCarran-Ferguson Act, federal courts have set out three elements for determining whether a state law controls over (reverse preempts) a federal statute: (1) The federal statute does not specifically relate to the business of insurance; (2) the state law was enacted for regulating the business of insurance; and (3) the federal statute operates to invalidate, impair, or supersede the state law. Applying this test, the only question for determining whether Nebraska law controls over the FAA is whether Nebraska's restriction of arbitration agreements in insurance policies regulates the business of insurance.

In *SEC v. National Securities, Inc.*, the Court first interpreted the McCarran-Ferguson Act in a dispute under the first clause of § 1012(b). It explained that in enacting the McCarran-Ferguson Act:

> Congress was concerned with the type of state regulation that centers around the contract of insurance.... The relationship between insurer and insured, *the type of policy which could be issued*, its reliability, interpretation, and enforcement—these were the core of the "business of insurance." ... But whatever the exact scope of the statutory term, it is clear where the focus was on the relationship between the insurance company and the policyholder. Statutes aimed at protecting or regulating this relationship, directly or indirectly, are laws regulating the "business of insurance."

In examining the act, the Court held that a state law that protected insurance stockholders from inequitable mergers was not a regulation of the insurance business: "The crucial point is that here the State has focused its attention on stockholder protection; *it is not attempting to secure the interests of those purchasing insurance policies.*" The Court recognized that the state had approved the merger at issue under a statute that also required it to find that the merger would not reduce the security of or services to policyholders. That part of the statute was a regulation of the insurance business and exempt from preemption by federal law. But to the extent the statute protected shareholders, it did not regulate the insurance relationship.

Later, in *Department of Treasury v. Fabe*, 508 U.S. 491 (1993), the Court held that a state priority statute for insurer liquidations was not preempted by a federal priority statute for bankruptcy obligations. To the extent that the state statute protected policyholders by giving their claims a higher priority than the federal government's claims, it regulated the business of insurance. In *Fabe*, the Court reemphasized its holding in *National Securities, Inc.* that the primary concern for disputes under the first clause of § 1012(b) is whether the state law regulates the core components of the business of insurance: the contractual relationship between the insurer and insured; the type of policy that can be issued; and its reliability, interpretation, and enforcement. It determined that the phrase "business of insurance" has a broader meaning under the first clause of § 1012(b) than under the second clause: "The broad category of laws enacted for the purpose of regulating the business of insurance consists of laws that possess the end, intention, or aim' of adjusting, managing, or controlling the business of insurance."

Every federal appellate court to address this issue has held that state laws restricting arbitration provisions in insurance contracts regulate the business of insurance and are not preempted by the FAA. These courts have reasoned that such state laws regulate core components of the insurance business by legislating how disputed claims can be resolved. Applying factors that the Supreme Court set out under the second clause of § 1012(b), these courts have also asked whether the law has the effect of transferring or spreading a policyholder's risk. They have reasoned that a state's restriction of arbitration clauses affects the transfer of risk by (1) placing limits on the parties' agreement to spread risk or (2) introducing the possibility of a jury verdict into the process for resolving disputed claims. Alternatively, they have simply stated that any contract of insurance is an agreement to spread risk.

Reasonable people might disagree whether statutes restricting arbitration agreements in insurance policies affect the transfer of risk. But we do not consider this issue dispositive. First, even for disputes under the second clause of § 1012(b), no factor is dispositive in itself whether an insurer's practice constitutes the "business of insurance." More important, the Court in *Fabe* explained that these factors were intended to define

> the scope of the antitrust immunity located in the second clause of § 101(2)(b). We deal here with the first clause, which is not so narrowly circumscribed.... To equate laws "enacted ... for the purpose of regulating the business of insurance" with the "business of insurance" itself ... would be to read words out of the statute. This we refuse to do.

We conclude that under *Fabe*, the *National Securities* test is the more relevant test for disputes under the first clause of § 1012(b). Applying that test, we conclude that a statute precluding the parties to an insurance contract from including an arbitration agreement for future controversies regulates the insurer-insured contractual relationship.

Thus, it regulates the business of insurance. So we agree with federal courts that the FAA does not preempt such statutes. Specifically, we hold that the FAA does not preempt Nebraska's § 25-2602.01(f)(4). But we are not done. The FAA is not the only federal law that we consider in determining whether § 25-2602.01(f)(4)'s preclusion of agreements to arbitrate future controversies in crop insurance policies is preempted.

RCIC issued this crop insurance policy under the FCIA, and the Federal Crop Insurance Corporation (the Corporation) is the reinsurer for all MPCI policies. All MPCI policies contain the same alternative dispute resolution provision. The Corporation is a wholly owned government corporation within the U.S. Department of Agriculture, established to regulate the crop insurance industry. Private insurance companies offer crop insurance and are then reinsured (and regulated) by the Corporation. Section 1506 authorize the Corporation to adopt rules and regulations necessary to conduct its business. Section 1508 (a)(1) authorizes the Corporation to "insure, or provide reinsurance for insurers of, producers of agricultural commodities ... under 1 or more plans of insurance determined by the Corporation to be adapted to the agricultural commodity concerned." Under this authority, the Corporation has promulgated regulations prescribing the terms for common crop insurance policies. The Corporation's regulations specifically require applicants to apply on one of the Corporation's prescribed policy forms. Those forms contain arbitration provisions for all policies reinsured by the Corporation. Also, 7 U.S.C. § 1506(1) provides in part:

> State and local laws or rules shall not apply to contracts, agreements, or regulations of the Corporation or the parties thereto to the extent that such contracts, agreements, or regulations provide that such laws or rules shall not apply, or to the extent that such laws or rules are inconsistent with such contracts, agreements, or regulations.

Under its statutory authority to regulate private crop insurance contracts, the Corporation has also promulgated regulations providing that state and local governments cannot pass laws or promulgate rules that affect or govern its agreements or contracts. And the regulations specifically preclude state and local governments from exercising approval authority over the policies it issues.

Under the Supremacy Clause of the U.S. Constitution, state law that conflicts with federal law is invalid. Federal law preempts state law when it conflicts with a federal statute or when the U.S. Congress, or an agency acting within the scope of its powers conferred by Congress, explicitly declares an intent to preempt state law. Preemption can also impliedly occur when Congress has occupied the entire field to the exclusion of state law claims.

We conclude that the FCIA and the Corporation's regulations express an intent to preempt state law that conflicts with the Corporation's regulations. Further, the Corporation's regulations requiring arbitration and the preclusion of the arbitration agreement under § 25-2602.01(f)(4) conflict because they cannot both be enforced.

And because the FCIA and the Corporation's regulations specifically deal with insurance, they invoke the exception under the McCarran-Ferguson Act's § 1012(b). That is, under the McCarran-Ferguson Act, Nebraska's § 25-2602.01(f)(4) does not reverse preempt federal law under the FCIA because the FCIA specifically relates to the business of insurance. Because the McCarran-Ferguson Act does not apply, the Corporation's regulations requiring arbitration preempt state law and are enforceable.

Moreover, the insureds cannot evade the arbitration requirement by claiming that they are enforcing settlement agreements with the adjuster. An agent's or loss adjuster's statement cannot bind the Corporation when the statement is inconsistent with governing federal law. And each crop insurance policy's arbitration provision is clearly broad enough to cover disputes over adjustment actions: "If you and we fail to agree on any determination *made by us*," the disagreement must be resolved through mediation or arbitration. We conclude that the district court did not err in determining that the insureds' disputes are subject to arbitration.

1. Comments and Questions

a. *Davister* and *Kremer* reflect courts' competing responses to the argument that the McCann-Ferguson Act reverse preempts the FAA. Until recently, many federal and state courts endorsed the reverse preemption doctrine in the FAA context, on the grounds that states have the right to dictate that courts, not arbitrators, resolve insurance disputes. Why would states be concerned about the arbitration of insurance disputes?

b. More recently, perhaps in response to the Supreme Court's recent FAA preemption cases, several state high courts have ruled the opposite — that the FAA preempts those state laws, as those laws regulate only the forum in which to resolve disputes, not the business of insurance directly. *See, e.g., Monarch Consulting, Inc. v. Nat'l Union Fire Ins. Co. of Pittsburgh, PA*, 256 N.E.2d 542 (N.Y. 2016); *Fredericksburg Care Co., L.P. v. Perez*, 461 S.W.3d 513 (Tex. 2015).

c. The Fourth Circuit recently held that the McCarran-Ferguson Act reverse preempted a *delegation clause* (delegating to arbitrators the authority to decide arbitrability) in a "reinsurance participation agreement." *See Minnieland Private Day School, Inc. v. Applied Underwriters Captive Risk Assur. Co., Inc.*, 867 F.3d 449 (4th Cir. 2017). In that case, the insured argued that their agreement was a "contract of insurance" within the meaning of Virginia law, and thus governed by Virginia's insurance law, which, among other things, voided arbitration clauses in insurance contracts. The Fourth Circuit voided the delegation clause, reasoning that the Virginia law

> reflects a state policy choice that insureds should have the option to seek enforcement of Virginia's insurance laws and regulations in court, rather than through arbitration. Enforcing contractual provisions that provide arbitrators with exclusive authority to determine whether a contract amounts to a 'contract of insurance' — a term defined by Virginia law — would undermine that

purpose by giving the arbitrators exclusive authority over a core question of Virginia insurance law.

Id. at 457.

Do you think the McCarran-Ferguson Act reverse preempts delegation clauses that are separable from arbitration clauses?

Chapter 4

Defenses to Arbitrability

A. Introduction

This Chapter explores a variety of defenses that parties reluctant to arbitrate can raise in opposition to a motion to compel arbitration or to stay litigation. Recall that section 2 of the FAA directs courts to enforce written agreements to arbitrate, "save upon such grounds as exist at law or in equity for the revocation of any contract." (FAA § 2) This last clause, sometimes known as the "savings clause," explicitly carves out from its mandate challenges to the validity of an arbitration clause based on traditional common law defenses to the enforcement of any contract. These defenses may include the lack of mutual assent, unconscionability, lack of authority, lack of consideration, duress/undue influence, lack of capacity, lack of due process, material breach, waiver, illusory provisions, statutes of limitations, failure to comply with conditions precedent (e.g., mediation or notice requirements), and lack of mutuality of obligation or remedies.

Sections B through E of this chapter examine how courts apply these standard "**contract formation**" or "**saving clause**" defenses to arbitration agreements. Specifically, Section B explores the defense of **lack of mutual assent** to an arbitration agreement. For example, do arbitration provisions contained in standard preprinted forms or purchase receipts constitute a valid assent to arbitrate? Can the contractual obligation to arbitrate arise from online transactions by the mere click of a mouse, or downloading of an app on a phone? Section C explores the defense of **unconscionability** — a defense you likely learned in your first-year contracts course. Do courts treat the defense any differently if the challenge is that an arbitration agreement is unconscionable? Section D explores the defense of **waiver**, that one party waived its right to arbitrate a dispute due to litigation conduct. Section E explores a unique twist to the **breach of contract** defense in the arbitration context.

In addition to traditional contract defenses, reluctant parties have asserted other defenses to arbitrability. Section F explores the "**effective vindication**" doctrine. Under this doctrine, reluctant parties argue that an arbitration agreement is not enforceable on the grounds that the resulting arbitration would deprive them of the ability to vindicate their statutory rights. The Supreme Court recently cast doubt on the vitality of that doctrine.

Section G addresses defenses to arbitrability that raise **constitutional** concerns, including assertions that a pre-dispute arbitration agreement (PDAA) violated a disputant's rights under the Due Process Clause or deprived a disputant of its Seventh Amendment right to a jury trial.

When reading this Chapter, evaluate whether the requisite elements of contractual arbitration are present in the cases that follow and identify whether the court or the arbitrator is the appropriate decision-maker to rule on the disputed issues.

B. Lack of Mutual Assent

Arbitration is premised upon the parties' agreement to arbitrate. An arbitration clause is frequently a non-negotiated term within a standard commercial contract and online purchase agreement. Suppose the arbitration provision is in the "Terms and Conditions" document located in the product's shipment invoice or on an account "sign-up" screen on a website or mobile app. Does this constitute assent to arbitration? Can the contractual obligation to arbitrate arise from online transactions by the mere click of a mouse, or downloading of an app on a phone?

Increasingly, issues surrounding arbitration provisions in form contracts continue to arise in the context of electronic commerce, rather than via in-store or telephone orders, as the following cases demonstrate.

Specht v. Netscape Communications Corp.
306 F.3d 17 (2d Cir. 2002)

SOTOMAYOR, CIRCUIT JUDGE.

This is an appeal from a judgment denying a motion by defendants Netscape and its corporate parent, America Online, Inc. (collectively, "defendants" or "Netscape"), to compel arbitration and to stay court proceedings. In order to resolve the central question of arbitrability presented here, we must address issues of contract formation in cyberspace. Principally, we are asked to determine whether plaintiffs by acting upon defendants' invitation to download free software made available on defendants' webpage, agreed to be bound by the software's license terms (which included the arbitration clause at issue), even though plaintiffs could not have learned of the existence of those terms unless, prior to executing the download, they had scrolled down the webpage to a screen located below the download button. We agree with the district court that a reasonably prudent Internet user in circumstances such as these would not have known or learned of the existence of the license terms before responding to defendants' invitation to download the free software, and that defendants therefore did not provide reasonable notice of the license terms. In consequence, plaintiffs' bare act of downloading the software did not unambiguously manifest assent to the arbitration provision contained in the license terms....

Defendants argue that plaintiffs must be held to a standard of reasonable prudence and that, because notice of the existence of SmartDownload license terms was on the next scrollable screen, plaintiffs were on "inquiry notice" of those terms. ["Inquiry notice" is actual notice of circumstances sufficient to put a prudent man upon inquiry.] We disagree with the proposition that a reasonably prudent offeree in plaintiffs' position would necessarily have known or learned of the existence of the license agreement prior to acting, so that plaintiffs may be held to have assented to that agreement with constructive notice of its terms. * * *

We conclude that in circumstances such as these, where consumers are urged to download free software at the immediate click of a button, a reference to the existence of license terms on a submerged screen is not sufficient to place consumers on inquiry or constructive notice of those terms.... Internet users may have, as defendants put it, "as much time as they need" to scroll through multiple screens on a webpage, but there is no reason to assume that viewers will scroll down to subsequent screens simply because screens are there. When products are "free" and users are invited to download them in the absence of reasonably conspicuous notice that they are about to bind themselves to contract terms, the transactional circumstances cannot be fully analogized to those in the paper world of arm's-length bargaining.

Defendants cite certain well-known cases involving shrinkwrap licensing and related commercial practices in support of their contention that plaintiffs became bound by the license terms by virtue of inquiry notice. For example, in *Hill v. Gateway 2000, Inc.*, 105 F.3d 1147 (7th Cir.1997), the Seventh Circuit held that where a purchaser had ordered a computer over the telephone, received the order in a shipped box containing the computer along with printed contract terms, and did not return the computer within the thirty days required by the terms, the purchaser was bound by the contract. In *ProCD, Inc. v. Zeidenberg*, the same court held that where an individual purchased software in a box containing license terms which were displayed on the computer screen every time the user executed the software program, the user had sufficient opportunity to review the terms and to return the software, and so was contractually bound after retaining the product.

These cases do not help defendants. To the extent that they hold that the purchaser of a computer or tangible software is contractually bound after failing to object to printed license terms provided with the product, *Hill* does not differ markedly from the cases involving traditional paper contracting discussed in the previous section. Insofar as the purchaser in *ProCD* was confronted with conspicuous, mandatory license terms every time he ran the software on his computer, that case actually undermines defendants' contention that downloading in the absence of conspicuous terms is an act that binds plaintiffs to those terms. Cases in which courts have found contracts arising from Internet use do not assist defendants, because in those circumstances there was much clearer notice than in the present case that a user's act would manifest assent to contract terms.

* * *

Meyer v. Uber Technologies, Inc.

868 F.3d 66 (2d Cir. 2017)

CHIN, CIRCUIT JUDGE:

In 2014, plaintiff-counter-defendant-appellee Spencer Meyer downloaded onto his smartphone a software application offered by defendant-counter-claimant-appellant Uber Technologies, Inc. ("Uber"), a technology company that operates, among other things, a ride-hailing service. Meyer then registered for an Uber account with his smartphone. After using the application approximately ten times, Meyer brought this action on behalf of himself and other similarly situated Uber accountholders against Uber's co-founder and former Chief Executive Officer, defendant-appellant Travis Kalanick, alleging that the Uber application allows third-party drivers to illegally fix prices. The district court joined Uber as a defendant and denied motions by Kalanick and Uber to compel arbitration. In doing so, the district court concluded that Meyer did not have reasonably conspicuous notice of and did not unambiguously manifest assent to Uber's Terms of Service when he registered. The district court held that Meyer therefore was not bound by the mandatory arbitration provision contained in the Terms of Service.

For the reasons set forth below, we vacate and remand for further proceedings consistent with this opinion.

BACKGROUND

A. The Facts

Uber offers a software application for smartphones (the "Uber App") that allows riders to request rides from third-party drivers. On October 18, 2014, Meyer registered for an Uber account with the Uber App on a Samsung Galaxy S5 phone running an Android operating system. After registering, Meyer took ten rides with Uber drivers in New York, Connecticut, Washington, D.C., and Paris.

In support of its motion to compel arbitration, Uber submitted a declaration from Senior Software Engineer Vincent Mi, in which Mi represented that Uber maintained records of when and how its users registered for the service and that, from his review of those records, Mi was able to identify the dates and methods by which Meyer registered for a user account. Attached to the declaration were screenshots of the two screens that a user registering in October 2014 with an Android-operated smartphone would have seen during the registration process.

The first screen, at which the user arrives after downloading the application and clicking a button marked "Register," is labeled "Register" and includes fields for the user to enter his or her name, email address, phone number, and a password (the "Registration Screen"). The Registration Screen also offers the user the option to register via a Google+ or Facebook account. According to Uber's records, Meyer did not sign up using either Google+ or Facebook and would have had to enter manually his personal information.

After completing the information on the Registration Screen and clicking "Next," the user advances to a second screen labeled "Payment" (the "Payment Screen"), on which the user can enter credit card details or elect to make payments using PayPal or Google Wallet, third-party payment services. According to Uber's records, Meyer entered his credit card information to pay for rides. To complete the process, the prospective user must click the button marked "REGISTER" in the middle of the Payment Screen.

Below the input fields and buttons on the Payment Screen is black text advising users that "[b]y creating an Uber account, you agree to the TERMS OF SERVICE & PRIVACY POLICY." *See* Addendum B. The capitalized phrase, which is bright blue and underlined, was a hyperlink that, when clicked, took the user to a third screen containing a button that, in turn, when clicked, would then display the current version of both Uber's Terms of Service and Privacy Policy. Meyer recalls entering his contact information and credit card details before registering, but does not recall seeing or following the hyperlink to the Terms and Conditions. He declares that he did not read the Terms and Conditions, including the arbitration provision.

When Meyer registered for an account, the Terms of Service contained the following mandatory arbitration clause:

Dispute Resolution

You and Company agree that any dispute, claim or controversy arising out of or relating to this Agreement or the breach, termination, enforcement, interpretation or validity thereof or the use of the Service or Application (collectively, **"Disputes"**) will be settled by binding arbitration, except that each party retains the right to bring an individual action in small claims court and the right to seek injunctive or other equitable relief in a court of competent jurisdiction to prevent the actual or threatened infringement, misappropriation or violation of a party's copyrights, trademarks, trade secrets, patents or other intellectual property rights. **You acknowledge and agree that you and Company are each waiving the right to a trial by jury or to participate as a plaintiff or class User in any purported class action or representative proceeding.** Further, unless both you and Company otherwise agree in writing, the arbitrator may not consolidate more than one person's claims, and may not otherwise preside over any form of any class or representative proceeding. If this specific paragraph is held unenforceable, then the entirety of this "Dispute Resolution" section will be deemed void. Except as provided in the preceding sentence, this "Dispute Resolution" section will survive any termination of this Agreement.

The Terms of Service further provided that the American Arbitration Association ("AAA") would hear any dispute, and that the AAA Commercial Arbitration Rules would govern any arbitration proceeding.

B. The District Court Proceedings

On December 16, 2015, Meyer, on behalf of a putative class of Uber riders, filed this action against Kalanick, alleging that the Uber App allows drivers to fix prices amongst themselves, in violation of the Sherman Act, 15 U.S.C. § 1, and the Donnelly

Act, N.Y. Gen. Bus. Law § 340. Meyer amended his complaint on January 29, 2016; the Amended Complaint also named only Kalanick, and not Uber, as the defendant.

The district court denied Kalanick's motion to dismiss the Amended Complaint for failure to state a claim. Kalanick filed a motion to join Uber as a necessary party, and Uber separately moved to intervene. On June 19, 2016, the district court granted Kalanick's motion and ordered that Uber be joined as a defendant. It subsequently denied Uber's motion as moot.

After the parties began to exchange discovery materials, Kalanick and Uber filed motions to compel Meyer to arbitrate. The district court denied the motions, concluding that Meyer did not have reasonably conspicuous notice of the Terms of Service and did not unambiguously manifest assent to the terms. Holding that no agreement had been formed, the district court did not reach Meyer's other defenses to arbitration, including whether defendants waived their right to arbitrate by actively participating in the litigation and whether Kalanick was also entitled to enforce an arbitration agreement to which he was not a signatory.

Defendants timely appealed the district court's July 29, 2016 order denying the motions to compel arbitration pursuant to 9 U.S.C. § 16, which permits interlocutory appeals from the denial of a motion to compel arbitration. The district court stayed the underlying action pending appeal on the joint motion of defendants, taking into account, *inter alia*, "the need for further appellate clarification of what constitutes adequate consent to so-called 'clickwrap,' 'browsewrap,' and other such website agreements." *Meyer v. Kalanick*, 203 F.Supp.3d 393 (S.D.N.Y. 2016).

DISCUSSION

We consider first whether there is a valid agreement to arbitrate between Meyer and Uber and then whether defendants have waived their right to enforce any such agreement to compel arbitration.

"State law principles of contract formation govern the arbitrability question." The district court applied California law in its opinion, but acknowledged that it "[did] not view the choice between California law and New York law as dispositive with respect to the issue of whether an arbitration agreement was formed." Defendants have not challenged the district court's choice of law but state that "if this Court concludes that New York law differs from California law with respect to any determinative issues, it should apply New York law." We agree with the district court's determination that California state law applies, and note that New York and California apply "substantially similar rules for determining whether the parties have mutually assented to a contract term."

To form a contract, there must be "[m]utual manifestation of assent, whether by written or spoken word or by conduct." California law is clear, however, that "an offeree, regardless of apparent manifestation of his consent, is not bound by inconspicuous contractual provisions of which he is unaware, contained in a document whose contractual nature is not obvious." "Thus, California contract law measures assent by an objective standard that takes into account both what the offeree said, wrote, or did and the transactional context in which the offeree verbalized or acted."

Where there is no evidence that the offeree had actual notice of the terms of the agreement, the offeree will still be bound by the agreement if a reasonably prudent user would be on inquiry notice of the terms. Whether a reasonably prudent user would be on inquiry notice turns on the "[c]larity and conspicuousness of arbitration terms,"; in the context of web-based contracts, as discussed further below, clarity and conspicuousness are a function of the design and content of the relevant interface.

Thus, only if the undisputed facts establish that there is "[r]easonably conspicuous notice of the existence of contract terms and unambiguous manifestation of assent to those terms" will we find that a contract has been formed.

"While new commerce on the Internet has exposed courts to many new situations, it has not fundamentally changed the principles of contract." "Courts around the country have recognized that [an] electronic 'click' can suffice to signify the acceptance of a contract," and that "[t]here is nothing automatically offensive about such agreements, as long as the layout and language of the site give the user reasonable notice that a click will manifest assent to an agreement."

With these principles in mind, one way in which we have previously distinguished web-based contracts is the manner in which the user manifests assent — namely, "clickwrap" (or "click-through") agreements, which require users to click an "I agree" box after being presented with a list of terms and conditions of use, or "browsewrap" agreements, which generally post terms and conditions on a website via a hyperlink at the bottom of the screen. Courts routinely uphold clickwrap agreements for the principal reason that the user has affirmatively assented to the terms of agreement by clicking "I agree." Browsewrap agreements, on the other hand, do not require the user to expressly assent. "Because no affirmative action is required by the website user to agree to the terms of a contract other than his or her use of the website, the determination of the validity of the browsewrap contract depends on whether the user has actual or constructive knowledge of a website's terms and conditions."

Of course, there are infinite ways to design a website or smartphone application, and not all interfaces fit neatly into the clickwrap or browsewrap categories. Some online agreements require the user to scroll through the terms before the user can indicate his or her assent by clicking "I agree." Other agreements notify the user of the existence of the website's terms of use and, instead of providing an "I agree" button, advise the user that he or she is agreeing to the terms of service when registering or signing up.

In the interface at issue in this case, a putative user is not required to assent explicitly to the contract terms; instead, the user must click a button marked "Register," underneath which the screen states "By creating an Uber account, you agree to the TERMS OF SERVICE & PRIVACY POLICY," with hyperlinks to the Terms of Service and Privacy Policy....

Following our precedent, district courts considering similar agreements have found them valid where the existence of the terms was reasonably communicated to the user. Classification of web-based contracts alone, however, does not resolve the notice inquiry. Insofar as it turns on the reasonableness of notice, the enforceability of a web-based agreement is clearly a fact-intensive inquiry. Nonetheless, on a motion to compel arbitration, we may determine that an agreement to arbitrate exists where the notice of the arbitration provision was reasonably conspicuous and manifestation of assent unambiguous as a matter of law.

Meyer attests that he was not on actual notice of the hyperlink to the Terms of Service or the arbitration provision itself, and defendants do not point to evidence from which a jury could infer otherwise. Accordingly, we must consider whether Meyer was on inquiry notice of the arbitration provision by virtue of the hyperlink to the Terms of Service on the Payment Screen and, thus, manifested his assent to the agreement by clicking "Register." ***

1. Reasonably conspicuous notice

In considering the question of reasonable conspicuousness, precedent and basic principles of contract law instruct that we consider the perspective of a reasonably prudent smartphone user. "[M]odern cell phones ... are now such a pervasive and insistent part of daily life that the proverbial visitor from Mars might conclude they were an important feature of human anatomy." *Riley v. California*, 134 S.Ct. 2473 (2014). As of 2015, nearly two-thirds of American adults owned a smartphone, a figure that has almost doubled since 2011. Consumers use their smartphones for, among other things, following the news, shopping, social networking, online banking, researching health conditions, and taking classes. In a 2015 study, approximately 89 percent of smartphone users surveyed reported using the internet on their smartphones over the course of the week-long study period. A purchaser of a new smartphone has his or her choice of features, including operating systems, storage capacity, and screen size.

Smartphone users engage in these activities through mobile applications, or "apps," like the Uber App. To begin using an app, the consumers need to locate and download the app, often from an application store. Many apps then require potential users to sign up for an account to access the app's services. Accordingly, when considering the perspective of a reasonable smartphone user, we need not presume that the user has never before encountered an app or entered into a contract using a smartphone. Moreover, a reasonably prudent smartphone user knows that text that is highlighted in blue and underlined is hyperlinked to another webpage where additional information will be found.

Turning to the interface at issue in this case, we conclude that the design of the screen and language used render the notice provided reasonable as a matter of California law. The Payment Screen is uncluttered, with only fields for the user to enter his or her credit card details, buttons to register for a user account or to connect the user's pre-existing PayPal account or Google Wallet to the Uber account, and the warning that "By creating an Uber account, you agree to the TERMS OF SERVICE

& PRIVACY POLICY." The text, including the hyperlinks to the Terms and Conditions and Privacy Policy, appears directly below the buttons for registration. The entire screen is visible at once, and the user does not need to scroll beyond what is immediately visible to find notice of the Terms of Service. Although the sentence is in a small font, the dark print contrasts with the bright white background, and the hyperlinks are in blue and underlined.

In addition to being spatially coupled with the mechanism for manifesting assent—*i.e.*, the register button+the notice is temporally coupled. As we observed in *Schnabel*, inasmuch as consumers are regularly and frequently confronted with non-negotiable contract terms, particularly when entering into transactions using the Internet, the presentation of these terms at a place and time that the consumer will associate with the initial purchase or enrollment, or the use of, the goods or services from which the recipient benefits at least indicates to the consumer that he or she is taking such goods or employing such services subject to additional terms and conditions that may one day affect him or her. *Schnabel*, 697 F.3d at 127. Here, notice of the Terms of Service is provided simultaneously to enrollment, thereby connecting the contractual terms to the services to which they apply. We think that a reasonably prudent smartphone user would understand that the terms were connected to the creation of a user account.

That the Terms of Service were available only by hyperlink does not preclude a determination of reasonable notice. Moreover, the language "[b]y creating an Uber account, you agree" is a clear prompt directing users to read the Terms and Conditions and signaling that their acceptance of the benefit of registration would be subject to contractual terms. As long as the hyperlinked text was itself reasonably conspicuous—and we conclude that it was—a reasonably prudent smartphone user would have constructive notice of the terms. While it may be the case that many users will not bother reading the additional terms, that is the choice the user makes; the user is still on inquiry notice.

Finally, we disagree with the district court's determination that the location of the arbitration clause within the Terms and Conditions was itself a "barrier to reasonable notice." In *Sgouros*, the Seventh Circuit determined that the defendant's website actively misled users by "explicitly stating that a click on the button constituted assent for TransUnion to obtain access to the purchaser's personal information," without saying anything about "contractual terms," and without any indication that "the same click constituted acceptance of the Service Agreement." The website did not contain a hyperlink to the relevant agreement; instead, it had a scroll box that contained the entirety of the agreement, only the first three lines of which were visible without scrolling, and it had no prompt for the reader to scroll for additional terms.

Here, there is nothing misleading. Although the contract terms are lengthy and must be reached by a hyperlink, the instructions are clear and reasonably conspicuous. Once a user clicks through to the Terms of Service, the section heading ("Dispute Resolution") and the sentence waiving the user's right to a jury trial on relevant claims are both bolded.

Accordingly, we conclude that the Uber App provided reasonably conspicuous notice of the Terms of Service as a matter of California law and turn to the question of whether Meyer unambiguously manifested his assent to those terms.

2. Manifestation of assent

Although Meyer's assent to arbitration was not express, we are convinced that it was unambiguous in light of the objectively reasonable notice of the terms, as discussed in detail above. As we described above, there is ample evidence that a reasonable user would be on inquiry notice of the terms, and the spatial and temporal coupling of the terms with the registration button "indicate[d] to the consumer that he or she is … employing such services subject to additional terms and conditions that may one day affect him or her." A reasonable user would know that by clicking the registration button, he was agreeing to the terms and conditions accessible via the hyperlink, whether he clicked on the hyperlink or not.

The fact that clicking the register button had two functions—creation of a user account and assent to the Terms of Service—does not render Meyer's assent ambiguous. The registration process allowed Meyer to review the Terms of Service prior to registration, unlike web platforms that provide notice of contract terms only after the user manifested his or her assent. Furthermore, the text on the Payment Screen not only included a hyperlink to the Terms of Service, but expressly warned the user that by creating an Uber account, the user was agreeing to be bound by the linked terms. Although the warning text used the term "creat[e]" instead of "register," as the button was marked, the physical proximity of the notice to the register button and the placement of the language in the registration flow make clear to the user that the linked terms pertain to the action the user is about to take.

The transactional context of the parties' dealings reinforces our conclusion. Meyer located and downloaded the Uber App, signed up for an account, and entered his credit card information with the intention of entering into a forward-looking relationship with Uber. The registration process clearly contemplated some sort of continuing relationship between the putative user and Uber, one that would require some terms and conditions, and the Payment Screen provided clear notice that there were terms that governed that relationship.

Accordingly, we conclude on the undisputed facts of this case that Meyer unambiguously manifested his assent to Uber's Terms of Service as a matter of California law.

3. Remand for trial

Finally, we see no need to remand this case for trial. Meyer offers no basis for his argument that we should remand for further factfinding if we vacate the district court's ruling, other than his assertion that no circuit has previously compelled arbitration in similar circumstances. Although Meyer purports to challenge the evidentiary foundation for the registration screens, defendants have submitted a declaration from an Uber engineer regarding Meyer's registration for and use of the Uber App, as well as the registration process and terms of use in effect at the time of his registration. Accordingly, we conclude on this record, as a matter of law, that Meyer agreed to arbitrate his claims with Uber. ***

1. Comments and Questions

a. The explosion of arbitration clauses contained in customer agreements for downloaded apps has brought this issue to the forefront in hundreds of court decisions in recent years. The ride-sharing service Uber has been no stranger to controversy, and has been sued by classes of both passengers and drivers on multiple grounds. These lawsuits have generated dozens of decisions around the country regarding the validity of its arbitration clause contained in the "Terms and Conditions" that a passenger as well as a driver must agree to in order to open an account via the Uber App. *See generally* Jill I. Gross, *The Uberization of Arbitration Clauses*, 9 Y.B. ON ARB. & MED. 43 (2017).

b. When evaluating a challenge to a consumer contract on the ground of lack of mutual assent, courts now distinguish among types of agreements depending on how the company claimed to obtain assent from the customer. Why do you think the courts treat these types of adhesive arbitration agreements differently from each other?

One federal judge described the categories as follows:

> "The '**shrinkwrap** license' gets its name from the fact that retail software packages are covered in plastic or cellophane 'shrinkwrap', and some vendors ... have written licenses that become effective as soon as the customer tears the wrapping from the package." Although it was not always the case, courts now generally enforce shrinkwrap agreements "on the theory that people agree to the terms by using the [product] they have already purchased." While shrinkwrap agreements, as the name suggests, formally apply only to tangible goods, agreements entered into online for both tangible goods and intangible goods and services have developed a body of terminology that borrows the word's suffix.

> "**Browsewrap**" agreements or licenses are those in which "the user does not see the contract at all but in which the license terms provide that using a Web site constitutes agreement to a contract whether the user knows it or not." Browsewrap agreements have been characterized as those "[w]here the link to a website's terms of use is buried at the bottom of the page or tucked away in obscure corners of the website where users are unlikely to see it." Normally, in a browsewrap agreement, "the website will contain a notice that—merely by using the services of, obtaining information from, or initiating applications within the website—the user is agreeing to and is bound by the site's terms of service."

> By contrast, a "**clickwrap**" agreement is an online contract "in which website users are required to click on an 'I agree' box after being presented with a list of terms and conditions of use." Courts view the clicking of an "I agree" or "I accept" box (or similar mechanism) as a requirement that "the user manifest

assent to the terms and conditions expressly" before she uses the website or services covered by the agreement. Clickwraps differ from browsewraps with respect to their enforceability under contract principles because, "[b]y requiring a physical manifestation of assent, a [clickwrap] user is said to be put in inquiry notice of the terms assented to." Clickwrap agreements permit courts to infer that the user was at least on inquiry notice of the terms of the agreement, and has outwardly manifested consent by clicking a box. As a result, "[b]ecause the user has 'signed' the contract by clicking 'I agree,' every court to consider the issue has held clickwrap licenses enforceable."

"**Sign-in-wrap**" couples assent to the terms of a website with signing up for use of the site's services. In a sign-in wrap, a user is presented with a button or link to view terms of use. It is usually not necessary to view the terms of use in order to use the web service, and sign-in-wrap agreements do not have an "I accept" box typical of clickwrap agreements. Instead, sign-in-wrap agreements usually contain language to the effect that, by registering for an account, or signing into an account, the user agrees to the terms of service to which she could navigate from the sign-in screen.

Cullinane v. Uber Techs., Inc., 2016 U.S. Dist. LEXIS 89540 at *13–15 (D. Mass. July 11, 2016). Other courts are slowly adopting this terminology as a means to analyze the enforceability of arbitration clauses contained in these wrap contracts. Are these meaningful legal distinctions?

c. Where the parties expect to have repeat dealings, notably banking and financial services, contracts also provide for unilateral change of the agreement by the provider institution. The institution provides notice to the customer of unilateral changes that will go into effect in the near future (usually 30 days), and that, by engaging in an account transaction, the customer has accepted the changes. The addition of an arbitration clause or alteration of an existing arbitration regime is a common unilateral change. That an arbitration agreement was signed electronically is not itself a defense. Under the Electronic Signatures in Global and National Commerce Act, "[a] contract ... may not be denied legal effect, validity, or enforceability solely because an electronic signature or electronic record was used in its formation." 15 U.S.C. §7001(2).

d. For additional commentary on electronic contract formation, *see* Peter A. Alces & Michael M. Greenfield, *They Can Do What!? Limitation on the Use of Change-of-Terms Clauses*, 26 GA. ST. U. L. REV. 1099 (2010); Theodore Eisenberg, *Arbitration's Summer Soldiers: An Empirical Study of Arbitration Clauses in Consumer and Nonconsumer Contracts*, 41 U. MICH. J.L. REFORM 871 (2008); David Horton, *The Shadow Terms: Contract Procedure and Unilateral Amendments*, 57 UCLA L. REV. 605 (2010); James J. White, *Warranties in the Box*, 46 SAN DIEGO L. REV. 733 (2010).

Problem

Locate an arbitration provision that you have entered into through an online commercial or consumer transaction. Did you know the contract contained an arbitration clause? Did you read it? Are there any provisions in the clause that concern you? Consider whether you have any grounds to challenge its validity.

C. Unconscionability

Arbitration provisions are frequently found in adhesion contracts, drafted by a party with superior bargaining power and presented on a "take it or leave it" basis. The drafting party may include a variety of provisions regarding the arbitration, such as designating the arbitrator, the provider, and the venue, as well as limiting remedies or the availability of class actions. While adhesion contracts are common in commercial transactions and are not *per se* unconscionable, at what point may the inclusion of harsh or one-sided provisions regarding the manner or substance of the arbitration render the arbitration unconscionable? Also, who should decide unconscionability claims—the court or arbitrator?

Chavarria v. Ralphs Grocery Co.
733 F.3d 916 (9th Cir. 2013)

CLIFTON, CIRCUIT JUDGE:

I. Background

Plaintiff Zenia Chavarria completed an employment application seeking work with Defendant Ralphs Grocery Company. Chavarria obtained a position as a deli clerk with Ralphs and worked in that capacity for roughly six months. After leaving her employment with Ralphs, Chavarria filed this action, alleging on behalf of herself and all similarly situated employees that Ralphs violated various provisions of the California Labor Code and California Business and Professions Code §§ 17200 et seq. Ralphs moved to compel arbitration of her individual claim pursuant to an arbitration policy incorporated into the employment application. Chavarria opposed the motion, arguing that the arbitration agreement was unconscionable under California law.

By completing an employment application with Ralphs, all potential employees agree to be bound by Ralphs' arbitration policy. The application contains an acknowledgment that the terms of the mandatory and binding arbitration policy have been provided for the applicant's review. Ralphs' policy contains several provisions central to this appeal.

Paragraph 7 governs the selection of the single arbitrator who will decide the dispute. It provides that, unless the parties agree otherwise, the arbitrator must be a retired state or federal judge. It explicitly prohibits the use of an administrator from either the American Arbitration Association ("AAA") or the Judicial Arbitration and Mediation Service ("JAMS"). If the parties do not agree on an arbitrator, the policy provides for the following procedure:

(1) Each party proposes a list of three arbitrators;

(2) The parties alternate striking one name from the other party's list of arbitrators until only one name remains;

(3) The party "who has not demanded arbitration" makes the first strike from the respective lists; and

(4) The lone remaining arbitrator decides the claims.

In practice, the arbitrator selected through this process will invariably be one of the three candidates nominated by the party that did not demand arbitration.

Paragraph 10 concerns attorney and arbitration fees and costs. It specifies that each party must pay its own attorney fees, subject to a later claim for reimbursement under applicable law. The provision regarding arbitration fees, including the amount to be paid to the arbitrator, is more than a little convoluted. Ultimately, it provides that the arbitrator's fees must be apportioned at the outset of the arbitration and must be split evenly between Ralphs and the employee unless a decision of the U.S. Supreme Court directly addressing the issue requires that they be apportioned differently.

Paragraph 13 of the policy permits Ralphs to unilaterally modify the policy without notice to the employee. The employee's continued employment constitutes acceptance of any modification.

The district court held that Ralphs' arbitration policy was unconscionable under California law, and it accordingly denied Ralphs' motion to compel arbitration. Ralphs appeals the district court's denial under 9 U.S.C. § 16.

II. Discussion

... Like other contracts, arbitration agreements can be invalidated for fraud, duress, or unconscionability. A defense such as unconscionability, however, cannot justify invalidating an arbitration agreement if the defense applies "only to arbitration or [derives its] meaning from the fact that an agreement to arbitrate is at issue." The U.S. Supreme Court has held that state rules disproportionately impacting arbitration, though generally applicable to contracts of all types, are nonetheless preempted by the FAA when the rule stands as an obstacle to the accomplishment of Congress's objectives in enacting the FAA.

No single rule of unconscionability uniquely applicable to arbitration is at issue in this case. We must therefore apply California's general principle of contract unconscionability. The parties dispute whether the Ralphs arbitration policy is unconscionable under California contract principles.

A. Unconscionability under California Law

Under California law, a contract must be both procedurally and substantively unconscionable to be rendered invalid. California law utilizes a sliding scale to determine unconscionability—greater substantive unconscionability may compensate for lesser procedural unconscionability. Applying California law, the district court held that the arbitration agreement in this case was both procedurally unconscionable and substantively unconscionable. We agree.

1. Procedural Unconscionability

Procedural unconscionability concerns the manner in which the contract was negotiated and the respective circumstances of the parties at that time, focusing on the level of oppression and surprise involved in the agreement. Oppression addresses the weaker party's absence of choice and unequal bargaining power that results in "no real negotiation." Surprise involves the extent to which the contract clearly discloses its terms as well as the reasonable expectations of the weaker party.

The district court held that Ralphs' arbitration policy was procedurally unconscionable for several reasons. The court found that agreeing to Ralphs' policy was a condition of applying for employment and that the policy was presented on a "take it or leave it" basis with no opportunity for Chavarria to negotiate its terms. It further found that the terms of the policy were not provided to Chavarria until three weeks after she had agreed to be bound by it. This additional defect, the court held, multiplied the degree of procedural unconscionability.

Ralphs argues that the policy is not procedurally unconscionable because Chavarria was not even required to agree to its terms. Ralphs bases this contention on a provision in the employment application that provides, "Please sign and date the employment application ... to acknowledge you have read, understand & agree to the following statements." The word "please," Ralphs contends, belies any suggestion of a requirement. Ralphs argues that Chavarria could have been hired without signing the agreement.

Ralphs' argument ignores the terms of the policy itself, which bound Chavarria regardless of whether she signed the application. The policy provides that "[n]o signature by an Employee or the Company is required for this Arbitration Policy to apply to Covered Disputes." That Ralphs asked nicely for a signature is irrelevant. The policy bound Chavarria and all other potential employees upon submission of their applications.

These circumstances are similar to others where we have held agreements to be procedurally unconscionable. In *Davis v. O'Melveny & Myers*, 485 F.3d 1066 (9th Cir. 2007), we held that an arbitration agreement was procedurally unconscionable under California law because it was imposed upon employees as a condition of their continued employment. We explained, "where ... the employee is facing an employer with 'overwhelming bargaining power' who 'drafted the contract and presented it to [the employee] on a take-it-or-leave-it basis,' the clause is procedurally unconscionable." Likewise, in *Pokorny v. Quixtar, Inc.*, 601 F.3d 987 (9th Cir. 2010), we held that "a contract is procedurally unconscionable under California law if it is 'a standardized contract, drafted by the party of superior bargaining strength, that relegates to the subscribing party only the opportunity to adhere to the contract or reject it.'" Chavarria could only agree to be bound by the policy or seek work elsewhere. Ralphs' policy meets the standard under which we have previously found arbitration provisions in employment contracts to be procedurally unconscionable.

Further, we have held that the degree of procedural unconscionability is enhanced when a contract binds an individual to later-provided terms. Ralphs did not provide

Chavarria the terms of the arbitration policy until her employment orientation, three weeks after the policy came into effect regarding any dispute related to her employment. The employment application merely contains a one-paragraph "notice" of the policy. The policy itself is a four-page, single-spaced document with several complex terms. *Harper v. Ultimo*, 113 Cal.App.4th 1402 (2003) (holding that a contract was procedurally unconscionable because the customer was forced to obtain the terms from another source "to find out the full import of what he or she is about to sign"). Ralphs' arbitration policy fits squarely within these decisions, so the district court did not err when it held that the policy was procedurally unconscionable.

2. Substantive Unconscionability

Chavarria must also demonstrate that Ralphs' arbitration policy is substantively unconscionable under California law. A contract is substantively unconscionable when it is unjustifiably one-sided to such an extent that it "shocks the conscience."

The district court found that several terms rendered Ralphs' arbitration policy substantively unconscionable. First, the court noted that Ralphs' arbitrator selection provision would always produce an arbitrator proposed by Ralphs in employee-initiated arbitration proceedings. Second, the court cited the preclusion of institutional arbitration administrators, namely AAA or JAMS, which have established rules and procedures to select a neutral arbitrator. Third, the court was troubled by the policy's requirement that the arbitrator must, at the outset of the arbitration proceedings, apportion the arbitrator's fees between Ralphs and the employee regardless of the merits of the claim. The court identified this provision as "a model of how employers can draft fee provisions to price almost any employee out of the dispute resolution process." The combination of these terms created a policy, according to the court, that "lacks any semblance of fairness and eviscerates the right to seek civil redress. . . . To condone such a policy would be a disservice to the legitimate practice of arbitration and a stain on the credibility of our justice system."

Ralphs contests the district court's conclusion and argues that the policy is not unconscionable. Indeed, Ralphs goes a step further and argues that the provisions relied upon by the district court actually disadvantage Ralphs and are intended to benefit the employee. Ralphs' strained construction of its policy is unpersuasive. In fact, the policy includes further provisions that add to its unconscionability.

Regarding the arbitrator selection provision, Ralphs does not deny that its policy precludes the selection of an arbitrator proposed by the party demanding arbitration. Nor does it deny that the party selecting the arbitrator gains an advantage in subsequent proceedings. Ralphs' opening brief affirmatively acknowledges as much: "Section 7 of the [arbitration policy] disadvantages the party seeking arbitration in the arbitrator selection process, by ensuring that the party resisting arbitration is guaranteed an arbitrator of its choosing." Ralphs simply argues that it won't always be the party that is guaranteed an arbitrator of its choosing.

In particular, Ralphs argues that the district court erred in assuming that an employee will always be the party that demands arbitration. Ralphs contends that the opposite is true. In Ralphs' view, Chavarria, the employee in this case, will wind up with an arbitrator of her choosing because it is Ralphs that demanded arbitration. Ralphs' logic is thus:

(1) Chavarria brought a claim in federal court;

(2) Ralphs filed a motion to compel arbitration;

(3) If the court grants the motion, then the case will go to arbitration; and

(4) Ralphs will have "demanded" arbitration and thereby relinquished the first strike to Chavarria.

Chavarria will, under Ralphs' scenario, strike all three of the arbitrators on Ralphs' list, and the last remaining arbitrator will necessarily be from Chavarria's list.

It doesn't take a close examination of Ralphs' argument to reveal its flaws. To begin with, Ralphs' argument invites an employee to disregard the arbitration policy and to file a lawsuit in court, knowing that the claim is subject to arbitration. Even if Ralphs is willing to waste its time and money for that detour, it is not one that makes any sense for the court. We cannot endorse an interpretation that encourages the filing of an unnecessary lawsuit simply to gain some advantage in subsequent arbitration.

Perhaps more to the point, Ralphs' argument relies on a fanciful interpretation of its arbitration policy. Ralphs' motion to compel arbitration does not constitute a "demand for arbitration" as provided in the policy. Paragraph 9 of the arbitration policy provides that "[a] demand for arbitration ... must be made in writing, comply with the requirements for pleadings under the [Federal Rules of Civil Procedure] and be served on the other party." Ralphs' motion to compel arbitration is not a demand for arbitration under the terms of Ralphs' policy because it does not comply with the Federal Rules of Civil Procedure requirements governing pleadings. See Fed.R.Civ.P. 7(a) (providing that "[o]nly these pleadings are allowed" before listing types of pleadings); Fed.R.Civ.P. 8 (stating the general rules of pleading).

A fair construction of the agreement suggests that an employee, even after filing a frivolous claim in federal court, nonetheless must serve on Ralphs a demand for arbitration that complies with the Federal Rules. Accordingly, as the district court found, Ralphs gets to pick the pool of potential arbitrators every time an employee brings a claim.

Even if it were the case that Ralphs' policy does not guarantee that Ralphs will always be the party with the final selection, the selection process is not one designed to produce a true neutral in any individual case. As noted above, Ralphs has not argued that the selection process is fair, acknowledging that the process "disadvantages the party seeking arbitration." Ralphs simply argues that sometimes the process may work to its disadvantage. But that is no consolation to the individual employee who is disadvantaged in her one and only claim. Forcing her into an arbitration process where Ralphs has an advantage cannot be justified by the possibility that some other employee might someday get the upper hand in that employee's arbitration against Ralphs.

Ralphs also argues that there is nothing of concern in its cost allocation provision because it simply follows the "American Rule" that each party shall bear its own fees and costs. Ralphs misses the point. The troubling aspect of the cost allocation provision relates to the arbitrator fees, not attorney fees.

The policy mandates that the arbitrator apportion those costs on the parties up front, before resolving the merits of the claims. Further, Ralphs has designed a system that requires the arbitrator to apportion the costs equally between Ralphs and the employee, disregarding any potential state law that contradicts Ralphs' cost allocation. Only a decision of the United States Supreme Court that directly addresses the issue can alter Ralphs' cost allocation term.... There is no justification to ignore a state cost-shifting provision, except to impose upon the employee a potentially prohibitive obstacle to having her claim heard. Ralphs' policy imposes great costs on the employee and precludes the employee from recovering those costs, making many claims impracticable.

The significance of this obstacle becomes more apparent through Ralphs' representation to the district court that the fees for a qualified arbitrator under its policy would range from $7,000 to $14,000 per day. Ralphs' policy requires that an employee pay half of that amount — $3,500 to $7,000 — for each day of the arbitration just to pay for her share of the arbitrator's fee. This cost likely dwarfs the amount of Chavarria's claims.[1]

[I]n this case, not only does the cost provision stand beside other unconscionable terms, there is nothing speculative about it. Ralphs' term requires that the arbitrator impose significant costs on the employee up front, regardless of the merits of the employee's claims, and severely limits the authority of the arbitrator to allocate arbitration costs in the award.

The district court focused its substantive unconscionability discussion on these terms, and it was correct in doing so because the terms lie far beyond the line required to render an agreement invalid. We therefore need not discuss at length the additional terms in Ralphs' arbitration policy, such as the unilateral modification provision, which we have previously held to support a finding of substantive unconscionability.

3. The Sliding Scale of Unconscionability

Excessive procedural or substantive unconscionability may compensate for lesser unconscionability in the other prong. But here we have both. Ralphs has tilted the scale so far in its favor, both in the circumstances of entering the agreement and its substantive terms, that it "shocks the conscience." Accordingly, Ralphs' arbitration policy cannot be enforced against Chavarria under California law.

---

1. [Ed: fn 5 in original] As the district court noted, Chavarria worked as a deli clerk for roughly five to six months and alleges she was not paid for rest and meal breaks as required by California law. Her monetary claims likely would not approach the cost of the arbitrator fees.

B. Preemption by the FAA

Federal law preempts state laws that stand as an obstacle to the accomplishment of Congress's objectives. Accordingly, the FAA preempts state laws that in theory apply to contracts generally but in practice impact arbitration agreements disproportionately. California's unconscionability doctrine applies to all contracts generally and therefore constitutes "such grounds at law or in equity for the revocation of [a] contract." 9 U.S.C. §2. But specific application of rules within that doctrine may be problematic.

In this case, California's procedural unconscionability rules do not disproportionately affect arbitration agreements, for they focus on the parties and the circumstances of the agreement and apply equally to the formation of all contracts. The application of California's general substantive unconscionability rules to Ralphs' arbitration policy, however, warrants more discussion.

The Supreme Court's recent decision in *American Express Corp. v. Italian Colors Restaurant*, 133 S.Ct. 2304 (2013), does not preclude us from considering the cost that Ralphs' arbitration agreement imposes on employees in order for them to bring a claim. In that case, plaintiffs argued that the class waiver term of the arbitration agreement at issue effectively foreclosed vindication of the plaintiffs' federal rights: specifically, their rights under the Sherman Antitrust Act. Plaintiffs could not pursue their antitrust claims, they argued, because the experts required to prove an antitrust claim would cost hundreds of thousands of dollars, while the individual recovery would not exceed $40,000. The class waiver provision did not foreclose effective vindication of that right, the Court reasoned, because "the fact that it is not worth the expense involved in proving a statutory remedy does not constitute an elimination of the right to pursue that remedy." The Court explicitly noted that the result might be different if an arbitration provision required a plaintiff to pay "filing and administrative fees attached to arbitration that are so high as to make access to the forum impracticable."

Ralphs' arbitration policy presents exactly that situation. In this case, administrative and filing costs, even disregarding the cost to prove the merits, effectively foreclose pursuit of the claim. Ralphs has constructed an arbitration system that imposes non-recoverable costs on employees just to get in the door.

The Supreme Court's holding that the FAA preempts state laws having a "disproportionate impact" on arbitration cannot be read to immunize all arbitration agreements from invalidation no matter how unconscionable they may be, so long as they invoke the shield of arbitration. Our court has recently explained the nuance: "*Concepcion* outlaws discrimination in state policy that is unfavorable to arbitration." We think this is a sensible reading of *Concepcion*.

This case illustrates the distinction. In addition to the problematic cost provision, Ralphs' arbitration policy contains a provision that unilaterally assigns one party (almost always Ralphs, in our view, as explained above) the power to select the arbitrator whenever an employee brings a claim. Of course, any state law that invalidated this provision would have a disproportionate impact on arbitration because the term is arbitration specific. But viewed another way, invalidation of this term is agnostic towards arbitration. It does not disfavor arbitration; it provides that the arbitration process must be fair.

If state law could not require some level of fairness in an arbitration agreement, there would be nothing to stop an employer from imposing an arbitration clause that, for example, made its own president the arbitrator of all claims brought by its employees. Federal law favoring arbitration is not a license to tilt the arbitration process in favor of the party with more bargaining power. California law regarding unconscionable contracts, as applied in this case, is not unfavorable towards arbitration, but instead reflects a generally applicable policy against abuses of bargaining power. The FAA does not preempt its invalidation of Ralphs' arbitration policy.

III. Conclusion

The arbitration policy imposed by Ralphs on its employees is unconscionable under California law. That law is not preempted by the FAA. We affirm the decision of the district court denying Ralphs' motion to compel arbitration, and we remand for further proceedings.

1. Comments and Questions

a. *Chavarria* is illustrative of the test for unconscionability used today in most states: a party challenging the validity of an agreement must show both procedural unconscionability (the bargaining process was unfair) and substantive unconscionability (the substantive terms resulting from the bargaining process are unfair) in order to be successful. In addition, many jurisdictions also employ a "sliding scale" in cases of extreme procedural or substantive unconscionability. Though the case provides an example of a reluctant party's *successful* unconscionability challenge to an arbitration agreement, the doctrine is rarely successful in commercial transactions. Why might that be?

b. Recall from Chapter 2, the Supreme Court in *Concepcion* held that the FAA preempted California's unconscionability doctrine as applied to class action waivers in consumer contracts. While the Supreme Court in *Concepcion* barred lower courts from finding class action waivers in arbitration agreements to be *per se* substantively unconscionable under a specific unconscionability test, lower courts still can strike down unfair arbitration clauses as unconscionable on other grounds using the general test for unconscionability. *Chavarria* is an example of a post-*Concepcion* case still finding an arbitration clause unconscionable. *See also Global Client Solutions, LLC. v. Ossello*, 367 P.3d 361 (Mont. 2016) (affirming lower court's finding that PDAA in a debt collection plan was unconscionable because obligations of parties to arbitrate disputes were not mutual). *Cf. Merkin v. Vonage Am., Inc.*, 639 F. App'x 481 (9th Cir. 2016) (enforcing arbitration clause but severing unconscionable language).

c. *Unconscionability and Ineffective Vindication.* The *Chavarria* court also rejected the argument that the Supreme Court's decision in *American Express Co. v. Italian Colors Restaurant*, 570 U.S. 228 (2013), foreclosed its consideration of the high costs of arbitration in finding the arbitration clause substantively unconscionable. The *Italian Colors* case is considered, *infra,* in Section F of this Chapter.

d. *Non-Mutuality: Must Arbitration Be a Two-Way Street?* Under the traditional contract doctrine of mutuality of remedies, serious disparities in the remedial provisions available to contracting parties provided a basis for courts not to enforce these provisions. Suppose that a contract requires one party to arbitrate, yet provides the other (drafting) party the option to seek judicial recourse. Should a court enforce this or other imbalanced agreements? Put another way, must arbitration be a two-way street, or at least not an entirely one-way street? To what extent should the answer depend on the use of form contracts, disparate bargaining power and similar "unfairness" factors?

Courts have largely discredited the nonmutuality defense in the arbitration context provided the contract is supported by consideration. For example, in *Fazio v. Lehman Bros., Inc.,* 340 F.3d 386 (6th Cir. 2003), the court ruled a PDAA was still valid despite the actions of a broker who stole $54 million from investors. The plaintiffs argued that there were no agreements because the accounts had been falsified, but the court said that because there was "no doubt" that the underlying contracts were supported by consideration, the arbitration clauses were enforceable. However, some courts still consider, or arguably recast, nonmutuality as a factor in assessing unconscionability. *See, e.g., Armendariz v. Foundation Health Psychcare Servs.,* 6 P.3d 669 (Cal. 2000); *Arnold v. United Cos. Lending Corp.,* 511 S.E.2d 854 (W. Va. 1998); *Iwen v. U.S. West Direct,* 977 P.2d 989 (Mont. 1999). For criticism of this application, see Christopher Drahozal, *Nonmutual Agreements to Arbitrate,* 27 Iowa J. Corp. L. 537, 547 (2002) (stating that "the ghost of mutuality has reappeared, this time cloaked in the garb of unconscionability").

e. *Who decides an unconscionability challenge to a delegation clause?* In *Mohamed v. Uber Techs., Inc.,* 848 F.3d 1201 (9th Cir. 2016), a class action filed by Uber drivers alleging they were improperly classified as independent contractors, the Ninth Circuit held that Uber's delegation clause was "clear and unmistakable evidence" that the parties wanted arbitrators to decide arbitrability questions. The Court of Appeals also considered, but rejected, plaintiffs' claims that the delegation clause was unconscionable, primarily because plaintiffs had the right to opt out of the arbitration provision, negating any argument of procedural unconscionability. For more discussion on these arguments, as well as the impact of opt-outs on unconscionability claims, see Jill I. Gross, *The Uberization of Arbitration Clauses,* 9 Y.B. on Arb & Med. 43 (2017).

D. Losing the Right to Arbitrate: Waiver

Another state law-based defense to the obligation to arbitrate is the waiver doctrine. Under this doctrine, even if a party initially had a contractual right to require arbitration of a claim, a party may lose that right by its own conduct. Consider the type of actions or failures to act that might constitute waiver, and who makes that determination.

Nicholas v. KBR, Inc.

565 F.3d 904 (5th Cir. 2009)

HAYNES, CIRCUIT JUDGE:

Geraldine Nicholas appeals the district court's denial of her motion to compel arbitration of her contract dispute with KBR, the successor corporation of her deceased husband's former employer. The district court found that Nicholas substantially invoked the judicial process to the prejudice of KBR.... We affirm the district court's judgment.

Nicholas, filed this lawsuit in Texas state court in January 2007, alleging that KBR breached the Agreement with her husband by failing to pay his life insurance benefits. Nicholas's petition neither mentioned the Agreement's arbitration clause nor gave any other indication that she wanted to arbitrate her claims. KBR removed the case to federal court in February. Thereafter, Nicholas filed a motion to remand, or, in the alternative, to amend the pleadings. In April the district court denied Nicholas's motion to remand, but granted her motion for leave to amend. Nicholas filed her first amended complaint May 2. Nicholas did not mention the Agreement's arbitration clause or otherwise indicate that she wanted to arbitrate her claims.

In June the parties filed their Joint Discovery/Case Management Plan. Shortly thereafter, the district court issued a scheduling order. The order set a discovery cutoff of February 1, 2008, a pretrial motions deadline of February 22, and a docket call for April 25. After the district court issued its scheduling order, KBR served written discovery on Nicholas. Nicholas responded to that discovery without raising arbitration or otherwise objecting. Nicholas also sat without objection for her deposition. On November 20, 2007—more than ten months after Nicholas sued KBR in Texas state court—Nicholas filed the underlying motion to compel arbitration. In the motion, Nicholas did not address the potential waiver of her right to arbitrate.

On December 4, 2007, Nicholas noticed the deposition of a third-party witness, Jim Wilhite, and proceeded to take his deposition on December 18, 2007. On January 4, 2008, KBR filed a response to Nicholas's motion to compel arbitration and argued that Nicholas waived her right to arbitration by substantially invoking the judicial process to the prejudice of KBR. In the motion, KBR specifically argued that Nicholas was aware of the Agreement's arbitration clause when she filed her original petition in Texas state court in January 2007. Nicholas did not respond to KBR's argument that she waived arbitration. Indeed, she filed no reply or evidence of any kind....

The right to arbitrate a dispute, like all contract rights, is subject to waiver. Although waiver of arbitration is a disfavored finding, "waiver will be found when the party seeking arbitration substantially invokes the judicial process to the detriment or prejudice of the other party." A party generally invokes the judicial process by initially pursuing litigation of claims then reversing course and attempting to arbitrate those claims. But "waiver can also result from some overt act in Court that evinces a desire to resolve the arbitrable dispute through litigation rather than arbitration." *Gulf Guar. Life Ins. Co. v. Conn. Gen. Life Ins. Co.*, 304 F.3d 476 (5th Cir. 2002). One of the primary goals of arbitration is to avoid the expense of litigation. In reviewing the question of whether the district court properly found waiver, then, we must look at two questions: (1) did Nicholas substantially invoke the judicial process, and if so (2) was KBR prejudiced thereby?

A. Invocation of the Judicial Process

In the vast majority of cases involving the question of waiver, it is the party being sued that belatedly seeks arbitration. Here, in contrast, it is the plaintiff, who, despite filing suit and pursuing her claims in court for more than ten months, now seeks to compel arbitration. Although this circuit has not expressly drawn a distinction between the waiver analysis when applied to a plaintiff and that applied to a defendant, we have recognized that the decision to file suit typically indicates a "disinclination" to arbitrate. *See Miller*, 781 F.2d at 497 (concluding that a party revealed a "disinclination to resort to arbitration" by, among other things, filing suit in state court without mentioning its desire to arbitrate). We have not, however, gone as far as the Seventh Circuit on this issue, and we do not do so here, as we continue to require a showing of prejudice, even if there is a substantial invocation of the process. *See Cabinetree of Wis., Inc. v. Kraftmaid Cabinetry, Inc.*, 50 F.3d 388 (7th Cir. 1995) (holding that a party's "election to proceed before a nonarbitral tribunal for the resolution of a contractual dispute is a presumptive waiver of the right to arbitrate").

We conclude that the act of a plaintiff filing suit without asserting an arbitration clause constitutes substantial invocation of the judicial process, unless an exception applies. Indeed, short of directly saying so in open court, it is difficult to see how a party could more clearly "evince a desire to resolve a ... dispute through litigation rather than arbitration," than by filing a lawsuit going to the merits of an otherwise arbitrable dispute. We emphasize that the legal standard for waiver is the same regardless of which party is the party alleged to have waived arbitration. Differences between the two sides arise from the voluntariness and timing of their actions, not the legal standard.

That is not to say there can be no exceptions. There are lawsuits that can be filed that would not be inconsistent with seeking arbitration. For example, a plaintiff might file suit solely to obtain a threshold declaration as to whether a valid arbitration agreement existed. *See Republic Ins. Co. v. Paico Receivables LLC*, 383 F.3d 341 (5th Cir. 2004) (determining that party's decision to file suit to determine whether a valid arbitration clause existed did not indicate a disinclination to arbitrate because filing suit for this purpose is not inconsistent with the right to arbitrate). A plaintiff might also have to file suit to obtain injunctive relief pending arbitration. Other situations may arise justifying an exception; the list here should not be seen as exhaustive.

This case presents no situation that would constitute an exception. Rather, as the district court concluded, Nicholas had no reason to file suit other than to litigate the claims she now seeks to arbitrate. Under these circumstances, we find that Nicholas's decision to file suit on her otherwise arbitrable claims constitutes substantial invocation of the judicial process as to those claims.

Other evidence supports the district court's conclusion that Nicholas engaged in substantial litigation activity before asserting her right to arbitration. She filed a motion to remand following removal, arguing that ERISA did not completely preempt her state law claims; the district court disagreed and denied that motion. Nicholas's belated decision to seek arbitration is particularly troubling given that it came on the heels of this adverse ruling. *See Cabinetree*, 50 F.3d at 391 (expressing particular concern with plaintiffs that want to test the waters in litigation before deciding whether they would be better off in arbitration). Moreover, after the district court denied the motion to remand, Nicholas filed an amended complaint, made initial disclosures, engaged in a meet-and-confer, and responded to KBR's discovery requests. The motion to compel arbitration also arrived shortly after a counsel change. Nicholas substantially invoked the judicial process.

B. Prejudice

In addition to invocation of the judicial process, the party opposing arbitration must demonstrate prejudice before we will find a waiver of the right to arbitrate. Prejudice in the context of arbitration waiver refers to delay, expense, and damage to a party's legal position. What constitutes a waiver of arbitration is a fact-dependent inquiry.

While delay in asserting the right to arbitrate will not alone result in waiver such delay "does bear on the question of prejudice, and may, along with other considerations, require a court to conclude that waiver has occurred." We have recognized that "where a party fails to demand arbitration..., and, in the meantime engages in pretrial activity inconsistent with an intent to arbitrate, the party later opposing a motion to compel arbitration may more easily show that its position has been compromised, i.e., prejudiced."

Nicholas's delay in asserting her right to arbitrate was substantial and wholly unexplained in the district court. She judicially pursued her claims for over ten months without mentioning the Agreement's arbitration clause or her desire for arbitration. In this relatively straightforward case, that delay virtually guaranteed that the district court would not rule on Nicholas's motion to compel until the parties had completed discovery and KBR had begun preparing its motion for summary judgment.

Although KBR did not put on evidence in terms of dollars and cents of its litigation costs in the district court, the record supports the district court's finding that KBR's litigation activities were significant in the context of this dispute: KBR removed the case to federal court based on ERISA preemption principles; successfully opposed

Nicholas's motion to remand; answered Nicholas's complaints; propounded discovery requests; and deposed Nicholas. After Nicholas filed her motion to compel arbitration but before the district court ruled on it, KBR participated in Nicholas's deposition of a third-party witness. While these litigation activities in the context of a larger, more complex case might be characterized as minimal, it was not unreasonable for the district court to find that they carry particular significance given the limited scope and relatively straightforward nature of Nicholas's denial-of-benefits claims. Indeed, by sitting on her rights for over ten months, Nicholas forced KBR to conduct the bulk of activity necessary to defend against her claims. Short of actually trying the case, it is unclear what additional litigation costs KBR could have incurred.

Moreover, it is questionable whether Nicholas would have been permitted to depose a third-party witness in arbitration. While Nicholas notes that Rule 9 of the AAA Employment Arbitration Rules grants arbitrators authority to order discovery, including depositions, the arbitrator's exercise of that authority is completely discretionary. Thus, Nicholas could not have obtained this deposition in arbitration as a matter of right. As we have recognized, "while discovery relating to non-arbitrable claims is not prejudicial, where the pretrial activity is related to all of the parties' claims, including those that [are] conceded to be arbitrable, compelling arbitration would result in prejudice."

1. Comments and Questions

a. *The test for waiver.* Waiver is an intensely fact-based inquiry. Courts typically consider factors such as whether:

1. the party's actions are inconsistent with the right to arbitrate;

2. "the litigation machinery has been substantially invoked" and the parties "were well into preparation of a lawsuit" before the party notified the opposing party of an intent to arbitrate;

3. a party either requested arbitration enforcement close to the trial date or delayed for a long period before seeking a stay;

4. a defendant seeking arbitration filed a counterclaim without asking for a stay of the proceedings;

5. important intervening steps [e.g., taking advantage of judicial discovery procedures not available in arbitration] had taken place; and

6. the delay "affected, misled, or prejudiced" the opposing party.

See In re Cox Enterprises, Inc. Set-top Cable Television Box Antitrust Litig., 790 F.3d 1112 (10th Cir. 2015). The Second Circuit considers: (1) the amount of time that has elapsed from the initiation of litigation to the demand for arbitration; (2) the amount and nature of litigation, including substantive motions and discovery; and (3) prejudice to the party opposing arbitration. *See Nat'l Union Fire Ins. Co. of Pittsburgh, P.A. v. NCR Corp.*, 376 F. App'x 70, 71 (2d Cir. 2010); *see also FPE Found. v. Cohen*, 801 F.3d 25 (1st Cir. 2015).

b. *Who decides waiver?* The majority of courts to address the question have concluded that courts, rather than arbitrators, decide whether a party has waived its right to arbitrate a claim by litigation conduct. *See Vine v. PLS Fin. Servs., Inc.,* 689 Fed. Appx. 800 (5th Cir. 2017) (citing recent decisions from First, Sixth, Ninth, and Eleventh Circuits); *see also Principal Investments v. Harrison,* 366 P.3d 688 (Nev. 2016). Legal commentators and the RUAA agree. *See* Stephen K. Huber, *The Arbitration Jurisprudence of the Fifth Circuit, Round II,* 37 Tex. Tech L. Rev. 531 (2005); RUAA, Commentary on Waiver (2000). Notably, section 3 of the FAA empowers courts to stay a litigation if the dispute is subject to a valid arbitration agreement, "providing the applicant for the stay is not in default in proceeding with such arbitration."

c. *Are courts willing to find waiver?* Courts do not so readily rule that a disputant has waived its right to arbitration. *See, e.g., LG Elecs., Inc. v. Wi-Lan USA, Inc.,* 623 F. App'x 568 (2d Cir. 2015) (patent licensor did not waive right to compel arbitration by bringing patent infringement claims in federal court because there was no substantive prejudice at the time of the arbitration demand); *Hill v. Ricoh Ams. Corp.,* 603 F.3d 766 (10th Cir. 2010) (holding that minimal litigation activity did not constitute waiver of right to arbitrate; employer did not waive its right to demand arbitration by delaying it demand for four months, a subsequent bonus retention agreement did not supersede the parties' employment agreement and its arbitration clause, and arbitration was not foreclosed by the Sarbanes-Oxley Act).

The Supreme Court of Texas has found a waiver of arbitration only once since Texas adopted its first arbitration statute in 1846, and that ruling was by a 5–4 vote. *Perry Homes v. Cull,* 258 S.W.3d 580 (Tex. 2008). On the other hand, courts will not tolerate a litigant who appears to be gaming the system by litigating first and then turning to arbitration when things do not go well. *See, e.g., Zuckerman Spaeder, LLP v. Auffenberg,* 646 F.3d 919 (D.C. Cir. 2011) ("By this opinion we alert the bar in this Circuit that failure to invoke arbitration at the first available opportunity will presumptively extinguish a client's ability later to opt for arbitration.").

d. *Prejudice.* Several federal courts have adopted attenuated standards regarding prejudice that may amount to little more than a fig leaf. For example, in the First Circuit "the prejudice showing required is tame at best." *Rankin v. Allstate Ins. Co.,* 336 F.3d 8 (1st Cir. 2003). Nothing more than a "modicum of prejudice" is required. *Tyco Int'l (U.S.) Ltd. v. Swartz (In re Tyco Int'l Ltd. Sec. Litig.),* 422 F.3d 41 (1st Cir. 2005). Prejudice is in practice difficult to separate from the court-related activity that results in a finding of waiver. After all, delay and cost are the central consequences of a failure by the other party to promptly seek arbitration. When a court determines that "expense and delay constitute prejudice," the two factors seem to collapse into one. *See, e.g., Nino v. Jewelry Exchange, Inc.,* 609 F.3d 191 (3d Cir. 2010). The Third Circuit has set forth factors to aid in the prejudice analysis. Those factors are: [1] the timeliness or lack thereof of a motion to arbitrate; [2] the degree to which the party seeking to compel arbitration [or to stay court proceedings pending arbitration] has contested the merits of its opponent's claims; [3] whether that party has informed its adversary of the intention to seek arbitration even if it has not yet filed a motion to stay the district court proceedings; [4] the extent of its non-merits motion practice; [5] its assent to the [trial] court's pretrial orders; and [6] the extent to which both parties have engaged in discovery. *Ehletier v. Grapetree Shores, Inc.*, 482 F.3d 207 (3d Cir. 2007). The Seventh Circuit does not require a showing of prejudice to find waiver, but will consider the degree of prejudice as a factor. *See Cooper v. Asset Acceptance, LLC*, 532 F. App'x 639 (7th Cir. 2013).

E. Breach of Contract

Hooters of America, Inc. v. Phillips

173 F.3d 933 (4th Cir. 1999)

WILKINSON, CHIEF JUDGE:

Annette R. Phillips alleges that she was sexually harassed while working as a bartender at a Hooters restaurant in Myrtle Beach, South Carolina [HOMB]. After quitting her job, Phillips threatened to sue Hooters in court. Alleging that Phillips agreed to arbitrate employment-related disputes, Hooters preemptively filed suit to compel arbitration under the FAA. Because Hooters set up a dispute resolution process utterly lacking in the rudiments of even-handedness, we hold that Hooters breached its agreement to arbitrate. Thus, we affirm the district court's refusal to compel arbitration.

The agreement to arbitrate ... provides that Hooters and the employee each agree to arbitrate all disputes arising out of employment, including "any claim of discrimination, sexual harassment, retaliation, or wrongful discharge, whether arising under federal or state law." The agreement further states that: "the employee and the company agree to resolve any claims pursuant to the company's rules and procedures for alternative resolution of employment-related disputes, as promulgated by the company from time to time ("the rules"). Company will make available or provide a copy of the rules upon written request of the employee."

The employees of HOMB were initially given a copy of this agreement at an all-staff meeting held on November 20, 1994. HOMB's general manager, Gene Fulcher, told the employees to review the agreement for five days and that they would then be asked to accept or reject the agreement. No employee, however, was given a copy of Hooters' arbitration rules and procedures. Phillips signed the agreement on November 25, 1994. When her personnel file was updated in April 1995, Phillips again signed the agreement. After Phillips quit her job in June 1996, Hooters sent to her attorney a copy of the Hooters rules then in effect. Phillips refused to arbitrate the dispute.

Hooters filed suit in November 1996 to compel arbitration under 9 U.S.C. § 4. Phillips defended on the grounds that the agreement to arbitrate was unenforceable. Phillips also asserted individual and class counterclaims against Hooters for violations of Title VII and for a declaration that the arbitration agreements were unenforceable against the class. In response, Hooters requested that the district court stay the proceedings on the counterclaims until after arbitration. The district court denied Hooters' motions to compel arbitration and stay proceedings on the counterclaims. The court found that there was no meeting of the minds on all of the material terms of the agreement and even if there were, Hooters' promise to arbitrate was illusory. In addition, the court found that the arbitration agreement was unconscionable and void for reasons of public policy. Hooters filed this interlocutory appeal.

The benefits of arbitration are widely recognized. Parties agree to arbitrate to secure "streamlined proceedings and expeditious results [that] will best serve their needs." Further, the adversarial nature of litigation diminishes the possibility that the parties will be able to salvage their relationship.... For these reasons parties agree to arbitrate and trade "the procedures and opportunity for review of the courtroom for the simplicity, informality, and expedition of arbitration." *Gilmer v. Interstate/Johnson Lane Corp.*, 500 U.S. 20 (1991). The FAA manifests "a liberal federal policy favoring arbitration agreements." When a valid agreement to arbitrate exists between the parties and covers the matter in dispute, the FAA commands the federal courts to stay any ongoing judicial proceedings, and to compel arbitration....

The threshold question is whether claims such as Phillips' are even arbitrable. The EEOC as amicus curiae contends that employees cannot agree to arbitrate Title VII claims in predispute agreements. We disagree. The Supreme Court has made it plain that judicial protection of arbitral agreements extends to agreements to arbitrate statutory discrimination claims. In *Gilmer*, the Court noted that "[b]y agreeing to arbitrate a statutory claim, a party does not forgo the substantive rights afforded by the statute; it only submits to their resolution in an arbitral, rather than a judicial, forum." Predispute agreements to arbitrate Title VII claims are valid and enforceable.

The question remains whether a binding arbitration agreement between Phillips and Hooters exists and compels Phillips to submit her Title VII claims to arbitration. The FAA provides that agreements "to settle by arbitration a controversy thereafter arising out of such contract or transaction ... shall be valid, irrevocable, and enforceable, save upon such grounds as exist at law or in equity for the revocation of any contract." 9 U.S.C. §2. "It is for the court, not the arbitrator, to decide in the first instance whether the dispute [i]s to be resolved through arbitration." Hooters argues that Phillips gave her assent to a bilateral agreement to arbitrate. That contract provided for the resolution by arbitration of all employment-related disputes, including claims arising under Title VII. Hooters claims the agreement to arbitrate is valid because Phillips twice signed it voluntarily. Thus, it argues, the courts are bound to enforce it and compel arbitration.

We disagree. The judicial inquiry, while highly circumscribed, is not focused solely on an examination for contractual formation defects such as lack of mutual assent and want of consideration. Courts also can investigate the existence of "such grounds as exist at law or in equity for the revocation of any contract." 9 U.S.C. §2. However, the grounds for revocation must relate specifically to the arbitration clause and not just to the contract as a whole. *Prima Paint Corp. v. Flood & Conklin Mfg. Co.*, 388 U.S. 395 (1967). In this case, the challenge goes to the validity of the arbitration agreement itself. Hooters materially breached the arbitration agreement by promulgating rules so egregiously unfair as to constitute a complete default of its contractual obligation to draft arbitration rules and to do so in good faith.

Hooters and Phillips agreed to settle any disputes between them not in a judicial forum, but in another neutral forum—arbitration. Their agreement provided that Hooters was responsible for setting up such a forum by promulgating arbitration rules and procedures.... The Hooters rules when taken as a whole, however, are so one-sided that their only possible purpose is to undermine the neutrality of the proceeding. The rules require the employee to provide the company notice of her claim at the outset, including "the nature of the Claim" and "the specific act(s) or omissions(s) which are the basis of the Claim." Hooters, on the other hand, is not required to file any responsive pleadings or to notice its defenses. Additionally, at the time of filing this notice, the employee must provide the company with a list of all fact witnesses with a brief summary of the facts known to each. The company, however, is not required to reciprocate.

The Hooters rules also provide a mechanism for selecting a panel of three arbitrators that is crafted to ensure a biased decisionmaker. The employee and Hooters each select an arbitrator, and the two arbitrators in turn select a third. Good enough, except that the employees' arbitrator and the third arbitrator must be selected from a list of arbitrators created exclusively by Hooters. This gives Hooters control over the entire panel and places no limits whatsoever on whom Hooters can put on the list. Under the rules, Hooters is free to devise lists of partial arbitrators who have existing relationships, financial or familial, with Hooters and its management. In fact, the rules do not even prohibit Hooters from placing its managers themselves on the list. Further, nothing in the rules restricts Hooters from punishing arbitrators who rule against the company by removing them from the list. Given the unrestricted control that one party (Hooters) has over the panel, the selection of an impartial decision maker would be a surprising result.

Nor is fairness to be found once the proceedings are begun. Although Hooters may expand the scope of arbitration to any matter, "whether related or not to the Employee's Claim," the employee cannot raise "any matter not included in the Notice of Claim." Similarly, Hooters is permitted to move for summary dismissal of employee claims before a hearing is held whereas the employee is not permitted to seek summary judgment. Hooters, but not the employee, may record the arbitration hearing "by audio or videotaping or by verbatim transcription." The rules also grant Hooters the right to bring suit in court to vacate or modify an arbitral award when it can show, by a preponderance of the evidence, that the panel exceeded its authority. No such right is granted to the employee.

In addition, the rules provide that, upon 30 days' notice, Hooters, but not the employee, may cancel the agreement to arbitrate. Moreover, Hooters reserves the right to modify the rules, "in whole or in part," whenever it wishes and "without notice" to the employee. Nothing in the rules even prohibits Hooters from changing the rules in the middle of an arbitration proceeding.

If by odd chance the unfairness of these rules were not apparent on their face, leading arbitration experts have decried their one-sidedness. George Friedman, senior vice president of the AAA, testified that the system established by the Hooters rules so deviated from minimum due process standards that the Association would refuse to arbitrate under those rules. George Nicolau, former president of both the National Academy of Arbitrators and the International Society of Professionals in Dispute Resolution, attested that the Hooters rules "are inconsistent with the concept of fair and impartial arbitration." He also testified that he was "certain that reputable designating agencies, such as the AAA and Jams/Endispute, would refuse to administer a program so unfair and one-sided as this one." Additionally, Dennis Nolan, professor of labor law at the University of South Carolina, declared that the Hooters rules "do not satisfy the minimum requirements of a fair arbitration system." He found that the "most serious flaw" was that the "mechanism [for selecting arbitrators] violates the most fundamental aspect of justice, namely an impartial decision maker." Finally, Lewis Maltby, member of the Board of Directors of the AAA, testified that "This is without a doubt the most unfair arbitration program I have ever encountered."

In a similar vein, two major arbitration associations have filed amicus briefs with this court. The National Academy of Arbitrators stated that the Hooters rules "violate fundamental concepts of fairness ... and the integrity of the arbitration process." Likewise, the Society of Professionals in Dispute Resolution noted that "[i]t would be hard to imagine a more unfair method of selecting a panel of arbitrators." It characterized the Hooters arbitration system as "deficient to the point of illegitimacy" and "so one sided, it is hard to believe that it was even intended to be fair."

We hold that the promulgation of so many biased rules — especially the scheme whereby one party to the proceeding so controls the arbitral panel — breaches the contract entered into by the parties. The parties agreed to submit their claims to arbitration — a system whereby disputes are fairly resolved by an impartial third party. Hooters by contract took on the obligation of establishing such a system. By creating a sham system unworthy even of the name of arbitration, Hooters completely failed in performing its contractual duty.

Moreover, Hooters had a duty to perform its obligations in good faith.... By agreeing to settle disputes in arbitration, Phillips agreed to the prompt and economical resolution of her claims. She could legitimately expect that arbitration would not entail procedures so wholly one-sided as to present a stacked deck. Thus we conclude that the Hooters rules also violate the contractual obligation of good faith.

Given Hooters' breaches of the arbitration agreement and Phillips' desire not to be bound by it, we hold that rescission is the proper remedy. Generally, "rescission will not be granted for a minor or casual breach of a contract, but only for those breaches which defeat the object of the contracting parties." Hooters' breach is by no means insubstantial; its performance under the contract was so egregious that the result was hardly recognizable as arbitration at all. We therefore permit Phillips to cancel the agreement and thus Hooters' suit to compel arbitration must fail.

We respectfully the Supreme Court's pronouncement that "questions of arbitrability must be addressed with a healthy regard for the federal policy favoring arbitration." Our decision should not be misread: We are not holding that the agreement before us is unenforceable because the arbitral proceedings are too abbreviated. An arbitral forum need not replicate the judicial forum.... Nor should our decision be misunderstood as permitting a full-scale assault on the fairness of proceedings before the matter is submitted to arbitration. Generally, objections to the nature of arbitral proceedings are for the arbitrator to decide in the first instance. Only after arbitration may a party then raise such challenges if they meet the narrow grounds set out in 9 U.S.C. § 10 for vacating an arbitral award. In the case before us, we only reach the content of the arbitration rules because their promulgation was the duty of one party under the contract. The material breach of this duty warranting rescission is an issue of substantive arbitrability and thus is reviewable before arbitration. This case, however, is the exception that proves the rule: fairness objections should generally be made to the arbitrator, subject only to limited post-arbitration judicial review as set forth in section 10 of the FAA.

By promulgating this system of warped rules, Hooters so skewed the process in its favor that Phillips has been denied arbitration in any meaningful sense of the word. To uphold the promulgation of this aberrational scheme under the heading of arbitration would undermine, not advance, the federal policy favoring alternative dispute resolution. This we refuse to do. The judgment of the district court is affirmed, and the case is remanded for further proceedings consistent with this opinion.

1. Comments and Questions

a. *Breach of contract.* The arbitration process set up by the Hooters franchise exemplifies how an employer can take advantage of an adhesive employment contract to tilt the dispute resolution process in its favor. That being said, why did the court invalidate the arbitration clause on the ground of breach of contract, as opposed to unconscionability or mutuality of obligations? Could the court have found the clause unconscionable? Why or why not?

b. The cases in this Section provide rare examples of courts refusing to enforce an arbitration agreement on the basis of a "savings clause" defense. Most challenges on these grounds, however, more frequently fail, as the arbitration clause is typically part of a larger contract for an underlying transaction.

c. A related defense to arbitrability is failure to satisfy a condition precedent to arbitration. Many contracts now include "laddered" or "stepped up" dispute resolution provisions, which may specify a precondition to the arbitration agreement, such as requiring mediation as a condition precedent to arbitration. Such provisions are commonly used, and are encouraged by the AAA and other providers of arbitration services. A standard AAA clause provides:

> If a dispute arises out of or relates to this contract, or the breach thereof, and if the dispute cannot be settled through negotiation, the parties agree first to try in good faith to settled the dispute by mediation by the AAA under its Commercial Mediation Procedures before resorting to arbitration, litigation, or other dispute resolution procedure.

Under the Supreme Court's mandate to enforce arbitration agreements as written, if a contract plainly sets up another dispute resolution process as a condition precedent to arbitration, courts will not compel arbitration unless the conditions are met. *See, e.g., HIM Portland, LLC v. DeVito Builders, Inc.*, 317 F.3d 41 (1st Cir. 2003) (affirming district court's refusal to compel arbitration because parties' contract conditioned arbitration upon either party's request for mediation, and neither party requested mediation).

F. Effective Vindication

In *Mitsubishi Motors Corp. v. Soler Chrysler-Plymouth, Inc.*, 473 U.S. 614 (1985), a Puerto Rican automobile dealer in a dispute with a Japanese auto manufacturer opposed a motion to compel arbitration of the dispute on the grounds that international arbitrators were not competent to decide its complex claims arising under the federal antitrust laws. The Court rejected the argument that arbitration was not an adequate dispute resolution mechanism for statutory claims, stating that "so long as the prospective litigant effectively may vindicate its statutory cause of action in the arbitral forum, the statute will continue to serve both its remedial and deterrent function." Subsequently, litigants have cited that *dictum* in support of their contention that a court should not enforce an arbitration agreement because doing so would deprive them of the ability to vindicate their statutory rights. The Court clarified the scope of the doctrine in the 5–3 opinion that follows.

American Express Co. v. Italian Colors Restaurant
570 U.S. 228 (2013)

JUSTICE SCALIA delivered the opinion of the Court.

We consider whether a contractual waiver of class arbitration is enforceable under the Federal Arbitration Act when the plaintiff's cost of individually arbitrating a federal statutory claim exceeds the potential recovery.

I

Respondents are merchants who accept American Express cards. Their agreement with petitioners—American Express and a wholly owned subsidiary—contains a clause that requires all disputes between the parties to be resolved by arbitration. The agreement also provides that "[t]here shall be no right or authority for any Claims to be arbitrated on a class action basis."

Respondents brought a class action against petitioners for violations of the federal antitrust laws. According to respondents, American Express used its monopoly power in the market for charge cards to force merchants to accept credit cards at rates approximately 30% higher than the fees for competing credit cards.[1] This tying arrange-

---

1. A charge card requires its holder to pay the full outstanding balance at the end of a billing cycle; a credit card requires payment of only a portion, with the balance subject to interest.

ment, respondents said, violated §1 of the Sherman Act. They sought treble damages for the class under §4 of the Clayton Act.

AMEX

Petitioners moved to compel individual arbitration under the Federal Arbitration Act (FAA). In resisting the motion, respondents submitted a declaration from an economist who estimated that the cost of an expert analysis necessary to prove the antitrust claims would be "at least several hundred thousand dollars, and might exceed $1 million," while the maximum recovery for an individual plaintiff would be $12,850, or $38,549 when trebled. The District Court granted the motion and dismissed the lawsuits. The Court of Appeals reversed and remanded for further proceedings. It held that because respondents had established that "they would incur prohibitive costs if compelled to arbitrate under the class action waiver," the waiver was unenforceable and the arbitration could not proceed.

We granted certiorari, vacated the judgment, and remanded for further consideration in light of *Stolt-Nielsen S.A. v. AnimalFeeds Int'l Corp.*, 559 U.S. 662 (2010), which held that a party may not be compelled to submit to class arbitration absent an agreement to do so. The Court of Appeals stood by its reversal, stating that its earlier ruling did not compel class arbitration. It then *sua sponte* reconsidered its ruling in light of *AT&T Mobility*, which held that the FAA pre-empted a state law barring enforcement of a class-arbitration waiver. Finding *AT&T Mobility* inapplicable because it addressed pre-emption, the Court of Appeals reversed for the third time. It then denied rehearing en banc with five judges dissenting. We granted certiorari to consider the question "[w]hether the Federal Arbitration Act permits courts ... to invalidate arbitration agreements on the ground that they do not permit class arbitration of a federal-law claim."

II

Congress enacted the FAA in response to widespread judicial hostility to arbitration.... [Section 2] reflects the overarching principle that arbitration is a matter of contract. And consistent with that text, courts must "rigorously enforce" arbitration agreements according to their terms, including terms that "specify *with whom* [the parties] choose to arbitrate their disputes," and the rules under which that arbitration will be conducted." That holds true for claims that allege a violation of a federal statute, unless the FAA's mandate has been "overridden by a contrary congressional command."

III

No contrary congressional command requires us to reject the waiver of class arbitration here....

IV

restaurant

Our finding of no "contrary congressional command" does not end the case. Respondents invoke a judge-made exception to the FAA which, they say, serves to harmonize competing federal policies by allowing courts to invalidate agreements that prevent the "effective vindication" of a federal statutory right. Enforcing the waiver of class arbitration bars effective vindication, respondents contend, because they have no economic incentive to pursue their antitrust claims individually in arbitration.

The "effective vindication" exception to which respondents allude originated as dictum in *Mitsubishi Motors,* where we expressed a willingness to invalidate, on "public policy" grounds, arbitration agreements that "operat[e] … as a prospective waiver of a party's *right to pursue* statutory remedies." Dismissing concerns that the arbitral forum was inadequate, we said that "so long as the prospective litigant effectively may vindicate its statutory cause of action in the arbitral forum, the statute will continue to serve both its remedial and deterrent function." Subsequent cases have similarly asserted the existence of an "effective vindication" exception, but have similarly declined to apply it to invalidate the arbitration agreement at issue.

And we do so again here. As we have described, the exception finds its origin in the desire to prevent "prospective waiver of a party's *right to pursue* statutory remedies." That would certainly cover a provision in an arbitration agreement forbidding the assertion of certain statutory rights. And it would perhaps cover filing and administrative fees attached to arbitration that are so high as to make access to the forum impracticable. *See Green Tree Financial Corp.-Ala. v. Randolph,* 531 U.S. 79 (2000) ("It may well be that the existence of large arbitration costs could preclude a litigant … from effectively vindicating her federal statutory rights"). But the fact that it is not worth the expense involved in *proving* a statutory remedy does not constitute the elimination of the *right to pursue* that remedy. The class-action waiver merely limits arbitration to the two contracting parties. It no more eliminates those parties' right to pursue their statutory remedy than did federal law before its adoption of the class action for legal relief in 1938. Or, to put it differently, the individual suit that was considered adequate to assure "effective vindication" of a federal right before adoption of class-action procedures did not suddenly become "ineffective vindication" upon their adoption.

A pair of our cases brings home the point. In *Gilmer,* we had no qualms in enforcing a class waiver in an arbitration agreement even though the federal statute at issue, the Age Discrimination in Employment Act, expressly permitted collective actions. We said that statutory permission did " 'not mean that individual attempts at conciliation were intended to be barred.' " And in *Vimar Seguros y Reaseguros, S.A. v. M/V Sky Reefer,* 515 U.S. 528 (1995), we held that requiring arbitration in a foreign country was compatible with the federal Carriage of Goods by Sea Act. That legislation prohibited any agreement " 'relieving' " or " 'lessening' " the liability of a carrier for damaged goods— which is close to codification of an "effective vindication" exception. The Court rejected the argument that the "inconvenience and costs of proceeding" abroad "lessen[ed]" the defendants' liability, stating that "[i]t would be unwieldy and unsupported by the terms or policy of the statute to require courts to proceed case by case to tally the costs and burdens to particular plaintiffs in light of their means, the size of their claims, and the relative burden on the carrier." Such a "tally[ing] [of] the costs and burdens" is precisely what the dissent would impose upon federal courts here.

Truth to tell, our decision in *AT&T Mobility* all but resolves this case. There we invalidated a law conditioning enforcement of arbitration on the availability of class procedure because that law "interfere [d] with fundamental attributes of arbitration." "[T]he switch from bilateral to class arbitration," we said, "sacrifices the principal advantage of arbitration — its informality — and makes the process slower, more costly, and more likely to generate procedural morass than final judgment." We specifically rejected the argument that class arbitration was necessary to prosecute claims "that might otherwise slip through the legal system."

The regime established by the Court of Appeals' decision would require — before a plaintiff can be held to contractually agreed bilateral arbitration — that a federal court determine (and the parties litigate) the legal requirements for success on the merits claim-by-claim and theory-by-theory, the evidence necessary to meet those requirements, the cost of developing that evidence, and the damages that would be recovered in the event of success. Such a preliminary litigating hurdle would undoubtedly destroy the prospect of speedy resolution that arbitration in general and bilateral arbitration in particular was meant to secure. The FAA does not sanction such a judicially created superstructure.

The judgment of the Court of Appeals is reversed.

It is so ordered.

Justice SOTOMAYOR took no part in the consideration or decision of this case.

Justice THOMAS, concurring.

I join the Court's opinion in full. I write separately to note that the result here is also required by the plain meaning of the Federal Arbitration Act. In *AT&T Mobility,* I explained that "the FAA requires that an agreement to arbitrate be enforced unless a party successfully challenges the formation of the arbitration agreement, such as by proving fraud or duress." In this case, Italian Colors makes two arguments to support its conclusion that the arbitration agreement should not be enforced. First, it contends that enforcing the arbitration agreement "would contravene the policies of the antitrust laws." Second, it contends that a court may "invalidate agreements that prevent the 'effective vindication' of a federal statutory right." Neither argument "concern[s] whether the contract was properly made." Because Italian Colors has not furnished "grounds ... for the revocation of any contract," 9 U.S.C. §2, the arbitration agreement must be enforced. Italian Colors voluntarily entered into a contract containing a bilateral arbitration provision. It cannot now escape its obligations merely because the claim it wishes to bring might be economically infeasible.

Justice KAGAN, with whom Justice GINSBURG and Justice BREYER join, dissenting.

Here is the nutshell version of this case, unfortunately obscured in the Court's decision. The owner of a small restaurant (Italian Colors) thinks that American Express (Amex) has used its monopoly power to force merchants to accept a form contract violating the antitrust laws. The restaurateur wants to challenge the allegedly unlawful provision (imposing a tying arrangement), but the same contract's arbitration clause prevents him from doing so. That term imposes a variety of procedural bars that would make pursuit of the antitrust claim a fool's errand. So if the arbitration clause is enforceable, Amex has insulated itself from antitrust liability — even if it has in fact violated the law. The monopolist gets to use its monopoly power to insist on a contract effectively depriving its victims of all legal recourse.

And here is the nutshell version of today's opinion, admirably flaunted rather than camouflaged: Too darn bad.

That answer is a betrayal of our precedents, and of federal statutes like the antitrust laws. Our decisions have developed a mechanism — called the effective-vindication rule — to prevent arbitration clauses from choking off a plaintiff's ability to enforce congressionally created rights. That doctrine bars applying such a clause when (but only when) it operates to confer immunity from potentially meritorious federal claims. In so doing, the rule reconciles the Federal Arbitration Act (FAA) with all the rest of federal law — and indeed, promotes the most fundamental purposes of the FAA itself. As applied here, the rule would ensure that Amex's arbitration clause does not foreclose Italian Colors from vindicating its right to redress antitrust harm.

The majority barely tries to explain why it reaches a contrary result. It notes that we have not decided this exact case before — neglecting that the principle we have established fits this case hand in glove. And it concocts a special exemption for class-arbitration waivers — ignoring that this case concerns much more than that. Throughout, the majority disregards our decisions' central tenet: An arbitration clause may not thwart federal law, irrespective of exactly how it does so. Because the Court today prevents the effective vindication of federal statutory rights, I respectfully dissent.

I

... And sure enough, our cases establish this proposition: An arbitration clause will not be enforced if it prevents the effective vindication of federal statutory rights, however it achieves that result.... If an arbitration provision "operated ... as a prospective waiver of a party's right to pursue statutory remedies," we emphasized, we would "condemn[ ]" it. Similarly, we stated that such a clause should be "set [ ] aside" if "proceedings in the contractual forum will be so gravely difficult" that the claimant "will for all practical purposes be deprived of his day in court." And in the decades since *Mitsubishi*, we have repeated its admonition time and again, instructing courts not to enforce an arbitration agreement that effectively (even if not explicitly) forecloses a plaintiff from remedying the violation of a federal statutory right.

Our decision in *Green Tree Financial Corp.-Ala. v. Randolph*, 531 U.S. 79 (2000), confirmed that this principle applies when an agreement thwarts federal law by making arbitration prohibitively expensive. The plaintiff there (seeking relief under the Truth in Lending Act) argued that an arbitration agreement was unenforceable because it "create[d] a risk" that she would have to "bear prohibitive arbitration costs" in the form of high filing and administrative fees. We rejected that contention, but not because we doubted that such fees could prevent the effective vindication of statutory rights. To the contrary, we invoked our rule from *Mitsubishi*, making clear that it applied to the case before us. Indeed, we added a burden of proof: "[W]here, as here," we held, a party asserting a federal right "seeks to invalidate an arbitration agreement on the ground that arbitration would be prohibitively expensive, that party bears the burden of showing the likelihood of incurring such costs." Randolph, we found, had failed to meet that burden: The evidence she offered was "too speculative." But even as we dismissed Randolph's suit, we reminded courts to protect against arbitration agreements that make federal claims too costly to bring.

Applied as our precedents direct, the effective-vindication rule furthers the purposes not just of laws like the Sherman Act, but of the FAA itself. That statute reflects a federal policy favoring actual arbitration—that is, arbitration as a streamlined "method of resolving disputes," not as a foolproof way of killing off valid claims. Put otherwise: What the FAA prefers to litigation is arbitration, not *de facto* immunity. The effective-vindication rule furthers the statute's goals by ensuring that arbitration remains a real, not faux, method of dispute resolution. With the rule, companies have good reason to adopt arbitral procedures that facilitate efficient and accurate handling of complaints. Without it, companies have every incentive to draft their agreements to extract backdoor waivers of statutory rights, making arbitration unavailable or pointless. So down one road: More arbitration, better enforcement of federal statutes. And down the other: Less arbitration, poorer enforcement of federal statutes. Which would you prefer? Or still more aptly: Which do you think Congress would?

The answer becomes all the more obvious given the limits we have placed on the rule, which ensure that it does not diminish arbitration's benefits. The rule comes into play only when an agreement "operate[s] ... as a prospective waiver"—that is, forecloses (not diminishes) a plaintiff's opportunity to gain relief for a statutory violation. So, for example, *Randolph* assessed whether fees in arbitration would be "prohibitive" (not high, excessive, or extravagant). Moreover, the plaintiff must make that showing through concrete proof: "[S]peculative" risks, "unfounded assumptions," and "unsupported statements" will not suffice. With the inquiry that confined and the evidentiary requirements that high, courts have had no trouble assessing the matters the rule makes relevant. And for almost three decades, courts have followed our edict that arbitration clauses must usually prevail, declining to enforce them in only rare cases. The effective-vindication rule has thus operated year in and year out without undermining, much less "destroy[ing]," the prospect of speedy dispute resolution that arbitration secures.

And this is just the kind of case the rule was meant to address. Italian Colors, as I have noted, alleges that Amex used its market power to impose a tying arrangement in violation of the Sherman Act. The antitrust laws, all parties agree, provide the restaurant with a cause of action and give it the chance to recover treble damages. Here, that would mean Italian Colors could take home up to $38,549. But a problem looms. As this case comes to us, the evidence shows that Italian Colors cannot prevail in arbitration without an economic analysis defining the relevant markets, establishing Amex's monopoly power, showing anticompetitive effects, and measuring damages. And that expert report would cost between several hundred thousand and one million dollars. So the expense involved in proving the claim in arbitration is ten times what Italian Colors could hope to gain, even in a best-case scenario. That counts as a "prohibitive" cost, in *Randolph's* terminology, if anything does. No rational actor would bring a claim worth tens of thousands of dollars if doing so meant incurring costs in the hundreds of thousands.

An arbitration agreement could manage such a mismatch in many ways, but Amex's disdains them all. As the Court makes clear, the contract expressly prohibits class arbitration. But that is only part of the problem. The agreement also disallows any kind of joinder or consolidation of claims or parties. And more: Its confidentiality provision prevents Italian Colors from informally arranging with other merchants to produce a common expert report. And still more: The agreement precludes any shifting of costs to Amex, even if Italian Colors prevails. And beyond all that: Amex refused to enter into any stipulations that would obviate or mitigate the need for the economic analysis. In short, the agreement as applied in this case cuts off not just class arbitration, but any avenue for sharing, shifting, or shrinking necessary costs. Amex has put Italian Colors to this choice: Spend way, way, way more money than your claim is worth, or relinquish your Sherman Act rights.

... Italian Colors proved what the plaintiff in *Randolph* could not—that a standard-form agreement, taken as a whole, renders arbitration of a claim "prohibitively expensive." The restaurant thus established that the contract "operate[s] ... as a prospective waiver," and prevents the "effective[ ] ... vindicat[ion]" of Sherman Act rights. I would follow our precedents and decline to compel arbitration. * * *

The Court today mistakes what this case is about. To a hammer, everything looks like a nail. And to a Court bent on diminishing the usefulness of Rule 23, everything looks like a class action, ready to be dismantled. So the Court does not consider that Amex's agreement bars not just class actions, but "other forms of cost-sharing ... that could provide effective vindication." In short, the Court does not consider—and does not decide—Italian Colors's (and similarly situated litigants') actual argument about why the effective-vindication rule precludes this agreement's enforcement.

As a result, Amex's contract will succeed in depriving Italian Colors of any effective opportunity to challenge monopolistic conduct allegedly in violation of the Sherman Act. The FAA, the majority says, so requires. Do not be fooled. Only the Court so requires; the FAA was never meant to produce this outcome. The FAA conceived of arbitration as a "method of *resolving* disputes"—a way of using tailored and streamlined procedures to facilitate redress of injuries. In the hands of today's majority, arbitration threatens to become more nearly the opposite—a mechanism easily made to block the vindication of meritorious federal claims and insulate wrongdoers from liability. The Court thus undermines the FAA no less than it does the Sherman Act and other federal statutes providing rights of action. I respectfully dissent.

1. Comments and Questions

a. The Supreme Court has yet to invalidate an arbitration agreement under the "effective vindication" doctrine. Thus, it remains to be seen precisely what type of right-stripping provision in an arbitration agreement the Court would view as rendering the agreement unenforceable. Can you envision one? What factors might a lower court consider when deciding a challenge to an arbitration clause under the doctrine as articulated in *Italian Colors*?

b. Even though *Italian Colors* sharply limited the use of the effective vindication doctrine to strike down class action waivers, several courts have refused to enforce other aspects of arbitration agreements under the newly articulated effective vindication doctrine. For example, in *Hayes v. Delbert Services Corp.*, 811 F.3d 666 (4th Cir. 2016), plaintiffs brought a putative class action against a payday lending company asserting that the company's lending practices violated various state and federal lending laws. The PDAA in the parties' loan agreement provided that the agreement was subject only to Indian law and not applicable state and federal law. The Fourth Circuit concluded that the clause, which expressly forbids plaintiffs from invoking protections guaranteed to them under federal law, was unenforceable under the effective vindication doctrine.

Likewise, in *Nesbitt v. FCNH, Inc.*, 811 F.3d 371 (10th Cir. 2016), a massage therapy student brought a putative class action in federal district court against the operator of massage therapy schools for violations of the Fair Labor Standards Act (FLSA) for failing to pay students for performing massages on customers. The student enrollment agreement contained a PDAA providing for arbitration at the American Arbitration Association pursuant to its commercial arbitration rules. Those rules provide, among other things, that each party bears its own arbitration expenses. The PDAA also stated that each party would bear its own attorney's fees.

The district court denied defendants' motion to compel arbitration, and the Tenth Circuit affirmed under the effective vindication doctrine. The Court of Appeals noted that plaintiff's affidavit stated that she could not afford the forum fees. The court also noted that the arbitration agreement was ambiguous as to whether the arbitrators were permitted to ignore the fee-shifting provisions of the FLSA. The court concluded that "it is unlikely that an employee in [the plaintiff's] position, faced with the mere possibility of being reimbursed for arbitrator fees in the future, would risk advancing those fees in order to access the arbitral forum." As a result, the court held that the arbitration agreement precluded plaintiff from vindicating her statutory rights and was thus unenforceable.

c. Scholars have been critical of the *Italian Colors* decision. *See* Hiro N. Aragaki, *The Federal Arbitration Act as Procedural Reform*, 89 N.Y.U. L. Rev. 1939, 2018–21 (2014) (describing the vindicating rights doctrine as an "equitable safety valve" and the *Italian Colors* holding as "surprising").

G. Constitutional Challenges

1. Fifth Amendment Challenges

Other defenses to arbitrability that reluctant parties have unsuccessfully asserted include challenges based on the U.S. Constitution. However, courts routinely strike down challenges under the Due Process Clause of the Fifth Amendment, as private arbitration institutions are private and not state actors. *See, e.g., Elmore v. Chicago & Illinois Midland Ry. Co.*, 782 F.2d 94 (7th Cir. 1986) ("[T]he fact that a private arbitrator denies the procedural safeguards that are encompassed by the term 'due process of law' cannot give rise to a constitutional complaint."); *Davis v. Prudential Sec., Inc.*, 59 F.3d 1186 (11th Cir. 1995) (finding securities industry arbitration proceeding did not constitute state action because it was the creature of a voluntary contractual agreement).

2. Seventh Amendment Challenges

Likewise, courts routinely reject arguments that arbitration clauses in an adhesive contract violate the Seventh Amendment's right to a jury trial. Rather, courts find that reluctant parties knowingly waived their Seventh Amendment right by agreeing to the PDAA. *See, e.g., Cooper v. MRM Inv. Co.*, 367 F.3d 493 (6th Cir. 2004); *Janiga v. Questar Capital Corp.*, 615 F.3d 735 (7th Cir. 2010).

3. Proposed Solutions to Perceived Unfairness of Adhesive Arbitration

Many of the unfairness claims surrounding arbitration derive from the FAA's application to arbitration required by adhesion contracts in employment and consumer cases in the context of no constitutional protections. Chapter 1, section D of this book mentions the Arbitration Fairness Act, a bill proposed, but not passed, to prohibit enforcement of pre-dispute arbitration agreements in employment, consumer, and franchise cases. *See also* Maureen A. Weston, *Preserving the Federal Arbitration Act by Reining in Judicial Expansion and Mandatory Use*, 8 Nev. L.J. 385 (2008).

One solution to the unfairness claims that has been implemented is the use of a "due process protocol" by arbitration providers. Adopted by providers such as AAA and JAMS, these protocols purport to ensure a fair process to those who use their services if the arbitration arose out of an adhesive contract. Although these standards do not in themselves have the force of law but are backed by the internal enforcement efforts of the providers, at least one of these standards, the AAA Consumer Due Process Protocol, includes in its commentary an invitation to courts to use the standards as a basis for assessing the fundamental fairness—and enforceability—of arbitration agreements.

You can find the AAA's Consumer Due Process Protocols on its website, at https://www.adr.org/sites/default/files/document_repository/Consumer%20Due%20Process%20Protocol%20(1).pdf. Do these AAA Protocols address disputants' fairness concerns? Why or why not?

Chapter 5

The Arbitration Process

A. Introduction

The first four chapters focused on the law governing arbitration and, in particular, the law governing the enforceability of an arbitration agreement. This chapter focuses on a very practical topic: what happens during the arbitration process itself?

Once parties have entered into an enforceable arbitration agreement, and a dispute within the scope of that agreement arises (or disputants agree post-dispute to arbitrate), one or both parties will likely pursue resolution of that dispute through the arbitration process. This chapter examines that arbitration process, from the initiation of the claim to the issuance of the award, and is designed to give the reader a general and objective sense of how an arbitration progresses. In contrast, **Chapter 7** views the process through the lens of the arbitration advocate.

Most of the material in this chapter is practice-oriented, rather than case law-oriented. Occasionally, however, issues arise during the arbitration process that require court intervention, such as requests for preliminary relief in aid of arbitration, or motions to quash arbitrator subpoenas. Court rulings resulting from these motions are addressed in this chapter as well.

Most arbitration institutions have their own unique procedural rules that apply to each of these phases, but they have many elements in common. The common elements of the commercial arbitration process can be described as a series of 10 steps:

1. *Initiation of the Claim*
2. *Pre-Appointment Administrative Conference*
3. *Arbitrator Selection*
4. *Post-Appointment Preliminary Hearing*
5. *Discovery*
6. *Dispositive Motions*
7. *The Hearing*
8. *Post-Hearing Submissions*
9. *Deliberation*
10. *Award*

This 10-step process, as it is practiced today in the United States, has been criticized recently for becoming more litigation-like, and resembling less and less the simple, efficient, and inexpensive arbitration process that Congress likely envisioned when it passed the Federal Arbitration Act (FAA). *See* Jill I. Gross, *Justice Scalia's Hat Trick and the Supreme Court's Flawed Understanding of Twenty-First Century Arbitration*, 81 BROOKLYN L. REV. 111, 119–20 (2015); Thomas J. Stipanowich, *Arbitration: The "New Litigation,"* 2010 U. ILL. L. REV. 1. As you read through the detailed description of each of the steps below, consider the differences between litigation and arbitration, and consider whether this critique is accurate.

B. The Ten Steps of Arbitration

1. Initiation of the Claim

When a dispute arises, a disputant who is a party to a valid arbitration agreement may submit the dispute to arbitration before a specific arbitrator or arbitration services provider (also known as an arbitration forum or institution), such as the American Arbitration Association (AAA) or JAMS, or to an arbitration institution designated by the parties in the arbitration agreement or required by applicable law (such as arbitration between securities customers and their brokerage firms at the Financial Industry Regulatory Authority (FINRA). Arbitration institutions can vary greatly in the degree of service they offer, the types of arbitrators on their rosters, the level of administrative support offered in individual cases, the procedural rules applicable to the case, and hearing locations offered.

To formally initiate a claim, most institutions ask the requesting party, known as the claimant, to complete a series of forms, such as a Demand for Arbitration. Accompanying that Demand typically is a Statement of Claim (SOC). Arbitration institutions impose virtually no pleading requirements on the SOC; it must include only basic information such as names of parties, contact information of all parties and their representatives, if known, a statement setting forth the nature of the claim including the type and amount of relief sought, and whether any particular location for the hearing is requested. *See, e.g.,* AAA Commercial Arbitration Rules and Mediation Procedures ("AAA R") R-4; FINRA Code of Arbitration Procedure for Customer Disputes ("FINRA R.") 12302. However, claimants often choose to include a more detailed narrative of the relevant facts and assertion of complaint-like causes of action. Some procedural rules also require that the claimant supply the provider organization with a copy of the applicable arbitration agreement. *See, e.g.,* AAA R-4. The claimant may, but is not required to, attach supporting documents or exhibits to the SOC. Most arbitration providers now offer electronic filing technology so claimants can upload the SOC and attachments to a website or portal.

Unless the arbitration provider has identified any administrative filing deficiencies, the provider will notify opposing parties, known as respondents, of the SOC, and may even serve (by mail or email) the respondent(s) with the SOC (some providers require the claimant to provide the SOC to the respondent(s)). Respondents then have an opportunity to file a Statement of Answer (Answer) and/or counterclaim, usually within a set period. *See, e.g.,* AAA R-5; FINRA R. 12303. Answers can also be brief or more detailed. Any counterclaim must include the same components as for a claim in a SOC. Claimants who are respondents on a Counterclaim then should file a Reply to the counterclaim in the same manner as an Answer. The institutions also have rules governing when and how a party can amend its SOC, Answer, and Counterclaim.

The forum may also have rules regarding the impact on a respondent of not filing an Answer or Reply to a counterclaim. For example, in the AAA, the respondent is deemed to deny a claim if it does not answer. AAA R-5(a). In contrast, at FINRA, failure to answer may subject a respondent to default proceedings. FINRA R. 12303(a).

If you were an arbitrator on a case, what information would you want the parties to include in their SOC and Answer? What are the advantages and disadvantages of the parties pleading causes of action or legalistic defenses? Would you want the parties to attach exhibits to their pleadings? Would your answers change if you knew that the arbitrator was or was not an attorney? Examples of a SOC and Answer are included in **Chapter 7**.

2. Pre-Appointment Administrative Conference

After the initial pleadings are filed, the forum may choose to hold, or the parties might request, an administrative conference, typically via telephone, to sort out administrative logistics even before the appointment of arbitrators. *See, e.g.,* AAA R-10. (Some forums skip this step altogether.)

Logistics to cover during this conference might include how the parties wish to go about selecting arbitrators, whether there are any timetables for resolution that the parties wish to impose on a panel, whether there are disputes about the hearing location, and issues as to payment of forum and arbitrator fees. In addition, the forum might want to assess the status of any parallel mediation. *See, e.g.,* AAA R-9 (requiring parties to every claim for $75,000 or more in damages to mediate the dispute, unless a party opts out). Because these issues might impact the type of arbitrator selected to hear the case, or the timetable for the process, the forum's administrator should resolve them before an arbitrator is chosen who might not be available on the parties' timetable or at the chosen location.

3. Arbitrator Selection

One of the most important and consequential decisions confronting the parties and their advocates during the arbitration process is the selection of the arbitrator(s). Once the parties select arbitrators, they cede an enormous amount of power to them, including the power to decide the validity and applicability of a contract containing an arbitration clause, the power to manage the arbitration process, the power to decide the dispute in accordance with applicable law and equitable principles, the power to bind the parties to an award, subject to only very limited review, and the power to award a broad range of remedies. Therefore, it is important that the parties choose arbitrators who can exercise those powers justly.

Unlike trial judges who are generalists and work full-time for a fixed salary, arbitrators are often specialists with subject matter and/or industry expertise who are paid by the case. Arbitrators are experienced professionals, but often they are not lawyers. Most arbitration institutions train their arbitrators on the basics of the arbitration process and arbitrator ethics; some even require continuing education.

In most arbitration institutions, parties have significant control over the selection of the arbitrators. Decisions parties have to make when they select arbitrators include the qualifications of the arbitrator(s), the method of selection the parties will use, and the number of arbitrators on a panel. Each of these is addressed in turn below.

Qualifications: Unless the parties have agreed to a particular individual or panel early on in the process, the parties will have to decide what kind of arbitrators they want. Generally, parties want experienced, trained, and unbiased arbitrators, but that is only a starting point. Each arbitration institution identifies specific criteria it requires arbitrators to have to be listed on their rosters (see, for example, the AAA's Qualification Criteria for Admittance to the AAA National Roster of Arbitrators, http://www.adr.org/aaa/ShowPDF?doc=ADRSTG_003878). Questions parties should ask themselves and discuss include: Should the arbitrators be experienced in substance, procedure, or both? How experienced? Do they want arbitrators who are lawyers? Parties might need to negotiate the answers to all of these questions before selecting any panelist. Can you think of other types of qualifications parties might want on a particular case?

Method of selection: The place to start for the means of arbitrator selection is the parties' agreement, as parties frequently specify in that agreement the selection method or, at least, the required qualifications for arbitrators. Occasionally an agreement will specify a particular individual, though that method is risky because that person might not be available at the time of the dispute.

If the parties did not agree on the method in advance, they may try to agree through post-dispute negotiation. The AAA now allows parties to search through its electronic database of arbitrator names and biographies to find mutually acceptable candidate(s). If this method does not work, then the forum typically has default selection rules. For example, absent party agreement, the AAA and FINRA use the list selection method. *See* AAA R-12; FINRA R. 12400. List selection involves the forum providing one or more lists of arbitrators who fit the required qualifications, and then the parties strike a certain number of "undesirable" names and rank the remaining names. The forum consolidates the lists and appoints the highest-ranked remaining name(s). Another way to select arbitrators from a list of candidates is to have each side alternatively strike names until only one person is left. Other methods of selection include tripartite, where each party selects one arbitrator and those two arbitrators select a third arbitrator to be the Chair. If the parties do not agree and there is no forum method available or forum methods failed, FAA § 5 provides a gap-filling procedure for a court to designate and appoint an arbitrator to hear the dispute. What are the advantages and disadvantages of each method of arbitrator selection?

Number of arbitrators: Sometimes the parties' arbitration agreement specifies the number of arbitrators to be on the panel; other times the forum rules govern. Unless it is a large-dollar-value dispute, panels consist of one arbitrator. *See, e.g.*, AAA R-16 ("If the arbitration agreement does not specify the number of arbitrators, the dispute shall be heard and determined by one arbitrator, unless the AAA, in its discretion, directs that three arbitrators be appointed."); FAA § 5 ("unless otherwise provided in the agreement the arbitration shall be by a single arbitrator"). What are the pros and cons of a one-arbitrator, as opposed to a three-arbitrator, panel?

Once the arbitrators are appointed, including the Chairperson for a three-arbitrator panel (see AAA Rule 16 on how the AAA selects the Chair), the arbitrators then have certain ethical obligations, primarily to disclose potential or actual conflicts of interest. *See, e.g.*, AAA R-17. These ethical obligations are addressed in **Chapter 8**.

4. Post-Appointment/Pre-Hearing Administrative Conference

Post-appointment, the arbitration panel conducts a preliminary conference with the parties, usually via telephone but occasionally in person, to discuss primarily procedural matters. All parties, or their counsel, attend this conference because separate phone calls to the different parties would violate ethical rules regarding *ex parte* communications. Substantive issues might also arise at this time. Before this conference, the arbitrators should read the parties' agreement to arbitrate very carefully, as it might specify certain rules or protocols the parties agreed to follow, particularly with respect to pre-hearing procedures, such as discovery.

Some arbitration institutions provide parties and arbitrators with tremendous guidance as to what to cover during this conference (*see, e.g.*, AAA R-21, P-1 and P-20); other institutions grant arbitrators broad discretion. The RUAA states that an arbitrator may conduct an arbitration "in such manner as the arbitrator considers appropriate for a fair and expeditious disposition of the proceeding." This authority "includes the power to hold conferences with the parties to the arbitration proceeding before the hearing and, among other matters, determine the admissibility, relevance, materiality, and weight of any evidence." RUAA § 15(a).

Procedural matters arbitrators routinely cover during this conference include:

- Securing the parties' acceptance of the composition of the panel;
- Setting discovery protocols (e.g., scope of e-discovery; expert discovery; subpoenas; whether depositions will be permitted) and deadlines;
- Addressing whether and how the parties can file dispositive motions and/or pre-hearing briefs;
- Scheduling pre-hearing exchange of witness lists and exhibits;

- Determining whether the parties want a protective order entered ensuring confidentiality;
- Determining the number of hearing dates needed;
- Selecting hearing location, dates and times; and
- Previewing any hearing-related procedures, such as whether the panel will permit telephonic or video testimony, or whether the parties will submit joint hearing binders.

At this conference, arbitrators can even hear arguments and rule on their own jurisdiction in the face of one party's objection. Finally, arbitrators may also entertain and decide requests for interim relief, such as requests for preservation of assets or preliminary injunctions.

An illustration of the scope of this conference is AAA's Commercial Arbitration Rules for "Preliminary Hearing Procedures." Rule P-1(a) states:

(a) In all but the simplest cases, holding a preliminary hearing as early in the process as possible will help the parties and the arbitrator organize the proceeding in a manner that will maximize efficiency and economy, and will provide each party a fair opportunity to present its case.

To minimize the risk that the outcome of the preliminary hearing will convert the arbitration into a litigation-like proceeding, Rule P-2(b) warns:

(b) Care must be taken to avoid importing procedures from court systems, as such procedures may not be appropriate to the conduct of arbitrations as an alternative form of dispute resolution that is designed to be simpler, less expensive and more expeditious.

Rule P-2(a) states:

(a) The following checklist suggests subjects that the parties and the arbitrator should address at the preliminary hearing, in addition to any others that the parties or the arbitrator believe to be appropriate to the particular case. The items to be addressed in a particular case will depend on the size, subject matter, and complexity of the dispute, and are subject to the discretion of the arbitrator:

The "checklist" has 19 subparts, some with further subdivisions, covering all of the topics that arbitrators should attempt to cover during the telephonic preliminary hearing. Topics listed include, *inter alia*, whether mediation is possible, the scope of and schedule for discovery, what law will apply to the case, logistics and scheduling for the merits hearing, and whether pre- or post-hearing submissions will be allowed. This detailed checklist exemplifies the tension arbitrators face: arbitrators want to manage the process to keep it moving as efficiently and inexpensively as possible; yet if they do not permit parties to engage in some discovery and other pre-hearing activities, the arbitrators risk having an award later vacated for being "guilty of misconduct in … refusing to hear evidence pertinent and material to the controversy; or of any other misbehavior by which the rights of any party have been prejudiced.…"

FAA, § 10(a)(3). Arbitrators tend to err on the side of permitting broad document exchange, unless the requests are immaterial or overly burdensome in cost or time.

After the conference, the panel issues an Order, which is known, depending on the forum, as a Scheduling Order, Pre-Hearing Conference Order, or a Case Management Order. *See, e.g.,* AAA Rule P-2(b) ("The arbitrator shall issue a written order memorializing decisions made and agreements reached during or following the preliminary hearing"). This Order governs the proceedings through the hearing unless and until the panel issues subsequent orders modifying or clarifying the initial order.

In some cases, one or more of the parties will request an extension of scheduled deadlines. Arbitrators have to balance the interest in conducting an efficient and speedy process with the parties' desire to control their own process. If the arbitrators do not grant requested postponements of scheduled deadlines, they risk having an award later vacated for being "guilty of misconduct in refusing to postpone the hearing, upon sufficient cause shown. . . ." FAA § 10(a)(3). The response of arbitrators is to be quite generous in granting postponements — and to almost always grant joint requests of the parties for a postponement. This can produce considerable delay because rescheduling requires the coordination of the schedules of arbitrators with busy professional lives with equally busy parties and counsel.

Below are excerpts from an article by an experienced arbitrator and mediator for AAA, FINRA, and the Counselors of Real Estate, on his approach to the pre-hearing conference.

Philip S. Cottone, Esq., *The Pre-Hearing Conference in Arbitration — A Step by Step Guide*

SECURITIES ARBITRATION 2012 COURSEBOOK (PLI)

FINRA (Financial Industry Regulatory Authority) calls it the *Initial Pre-Hearing Conference* in its securities arbitrations, and AAA (American Arbitration Association) the *Preliminary Hearing,* but despite the subtle differences in nomenclature this pretrial conference with counsel, the arbitration panel and the case manager, usually by phone and usually without the parties present, is a critical part of the process because it lays the foundation for all that will follow. It is not just about setting dates, and if that is all that is accomplished an opportunity has been wasted to establish the proper tone for the subsequent proceedings and for the arbitrators to take control of and begin to manage the process. This article will describe the customary procedures in what I will call the Pre-Hearing Conference herein, and some do's and don'ts for counsel and arbitrators to help ensure an arbitration that respects party choice and is fair and attentive to conserving time and money where possible.

Who Should Attend

Especially in larger commercial cases, . . . counsel for each of the parties should be present at the Pre-Hearing conference. This is so because many decisions will be made that affect the costs to be incurred and the speed with which the matter will proceed and the parties have a real interest in those subjects. The presence of in-house counsel also commits the client more directly to the philosophy to be discussed and hopefully subscribed to by everyone present that arbitration is not litigation, and the objectives of cost and time efficiencies as well as fairness and party choice are to be respected. At best, again for the larger cases, this should done in person because developing agreement and cooperation to the extent possible among counsel and the parties and getting a commitment to achieving the shared objectives that should be articulated at the Pre-Hearing Conference is much better accomplished face to face than by phone.

. . .

Introductions and Preliminaries

After roll call has been taken and the parties have introduced themselves it is appropriate for the Chair to ask the panel if there are any disclosures they have to make in addition to those previously made on any Oath and written disclosures that may have been filed. After that the FINRA script has the Chair ask if counsel accepts the composition of the panel, and I believe that is good practice in all cases, namely to get an affirmative representation on the record from counsel that they have no problem with the designated arbitrators proceeding, notwithstanding any disclosures made.

In FINRA cases the panel will usually have the pleadings and often other documents to review prior to the Pre-Hearing Conference so it will have some idea what the controversy is all about. That is usually not the case with AAA and private matters where the panel might have only a Demand for Arbitration, if anything at all. In those cases it is always a good idea to ask counsel for the moving party (Claimant herein) to briefly review the cause of action that has been asserted (what the AAA calls Statements of Claims and Issues), and to ask the Respondent to answer. The FINRA outline then has the arbitrators confirm the documents they have received, and I think this is also good practice. Occasionally it turns out that the panelists do not all have the same materials and this is a good time to find out and get everyone on the same page.

Dates

The AAA Preliminary Hearing Checklist then proceeds directly to establishing dates for the hearing. The FINRA checklist does the same, but after having the Chair remind the parties of its highly successful, voluntary mediation program. My practice at this juncture is to ask counsel if they have had a discussion about dates in preparation for the call. Often they have, about trial dates and/or discovery dates, and in that case I hear them out. It is always best for counsel to confer privately before the call and to agree where possible on how they would like the arbitration to be conducted. Asking if they did that, and maybe saying a few words to encourage that kind of dialogue between and among counsel as we proceed, is always useful. The best way for them to protect themselves against arbitral rulings they might not like is to work it out themselves if they can. If they have not talked I ask if they want to discuss dates for exchanging information first, and then trial dates, or the other way around.

I do it this way to see what the parties have in mind and to let them steer the discussion based on what is most important to them. Some start talking about the need for prompt trial dates and may suggest a number of weeks or months out; others are more concerned with getting on with discovery and setting dates for the filing of requests, subpoenas, and Motions to Compel. This is the parties' process, after all, and letting them direct the discussion at the Pre-Hearing Conference does not at all mean the arbitrators are giving up control but, rather, that they are listening to the concerns of counsel to help them structure a calendar that will accomplish their objectives.

Discovery

"The expansion of discovery stands out as the primary contributor to greater expense and longer cycle time (in arbitration)" concluded a poll of participants in the 2010 National Summit on Business to Business Arbitration.... Historically discovery in arbitration was not an entitlement beyond the exchange of the most basic documents between the parties. As years have gone by and arbitration is increasingly used for larger commercial cases, discovery has increased accordingly, and institutional rules have developed to include required or optional Information exchanges....

Managing the discovery process is absolutely essential for a just, expeditious and comparatively inexpensive arbitration. The panel has to control the process to stop the increasing "litigitization" of arbitration and to make sure proportionality is achieved so the parties get what they need and no more, and at a reasonable cost in terms of money and delay.... Discovery in arbitration is generally much more limited than under the Federal Rules of Civil Procedure or state discovery rules, and an out-of-control discovery process is certain to derail any arbitration. Limits need to be discussed and agreed to at the Pre-Hearing Conference.

If it is a large case the parties can be encouraged to meet and confer on limits themselves and come back with recommendations to the panel. If subpoenas have to be used there must be a limitation on how many for both sides; if depositions need to be conducted to save time at trial they also should be limited in both number and in the time allotted for each (or overall).... In a recent AAA commercial case I chaired the parties agreed at the Preliminary Hearing to a limitation of no more than five depositions and a total of fifteen hours of total deposition time, with all of them to be completed by a date certain....

It is usual for the Chair to handle any discovery disputes and to rule on Motions to Compel, and for a date to be fixed at the Pre-Hearing Conference for that to be done. It is important that a careful balance be struck and that concerns about cost and time do not unfairly restrict a party's ability to get relevant and material information that will be essential to its case. Moreover, there are no hard and fast rules applicable to all cases, and one size does not fit all. The panel must consider the unique circumstances of the case before them and work with the parties to tailor the discovery limitations in a manner that is fair and equitable and achieves the cost and time objectives that are appropriate....

In the troublesome area of electronic documents (ESI) there should be agreement that, absent compelling reasons, production will be limited to sources in the ordinary course of business, not back-up information; that only generally available technology will be used; and that where the cost and burden of production is great the arbitrator will consider cost shifting to the requesting party, subject to the allocation of costs in the final award.... Here too the concept of proportionality is critical....

Motions

Sixty five percent of those polled at the National Arbitration Summit by CCA concluded that excessive, inappropriate or mismanaged motion practice was "moderately" to "very much" responsible for failing to meet their desires for arbitration efficiency and economy.... Like discovery, motion practice must be managed and controlled by the panel.

Some motions, such as those based upon statutes of limitation, release, contractual limits on damages, statutory remedies and other legal limitations on causes of action may be entirely in order early on if there are no major questions of fact to be decided. They would potentially save time and money by limiting the scope of the litigation and disposing of matters that advance the case to resolution more quickly. However, if there are factual issues which require extensive discovery or testimony, and which would require the arbitrators to reserve decision perhaps until the end of the trial, such motions should not be permitted.

...

It has been suggested in the CCA Guide that if motions are to be considered they should be fleshed out at the Pre-Hearing Conference, and not be presented without advance permission from the arbitrators. Oral argument without written submissions is preferred, as well as requiring counsel to confer about whether the motion is really necessary.... Then the panel decides, and if they go forward with the motion they would place page limits on the briefs and set an accelerated schedule for argument, if any, and disposition. Some common types of motions include those for preliminary relief or interim measures; discovery; bifurcation; motions in limine (not favored under most circumstances); for sanctions, or continuance. In most cases the criterion is whether considering them will reduce costs and streamline the process.

* * *

Hearing Preparation

The Pre-Hearing Conference must also set dates, location and the first day starting time for the hearing, and for the exchange of information regarding witness and exhibit lists, usually 15 to 20 days before the first day of the hearing. It is good practice to specify whether business or calendar days so everyone knows exactly what is required. As to the hearing dates, it is prudent, after asking counsel how many days they will need and reaching agreement, to consider adding one extra day for safety and/or for the panel to meet and have an initial conference on the case. This is especially important if the panelists are from different cities. You don't want an adjourned hearing if you can avoid it because it is very disruptive to an orderly trial and decision making process. On the other hand, because work often expands to fill the time available, it is important that counsel understand the dates are firm and they will be held to their estimates of time. Moreover, it should be made clear that the trial dates will not be changed unless there is good cause shown, and some arbitrators and providers specify in their agreements that the neutrals will be paid in full for scheduled time if a cancellation is not requested and approved within thirty or more days in advance.

Most pre-hearing checklists specify that witness lists must include the name and title of the witness and a short summary of anticipated testimony, together with a CV if it is an expert. Exhibits have to include everything that is to be offered at the hearing (reports, summaries, diagrams and charts, says the AAA Checklist), pre-marked for identification. The parties should be directed to confer on preparation of joint exhibits as well.

In my experience, though some arbitrators and counsel disagree, I find a Stipulation of Uncontested Facts to be unnecessary and rarely ask for it unless counsel or my fellow panelists think it is desirable. It occasionally leads to contentious disagreements between and among counsel, and in my view has limited value, and often requires a lot of work and time by counsel that can be put to better use. The panel usually learns very quickly what facts are disputed and what are agreed without such a Stipulation.

While FINRA provides for digital recording of hearings, in other fora there must be a discussion of whether any party desires and is prepared to pay for a stenographic record. In many instances the decision on that subject is reserved until closer to trial, and in that case it is good practice is to specify a firm date by which the parties will discuss the subject and advise the panel.

The form of award should be discussed and definitions for each (e.g., Standard, Reasoned, or Findings of Fact and Conclusions of Law), should be reviewed by the Chair to make sure everyone knows exactly what they will be getting.

* * *

Case Management Order

The Pre-Hearing Conference results in a Case Management Order that records the agreements reached.... I think it is good practice for the Chair to circulate a form of order to the co-panelists for review and comments, and, when it is agreed to, forward it to the Case Manager for distribution to the parties (unless it is a FINRA case where direct communication has been selected). If the Order specifies a time line extending out over many months, the panel may want to consider scheduling an additional Pre-Hearing Conference or two if needed to check on progress and make sure things are on track.

Closing Comments

This article and most contemporary commentary on best practices in arbitration emphasize the need for what has been characterized in a number of places as "muscular" management by the arbitrators to make sure the objectives of party autonomy and choice are balanced by those of fairness, and cost and time control, and that a litigation mind-set does not take control of events. The place to lay the foundation for that is the Pre-Hearing Conference, and then to follow up on it during the hearings themselves. While this article is not about management of the hearing, it is clear that the arbitrator has the ability to assert control if necessary to keep counsel on track regarding deadlines and commitments made during the Pre-Hearing Conference....

While at the Pre-Hearing Conference the theme should be one of cooperation and respect between and among counsel and the use of "meet and confer" to resolve issues if they can themselves. But, as noted earlier, they must also be reminded that dates are firm and the agreements reached in the Case Management Order are to be kept unless there is good cause shown. If necessary they can also be reminded of the possible sanctions they will face if they do not live up to their commitments.

a. Comments and Questions

Having read this excerpt, how would you describe the arbitrator's role of managing the time and expense of arbitration? How much control should the parties have in defining their own process? Courts rarely second-guess an arbitrator's procedural rulings related to or stemming from this preliminary conference. *See, e.g., Cumberland Valley Ass'n v. Antosz,* No. 294799, 2011 WL 2119664, at *3 (Mich. Ct. App. May 26, 2011) ("We decline to interfere with the arbitrator's resolution of the procedural issue [regarding the preliminary conference]").

5. Discovery

The availability of discovery—the pre-hearing process in which parties request and disclose relevant evidence and other information to opposing parties—is one of the defining characteristics of litigation in the United States. Discovery is also the most expensive and time-consuming component of litigation, as attorneys have to devote an enormous amount of time (and thus cost) to document collection, review and production, as well as taking and defending witness depositions.

At least historically, restricting the scope of discovery was one of the hallmarks of commercial arbitration, and one of the main reasons the process was less costly and more efficient. Parties accepted the tradeoff of less discovery, in exchange for a process involving lower costs and quicker resolution of disputes. However, the limited discovery also reduced parties' ability to discover relevant facts in advance of hearing. As a result, a trend in modern arbitration is to expand discovery to a point where it can approach the scope and volume of that in litigation.

During the discovery phase in commercial arbitration, parties may exchange documents and information, seek documents and information from third-party witnesses via subpoenas, exchange expert reports, possibly take a limited number of depositions, and seek arbitrator intervention to resolve discovery disputes. While most forums permit parties to begin the discovery process once responsive pleadings are filed, no means of enforcement of discovery obligations exist until an arbitration panel is appointed. Thus, as a practical matter, most arbitration discovery takes place post-appointment.

Discovery From Parties. What laws govern discovery in arbitration? Most arbitration agreements do not address discovery issues, although parties can and sometimes do consent to either a broader or narrower scope of discovery in their agreements. While the FAA does not address the scope of party discovery in arbitration, the RUAA (§ 17) provides that arbitrators may permit discovery and issue subpoenas to order depositions. RUAA section 17(g) provides for judicial enforcement of those subpoenas.

Some non RUAA-based state statutes permit courts to order discovery in aid of arbitration. For example, New York's civil procedure rules (Article 31 — Disclosure) provide:

> § 3102(c). Before action commenced. Before an action is commenced, disclosure to aid in bringing an action, to preserve information or to aid in arbitration, may be obtained, but only by court order. The court may appoint a referee to take testimony.

Although the language appears broad, New York courts have construed this provision to provide for discovery in aid of arbitration only under extraordinary circumstances, and only when absolutely necessary for the protection of the rights of a party. Federal courts apply similar principles, strictly limiting court involvement in discovery when there is a pending arbitration and no litigation. *See, e.g.,* McIntire v. China Media-Express Holdings, 252 F. Supp. 3d 328, 331 (S.D.N.Y. 2017) (stating that courts should deny requests for discovery on the subject matter of a dispute to be arbitrated absent extraordinary circumstances, such as "where a party's ability to properly present its case to the arbitrators will be irreparably harmed absent court ordered discovery" or "to preserve the relevant evidence and to promote efficiency in the proceedings when there may be a long wait for an arbitration panel to be appointed").

Due to the lack of statutory authority, arbitration institutions have promulgated their own procedural rules governing discovery. Each forum has slightly different rules permitting the use of different discovery devices, in particular document and information exchange and identification of relevant witnesses, but none provides for the full range of devices available under the Federal Rules of Civil Procedure or similar state discovery rules. Forum rules confirm that depositions are rarely available in arbitration, especially for low-dollar-value disputes. For example, JAMS Rule 17(c) allows each party to take one deposition of an opposing party or of one individual representing the opposing party; arbitrators determine the need for additional depositions. The AAA expressly allows for depositions, but only in large, complex cases. *See* AAA R L-3(f). Of course, the parties are free to engage in consensual deposition discovery without the aid of the arbitrator or the need to resort to an institutional rule.

Many arbitration institutions now contemplate electronic discovery, or e-discovery, and provide arbitrators with guidance on how to manage that process. The Chairperson may be called upon to set limits on e-discovery, as too wide a scope can overwhelm the process and remove any efficiencies otherwise expected. The Chair has to make tough calls and balance the needs of the parties against the promise of arbitration as speedy and cost-effective.

Forum rules also authorize arbitrators to impose sanctions on parties for non-compliance with discovery orders (*see, e.g.,* AAA R-23; JAMS R. 29), and courts uphold those sanctions. *See, e.g., First Pres. Capital, Inc. v. Smith Barney, Harris Upham*

& Co., 939 F. Supp. 1559, 1565 (S.D. Fla. 1996) ("Parties in arbitration must understand that willful violations of the discovery process can have severe consequences."); *Superadio Ltd. P'ship v. Winstar Radio Prods., LLC*, 844 N.E.2d 246, 253 (Mass. 2006) ("To give arbitrators control over discovery and discovery disputes without the authority to impose monetary sanctions for discovery violations and noncompliance with appropriate discovery orders, would impede the arbitrators' ability to adjudicate claims effectively in the manner contemplated by the arbitration process.").

Discovery From Non-Parties. Discovery from non-parties in arbitration provides different challenges than from parties. Because arbitrators derive their powers strictly from the parties' agreement, arbitrators have no contractual authority over third parties, who are not a party to the arbitration agreement and have not consented to the arbitrators' authority.

As a result, in arbitration, the only means to obtain information and documents from third parties is through the issuance of a subpoena. The FAA explicitly imbues arbitrators (but not attorneys) with subpoena power in arbitration, though the circuits are split as to how far that subpoena power goes. Section 7 provides:

> The arbitrators ... may summon in writing any person to attend before them or any of them as a witness and in a proper case bring with him or them any book, record, document, or paper which may be deemed material as evidence in the case.

9 U.S.C. §7. The permissible fees and methods of service are the same as those for court subpoenas under the Federal Rules of Civil Procedure. Additionally, some arbitration institutions permit arbitrators to issue third-party subpoenas. *See, e.g.,* FINRA R. 12512.

Does section 7 authorize arbitrators to issue a subpoena *duces tecum* (subpoena to produce documents pre-hearing) or just for a subpoena *ad testificandum* (to testify before the arbitrators at the hearing itself and bring documents)? Consider the case below, authored by Justice Alito when he was a judge on the Third Circuit.

Hay Group, Inc. v. E.B.S. Acquisition Corp.
360 F.3d 404 (3d Cir. 2004)

ALITO, CIRCUIT JUDGE.

PriceWaterhouseCoopers ("PwC") and E.B.S., non-parties to an arbitration, seek to avoid compliance with an arbitration panel's subpoena requiring them to turn over documents prior to the panel's hearing. The District Court enforced the subpoena. We reverse.

Hay Group ("Hay") is a management consulting firm. David A. Hoffrichter left Hay's employment and joined PwC in September 1999. In early 2002, PwC sold the division employing Hoffrichter to E.B.S. Hoffrichter's separation agreement from Hay contained a clause that forbade him from soliciting any of Hay's employees or clients for one year. The agreement further provided for arbitration to resolve any dispute arising under the agreement. In February 2000, Hay commenced such an arbitration proceeding in Philadelphia, Pennsylvania, against Hoffrichter, claiming that he had violated the non-solicitation clause.

In an attempt to obtain information for the arbitration, Hay served subpoenas for documents on E.B.S. at its Pittsburgh office and on PwC at its Philadelphia office. Hay sought to have the documents produced prior to the panel's arbitration hearing. PwC and E.B.S. objected to these subpoenas, but the arbitration panel disagreed. When PwC and E.B.S. still refused to comply with the subpoenas, Hay asked the United States District Court to enforce the subpoenas. PwC and E.B.S. again objected, claiming that the FAA did not authorize the panel to issue subpoenas to non-parties for pre-hearing document production and that the Federal Rules of Civil Procedure prohibited the District Court from enforcing a subpoena on a non-party for documents outside the Courts' territorial jurisdiction.

In November 2002, the District Court issued a decision enforcing the subpoenas and ordering the parties to resolve any remaining differences. In doing so, the District Court accepted the view of the Eighth Circuit and several district courts that the FAA authorizes arbitration panels to issue subpoenas on non-parties for pre-hearing document production. The District Court also held that even under the view of the Fourth Circuit, which permits such production only when there is a "special need," the panel's subpoenas would be valid. In addition, the District Court held that it had the power to enforce subpoenas on non-parties for document production even if the documents were located outside the territory within which the court's subpoenas could be served. PwC and E.B.S. then filed the present appeal....

In interpreting a statute, we must, of course, begin with the text.... Section 7 of the FAA ... speaks unambiguously to the issue before us. The only power conferred on arbitrators with respect to the production of documents by a non-party is the power to summon a non-party "to attend before them or any of them as a witness *and* in a proper case *to bring with him or them* any book, record, document or paper which may be deemed material as evidence in the case." The power to require a non-party "to bring" items "with him" clearly applies only to situations in which the non-party accompanies the items to the arbitration proceeding, not to situations in which the items are simply sent or brought by a courier. In addition, the use of the word "and" makes it clear that a non-party may be compelled "to bring" items "with him" only when the non-party is summoned "to attend before [the arbitrator] as a witness." Thus, Section 7's language unambiguously restricts an arbitrator's subpoena power to situations in which the non-party has been called to appear in the physical presence of the arbitrator and to hand over the documents at that time.[7]

...

---

7. Some states have recently adopted versions of the UAA which differ from the FAA. Some of these state statutes explicitly grant arbitrators the power to issue pre-hearing document production subpoenas on third parties. *See, e.g.,* 10 Del. Code §5708(a) (2003) ("The arbitrators may compel the attendance of witnesses and the production of books, records, contracts, papers, accounts, and all other documents and evidence, and shall have the power to administer oaths."); 42 Pa.C.S.A. §7309

Some courts have argued that the language of Section 7 implies the power to issue such pre-hearing subpoenas. *See In re Security Life Insurance Co. of America*, 228 F.3d 865, 870–71 (8th Cir.2000) ("We thus hold that implicit in an arbitration panel's power to subpoena relevant documents for production at a hearing is the power to order the production of relevant documents for review by a party prior to the hearing.").

We disagree with this power-by-implication analysis. By conferring the power to compel a non-party witness to bring items to an arbitration proceeding while saying nothing about the power simply to compel the production of items without summoning the custodian to testify, the FAA implicitly withholds the latter power. If the FAA had been meant to confer the latter, broader power, we believe that the drafters would have said so, and they would have then had no need to spell out the more limited power to compel a non-party witness to bring items with him to an arbitration proceeding. . . .

Since the text of Section 7 of the FAA is straightforward, we must see if the result is absurd. . . . [W]e believe that a reasonable argument can be made that a literal reading of Section 7 actually furthers arbitration's goal of resolving disputes in a timely and cost efficient manner. First, as noted above, until 1991 the Federal Rules of Civil Procedure themselves did not permit a federal court to compel pre-hearing document production by non-parties. That the federal courts were left for decades to operate with this limitation of their subpoena power strongly suggests that the result produced by interpreting Section 7 of the FAA as embodying a similar limitation is not absurd. Second, it is not absurd to read the FAA as circumscribing an arbitration panel's power to affect those who did not agree to its jurisdiction. The requirement that document production be made at an actual hearing may, in the long run, discourage the issuance of large-scale subpoenas upon non-parties. This is so because parties that consider obtaining such a subpoena will be forced to consider whether the documents are important enough to justify the time, money, and effort that the subpoenaing parties will be required to expend if an actual appearance before an arbitrator is needed. Under a system of pre-hearing document production, by contrast, there is less incentive to limit the scope of discovery and more incentive to engage in fishing expeditions that undermine some of the advantages of the supposedly shorter and cheaper system of arbitration. *See COMSAT Corp. v. Natl. Science Foundation*, 190 F.3d at 269 (4th Cir.1999) ("The rationale for constraining an arbitrator's subpoena power is clear. Parties to a private arbitration agreement forego certain procedural rights attendant to formal litigation in return for a more efficient and cost-effective

---

("The arbitrators may issue subpoenas in the form prescribed by general rules for the attendance of witnesses and for the production of books, records, documents and other evidence.") The language of these state statutes clearly shows how a law can give authority to an arbitrator to issue pre-hearing document-production orders on third parties.

resolution of their dispute. A hallmark of arbitration—and a necessary precursor to its efficient operation—is a limited discovery process.")....

We have carefully considered but must respectfully disagree with the Eighth Circuit's holding in *Security Life* that Section 7 authorizes arbitrators to issue pre-hearing document-production subpoenas on non-parties. In *Security Life*, the Eighth Circuit reasoned that the "the interest in efficiency is furthered by permitting a party to review and digest relevant documentary evidence prior to the arbitration hearing." 228 F.3d at 870. In our view, however, this policy argument cannot supersede the statutory text.

In sum, we hold that the FAA did not authorize the panel to issue a pre-hearing discovery subpoena to PwC and E.B.S. We further reject any "special needs exception" to this rule. If Hay wants to access the documents, the panel must subpoena PwC and E.B.S. to appear before it and bring the documents with them.

[The court then rejects PwC's additional argument that the subpoenas at issue in this case were improper "because they sought the production of documents that were located outside the territorial jurisdiction of the District Court."]

For the reasons set out above, the order of the District Court is reversed.

CHERTOFF, CIRCUIT JUDGE, concurring:

I join Judge Alito's opinion in full. But I appreciate the reason that a number of courts have been motivated to read a pre-hearing discovery power into the arbitration rules. I write separately to observe that our opinion does not leave arbitrators powerless to require advance production of documents when necessary to allow fair and efficient proceedings.

Under section 7 of the FAA, arbitrators have the power to compel a third-party witness to appear with documents before a single arbitrator, who can then adjourn the proceedings. This gives the arbitration panel the effective ability to require delivery of documents from a third-party in advance, notwithstanding the limitations of section 7 of the FAA. In many instances, of course, the inconvenience of making such a personal appearance may well prompt the witness to deliver the documents and waive presence.

To be sure, this procedure requires the arbitrators to decide that they are prepared to suffer some inconvenience of their own in order to mandate what is, in reality, an advance production of documents. But that is not necessarily a bad thing, since it will induce the arbitrators and parties to weigh whether advance production is really needed. And the availability of this procedure within the existing statutory language should satisfy the desire that there be some mechanism "to compel pre-arbitration discovery upon a showing of special need or hardship." *COMSAT Corp. v. Nat'l Sci. Found.*, 190 F.3d 269 (4th Cir.1999).

a. Comments and Questions

Circuit split. Since *Hay Group*, other circuits have agreed with the Third Circuit (and the Fourth Circuit in *COMSAT Corp. v. Nat'l Sci. Found.*, 190 F.3d 269 (4th Cir.1999)) that the FAA does not empower arbitrators to issue a subpoena *duces tecum* to a third-party witness for documents only without requiring in-person attendance.

See Life Receivables Trust v. Syndicate 102 at Lloyd's of London, 549 F.3d 210 (2d Cir. 2008) (reversing enforcement of discovery subpoena to non-parties for production of documents in an arbitration); *CVS Health Corp. v. Vividus*, LLC, 878 F.3d 703, 708 (9th Cir. 2017). These circuits all disagreed with the opinion of the Eighth Circuit as cited in *Hay Group*, further contributing to the circuit split. Which interpretation of the FAA do you think is better?

What about state law? As noted in footnote 7 in *Hay Group*, some state arbitration statutes provide arbitrators and/or attorneys with subpoena power in arbitration. *See* RUAA § 17 (giving arbitrators subpoena power over third parties for discovery matters); N.Y. CPLR § 7505 (empowering arbitrators and any attorney of record in the arbitration proceeding to issue subpoenas). To what extent might the FAA preempt these state statutes?

6. Dispositive Motions

As illustrated by the case below, courts permit arbitrators to grant dispositive motions in arbitration. *See also* RUAA § 15(b) (authorizing arbitrators to summarily dismiss claims if opposing party given notice and opportunity to respond). The AAA Commercial Rules used to be silent with respect to dispositive motions, and arbitrators discouraged them. Rule 33, revised in 2013, now expressly addresses them: "The arbitrator may allow the filing of and make rulings upon a dispositive motion only if the arbitrator determines that the moving party has shown that the motion is likely to succeed and dispose of or narrow the issues in the case." In addition, the AAA's preliminary hearing checklist mentions pre-hearing procedures to dismiss part or all of claims. Other forums may not permit dispositive motions. After reading the cases below, consider the advantages and disadvantages of permitting dispositive motions in arbitration.

Vento v. Quick & Reilly, Inc.

128 Fed. Appx. 719 (10th Cir. 2005)

SEYMOUR, CIRCUIT JUDGE.

Plaintiff Joseph A. Vento appeals from a district court order denying his motion to vacate an unfavorable decision issued by an arbitration panel for the National Association of Securities Dealers, Inc. (NASD). Although Mr. Vento raised several subsections of the statute governing judicial review of arbitration, see 9 U.S.C. § 10(a)(1)–(4), his objections related primarily to the arbitration panel's refusal to hold a hearing and dismissal of his action on the pleadings. The district court granted summary judgment for Defendant Quick & Reilly, Inc. (Q&R)....

Mr. Vento had a securities account with Q&R that became the subject of garnishment proceedings relating to a state court judgment obtained against him in Colorado. Q&R responded to a writ of garnishment by affirming that it held for Mr. Vento $108,074.42 in a money market fund and $1,300,000 in treasury bills. Thereafter, Q&R received an order directing it to pay $93,847.25 to the court clerk, who was to turn the sum over to the party collecting the judgment against Mr. Vento. After Q&R

complied, Mr. Vento filed a claim with the NASD arbitration panel contending Q&R violated various legal duties when it revealed his assets and turned them over to the state court clerk.

Mr. Vento claimed that Q&R improperly complied with procedure appropriate in cases where "the garnishee is indebted to the judgment debtor," Colo. R. Civ. P. 103, §2(g)(1), whereas the proper procedure, he asserted, was for the court to "order the garnishee to deliver such property to the sheriff to be sold as upon execution," with the proceeds applied to the judgment debt and any surplus returned to Mr. Vento, because Q&R "possess[ed] or control[led] intangible personal property or personal property capable of manual delivery owned by the judgment debtor." Q&R moved to dismiss the arbitration action, asserting that it had followed a facially valid order and that "[i]f, in fact, there were procedural irregularities in the processing of the garnishment, Mr. Vento should have brought them to the attention of the court." In response, Mr. Vento reasserted his position that the order Q&R followed was invalid under Rule 103, but did not claim Q&R had any duty to challenge the garnishment on this basis on his behalf. He also contended "[t]here is no provision in the Code of arbitration Procedure for a motion to dismiss comparable to the one filed by Q&R."

After the motion to dismiss was set for hearing, Mr. Vento submitted an "Advisement" stating he would not attend the hearing but would "continue[ ] to advocate and rely upon" his previously filed response to the motion. On the hearing date, the arbitration panel "f[ound] itself in need of additional information, and request[ed] an additional brief from each of the parties," on such matters as Q&R's legal duty upon receipt of the garnishment order to investigate its validity, and whether Mr. Vento did anything to challenge the garnishment order himself. The panel noted Mr. Vento's decision to forego attendance at the hearing on the motion to dismiss and "strongly recommend[ed] that [he] secure the advice and services of an attorney experienced in matters involving NASD arbitration." Mr. Vento filed a pro se brief in response to the order.

The arbitration panel saw the dispute framed by the parties as purely legal, concerning the respective duties of a broker-dealer and its client when faced with a garnishment order ... The panel held it was "compelled to find in favor of Q&R as a matter of law," and dismissed the case with prejudice pursuant to NASD Code of Arbitration Rule 10305.[2]

[T]he circumstances presented here did not warrant any interference with the arbitration panel's decision under the "highly deferential standard" that federal courts must employ in this area. *Bowen*, 254 F.3d at 932 (noting standard governing judicial

---

2. NASD Code of Arbitration Rule 10305 provides: (a) At any time during the course of an arbitration, the arbitrators may either upon their own initiative or at the request of a party, dismiss the proceeding and refer the parties to their judicial remedies, or to any dispute resolution forum agreed to by the parties, without prejudice to any claims or defenses available to any party. (b) The arbitrators may dismiss a claim, defense, or proceeding with prejudice as a sanction for willful and intentional material failure to comply with an order of the arbitrator(s) if lesser sanctions have proven ineffective. (c) The arbitrators shall at the joint request of all parties dismiss the proceedings.

review of arbitration decisions is "among the narrowest known to law." Mr. Vento's primary objection, regarding the lack of authorization for a dismissal on the pleadings under Rule 10305, was explicitly rejected by this court in *Sheldon v. Vermonty*, 269 F.3d 1202 (10th Cir. 2001): Although NASD's procedural rules do not specifically address whether an arbitration panel has the authority to dismiss facially deficient claims with prejudice based solely on the pleadings, there is no express prohibition against such a procedure. In addition, NASD's procedural rules expressly provide that "[t]he arbitrator(s) shall be empowered to award any relief that would be available in a court of law." NASD Manual § 10214.

Logically, this broad grant of authority should include the authority to dismiss facially deficient claims with prejudice, and we hold that a NASD arbitration panel has full authority to grant a pre-hearing motion to dismiss with prejudice based solely on the parties' pleadings so long as the dismissal does not deny a party fundamental fairness.

Like the plaintiff in *Sheldon*, Mr. Vento "was provided with a fundamentally fair arbitration proceeding in that he was provided with the opportunity to fully brief and argue the motion[ ] to dismiss." Given that his "claims [were] facially deficient and [he] therefore ha[d] no relevant or material evidence to present at an evidentiary hearing, the arbitration panel ha[d] full authority to dismiss the claims without ... holding an evidentiary hearing."

Mr. Vento's attempts to avoid the rule of *Sheldon* are plainly meritless. He argues that Q&R's motion to dismiss "was not based on the parties' pleadings as required by [*Sheldon*]," because it rested on the assertion "that Q&R followed an order by a court clerk." But the latter point was not beyond the scope of Mr. Vento's arbitration claims; it was essential to them. The alleged misconduct of Q&R *consisted in* its compliance with the garnishment writ and ensuing order. When the arbitration panel concluded that such compliance was proper as a matter of law, dismissal on the pleadings was precisely the appropriate procedural disposition.

Mr. Vento contends the panel's decision was not on the pleadings as in *Sheldon* because the panel's rationale rested on a legal ground omitted from Q&Rs' motion to dismiss. This argument is unavailing. Although Mr. Vento acknowledges the motion asserted Q&R acted properly in complying with the garnishment order because Mr. Vento had not challenged it, he insists the panel's rationale—that it was his, not Q&R's, duty to challenge the order—reflects a distinct legal proposition. But the latter is obviously inherent in (if not a mere paraphrase of) the defense advanced by Q&R in its motion and, in any event, the panel's decision clearly encompassed both: "The duty to timely file a motion to quash ... an improper garnishment order properly falls on the shoulders of the person garnished.... [E]xpending attorney's fees and costs to oppose the garnishment by filing a motion to quash on his behalf ... is not within the scope of a broker-dealer's fiduciary duty to its customer." The whole point of holding that Q&R was not duty-bound to oppose the garnishment order is to explain why it acted properly in complying with it.

Mr. Vento's accusation of bias on the part of the arbitration panel is equally meritless. The panel's recommendation that Mr. Vento consult with an attorney experienced in NASD arbitration was just prudent advice. There is nothing in the record to suggest any basis for questioning the panel's impartiality.

As for Mr. Vento's challenge to the validity of the garnishment order under specific provisions of state procedural law, the arbitration panel accepted that premise for purposes of its analysis and therefore cannot be said to have disregarded that law. As for the legal point that was ultimately dispositive of the case, regarding a broker-dealer's duty to challenge garnishment process on behalf of a client, the panel asked Mr. Vento to cite the legal precedent supporting his claim to which he responded only that he "ha[d] researched ... whether the broker dealer is obligated to investigate the validity of that court order or may it merely accept the order as written, and [had] found no legal precedents about the matter." His appellate briefing is likewise deficient.

Fed. R. Civ. P. 12 and 56 is specious. The civil rules apply in arbitration cases "to the extent that matters of procedure are not provided for in [the federal arbitration] statutes." Fed.R.Civ.P. 81(a)(3). Because the arbitration statutes do not provide procedures to displace Rules 12 and 56 and M r. Vento offers no "reason why normal procedures should be subverted," the district court properly adhered to these rules. The judgment of the district court is affirmed. Q&R's motion for sanctions is granted....

a. Comments and Questions

Vento involved an arbitration before the NASD, now known as FINRA. In the years after *Vento*, other courts similarly upheld an NASD arbitrator's dismissal of a claim before the merits hearing. *See, e.g., Reinglass v. Morgan Stanley Dean Witter, Inc.,* 2006-Ohio-1542, ¶ 17 (imposing Fed. R. Civ. P. 9(b) pleading requirements on NASD statement of claim and stating "where a party's claims are facially deficient and the party therefore has no relevant or material evidence to present at an evidentiary hearing, an arbitration panel may dismiss the claims without permitting discovery or holding an evidentiary hearing"). *But see Pennington v. Cuna Brokerage Sec., Inc.,* 5 So. 3d 172, 177 (La. App. 1 Cir. 2008) (vacating an NASD award on the grounds that the arbitrators' dismissal of the claimant's claims at a telephonic pre-hearing conference before the merits hearing and without giving the claimant an opportunity to amend his claims denied the claimant a fundamentally fair hearing). Subsequent to these cases, FINRA amended its Code of Arbitration to sharply limit the grounds on which an arbitrator can grant a motion to dismiss a FINRA arbitration before the merits hearing. *See* FINRA R. 12504.

Pleading requirements? Should arbitrators impose pleading requirements on arbitration statements of claim similar to those in the rules of civil procedure? Should arbitrators be able to dismiss an arbitration before a merits hearing? If so, on what grounds? What policy goals might this kind of dismissal advance?

Ethical Consideration. Unlike judges, arbitrators are usually paid by the hour. If arbitrators grant motions to dismiss, they end the case early and effectively act against their own interests. Do you see any way to alleviate the underlying economic motivations that might consciously or unconsciously create a bias in favor of denying dispositive motions?

7. The Hearing

The merits hearing is the stage where parties may present testimony and evidence to the arbitrator(s) in order to arrive at a (nearly always final) decision that is binding on the parties. At the time the hearing begins, the arbitrators have: (1) read the Demand and Answer; (2) had a preliminary telephonic hearing primarily for administrative purposes; and (3) possibly read pre-hearing briefs. Thus, the parties and/or their representatives have had little in-person interaction with their decision-makers before the merits hearing begins.

An arbitration hearing in some ways is like a judicial trial, but there is no jury, and the rules of civil procedure and evidence do not strictly apply. Depending on the size and complexity of the case, hearings may extend to several days, weeks or, in rare cases, months. Although a hearing usually occurs on sequential days (other than weekend days), some hearings occur over a matter of months (or years) because the parties could not complete the hearing and must reconvene at a mutually convenient time in the future. Hearings may involve a number of separate claims or disputes. In some cases, the parties may bifurcate the hearing and focus on specific items at specific times. For example, the parties may hold a hearing on liability and await a ruling on liability before having a hearing on damages, if necessary.

In addition, an arbitration hearing takes place in whatever physical location is available: a law office, a hotel conference room, or on business premises — often there is not a dedicated location like a courtroom. The hearing is conducted around a meeting table with the arbitrators at one end — a less formal atmosphere than the typical courtroom trial. The witness usually, but not always, sits directly across from the arbitrators, and the parties sit on either side of the table. Some cases require large facility space, particularly in cases involving multiple parties, in-house counsel, outside counsel, expert witnesses, arbitrators, and other support personnel such as paralegals, translators, and court reporters. Geographically, most forums allow the parties to agree on a locale; if they cannot agree, the forum will set the locale as the place with the most connection to the dispute and/or the parties. *See, e.g.,* AAA R-11. *Ex parte* contacts with the arbitrators are forbidden (with limited exceptions for party arbitrators). Though lawyers are not required, most parties in a commercial case of any significant value are represented in an arbitration.

Arbitrators can conduct the hearing in-person, telephonically, via video conferencing technology, online, or on the papers. Some cases involve a combination of these technologies, particularly when an in-person hearing is scheduled, but some witnesses must appear via telephone or by video conference. In addition, the arbitrator has discretion to conduct a hearing in as expeditious and cost-effective a manner as is feasible. *See* AAA R-32(b). To that end, courts have approved of "paper" hearings (called "desk arbitration" at AAA and "simplified arbitration" at FINRA) as sufficient to provide a fundamentally fair process under the FAA. *See, e.g., FDIC v. Air Fla. Sys., Inc.,* 822 F.2d 833, 842 (9th Cir. 1987); *In the Matter of the Arbitration between Intercarbon Bermuda, Ltd. and Caltex Trading and Transport Corp.,* 146 F.R.D. 64, 74 (S.D.N.Y. 1993); *see also Gray Panthers v. Schweiker,* 652 F.2d 146, 168 n.3 (D.C. Cir. 1980) ("A 'hearing' means *any* confrontation, oral or otherwise, between an affected individual and an agency decisionmaker sufficient to allow the individual to present his case in a meaningful manner. Hearings may take many forms, including a 'formal,' trial-type proceeding, an 'informal discuss[ion]' ... or a 'paper hearing,' without any opportunity for oral exchange"). That being said, most arbitrations resolve via an in-person hearing.

Phases of the hearing. A typical merits hearing proceeds in the following phases:

a. *Arbitrator's Opening.* Typically the Chair opens the hearing by:

- Introducing the panel,
- Identifying the parties in the room and the case file name and number (in case an audio recording becomes separated from the case file),
- Repeating and updating any arbitrator disclosures,
- Addressing any preliminary and/or administrative matters before the attorneys' opening statements, such as potential evidentiary stipulations, outstanding discovery issues, pending subpoenas, separating witnesses, or scheduling telephonic testimony of out-of-town witnesses, if applicable, and
- Administering an oath to any party or witness present who will be testifying at the hearing.

b. *Parties' opening statements.* Claimant opens first, then Respondent opens.

c. *Presentation of claimant's and respondent's case.* Each party presents witness testimony—either live, in-person or telephonic, testimony, or via affidavit. Adverse parties may cross-examine witnesses. Parties also offer documents into evidence, possibly via a joint exhibit binder agreed to in advance by the parties. The Chair usually handles lawyers' evidentiary objections, keeping in mind that the rules of evidence do not govern the hearing. Arbitrators are permitted to ask witnesses questions, but should reserve those questions to the end of that witness' testimony.

d. *Presentation of rebuttal case, if any.*

e. *Closing statements.* Typically, respondent delivers the closing statement first, as the claimant can (and almost always does) reserve its entire closing for rebuttal.

f. *Chair closes hearing.* The Chair should ask all parties to affirm that they have had a full and fair opportunity to be heard, and have no further evidence to present. The Chair can keep the record open pending receipt of post-hearing briefs, if parties requested to submit them and the panel agreed.

With respect to evidence, arbitrators have wide latitude in conducting an arbitration subject to the parties' agreement and to determine what evidence should be considered. *See* RUAA § 15(a). Among the very few grounds for vacating an arbitration award is that the arbitrators refused to hear "evidence pertinent and material to the controversy...." FAA, § 10(a)(3). The response of arbitrators, and arbitral organizations, is entirely predictable: the exclusionary rules of the law of evidence are ignored, and virtually everything is admitted into evidence. Additional guidance for arbitration advocates at the merits hearing is addressed in **Chapter 7.**

If a respondent does not appear or participate in the hearing, the claimant is still put to its proof, and cannot obtain a default award without such proof. The arbitration "may proceed in the absence of any party who, after due notice, fails to attend or obtain a postponement." AAA R-31. In this way, arbitration practice is different from litigation practice, which does allow for default rulings.

Confidentiality in Arbitration. It is a common myth that arbitrations are confidential. While arbitrations are *private* (as opposed to public) and the forum can restrict access to the hearing room, *see, e.g.,* AAA R-25, no state or federal law provides confidentiality protection for arbitration communications (unlike for mediation). Forum rules usually require the arbitrator and forum staff to keep arbitration proceedings confidential, but, absent a specific agreement among parties or a case-specific protective order, parties and their agents have no obligation of confidentiality. If requested by the parties, arbitrators typically will sign a protective order governing the case, ensuring confidentiality and protection of proprietary information or trade secrets going forward. *See* AAA R-23(a) (explicitly authorizing arbitrators to sign confidentiality orders). In many cases, the arbitration agreement includes a confidentiality provision, and the parties' duty of confidentiality flows from their own agreement, not from outside law.

8. Post-Hearing Submissions

This stage of the process provides parties with an opportunity to submit additional documentation after the merits hearing is over but before the arbitrators close the record, if allowed or requested by the arbitrator. Under AAA R-35(c), arbitrators can direct post-hearing submissions. If arbitrators are unsure about applicable legal rules, or want the parties to summarize lengthy testimony for them, they may request post-hearing briefs. Post-hearing briefs can range in length; the more money at stake, the longer and more complex these submissions tend to be. To prevent unnecessarily detailed post-hearing submissions, arbitrators can and should direct the parties to focus on the issues that lie at the core of the dispute.

If this stage is necessary, it usually occurs shortly after the hearing closes. The arbitrators keep the record open to receive these submissions until they deliberate and issue an award.

9. Deliberation

If only one arbitrator is deciding a case, then that sole arbitrator presumably considers all of the testimonial and documentary evidence and legal argument, and renders a decision. If a panel has more than one arbitrator, the panel deliberates outside the presence of the parties. Even if the hearing is recorded or transcribed, the panel deliberations are usually not recorded. If the panel closes the record immediately at the close of the hearing, the arbitrators may stay in the room and deliberate after everyone else has left the hearing room. If the record remains open pending post-hearing submissions, the arbitrators will get together and deliberate either in person or telephonically as soon as possible after receipt and review of final submissions.

How arbitrators deliberate remains a mystery to many. At least theoretically, they fully consider all evidence presented in light of the legal and factual arguments, and reason through a decision that considers (and does not disregard) applicable law, as well as achieves equity for all. Practically speaking, like jurors, panelists bring to the deliberation very different backgrounds and perspectives on the same facts and issues. Unlike jurors, they may not receive neutral "instructions" on the applicable legal rules; rather, they rely on the parties' advocacy-based presentations of applicable law. They may or may not be able to revisit testimony via daily transcripts, depending on the value of the case and the resources the parties choose to devote to stenographic transcription of the hearing.

Deliberations leading to an award can also resemble a form of negotiation, and arbitrators may bring different bargaining styles and strategies to the table. Some — especially those who are identified as the chair or head of the panel — may feel a need to play a facilitative (mediator) role. Because some arbitrators are lawyers and others not, the non-lawyer arbitrators may choose to defer to the lawyer-arbitrators on issues of law. By contrast, attorney arbitrators may defer to industry arbitrators on issues of cultural norms or business expectations within an industry.

Some theorize that arbitration awards are more a product of compromise — hence the metaphor that arbitrators, like King Solomon in the bible story, "split the baby." However, empirical evidence has not supported that theory. *See, e.g.,* AAA White Paper, *AAA®/ICDR® Awards Do Not Split the Baby: Countering Counsel Perception in Commercial B2B Arbitration Cases* (2016) (finding arbitrators issued decisions "clearly in favor of one party" in more than 93 percent of the cases surveyed); Securities Arbitration Alert 2016–17 (July 20, 2016) (finding similar results in FINRA arbitration awards).

Other empirical evidence regarding arbitrator decision-making suggests that arbitrators have the same capacity to decide as judges. *See* Rebecca K. Helm, Andrew J. Wistrich, and Jeffrey J. Rachlinski, *Are Arbitrators Human?,* 13 J. Emp. St. 666 (2016) (reporting that "arbitrators perform about the same as judges in experiments designed to detect the presence of common cognitive errors and excessive reliance on intuition"); *see also* Edna Sussman, *Arbitrator Decision-Making: Unconscious Psychological Influences and What You Can Do About Them*, 24 Am. Rev. Int'l. Arb. 487, 490 (2013) (reporting on results of survey examining arbitrators' unconscious intuitive processes in their decision-making and suggesting ways "to foster a more robust deliberative overlay and improve the quality of decisions by arbitrators").

10. Award

The arbitrator closes the record regarding the case and issues a decision, inclusive of an award. For a panel of more than one arbitrator, only a majority of arbitrators need be in favor of the award. *See, e.g.,* AAA R-44.

Time of award. Though the FAA sets no time limit, most arbitration institutions designate a time limit for issuing an award measured from when the arbitrators close the record. A common time limit is 30 calendar days from the closing of the hearing. *See* AAA R-45.

Form of Award. The FAA does not require the award to be in writing, though most arbitration institutions require it to be in writing and signed by the arbitrators. *See, e.g.,* AAA R-46(a) ("Any award shall be in writing and signed by a majority of the arbitrators. It shall be executed in the form and manner required by law."). Each institution has its own requirements for other components of the award to be included, such as whether the award identifies the parties, the hearing dates, the claims and defenses, and the allocation of forum costs and fees. Some forums use templates for the form of award; other forums allow the arbitrator to create the form.

Scope of award. At a minimum, the award should include the relief awarded, including what compensatory damages are awarded, and whether pre- or post-award interest, attorney's fees and/or punitive damages are included.

Partial, Interim or Final Award? "Arbitrators should strive to ensure that a final award: (1) clearly determines every issue submitted and does not decide issues that were not submitted; (2) is timely issued; and (3) contains full and complete relief as authorized by the arbitration agreement and the applicable law and rules." The College of Commercial Arbitrators, *Awards: Getting An Arbitration Award That Meets The Needs of The Parties* (2015).

While most awards are "final" in that they conclusively resolve all issues the parties submitted to the arbitrators, some awards dispose of only some of the outstanding issues. If a panel issues either a "partial final award" that resolves only some of the issues in dispute, or an "interim award" that preliminarily determines some issues (such as when liability and damages are bifurcated), legal consequences can flow that might frustrate the parties' intent. For example, a "partial final award" may be subject to confirmation or vacatur motions and may trigger the doctrine of *functus officio,* which strips the arbitrators' authority to decide any further issues. Under the doctrine of *functus officio,* once an arbitrator has issued a final award, the arbitrator's power to act further in the case ceases. (For more on this doctrine, see **Chapter 9.**) Although issuing an interim award avoids the application of the *functus officio* doctrine, an interim award still may be subject to a motion to vacate, thus further delaying a final resolution.

Reasoned award. Unless mandated by the parties' agreement or a forum rule, arbitrators have discretion as to whether the award contains any explanation. The FAA does not require the award to include reasons or an explanation. Most forums do not require arbitrators to include reasons either, unless the parties jointly request an explanation or the arbitrators decide to include one. *See, e.g.,* AAA R-46(b).

As a result, some awards are barebones, identifying the relief granted without any reasons for the outcome. At the other extreme, in large, complex commercial cases, arbitrators may issue an award that includes detailed Findings of Fact and Conclusions of Law. In between is the "reasoned award," which might include a brief explanation for the outcome, but does not resemble a lengthy judicial opinion. What exactly is a reasoned award? Here is one definition offered by the Court of Appeals for the Second Circuit:

> We agree with our sister Circuits, and hold today that a reasoned award is something more than a line or two of unexplained conclusions, but something less than full findings of fact and conclusions of law on each issue raised before the panel. A reasoned award sets forth the basic reasoning of the arbitral panel on the central issue or issues raised before it. It need not delve into every argument made by the parties.

Leeward Constr. Co., Ltd. v. Am. Univ. of Antigua-College of Med., 826 F.3d 634, 640 (2d Cir. 2016). Whether an award should include reasons is a hotly debated issue. What are the pros and cons of including reasons in the award? Why might parties want an explanation as to the outcome? Why might other parties *not* want any explanation?

Modification of award. Once an award is issued, some forums permit clarification or modification of the award, but only within a short time frame. *See, e.g.,* AAA R-50 ("Within 20 calendar days after the transmittal of an award, any party, upon notice to the other parties, may request the arbitrator, through the AAA, to correct any clerical, typographical, or computational errors in the award. The arbitrator is not empowered to redetermine the merits of any claim already decided.") **Chapter 9** addresses the scope of post-award relief parties can seek from courts.

C. Remedial Powers of Arbitrator

Arbitrators have virtually unlimited power to issue any relief that is within the scope of the parties' arbitration agreement. (Whether they should or not is a separate policy question.) The FAA does not contain specific provisions listing arbitral remedial powers; however, courts have interpreted the federal policy favoring arbitration to confer upon arbitrators broad powers to fashion both legal and equitable remedies, including compensatory damages, specific performance, injunctions, and punitive damages. *See Mastrobuono v. Shearson Lehman Hutton, Inc.,* 514 U.S. 52 (1995) (ruling that arbitrators have authority to award punitive damages under the FAA and preempting New York's *Garrity* rule barring arbitrators from awarding punitive damages).

Likewise, courts construe broadly worded arbitration clauses to confer upon the arbitrator broad authority to issue a plethora of remedies, both legal and equitable. With exceptions, arbitrators may even issue some remedies a court could not.

Additionally, commercial arbitration agreements typically incorporate the rules of a particular arbitration provider, most of which confer on arbitrators broad remedial authority. For example, AAA Commercial Arbitration Rule 47(a) states: "The arbitrator may grant any remedy or relief that the arbitrator deems just and equitable and within the scope of the agreement of the parties, including, but not limited to, specific performance of a contract." Rules 47(b), (c), and (d) authorize arbitrators to issue interim, interlocutory, or partial rulings, orders, and awards; fees, expenses, and compensation; and attorney's fees and interest. JAMS, CPR, and FINRA have similarly broad rules. However, in the absence of a provision in the arbitration agreement, a forum rule, or an applicable statute, the prevailing view is that arbitrators do not have authority to award attorneys' fees to a prevailing party.

The RUAA specifically provides for broad arbitral remedial powers. *See* RUAA §21(c) ("an arbitrator may order such remedies as the arbitrator considers just and appropriate under the circumstances of the arbitration proceeding"). If an arbitrator decides to award punitive damages under Section 21(a), not only must such an award be authorized by law as if the claim were made in a civil action, but the arbitrator also must apply the same legal standards to the claim as required in a civil action and the evidence must be sufficient to justify an award of punitive damages.

In many, but not all, jurisdictions, arbitrators also have the power to impose sanctions for abusive or bad faith conduct in the arbitration. *See ReliaStar Life Ins. Co. of N.Y. v. EMC Nat. Life Co.*, 564 F.3d 81, 86 (2d Cir. 2009) (reversing order vacating award of attorney's fees as a sanction and holding that "a broad arbitration clause ... confers inherent authority on arbitrators to sanction a party that participates in the arbitration in bad faith and that such a sanction may include an award of attorney's or arbitrator's fees"). *But see Grynberg v. BP Expl. Operating Co.*, 938 N.Y.S. 2d 439 (N.Y. App. Div. 2012) (affirming vacatur of sanctions award of $3 million because it "was punitive in nature" and thus "violated public policy"). Sanctions may be monetary, or may involve making adverse inferences based on a party's improper behavior or, in extreme cases, issue preclusion sanctions.

Of course, contracts may include a detailed provision about remedies circumscribing the arbitrator's authority. For example, in "baseball arbitration," the parties limit the arbitrator to selecting either the dollar figure offered by the team or the amount demanded by the player. More troubling are "remedy-stripping" provisions in arbitration contracts that, by purported agreement, limit an arbitrator's authority to issue, and a party's right to seek, certain forms of relief, including but not limited to punitive damages or rights to attorney fees, which are otherwise available by statute or in a court of law. If egregious, courts might strike down such remedy-stripping provisions as unconscionable, against public policy, or preventing effective vindication of rights. *See* **Chapter 4.**

What policies support the broad remedial powers of arbitrators? What policies might support restricting the scope of arbitrators' authority?

D. Comments and Questions

1. As mentioned at the beginning of this chapter, and, as you might have gathered after learning about the various steps of the arbitration process, users of modern commercial arbitration in the United States have roundly criticized the increasingly litigation-like nature of the entire process. Do you agree with this critique?

Arbitration institutions have responded to this critique in a variety of ways — either by promoting ways to expedite the process or rebutting the critique with empirical evidence. For example, in 2009, the College of Commercial Arbitrators convened a national summit and developed Protocols for Expeditious, Cost-Effective Commercial Arbitration, in response to mounting concerns about the protracted nature and cost of arbitration. *See* Edna Sussman & Christi Underwood, *Time & Cost Solutions for Commercial Arbitration*, Disp. Resol. J. 23 (Feb./Apr. 2011) (highlighting the summit's recommendations and the resulting protocols). In 2017, the AAA released a "study by the economic research firm Micronomics [that] quantifies the significant time differences between litigation and AAA arbitration from initiation of a case to the final determination — and concludes that arbitration accelerates the pace of dispute resolution." *See* Roy Weinstein, Cullen Edes, Joe Hale, and Nels Pearsall, *Efficiency and Economic Benefits of Dispute Resolution through Arbitration Compared with U.S. District Court Proceedings*, http://go.adr.org/impactsofdelay.html (Mar. 2017); *see also*; Christine L. Newhall, *The AAA's War on Time and Cost*, Disp. Resol. J. 20 (Aug./Oct. 2012) (detailing the AAA's efforts to combat users' time and cost concerns).

Can you think of other possible responses to the critique? Can you think of reforms to the arbitration process that would reduce these time and cost concerns without impairing the disputants' rights to a fundamentally fair hearing?

2. While concerns remain in the "mandatory arbitration" context (see **Chapter 4**), users of business-to-business arbitration remain supportive of the process. Recent surveys reveal that corporate counsel intend to continue to use the process to resolve business disputes. *See* Thomas Stipanowich and J. Ryan Lamare, *Living with ADR: Evolving Perceptions and Use of Mediation, Arbitration and Conflict Management in Fortune 1000 Corporations*, 19 Harv. Negot. L. Rev. 1, 49 (2014) (reporting that half of survey respondents indicated their company was likely or very likely to use commercial arbitration for company disputes in the future). If you were an in-house counsel at a company, would you recommend that the company submit to arbitration of commercial disputes with other entities? Why or why not? What about for employment disputes with company employees?

Chapter 6

The Arbitration Agreement

A. Introduction

As we learned in **Chapter 2**, the Federal Arbitration Act requires courts to enforce a *written* arbitration agreement. And, as we learned in **Chapter 4**, the arbitrators derive all of their authority over the disputants from the written arbitration agreement. The arbitration agreement thus sets the stage for all that follows in the arbitration process.

This chapter focuses on practical aspects of the written agreement to arbitrate, including its components, functions, and variations. The chapter also provides useful practice tips on how to draft an enforceable and effective agreement to arbitrate a dispute and concludes with a drafting exercise for students.

Before turning to the actual drafting process, however, it is critical to understand *why* a lawyer (or client) would be in the position of drafting an arbitration agreement. If drafting takes place *after* a dispute has arisen, then the dispute triggered the parties to turn to arbitration as the dispute resolution mechanism. If drafting takes place *before* a dispute has arisen, something else must have prompted the drafter(s) to consider arbitration as a means of resolving a future dispute that might arise out of the underlying transaction. To better understand what might have triggered the parties' decision to draft an arbitration agreement, consider the following questions:

- Why might arbitration be better for the parties than litigation?
- What kinds of disputes are appropriate to be resolved in arbitration?
- When should parties enter into arbitration agreements: before a dispute arises or afterward?
- Which parts of the arbitration process, if any, should be addressed in the arbitration agreement?
- Are the parties of equal bargaining power and negotiating this agreement?
- Is a party presenting the agreement as a take-it-or-leave-it contract of adhesion?

B. Components of an Arbitration Agreement

Parties often enter into an arbitration agreement before a dispute arises (pre-dispute arbitration agreement or PDAA). Consider the following typical pre-dispute arbitration agreement in a commercial contract:

> Any controversy or claim arising out of or relating to this contract, or the breach thereof, shall be settled by arbitration administered by the American Arbitration Association in accordance with its Commercial Arbitration Rules, and judgment on the award rendered by the arbitrator(s) may be entered in any court having jurisdiction thereof.

Though only 52 words in length, the clause above serves several key functions. Before reading ahead, can you think what those functions might be?

Agreement. At its core, the clause functions as each signatory's consent in writing to arbitrate disputes within its scope.

Scope. The arbitration agreement is the starting point for determining whether a particular dispute is covered by the agreement. Thus, the language should clearly designate what types of disputes are included within its scope. Does it cover claims alleging breach of contract only, or does it cover disputes alleging other causes of action? Does this arbitration agreement delegate arbitrability disputes to the arbitrator? Ambiguous language can leave these questions unsettled, which means a court might have to get involved to resolve them. When deciding whether a particular dispute falls within the scope of an arbitration agreement, courts apply common law principles governing the interpretation of contracts.

Forum selection. Contracting parties should designate a particular arbitration institution to administer the arbitration. Designating a forum with overly unfair arbitration procedures or one that no longer exists can have severe consequences for the parties, including non-enforceability of the arbitration agreement. *See* Chapter 2.

Why did the parties above select the AAA as the arbitration forum? How is the AAA different from other arbitration institutions? By examining their respective websites, you can infer some key differences among them. For example, JAMS (www.jamsadr.com) offers strong administrative support, while CPR Institute for Dispute Resolution (www.cpradr.org) offers very limited administrative support, instead promoting a party-administered process. AAA's commercial arbitration process (www.adr.org) falls somewhere in between, offering some support according to the parties' specific needs.

Procedural rule selection. Separate and apart from forum selection, the arbitration agreement should also designate which set of rules within the forum the parties agree to use, as several forums offer many different kinds of rules. For example, AAA has different rules for commercial, construction, and consumer disputes. If rules are designated, parties will have fewer disputes about the rules and procedures that apply. In addition, the parties might supplement or supersede certain forum rules that might not be desirable for them, such as the rules governing arbitrator selection, or location of a hearing.

The default rules for a commercial arbitration are found, in order of priority, in the agreement of the parties, the rules of the administering organization (if any), and the discretion of the arbitrator(s). The AAA Commercial Arbitration Rules for administered arbitration are available at https://www.adr.org/sites/default/files/Commercial%20Rules.pdf, and the parallel CPR Rules are available at https://www.cpradr.org/resource-center/rules/arbitration/administered-arbitration-rules.

Choice of Law. As mentioned in Chapter 2, drafters should consider whether to include a choice of law clause, designating a particular state's substantive law to govern the arbitration agreement. Choice of law clauses can avoid expensive and time-consuming arguments with adverse parties about which law an arbitrator should apply to the construction and interpretation of the respective obligations arising under the agreement to arbitrate. If the underlying contract includes a general choice of law clause, does it/should it govern the arbitration proceeding? Recall the legal ramifications for such a clause from Chapter 2.

Post-award enforcement. The final phrase of the clause submits the parties to the jurisdiction of a court for post-award proceedings, and it signals the parties' consent that the award is final and binding.

Other issues contracting parties should consider when drafting their arbitration agreements include:

- Should the clause specify only arbitration—which yields a binding decision—or also provide an opportunity for non-binding negotiation or mediation as steps in the process (also known as a multistep or stepped dispute resolution clause)?
- Should the parties incorporate a forum's procedures for large or complex disputes in the event the parties end up in a complicated case?
- Conversely, should the parties incorporate expedited procedures for smaller, simpler claims?
- Without knowing the nature of the dispute that might arise, should the parties designate specialized rules for disputes in a specialized subject matter area, such as construction, intellectual property, healthcare, or employment?
- Should the agreement include language barring the parties from bringing claims collectively or as a class (a class action waiver)?
- Should the agreement include a delegation clause, delegating to the arbitrators the power to decide questions of arbitrability? Recall from Chapter 3 the amount of power given to arbitrators when the delegation clause is part of the arbitration agreement.

By thinking about these issues when drafting a contract rather than after a dispute has arisen, the parties can control aspects of the arbitration process to a far greater degree than is true of litigation.

The Drafting Process. Lawyers who need to draft contracts, wills, or other documents do not begin by writing on a blank screen or page. Rather, they begin with existing forms and adjust them to suit the particular circumstances. Often this amounts to little more than filling in the blanks for the few negotiated terms in a form transaction.

A good place to start when drafting an arbitration agreement is the website of one of the numerous arbitration institutions. For example, the AAA suggestions for drafting arbitration provisions, excerpted below, address most, if not all, of the issues that require attention, particularly for domestic commercial arbitration. The AAA provisions are time-tested and should not be changed lightly.

Other prominent commercial arbitration forums publish similar guides, which can be found on their respective websites. *See, e.g.,* JAMS Clause Workbook, A Guide to Drafting Dispute Resolution Clauses for Commercial Contracts (Apr. 2015), *available at* https://www.jamsadr.com/clauses/; CPR Model Arbitration Clauses, *available at* https://www.cpradr.org/resource-center/model-clauses/arbitration-model-clauses; NAM, Sample ADR Contract Clauses, *available at* http://www.namadr.com/adr clauses.cfm.

For securities arbitrations, FINRA Rules mandate broker-dealer firms with an arbitration clause in their customer agreements to include prescribed language. *See* FINRA R. 2268. Broker-dealers can add to that language, as long as those additions do not limit or waive customers' rights. See FINRA R. 2268(d).

Some arbitration institutions also offer very useful clause-building tools. These are online, interactive tools that allow parties to contracts to pick and choose the features of the process they would want, and to custom design the clause easily. The tool then generates an easily adoptable word file. *See, e.g.,* AAA, ClauseBuilder®, *available at* www.clausebuilder.org; The CPR Dispute Resolution Clause Selection Tool, *available at* https://www.cpradr.org/resource-center/model-clauses/clause-drafting/clause-selection-completion-tool.

One caveat: Though the mindless use of a standardized form may disserve your client, or even amount to malpractice, crafting a customized arbitration provision also has dangers. Quality model provisions have been created by experienced experts and changed periodically to reflect experience with their use and should not be altered without good reason. Before making changes to standard arbitration provisions, such as those provided by the AAA, be certain that you understand what was intended by the drafters and that an alternative approach is beneficial for your client.

As you recall from Chapter 4, the parties have great latitude in process design in each case. Even if the parties have a standard arbitration clause, they can still customize the process to meet their particular needs. For example, parties with a standard arbitration clause could agree before or during a pre-hearing conference that an aggressive hearing schedule with a limited discovery window is appropriate. In another case with a standard clause, the parties could agree to longer timeframes and great latitude for expert witness discovery. Because the dispute resolution needs of the parties are unknown at the time of drafting a pre-dispute arbitration agreement, a best practice may be to leave some latitude for post-dispute process design.

Finally, if disputants want to enter into arbitration and no pre-dispute arbitration agreement exists, they can still agree after the dispute has arisen to submit to arbitration to resolve the dispute. In that circumstance, the language of the agreement will be different, and will be subject to negotiation by the disputants knowing precisely what the nature of the dispute is. An example of a post-dispute submission agreement is included in the AAA Drafting Guide, reproduced below.

American Arbitration Association, Drafting Dispute Resolution Clauses

(2013)[*]

Millions of business contracts provide for ... arbitration as ways of resolving disputes. A large number of these contracts provide for administration by the American Arbitration Association® (AAA), a public-service, not-for-profit organization offering a broad range of conflict management procedures.

The agreement to arbitrate or mediate can empower the parties with a great deal of control—over the process and the arbitrator who hears the case, or the mediator who assists the parties in settlement efforts. A well-constructed AAA dispute resolution clause can provide certainty by defining the process prior to a dispute, after which agreement becomes more problematic. This Guide is designed to assist drafters in constructing basic clauses for negotiation, mediation, and arbitration, as well as more comprehensive clauses that address a variety of issues.

* * *

Typically, the parties' agreement to mediate or arbitrate is contained in a future-disputes clause in their contract; the clause may provide that any disagreement will be resolved under the mediation or arbitration rules of the AAA.

* * *

I. A Checklist for the Drafter of ADR Clauses

Drafting clear, unambiguous clauses contributes to the efficiency of the ADR process. For example, arbitration agreements require a clear intent to arbitrate. It is not enough to state that "disputes arising under the agreement shall be settled by arbitration." While that language indicates the parties' intention to arbitrate and may authorize a court to enforce the clause, it leaves many issues unresolved. Issues such as when, where, how and before whom a dispute will be arbitrated are subject to disagreement once a controversy has arisen, with no way to resolve them except to go to court.

Some of the more important elements a practitioner should keep in mind when drafting, adopting or recommending a dispute resolution clause follow.

- The clause might cover all disputes that may arise, or only certain types.
- It could specify only arbitration—which yields a binding decision—or also provide an opportunity for non-binding negotiation or mediation.

- The arbitration clause should be signed by as many potential parties to a future dispute as possible.
- To be fully effective, "entry of judgment" language in domestic cases is important.
- It is normally a good idea to state whether a panel of one or three arbitrator(s) is to be selected, and to include the place where the arbitration will occur.
- If the contract includes a general choice of law clause, it may govern the arbitration proceeding. The consequences should be considered.
- Consideration should be given to incorporating the AAA's Procedures for Large, Complex Commercial Disputes for potentially substantial or complicated cases. For smaller, simpler cases the drafter may want to call for the Expedited Procedures that limit the extent of the process.
- The drafter should keep in mind that the AAA has specialized rules for arbitration in the construction, patent, payor provider (healthcare), and certain other fields. If anticipated disputes fall into any of these areas, the specialized rules should be considered for incorporation in the arbitration clause. A panel with specialized subject matter expertise and an experienced AAA administrative staff manages the processing of cases under AAA rules.
- The parties are free to customize and refine the basic arbitration procedures to meet their particular needs. If the parties agree on a procedure that conflicts with otherwise applicable AAA rules, the AAA will almost always respect the wishes of the parties.

* * *

III. Clauses Approved by the AAA for General Commercial Use

Arbitration

* * *

The parties can provide for arbitration of future disputes by inserting the following clause into their contracts (the language in the brackets suggests possible alternatives or additions).

> STD 1. Any controversy or claim arising out of or relating to this contract, or the breach thereof, shall be settled by arbitration administered by the American Arbitration Association in accordance with its Commercial [or other] Arbitration Rules, and judgment on the award rendered by the arbitrator(s) may be entered in any court having jurisdiction thereof.

Arbitration of existing disputes may be accomplished by use of the following:

> STD 2. We, the undersigned parties, hereby agree to submit to arbitration administered by the American Arbitration Association under its Commercial [or other] Arbitration Rules the following controversy: [describe briefly]. We further agree that a judgment of any court having jurisdiction may be entered upon the award.

The preceding clauses, which refer to the time-tested rules of the AAA, have consistently received judicial support. The standard clause is often the best to include in a contract. By invoking the AAA's rules, such a clause meets the following requirements of an effective arbitration clause:

- It makes clear that all disputes are arbitrable. Thus, it minimizes dilatory court actions to avoid the arbitration process.

- It is self-enforcing. Arbitration can continue despite an objection from a party, unless the proceedings are stayed by court order or by agreement of the parties.

- It provides a complete set of rules and procedures. This eliminates the need to spell out dozens of procedural matters in the parties' agreement.

- It provides for the selection of a specialized, impartial panel. Arbitrators are selected by the parties from a screened and trained pool of available experts. Under the AAA rules, a procedure is available to disqualify an arbitrator for bias.

- It settles disputes over the locale of proceedings. When the parties disagree, locale determinations are made by the AAA as the administrator, precluding the need for intervention by a court.

- It makes possible administrative conferences. If the clause incorporates the AAA commercial, construction industry or related arbitration rules, an administrative conference with the parties' representatives and AAA case management to expedite the arbitration proceedings is available when appropriate.

- It makes available preliminary hearings in all but the simplest cases and provides arbitrators with a checklist of items to be discussed at the conference if the clause provides for AAA Commercial Rules. A preliminary hearing can be arranged in cases of any size to specify the issues to be resolved, clarify claims and counterclaims, provide for a pre-hearing exchange of information, and consider other matters that will expedite the arbitration proceedings.

- It also makes mediation available. The AAA Commercial Arbitration Rules and Mediation Procedures require parties to mediate or opt-out of the process. If the clause provides for any of the AAA's various commercial arbitration rules, mediation conferences can be arranged to facilitate a voluntary settlement, without additional administrative cost to the parties.

- It establishes time limits to ensure prompt resolution for all disputes. An additional feature of the various AAA rules is a special expedited procedure, which may be used to resolve smaller claims and other disputes that need more speedy resolutions.

- It provides for AAA administrative assistance to the arbitrator and the parties. To protect neutrality and avoid unilateral contact, most rules provide for the AAA to channel communications between the parties and the arbitrator. An AAA case manager may also provide guidance to help ensure the prompt conclusion of a proceeding.

- It establishes a procedure for serving notices. Depending on the rules used and the type of the case, notices may be served by regular mail, addressed to the party or its representative at the last known address. Under the rules, the AAA and the parties may use facsimile transmission or other written forms of electronic communication to give the notices required by the rules.

- Unless otherwise provided, it gives the arbitrator the power to decide matters equitably and to fashion appropriate relief. The AAA commercial rules allow the arbitrator to grant any remedy or relief that the arbitrator deems just and equitable and within the scope of the agreement of the parties, including specific performance.

- It allows ex parte hearings. A hearing may be held in the absence of a party who has been given due notice. Thus, a party cannot avoid an award by refusing to appear.

- It provides for enforcement of the award. The award can be enforced in any court having jurisdiction, with only limited statutory grounds for resisting the award. If, in a domestic transaction, as distinguished from an international one, the parties desire that the arbitration clause be final, binding and enforceable, it is essential that the clause contain an "entry of judgment" provision such as that found in the standard arbitration clause ("and judgment on the award rendered by the arbitrator may be entered in any court having jurisdiction thereof").

Negotiation

The parties may wish to attempt to resolve their disputes through negotiation prior to arbitration. A sample clause which provides for negotiation follows.

> **NEG 1** In the event of any dispute, claim, question, or disagreement arising from or relating to this agreement or the breach thereof, the parties hereto shall use their best efforts to settle the dispute, claim, question, or disagreement. To this effect, they shall consult and negotiate with each other in good faith and, recognizing their mutual interests, attempt to reach a just and equitable solution satisfactory to both parties. If they do not reach such solution within a period of 60 days, then, upon notice by either party to the other, all disputes, claims, questions, or differences shall be finally settled by arbitration administered by the American Arbitration Association in accordance with the provisions of its Commercial Arbitration Rules.

Mediation

The parties may wish to attempt mediation before submitting their dispute to arbitration. This can be accomplished by agreeing to mediation, a voluntary process that may be entered into either by a standalone agreement or incorporated into an arbitration clause as a first step and may be terminated at any time by either party.

The AAA Commercial Rules call for mediation to take place as part of the arbitration with parties given the choice to unilaterally opt out of the mediation step. Parties may desire to customize their mediation step in their agreement. Example

Mediation 1 can be used for a customized clause and example Mediation 2 can be used to submit a dispute to mediation.

> **MED 1** If a dispute arises out of or relates to this contract, or the breach thereof, and if the dispute cannot be settled through negotiation, the parties agree first to try in good faith to settle the dispute by mediation administered by the American Arbitration Association under its Commercial Mediation Procedures before resorting to arbitration, litigation, or some other dispute resolution procedure.

> **MED 2** The parties hereby submit the following dispute to mediation administered by the American Arbitration Association under its Commercial Mediation Procedures [the clause may also provide for the qualifications of the mediator(s), the method for allocating fees and expenses, the locale of meetings, time limits, or any other item of concern to the parties].

An AAA administrator can assist the parties regarding selection of the mediator, scheduling, pre-mediation information exchange and attendance of appropriate parties at the mediation conference.

It is prudent to include time limits on steps prior to arbitration. Under a broad arbitration clause, the question of whether a claim has been asserted within an applicable time limit is generally regarded as an arbitrable issue, suitable for resolution by the arbitrator.

Large, Complex Cases

The large, complex case framework offered by the AAA is designed primarily for business disputes involving claims of at least $500,000, although parties are free to provide for use of the LCC Rules in other disputes. The key elements of the program are (1) selection of arbitrators who satisfy rigorous criteria to insure that the panel is an extremely select one; (2) training, orientation, and coordination of those arbitrators in a manner designed to facilitate the program; (3) establishment of procedures for administration of those cases that elect to be included in the program; (4) flexibility of those procedures so that parties can more speedily and efficiently resolve their disputes; and (5) administration of large, complex cases by specially trained, experienced AAA staff.

The procedures provide for an early administrative conference with the AAA, and a preliminary hearing with the arbitrators. Documentary exchanges and other essential exchanges of information are facilitated. The procedures also provide that a statement of reasons may accompany the award, if requested by the parties. The procedures are meant to supplement the applicable rules that the parties have agreed to use. They include the possibility of the use of mediation to resolve some or all issues at an early stage.

The parties can provide for future application of the procedures by including the following arbitration clause in their contract.

> **LCCP 1** Any controversy or claim arising from or relating to this contract or the breach thereof shall be settled by arbitration administered by the American

Arbitration Association under its [applicable] Procedures for Large, Complex Commercial Disputes, and judgment on the award rendered by the arbitrator(s) may be entered in any court having jurisdiction thereof.

A pending dispute can be referred to the program by the completion of a Submission to Dispute Resolution form if the underlying contract documents do not provide for AAA administration.

LCCP 2 We, the undersigned parties, hereby agree to submit to arbitration administered by the American Arbitration Association under its [applicable] Procedures for Large, Complex Commercial Disputes the following controversy [describe briefly]. Judgment of any court having jurisdiction may be entered on the award. An AAA administrator can assist the parties regarding selection of the mediator, scheduling, pre-mediation information exchange and attendance of appropriate parties at the mediation conference.

V. Other Provisions That Might Be Considered

This section contains various provisions which expand upon and are supplemental to the basic dispute resolution clauses set forth in Sections III and IV. The listing of such provisions is not intended to be all-inclusive and does not necessarily indicate that the AAA endorses the use of such additional language. The AAA recognizes, however, that some drafters choose to expand their dispute resolution clauses to reflect at least some of these ideas. Since it is important that practitioners be well informed when making choices in drafting, the section also sets forth, where appropriate, certain of the pros and cons of adopting the various supplemental provisions.

A. Specifying a Method of Selection and the Number of Arbitrators

Under the AAA's arbitration rules, arbitrators are generally selected using a listing process. The AAA case manager provides each party with a list of proposed arbitrators who are generally familiar with the subject matter involved in the dispute. Each side is provided a number of days to strike any unacceptable names, number the remaining names in order of preference, and return the list to the AAA. The case manager then invites persons to serve from the names remaining on the list, in the designated order of mutual preference. The parties may agree to have one arbitrator or three (which significantly increases the cost). If parties do not agree on the number of arbitrator(s), it will be left to the discretion of the AAA to decide the appropriate number of arbitrators.

The parties may use other arbitrator appointment systems, such as the party-appointed method in which each side designates one arbitrator and the two thus selected appoint the chair of the panel.

The Commercial Arbitration Rules, Construction Industry Arbitration Rules, Employment Arbitration Rules along with other domestic specialty rules provide that unless the parties specifically agree in writing that the party-appointed arbitrators are to be non-neutral, arbitrators appointed by the parties must meet the impartiality and independence standards set forth within the rules. The AAA's International Arbitration Rules indicate that all arbitrators acting under their rules shall be impartial and independent.

If parties intend that their party-appointed arbitrators serve in a non-neutral capacity, this should be clearly stated within their clause.

The arbitration clause can also specify by name the individual whom the parties want as their arbitrator. However, the potential unavailability of the named individual in the future may pose a risk.

All of these issues and others can be dealt with in the arbitration clause. Some illustrative provisions follow.

> **ARBSEL 1** The arbitrator selected by the claimant and the arbitrator selected by respondent shall, within 10 days of their appointment, select a third neutral arbitrator. In the event that they are unable to do so, the parties or their attorneys may request the American Arbitration Association to appoint the third neutral arbitrator. Prior to the commencement of hearings, each of the arbitrators appointed shall provide an oath or undertaking of impartiality.
>
> **ARBSEL 2** Within 14 days after the commencement of arbitration, each party shall select one person to act as arbitrator and the two selected shall select a third arbitrator within 10 days of their appointment. [The party-selected arbitrators will serve in a non-neutral capacity.] If the arbitrators selected by the parties are unable or fail to agree upon the third arbitrator, the third arbitrator shall be selected by the American Arbitration Association.
>
> **ARBSEL 3** In the event that arbitration is necessary, [name of specific arbitrator] shall act as the arbitrator. When providing for direct appointment of the arbitrator(s) by the parties, it is best to specify a time frame within which it must be accomplished. Also, in many jurisdictions, the law permits the court to appoint arbitrators where privately-agreed means fail. Such a result may be time consuming, costly, and unpredictable. Parties who seek to establish an ad-hoc method of arbitrator appointment might be well advised to provide a fallback, such as, should the particular procedure fail for any reason, "arbitrators shall be appointed as provided in the AAA Commercial Arbitration Rules."

When providing for direct appointment of the arbitrator(s) by the parties, it is best to specify a time frame within which it must be accomplished. Also, in many jurisdictions, the law permits the court to appoint arbitrators where privately-agreed means fail. Such a result may be time consuming, costly, and unpredictable. Parties who seek to establish an ad-hoc method of arbitrator appointment might be well advised to provide a fallback, such as, should the particular procedure fail for any reason, "arbitrators shall be appointed as provided in the AAA Commercial Arbitration Rules."

B. Arbitrator Qualifications

The parties may wish that one or more of the arbitrators be a lawyer or an accountant or an expert in computer technology, etc. In some instances, it makes more sense to specify that one of three arbitrators be an accountant, for example, than to turn the entire proceeding over to three accountants. Sample clauses providing for specific qualifications of arbitrators are set forth below.

QUAL 1 The arbitrator shall be a certified public accountant.

QUAL 2 The arbitrator shall be a practicing attorney [or a retired judge] of the [specify] [Court].

QUAL 3 The arbitration proceedings shall be conducted before a panel of three neutral arbitrators, all of whom shall be members of the bar of the state of [specify], actively engaged in the practice of law for at least 10 years.

QUAL 4 The panel of three arbitrators shall consist of one contractor, one architect, and one construction attorney.

QUAL 5 The arbitrators will be selected from a panel of persons having experience with and knowledge of electronic computers and the computer business, and at least one of the arbitrators selected will be an attorney.

QUAL 6 In the event that any party's claim exceeds $1 million, exclusive of interest and attorneys' fees, the dispute shall be heard and determined by three arbitrators.

Parties might wish to specify that the arbitrator should or should not be a national or citizen of a particular country. The following examples can be added to the arbitration clause to deal with this concern.

NATLY 1 The arbitrator shall be a national of [country].

NATLY 2 The arbitrator shall not be a national of either [country A] or [country B].

NATLY 3 The arbitrator shall not be of the nationality of either of the parties.

C. Locale Provisions

Parties might want to add language specifying the place of the arbitration. The choice of the proper place to arbitrate is most important because the place of arbitration implies generally a choice of the applicable procedural law, which in turn affects questions of arbitrability, procedure, court intervention and enforcement.

In specifying a locale, parties should consider (1) the convenience of the location (e.g., availability of witnesses, local counsel, transportation, hotels, meeting facilities, court reporters, etc.); (2) the available pool of qualified arbitrators within the geographical area; and (3) the applicable procedural and substantive law. Of particular importance in international cases is the applicability of a convention providing for recognition and enforcement of arbitral agreements and awards and the arbitration regime at the chosen site.

An example of locale provisions that might appear in an arbitration clause follows.

LOC 1 The place of arbitration shall be [city], [state], or [country].

D. Language

In matters involving multilingual parties, the arbitration agreement often specifies the language in which the arbitration will be conducted. Examples of such language follow.

LANG 1 The language(s) of the arbitration shall be [specify].

LANG 2 The arbitration shall be conducted in the language in which the contract was written.

Such arbitration clauses could also deal with selection and cost allocation of an interpreter.

E. Governing Law

It is common for parties to specify the law that will govern the contract and/or the arbitration proceedings. Some examples follow.

GOV 1 This agreement shall be governed by and interpreted in accordance with the laws of the State of [specify]. The parties acknowledge that this agreement evidences a transaction involving interstate commerce. The United States Arbitration Act shall govern the interpretation, enforcement, and proceedings pursuant to the arbitration clause in this agreement.

GOV 2 Disputes under this clause shall be resolved by arbitration in accordance with Title 9 of the US Code (United States Arbitration Act) and the Commercial Arbitration Rules of the American Arbitration Association.

GOV 3 This contract shall be governed by the laws of the state of [specify].

In international cases, where the parties have not provided for the law applicable to the substance of the dispute, the AAA's International Arbitration Rules contain specific guidelines for arbitrators regarding applicable law....

F. Conditions Precedent to Arbitration

Under an agreement of the parties, satisfaction of specified conditions may be required before a dispute is ready for arbitration. Examples of such conditions precedent include written notification of claims within a fixed period of time and exhaustion of other contractually established procedures, such as submission of claims to an architect or engineer. These kinds of provisions may, however, be a source of delay and may require linkage with a statute of limitations waiver (see below). An example of a "condition precedent" clause follows.

CONPRE 1 If a dispute arises from or relates to this contract, the parties agree that upon request of either party they will seek the advice of [a mutually selected engineer] and try in good faith to settle the dispute within 30 days of that request, following which either party may submit the matter to mediation under the Commercial Mediation Procedures of the American Arbitration Association. If the matter is not resolved within 60 days after

initiation of mediation, either party may demand arbitration administered by the American Arbitration Association under its [applicable] rules.

G. Preliminary Relief

While preliminary relief is provided for in the AAA's Commercial Rules, when a clause calls for other rules it is appropriate to provide specifically for it if a need for an interim remedy is anticipated. One way to do so is to incorporate the Emergency Measures of Protection (R-38) of the AAA Commercial Arbitration Rules and Mediation Procedures, discussed above. Alternatively, if the parties foresee the possibility of needing emergency relief akin to a temporary restraining order, they might specify an arbitrator by name for that purpose in their arbitration clause or authorize the AAA to name a preliminary relief arbitrator to ensure an arbitrator is in place in sufficient time to address appropriate issues.

Specific clauses providing for preliminary relief are set forth below.

PRELIM 1 Either party may apply to the arbitrator seeking injunctive relief until the arbitration award is rendered or the controversy is otherwise resolved. Either party also may, without waiving any remedy under this agreement, seek from any court having jurisdiction any interim or provisional relief that is necessary to protect the rights or property of that party, pending the establishment of the arbitral tribunal (or pending the arbitral tribunal's determination of the merits of the controversy).

Note that the AAA's rules provide for interim relief by the arbitrator upon application of a party.

Pending the outcome of the arbitration, parties may agree to hold in escrow money, a letter of credit, goods, or the subject matter of the arbitration. A sample of a clause providing for such escrow follows.

ESCROW 1 Pending the outcome of the arbitration [name of party] shall place in escrow with [law firm, institution, or AAA] as the escrow agent, [the sum of _____, a letter of credit, goods, or the subject matter in dispute]. The escrow agent shall be entitled to release the [funds, letter of credit, goods, or subject matter in dispute] as directed by the arbitrator(s) in the award, unless the parties agree otherwise in writing.

H. Consolidation

Where there are multiple parties with disputes arising from the same transaction, complications can often be reduced by the consolidation of all disputes. Since arbitration is a process based on voluntary contractual participation, parties may not be required to arbitrate a dispute without their consent. However, parties can provide for the consolidation of two or more separate arbitrations into a single proceeding or permit the joinder of a third party into an arbitration. In a construction dispute, consolidated proceedings may eliminate the need for duplicative presentations of claims and avoid the possibility of conflicting rulings from different panels of arbitrators. However, consolidating claims might be a source of delay and expense. An example of language that can be included in an arbitration clause follows.

> **CONSOL 1** The owner, the contractor, and all subcontractors, specialty contractors, material suppliers, engineers, designers, architects, construction lenders, bonding companies, and other parties concerned with the construction of the structure are bound, each to each other, by this arbitration clause, provided that they have signed this contract or a contract that incorporates this contract by reference or signed any other agreement to be bound by this arbitration clause. Each such party agrees that it may be joined as an additional party to an arbitration involving other parties under any such agreement. If more than one arbitration is begun under any such agreement and any party contends that two or more arbitrations are substantially related and that the issues should be heard in one proceeding, the arbitrator(s) selected in the first-filed of such proceedings shall determine whether, in the interests of justice and efficiency, the proceedings should be consolidated before that (those) arbitrator(s).

I. Document Discovery

Under the AAA rules, arbitrators are authorized to direct a prehearing exchange of documents. The parties typically discuss such an exchange and seek to agree on its scope. In most (but not all) instances, arbitrators will order prompt production of limited numbers of documents which are directly relevant to the issues involved. In some instances, parties might want to ensure that such production will in fact occur and thus provide for it in their arbitration clause. In doing so, however, they should be mindful of what scope of document production they desire. This may be difficult to decide at the outset. If the parties address discovery in the clause, they might include time limitations as to when all discovery should be completed and might specify that the arbitrator shall resolve outstanding discovery issues. Sample language is set forth below.

> **DOC 1** Consistent with the expedited nature of arbitration, each party will, upon the written request of the other party, promptly provide the other with copies of documents [relevant to the issues raised by any claim or counterclaim] [on which the producing party may rely in support of or in opposition to any claim or defense]. Any dispute regarding discovery, or the relevance or scope thereof, shall be determined by the [arbitrator(s)] [chair of the arbitration panel], which determination shall be conclusive. All discovery shall be completed within [45] [60] days following the appointment of the arbitrator(s).

The AAA's various commercial arbitration rules provide an opportunity for an administrative conference with the AAA staff and/or a preliminary hearing with the arbitrator. The purposes of such meetings include establishing the extent of and a schedule for production of relevant documents and other information.

J. Depositions

Generally, arbitrators prefer to hear and be able to question witnesses at a hearing rather than rely on deposition testimony. However, parties are free to provide in their arbitration clause for a tailored discovery program, preferably to be managed by the arbitrator. This might occur, for example, if the parties anticipate the need for distant witnesses who would not be able to testify except through depositions or, in the alternative, by the arbitrator holding a hearing where the witness is located and subject to subpoena. In most cases where parties provide for depositions, they do so in very limited fashion, i.e., they might specify a 30-day deposition period, with each side permitted three depositions, none of which would last more than three hours. All objections would be reserved for the arbitration hearing and would not even be noted at the deposition except for objections based on privilege or extreme confidentiality. Sample language providing for such depositions is set forth below.

> **DEP 1** At the request of a party, the arbitrator(s) shall have the discretion to order examination by deposition of witnesses to the extent the arbitrator deems such additional discovery relevant and appropriate. Depositions shall be limited to a maximum of [three] [insert number] per party and shall be held within 30 days of the making of a request. Additional depositions may be scheduled only with the permission of the [arbitrator(s)] [chair of the arbitration panel], and for good cause shown. Each deposition shall be limited to a maximum of [three hours] [six hours] [one day's] duration. All objections are reserved for the arbitration hearing except for objections based on privilege and proprietary or confidential information.

K. Duration of Arbitration Proceeding

While AAA Commercial Arbitration Rules normally provide for an award within 30 days of the closing of the hearing, parties sometimes underscore their wish for an expedited result by providing in the arbitration clause, for example, that there will be an award within a specified number of months of the notice of intention to arbitrate and that the arbitrator(s) must agree to the time constraints before accepting appointment. Before adopting such language, however, the parties should consider whether the deadline is realistic and what would happen if the deadline were not met under circumstances where the parties had not mutually agreed to extend it (e.g., whether the award would be enforceable). It thus may be helpful to allow the arbitrator to extend time limits in appropriate circumstances. Sample language is set forth below.

> **TIME 1** The award shall be made within nine months of the filing of the notice of intention to arbitrate (demand), and the arbitrator(s) shall agree to comply with this schedule before accepting appointment. However, this time limit may be extended by agreement of the parties or by the arbitrator(s) if necessary.

L. Remedies

Under a broad arbitration clause and most AAA rules, the arbitrator may grant "any remedy or relief that the arbitrator deems just and equitable" within the scope of the parties' agreement. Sometimes parties want to include or exclude certain specific remedies. Examples of clauses dealing with remedies follow.

REM 1 The arbitrators will have no authority to award punitive or other damages not measured by the prevailing party's actual damages, except as may be required by statute.

REM 2 In no event shall an award in an arbitration initiated under this clause exceed $_____.

REM 3 In no event shall an award in an arbitration initiated under this clause exceed $_____ for any claimant.

REM 4 The arbitrator(s) shall not award consequential damages in any arbitration initiated under this section.

REM 5 Any award in an arbitration initiated under this clause shall be limited to monetary damages and shall include no injunction or direction to any party other than the direction to pay a monetary amount.

REM 6 If the arbitrator(s) find liability in any arbitration initiated under this clause, they shall award liquidated damages in the amount of $_____.

REM 7 Any monetary award in an arbitration initiated under this clause shall include pre-award interest at the rate of ____% from the time of the act or acts giving rise to the award.

M. "Baseball" Arbitration

"Baseball" arbitration is a methodology used in many different contexts in addition to baseball players' salary disputes, and is particularly effective when parties have a long-term relationship.

- The procedure involves each party submitting a number to the arbitrator(s) and
- serving the number on his or her adversary on the understanding that,
- following a hearing, the arbitrator(s) will pick one of the submitted numbers, nothing else.

A key aspect of this approach is that there is incentive for a party to submit a highly reasonable number, since this increases the likelihood that the arbitrator(s) will select that number. In some instances, the process of submitting the numbers moves the parties so close together that the dispute is settled without a hearing. Sample language providing for "baseball" arbitration is set forth below.

BASEBALL 1 Each party shall submit to the arbitrator and exchange with each other in advance of the hearing their last, best offers. The arbitrator shall be limited to awarding only one or the other of the two figures submitted.

N. Arbitration Within Monetary Limits

Parties are often able to negotiate to a point but are then unable to close the remaining gap between their respective positions. By setting up an arbitration that must result in an award within the gap that remains between the parties, the parties are able to eliminate extreme risk, while gaining the benefit of the extent to which their negotiations were successful.

There are two commonly-used approaches. The first involves informing the arbitrator(s) that the award should be somewhere within a specified monetary range. Sample contract language providing for this methodology is set forth below.

> **LIMITS 1** Any award of the arbitrator in favor of [specify party] and against [specify party] shall be at least [specify a dollar amount] but shall not exceed [specify a dollar amount]. [Specify a party] expressly waives any claim in excess of [specify a dollar amount] and agrees that its recovery shall not exceed that amount. Any such award shall be in satisfaction of all claims by [specify a party] against [specify a party].

A second approach is for the parties to agree but not tell the arbitrator(s) that the amount of recovery will, for example, be somewhere between $500 and $1,000. If the award is less than $500, then it is raised to $500 pursuant to the agreement; if the award is more than $1,000, then it is lowered to $1,000 pursuant to the agreement; if the award is within the $500–1,000 range, then the amount awarded by the arbitrator(s) is unchanged. Sample contract language providing for this methodology is set forth below.

> **LIMITS 2** In the event that the arbitrator denies the claim or awards an amount less than the minimum amount of [specify], then this minimum amount shall be paid to the claimant. Should the arbitrator's award exceed the maximum amount of [specify], then only this maximum amount shall be paid to the claimant. It is further understood between the parties that, if the arbitrator awards an amount between the minimum and the maximum stipulated range, then the exact awarded amount will be paid to the claimant. The parties further agree that this agreement is private between them and will not be disclosed to the arbitrator.

O. Assessment of Attorneys' Fees

The AAA rules generally provide that the administrative fees be borne as incurred and that the arbitrators' compensation be allocated equally between the parties and, except for international rules, are silent concerning attorneys' fees; but this can be modified by agreement of the parties. Fees and expenses of the arbitration, including attorneys' fees, can be dealt with in the arbitration clause. Defining the term 'prevailing party' within the contract is recommended to avoid misunderstanding. Some typical language dealing with fees and expenses follows.

> **FEE 1** The prevailing party shall be entitled to an award of reasonable attorney fees.

FEE 2 The arbitrators shall award to the prevailing party, if any, as determined by the arbitrators, all of its costs and fees. "Costs and fees" mean all reasonable pre-award expenses of the arbitration, including the arbitrators' fees, administrative fees, travel expenses, out-of-pocket expenses such as copying and telephone, court costs, witness fees, and attorneys' fees.

FEE 3 Each party shall bear its own costs and expenses and an equal share of the arbitrators' and administrative fees of arbitration.

FEE 4 The arbitrators may determine how the costs and expenses of the arbitration shall be allocated between the parties, but they shall not award attorneys' fees.

P. Reasoned Opinion Accompanying the Award

In domestic commercial cases, arbitrators usually will write a reasoned opinion explaining their award if such an opinion is requested by all parties. While some take the position that reasoned opinions detract from finality if they facilitate post-arbitration resort to the courts, parties sometimes desire such opinions, particularly in large, complex cases or as already provided by most applicable rules in international disputes. If the parties want such an opinion, they can include language such as the following in their arbitration clause.

OPIN 1 The award of the arbitrators shall be accompanied by a reasoned opinion.

OPIN 2 The award shall be in writing, shall be signed by a majority of the arbitrators, and shall include a statement setting forth the reasons for the disposition of any claim.

OPIN 3 The award shall include findings of fact [and conclusions of law].

OPIN 4 The award shall include a breakdown as to specific claims.

Q. Confidentiality

While the AAA and arbitrators adhere to certain standards concerning the privacy or confidentiality of the hearings (see the AAA-ABA Code of Ethics for Arbitrators in Commercial Disputes, Canon VI), parties might also wish to impose limits on themselves as to how much information regarding the dispute may be disclosed outside the hearing. The following language might help serve this purpose.

CONF 1 Except as may be required by law, neither a party nor an arbitrator may disclose the existence, content, or results of any arbitration hereunder without the prior written consent of both parties.

The preceding language could also be modified to restrict only disclosure of certain information (e.g., trade secrets).

R. Appeal

The basic objective of arbitration is a fair, fast and expert result, achieved economically. Consistent with this goal, an arbitration award traditionally will be set aside only in egregious circumstances such as demonstrable bias of an arbitrator. Sometimes, however, the parties desire a more comprehensive appeal, most often in the setting of legally complex cases. Parties may include the AAA Appellate Rules in their agreement by including the following clause.

> **APP 1** "Notwithstanding any language to the contrary in the contract documents, the parties hereby agree: that the Underlying Award may be appealed pursuant to the AAA's Optional Appellate Arbitration Rules ("Appellate Rules"); that the Underlying Award rendered by the arbitrator(s) shall, at a minimum, be a reasoned award; and that the Underlying Award shall not be considered final until after the time for filing the notice of appeal pursuant to the Appellate Rules has expired. Appeals must be initiated within thirty (30) days of receipt of an Underlying Award, as defined by Rule A-3 of the Appellate Rules, by filing a Notice of Appeal with any AAA office. Following the appeal process the decision rendered by the appeal tribunal may be entered in any court having jurisdiction thereof ..."

S. Mediation-Arbitration

A clause may provide first for mediation under the AAA's mediation procedures. If the mediation is unsuccessful, the mediator could be authorized to resolve the dispute under the AAA's arbitration rules. This process is sometimes referred to as "Med-Arb." Except in unusual circumstances, a procedure whereby the same individual who has been serving as a mediator becomes an arbitrator when the mediation fails is not recommended, because it could inhibit the candor which should characterize the mediation process and/or it could convey evidence, legal points or settlement positions ex parte, improperly influencing the arbitrator. The AAA Commercial Arbitration Rules and Mediation Procedures (effective October 1, 2013) provide for a mediation/arbitration process that runs concurrently. A sample of a med-arb clause follows that runs sequentially can be used to submit a present dispute or to vary the revised AAA Commercial Rules in a dispute resolution clause.

> **MEDARB 1** If a dispute arises from or relates to this contract or the breach thereof, and if the dispute cannot be settled through direct discussions, the parties agree to endeavor first to settle the dispute by mediation administered by the American Arbitration Association under its Commercial Mediation Procedures before resorting to arbitration. Any unresolved controversy or claim arising from or relating to this contract or breach thereof shall be settled by arbitration administered by the American Arbitration Association in accordance with its Commercial Arbitration Rules, and judgment on the award rendered by the arbitrator may be entered in any court having jurisdiction thereof. If all parties to the dispute agree, a mediator involved in the parties' mediation may be asked to serve as the arbitrator.

T. Statute of Limitations

Parties may wish to consider whether the applicable statute of limitations will be tolled for the duration of mediation proceedings, and can refer to the following language.

STATLIM 1 The requirements of filing a notice of claim with respect to the dispute submitted to mediation shall be suspended until the conclusion of the mediation process.

* * *

Conclusion

A dispute resolution clause should address the special needs of the parties involved. An inadequate ADR clause can produce as much delay, expense, and inconvenience as a traditional lawsuit. When writing a dispute resolution clause, keep in mind that its purpose is to resolve disputes, not create them. If disagreements arise over the meaning of the clause, it is often because it failed to address the particular needs of the parties. Use of standard, simple AAA language may avoid difficulties. Drafting an effective ADR agreement is the first step on the road to successful dispute resolution.

C. Arbitration Clause Drafting Exercise

A Grainy Situation

Consider the following factual scenario:

Two companies, Good Grains and All Ears, are about to enter into a long-term supply contract. The two companies are just about ready to wrap up their deal, but, after talking to their lawyers, want to include a dispute resolution clause in their contract. They are particularly interested in arbitration, but they are willing to consider a multistep process, provided that the dispute ultimately be settled by arbitration.

Good Grains is a leading manufacturer of breakfast cereal. Good Grains is located in the fictional state of Dover,[1] which is located on the east coast of the United States, near New York. Good Grains is one of the three largest breakfast cereal manufacturers in the United States, and it is widely known that it is proud of its reputation and its market share. To make breakfast cereal, Good Grains uses a variety of natural grains, including corn, rice, bran, and wheat, to name a few.

Good Grains has contracts with multiple suppliers for the sale of grains. Good Grains approximates that it has contracts with about 75 different grain supply companies, none of which has an exclusive contract with Good Grains. Making matters worse, Good Grains has no uniform contracts with any of its grain suppliers. Good Grains recently had a change in corporate management, and the new CEO has made it a priority that all future contracts will be uniform.

---

1. Dover law is business-friendly, similar to Delaware law.

All Ears is a corn supplier from the fictional state of Springfield,[2] which is located in the Midwest of the United States. All Ears has a large presence in the Midwest, but it has yet to have much, if any, presence on the coasts. All Ears has a large-scale operation and insists on having exclusivity contracts with all of its customers.

All Ears and Good Grains negotiated a 20-year exclusive contract for the sale of corn from All Ears to Good Grains. The exclusive contract means that Good Grains will only buy corn from All Ears. All Ears, however, is still free to sell corn to other companies. This agreement is a blockbuster deal for All Ears, who manages to gain a foothold into the northeast region of the country. Good Grains is also excited about this deal because it takes care of all of its corn needs from one supplier. The contract provides that the price of corn is tied to the Grain Index.

Given these facts, assume that the first paragraph of the arbitration agreement will be the following:

> **Scope:** Good Grains and All Ears agree to submit any and all disputes arising out of or relating to this contract to arbitration, including questions of contract validity, arbitrability, and potential defenses.

Given this scope, draft provisions for the arbitration agreement covering the following topics:

1. The process to employ (arbitration only or another procedure).

2. Arbitrator selection process

3. Number of arbitrators

4. Arbitrator qualifications

5. Arbitration locale

6. Governing law

7. Discovery

8. Available remedies

9. Witnesses and Evidence

10. Reasoned Opinion or Other Type of Award

11. Confidentiality

[Your instructor may provide you additional instructions regarding your role.]

---

2. Springfield law is also business friendly, but less business friendly than New Dover law. Springfield law, however, does have some farm-friendly laws.

Chapter 7

Arbitration Advocacy

A. Introduction

While **Chapter 5** examined the arbitration process from the arbitrator's perspective, this chapter focuses on the **role of the advocate** in the arbitration process. This chapter also is practice-oriented and contains a number of exercises for students to practice representing a client in an arbitration matter. As with litigation, arbitration advocacy starts with the very decision to initiate a case, continues through to the hearing, and may even include a post-hearing tasks. Approaching these various stages as an advocate, as opposed to an arbitrator, requires different preparation and strategies. In addition to the materials in this chapter, this book provides students with a complete case file and instructions for conducting an arbitration simulation.

This chapter considers advocacy within the arbitral forum as well as in seeking judicial relief ancillary to, or as part of, an arbitration case. For example, parties may seek from a court emergency relief, the appointment of an arbitrator, or even intervention in discovery.

The first step of arbitration advocacy is actually the decision to draft an arbitration agreement, which has already been discussed in the previous chapter. This chapter, then, picks up when a dispute arises under an arbitration agreement and the parties decide to submit the claim to arbitration. This chapter takes students from the initiation of a claim through submission of the claim to the arbitrators following a hearing. Award enforcement and judicial review are discussed later in this book.

This chapter proceeds similarly to **Chapter 5**, considering arbitration advocacy as a series of steps. Many of these steps will look familiar, and those that are different are highlighted:

1. *Initiation of the Claim*

2. *Arbitrator Selection*

3. **Preliminary and Interim Relief**

4. *Post-Appointment Preliminary Hearing*

5. *Discovery*

6. *Dispositive (and Other) Motions*

7. *The Hearing*

8. **Pre- and** *Post-Hearing Submissions*

In addition to these steps, this chapter considers the attorney's ethical obligations within the arbitral forum. Lawyers may have a duty to advise clients of alternative methods to resolve their disputes, including arbitration. In addition, attorneys have obligations of truthfulness and fairness to the forum, similar to obligations to other tribunals. Finally, this chapter raises the issue of whether non-attorney representatives are engaged in the unauthorized practice of law if they assist a party in pursuing a claim or defense in arbitration.

B. Initiation of the Claim

Initiating a claim in arbitration is a relatively simple process. The initiating party (the "claimant") typically files a Demand for Arbitration and a Statement of Claim. The claimant should also attach a copy of the parties' arbitration agreement. For some provider organizations, such as the American Arbitration Association, the Demand for Arbitration is a fillable form asking for the names and contact information of the parties and their representatives, if any; the nature of the claim and including the amount involved and other type of relief sought; and locale requested. The AAA has a different demand form depending on the type of case, such as for a consumer, commercial, employment, or international case. Advocates should be careful to use the appropriate form for their cases. The AAA's forms are available online at: www.adr.org/Forms.

The Statement of Claim is a written narrative that sets forth the essential facts of the dispute. The Statement of Claim can be a short document with minimal factual allegations, legal claims, and request for relief, or it can be a more complex factual narrative accompanied by detailed causes of action and a request for multiple remedies. The level of detail provided can vary depending on the type and size of the dispute, the forum, and the advocates' practice. Either way, arbitration counsel need not be concerned about satisfying pleading requirements that govern complaints in civil litigation, such as the Federal Rule of Civil Procedure Rule 8, as interpreted in *Ashcroft v. Iqbal*, 556 U.S. 662 (2009), and *Bell Atlantic Corp. v. Twombly*, 550 U.S. 554 (2007). Arbitrators rarely entertain motions to dismiss, and they would likely deny any such motion and allow the discovery process to proceed.

In addition to filing these documents, the claimant will also likely have to pay the corresponding fees. Parties using a provider organization must pay an administrative filing fee to the organization. The administrative fees do not include arbitrator compensation or expenses. Although a claimant is generally responsible for the fee, some consumer and employment agreements shift fees to the respondent company. Provider organizations that have separate rules for consumers may have reduced filing fees for the consumer party. Parties who do not use a provider organization and instead directly select a specific arbitrator (i.e., an "ad hoc" arbitration) may need to pay a retainer to secure the arbitrator's services. Parties may be able to file their claims online or by submitting their claims to the administering organization, which then provides notice to the parties and their representatives.

To respond to a Statement of Claim, similar to answering a complaint in litigation, a respondent submits an Answer to the claimant's factual allegations, legal claims and request for relief. No particular level of specificity is required. Advocates have considerable leeway in deciding whether to respond with a counter-narrative or just general denials of claimant's allegations. A respondent may also file a counterclaim, which sets forth the nature of relief sought.

What should you do if you receive a Demand and/or Statement of Claim, but do not believe your client is subject to a valid arbitration agreement? Because arbitrators derive their power solely and exclusively from the parties' agreement, the arbitrators do not have jurisdiction over the parties absent such an agreement. A respondent can respond to the Statement of Claim by filing a motion to dismiss the arbitration for lack of jurisdiction. If a party does not file an Answer, the arbitration could proceed without the respondent present, and the respondent might be bound to any award, assuming it received adequate notice of the process, similar to a default judgment. On the other hand, not answering is not deemed a waiver of an objection to the arbitration agreement, and the respondent can seek court relief in the form of a motion to stay arbitration. Depending on the applicable law, the objection to jurisdiction might be an issue for the arbitrator or an issue for the court. See Chapter 3.B on "Who Decides."

When drafting a Statement of Claim or Answer, advocates or parties should consider the following questions:

- How much information do I know at this time?

- How much information do I want to disclose at this time?

- What claims do I think I will be able to prove based on what I know now and what I expect to learn in discovery?

Consider the following sample combined Demand for Arbitration and Statement of Claim and sample Answer.

United Arbitration Board

Name and address for **Claimant(s)**   **Demand for Arbitration and Statement of Claim**

Julie Richardson
3131 Third Avenue, Apt. 312
Central, Dover 18412   2018-0012345

Record Number: _____

Name and address for **Respondent(s)**   October 12, 2018

Metro Care, Inc.   Filing Date: _____
45 Spruce Street
Central, Dover 18412

RESPONDENT: A demand for arbitration has been filed with the United Arbitration Board. Respondent has 15 days to file an answering statement or counter claim.

Claimant states:

1. Julie Richardson ("Richardson") is a citizen of Dover currently residing in Central, Dover. Metro Care, Inc. ("Metro Care") is a not-for-profit Dover corporation headquartered in Central, Dover. At all times relevant to this arbitration, Metro Care owned and operated Metro Care Memorial Hospital. The parties agree to arbitrate this dispute by neutral binding arbitration. The parties' agreement to arbitrate is attached as Exhibit A. [Attachment omitted]

2. In June of 2014, Richardson began employment with Metro Care as a nurse in the Emergency Room. Her duties included making assessments of patient needs upon being admitted to the emergency room, assisting doctors in emergency room procedures, and making arrangements for the patients' discharge or future care following their stay in the emergency room.

3. Prior to starting with Metro Care, Richardson had 20 years of nursing experience as a traveling nurse, working in emergency care across the United States.

4. During her employment with Metro Care, Richardson received yearly employment evaluations. Her supervisor, Nancy Neville, gave Richardson an "exemplary" review in October 2014, October 2015, October 2016, and October 2017. Richardson also received pay raises each year based on her performance.

5. In June 2018, Richardson applied for the position of "Managing Nurse," which is the lowest level of management for nursing staff at Metro Care. At the time of her application, Richardson was 57 years old.

6. On July 10, 2018, Richardson learned that Metro Care hired Susan Bricker for the position of Managing Nurse. Bricker was 35 years old at the time of her promotion. The two other Managing Nurses in the Metro Care Emergency Room are in their 40s.

7. Metro Care violated the Age Discrimination in Employment Act, 29 U.S.C. §621 *et seq.*, in not promoting Richardson to Managing Nurse. Richardson is a member

of a protected class by virtue of her age. She was qualified for the position of Managing Nurse. She suffered an adverse employment action when she was not promoted, and Metro Care was motivated to hire younger, less qualified Managing Nurses.

8. Claimant has filed the required discrimination charges with the Equal Employment Opportunity Commission (EEOC) and complied with the 60-day filing period to file this claim.

9. As a result of the discrimination, Richardson is entitled to receive a promotion to Managing Nurse. Alternatively, Richardson is entitled to recover damages in excess of $250,000, plus interest and costs. Richardson requests Metro Care pay all forum fees, arbitrator fees, and Richardson's attorney's fees.

Claimant's Oath of Authenticity:

I, Julie Richardson, under penalty of perjury, affirm that the facts supporting the Claim, the supporting Documents, and the Arbitration Agreement are accurate and correct.

Claimant's Signature: /s/   Date: 10/12/2018

United Arbitration Board

Respondent(s):   **ANSWERING STATEMENT**

Metro Care, Inc.
45 Spruce Street
Central, Dover 18412

Initial Claimant(s):

Julie Richardson   Record Number: 2018-0012345
3131 Third Avenue, Apt. 312   _____
Central, Dover 18412   *(As it appears on Initial Claim)*

Respondent states:

1. Metro Care, Inc. ("Metro Care") is a not-for-profit Dover corporation headquartered in Central, Dover, which operates the Metro Care Emergency Room in Dover.

2. Metro Care hired Julie Richardson ("Richardson") as an Emergency Room nurse in June 2014. At the time of her hire, Richardson had been a traveling nurse for many years, and she had not worked for the same hospital for more than 24 months at a time.

3. Metro Care hired Susan Bricker ("Bricker") in 2007 as an Emergency Room Nurse. Bricker received exemplary yearly performance evaluations, and she had a longer term of service with Metro Care than Richardson.

4. Metro Care did not discriminate against Richardson when it promoted Bricker to Managing Nurse.

5. Metro Care is not liable for any damages to Richardson. Metro Care requests Richardson pay all forum fees, arbitrator fees, and Metro Care's attorney's fees.

Respondent's Oath of Authenticity:

I, Richard Journeyman, Chief of Operations for Metro Care, Inc., assert, under penalty of perjury, that the facts supporting this Answering Statement are accurate and correct.

Respondent's Signature: /s/　　　　　　Date: 10/22/2018

Problem

After Good Grains and All Ears finalized their contract, including the arbitration clause, their business relationship proceeded as planned during the first year. Good Grains bought all of the corn it needed for production from All Ears and paid all of its invoices within the time provided. During this period, the price of corn increased at a pace slightly higher than inflation. The parties worked well together, and the executives from both companies were glad to have made this agreement.

Unfortunately, roughly 14 months after the parties entered into their contract, a great drought occurred, hitting the Midwestern portion of the country more than any other part. The drought severely limited All Ears' ability to produce all of the corn necessary to meet the demands on its many contracts.

All Ears' corn production decreased by approximately 20 percent over the last few months. As a response, All Ears decided that it would ship enough corn to meet 80 percent of its obligations on all of its contracts. All Ears considered this to be an equitable solution to the problem, as opposed to completely satisfying some of its obligations, while not satisfying others.

Over the last three months, Good Grains received only 80 percent of its promised corn shipment from All Ears. Good Grains, upset by the situation, withheld all payment to All Ears. In addition, Good Grains had to "cover" and buy the remaining 20 percent of its corn requirements on the temporary market at a price nearly twice what Good Grains would have paid under the contract, given the current market situation.

Using the templates in the *Metro Care v. Richardson* filing:

(a) Representing Good Grains, draft a Demand for Arbitration/Statement of Claim;

(b) Representing All Ears, draft an Answer and Counterclaim (if applicable).

C. Arbitrator Selection

Unlike litigation, parties in arbitration select and employ their panel of arbitrators. The ability to select one's own decision-maker, with known qualifications, expertise, and reputation, is seen as a chief advantage of arbitration. Yet the process of mutually selecting an arbitrator by parties already in dispute, may not run smoothly or quickly. The parties' contract may stipulate the process for selecting the arbitrator(s) and the qualifications required of the arbitrator (such as expertise in a particular subject matter), as well as name an administering organization, such as AAA or JAMS. In some cases, the contract may designate a specific person or administering organization in advance of the dispute (which may raise "repeat player" concerns of bias). Generally, when the parties have agreed to a panel of arbitrators, each party may select an arbitrator and the third arbitrator is selected by the two party-appointed arbitrators. In the event that the parties cannot agree on an arbitrator, provider rules incorporated in the contract provide default means of selecting an arbitrator, or the court may appoint an arbitrator under the FAA. Obviously, arbitrator selection is a crucial decision for the parties because, once selected, the arbitrator has tremendous power throughout the process. Thus, ensuring arbitral competence, fairness, and neutrality is paramount.

Selecting an arbitrator is one of the most important decisions that an advocate can make throughout the process. As discussed in the previous section, arbitrators are most often chosen from a list generated by a provider organization. When a lawyer receives a list of arbitrators, how should he or she learn about those arbitrators? Certainly, advocates should conduct Internet searches to see what type of information is readily available about those arbitrators. Most arbitrators maintain an online presence and post an online resume or bio, and sometimes Internet searches reveal news articles or blog posts either by or about arbitrators. In addition, lawyers can run searches of the arbitrators' names in legal databases, to see if the arbitrator worked as an advocate for particular parties or to determine if the arbitrator has ever issued an award that was challenged in court. In addition to Internet sources, advocates can also talk to colleagues and ask if any of them have experience with the arbitrators on the list to receive less formal feedback and candid advice about the arbitrators on the list.

In some instances, parties can find awards previously issued by the arbitrators. For securities industry disputes, FINRA maintains a public database of arbitration awards. AAA's class action docket is available online, although most of the AAA awards are non-public. BNA publishes labor arbitration awards, which are accessible to subscribers for a fee. In addition, the arbitrators will provide disclosures to the potential clients, and those disclosures should be carefully reviewed by the parties.

In examining the list, the advocate should consider the qualifications of the arbitrators and what type of arbitrator he or she would like to serve. Do you want an arbitrator with subject matter expertise? Extensive process experience? Geographical proximity to the underlying dispute? Consider the following types of arbitrator qualifications and the pros and cons of the following types of arbitrators:

- Retired Judges
- Attorneys
- Academics
- Industry Experts
- "Public" Arbitrators (those without specific industry experience)

Different cases and different clients may lead to different strategic decisions regarding the type of arbitrator that would be best.

The teacher's manual contains fictional biographies of potential arbitrators for the Good Grains case. Representing Good Grains and All Ears, students can try different arbitrator selection techniques to arrive at a single arbitrator, including:

- Eliminating arbitrators one by one until only one is left;
- Ordering the arbitrator in terms of preference, and the one with the lowest combined score is picked;
- Eliminating undesirable arbitrators from the list and then rank-ordering the rest; or
- Trying other selection methods discussed in Chapter 5(B)(3).

D. Preliminary, Interim, and Emergency Relief

In some cases, parties to arbitration need preliminary injunctive, interim, or emergency relief to preserve the status quo while the dispute is being arbitrated. The need for this type of relief occurs in a wide variety of situations, such as to preserve perishable goods or other assets, to freeze funds that otherwise may be transferred beyond the reach of creditors; to protect intellectual property or to otherwise maintain the status quo pending the completed arbitration process.

Courts are empowered to issue this type of interim relief. But how should a party *in, or seeking to compel, arbitration* proceed in obtaining preliminary, interim, or emergency relief? Does arbitration restrict a party from enlisting this relief from the courts? Does an arbitrator have such powers? Historically, parties bound by arbitration have nonetheless been able to access the courts for this type of injunctive relief. Why do you think that is? Today, many of the major arbitration providers have special rules for arbitrators to provide this type of relief. This section considers the availability of relief first from courts and then from arbitrators.

1. Preliminary Relief from Courts

Consider the following case that examines the interplay between a court's powers to issue preliminary injunctive relief in a case otherwise subject to an arbitrator's powers.

Ortho Pharmaceutical Corp. v. Amgen, Inc.
882 F.2d 806 (3d Cir. 1989)

SIRICA, Circuit Judge:

The primary issues in this appeal are whether the Federal Arbitration Act, 9 U.S.C. §§ 1–15 (1982), abrogates the district court's power to issue a preliminary injunction in an arbitrable dispute, and whether the district court erred in deciding that Ortho had met the prerequisites for a preliminary injunction.... The district court determined that under the Federal Arbitration Act, it had the authority to issue a preliminary injunction "to preserve the status quo pending arbitration." ...

Whether a district court has subject matter jurisdiction to grant injunctive relief in an arbitrable dispute presents a question of first impression for this court. We find guidance, however, in the reasoning of the Courts of Appeals for the First, Second, Fourth, Seventh, and Ninth Circuits, all of which have determined that the Arbitration Act does not deprive the district court of the authority to grant interim relief in an arbitrable dispute, provided the court properly exercises its discretion in issuing the relief. Only the Court of Appeals for the Eighth Circuit appears to have expressly held otherwise. See Merrill Lynch, Pierce, Fenner & Smith v. Hovey, 726 F.2d 1286, 1291–92 (8th Cir.1984) ("where the Arbitration Act is applicable and no qualifying contractual language has been alleged, the district court errs in granting injunctive relief").

We first consider Amgen's claim that the language of § 3 of the Arbitration Act expressly prevents the district court from entering preliminary injunctive relief. Section 3 provides:

§ 3. Stay of proceedings where issue therein referable to arbitration

If any suit or proceeding be brought in any of the courts of the United States upon any issue referable to arbitration under an agreement in writing for such arbitration, the court in which such suit is pending, upon being satisfied that the issue involved in such suit or proceeding is referable to arbitration under such an agreement, shall on application of one of the parties stay the trial of the action until such arbitration has been had in accordance with the terms of the agreement, providing the applicant for the stay is not in default in proceeding with such arbitration.

9 U.S.C. § 3. Amgen asserts that the language providing that the district court "shall" stay "any suit or proceeding" regarding an issue that is referable to arbitration, expressly prohibits the district court from issuing a preliminary injunction in an arbitrable dispute. We disagree that the Arbitration Act expressly addresses the issue. As the Fourth Circuit explained in *Bradley*, § 3 declares only that the court shall stay the "trial of the action"; it does not mention preliminary injunctions or other pre-trial proceedings. Indeed, "nothing in the statute's legislative history suggests that the word 'trial' should be given a meaning other than its common and ordinary usage." *Id.*

Consequently, we must decide whether the exercise of the district court's equitable powers would undermine the operation of the Arbitration Act, and is therefore implicitly prohibited. Like the majority of courts that have examined the issue, we find no conflict and thus no implicit prohibition. After an exhaustive discussion of various circuit and Supreme Court authority, the First Circuit in Teradyne summarized the rationale for the majority rule:

> [T]his approach reinforces rather than detracts from the policy of the Arbitration Act.... We believe that the congressional desire to enforce arbitration agreements would frequently be frustrated if the courts were precluded from issuing preliminary injunctive relief to preserve the status quo pending arbitration and, ipso facto, the meaningfulness of the arbitration process.

Teradyne, 797 F.2d at 51. We find this reasoning convincing. As the Supreme Court stated in *Dean Witter Reynolds, Inc. v. Byrd,* 470 U.S. 213 (1985), the Arbitration Act was "motivated by a congressional desire to enforce agreements into which parties had entered." We believe that an arbitration agreement reflects the parties' intention to adhere to an orderly process of alternative dispute resolution. Therefore, we do not construe such an agreement as constituting a "waiver" by either party of the right to seek preliminary injunctive relief necessary to prevent one party from unilaterally eviscerating the significance of the agreed-upon procedures.

Therefore, we hold that a district court has the authority to grant injunctive relief in an arbitrable dispute, provided that the traditional prerequisites for such relief are satisfied. This court has consistently identified four factors that a court must consider in ascertaining the propriety of a preliminary injunction: (1) whether the movant has demonstrated reasonable probability of eventual success in the litigation; (2) whether the movant has demonstrated that it will be irreparably injured pendente lite if relief is not granted to prevent a change in the status quo; (3) the possibility of harm to other interested persons from the grant or denial of the injunction, and (4) the public interest. Absent an error of law or serious mistake in the consideration of proof, the district court's decision will be reversed only for an abuse of discretion. A reviewing court will find an abuse of discretion only when the district court has committed a "clear error of judgment," not simply because that reviewing court, applying the law to the facts of the case, could arguably reach a different result. When reviewing the grant of a preliminary injunction, we accord deference to the judgment of the district court "because of the infinite variety of situations which may confront it."

Our conclusion here—that in the case of an arbitrable dispute, the district court should apply the traditional test to determine whether the case is an appropriate one to issue injunctive relief, and that a reviewing court should accord deference to the district court's balancing of these traditional factors—comports with the views of other courts of appeals. After holding that "a district court can grant injunctive relief in an arbitrable dispute pending arbitration, provided the [traditional] prerequisites for injunctive relief are satisfied," the *Teradyne* court then reiterated that "[t]he decision to grant or deny a preliminary injunction is a matter for the discretion of the district court." Similarly, in *Roso-Lino Beverage Distributors,* 749 F.2d 124, the Second Circuit explained that the reviewing court must "determine whether the dispute is a 'proper case' for an injunction." Accordingly, that court applied the circuit's traditional test for determining whether to issue a preliminary injunction.

Nevertheless, Amgen contends that even if the Arbitration Act does not abrogate entirely the district court's subject matter jurisdiction over arbitrable disputes, it at least limits that jurisdiction to "preservation of the status quo." Accordingly, Amgen argues that in this case, the district court "exceeded the scope of its jurisdiction" by: (1) "misperceiving" the status quo; (2) addressing the merits of the contractual dispute; and (3) granting relief that resolved the pending dispute. Central to Amgen's analysis is the belief that the "status quo" at the time arbitration was filed was that the FDA was considering Amgen's own PLA that did not include Ortho clinical data. Whether the district court exceeded the scope of its jurisdiction is an issue of law subject to plenary review by this court.

As our previous discussion indicates, we disagree that the "preservation of the status quo" operates as a separate test for determining whether the district court acted within its jurisdictional authority. Rather, the "preservation of the status quo" represents the goal of preliminary injunctive relief in any litigation, including in an arbitrable dispute. It is the balancing of the various factors of the traditional four-pronged test that bear upon the court's exercise of discretion:

> [T]he most compelling reason in favor of ... [issuing a preliminary injunction] is the need to prevent the judicial process from being rendered futile by defendant's action or refusal to act. On the other hand, judicial intervention before the merits have been finally determined frequently imposes a burden on defendant that ultimately turns out to be unjustified. Consequently, the preliminary injunction is appropriate whenever the policy of preserving the court's power to decide the case effectively outweighs the risk of imposing an interim restraint before it has done so. Thus, the function of this traditional test is to enable the court, on the basis of the data before it, "to attempt to minimize the probable harm to legally protected interests between the time that the motion for a preliminary injunction is filed and the time of the final hearing."

In sum, courts invoke the phrase "preservation of the status quo" as a summary explanation of the need to protect the integrity of the applicable dispute resolution process. Thus, the court granting an injunction has the power—and indeed is required—to make all factual findings necessary to "set forth the reason for ... issuance [of injunctive relief]." Fed.R.Civ.P. 65(d). Moreover, because the district court must focus on preservation of the integrity of the arbitration process, the relief granted need not be limited to restoring the parties precisely to their pre-litigation position without regard to the irreparable injury that movant faces. If the existing "status quo" is currently causing one of the parties irreparable injury and thereby threatens to nullify the arbitration process, then it is necessary to alter the situation to prevent the injury.

In support of its position that the "preservation of the status quo" serves as a jurisdictional test, Amgen relies principally on *Merrill Lynch, Pierce, Fenner & Smith, Inc. v. Bradley*, 756 F.2d 1048. This reliance is misplaced. In *Bradley*, the Fourth Circuit held that

> where a dispute is subject to mandatory arbitration under the Federal Arbitration Act, a district court has the discretion to grant a preliminary injunction to preserve the status quo pending the arbitration of the parties' dispute if the

enjoined conduct would render that process a "hollow formality." The arbitration process would be a hollow formality where "the award when rendered could not return the parties substantially to the status quo ante. [citation omitted]."

The *Bradley* court concluded, however, that by finding that the movant faced irreparable harm, "the district court implicitly found that arbitration of this dispute would be a hollow formality absent preliminary relief." As we noted above, the First Circuit's *Teradyne* decision took a similar view. While explaining that the district court "can, and should, grant a preliminary injunction in an arbitrable dispute to preserve the status quo pending arbitration," the *Teradyne* court held that "a district court can grant injunctive relief in an arbitrable dispute pending arbitration, provided the [traditional] prerequisites for injunctive relief are satisfied." Accordingly, we next consider whether injunctive relief was properly issued in this case....

a. Comments and Questions

1. Are courts equipped to deal with interim and preliminary matters? What are the benefits and drawbacks of asking courts to step into the role of deciding interim matters when the merits of the case will be arbitrated? *See Janvey v. Alguire*, 647 F.3d 585 (5th Cir. 2011) (holding that a court had the power to rule on interim relief prior to ruling on a motion to compel arbitration).

2. For a more recent look at the issue, see Bruce Meyerson, *Interim Relief in Arbitration: What Does the Case Law Teach Us?*, 34 ALTERNATIVES TO THE HIGH COST OF LITIG. 131 (Oct. 2016).

2. Preliminary Relief from Arbitrators

In recent years, arbitration providers have begun to institute rules for preliminary relief and populated panels of arbitrators who can be deployed in a short amount of time to rule on a preliminary matter.

American Arbitration Association, Commercial Arbitration R-38

(b) A party in need of emergency relief prior to the constitution of the panel shall notify the AAA and all other parties in writing of the nature of the relief sought and the reasons why such relief is required on an emergency basis....

(c) Within one business day of receipt of notice as provided in section (b), the AAA shall appoint a single emergency arbitrator designated to rule on emergency applications....

(d) The emergency arbitrator shall as soon as possible, but in any event within two business days of appointment, establish a schedule for consideration of the application for emergency relief. Such a schedule shall provide a reasonable opportunity to all parties to be heard....

(e) If after consideration the emergency arbitrator is satisfied that the party seeking the emergency relief has shown that immediate and irreparable loss or damage shall result in the absence of emergency relief, and that such party is entitled to such relief, the emergency arbitrator may enter an interim order or award granting the relief and stating the reason therefore.

JAMS Comprehensive Arbitration Rules & Procedures Rule 2

(c) Emergency Relief Procedures. These Emergency Relief Procedures are available in Arbitrations filed and served after July 1, 2014, and where not otherwise prohibited by law. Parties may agree to opt out of these Procedures in their Arbitration Agreement or by subsequent written agreement.

(i) A Party in need of emergency relief prior to the appointment of an Arbitrator may notify JAMS and all other Parties in writing of the relief sought and the basis for an Award of such relief. This Notice shall include an explanation of why such relief is needed on an expedited basis....

(ii) JAMS shall promptly appoint an Emergency Arbitrator to rule on the emergency request. In most cases the appointment of an Emergency Arbitrator will be done within 24 hours of receipt of the request....

(iii) Within two business days, or as soon as practicable thereafter, the Emergency Arbitrator shall establish a schedule for the consideration of the request for emergency relief. The schedule shall provide a reasonable opportunity for all Parties to be heard taking into account the nature of the relief sought....

(iv) The Emergency Arbitrator shall determine whether the Party seeking emergency relief has shown that immediate and irreparable loss or damage will result in the absence of emergency relief and whether the requesting Party is entitled to such relief. The Emergency Arbitrator shall enter an order or Award granting or denying the relief, as the case may be, and stating the reasons therefor.

Comments and Questions

1. Do you think that parties to an arbitration agreement intend for an arbitrator to decide issues of preliminary, interim, or emergency relief? Do these new rules give parties the services that they would need in emergency situations? As a party to an arbitration, would you prefer to have a court or an arbitrator decide these preliminary matters?

2. In what ways do the AAA and JAMS rules meet the parties' need for expediency?

3. Emergency relief by arbitrators has a longer history in international arbitration than in domestic arbitration. Does emergency relief in international arbitration make more sense than in domestic arbitration? In international arbitration, questions may

arise regarding which courts have jurisdiction, how to serve parties, and whether the relief sought is even available in the foreign court. For more information on this topic, see Erin Collins, *Pre-Tribunal Emergency Relief in International Commercial Arbitration*, 10 Loy. U. Chi. Int'l L. Rev. 105 (2012) (regarding international arbitration); Ben H. Sheppard Jr. & John M. Townsend, *Holding the Fort Until the Arbitrators Are Appointed: The New ICDR International Emergency Rule*, 61 Disp. Resol. J. 75 (July 2006).

E. Post-Appointment/ Pre-Hearing Conference

Once the arbitral panel is established, it is generally helpful to schedule a pre-hearing administrative conference to discuss and establish a procedure for the administration of the arbitration. The hearing may be conducted by telephone or in person. As with any meeting with the arbitrators, an effective advocate should be prepared to discuss:

- How much discovery needs to take place.
- How long the discovery will take to complete.
- Whether and when the parties should file pre-hearing motions.
- Whether and when the parties should attempt mediation.
- How many hearing days the parties will need to present their case.
- Whether there are any witnesses who might need to testify other than in-person, such as telephonically or via videoconference.
- Whether the parties need the arbitrators to issue third-party subpoenas.

At this conference, the parties and arbitrator(s) set a schedule with important dates, such as discovery cut-offs, motion filing dates, and hearing dates. Although the dates may be adjusted (and FAA § 10(a)(3) gives arbitrators an incentive to allow extensions), rescheduling with multiple parties and arbitrators can become a daunting task and delay a case substantially.

Some scheduling and administrative matters may have a significant impact on clients and should be considered as early as possible. For instance, the parties may need to decide on a location for the arbitration hearing. In some cases, the hearing location is set through a series of provider organization rules or practices. In other cases, the hearing location may be designated by the contract. In the absence of these circumstances, the parties should quickly determine where the arbitration will occur if the parties are located in different places, or if the subject matter of the arbitration is in another locale completely. Some clients prefer to stay close to home, especially during a stressful time, such as an arbitration hearing. This first conference might also be a good time to alert the arbitrator to any special accommodations that need to be made for a client, such as securing a facility with wheelchair access or the need for translation services.

This early meeting may also be a good time to have a discussion about the use of technology, both during discovery and during the hearing. If parties, lawyers, and witnesses are separated by a great distance, the initial hearing may be a time to raise the issue of telephonic or video depositions or hearing testimony. In rare cases, key witnesses may be infirm or close to death, and special arrangements may need to be made in a timely manner to secure testimony or other evidence relevant to the matter.

The prepared advocate will attend the pre-hearing administrative conference with her calendar. One of the most important items to come out of this hearing is the schedule of important dates. The arbitrators will likely come to agreement on the dates by consensus, and everyone should know those dates by the time the conference call is complete. In the days following the conference, the arbitrators also will likely issue a formal schedule to confirm with the parties and attorneys.

F. Discovery

Traditionally, advocates did little discovery work in arbitrations and presented their cases based largely on their own documents and witnesses. Advocates did not depose more than a small handful of parties or witnesses in a case, and the lawyers did not necessarily know what the witnesses called by the opposing party would say. What are the benefits and drawbacks to this type of approach?

Today's arbitration discovery can look very similar to litigation discovery, and the explosion of modern discovery into arbitration has helped advocates better prepare for the hearing—but at what cost? The question of discovery is essentially a question of advocacy and a question of costs. Today's discovery consists largely of retrieving and evaluating large sums of electronically stored data, i.e., "e-discovery." *See* Charles Yablon & Nick Landsman-Roos, *Discovery About Discovery: Sampling Practice and the Resolution of Discovery Disputes in an Age of Ever-Increasing Information*, 34 Cardozo L. Rev. 719 (2012) (providing both theoretical and empirical analysis of modern discovery issues).

Unsurprisingly, arbitrators manage the discovery process as necessary. Parties who are dissatisfied with the course of discovery can ask the Chair to intervene and guide, or even control, aspects of the discovery process. It is not uncommon for parties in commercial arbitration to file motions to compel discovery, as well as requests for subpoenas of third parties for depositions or documents. Arbitration provider organization rules generally require the parties to attempt to resolve their discovery disputes between themselves before enlisting the services of the arbitrator. Arbitrators generally issue discovery orders, ruling on matters as they arise.

What if a party is unsatisfied with the outcome? What if the arbitrator orders the production of a document that one party believes is covered by the attorney-client privilege? Consider the following case.

Tenet Healthcare Corp. v. Maharaj

859 So. 2d 1209 (Fla. Dist. Ct. App. 2003)

FARMER, Chief Judge:

This attempted appeal arises from our decision in Tenet Healthcare Corp. v. Maharaj, 787 So.2d 241 (Fla. 4th DCA 2001). There we held that the agreement between the parties requires the controversy to be settled by arbitration. During the course of the ensuing arbitration proceedings, the arbitrator ordered appellants to produce a certain document. Appellants in turn sought review of the arbitrator's order in the circuit court. Appellees asked the circuit court to dismiss the attempt on the grounds that the arbitrator's discovery orders were unreviewable. The circuit court agreed with appellees and dismissed the attempt. Appellants then filed the present appeal.

Appellees now seek to have this appeal dismissed, again arguing that the arbitrator's decision is not reviewable. We read appellees' motion effectually to seek enforcement of our Mandate from the prior appeal requiring the entire matter to be arbitrated, not litigated in court. In response to this motion, appellants argue that all they have done is to seek conventional review of a trial court's order concluding that it lacks jurisdiction and that such orders have been widely understood to be subject to review by appeal.

We disagree with appellants. First, the order of the arbitrator for which appellants seek judicial review is an order compelling production of a document, a routine discovery order. Appellants argue that the arbitrator erred in compelling production of the document because, they claim, it is covered by the attorney/client privilege. They presented their privilege claim to the arbitrator, who rejected it. Nothing they have cited would allow for judicial review of such a discovery decision by an arbitrator.

The Florida Arbitration Code authorizes an arbitrator to order discovery. Section 682.08 explicitly allows the arbitrator to compel production of documents and to issue subpoenas for that purpose. § 682.08, Fla. Stat. (2003). The statute provides for enforcement of such subpoenas "in the manner provided by law," but it says nothing about judicial review of arbitrator orders compelling discovery. Similarly, although section 682.20 provides for some judicial review in arbitration cases, it carefully limits such review to specified final decisions, none of which include review of discovery orders. § 682.20, Fla. Stat. (2003). We take that silence to represent a decision not to provide for such review.

We note the anomaly appellants' argument would create. In ordinary civil litigation, there is no right of appeal of discovery orders; any review is discretionary and subject to severe limitations. But arbitration is an alternative to court proceedings, in which the parties have elected to forego the usual civil procedures—including, for example, discovery and the rules of evidence—in favor of a swifter, less expensive resolution of their disputes. Appellants' position in this case would introduce a judicial remedy into arbitration discovery disputes that does not exist even in civil cases. While we recognize that certiorari is sometimes granted in civil cases to review discovery orders affecting privileged matters, a party to an arbitration agreement could plausibly argue that it was precisely to avoid this kind of judicial intervention that the parties chose arbitration. As we held some years ago, "[o]nce the parties agree[ ] to submit to arbitration, the code limits the authority of the court to interfere in the process prematurely." *Air Conditioning Equip., Inc. v. Rogers*, 551 So.2d 554, 557 (Fla. 4th DCA 1989).

Appellants strive to support their position with *State ex rel. Gaines Constr. Co. v. Pearson*, 154 So.2d 833 (Fla.1963). We think their contended interpretation of *Pearson* would vastly overreach its essential holding. *Pearson* simply recognized final review as to decisions that decide the essential claim of right even though they technically seem to leave something else unresolved. *Pearson* does not purport to expand court intervention into arbitration cases. In fact it emphasizes the narrow basis for such intervention.

In *Pearson* the order did not itself determine the amount due, but specified the formula to ascertain that amount. *Pearson* regards such an outcome as final enough for review. As we noted in *Rogers*, *Pearson* "clearly expressed disapproval of confirmation of such orders other than in exceptional circumstances." 551 So.2d at 557. Judicial intervention to review discovery orders would greatly disrupt the primacy of the arbitration process. We certainly do not read *Pearson* to allow review of discovery orders in arbitration.

The trial court order in this case was manifestly not a conventional order determining subject matter jurisdiction. In fact the court was simply enforcing our Mandate that the arbitration of this controversy should proceed to a final result. Appellants are not entitled to review of the trial court's refusal to intervene in the arbitration discovery order.

APPEAL DISMISSED.

1. Comments and Questions

a. Cases involving review of discovery orders are relatively rare. In the usual case, they are not worth the time and expense of fighting the jurisdictional challenges. Is the general rule that discovery orders are not immediately appealable a good rule? When, if ever, can a party challenge a discovery order?

b. The *Tenet Healthcare* case involved the potential disclosure of materials governed by the attorney-client privilege. Should courts treat arbitration discovery disputes involving the privilege differently?

G. Dispositive Motions

Until recently, parties did not even consider filing dispositive motions in arbitration. Arbitration institutions did not historically have rules expressly allowing parties to file dispositive motions. Despite the lack of clear rules, parties would request dispositive relief by filing motions to dismiss or motions for summary judgment. More modern versions of codes of arbitration procedure include specific reference to dispositive motions. Some forums, such as FINRA, strictly limit them. Traditional advice for advocates has been to refrain from filing dispositive motions because arbitrators rarely grant them. On the other hand, advocates can argue to the panel that granting the motion could narrow or even dispose of some of the issues for the merits hearing, thus promoting efficiency.

In 2010, the College of Commercial Arbitrators issued *Protocols for Expeditious, Cost-Effective Commercial Arbitration* to respond to the rising costs of arbitration. The *Protocols* recognize that as trial lawyers transitioned into becoming arbitration lawyers, they "nonetheless generally want to try cases in arbitration with the same intensity and the same tactics with which they were conducted in court. Thus, expanded arbitral motion practice and discovery have developed within the framework of standard commercial arbitration rules, which tend to afford arbitrators and parties considerable 'wiggle room' on matters of procedure." *Protocols*, at 5. The increased use of dispositive motions, however, has mixed benefits. On the one hand, the use of dispositive motions can narrow "arbitral issues prior to hearings and full-blown discovery, thus avoiding unnecessary preparation and hearing time." *Protocols*, at 9. On the other hand, "motion practice often contributes significantly to arbitration cost and cycle time without clear benefits. The filing of motions leads to the establishment of schedules for briefing and argument entailing considerable effort by advocates, only to have the arbitrators postpone a decision until the close of the hearing because of the existence of unresolved factual disputes raised by the motion papers." *Id.* The Protocols suggest a number of solutions for advocates in considering the question of motion practice. Consider the following protocols.

College of Commercial Arbitrators, Protocols for Expeditious, Cost-Effective Commercial Arbitration

(2010)

A Protocol For Business Users and In-House Counsel

Protocol 9. Control motion practice

Businesses should also consider agreeing to procedures for limiting "reflexive" motion practice and expediting the presentation and hearing of motions that have the potential to promote cost- and time-saving in arbitration.

Comments

* * *

While it is generally appropriate for arbitrators to steer clear of dispositive motions involving extensive factual issues, there are certain matters that may be forthrightly addressed early on with little or no discovery or testimony, such as contractual limitations on damages, statutory remedies, or statutes of limitations and other legal limitations on causes of action. If dispositive action is foreseen as a useful element in arbitration, there should be an appropriate provision in the arbitration procedure.

A Protocol for Outside Counsel

Protocol 8. Recognize and exploit the difference between arbitration and litigation

Counsel should recognize the many differences between litigation and arbitration, including the absence of a jury on whom rhetorical displays and showboating may have some effect. Arbitrators are generally experienced and sophisticated professionals with whom posturing and grandstanding are almost always inappropriate, counter-productive, and wasteful of the client's time, money and credibility with the arbitrators. Counsel should keep in mind that dispositive motions are rarely granted in arbitration, and should employ such motions only where there will be a clear net benefit in terms of time and cost savings. Counsel should be aware that arbitrators tend to employ more relaxed evidentiary standards, and should therefore avoid littering the record with repeated objections to form and hearsay. An advocate who objects at every turn is likely to try the patience of a tribunal and undermine his or her own credibility.

1. Comments and Questions

a. What do you think about the *Protocols'* discussion of dispositive motions? Do the suggestions go far enough? Too far? Do you agree with the *Protocols'* decision to give separate guidance to in-house and outside counsel? The *Protocols* also include guidance for arbitrators and provider organizations, but those are not reproduced here.

b. Why do you think that advocates file motions to dismiss and motions for summary judgment in arbitration? Are there any benefits to filing a dispositive motion, even if the motion is unlikely to succeed?

H. Representing Clients at the Hearing

In many ways, representing clients at an arbitration hearing is similar to representing clients at trial. A law school trial advocacy class will teach students many important skills that are largely transferrable to arbitration advocacy. Some important differences exist, though, and good trial tactics may fall flat in arbitration. The key difference in trial practice and arbitration practice lies in the nature of the decision-maker. Convincing a generalist jury is very different from convincing an expert arbitrator.

This section consists of advice by our casebook authors, all of whom are practicing arbitrators. Some of this advice may seem obvious. It is our experience, however, that lawyers underappreciate the differences between arbitration and litigation and simply import trial tactics into their arbitration advocacy. We hope to leave you with some practical tips to lead to more arbitration success.

Preliminary Motions

Preliminary motions are those raised immediately after the arbitrators' introduction. These motions usually involve procedural and evidentiary matters that would affect the hearing. Arbitrators routinely grant stipulations if both parties already agree. Stipulations might cover issues such as hearing witness testimony by telephone or pre-arranging the testimony of certain witnesses on certain days (i.e., "out of order") to accommodate the witness' travel schedule. The parties might also stipulate in advance to the admissibility of all documentary evidence, or at least some joint exhibits.

In some instances, parties may move *in limine* to exclude certain evidence. *In limine* motions are rarely granted, and they may be an inefficient use of time and client resources. Arbitrators rarely exclude evidence, and more commonly arbitrators will admit the evidence "for what it's worth." If a piece of evidence is arguably covered by a privilege or if the evidence is extraordinarily inflammatory, filing a motion *in limine* may make sense. Otherwise, most evidentiary issues should be handled as they arise during the hearing.

Party Opening Statements

Unlike in court, advocates deliver party opening statements while sitting at the table, rather than while standing up. Claimant should expect to go first. Usually, claimant will not have a "rebuttal" opening statement, but if the respondent also has a counterclaim, the arbitrators may allow for a rebuttal statement on the counterclaim issues.

The duration of opening statements can vary widely, but they generally last between 15 minutes and two hours. Before opening statements begin, the arbitrator will likely ask how much time each party needs for its opening statement, and the arbitrator will try to limit each opening to that time period. The duration of an opening statement will also be impacted by the number of days the hearing is expected to take. A one- or two-day hearing requires significantly shorter opening statements than a hearing expected to last several weeks or even months.

The opening statements should be brief (for the circumstances), concise, yet still complete to give the arbitrators a picture of what to expect throughout the rest of the hearing. As with trial practice, many attorneys will develop themes, and those themes may be helpful, so long as they are not too outlandish or unrealistic. In a medical malpractice case, a claimant's theme might be the "surgeon's inexperience," while the respondent's theme might be the "claimant's failure to provide a complete medical history." Over-the-top themes, such as the "millennial doctor's heartlessness and greed" or the "claimant's money-grubbing nature while trying to destroy the career of the young surgeon" are easily dismissed by arbitrators.

Many advocates choose to use trial technology in their opening statements. Advocates can use projectors to showcase certain documents, or they can use a Power-Point presentation or more sophisticated software to create a visual effect for their case. Lawyers choosing to use this type of technology should bring their own equipment (computers, projectors, screens, etc.) and ensure that the room is large enough to accommodate the presentation equipment without rendering the room uncomfortably cramped.

Witness Presentation and Making Objections

Following opening statements, claimant begins its presentation of evidence. In the usual course, claimant presents all of its witnesses and then rests. After claimant has rested, respondent presents its witnesses and then rests. Whether a rebuttal case may be presented is often a matter of arbitrator discretion. Any number of exceptions to this usual procedure are not uncommon. Witnesses may testify out of order if travel arrangements necessitate it. For example, consider an out-of-town witness for respondent that has travel plans to be at the hearing between Wednesday and Friday of the first hearing week. The hearing is progressing more slowly than planned, and claimant is still presenting witnesses on Friday morning. With everyone's permission, respondent's witness could be heard out of turn in the middle of claimant's case so that the witness can keep her travel plans and not incur a large cost. Alternatively, witnesses can testify via telephone or video connection.

The content of the witness presentation in domestic arbitration is very similar to trial practice.[1] The witness will be subject to both direct and cross-examination. In many instances, the arbitrator will also allow for limited re-direct and re-cross. On direct, the witness should provide answers to the advocate's questions in narrative form. Hopefully, the advocates have prepared the witnesses so that they know what to expect and what questions will be asked. Witnesses are also likely to be asked questions about documents and their knowledge of those documents. Advocates who ask a combination of open-ended factual questions and closed-ended confirmation questions generally put their witnesses in the best light on direct examination.

On cross-examination, witnesses perform best when they answer in a concise manner, responding to the attorney's (typically) leading questions. Witnesses who are combative, elusive, or who fail to answer the question posed do not present well to the arbitrators. On cross-examination, lawyers should ask closed-ended questions to uncover inconsistencies, create holes in the direct testimony, make succinct points for the other side, and explore biases. Cross-examination is usually most effective when advocates ask short questions that garner short responses. Arbitrators can easily see through trial tactics, such as using compound questions to cause a witness to slip and admit to something he or she did not intend.

Advocates generally make far fewer objections in arbitration than in trial practice. Most objections are overruled, particularly if they relate to the form of a question. Questions can easily be rephrased, and many arbitrators allow the question to stand

---

1. As will be discussed in Chapter 11, international arbitration has many different procedures. In many European traditions, lawyers do not engage in a direct examination of their witnesses. Instead, the witnesses will present a written declaration that serves as their direct testimony. Live witness presentation, then, is limited to cross-examination and rebuttal.

rather than asking the advocate to go through the academic exercise of reframing it. Even in the face of a facially valid objection, many arbitrators state that they will allow the evidence in "for what it's worth," and consider the question a matter of the weight of the evidence. The more successful objections are those regarding the content of material presented (as compared to the form of the question), although those are often overruled, too. Attorneys should only make objections that matter, such as objections to potentially privileged material, sensitive information, or highly damaging testimony.

Because few objections are made or sustained, questioning techniques in arbitration are considerably lax as compared to those in litigation. Attorneys often ask leading questions on direct examination, ask for hearsay evidence, and ask questions relating to a document that the witness may not have authored or received. As in trial practice, generally only the lawyer who questions the witness can interpose objections.

Another major difference in witness presentations is that arbitrators can, and often do, ask questions of the witnesses. The traditional place for arbitrator questions is at the end of the attorneys' presentation of that witness. In other words, the arbitrators ask questions after the conclusion of any re-direct testimony and before the witness is dismissed. If a witness's testimony is lengthy (more than a day), however, the arbitrators may ask questions during the lawyer's presentation (direct or cross) so as to not risk forgetting the questions by the time the witness' testimony concludes.

Evidentiary Submissions

In addition to live testimony, arbitrators also consider documentary and physical evidence. Documentary and physical evidence includes a wide variety of items, including emails, balance sheets, and other financial information, contracts, pictures, reports, charts and graphs, and sometimes physical objects, such as alleged defective products. Some cases also involve a physical inspection, such as the inspection of a building in a construction dispute or the inspection of a damaged vehicle in an insurance dispute. In cases involving a physical inspection, the arbitrators will visit the site accompanied by attorneys from both sides so as to preclude the possibility of ex parte communications.

As with testimonial evidence, arbitrators overrule most objections to the introduction of documentary and physical evidence. Objections to the introduction of evidence should be made sparingly, if at all. In some cases, the parties will stipulate to all documents listed on their previously exchanged exhibit lists. In those cases, the parties need not establish any type of foundation before documents are admitted.

In addition to "real" evidence, advocates should also consider the use of demonstrative evidence. Timelines, charts, graphs, simulated videos, and the like can all be very persuasive, if used correctly and sparingly. At the conclusion of the hearing, parties can move to admit the demonstrative evidence so that the arbitrators can use it while they deliberate.

Expert Testimony

In appropriate cases, advocates should consider calling expert witnesses in addition to factual witnesses. Arbitrators rarely exclude expert testimony, and the requirements for expert testimony in federal and state courts do not govern arbitration. Advocates should work with their experts in advance and provide any written expert reports by applicable deadlines in their discovery schedules.

Despite the lax rules, expert practice in arbitration is quite similar to litigation. Lawyers are still expected to ask the expert about his or her qualifications prior to "offering" the witness as an expert. On direct examination, experts usually testify about their expert opinions and the support for their conclusions. All of this information is usually also available in the expert's report.

On cross-examination, lawyers generally look for flaws in the experts' analysis, opinions based on incomplete information, and bias. At some point on direct or cross-examination, the expert will likely be asked about his or her expert fees, how often the expert is engaged, and whether the expert has a reputation for engagement by claimants' side attorneys or respondents' side attorneys. For example, some expert witnesses are routinely engaged by investors, while other experts routinely are routinely engaged by broker-dealers.

Expert witness testimony can be useful on a wide variety of topics. Experts are probably most often retained to calculate damages and opine on breaches of professional duties, but experts can testify on any number of liability or damages issues.

Closing Statements

The final portion of the arbitration hearing for the advocates is the closing statements. As with opening statements, advocates should expect to deliver closing statements from a seated position. Respondents usually close first, as claimants can reserve their entire closing for rebuttal. This order gives the claimant the "first and last" chance to present. Closing statements generally last from 15 minutes to two hours, again depending on the length of the hearing. Attorneys rarely object during the closing statements, and arbitrators may ask an occasional question of the attorneys.

While the opening statement explains what to expect from the hearing, the closing statement summarizes the key factual issues and legal arguments proven during the hearing. Advocates should also clearly reiterate any requests for relief, so the arbitrators know precisely what remedies they should consider awarding.

As with opening statements, attorneys should continue to avoid hyperbole, as arbitrators will easily see through the rhetoric and rely on the factual information already presented. Additionally, if there are legal issues in dispute, advocates should bring to the arbitrators' attention during closing argument any authorities that the parties would like the panel to consider when deliberating. Thus, it is the lawyers' responsibility to provide copies of any cases, statutes, or secondary authorities to the panelists, as most arbitrators in domestic commercial arbitration will not conduct their own independent legal research. Alternatively, if the parties want to argue complex factual and legal theories, including those in pre- or post-hearing briefs might make it easier for the panelists to follow. These briefs are discussed in the next section.

I. Pre- and Post-Hearing Briefing

Pre- and post-hearing briefing is a relatively common practice in arbitration. Although pre-hearing briefing has a trial counterpart (i.e., the "trial brief), post-hearing briefing is more common in arbitration than any other type of dispute resolution process. This section gives an overview of the purpose of these documents and examples of what they should include.

1. Pre-Hearing Briefing

Pre-hearing briefs allow advocates to give the arbitrators an overview of the dispute, a general description of the applicable law, and a preview of the evidence that the advocate expects to present at the hearing. Although the audience for the pre-hearing brief is the arbitrator, advocates will also exchange their pre-hearing briefs with opposing counsel. Not all cases require pre-hearing briefing. Parties may forego this step entirely in cases that are not particularly complex or that do not require more than one or two hearing days.

As a practical matter, pre-hearing briefs resemble trial submissions. They begin with a case caption, including the parties' names, case number, arbitrators' names, and the like. The document varies in length, depending on the case, and can be as short as five pages or as long as 25 pages, and contain attached exhibits. Arbitrators are rarely impressed with voluminous briefing, and brevity is often appreciated. The tone of the pre-hearing brief should be professional and similar to trial and appellate filings.

Pre-hearing briefing has two primary components. The first is a statement of the facts that the party expects to prove at the hearing. The second is an overview of the relevant law. The legal overview need not be extensive, but it should give the arbitrators a general understanding of the legal landscape surrounding the dispute. Pre-hearing briefing is also a good time to introduce the themes that the advocate intends to present at the hearing. Consider the following example of a short prehearing brief in the fictitious age discrimination case of *Richards v. Metro Care*. Unlike the example below, the brief would normally cite to evidentiary materials and also contain exhibits or attachments.

United Arbitration Board

Julie Richardson

and   2018-0012345

Record Number: _____

Metro Care, Inc.

August 24, 2019

Filing Date: _____

Pre-Hearing Brief of Julie Richardson

Claimant Julie Richardson ("Richardson") brings this Age Discrimination claim against her employer, Respondent Metro Care, Inc. ("Metro Care"). This case is set for a four-day arbitration hearing commencing on September 16, 2019. The primary issue in this case is whether Metro Care violated the Age Discrimination in Employment Act, 29 U.S.C. § 621 *et seq.* ("ADEA"), and the Dover Age Discrimination Act, 26 Dov. St. § 1560 *et seq.* ("DADA"), when it promoted Susan Bricker ("Bricker") to the new position as Managing Nurse when Richardson was the more qualified, albeit older, candidate.

Summary of Facts

Richardson is currently 58 years old, and has been a nurse for 28 years. Richardson received her Bachelors of Science in Nursing in 1991 from New State University in Atlanta, Georgia. She graduated in the top 10 percent of her class, and received multiple job offers upon her graduation.

Julie spent most of the first 20 years following graduation as a Traveling Emergency Room Nurse. A traveling nurse is a nurse that works in a specific location, but only for a limited amount of time. Traveling nurses work between 15 and 25 weeks in a given location before moving on to the next location. Traveling nurses are paid significantly more than their permanent counterparts. They can be located in both urban and rural areas throughout the country. Richardson's career took her throughout the United States, and she worked in hospitals in places including Boston, Massachusetts, Cleveland, Ohio, Minot, North Dakota, and Billings, Montana. Her last stint as a traveling nurse was in Central, Dover. There, she met her husband, and she decided to make Dover her permanent home.

In June 2014, Metro Care hired Richardson, then 53 years old, as an Emergency Room nurse. When Nancy Neville ("Neville") hired Richardson, Neville claimed that she was highly impressed with Richardson's experience across the country. During the interview process, Richardson asked Neville about opportunities for advancement. Neville noted that Richardson had excellent experience and should consider applying for management positions as they arise.

Each and every year after she was hired, Richardson received "exemplary" performance reviews, as well as merits-based pay raises. At her annual reviews, Richardson and Neville discussed the possibility of advancement into management, and Neville always gave Richardson the impression that she would be an excellent candidate.

In 2018, Metro Care posted a Managing Nurse opening. This was the first management position to come open since Metro Care hired Richardson. Richardson was very excited about the opportunity to apply, but she had some trepidations. She is at least a decade older than every other Managing Nurse at Metro Care, and she had heard some gossip from some of the other nurses that she "didn't have a chance" because Metro Care prefers to have a young management team. The management team has a reputation of going out after work and participating in social events, while Richardson prefers to go home after work and spend time with her husband.

Richardson was disappointed, but not surprised, when Metro Care hired Bricker to fill the Managing Nurse opening. Bricker was only 35 years old at the time of her promotion, and she had roughly 15 years less experience than Richardson and had only ever worked in Dover. Almost immediately after her promotion, Richardson heard rumors that Bricker was already going out to bars and clubs with the other Managing Nurses. Metro Care's hiring choices have created a "culture of youth" to the detriment of the more experienced and mature workers. None of the Metro Care Managing Nurses are more than 45 years old, and most of them were hired into management in their early to mid-30s.

Richardson continues to work in the Emergency Room as a nurse at Metro Care. The atmosphere at work has become tense since she filed this claim, but she has earned and deserves a promotion to Managing Nurse.

Legal Argument

Metro Care violated both the ADEA and the DADA when it promoted Bricker over Richardson for the position of Managing Nurse. At the hearing, Richardson will prove that Metro Care's "culture of youth" and promotion of younger employees over more qualified older employees violated both of these statutes.

At the hearing, Richardson will show that she meets each of the elements of a prima facia case of age discrimination. To prove the claim, Richardson will show that she: (1) was at least 40 years old; (2) was qualified for the position; (3) suffered an adverse employment action; and (4) was rejected for someone sufficiently younger to permit the inference of age discrimination. *Aulick v. Skybridge Americas, Inc.*, 860 F.3d 613 (8th Cir. 2017). Richardson will easily prove all of these elements.

First, Richardson was 58 years old at the time Metro Care hired Bricker instead of her. Richardson was more than qualified for the promotion. She had been working as a nurse for 28 years, and her experience as a traveling nurse gave her a wide perspective on different types of hospitals, regional care issues, and working with a wide variety of people.

Further, Richardson suffered an adverse employment action when she was denied the promotion. Finally, Richardson was rejected in favor of someone sufficiently younger to permit the inference of age discrimination. Bricker was only 35 years old at the time of her hire, and the 20+ years between them meets the requirement of Dover law to prove a prima facia case. *See Johnson v. Tullbear Indus.*, 57 Dov. 127, 130 (1997) (holding that an age difference of 15 or more years meets the prima facia test).

Richardson expects Metro Care to articulate legitimate, non-discriminatory reasons for hiring Bricker over Richardson. Metro Care will likely argue that Bricker had roughly 10 years of experience at Metro Care and that Metro Care promoted Bricker because she had more years of service to Metro Care than Richardson.

Richardson will prove at the hearing that these proffered reasons are merely a pretext for age discrimination. *See Martinez v. MagnaCorp.*, 120 Dov. 89, 100 (2016). Richardson will present documents and testimony to prove that: (1) Metro Care only hires managers in their 30s; (2) Metro Care misled Richardson into taking her nursing position by implying it would promote her to a management role; (3) Metro Care's management team has a social culture intended to attract younger talent than more experienced talent; and (4) Richardson heard many Metro Care employees tell her that she "didn't have a chance" for the promotion because of her age.

This case is factually similar to the Dover Court of Appeals case of *Long v. First Second Bank*, 98 Dov. 225 (Dov. Ct. App. 2005). In that case, plaintiff Sarah Long, 55, applied for a position as a mortgage lender after spending 30 years as a teller at First Second Bank. Long did not receive the promotion, and First Second Bank hired Brittney Forrester, 32, instead. Similar to Richardson, Long had significantly more experience in the field, though not as long a tenure at the employer, than the person hired for the job. After a trial, the jury awarded Long $250,000 in damages, and the Dover Court of Appeals affirmed the judgment.

At the hearing, Richardson will show not only the prima facie elements of age discrimination under federal and state law but also demonstrate that any proffered reasons by Metro Care are merely pretext. Metro Care's culture of youth is not a bad business practice, but it violates well-established anti-discrimination laws.

Conclusion

Based on the foregoing, Richardson is entitled to receive the promotion to Managing Nurse. Alternatively, Richardson is entitled to recover damages in excess of $250,000, plus interest and costs. Finally, Richardson requests Metro Care pay all forum fees, arbitrator fees, and Richardson's attorney's fees, pursuant to the fee-shifting provision in the age discrimination statutes.

Respectfully Submitted,

2. Post-Hearing Briefing

Unlike jury trial practice, some advocates ask to submit post-hearing briefs after the conclusion of the hearing. As noted in Chapter 4, the post-hearing brief can be an opportunity for advocates to submit additional documentary evidence, but, most often, it is an opportunity to provide the arbitrators with a written summary of the evidence admitted at the arbitration, the law, and legal analysis.

The pre-hearing and post-hearing briefs are similar in terms of length, tone, and even purpose. The biggest difference between the two is that the pre-hearing brief describes what the parties plan to prove while the post-hearing brief describes what the parties actually proved. If the parties have paid for a transcript, they can reference specific transcript pages. Whether or not the parties have a transcript, they can attach specific exhibits to their briefs.

In particularly lengthy hearings that span multiple months or years—usually because they can only meet for a few hearing days at a time with long breaks in between—post-hearing briefs are helpful to refresh the arbitrators' recollections if the evidence was presented many months prior. In some instances, parties may forego closing arguments altogether and submit post-hearing briefs instead.

J. Participant Ethics

Participant ethics is an often-overlooked part of arbitration law. While arbitrators have codes of ethics and guidelines for practice, *see* Chapter 8, the rules surrounding attorney and participant behavior are less clear. This section considers the ethical rules governing lawyer and non-lawyer participants, such as clients and witnesses. In addition, this section considers whether non-lawyer representatives violate the prohibition on the unauthorized practice of law.

1. Duty to Advise About ADR Options

If the parties do not have a pre-dispute arbitration agreement, should attorneys have a duty to suggest that the parties consider ADR options, such as arbitration? Consider the following article excerpt.

Kristen M. Blankley, *The Ethics and Practice of Drafting Pre-Dispute Resolution Clauses*
49 Creighton L. Rev. 743 (2016)

The role of the lawyer is more than merely that of an advocate. Equally important, however, is the role of lawyer as counselor. Chapter Two of the Model Rules of Professional Responsibility covers the role of lawyer as counselor. Regarding the role of counselor and advisor, Rule 2.1 states: "In representing a client, a lawyer shall exercise independent professional judgment and render candid advice. In rendering advice, a lawyer may refer not only to law but to other considerations such as moral, economic, social and political factors that may be relevant to the client's situation."

The purpose of this rule is to be clear that lawyering is not all about the law. Lawyering also involves non-legal advice, depending on the client's circumstances. ...

[A]dvising clients of the practical consequences of the advice is well within the scope of a lawyer's duties, as well as a best practice.

Lawyers have the right and the ability to advise about many of these non-legal considerations even if the client does not directly ask for such advice. Comment five notes that:

> a lawyer is not expected to give advice until asked by the client. However, when a lawyer knows that a client proposes a course of action that is likely to result in substantial adverse legal consequences to the client, the lawyer's duty to the client under Rule 1.4 may require that the lawyer offer advice if the client's course of action is related to the representation.

Rule 1.4 (referenced above) is the lawyer's general duty of communication and ensuring that the client is informed. Under Rule 1.4, the lawyer is also responsible for "reasonably consult[ing] with the client about the means by which the client's objectives are to be accomplished" and "explain[ing] a matter to the extent reasonably necessary to permit the client to make informed decisions regarding the matter." In other words, the lawyer may have a duty to broach the idea of dispute resolution and explain the options....

1. Duty to Advise About Alternative Dispute Resolution Options?

In the realm of litigation options, the Model Rules suggest that lawyers may need to inform clients of alternate dispute resolution ("ADR") options compared to the traditional litigation option. Comment five to Rule 2.1 states that "when a matter is likely to involve litigation, it may be necessary under Rule 1.4 to inform the client of the available forms of dispute resolution that might constitute reasonable alternatives to litigation." The Model Rule does not create a requirement of discussion of ADR options with litigation clients, but some other jurisdictions make such a requirement mandatory.

In Michigan, for example, the State Bar of Michigan Standing Committee on Professional and Judicial Ethics ("Michigan State Bar") stated in 1996 that a lawyer has such an obligation. The Michigan State Bar stated that the lawyer generally has "an ethical duty to inform the client of any options or alternative which are reasonable in pursuing the client's lawful interests," and while not all available options "need be discussed, any doubt about whether a possible option is reasonably likely to promote the client's interests ... should be ... resolved in favor of providing the information to the client and allowing the client to render a decision." This duty stems from the lawyer's duty to attend to the client's "subjective desires and objectives" and to "communicate any and all information necessary to allow the lawyer to be confident that these goals and objectives are those which the lawyer seeks to accomplish." The Michigan State Bar recommends that the lawyer communicate the "costs of any available option [of dispute resolution] as well as the likely benefits of such [processes.]"

In a separate opinion, the Michigan State Bar also stated that if opposing counsel suggests using an ADR option, the lawyer receiving that option must take the offer to the client for consideration. This opinion's holding that a lawyer has a duty to report ADR proposals from the other side to the client is particularly interesting. This opinion introduces the idea that ADR options are particular client "ends" to which the client decides — as opposed to the lawyer. The question of whether ADR options are a client "ends" or a decision regarding lawyer "means" is analyzed below. The Model Rule and the Michigan opinions suggest that when a lawyer is involved in litigation matters, the lawyer may have the duty to suggest alternative options.

Comments and Questions

1. Should lawyers have a duty to counsel clients to consider alternative dispute resolution mechanisms to resolve their disputes? If so, do you think the advice should be limited to consensual forms of dispute resolution, such as mediation? Or also adjudicatory process, such as arbitration?

2. Under what circumstances would you suggest that parties arbitrate their dispute if they were not already bound by a pre-dispute arbitration agreement?

2. Participant Ethics

Litigation practice has clear rules regarding unethical conduct such as lying, destroying documents, and providing false testimony. Witnesses who testify before a court take an oath and testify under the penalty of perjury. Although criminal trials for perjury and document destruction are rare, most attorneys, clients, and witnesses comply with these rules, either out of fear of repercussion or out of respect for the judiciary.

Is arbitration different? Do the rules of perjury, document destruction, and honesty apply to the same extent — or at all — in the arbitral forum? Over the years, some arbitration horror stories have emerged about witnesses or lawyers behaving in a highly unethical manner. For instance, following the 9/11 tragedies, broker-dealer Morgan Stanley falsely claimed in numerous FINRA arbitrations that it had lost millions of pre-9/11 emails because of the destruction of its e-mail servers at the World Trade Center. In fact, those e-mails existed on backup tapes stored at another location. As a result of its discovery abuse, FINRA initiated an enforcement action and, in 2007, Morgan Stanley agreed to pay FINRA a $12.5 million penalty. Of that payment, $9.5 million compensated victims, and $3 million was a fine imposed by FINRA. *See* FINRA Press Release, *Morgan Stanley to Pay $12.5 Million to Resolve FINRA Charges that it Failed to Provide Documents to Arbitration Claimants, Regulators*, available at http://www.finra.org/newsroom/2007/morgan-stanley-pay-125-million-resolve-finra-charges-it-failed-provide-documents (Sept. 27, 2007).

In 2015, an arbitration panel imposed significant sanctions on Tour de France-winning cyclist Lance Armstrong for lying under oath during a 2007 arbitration. The earlier arbitration surrounded doping allegations and whether prize money for the 2004 Tour should be dispersed. Consider the following opinion excerpts.

Lance Armstrong and Tailwind Sports Corp. v. SCA Promotions, Inc., et al.

Arbitration Tribunal (2015)

Hon. Richard D. Faulkner and Richard Chernick.

[SCA Promotions contracted to pay Lance Armstrong prize money if he won the 2004 Tour de France. After Armstrong won, he sought the prize money, but SCA did not initially pay due to the disputed nature of the win. In 2007, the parties arbitrated the dispute, and the panel heard extensive testimony and evidence. Prior to the panel issuing a ruling, the parties settled, and SCA agreed to pay Armstrong $7.5 million. The settlement agreement contained an arbitration clause applicable to disputes under the contract.

Armstrong later admitted to doping, and the United States Anti-Doping Agency ("USADA") revoked Armstrong's 2004 title. SCA thereafter moved to re-open the arbitration and move for sanctions. The tribunal considered a number of questions, including "[i]f sanctions are appropriate, what sanctions should this Arbitration Tribunal award?"]

XII. SANCTIONS

C. Party Obligations Not to Frustrate or Impede Contracts

Claimants object to jurisdiction and correctly advise that Texas does not accept or follow the contract doctrine of "good faith and fair dealing." English v. Fischer, 660 S.W.2d 521, 522 (Tex. 1983). Therefore, Claimants assert that no jurisdiction to sanction wrongdoing exists. Fortunately, Texas, and other jurisdictions, recognize and accept the more limited subsidiary concept of an implied covenant that parties must not "frustrate or impede" any other parties' performance of their contract. Though disfavored in Texas law, application of an implied covenant is appropriate where necessary to effectuate the parties' intentions where the obligation is "so clearly within the contemplation of the parties that they deemed it unnecessary to express it." We conclude that the obligations of parties to be truthful, to not commit perjury and to not intentionally submit fraudulent evidence in arbitrations of their disputes arising from their agreements are precisely such implied covenants and obligations.

Thus parties' duty to cooperate is implied in every contract in which cooperation is necessary for performance of the contract. Where applicable, this implied duty requires that a party to a contract may not hinder, prevent, or interfere with another party's ability to perform its duties under the contract. Furthermore, as explained by the Fifth Circuit Court of Appeal, an implied covenant to cooperate differs from the broader covenant of good faith and fair dealing that the Texas Supreme Court rejected in English v. Fischer.

> "An implied covenant of good faith and fair dealing places duties of 'good faith,' 'fairness,' 'decency,' and 'reasonableness' upon all parties in regard to actions construing the contract. Implying a promise on the part of one party

not to prevent the other party from performing the contract falls short of implying a covenant of good faith and fair dealing."

Tex. Nat'l Bank v. Sandia Mortgage Corp., 872 F.2d 692, 698–99 (5th Cir. 1989)....

D. Claimants Frustrated and Impeded CSA Contract Performance

The Tribunal here affirmatively finds that Claimants' actions improperly prevented SCA from performing its duties under the parties' contracts and the agreements to arbitrate. Claimants further intentionally breached their obligations to arbitrate their disputes with SCA. Breach of a party's contractual duty to honor an agreement for use of a dispute resolution process or arbitration has been recognized in Texas as imposing liability and damages for over 160 years.

E. Claimants Frustrated and Impeded Arbitration Tribunal Performance

This Tribunal further affirmatively finds that Claimants also intentionally prevented this arbitration Tribunal from properly discharging the contractual duties it was obligated to perform for the benefit of all of the parties by knowingly presenting perjury and fraudulent evidence. A thorough analysis of arbitration reveals the reality is that every contract with an arbitration clause is a primary contract containing within it multiple subsidiary agreements imposing additional sets of obligations upon the parties and the arbitrator(s). There is first the agreement of the parties to arbitrate with their counterparty. Breach of that obligation can lead to damages. There are also agreements between the parties and the arbitrator(s) to participate in any arbitration according to any agreed rules, to comply with validly issued awards and to pay arbitrators for their services. These obligations of the parties are reciprocated by the arbitrators' agreeing to dedicate sufficient time and judgment to resolving the parties' dispute according to their disagreement with the designated law. The Claimants' employment of perjured testimony and fraudulent [sic] prevented the Tribunal from performing those obligations which were owed to all of the parties participating in this arbitration.

XIII. DETERMINATION OF SANCTIONS

Ample evidence was adduced at the hearing through documents and witnesses that Claimants commenced this proceeding knowing and intending to lie; committed perjury before the Panel with respect to every issue in the case; intimidated and pressured other witnesses to lie; or influenced others to help them lie and hide the truth; used a false personal and emotional appeal to perpetuate their lies to the Panel; used perjury and other wrongful conduct to secure millions of dollars of benefits from the Respondents; used lies and fraud to falsely claim that the Panel exonerate them, thereby further allowing them to profit further from additional endorsements and sponsorships; expressed no remorse to the Panel for their wrongful conduct; and continued to lie to the Panel throughout the final hearing even while admitting to prior falsehoods and other wrongful conduct. Claimants admitted in substantial part the substantial part the substance of all (but the last) of the foregoing conduct.

The evidence placed before the Tribunal established that SCA paid Claimants $7,500,000.00 pursuant to the "Consent" Final Award of February 8, 2006. The evidence adduced in the recent arbitration hearing established that SCA has reasonably incurred attorneys' fees and costs in excess of $2,000,000.00, which fees and costs continue. Claimants' actions have further imposed upon SCA additional costs insusceptible of precise calculation. These figures are not cited as a calculation of "damages" but rather as one measure of the harm generally caused by Claimants' conduct. Considering that the Claimants must take full responsibility for the consequences of their actions, sanctions in the sum of $10,000,000.00 are appropriate and are awarded against Claimants.

a. Comments and Questions

1. The *Armstrong* arbitration award was 2–1 in favor of SCA and against Armstrong. The dissent mostly concerned the panel's authority to reconvene and the doctrine of *functus officio*, which is covered in more detail in Chapter 9. As to damages, the dissent stated: "The amount of the sanction is almost exactly that which SCA paid to settle with Claimants and what SCA paid in attorneys' fees and costs. To say that this is a sanction when it mirrors almost exactly what SCA paid is incorrect. In substance, the majority's sanction is an unwarranted, unlawful reversal of a settlement agreement that was made and effectuated nine years ago. There is an old saying that if it looks like a duck, walks like a duck and quacks like a duck, it's a duck. This is a duck and it is no more or less than SCA trying to overturn an agreement SCA voluntarily entered into in February 2006 to get its money back because Armstrong lied about performance enhancing drugs in the 2005–2006 proceedings."

2. Do you agree with the award of sanctions? What about the amount? Although arbitration awards are not intended to create precedent, do you think that this award, which is publicly available online, emboldens arbitrators to issue similar awards?

3. The Model Rules of Professional Conduct make clear that lawyers' obligations toward arbitrators are identical to those obligations toward courts. The Model Rules refer to obligations towards "tribunals," and the definition of "tribunal" includes an arbitral tribunal. Model R. of Prof'l Conduct R. 1.0(m). Lawyers have a duty of "Candor Toward the Tribunal" in Rule 3.3 that prohibits lawyers from making false statements of law or fact, failing to disclose adverse controlling authority, and offering evidence the lawyer knows to be false. These legal ethics rules, however, only apply to lawyers, and not to non-lawyer participants in arbitration, such as clients, witnesses, and expert witnesses.

4. Professor Kristen Blankley has spent considerable time researching issues regarding participant ethics in arbitration. She discovered that traditional rules of perjury, document destruction, and falsifying evidence do not directly apply to unethical behavior in the arbitral forum. She recommends that states update their laws to make them explicitly applicable to arbitration. *See* Kristen M. Blankley, *Lying, Stealing, and Cheating: The Role of Arbitrators as Ethics Enforcers*, 52 U. LOUISVILLE L. REV. 443 (2014); Kristen M. Blankley, *Advancements in Arbitral Immunity and Judicial Review of Arbitral Awards Create Ethical Loopholes in Arbitration*, in JUSTICE, CONFLICT, AND WELL-BEING (2014); and Kristen M. Blankley, *Taming the Wild West of Arbitration Ethics*, 60 KAN. L. REV. 925 (2012).

3. Unauthorized Practice of Law for Non-Lawyer Representatives

Arbitration has a long tradition of permitting non-lawyers to serve as party representatives in certain contexts. Non-lawyer representatives are most frequently used in the labor-management context. Non-attorney union representatives historically have represented other union members in workplace grievances. Some states specifically permit these non-lawyer representatives as an exception to unauthorized practice of law rules. *See, e.g.,* Ne. S. Ct. R. §3-1004(E) (2017).

Are statutory claims different from garden-variety workplace grievances or industry disputes? Professor Sarah R. Cole considered whether non-attorneys should be permitted to represent clients in arbitrations involving statutory matters.

Sarah R. Cole, *Blurred Lines: Are Non-Attorneys Who Represent Parties in Arbitration Involving Statutory Claims Practicing Law?*
48 U.C. Davis L. Rev. 921 (2015)

Historically, parties in arbitration did not need and were not required to utilize representation in arbitration because arbitrators used customs and norms to evaluate and resolve parties' claims. Modern arbitration differs considerably from this model. Over the last thirty years, businesses have increased their use of arbitration, while, at the same time, expanding the types of disputes that are subject to arbitration. At one time, arbitrators primarily resolved contractual interpretation disputes. Today, however, arbitration agreements routinely cover a wide variety of statutory claims including Title VII, the Family and Medical Leave Act ("FMLA"), the Age Discrimination in Employment Act ("ADEA"), the Americans with Disabilities Act ("ADA"), the Truth in Lending Act, and many more. Moreover, many modern arbitration hearings involve expansive discovery. The rules businesses typically utilize in arbitration also anticipate the use of motions and pre-trial hearings, as well as extensive examination and cross-examination of witnesses. If, as a practical matter, the majority of consumer and employee claims against businesses will now be removed to arbitration, representation of parties in arbitration is likely to require considerably greater legal knowledge and expertise than it has in the past. Disputants attempting to arbitrate statutory claims will need legal counsel to properly present their cases in the arbitration forum.

The need for more frequent legal representation in arbitration likely extends to all forms of arbitration, including consumer, labor, securities, and employment arbitration. While critics focus on whether arbitrators are capable of adjudicating such claims, scant attention has been paid to whether non-lawyer representatives, who commonly appear in these kinds of arbitral proceedings, can properly traverse the increasingly complex landscape of legal claims at issue in arbitration. As statutory claims become increasingly prevalent in arbitration, concern and focus on who is representing parties in arbitration must change. If the vast majority of consumer, employee, and investor claims are to be arbitrated, and the subject matter of arbitration involves statutory, as well as contract, interpretation, it may be that lawyers, not lay advocates, are necessary to provide adequate representation to arbitration disputants. While this change runs counter to traditional arbitration practice, which routinely permitted party representation by non-lawyer advocates, modern arbitration practice demands that advocates be able to understand and apply the law. Continuing to permit non-lawyer representation in arbitration is sanctioning the unauthorized practice of law ("UPL").

But addressing this issue may raise a variety of concerns. First, if lawyers are necessary to the arbitration process, undoubtedly the cost of arbitration will increase for the vast majority of one-shot player litigants, such as consumers and employees. Second, if a state acknowledged that lawyers were necessary to the arbitration process, and enacted legislation to require the presence of lawyers in arbitration, the state legislation would likely be subject to challenge on preemption grounds. The Supreme Court interprets the Federal Arbitration Act ("FAA") to preempt state legislation or judicial decisions that alter fundamental attributes of arbitration. Thus, the Court in *Concepcion* held that the FAA preempted a California Supreme Court decision that conditioned enforceability of an arbitration agreement between a consumer and a business on the availability of class arbitration. The *Concepcion* Court concluded that class arbitration interferes with fundamental attributes of arbitration such as lower expected costs and higher efficiency. If, in the instant case, the Court determined that the possibility of non-lawyer representation in arbitration is a fundamental aspect of arbitration, then state legislative or judicial attempts to limit this fundamental attribute would be subject to a challenge on preemption grounds. Given the track record for preemption challenges in the Supreme Court, it seems likely that attempts to alter a fundamental attribute of arbitration through state legislation or judicial decision would fail. This conclusion would leave states unable to implement their view of appropriate public policy through state legislation or judicial decisions. The states would be forced to wait for Congress to amend the FAA to require legal representation in disputes involving statutory claims. The states would likely wait a long time for such action, since Congress has routinely rejected attempts to amend the FAA. Alternatively, non-lawyers might work within the existing system, avoiding unauthorized practice of law charges by representing clients in the arbitration of statutory disputes under the guidance of an experienced lawyer.

Interestingly, if the possibility of non-lawyer representation in arbitration is a fundamental attribute of arbitration, neither state legislatures nor state courts could legislate or decide that non-lawyers were engaged in the unauthorized practice of law during arbitration. If that is so, states would be unable to address the potential harm to consumers from incompetent non-lawyer representation in arbitration of statutory claims using existing state UPL laws. Federal attention to this issue, if this prediction is correct, would then be the only possible solution available to address this growing problem. If non-lawyers conclude that states are unable to prosecute them, they would have little incentive to join with lawyers, who might be able to provide appropriate supervision for them in cases involving statutory claims.

This burgeoning problem, perhaps unlike those that have come before it, may provide the impetus needed for Congress to consider realistic reform of the Federal Arbitration Act to ensure that arbitration agreements do not become a mechanism by which vulnerable populations are further harmed.

Chapter 8

The Role of the Arbitrator: Ethics, Neutrality, and Immunity

A. Introduction

Arbitration is typically a private, consensual method of dispute resolution, and its legitimacy depends on a fair and ethical process. Traditionally, arbitrators were volunteers who served as dedicated and respected industry members. As the use of arbitration has expanded significantly, the need for professional arbitration services has correspondingly increased. For example, the American Arbitration Association (AAA) and JAMS are major provider institutions that administer hundreds of thousands of domestic and international cases each year. The business of arbitration is selling the services of case administrator and decision-maker (who is potentially an expert) in a private setting. Given the accessibility of a public system of dispute resolution, i.e., the court system, arbitration must offer parties something they cannot get from that public system or, at a minimum, be accountable to adhere to standards that ensure arbitration can provide a fair and ethical process.

The reasons that parties choose arbitration vary, but many of the most common reasons have their roots in professionalism and ethics. For example, for parties who choose arbitration because of the privacy that arbitration confers, the duty to maintain that privacy (or confidentiality) is an ethical obligation. For parties who choose arbitration because of the ability to choose their decision-maker, those parties trust that their arbitrator will act with professionalism and rule on the case in accordance with the law and equity, and not out of self-interest or bias.

To what extent must arbitrators follow standards of professionalism and ethics? What are those standards? What happens if they fail to do so? This chapter seeks to answer these three broad questions, while not losing sight of the practical implications of good and bad arbitration practice.

Section B begins the discussion by addressing the sources of ethical and professional standards for arbitrators. Although the field of arbitration is often described as unregulated, ethical standards and norms arise from a number of sources. Most, but not all, arbitrators are listed on a roster and associated with a provider organization, such as the AAA or JAMS. These provider organizations have their own ethical standards that arbitrators must follow. If arbitrators violate the standards, they could be removed from the rosters and no longer receive business from those organizations. A second source of ethical rules stems from state law. Only a minority of states regulate arbitrator conduct, but where such laws exist, arbitrators have a duty to follow the law of the jurisdiction. A third consideration to note is the force of the marketplace. Unlike judges and other public decision-makers, parties must choose their arbitrator. Presumably, unethical arbitrators will not receive repeat business, so market factors are a consideration that should not be overlooked.

Next, Section C explores the substance of the most common ethical rules for neutral arbitrators. Certain ethics rules require them to remain free from bias and conflicts of interest, engage in independent decision-making, and market and advertise their services in an ethical manner. Section D turns to the substance of ethical rules for non-neutral arbitrators. In the United States, the system of tripartite arbitration is still popular among some businesses, although this form of arbitration is not common worldwide. As mentioned in Chapter 4, in tripartite arbitration, each party appoints an arbitrator to a three-arbitrator panel, but those party-appointed arbitrators are not necessarily expected to be neutral. In fact, many of these arbitrators are intended to be an advocate for the party appointing the arbitrator. Despite being party-appointed and non-neutral, those arbitrators are still expected to abide by certain ethical standards. Section D considers the ethical obligations for these party-appointed arbitrators. Specifically, this section considers how their duties of neutrality are relaxed.

Section E considers a different type of neutrality issue. In some instances, the parties specify at the onset of their relationship that a person associated with one of the parties will be the decision-maker of any resulting disputes. These arbitrations involve "structural bias." For instance, in public construction matters, the parties may agree that a person employed by the city who is familiar with construction will be the arbitrator. Although the arbitrator is aligned with one of the parties, the arrangement makes sense for expediency and expertise reasons. Section E provides examples of cases involving structural bias, as well as explores the legal boundaries of this concept.

Finally, Section F deals with the issues of arbitrator liability and arbitrator immunity. This Section considers the question—what happens if an arbitrator breaks ethical rules? What, if any, recourse do parties have against bad arbitrators or bad provider organizations? Because arbitrators have a functional equivalency to judges, the cases in this section consider the extent to which the immunity that applies to the judiciary should also apply to judges.

Problem

Alba Averez served as Arbitrator in a dispute between Business Supplier ("Supplier") and Gadget Maker ("Gadget") involving an alleged breach of contract. Gadget contended that widgets it bought were not of sufficient quality, and, in response, did not pay Business Supplier. Claimant Supplier initiated the arbitration for payment of the debt. Respondent Gadget denied the contractual breach and counterclaimed for damages based on the defective widgets.

Alba is an arbitrator associated with United Arbitration Association (UAA). The parties selected Alba from a list of seven arbitrators by ranking them in order of preference. During the discovery phase, Alba granted a motion to compel discovery filed by Supplier and denied a similar motion to compel by Gadget. Prior to ruling on Supplier's motion, Alba took a private phone call about the motion from Supplier's attorney, and neither Alba nor the attorney told Gadget about the phone call.

UAA mailed notices of the hearing to the parties, but due to a glitch in the address, Gadget did not receive the notice until seven days before the hearing. The hearing was scheduled for five business days. Supplier's presentation of evidence took more than three days, and Gadget asked for more time to present its case, but Alba denied that request. Upon completion of the hearing and considering the evidence, Alba awarded Supplier $25 million in damages.

Two months after Alba issued the award, Gadget learned that Alba was college roommates with the lawyer for Supplier. In addition, Gadget learned that Alba misrepresented her credentials on her resume that the parties reviewed before hiring her. Alba claimed on her resume that she had a Master's of Business Administration degree (MBA), but, in fact, the highest degree she earned was a Bachelor's Degree. Gadget claims it would not have ranked Alba so highly if it had known she did not have an MBA.

What ethical questions arise under these facts? What recourse, if any, should be available to the parties to remedy any ethical violations?

B. Sources of Ethical Standards for Arbitrators

If arbitration is a largely unregulated profession, why are there ethical rules and who enforces them? This Section considers the sources of ethical rules, such as provider organization rules, state statutes, and market forces. Next, Section C examines the content and application of these ethical standards.

1. Provider Organization Rules

Arbitrators gain many benefits from being associated with provider organizations such as the AAA, JAMS, FINRA, or others. When provider organizations administer a case, they use neutrals from their rosters, so provider organizations are a referral source of new business for arbitrators. In addition, the leading provider organizations lend credibility to the arbitrators on their roster.

Provider organizations, too, have an interest in maintaining their own reputations. The stellar reputations of the arbitrators on the panel also lend credibility back to the provider organizations. Provider organizations are only as good as the arbitrators on their roster, so ethical practice is beneficial not only for the parties, but also for the arbitrators and the provider organizations.

In 1977, a joint committee of the American Arbitration Association and a special committee of the American Bar Association created the *Code of Ethics for Arbitrators in Commercial Disputes*, which was later revised in 2003 (and went into effect in the AAA on March 1, 2004) ("Code of Ethics"). This Code of Ethics governs the conduct of arbitrators working on cases administered by the AAA. In addition, other provider organizations, such as FINRA, require arbitrators working on their administered cases to abide by the Code of Ethics. Other organizations, such as JAMS, have a distinct, but similar, code of ethics.

Consider the following rationale for the ABA/AAA Code of Ethics for Arbitrators in Commercial Disputes. Do you agree with the stated rationales? Are there other reasons a provider organization would want to have a code of ethics?

American Bar Association/American Arbitration Association Code of Ethics for Arbitrators in Commercial Disputes
(2004)

Preamble

The use of arbitration to resolve a wide variety of disputes has grown extensively and forms a significant part of the system of justice on which our society relies for a fair determination of legal rights. Persons who act as arbitrators therefore undertake serious responsibilities to the public, as well as to the parties. Those responsibilities include important ethical obligations.

Few cases of unethical behavior by commercial arbitrators have arisen. Nevertheless, this Code sets forth generally accepted standards of ethical conduct for the guidance of arbitrators and parties in commercial disputes, in the hope of contributing to the maintenance of high standards and continued confidence in the process of arbitration....

There are many different types of commercial arbitration. Some proceedings are conducted under arbitration rules established by various organizations and trade associations, while others are conducted without such rules. Although most proceedings are arbitrated pursuant to voluntary agreement of the parties, certain types of disputes are submitted to arbitration by reason of particular laws. This Code is intended to apply to all such proceedings in which disputes or claims are submitted for decision to one or more arbitrators appointed in a manner provided by an agreement of the parties, by applicable arbitration rules, or by law. In all such cases, the persons who have the power to decide should observe fundamental standards of ethical conduct. In this Code, all such persons are called "arbitrators," although in some types of proceeding they might be called "umpires," "referees," "neutrals," or have some other title.

Arbitrators, like judges, have the power to decide cases. However, unlike full-time judges, arbitrators are usually engaged in other occupations before, during, and after the time that they serve as arbitrators. Often, arbitrators are purposely chosen from the same trade or industry as the parties in order to bring special knowledge to the task of deciding. This Code recognizes these fundamental differences between arbitrators and judges.

In those instances where this Code has been approved and recommended by organizations that provide, coordinate, or administer services of arbitrators, it provides ethical standards for the members of their respective panels of arbitrators. However, this Code does not form a part of the arbitration rules of any such organization unless its rules so provide.

2. State Rules for Arbitrators and Provider Organizations

In a minority of jurisdictions, state law also provides ethical rules for arbitrators practicing within the jurisdiction. In 2001, California became the first state to implement a mandatory code of conduct for private contractual arbitrators. The *Ethics Standards for Neutral Arbitrators in Contractual Arbitration* (Ethics Standards) are comprised of 17 standards set forth in the Appendix to the California Rules of Court (2017). The Standards address arbitrator duties regarding, among other things, disclosure, confidentiality, compensation, disqualification, ex parte proceedings, and marketing. The purpose of the Ethics Standards is to establish minimum standards of conduct and "to guide the conduct of arbitrators, to inform and protect participants in arbitration, and to promote public confidence in the arbitration process." (Standard 1) The Ethics Standards apply to all neutral arbitrators appointed pursuant to an arbitration agreement subject to the California Arbitration Act and where the arbitration hearing is to be conducted in California. The Ethics Standards remain in effect from the arbitrator's acceptance of appointment until the conclusion of the arbitration.

Although the California Ethics Standards are mandatory, the penalty for violation is not entirely clear. Standard 7 provides for disqualification where an arbitrator fails to make required disclosures or cannot maintain impartiality. An arbitrator's violation of the Ethics Standards, under some circumstances, may fall within statutory grounds for vacating an arbitration award, provided the aggrieved party demonstrates that its rights were "substantially prejudiced." Civil liability for ethical breaches is also doubtful, as arbitrators are generally cloaked with arbitral immunity.

The overall objective of the California Ethics Standards is to address concerns about the private dispute resolution process, particularly the contention that financial incentives compel arbitrators to favor "repeat players" over "one-shot" arbitration users. As stated in the Ethics Standards, "[f]or arbitration to be effective, there must be broad public confidence in the integrity and fairness of the process. Arbitrators are responsible to the parties, the other participants, and the public for conducting themselves in accordance with these standards so as to merit that confidence." (Standard 1) Despite laudable objectives, the Ethics Code is not without controversy or its critics. A number of individuals and service providers in the arbitration community are concerned that the standards impose undue and unrealistic administrative burdens on individual arbitrators.

While the Code of Ethics and the California Ethics Standards apply specifically to individual arbitrators, the California legislature also focused on the role that provider organizations have in the arbitration process. In California, specific statutory provisions are directed at ADR provider organizations. Accordingly, arbitration providers in California are prohibited from administering consumer arbitrations in which the provider has had any type of financial involvement with a party or attorney within the past year, or if they have a financial interest in the provider. CAL. CODE CIV. PROC. § 1281.92. Providers must also collect and publish information regarding consumer arbitrations they have administered in the past five years. The information must include the name of the nonconsumer party, the type of dispute involved, the number of times, if any, the nonconsumer party has previously been a party in an arbitration or mediation administered by the provider, whether the consumer party was represented by an attorney, the amount of the claim, award and relief granted, and the name and fee of the arbitrator. CAL. CODE CIV. PROC. § 1281.96. For more information on the California statutes, see Maureen Weston, *California's New Arbitrator Ethics Standards: A Primer for Compliance and Confusion?*, DISP. RESOL. NEWS (2002). For additional commentary on the California arbitration legislation, see Jay Folberg, *Arbitration Ethics — Is California the Future?*, 18 OHIO ST. J. DISP. RESOL. 343 (2003); Ruth V. Glick, *California Arbitration Reform: The Aftermath*, 38 U.S.F. L. REV. 119 (2003).

Following the lead of California, the 2009 Montana Legislature enacted the "Fairness in Arbitration Act" as part of the Montana Uniform Arbitration Act, Title 27, Chapter 5, codified at §§ 27-5-116, 27-5-211 and 27-5-312, MCA. As will be discussed in more detail below, this Act also focuses on arbitrator disclosure laws and conflicts of interest. Ross W. Cannon, *New Act Requires Disclosures by Neutral Arbitrators*, 35-JAN MONT. LAW. 19 (2010); see also Minn. Stat. 572B.12 (2010) (Minnesota arbitrator disclosure law). Lawyers and arbitrators should always consult local law to understand the ethical rules within their given jurisdiction.

Recall from Chapter 2 the breadth of the preemption of the FAA. Do you think that the FAA preempts these state ethics statutes? See *Credit Suisse First Boston Corp. v. Grunwald*, 400 F.3d 1119 (9th Cir. 2005) (preempting California ethics procedures in NASD — i.e., securities — arbitrations). Should more states regulate arbitration ethics? Some scholars think so. See Shari Maynard, *The Current State of Arbitrator Ethics and Party Recourse Against Grievances*, 8 Y.B. ON ARB. & MEDIATION 204 (2016).

3. Market Forces

No state or federal law sets forth specific requirements with respect to the certification, licensing, or particular qualifications of arbitrators. That the regulation of who may serve as an arbitrator for disputes is entirely a private matter is hardly a self-evident proposition, considering that barbers, beekeepers, and many other categories of workers are subject to licensure. Arbitrators are generally selected by the parties or the administering agency. Thus, education, professional experience, or other desired qualifications for the selected arbitrator are determined by the contracting parties or by the affiliated provider organization.

Is the lack of regulation a good thing? Economists might argue that the market for arbitration services will ensure that competent and ethical arbitrators get work while incompetent and unethical arbitrators will not be hired at all, and certainly not hired for repeat services. Is that idea convincing to you? In some arbitration cases, a repeat player may be arbitrating against a one-shot player. Can market forces effectively screen out bad arbitrators if one disputant (i.e., the repeat player) has more information about a particular arbitrator than the adverse party (i.e., the single-shot player)? What if one or more of the parties are pro se? A recent study of FINRA arbitration cases found that an arbitrator's background in the securities industry is correlated with increased awards for industry parties. The outcome was more pronounced in cases in which the non-industry party was *pro se. See* Stephen J. Choi et al., *The Influence of Arbitrator Background and Representation on Arbitrator Outcomes*, 9 Va. L. & Bus. Rev. 43 (2014).

Recent research shows that arbitrators fall victim to similar cognitive biases that plague the general population as well as the judiciary, such as biases associated with anchoring, framing, hindsight, and the like. *See* Jan-Philip Elm, *Behavioral Insights Into International Arbitration: An Analysis of How to De-Bias Arbitrators*, 27 Am. Rev. Int'l Arb. 75 (2016). Can market forces alone combat some of the cognitive biases present in individual arbitrators across the marketplace of arbitrators?

C. Ethical Obligations for Neutral Arbitrators

This section considers the most common ethical obligations for neutral arbitrators. This Chapter separates these obligations into three categories of obligations: (1) bias and conflicts of interest, (2) independent decision-making, and (3) business and advertising ethics. These obligations are generally considered to be the cornerstone of good arbitration practice. Because of the development and prevalence of tripartite arbitration, the different ethical obligations for party-appointed arbitrators under that system will be discussed in the next section.

1. Bias and Conflicts of Interest

Freedom from bias and the appearance of bias are often considered the most important ethical obligations for all neutrals, and especially arbitrators. Unlike judges, arbitrators are private individuals, many of whom hold full-time employment within the industry they arbitrate. Unlike mediators, arbitrators have adjudicative authority to issue a binding resolution in the controversy submitted to them. The role of the arbitrator, then, must be one of integrity. Consider the following ethical obligations regarding bias and conflicts of interest. Do these standards protect the arbitration process and lend credibility to the institution?

American Bar Association/American Arbitration Association, The Code of Ethics for Arbitrators in Commercial Disputes
Canons I & II (2004)

Canon I. An Arbitrator Should Uphold the Integrity and Fairness of the Arbitration Process.

A. An arbitrator has a responsibility not only to the parties but also to the process of arbitration itself, and must observe high standards of conduct so that the integrity and fairness of the process will be preserved. Accordingly, an arbitrator should recognize a responsibility to the public, to the parties whose rights will be decided, and to all other participants in the proceeding. This responsibility may include pro bono service as an arbitrator where appropriate.

B. One should accept appointment as an arbitrator only if fully satisfied: (1) that he or she can serve impartially; (2) that he or she can serve independently from the parties, potential witnesses, and the other arbitrators; (3) that he or she is competent to serve; and (4) that he or she can be available to commence the arbitration in accordance with the requirements of the proceeding and thereafter to devote the time and attention to its completion that the parties are reasonably entitled to expect.

C. After accepting appointment and while serving as an arbitrator, a person should avoid entering into any business, professional, or personal relationship, or acquiring any financial or personal interest, which is likely to affect impartiality or which might reasonably create the appearance of partiality. For a reasonable period of time after the decision of a case, persons who have served as arbitrators should avoid entering into any such relationship, or acquiring any such interest, in circumstances which might reasonably create the appearance that they had been influenced in the arbitration by the anticipation or expectation of the relationship or interest....

F. An arbitrator should conduct the arbitration process so as to advance the fair and efficient resolution of the matters submitted for decision. An arbitrator should make all reasonable efforts to prevent delaying tactics, harassment of parties or other participants, or other abuse or disruption of the arbitration process.

G. The ethical obligations of an arbitrator begin upon acceptance of the appointment and continue throughout all stages of the proceeding.... [C]ertain ethical obligations [as specified in this Code] begin as soon as a person is requested to serve as an arbitrator and certain ethical obligations continue after the decision in the proceeding has been given to the parties....

CANON II. An Arbitrator Should Disclose Any Interest or
Relationship Likely to Affect Impartiality or Which
Might Create an Appearance of Partiality.

A. Persons who are requested to serve as arbitrators should, before accepting, disclose: (1) any known direct or indirect financial or personal interest in the outcome of the arbitration; (2) any known existing or past financial, business, professional or personal relationships which might reasonably affect impartiality or lack of independence in the eyes of any of the parties ...

C. The obligation to disclose interests or relationships described in paragraph A is a continuing duty which requires a person who accepts appointment as an arbitrator to disclose, as soon as practicable, at any stage of the arbitration, any such interests or relationships which may arise, or which are recalled or discovered....

F. When parties, with knowledge of a person's interests and relationships, nevertheless desire that person to serve as an arbitrator, that person may properly serve.

G. If an arbitrator is requested by all parties to withdraw, the arbitrator must do so. If an arbitrator is requested to withdraw by less than all of the parties because of alleged partiality, the arbitrator should withdraw unless an agreement of the parties, or arbitration rules agreed to by the parties, or applicable law establishes procedures for determining challenges to arbitrators, in which case those procedures should be followed ...

State Disclosure Statutes

Some states have ethics laws that require arbitrators to make disclosures of conflicts of interest. These requirements apply to *all* arbitrators, whether or not those arbitrators are associated with a specific arbitration institution, such as the AAA or FINRA. Consider the state statutes excerpted below.

California Ethics Standards for Neutral Arbitrators in Contractual Arbitration

Standard 7. Disclosure

(d) Required disclosures

A proposed arbitrator or arbitrator must disclose all matters that could cause a person aware of the facts to reasonably entertain a doubt that the arbitrator would be able to be impartial, including, but not limited to, all of the following:

(1) Family relationships with party

The arbitrator or a member of the arbitrator's immediate or extended family is:

(A) A party;

(B) The spouse or domestic partner of a party; or

(C) An officer, director, or trustee of a party

(2) Family relationships with lawyer in the arbitration

(A) Current relationships

The arbitrator, or the spouse, former spouse, domestic partner, child, sibling, or parent of the arbitrator or the arbitrator's spouse or domestic partner is:

(i) A lawyer in the arbitration;

(ii) The spouse or domestic partner of a lawyer in the arbitration; or

(iii) Currently associated in the private practice of law with a lawyer in the arbitration.

(B) Past relationships ...

(3) Significant personal relationship with party or lawyer for a party.

The arbitrator or a member of the arbitrator's immediate family has or has had a significant relationship with a party or lawyer for a party.

(4) Service as arbitrator for a party or lawyer for a party

(A) The arbitrator is serving or, within the preceding five years, has served [as an arbitrator in another case involving a party or lawyer to the current arbitration]:

(B) Case information

If the arbitrator is serving or has served ... under (A), he or she must disclose:

(i) The names of the parties in each prior or pending case and, where applicable, the name of the attorney representing the party in the current arbitration who is involved in the pending case, who was involved in the prior case, or whose current associate is involved in the pending case.

(ii) The results of each case arbitrated to conclusion, including the date of the arbitration award, identification of the prevailing party, the amount of monetary damages awarded, if any, and the names of the parties' attorneys.

(C) Summary of case information

If the total number of the cases disclosed under (A) is greater than five, the arbitrator must provide a summary of these cases that states:

(i) The number of pending cases in which the arbitrator is currently serving in each capacity;

(ii) The number of prior cases in which the arbitrator previously served in each capacity;

(iii) The number of prior cases arbitrated to conclusion; and

(iv) The number of such prior cases in which the party to the current arbitration, the party represented by the lawyer for a party in the current arbitration or the party represented by the party-arbitrator in the current arbitration was the prevailing party.

(5) Compensated service as other dispute resolution neutral

The arbitrator is serving or has served as a dispute resolution neutral other than an arbitrator in another pending or prior noncollective bargaining case involving a party or lawyer for a party and the arbitrator received or expects to receive any form of compensation for serving in this capacity....

(6) Current arrangements for prospective neutral service

Whether the arbitrator has any current arrangement with a party concerning prospective employment or other compensated service as a dispute resolution neutral or is participating in or, within the last two years, has participated in discussions regarding such prospective employment or service with a party.

(7) Attorney-client relationship

Any attorney-client relationship the arbitrator has or has had with a party or lawyer for a party....

(8) Employee, expert witness, or consultant relationships

The arbitrator or a member of the arbitrator's immediate family is or, within the preceding two years, was an employee of or an expert witness or a consultant for a party or for a lawyer in the arbitration.

(9) Other professional relationships

Any other professional relationship not already disclosed under paragraphs (2)–(8) that the arbitrator or a member of the arbitrator's immediate family has or has had with a party or lawyer for a party.

(10) Financial interests in party

The arbitrator or a member of the arbitrator's immediate family has a financial interest in a party.

(11) Financial interests in subject of arbitration

The arbitrator or a member of the arbitrator's immediate family has a financial interest in the subject matter of the arbitration.

(12) Affected interest

The arbitrator or a member of the arbitrator's immediate family has an interest that could be substantially affected by the outcome of the arbitration.

(13) Knowledge of disputed facts

The arbitrator or a member of the arbitrator's immediate or extended family has personal knowledge of disputed evidentiary facts relevant to the arbitration. A person who is likely to be a material witness in the proceeding is deemed to have personal knowledge of disputed evidentiary facts concerning the proceeding.

(14) Membership in organizations practicing discrimination

The arbitrator is a member of any organization that practices invidious discrimination on the basis of race, sex, religion, national origin, or sexual orientation. Membership in a religious organization, an official military organization of the United States, or a nonprofit youth organization need not be disclosed unless it would interfere with the arbitrator's proper conduct of the proceeding or would cause a person aware of the fact to reasonably entertain a doubt concerning the arbitrator's ability to act impartially.

(15) Any other matter that:

> (A) Might cause a person aware of the facts to reasonably entertain a doubt that the arbitrator would be able to be impartial;

> (B) Leads the prospective arbitrator to believe there is a substantial doubt as to his or her capacity to be impartial, including, but not limited to, bias or prejudice toward a party, lawyer, or law firm in the arbitration; or

> (C) Otherwise leads the arbitrator to believe that his or her disqualification will further the interests of justice....

(f) Continuing duty

An arbitrator's duty to disclose the matters described in subdivisions (d) and (e) of this standard is a continuing duty, applying from service of the notice of the arbitrator's proposed nomination or appointment until the conclusion of the arbitration proceeding.

Minnesota Statutes 572b.12

Disclosure by Arbitrator

(a) Before accepting appointment, an individual who is requested to serve as an arbitrator, after making a reasonable inquiry, shall disclose to all parties to the agreement to arbitrate and arbitration proceeding and to any other arbitrators any known facts that a reasonable person would consider likely to affect the impartiality of the arbitrator in the arbitration proceeding, including: (1) a financial or personal interest in the outcome of the arbitration proceeding; and (2) an existing or past relationship with any of the parties to the agreement to arbitrate or the arbitration proceeding, their counsel or representatives, witnesses, or the other arbitrators.

(b) An arbitrator has a continuing obligation to disclose to all parties to the agreement to arbitrate and arbitration proceedings and to any other arbitrators any facts that the arbitrator learns after accepting appointment which a reasonable person would consider likely to affect the impartiality of the arbitrator.

a. Comments and Questions

1. What is the difference between bias and the appearance of bias? Should the ethical codes regulate both actual and appearance of bias?

2. Compare the disclosure laws in the AAA/ABA Code of Ethics with the state statutes excerpted. Do you think one is better than the other?

3. What should the remedy be if an arbitrator does not disclose a conflict of interest? Below, this chapter addresses specific remedies against arbitrators for arbitrator malpractice. In contrast, Chapter 9, dealing with post-award judicial review, discusses how a court can vacate an arbitration award based on an arbitrator's undisclosed conflict of interest. The Minnesota statute specifically gives the parties the right to seek vacatur based on either a disclosed or undisclosed conflict of interest. Minn. Stat. 572B-12 (c)–(e).

4. Consider the following situations:

a. An arbitrator issues an award in favor of a local nonprofit organization in a relatively small breach of contract claim. Three months later, the nonprofit asks the arbitrator to sit on its board of directors. What should the arbitrator do? What if the invitation comes nine months after the award? Twelve? Eighteen?

b. An arbitrator discloses all relevant and legally required conflicts of interest prior to appointment as arbitrator. When the arbitrator receives the parties' witness lists, the arbitrator recognizes one of the witness names as a former co-worker. What should the arbitrator do?

c. An arbitrator who sits on the board of directors of the local animal rights advocacy organization is asked to arbitrate a dispute between a pharmaceutical company and a former employee. The former employee is being sued for damages when she covertly "freed" a dozen monkeys from a testing laboratory. What should this proposed arbitrator do?

d. Respondent moves to postpone an arbitration hearing. The arbitrator — normally willing to grant such motions — previously granted two motions to postpone in this very case. However, this is the third such motion that respondent filed in this matter and, unlike for the first two motions, claimant opposes this request. What should the arbitrator do?

e. An arbitrator holds less than one percent of respondent's company's stock in a mutual fund. Does it matter if the arbitrator is unaware of exactly what stocks are in the arbitrator's mutual funds? May the arbitrator take this appointment?

f. An arbitrator has an extensive presence on social media, including accounts on Facebook, Twitter, Instagram, and LinkedIn. Must the arbitrator search all social media contacts to determine what must be disclosed?

2. Independent Decision-Making

In addition to reducing bias and conflicts of interest on the part of the neutral, the Code of Ethics seeks to ensure that the process is fair, the arbitrator makes a determination based on the presentations by the parties and no other factors, all parties have an equal opportunity to participate in the arbitration, and the parties have the time and ability to present their case adequately. Canons III through IV of the AAA/ABA Code of Ethics for Arbitrators in Commercial Disputes cover these, and other issues, relating to the fairness of the process and independent decision-making of the arbitrator.

American Bar Association/American Arbitration Association, The Code of Ethics for Arbitrators in Commercial Disputes

Canons III–VI (2004)

CANON III. An Arbitrator Should Avoid Impropriety or the Appearance of Impropriety in Communicating with Parties.

A. If an agreement of the parties or applicable arbitration rules establishes the manner or content of communications between the arbitrator and the parties, the arbitrator should follow those procedures ...

B. [Arbitrators] should not discuss a proceeding with any party in the absence of any other party, [a listing of exceptions is omitted]

C. [W]henever an arbitrator communicates in writing with one party, the arbitrator should at the same time send a copy of the communication to every other party ...

CANON IV. An Arbitrator Should Conduct the Proceedings Fairly and Diligently.

B. The arbitrator should afford to all parties the right to be heard and due notice of the time and place of any hearing. The arbitrator should allow each party a fair opportunity to present its evidence and arguments.

C. The arbitrator should not deny any party the opportunity to be represented by counsel or by any other person chosen by the party.

D. If a party fails to appear after due notice, the arbitrator should proceed with the arbitration when authorized to do so, but only after receiving assurance that appropriate notice has been given to the absent party.

E. When the arbitrator determines that more information than has been presented by the parties is required to decide the case, it is not improper for the arbitrator to arbitrator to ask questions, call witnesses, and request documents or other evidence, including expert testimony.

F. Although it is not improper for an arbitrator to suggest to the parties that they discuss the possibility of settlement or the use of mediation, or other dispute resolution processes, an arbitrator should not exert pressure on any party to settle or to utilize other dispute resolution processes. An arbitrator should not be present or otherwise participate in settlement discussions or act as a mediator unless requested to do so by all parties.

CANON V. An Arbitrator Should Make Decisions in a Just, Independent and Deliberate Manner.

A. The arbitrator should, after careful deliberation, decide all issues submitted for determination. An arbitrator should decide no other issues....

D. In the event that all parties agree upon a settlement of issues in dispute and request the arbitrator to embody that agreement in an award, the arbitrator may do so, but is not required to do so unless satisfied with the propriety of the terms of settlement....

CANON VI. An Arbitrator Should be Faithful to the Relationship of
Trust and Confidentiality Inherent in that Office.

A. An arbitrator is in a relationship of trust to the parties and should not, at any time, use confidential information acquired during the arbitration proceeding to gain personal advantage or advantage for others, or to affect adversely the interest of another....

a. Comments and Questions

1. A party appears *pro se* in a commercial arbitration against a credit card company. She does not have a college degree, but her husband does. They do not have enough money to hire an attorney. She asks the arbitrator if her husband can attend the arbitration and help her make arguments and question witnesses. What should the arbitrator do? *See* Sarah R. Cole, *Blurred Lines: Are Non-Attorneys Who Represent Parties in Arbitration Involving Statutory Claims Practicing Law?*, 48 U.C. DAVIS L. REV. 921 (2015).

2. An arbitrator is handling a multimillion-dollar case involving a publicly traded company. Although the arbitrator (or anyone in the arbitrator's family) does not own any of the company's stock, the arbitrator's neighbor does. The arbitrator periodically receives gifts from the neighbor, such as sporting event tickets and homemade goods. The arbitrator knows that the publicly traded company is going to lose this case, and badly. Can the arbitrator warn the neighbor of the upcoming decision? Why or why not?

3. A *pro se* claimant writes a long, angry letter to the arbitrator about alleged injustices suffered by the claimant and caused by the respondent bank. The 10-page, handwritten letter discusses the merits of the case and complains about how the respondent bank treated the claimant during the arbitration process. What should the arbitrator do with the letter?

4. An arbitrator sends notice of a hearing date by certified mail, return receipt requested, to all of the parties. The arbitrator received return receipts from all of the parties. On the day of the hearing, the respondent does not appear. What should the arbitrator do?

5. During the course of the arbitration, the parties briefed, argued, and presented evidence on a tort claim that the parties admit falls outside the scope of the arbitration agreement. What should the arbitrator do?

3. Business Ethics

As with any profession, arbitrators must be clear and truthful in advertising and making fee arrangements. Canons VII and VIII of the AAA/ABA Code of Ethics for Arbitrators in Commercial Disputes cover these important topics.

American Bar Association/American Arbitration Association, The Code of Ethics for Arbitrators in Commercial Disputes
Canons VII & VIII (2004)

CANON VII. An Arbitrator Should Adhere to Standards of
Integrity and Fairness When Making Arrangements for
Compensation and Reimbursement of Expenses

A. Arbitrators who are to be compensated for their services or reimbursed for their expenses shall adhere to standards of integrity and fairness in making arrangements for such payments.... Arbitrators should not, absent extraordinary circumstances, request increases in the basis of their compensation during the course of a proceeding.

CANON VIII. An Arbitrator May Engage in Advertising or Promotion of
Arbitral Services Which is Truthful and Accurate

A. Advertising or promotion of an individual's willingness or availability to serve as an arbitrator must be accurate and unlikely to mislead. Any statements about the quality of the arbitrator's work or the success of the arbitrator's practice must be truthful.

B. Advertising and promotion must not imply any willingness to accept an appointment otherwise than in accordance with this Code.

a. Comments and Questions

1. Do these provisions apply to arbitration institutions? Should they?

2. Consider the following scenarios:

a. An arbitrator negotiates a flat fee of $7,000 for services provided in a case that is expected to last two hearing days, inclusive of pre-hearing motions, study time, and award writing. Within the first six months following appointment, the parties filed 10 motions (some discovery, some dispositive) and submitted witness lists naming more than 15 witnesses the parties expect to call at the hearing. The arbitrator now feels underpaid. What should the arbitrator do?

b. An arbitrator listed on her resume that she was the CEO of StartMeUp, Co., a company that created an app for fitness and calorie counting. Although the arbitrator listed this position under "former employment," she did not disclose the dates of employment. In fact, the company foundered in only eight months. Did the arbitrator violate any ethical rules?

D. Ethical Obligations of Party-Appointed Arbitrators

Party-appointed arbitrators in a tripartite arbitration are not expected to abide by the same ethical standards as neutral arbitrators. These arbitrators are permitted to have bias in favor of the appointing party, and the arbitrator can have ex parte conversations with the appointing party under certain circumstances. Consider carefully the ethics rules regarding party-appointed arbitrators. Also consider whether this is a practice that should be continued in the United States.

American Bar Association/American Arbitration Association, The Code of Ethics for Arbitrators in Commercial Disputes

Canons IX and X (2004)

CANON IX. Arbitrators Appointed by one Party Have a Duty to Determine and Disclose their Status and to Comply with this Code, Except as Exempted by Canon X.

A. In some types of arbitration in which there are three arbitrators, it is customary for each party, acting alone, to appoint one arbitrator. The third arbitrator is then appointed by agreement either of the parties or of the two arbitrators, or failing such agreement, by an independent institution or individual. In tripartite arbitrations to which this Code applies, all three arbitrators are presumed to be neutral and are expected to observe the same standards as the third arbitrator.

B. Notwithstanding this presumption, there are certain types of tripartite arbitration in which it is expected by all parties that the two arbitrators appointed by the parties may be predisposed toward the party appointing them. Those arbitrators, referred to in this Code as "Canon X arbitrators," are not to be held to the standards of neutrality and independence applicable to other arbitrators. Canon X describes the special ethical obligations of party-appointed arbitrators who are not expected to meet the standard of neutrality.

C. A party-appointed arbitrator has an obligation to ascertain, as early as possible but not later than the first meeting of the arbitrators and parties, whether the parties have agreed that the party-appointed arbitrators will serve as neutrals or whether they shall be subject to Canon X, and to provide a timely report of their conclusions to the parties and other arbitrators ...

D. Party-appointed arbitrators not governed by Canon X shall observe all of the obligations of Canons I through VIII unless otherwise required by agreement of the parties, any applicable rules, or applicable law.

CANON X. Exemptions for Arbitrators Appointed by One Party Who Are Not Subject to Rules of Neutrality.

Canon X arbitrators are expected to observe all of the ethical obligations prescribed by this Code except those from which they are specifically excused by Canon X.

[Canon X arbitrators should observe all of the obligations of Canon IV, Canon VI, Canon VII, and Canon VIII.]

A. Obligations under Canon I. Canon X arbitrators should observe all of the obligations of Canon I subject only to the following provisions:

(1) Canon X arbitrators may be predisposed toward the party who appointed them but in all other respects are obligated to act in good faith and with integrity and fairness. For example, Canon X arbitrators should not engage in delaying tactics or harassment of any party or witness and should not knowingly make untrue or misleading statements to the other arbitrators; and

(2) The provisions of subparagraphs B(1), B(2), and paragraphs C and D of Canon I, insofar as they relate to partiality, relationships, and interests are not applicable to Canon X arbitrators.

B. Obligations under Canon II

(1) Canon X arbitrators should disclose to all parties, and to the other arbitrators, all interests and relationships which Canon II requires be disclosed. Disclosure as required by Canon II is for the benefit not only of the party who appointed the arbitrator, but also for the benefit of the other parties and arbitrators so that they may know of any partiality which may exist or appear to exist; and

(2) Canon X arbitrators are not obliged to withdraw under paragraph U of Canon 11 if requested to do so only by the party who did not appoint them.

C. Obligations under Canon III. Canon X arbitrators should observe all of the obligations of Canon III subject only to the following provisions:

(1) Like neutral party-appointed arbitrators, Canon X arbitrators may consult with the party who appointed them to the extent permitted in paragraph B of Canon III;

(2) Canon X arbitrators shall, at the earliest practicable time, disclose to the other arbitrators and to the parties whether or not they intend to communicate with their appointing parties. If they have disclosed the intention to engage in such communications, they may thereafter communicate with their appointing parties concerning any other aspect of the case, except as provided in paragraph (3);

(3) If such communication occurred prior to the time they were appointed as arbitrators, or prior to the first hearing or other meeting of the parties with the arbitrators, the Canon X arbitrator should, at or before the first hearing or meeting of the arbitrators with the parties, disclose the fact that such communication has taken place. In complying with the provisions of this subparagraph, it is sufficient that there be disclosure of the fact that such communication has occurred without disclosing the content of the communication. A single timely disclosure of the Canon X arbitrator's intention to participate in such communications in the future is sufficient;

(4) Canon X arbitrators may not at any time during the arbitration: (a) disclose any deliberations by the arbitrators on any matter or issue submitted to them for de-

cision; (b) communicate with the parties that appointed them concerning any matter or issue taken under consideration by the panel after the record is closed or such matter or issue has been submitted for decision; or (c) disclose any final decision or interim decision in advance of the time that it is disclosed to all parties;

(5) Unless otherwise agreed by the arbitrators and the parties, a Canon X arbitrator may not communicate orally with the neutral arbitrator concerning any matter or issue arising or expected to arise in the arbitration in the absence of the other Canon X arbitrator. If a Canon X arbitrator communicates in writing with the neutral arbitrator, he or she shall simultaneously provide a copy of the written communication to the other Canon X arbitrator;

(6) When Canon X arbitrators communicate orally with the parties that appointed them concerning any matter on which communication is permitted under this Code, they are not obligated to disclose the contents of such oral communications to any other party or arbitrator; and

(7) When Canon X arbitrators communicate in writing with the party who appointed them concerning any matter on which communication is permitted under this Code, they are not required to send copies of any such written communication to any other party or arbitrator....

E. Obligations under Canon V. Canon X arbitrators should observe all of the obligations of Canon V, except that they may be predisposed toward deciding in favor of the party who appointed them....

I. Obligations Under Canon IX. The provisions of paragraph D of Canon IX are inapplicable to Canon X arbitrators, except insofar as the obligations are also set forth in this Canon.

Bruce Meyerson & John M. Townsend, *Revised Code of Ethics for Commercial Arbitrators Explained*
59 Disp. Resol. J. 10 (2004)

The revised Code of Ethics for Arbitrators in Commercial Disputes brings the 1977 Code more in line with modern practice.... Because the practice of arbitration has developed significantly since 1977, [the ABA and AAA] began to review whether changes in the laws governing arbitration, the increasing globalization of commercial transactions, and changes in the public perception and expectations of arbitration required revisions to the 1977 Ethics Code....

The 2004 Revision preserves the style and format, and much of the language, of the 1977 Ethics Code. It is called a revision, rather than a new document, to signal its continuity with the many unchanged provisions of the 1977 Ethics Code and respect for the degree of judicial acceptance that it has achieved. All provisions of the 2004 Revision are subject to any contrary principles that may be found in governing law or applicable arbitration rules and also to the right of the parties to any arbitration to reach agreement on different rules and standards.

Presumption of Neutrality

The most fundamental and far-reaching change contained in the 2004 Revision is the application of a presumption of neutrality to all arbitrators, including party-appointed arbitrators. By contrast, the 1977 Ethics Code presumed that the party-appointed arbitrators to a three-person panel (tripartite arbitration) would not be neutral. This meant that, in practice, they were not only free to act as advocates for the positions of the party that appointed them, they were expected to act that way. Under the 1977 Ethics Code, party-appointed arbitrators were to be considered "non-neutral unless both parties inform the arbitrators that all three arbitrators are to be neutral or unless the contract, the applicable arbitration rules, or any governing law requires that all three arbitrators be neutral."

Thus, absent contrary indications in the parties' agreement, the governing law or arbitral rules, the default rule was that all party-appointed arbitrators were considered nonneutral when no agreement for their neutrality had been made.

The 2004 Revision reverses the presumption of nonneutrality for party-appointed arbitrators. Instead, it establishes a presumption of neutrality for all arbitrators. Thus, they will all be held to the same standard.... This presumption is reaffirmed in Canon IX.A of the 2004 Revision.

The concept of neutrality embodied in the 2004 Revision encompasses both independence and impartiality. This is codified in Canon I.B, which provides that an arbitrator should accept appointment only if fully satisfied that he or she can serve "impartially" and "independently" from the parties, potential witnesses, and the other arbitrators. The Comment to Canon I explains that arbitrators do not contravene the Canon if by virtue of experience or expertise they have views on certain general issues likely to arise in an arbitration, but emphasizes that "an arbitrator may not have prejudged any of the specific legal or factual determinations to be addressed during the arbitration."

The 2004 Revision continues to permit party-appointed arbitrators to be partisan, but only when it is shown that "all parties" intended that they may be "predisposed" toward the party who appointed them. This balance is struck by two provisions of new Canon IX. First, Canon IX.A provides: "In tripartite arbitrations to which this Code applies, all three arbitrators are presumed to be neutral and are expected to observe the same standards as the third arbitrator." ... The 2004 Revision refers to nonneutral arbitrators as "Canon X arbitrators" because that Canon establishes the special ethical obligations of party-appointed arbitrators who are not expected to meet the standards of neutrality.

The grouping of provisions applicable to non-neutral party-appointed arbitrators in Canon X represents an architectural solution designed to reconcile different points of view on the subject of non-neutral arbitrators. On one side, there were strong feelings that the endorsement of non-neutral party-appointed arbitrators in the 1977 Ethics Code had taken American domestic arbitration out of the mainstream of international arbitration, where the prevailing view is that all arbitrators, including party-appointed arbitrators, should be independent of the parties and impartial to the extent possible. Those sharing this position argued that a code of ethics could achieve international respect only if it required all arbitrators to be neutral. On the countervailing side was the view that use of nonneutral party-appointed arbitrators was an accepted, well established practice in many types of American domestic arbitration, and American courts have accepted the practice as consistent with legal standards established by the Federal Arbitration Act.

The solution represented by the 2004 Revision demonstrates a firm preference for arbitrator neutrality, while providing a tent large enough to accommodate those who have specifically agreed otherwise. The 2004 Revision, therefore, provides that Canon X arbitrators are expected to observe all of the ethical obligations prescribed by Code, except those from which they are expressly excused. However, these ethical obligations differ from those of neutral party-appointed arbitrators in several carefully defined respects. Canon X.A permits Canon X arbitrators to be "predisposed" toward the party who appointed them. Canon X.B provides that Canon X arbitrators are not obliged to withdraw because of alleged partiality when requested to do so by the non-appointing party. And Canon X.C allows Canon X arbitrators to generally engage in ex parte communications with their appointing party.

On the other hand, Canon X.A requires Canon X arbitrators to act in good faith and with integrity and fairness. These arbitrators may not, for example, engage in delaying tactics or harassment. They are required to make the same disclosures of interests and relationships that was previously required ... only of neutral arbitrators. And they are subject to specific limitations on the scope of their ex parte communications with the appointing parties and with the third arbitrator, although they are permitted far more freedom to engage in such communications than are neutral arbitrators.

Effect on Drafting

From now on, attorneys who draft such agreements will be well advised to clarify in the arbitration provision the parties' understanding regarding the "status" of party-appointed arbitrators, particularly if they desire them to act as Canon X arbitrators (i.e., to act as partisan arbitrators for the appointing parties).

Duties of Party-Appointed Arbitrators

Investigation and Disclosure of Status

One of the significant features of the 2004 Revision is contained in Canon IX, which imposes a duty on every party-appointed arbitrator to ascertain and disclose whether he or she will be acting as a neutral arbitrator or as a Canon X arbitrator. Canon IX.C(3) provides that, in the event of doubt or uncertainty, all party-appointed arbitrators should serve in a neutral capacity until such doubt or uncertainty is resolved. This ethical requirement is new.

Under Canon IX.C, each party-appointed arbitrator now has an obligation to (1) ascertain his or her status as early as possible (and not later than the first meeting of the arbitrators and the parties), and (2) provide a timely report on the subject to the parties and the other arbitrators....

Disclosure of Interests and Relationships

The 2004 Revision subjects all arbitrators to the same obligations to disclose interests or relationships likely to affect impartiality or which might create an appearance of partiality. This is new.... [S]pecifically, Canons II.A, X.B, all arbitrators, including Canon X arbitrators, are required to disclose any interest or relationship likely to affect their impartiality or which might create an appearance of partiality. This duty encompasses "any known ... financial or personal interest in the outcome of the arbitration" or existing or past relationships.

The standard for disclosure of relationships in the Canon II.A(2) of the 2004 Revision is new. It is whether known financial, business, professional or personal relationships "might reasonably affect impartiality or lack of independence in the eyes of any of the parties. Canon II.B requires prospective arbitrators to make a reasonable effort to inform themselves of relevant interests or relationships. And any doubt as to whether or not disclosure is to be made should be resolved in favor of disclosure. The disclosure obligation defined by Canon II.A continues ... throughout the arbitration....

Consistent with the principle of party autonomy, the 2004 Revision expressly states in Canon I.C that the existence of any relationship or interest "does not render it unethical for one to serve as an arbitrator where the parties have consented to the arbitrator's appointment or continued services following full disclosure of the relevant facts" in accordance with the Code. So long as the arbitrator makes a full disclosure of the interest or relationship, the parties are free to consent to continued service or appointment and the arbitrator may ethically accept the appointment or continue to serve.

Communications with the Parties and the Other Arbitrators

The 2004 Revision clarifies the limits on permissible communications between arbitrators and the parties, and establishes new guidelines on communications between party-appointed arbitrators and the chair of the tribunal in tripartite arbitrations.

The 2004 Revision provides guidance ... on what a prospective arbitrator may discuss on an ex parte basis with the appointing party concerning the potential appointment. Canon III.B(1) limits the discussion to three general subjects: (1) the identities of the parties, counsel or witnesses, (2) the general nature of the case, and (3) the arbitrator's suitability or availability for the appointment. Discussion of the merits of the case is specifically prohibited, except to a limited extent for Canon X arbitrators.

In addition, Canon III.B allows a party-appointed arbitrator to consult with the appointing party concerning (a) the choice of the third arbitrator, (b) compensation, and (c) the status of the arbitrator as a neutral arbitrator or as a Canon X arbitrator.

Canon III.B(3) and (4) allows both neutral and Canon X arbitrators to discuss with the party who appointed them the selection of the third arbitrator. By contrast, the 1977 Ethics Code only allowed nonneutral party-appointed arbitrators to discuss selection of the third arbitrator with the party who appointed them.

Provided a Canon X arbitrator has disclosed the intention to engage in such communications, Canon X.C(2) permits this arbitrator to communicate with the appointing party concerning the merits or "any other aspect of the case," subject to certain enumerated exceptions. If these communications occurred prior to the arbitrator's appointment, or prior to the first hearing or the parties' first meeting with the arbitrators, a Canon X arbitrator is to disclose, at or before the first hearing or meeting, the fact that the communication took place. There is no obligation to disclose the content of the communication. Canon X.C(4) of the 2004 Revision clarifies that Canon X arbitrators may not, at any time during the arbitration, communicate with the appointing party concerning the deliberations of the arbitrators or "any matter or issue taken under consideration by the panel after the record is closed or such matter or issue has been submitted for decision." It also carries forward the prohibitions contained in the 1977 Ethics Code against disclosure of the deliberations of the arbitrators or of any "final or interim decision" in advance of the time it is given to all parties.

Moreover, there are new restrictions on communications between Canon X arbitrators and the neutral arbitrator. The 2004 Revision prohibits these arbitrators from communicating orally with a neutral arbitrator concerning "any matter or issue" arising or expected to arise in the arbitration in the absence of the other Canon X arbitrator. Canon X.C(5) provides that if a Canon X arbitrator communicates in writing with the neutral arbitrator, that arbitrator must simultaneously provide a copy of the written communication to the other Canon X arbitrator....

Conclusion

The 1977 Ethics Code remains an historic document that greatly enhanced the integrity of and respect for arbitration process throughout the United States and the world. The 2004 Revision makes this Code even better and even more in tune with modern, contemporary practice. It also brings American standards closer to standards accepted in international commercial arbitration.

1. Comments and Questions

a. When is tripartite arbitration a good option for parties? What are its benefits? What are its shortcomings?

b. For scholarly opinions on tripartite arbitration, *see, e.g.*, David J. Branson, *American Party-Appointed Arbitrators — Not the Three Monkeys*, 30 U. Dayton L. Rev. 1 (2004); David McLeon & Sean-Patrick Wilson, *Is Three a Crowd? Neutrality, Partiality and Partisanship in the Context of Tripartite Arbitration*, 9 Pepp. Disp. Resol. L.J. 167 (2008); Daniel Yamshon, *Do Party Arbitrators Have Ethical Duties of Neutrality?*, 17 Disp. Resol. Mag. 21 (Summer 2011).

c. Consider the following scenarios:

1. Respondent challenges claimant's party-appointed (Canon X) arbitrator on the basis of bias. Must the party-appointed arbitrator withdraw from the panel?

2. A Canon X arbitrator discusses hearing strategy with the appointing party before and during the arbitration hearing. Is this permissible? Under what circumstances?

3. A Canon X arbitrator calls the neutral arbitrator on the telephone to discuss the merits of the case. What should the neutral arbitrator do?

4. A software company appoints an attorney on its Board of Directors to be its Canon X arbitrator. The attorney and the company have routine conversations on matters relating to this dispute and on other matters involving business, strategy, and finances. The arbitrator understands that he must make certain disclosures about these conversations with the software company. What should those disclosures be?

5. Two businesses arbitrate a dispute before a three-arbitrator panel. Each party chooses one arbitrator, and those two arbitrators choose a third arbitrator. At the hearing, one of the parties wants to have a conference with its appointed arbitrator. Is that permissible?

E. Structural Bias

So far, this chapter has assumed that, unless parties designate a non-neutral as a party-appointed arbitrator, the parties want arbitrators who are neutral and free from connections (personal, business, professional, or otherwise) with any of the parties. But what if the parties wanted their arbitrator to be someone who is affiliated with one party or another? Is that permissible? Wise? Ethical?

This section considers what is known as *structural bias*. Structural bias occurs when the parties, at the onset, agree that the decision-maker should be someone affiliated with one of the sides. Both parties agree, with eyes wide open, that the decision-maker is not going to be someone independent of the parties, but someone whose connection to the underlying dispute provides the requisite knowledge and expertise and who can resolve the dispute efficiently. As the cases below demonstrate, these types of situations occur most often in the case of public contracts, such as construction contracts, and employment contracts.

National Football League Management Council v.
National Football Players Association & Tom Brady
820 F.3d 527 (2d Cir. 2016)

PARKER, CIRCUIT JUDGE.

This case involves an arbitration arising from New England Patriots quarterback Tom Brady's involvement in a scheme to deflate footballs used during the 2015 American Football Conference Championship Game to a pressure below the permissible range. Following an investigation, the NFL suspended Brady for four games. Brady requested arbitration and League Commissioner Roger Goodell, serving as arbitrator, entered an award confirming the discipline. The parties sought judicial review and the district court vacated the award, reasoning that Brady lacked notice that his conduct was prohibited and punishable by suspension, and that the manner in which the proceedings were conducted deprived him of fundamental fairness. The League has appealed and we now reverse....

We must simply ensure that the arbitrator was "even arguably construing or applying the contract and acting within the scope of his authority" and did not "ignore the plain language of the contract." These standards do not require perfection in arbitration awards. Rather, they dictate that even if an arbitrator makes mistakes of fact or law, we may not disturb an award so long as he acted within the bounds of his bargained-for authority.

Here, that authority was especially broad. The Commissioner was authorized to impose discipline for, among other things, "conduct detrimental to the integrity of, or public confidence, in the game of professional football." In their collective bargaining agreement, the players and the League mutually decided many years ago that the Commissioner should investigate possible rule violations, should impose appropriate sanctions, and may preside at arbitrations challenging his discipline. Although this tripartite regime may appear somewhat unorthodox, it is the regime bargained for and agreed upon by the parties, which we can only presume they determined was mutually satisfactory.

Given this substantial deference, we conclude that this case is not an exceptional one that warrants vacatur. Our review of the record yields the firm conclusion that the Commissioner properly exercised his broad discretion to resolve an intramural controversy between the League and a player. Accordingly, we REVERSE the judgment of the district court and REMAND with instructions to confirm the award....

B. Evident Partiality

The Association's final contention is that the Commissioner was evidently partial with regard to the delegation issue and should have recused himself from hearing at least that portion of the arbitration because it was improper for him to adjudicate the propriety of his own conduct. This argument has no merit.

We may vacate an arbitration award "where there was evident partiality ... in the arbitrator[ ]." 9 U.S.C. § 10(a)(2). "Evident partiality may be found only 'where a reasonable person would have to conclude that an arbitrator was partial to one party to the arbitration.'" The party seeking vacatur must prove evident partiality by "clear and convincing evidence." However, arbitration is a matter of contract, and consequently, the parties to an arbitration can ask for no more impartiality than inheres in the method they have chosen.

Here, the parties contracted in the CBA to specifically allow the Commissioner to sit as the arbitrator in all disputes brought pursuant to Article 46, Section 1(a). They did so knowing full well that the Commissioner had the sole power of determining what constitutes "conduct detrimental," and thus knowing that the Commissioner would have a stake both in the underlying discipline and in every arbitration brought pursuant to Section 1(a). Had the parties wished to restrict the Commissioner's authority, they could have fashioned a different agreement.

CONCLUSION

For the foregoing reasons, we REVERSE the judgment of the district court and REMAND with instructions for the district court to confirm the arbitration award.

Westinghouse Electric Corp. v. New York City Transit Auth.

623 N.E.2d 531 (N.Y. 1993)

BELLACOSA, JUSTICE [for a unanimous court].

The issue in this case, certified to this Court by the United States Court of Appeals for the Second Circuit so that we might resolve a question of New York law, is whether New York public policy prohibits an "ADR provision that authorizes an employee of a party [the New York City Transit Authority] to a contract dispute, where such employee is personally involved in the dispute, to make conclusive, final, and binding decisions on all questions arising under the contract" We answer the certified question in the negative and conclude that the challenged ADR provision, which expressly provides for judicial review, does not in these circumstances violate New York public policy.

In 1983, Westinghouse won and entered into a contract with the New York City Transit Authority (NYCTA) for the sale, delivery, and installation of power rectifier equipment to five substations for the New York City subway system. [N]umerous disputes arose between the parties concerning whether Westinghouse was entitled to damages for delay or compensation for additional work; whether NYCTA could properly delete certain portions of the work from the contract; whether Westinghouse was being restrained from performing under the contract; and whether Westinghouse was entitled to unilaterally stop work under the contract. The alternative dispute resolution provision, article 8.03, provides:

> (c) The parties to this contract authorize the Superintendent, acting personally, to decide all questions of any nature whatsoever arising out of, under, or in connection with, or in any way related to or on account of, this Contract ... and his decision shall be conclusive, final and binding on the parties.

Westfall (whose title is Chief Electrical Officer) is a NYCTA employee and functioned as the Superintendent and ADR adjudicator. By letter dated November 3, Westinghouse notified Westfall that the NYCTA's failure to resolve numerous longstanding design problems and other restraints and prohibitions on Westinghouse's work constituted a constructive stop work order. The letter requested that the NYCTA resolve all outstanding performance problems within 90 days. In a subsequent letter dated February 3, 1989, Westinghouse advised Westfall that it was suspending further performance effective February 3, 1989, because the NYCTA did not respond to the problems set forth in the earlier letter. Westfall responded by letter dated February 8, 1989, acknowledging Westinghouse's formal advice that it was suspending performance under the contract. Westfall further stated that this was a breach of contract and directed Westinghouse to discontinue all work. In addition, Westfall advised Westinghouse that a recommendation would be made that it be held in default and, on June 13, the NYCTA advised Westinghouse that that had been formally effectuated. On June 21, 1989, Westinghouse submitted to Westfall a "Request for Additional Compensation and Time Extension," including the costs of additional labor, equipment, and general and administrative expenses Westinghouse claimed it incurred to perform the contract due to the NYCT A's alleged failure to discharge its contract obligations. Westinghouse asked that the NYCTA's default declaration be rescinded and for a Superintendent's decision, as required by article 8.03. It thus submitted itself to the ADR mechanism. By letter dated July 26, 1989, Westfall advised Westinghouse that he rejected its claims. ...

Matter of Astoria Med. Group (Health Ins. Plan), 182 N.E.2d 85 and *Matter of Siegel*, provide persuasive authority. ... In *Matter of Siegel*, the parties designated a lawyer and an accountant of one of the parties as the arbitrators of any dispute arising from a stock purchase agreement. A dispute arose resulting in a demanded arbitration, but before a decision was rendered, one party refused arbitration and brought a proceeding to vacate the designation of the lawyer and the accountant as arbitrators. This Court dismissed the action, stating that as it has long been the policy of New York courts to interfere as little as possible with the freedom of consenting parties, "[t]herefore, strange as it may seem ... a fully known relationship between an arbitrator and a party, including one as close as employer and employee ... will not in and of itself disqualify the designee." ...

Westinghouse chose, with its business eyes open, to accept the terms, specifications and risk of the bid contract, including the ADR clause. It subsequently came to believe and feel aggrieved that having an employee of the NYCTA alone decide the ongoing disputes during the performance of the contract led ultimately to decisions unfavorable to it. Without doubt, Westinghouse understood the implications of the ADR clause prior to undertaking its business and legal risks under the whole of the multimillion dollar agreement. To allow it, after the fact, to secure the assistance and power of the courts to relieve it of a particular procedural provision, while retaining the benefits of the rest of the publicly bid public works contract, is not compelled by our precedents and would have destabilizing commercial law consequences.

Focusing on the instant case, we recognize the commercial and competing public policy realities when parties freely contract and select their own ADR process and adjudicator with some judicial review. Most importantly, we conclude only that public policy has not been transgressed in this case, particularly because of the provision for judicial review of the adjudicator's decision. That review, under the terms of the agreement, is by CPLR article 78 and thus allows broader review than the usual and stricter standards of arbitration award review in article 75.

Westinghouse, nevertheless, emphasizes that this case should not rest on freedom of contract principles because of the inhibiting nature of the bid process. But Westinghouse pushes the argument too far when it urges that public policy requires that in contractual relations public entities cannot, as a matter of law, require by bid specification that private contractors (often economic giants in their own right) must allow a Chief Engineer as Superintendent to serve as the ADR adjudicator of contractual disputes, when the ADR provision itself imposes some independent review mechanism.

Relative one-sidedness is a proposition of too general a nature to resolve, by itself, such an important public contract issue. To be sure, when powerful municipalities put their public works jobs out for bid and require competition, low cost and performance in accordance with published specifications, they enjoy a virtual monopolistic-kind of power. But that does not make those contracts adhesion agreements. The courts should not, except for compelling reasons, wrest away from contracting parties a superior marketplace bargaining hand and try to equalize relatively arm's length commercial dealings. The judicial review check provided for in this ADR provision should be sufficient to regulate and remedy intolerable abuses and one-sided economic oppression. Thus, the parties should be left to their own ingenuity to enter such agreements and solve their differences with appropriate ADR mechanisms, such as the one here.

Our public policy evaluation is also relevantly affected by the realization that billions of dollars of commercial transactions and thousands of public work contracts are outstanding containing identical or similar ADR provisions. They are entitled to some stability because they were entered into with reliance on reasonable predictability factors. These contracts were let, bid and made under what was evidently perceived to be the state of the law and valid public policy in New York, promoted and induced by judicial decisions and extant policies, such as they were, which not only tolerated but encouraged parties to freely contract generally and especially with ADR mechanisms. Altering the path taken through the forest in the fashion urged here by Westinghouse by relocating trees across the roadway would not be prudent or sound public policy. The rule of law should not suddenly be changed to dislodge reliably perceived public policy in New York, which encourages parties to agree to submit their disputes to forums and persons for prompt, efficient and fair resolution, by their reckoning, not that of the courts, after the fact.

Harter v. Iowa Grain
220 F.3d 544 (7th Cir. 2000)

CUDAHY, CIRCUIT JUDGE

Lowell Harter was, until his retirement, a corn farmer in Grant County, Indiana. "The Andersons" is a corporation that operates grain elevators around the Midwest. [The parties' disagreement stems from a contract to deliver corn at a future date. Harter never delivered the corn in question, and The Andersons sought damages for the corn that was not delivered.]

Harter filed a class action lawsuit in the Northern District of Illinois against The Andersons, its subsidiary AISC and introducing broker Iowa Grain. Harter later dropped Iowa Grain, which Harter had erroneously believed to be The Andersons' principal, from the suit. Harter alleged that The Andersons had violated the Commodity Exchange Act, the federal Racketeer Influenced and Corrupt Organizations Act (RICO), the Indiana RICO statute, and had committed common law fraud, breach of fiduciary duty and intentional infliction of emotional distress. The contracts Harter had signed expressly provided that in the event of a dispute, the National Grain & Feed Association (NGFA) would arbitrate. After Harter filed suit, The Andersons petitioned the district court, pursuant to the Federal Arbitration Act, 9 U.S.C. § 1 et seq., to stay proceedings and to compel arbitration. The district judge granted the motion. The NGFA arbitrators entered an award in favor of The Andersons, and ordered Harter to pay contract damages of $55,350 plus interest, as well as $85,000 in attorney's fees plus interest. Harter moved to vacate or modify the award; The Andersons moved to confirm it. On July 24, 1998, the district court entered an order confirming the arbitration award in its entirety. It subsequently granted The Andersons' request that Harter bear the attorney's fees that The Andersons incurred in non-arbitration portions of the litigation. Harter now appeals the district court's order compelling arbitration, its order affirming the award and its order regarding attorney's fees....

IV. Structural Bias of the NGFA Arbitration Panel

The Andersons asked the district court to confirm the NGFA panel's award, which it did. Harter now argues to us, as he did below, that this decision was erroneous because the NGFA panel was biased against him. When reviewing the district court's confirmation of the arbitration award, we decide questions of law de novo and review findings of fact for clear error. The Federal Arbitration Act permits us to upset the parties' bargain by vacating an arbitration award only in very specific situations. See 9 U.S.C. § 10. Harter argues that this arbitration is such a situation because there was "evident partiality ... in the arbitrators ..." in violation of section 10(a)(2) of the Act. 9 U.S.C. § 10(a)(2). We have stated that "evident partiality" exists when an arbitrator's bias is "direct, definite and capable of demonstration rather than remote, uncertain, or speculative." Harter now asks us to recognize a subset of arbitral partiality, "structural bias." He contends that the NGFA is "structurally biased" against farmers because its members include grain elevators like The Andersons. Thus, he was "placed in the unenviable position of having to attempt to persuade NGFA members that a widespread practice of the association's membership is illegal." Harter no doubt feels that the farmers' traditional adversaries were sitting in judgment over him.

Some notable jurists have harbored similar suspicions about the fate of customers appearing before arbitration panels populated by industry "insiders." For instance, when the Second Circuit required a securities buyer to arbitrate a fraud claim under the 1933 Securities Act against his broker, Judge Clark dissented. Judge Clark stated that "the persons to [adjudicate the dispute] would naturally come from the regulated business itself. Adjudication by such arbitrators ... is surely not a way of assuring the customer that objective and sympathetic consideration of his claim which is envisaged by the Securities Act." The Supreme Court adopted Judge Clark's point of view, stating that Congress's intent in passing section 14 of the Securities Act was to "assure that sellers could not maneuver buyers into a position that might weaken their ability to recover under the Securities Act." Wilko v. Swan, 346 U.S. 427, 432, (1953). Section 14 created a non-waivable right to bring suit in federal court for such maneuvers, the Court determined.

The Seventh Circuit adopted this reasoning in *Weissbuch v. Merrill Lynch, Pierce, Fenner & Smith, Inc.*, 558 F.2d 831 (7th Cir.1977). In *Weissbuch*, we relied on *Wilko* to find that a Rule 10b-5 consumer fraud claim was not arbitrable. The same year we decided *Weissbuch*, we held that an analogous CEA claim was arbitrable. We reasoned that unlike the Securities Act of 1933 at issue in *Wilko*, the CEA had no non-waivable consumer protection provision. Judge Swygert, in a persuasive dissent, relied on *Wilko* and *Weissbuch* to argue that commodities investors, like securities investors, were "vulnerable to fraudulent schemes perpetrated by industry insiders," and thus deserved a judicial forum for their claims.

However perceptive Judge Swygert and Judge Clark may have been, the opposing view favoring arbitration has firmly won out. In 1989, the Supreme Court explicitly overruled *Wilko*, stating that it had "fallen far out of step with our current strong endorsement of the federal statutes favoring [arbitration as a] method of resolving disputes." *Rodriguez de Quijas* was the culmination of a series of pro-arbitration cases decided in the 1980s....

To avoid the arbitration pitfalls identified by Judges Swygert and Clark, we have required arbitrators to provide a "fundamentally fair hearing." We guarantee fairness by steering clear of "evident partiality." And, in settings where arbitrators and litigants were structural adversaries, as Harter suggests they are here, we have never found evident partiality. For instance, we refused to set aside an award rendered in favor of a financial services company by a panel whose members were "drawn from persons in the commodities business." *Tamari v. Bache Halsey Stuart, Inc.*, 619 F.2d 1196, 1201 (7th Cir.1980). We reasoned that disqualifying arbiters with experience in the business would eviscerate the goals of arbitration. We also noted in *Tamari* that the customer had agreed to arbitrate before the "industry" panel. We have elsewhere stated that by virtue of their expertise in a field, arbitrators may have interests that overlap with the matter they are considering as arbitrators. Such overlap has not amounted to prima facie partiality. Thus, even a prior business association between an arbitrator and a party is not sufficient evidence of bias to vacate an award. Reviewing these cases, we find it difficult to imagine how courts might apply the "structural bias" standard Harter advocates. In an economy increasingly populated by large conglomerates with diverse interests, many individual arbitrators could be affiliated with companies only arguably adverse to one of the parties. Harter's standard would require disqualification, despite the practical reality that the arbitrators themselves would quite likely be impartial.

Although as a matter of first impression we might sympathize with Harter's frustration, we are in the mainstream in rejecting his "structural bias" argument. The First Circuit recently rejected an argument that an arbitration panel comprising financial employers was so inclined to side with employers that it could not adjudicate the claim of a female worker alleging gender discrimination. The Eleventh Circuit has affirmed the impartiality of a panel whose members were in the business of collecting futures debit balances from customers in a situation where the panel held a customer liable for such obligations. And, of particular relevance to us, the Sixth Circuit recently found in favor of The Andersons in a challenge to an NGFA arbitral award involving an HTA [hedge-to-arrive, i.e., "futures"] contract almost identical to Harter's. So precedent in this circuit and others, as well as the broad policy goals served by arbitration, require us to reject Harter's argument of "structural bias" in the NGFA. This issue is no longer open.

Thus, we will vacate the arbitration award only if Harter can show that the NGFA panel had direct bias against him. This standard is difficult to meet. For instance, in one of the few cases vacating an award because of arbitral bias, the Second Circuit objected when a son served as arbitrator of a dispute involving a local unit of an international union of which his father was president.

Harter observes that the NGFA is an organization of grain merchandisers and their affiliates. Apparently, however, a number of farmer-owned cooperatives are also NGFA members. On the other hand, one of The Andersons' top employees sits on the NGFA board. The Andersons pays more than $26,000 in dues annually to the NGFA. And the NGFA has taken the public position that HTA contracts are not futures instruments. Harter charges that a significant portion of NGFA members have written HTA contracts, and that NGFA arbitration rules do not disqualify arbitrators who have written HTA contracts. Harter also charges that, prior to the influx of HTA cases, the NGFA arbitrated fewer than 20 cases involving farmers, and only vindicated farmers twice. Harter alleges that almost half of the NGFA's members have written HTA contracts, while the NGFA points out that just half of those members responding to an HTA survey have done so. Even if all of these facts are true, they do not establish the direct, definite, demonstrable bias required by *United States Wrestling Federation*.

Under NGFA arbitration rules, an aggrieved party must first file a complaint with the NGFA national secretary. The parties then fully brief the dispute, and either party may request oral argument, though the requesting party bears the cost. The NGFA national secretary then appoints a three-member arbitration committee selected from the membership. The individual arbitrators must have expertise in the industry sector at issue, but must be commercially disinterested in the particular dispute. Arbitrators must disclose any bias or financial interest that could influence their analysis; either party may object to any of the arbitrators. The panel issues written opinions, and the parties may appeal. These facts suggest significant procedural safeguards for the parties.

Finally, Harter argues that the panel demonstrated its bias by granting an unsubstantiated request by The Andersons for attorney's fees, and delegating to the NGFA national secretary the task of verifying The Andersons' expenditures. It is true that, when a party claims arbitral bias, we must "scan the record" for evidence of partiality.

Here, the NGFA panel unanimously found in favor of The Andersons, and awarded damages reflecting The Andersons' actual market loss, plus cancellation fees, plus compound interest calculated at nine percent. It also cited a provision in Harter's contract stating that "seller shall also be liable for The Andersons' attorney's fees ..." and stated that the Andersons "indicated that outside counsel fees and costs totaled approximately $85,000 through November 1996 in connection with the federal court case resulting from Harter's refusal to arbitrate the dispute...." The arbitration panel's written decision also recounted the ongoing court battle between the parties. Thus, although The Andersons had not submitted actual billing records, the panel had before it contract language calling for Harter to pay The Andersons' legal fees, The Andersons' estimate of its legal fees and evidence of the court battle giving rise to those fees. The decision to award attorney's fees subject to a detailed review by the NGFA national secretary was reasonable, and certainly does not prove direct bias against Harter. We therefore affirm the district court's confirmation of the arbitral award.

1. Comments and Questions

a. The case involving Tom Brady arose in the labor law context. Does allowing structural bias in cases involving collective bargaining agreements make more sense than in a non-labor situation? How sophisticated were the respective parties in that case? Do you think that the union and players gained anything of value when they agreed that the Commissioner will be the arbitrator in disputes between them?

b. The *Westinghouse* case remains good and influential law more than two decades after its publication in New York and elsewhere. *See Staviski v. Christa Constr.*, 124 A.D.3d 1126 (N.Y. App. Div. 2015); *Yonkers Contracting Co., Inc. v. Port Authority Trans-Hudson Corp.*, 87 N.Y.2d 927 (1996); *City and Council of Denver v. District Court in and for City and County of Denver*, 939 P.2d 1353 (Colo. 1997).

c. BDO Seidman, a national accounting firm, and its partners—all educated, licensed, and highly compensated persons, entered into the following arbitration agreement when joining the partnership:

> Any dispute or controversy shall be considered and decided by an arbitration panel consisting of two (2) members of the Board of Directors (other than the Chairman and Chief Executive Partner) selected by the Board of Directors and three (3) Partners from the Partnership's practice office who are not members of the Board of Directors. The members of the arbitration panel shall be mutually agreed to by the Board of Directors and the parties to the controversy or dispute, provided that no member of the panel shall be from an office in which any complaining Partner was located at the time of the filing of the complaint, nor be otherwise involved in the controversy or dispute ...

What do you think of this type of employment arbitration agreement? How sophisticated are the parties to this contract? Does that matter in your analysis of whether you think the agreement should be enforced? Do economic incentives influence your thinking on the issue?

This particular contract has been subject to a significant amount of litigation. Most courts upheld the arbitration agreement. *See Hottle v. BDO Seidman, LLP,* 846 A.2d 862 (Conn. 2004); *Greenwald v. Weisbaum,* 785 N.Y.S.2d 664 (Sup. Ct. N.Y. Co. 2004); *Selznik v. BDO Seidman,* No. 507/95 (Sup. Ct. Westchester Co. June 12, 1995); *Brown v. BDO Seidman,* File No. 91-9343 (Circuit Court of Grand Travers County, Mich. Dec. 18, 1992); *Pieso v. Abernathy,* No. 90-1637 (Wis. Ct. App. Aug. 28, 1990). This finding, however, has not been universal. *See BDO Seidman v. Miller,* 949 S.W.2d 858 (Tex. App. 1997) (finding agreement illusory); *Buhrer v. BDO Seidman, L.L.P.,* 2003 Mass. Super. LEXIS 235 (July 7, 2003) (finding agreement "offensive to basic notions of fairness").

d. How are these cases involving structural bias different from the cases presented in Chapter 4, like the *Hooters* case, regarding allegedly biased arbitrators?

F. Liability of Arbitrators and Arbitral Organizations

The good news for arbitrators, and for the organizations that appoint them, is that quasi-judicial immunity is a relatively established principle for any actions reasonably related to the arbitration process. In addition to the chilling effect that lawsuits might have on arbitration and arbitrators, such suits can be seen as an impermissible collateral attack on the process, because the FAA and UAA specify procedures for judicial review of arbitration awards and arbitrator neutrality.

Unsurprisingly, the FAA is silent on the issue of arbitrator immunity. RUAA § 14, reprinted below, would make specific provision for immunity. Consider whether, with the expanded use of arbitration in corporate-consumer transactions, the justifications for arbitral immunity are still valid. Also, consider the following cases and their rationales for when to apply or not apply the doctrine of immunity to the arbitrator, the provider organization, or both.

Revised Uniform Arbitration Act
Section 14. Immunity of Arbitrator (2000)

Section 14 of the RUAA proposes that:

(a) An arbitrator or an arbitration organization acting in that capacity is immune from civil liability to the same extent as a judge of a court of this State acting in a judicial capacity.

(b) The immunity afforded by this section supplements any immunity under other law.

(c) The failure of an arbitrator to make a disclosure required by Section 12 does not cause any loss of immunity under this section....

(e) If a person commences a civil action against an arbitrator, arbitration organization, or representative of an arbitration organization arising from the services of the arbitrator, organization, or representative or if a person seeks to compel an arbitrator or a representative of an arbitration organization to testify or produce records in violation of subsection (d), and the court decides that the arbitrator, arbitration organization, or representative of an arbitration organization is immune from civil liability or that the arbitrator or representative of the organization is not competent to testify, the court shall award to the arbitrator, organization, or representative reasonable attorney's fees and other reasonable expenses of litigation.

Corey v. New York Stock Exchange
691 F.2d 1205 (6th Cir. 1982)

KENNEDY, CIRCUIT JUDGE.

Corey appeals from the District Court's dismissal of his lawsuit against the New York Stock Exchange (NYSE) in which he claimed that the procedures followed in an arbitration proceeding sponsored by the NYSE and to which he was a party were wrongful and caused him injury. Corey sought to hold the NYSE liable for the conduct of the arbitrators and the NYSE's arbitration director, Cavell. We agree with the District Court that Corey's claims against the NYSE for the acts of the arbitrators are barred by arbitral immunity and those based on Cavell's acts constitute no more than an impermissible collateral attack on the arbitrators' award....

I. Arbitral Immunity

To the extent that Corey's complaint may be construed to allege wrongdoing by the arbitrators for which the NYSE is liable, we agree with the District Court that the NYSE, acting through its arbitrators, is immune from civil liability for the acts of the arbitrators arising out of contractually agreed upon arbitration proceedings. Our decision to extend immunity to arbitrators and the boards which sponsor arbitration finds support in the case law, the policies behind the doctrines of judicial and quasi-judicial immunity and policies unique to contractually agreed upon arbitration proceedings.

The Supreme Court has long recognized that there are certain persons whose special functions require a full exemption from liability for acts committed within the scope of their duties. The rationale behind the Supreme Court decisions is that the independence necessary for principled and fearless decision-making can best be preserved by protecting these persons from bias or intimidation caused by the fear of a lawsuit arising out of the exercise of official functions within their jurisdiction. *Butz v. Economou*, 438 U.S. 478 (1978). In *Butz*, the Court stated that immunity is not extended to individuals because of their particular location in government but because of the special nature of their responsibilities. The Court said that the relevant consideration in evaluating whether immunity should attach to the acts of persons in certain roles and with certain responsibilities was the "functional comparability" of their judgments to those of a judge. In each instance, safeguards were present to protect other participants and the integrity of the decision-making process. Paramount among these safeguards is the right of judicial review.

We believe that determinations made by the panel of arbitrators in the case on appeal are functionally comparable to those of a judge or an agency hearing examiner even though this was not a statutory arbitration or one where the arbitrators were court appointed.... The submission of the parties replaces a statute or court order as the source of the arbitrators' power with regard to subject matter and procedural rules.

Several safeguards exist to protect the participants in the decision-making process and the integrity of the arbitration proceedings. First, arbitration proceedings resemble judicial proceedings in several respects. Arbitration is adversarial. Both parties had a right to be represented by an attorney—a right Corey did not exercise. Discovery was available and hearings were held at which the arbitrators received evidence and entertained arguments. Both parties had the opportunity to present witnesses and other evidence and to cross-examine or impeach those of their adversary. After a period of deliberation, the arbitrators issued a written opinion deciding the claim. The second safeguard is the automatic right of judicial review provided by the FAA applicable because of the commerce clause nexus present in transactions involving the purchase and sale of securities.... In light of these safeguards, the risk of a wrongful act by the arbitrators is outweighed by the need for preserving the independence of their decision-making.

A number of policy arguments support our decision. From *Butz* it is clear that immunity does not depend upon the source of the decision-making power but rather upon the nature of that power. Accordingly, the limits of immunity should be fixed in part by federal policy. The functional comparability of the arbitrators' decision-making process and judgments to those of judges and agency hearing examiners generates the same need for independent judgment, free from the threat of lawsuits. Immunity furthers this need. As with judicial and quasi-judicial immunity, arbitral immunity is essential to protect the decision-maker from undue influence and protect the decision-making process from reprisals by dissatisfied litigants. Federal policy, as manifested in the Arbitration Act and case law, favors final adjudication of differences by a means selected by the parties. Because federal policy encourages arbitration and arbitrators are essential actors in furtherance of that policy, it is appropriate that immunity be extended to arbitrators for acts within the scope of their duties and within their jurisdiction. The extension of immunity to arbitrators where arbitration is pursuant to a private agreement between the parties is especially compelling because arbitration is the means selected by the parties themselves for disposing of controversies between them. By immunizing arbitrators and their decisions from collateral attacks, arbitration as the contractual choice of the parties is respected yet the arbitrators are protected. Arbitrators have no interest in the outcome of the dispute and should not be compelled to become parties to that dispute. "[I]ndividuals cannot be expected to volunteer to arbitrate disputes if they can be caught up in the struggle between the litigants and saddled with the burdens of defending a lawsuit."

An aggrieved party alleging a due process violation in the conduct of the proceedings, fraud, misconduct, a violation of public policy, lack of jurisdiction, etc., by arbitrators should pursue remedies against the "real" adversary through the appeal process. To allow a collateral attack against arbitrators and their judgments would also emasculate the appeal provisions of the FAA. For these reasons we believe that arbitral immunity is essential to the maintenance of arbitration by contractual agreement as a viable alternative to the judicial process for the settlement of controversies and must be applied in this case.

Extension of arbitral immunity to encompass boards which sponsor arbitration is a natural and necessary product of the policies underlying arbitral immunity; otherwise the immunity extended to arbitrators is illusionary. It would be of little value to the whole arbitral procedure to merely shift the liability to the sponsoring association.

II. Arbitration Act as Exclusive Remedy

Corey's complaint may also be construed as alleging wrongdoing by Cavell for which the NYSE is liable, such as improper selection of the panel of five arbitrators so that they were biased against Corey and adjournments of Corey's hearing dates which caused him prejudice. It is implicit in Corey's complaint that these acts compromised the arbitration award thereby causing him mental anguish and physical problems. We agree with the District Court that the FAA provides the exclusive remedy for challenging acts that taint an arbitration award and that Corey's attempt to sue the NYSE for the acts of Cavell is no more, in substance, than an impermissible collateral attack on the award itself.

Corey's claims constitute a collateral attack against the award even though Corey is presently suing a different defendant than his original adversary in the arbitration proceeding and is requesting damages for the acts of wrongdoing rather than the vacation, modification or correction of the arbitration award. Corey was not harmed by the selection of the arbitrators and the adjournments of the hearings in and of themselves; he did not and cannot raise a constitutional due process claim. Rather, he was harmed by the impact these acts had on the award. Corey's complaint has no purpose other than to challenge the very wrongs affecting the award for which review is provided under section 10 of the Arbitration Act. The mere presence of the NYSE, Cavell or the arbitrators or the prayer for damages does not change the substance of his claim. Very simply, Corey did not avail himself of the review provisions of section 10 of the Arbitration Act and may not transform what would ordinarily constitute an impermissible collateral attack into a proper independent direct action by changing defendants and altering the relief sought.

Baar v. Tigerman

140 Cal. App. 3d 979, 189 Cal. Rptr. 834 (1983)

KLEIN, PRESIDING JUSTICE.

Plaintiffs … appeal from orders dismissing their complaints after the trial court sustained defendants American Arbitration Association (AAA) and Bert Z. Tigerman demurrers. We decline to grant quasi-judicial immunity to an arbitrator who breaches his contract to render a timely award. Further, we hold that arbitral immunity does not extend to a private arbitration association for its administrative actions.…

In 1975, pursuant to the arbitration clause of their limited partnership agreement, appellants engaged the AAA to administer arbitration proceedings. The AAA agreed to provide such services and selected Tigerman to act as arbitrator. Appellants agreed to pay both Tigerman and the AAA and did so.

Hearings commenced in November 1976, and concluded in March 1980. During this four year period, Tigerman held about 43 days of evidentiary hearings as well as 10 days of closing arguments. Both sides submitted final briefs on July 17, 1980 and on July 18, 1980, the AAA deemed the arbitration submitted. The AAA set Tigerman's arbitration award deadline at August 17, 1980, 30 days after the final submission, as required by the AAA's [Commercial Arbitration] rules. On August 20, 1980, the AAA by letter requested and received an extension until November 30, 1980, for Tigerman to make an award.

However, Tigerman did not meet this deadline. In fact, as Tigerman had yet to make an award some seven months after the submission, appellants filed written objection to Tigerman's making any award. As a result, Tigerman lost the authority vested in him by the AAA contract and the statutory law to make an award.

Appellants filed complaints against Tigerman and the AAA alleging among other causes of action breach of contract and negligence. The trial court held that arbitral immunity protected the respondents and sustained demurrers to all three complaints. Orders of dismissal followed, and these appeals were timely filed.

1. Arbitral immunity covers only the arbitrator's quasi-judicial actions, not failure to render an award.

Courts of this country have long recognized immunity to protect arbitrators from civil liability for actions taken in the arbitrator's quasi-judicial capacity. Arbitral immunity, like judicial immunity, promotes fearless and independent decision making. To this end, the courts have refused to hold judges and arbitrators liable for their judicial actions.

By contrast, the present case involves Tigerman's failure to make an award without any allegation of misconduct similar to that charged in the above cases. Respondents' contention that this court should extend immunity to an arbitrator who never renders an award fails to appreciate the nature of the arbitrator-party relationship and mis-perceives the policy underlying arbitral immunity....

Although the courts have looked favorably upon arbitration as an alternative to lit-igation in the courts arbitration remains essentially a private contractual arrangement between parties.... "Arbitration is essentially a creature of contract, a contract in which the parties themselves charter a private tribunal for the resolution of their disputes."

The contractual agreement in this case specifically sets forth the time period within which Tigerman had to render his award. A judge has discretion in terms of when a decision is made, but an arbitrator loses jurisdiction if a timely award is not forth-coming. While we must protect an arbitrator acting in a quasi-judicial capacity, we must also uphold the contractual obligations of an arbitrator to the parties involved....

Remembering that an arbitrator is not a judge and that arbitration is not a judicial proceeding, and assuming as we must the truth of the allegations contained in the complaints, a cause of action at the least was stated in breach of contract thus requiring that the demurrer be overruled.

2. Arbitral immunity does not protect the sponsoring organization when the arbitrator is not immune from liability.

Few courts have addressed the question of immunity for organizations that sponsor and administer arbitrations. Nevertheless, the cases provide that these organizations derive their immunity from the arbitrator. *Corey v. New York Stock Exchange*, 691 F.2d 1205 (6th Cir. 1982).... Thus, when immunity does not attach to the arbitrator, it cannot protect the sponsor. We declined to grant immunity to Tigerman and so find no immunity for the AAA.

Further, even had we found Tigerman immune, we would not be compelled to extend it to the AAA because of the factual differences between *Corey* and the present case. Here, appellants do not seek to circumvent the arbitrator's immunity in order to attack the award. Indeed, there is no award to attack. Rather, the appellants seek to hold the AAA liable for Tigerman's inaction and the AAA's alleged improper ad-ministration.

Assuming for the purpose of this appeal the truth of appellants' allegations, a trial court could easily find that Tigerman and the AAA affected the appellants adversely rather than merely withholding a benefit.

3. The AAA did not act in an arbitral capacity and therefore its actions standing alone do not merit immunity.

The AAA also cites *Rubenstein v. Otterbourg*, 357 N.Y.S.2d 62 (1973), as precedent for a claim of immunity. We find *Rubenstein* inapposite. The plaintiff therein sought to hold an arbitrator and the AAA liable for damages for improper conduct in an ar-bitration. The plaintiff charged that after the arbitrator refused to disqualify himself for conflict of interest, the AAA failed to intervene despite knowledge of all the facts which presumably showed that the conflict existed. The New York court granted im-munity to the AAA. It reasoned that the AAA's determination not to intervene was itself quasi-judicial in nature. In other words, the *Rubenstein* court granted immunity to the AAA to protect the AAA's own decision making.... The appellants do not seek to hold the AAA liable for any discretionary act similar to that taken in *Rubenstein*. The AAA was not involved in the decision making process, but instead acted only to oversee that process.

Appellants alleged in their complaints that the AAA failed to exercise reasonable care in the selection of Tigerman as an arbitrator in the first instance, and that the AAA thereafter failed to properly administer the arbitration, and thereby stated a cause of action as against demurrers. The orders of dismissal are reversed and remanded.

Owens v. American Arbitration Association

670 Fed. Appx. 441 (8th Cir. 2016)

PER CURIAM

Plaintiff Timothy Owens sued the American Arbitration Association (AAA) for removing an arbitrator from an arbitration panel that had issued him an award. The district court dismissed Owens' claims based on arbitral immunity. Owens appeals, and we affirm.

I.

Timothy Owens was the president and CEO of Voyager Bank. After Voyager terminated him, Owens filed for arbitration against Voyager before the AAA. The law firm of Anthony Ostlund Baer & Louwagie represented Owens, and the firm of Lindquist & Vennum represented Voyager. AAA chose a three member arbitration panel that included Allen Saeks. After the three arbitrators disclosed possible conflicts of interest, Saeks filed a supplemental disclosure in which he said that he had been "briefly consulted" by an attorney at his firm about an already resolved matter in which both Anthony Ostlund and Lindquist & Vennum had been involved. No party to the arbitration sought more information about Saeks' disclosures or objected to the arbitration panel.

The arbitration panel issued an initial award of more than $3 million to Owens. Voyager then claimed that Saeks had been more involved in the earlier matter than he had disclosed. AAA did not have a published procedure governing removal of an arbitrator. It ordered Owens to respond to Voyager's claims and not contact any of the arbitrators. AAA did not hold a hearing, consult Saeks, or inform Owens about the procedure for deciding Voyager's claim before it removed Saeks from the arbitration panel without explanation. The two remaining arbitrators then issued a final award in Owens' favor.

Next, Owens and Voyager filed cross motions in Hennepin County District Court, one to confirm the award and one to vacate it. The district court decided to vacate the arbitration award, and then Owens sued AAA in state court for breach of contract, unjust enrichment, tortious interference with contract, and tortious interference with prospective economic advantage. AAA removed the case to federal court, where the district court determined that Owens' claims were barred by arbitral immunity. AAA's motion to dismiss was granted, and Owens now appeals.

II.

We review the district court's grant of a motion to dismiss de novo, assuming the facts alleged in the complaint are true. To survive a motion to dismiss, a complaint must "state a claim to relief that is plausible on its face." Arbitrators can be entitled to immunity because their role in deciding disputes is "functionally equivalent" to the role of judges. *Olson v. Nat'l Ass'n of Sec. Dealers*, 85 F.3d 381, 382 (8th Cir. 1996). Courts extend immunity to arbitrators to protect them from "undue influence" and the arbitration process "from attack by dissatisfied litigants." Arbitral immunity may extend "to organizations that sponsor arbitrations" and "all acts within the scope of the arbitral process" are protected.

In *Olson*, the plaintiff sued an arbitration sponsoring organization for allegedly appointing a biased arbitrator. We affirmed the dismissal of the plaintiff's claims and concluded that arbitral immunity bars claims against a sponsoring organization based on the appointment of a biased arbitrator. We also concluded that a sponsoring organization is entitled to immunity even if a claim arises from the organization's failure to follow its own rules when selecting an arbitration panel. Id. Such immunity is broad and protects sponsoring organizations from civil liability at all stages of the arbitration process. The appointment of arbitrators is protected because it is an important part of the arbitral process.

We conclude that the removal of arbitrators is similarly protected by arbitral immunity because it is just as much a part of the arbitration process as the appointment of arbitrators. Because Owens' claims are barred by arbitral immunity, the district court did not err in dismissing his action. For these reasons we affirm the judgment of the district court.

Maureen A. Weston, *Reexamining Arbitral Immunity in an Age of Mandatory and Professional Arbitration*
88 MINN. L. REV. 449 (2004)

Arbitration, as a form of private dispute resolution, has been used for centuries in various commercial and labor-management sectors. Traditionally, entities with relatively equal bargaining power used arbitration primarily in specialized industries. In the past ten to twenty years, however, arbitration has gained acceptance in other areas, notably proliferating as a result of mandatory predispute and form arbitration contracts between corporate entities and their customers, patients, or employees. As the use of arbitration has increased, the need for arbitration services has correspondingly risen and spawned a market for professional private arbitrators and an industry of private businesses that provide arbitration support and administrative services (provider institutions). For example, major provider institutions such as the American Arbitration Association (AAA), National Arbitration Forum (NAF), and Judicial Arbitration and Mediation Services, Inc. (JAMS), continue to report growth in caseload and neutral membership. In 2002, the AAA administered more than 230,255 cases through mediation or arbitration. In 2001, the AAA reported its seventh consecutive year of growth, with over 218,000 cases administered. This is up from a caseload of approximately 61,000 between 1991 and 1995. JAMS likewise reports that its caseload has increased 2300% from 1987 to 1993. The decision makers operating within the private arbitration industry range from individual arbitrators operating out of their homes to multinational corporate provider institutions. Arbitrators are not restricted to individuals trained in the law or a particular area of expertise. Likewise, arbitration provider institutions or entities have no particular standard for entry. Statistics on the number of private arbitrators are difficult to track, as there is neither an official registry nor a need for affiliation with a particular organization. The AAA, however, reports a roster of over 8000 neutrals in diverse fields and professions that represent a broad spectrum of expertise. A single Internet search of "arbitrators" results in a list of over 300,000 entries. The number, size, and quality of private entities operating as alternative dispute resolution (ADR) providers also vary. Provider institutions can offer an array of arbitration administrative services, as well as other consulting and training services. In some cases, a provider organization may have an exclusive contractual arrangement with a company to administer all of the company's arbitrations or dispute resolution processes; a party may also unilaterally include a provision in its contracts requiring that all disputes subject to arbitration be filed with a particular provider organization.

Arbitration is customarily defined as "a simple proceeding voluntarily chosen by parties who want a dispute determined by an impartial judge of their own mutual selection, whose decision, based on the merits of the case, they agree in advance to accept as final and binding." The process is touted as an inexpensive, speedy, informal, and private alternative to the judicial system. Whether one agrees that these traditional characterizations of arbitration have continued vitality in a prevailing environment of mandatory predispute consumer and employment arbitration, it is clear that private arbitrators have significant power to determine not only contractual, but also statutory and other legal rights and liabilities of the parties involved, and that judicial review is quite limited. Arbitration provider institutions can also play a significant role in the conduct and outcome of the arbitration process by designing rules and procedures, setting fees, and determining who may be on the list of potential arbitrators, in addition to selecting the arbitrator in the event of default.

Arbitration is used on a variety of scales, yet in many ways, arbitration itself has become a profession, if not big business. Although some arbitrators work for reduced or no compensation in certain cases, the costs of a private arbitration typically include the fees paid to the arbitrator (or panel of arbitrators) on a flat fee or hourly (which can range from $75 to well over $500 per hour) basis. Parties may also be responsible for paying a provider institution fee for a range of administrative support services, such as for filing claims, motions, or responses, for case management, for the use of conference rooms, or for participating in a hearing. According to a report by Public

Citizen, a nonprofit public interest research organization, the administrative fees charged by provider institutions can cost approximately 700% more than courts charge for similar services.

Federal legislation, specifically the Federal Arbitration Act of 1925 (FAA), provides for the judicial enforcement of written contracts to resolve disputes by arbitration. Although initially reluctant to interpret the FAA expansively, the United States Supreme Court now regularly relies on the statute as the basis to preempt state laws regulating arbitration and to uphold the enforcement of mandatory predispute arbitration agreements in a variety of contexts, including resolution of statutory and common law claims in employment and consumer transactions. According to the Court, the FAA evinces a "federal policy favoring arbitration."

The FAA's statutory framework primarily addresses procedural matters providing for the judicial enforcement of arbitration agreements and awards, but also identifies specific grounds for vacating such awards. However, the FAA does not address increasingly important issues in contemporary arbitration. For example, the FAA is silent on whether, if at all, parties are entitled to minimum standards of due process in mandatory consumer and employment arbitration; what standards of ethics, disclosure, or conduct apply to arbitrators and provider institutions; or whether arbitrators or provider institutions are or should be accorded immunity from civil actions to the same extent as public judges. State arbitration legislation typically mirrors the FAA's structure, leaving these questions unanswered or addressed by ad hoc judicial decisions, precatory standards set by the arbitration community, or by contract between the private arbitral institutions or the individual arbiter and the parties.

Prominent national ADR professionals and provider institutions have been at the forefront in promulgating aspirational rules and standards for the professional ethics, disclosure, and conduct of private arbitrators and provider institutions. Some provider institutions maintain internal policies and standards in an attempt to ensure a fair arbitration process for their users. At least one state, California, has enacted specific conduct and disclosure standards for arbitrators, but does not provide an independent mechanism for enforcement or oversight. Due to the unregulated nature of the arbitration practice, however, enforcement of these rules is difficult, if not impossible, leaving compliance largely voluntary. Moreover, even though many providers set forth standards and rules for an arbitration under their auspices, these rules or contractual agreements typically contain provisions exculpating them from "any and all" liability, including liability for failing to follow the provider's own rules, policies, and contractual obligations. Some providers even condition their services upon the parties' agreement to waive compliance with internal rules or applicable laws. Irrespective of the efforts for, or legality of, contractual immunity for arbitrators and providers, the law in various guises confers substantial protection from civil liability through the doctrine of arbitral immunity. As a result, parties injured by arbitral misconduct have limited recourse and effectively no remedy.

While codes for arbitrator and provider ethics provide important guidelines, their impact is questionable if true enforcement is unavailable. Ensuring the enforcement of standards and providing meaningful remedies to those injured by arbitral misconduct is equally as important as articulating standards of conduct and professional ethics for arbitrators and provider institutions. The availability of judicial recourse, a key step towards this objective, is restricted not only by the FAA's limited vacatur remedy but also by broad arbitral immunity doctrines recognized by state statute or common law. The Revised Uniform Arbitration Act (RUAA) ... proposes not only to codify this immunity for arbitrators and provider institutions but also to penalize audacious challenges.

Despite a seemingly entrenched rule of arbitral immunity, numerous individuals have alleged a range of claims against arbitrators and provider institutions, including breach of contract, failure to follow internal policies, failing to disclose conflicts of interest, negligence, bias, deceptive advertising, conspiracy, and antitrust violations. In all of these cases, plaintiffs lost due to the seemingly impenetrable doctrine of arbitral immunity. The changing nature of the arbitration industry and the fact that so many individuals have been discouraged from asserting arbitral misconduct claims, combined with the RUAA's proposal to effectively bar and penalize mere challenges, necessitates an examination of the continued propriety of the doctrine.

The use of arbitration has changed significantly since the FAA's inception in 1925, from the traditional model involving voluntary arbitration between parties of relatively equal bargaining power, to a system where arbitration has become a profession and a commercialized industry that is imposed upon consumers and employees. Meanwhile, a significant body of federal and state laws has since developed to protect civil rights, market competition, employees, and consumers. Presumably, the policy of enforcing agreements to arbitrate does not supplant laws requiring individuals engaging in contracts, albeit contracts to provide arbitral services, to comply with their promises and to be held accountable for their conduct. Individuals of nearly every profession are held accountable for complying with their contractual obligations and for exercising a reasonable degree of competency. Does it continue to make sense to exempt from the law the entire arbitration industry?

This Article [questions] the assumption that arbitrators and provider institutions should be per se immune from civil liability.... [and] argues against the broad and uncritical expansion of arbitral immunity.... Significant differences exist between public judges operating in an open judicial process and the private judging world of arbitration, which necessitates a more exacting scope of immunity.... [A] standard of qualified immunity appropriately balances the competing policy concerns of protecting arbitrators in their decisional roles, while also holding the arbitration industry accountable to parties and the public....

1. Comments and Questions

a. The National Arbitration Forum (NAF) closed down its administration of consumer arbitration services amid charges of conflict of interest, as well as fraud, deceptive trade practices, and false advertising raised by the Minnesota Attorney General in 2009. A lawsuit against the NAF claims the corporate relationship between NAF and lending and debt collection companies brought into serious doubt NAF's neutrality in administering consumer collection arbitrations. The district court denied NAF's motion to dismiss the lawsuit on grounds of arbitral immunity, reasoning that if the allegations of bias were true, NAF's actions were "outside of the arbitral process." *In re Nat'l Arbitration Forum Trade Practices Litig.*, 2010 U.S. Dist. LEXIS 35655 (D. Minn. Apr. 12, 2010) (holding that immunity ruling was not immediately appealable by a private arbitral entity); *see also* Nancy A. Welsh, *Funding Justice: What Is "(Im)partial Enough" in a World of Embedded Neutrals?*, 52 ARIZ. L. REV. 395 (2010). Are allegations of bias really "outside of the arbitral process?"

b. What if an arbitrator allegedly lies on her resume? In 2013, California resident Kevin Kinsella used the services of arbitrator Sheila Prell Sonenshine, hired through JAMS, to arbitrate certain terms of his divorce. During the arbitrator selection process, Kinsella allegedly rated Sonenshine highly on the list due to her experience co-founding an investment bank and equity fund. Kinsella later learned that Sonenshine's private equity fund was unsuccessful, short-lived, and only involved Sonenshine's family's personal funds. Kinsella sued both Sonenshine and JAMS the arbitrator and provider organization under consumer protection statutes and false advertising. The California Superior Court, San Diego Division (No. 37-2015-00026133-CU-FR-CTL) denied Sonenshine's and JAMS' motion for summary judgment on the basis of immunity. The case went to trial, and, after three weeks of trial, a jury found that Kinsella had not proven any damages. The jury could not agree on whether Sonenshine falsified her credentials, but it could agree that no damages resulted. Should these types of cases go to trial, or should immunity have been granted?

c. Do you think that arbitral immunity is a good policy? What recourse should a party have if an arbitrator commits an error, perhaps an ethical error or an egregious error in decision-making? Do you think that ethical errors, such as non-disclosure of a conflict of interest, should be treated differently from errors in ruling on the merits, such as deciding a motion or an issue incorrectly? Are there other remedies available for either the participants or a provider organization?

d. Consider whether immunity should be given in the following situations:

1. The United Arbitration Association (UAA) sends a notice of hearing to John Smith, 48th N. Rd. In fact, John Smith lives at 48th S. Rd. The letter was delivered to 48th N. Rd, someone signed for it, and the signature is illegible. The arbitration proceeded to a default judgment. Is immunity available if John Smith institutes an action against UAA or the arbitrator?

2. Party A and Party B submit motions for summary judgment to Arbitrator Alicia. Arbitrator Alicia takes them under advisement but never rules on them.

She ultimately issued a decision in favor of Party B. Party A sues Arbitrator Alicia for not ruling on the summary judgment motion. Is immunity available for Arbitrator Alicia?

3. Parties C and D agree on Arbitrator Alec, and the UAA appoints him to arbitrate their dispute. Arbitrator Alec then discloses additional conflicts. Party C moves for Arbitrator Alec to remove himself from the case on the basis of those newly disclosed conflicts. Arbitrator Alec denies the motion. Party C also asks the UAA to remove Arbitrator Alec, but the UAA does not remove him. Arbitrator Alec issues a ruling in favor of Party D. Party C sues Arbitrator Alec and the UAA. Are they entitled to immunity?

Chapter 9

Judicial Enforcement and Review of Arbitration Awards

A. Introduction

This chapter examines the processes that take place *after* an arbitration panel issues an award, where a party requests a court to enforce, modify, or vacate an arbitration award. In addition to providing for the enforcement of arbitration agreements, the FAA authorizes judicial confirmation, vacatur, and modification of arbitral awards in sections 9, 10, and 11, respectively. Relevant provisions of the UAA (1955) and RUAA (2000) closely track those of the FAA, so the procedures and grounds for judicial enforcement and review of arbitral awards—albeit not necessarily the judicial interpretation of them—are *usually* the same under state and federal law. Many of these standards for vacatur also have been mentioned in earlier chapters. For example, the materials from **Chapter 8** on arbitrator selection and ethics addressed arbitrator duties to disclose actual or potential conflicts of interest. Inadequate disclosures may indicate arbitral bias or "evident partiality" and thus may be not only grounds upon which to disqualify an arbitrator, but also an important basis for vacating an arbitration award. Earlier chapters also emphasized that an arbitrator's powers are derived from, and thus circumscribed by, the arbitration agreement. Accordingly, an arbitrator who fails to follow those contractual parameters or other statutory standards may have exceeded her authority.

Courts subject arbitrator decisions to extremely limited judicial review. What practical and policy justifications support this deference? Suppose, however, that an arbitral award rendered is contrary to public policy, lacked fundamental fairness, an impartial arbitrator, or simply "manifestly disregards" the law?

This chapter discusses two primary U.S. Supreme Court decisions addressing judicial review of arbitration awards. First, *Commonwealth Coatings Corp. v. Continental Casualty Co.*, 393 U.S. 145 (1968), acknowledges that arbitrators often are active members of the business industry in which they preside as arbitrators. Parties often select these arbitrators because of their specialized knowledge and, historically, these arbitrators volunteered out of service to their industry. Considering, however, that arbitrators "[h]ave completely free rein to decide the law as well as the facts and are not subject to appellate review," *Commonwealth* examines whether the requirements for impartiality that apply in public judicial proceedings should be suspended, or perhaps be more stringent, for arbitrators presiding in commercial arbitration cases.

Second, the Supreme Court's decision in *Hall Street Assocs., L.L.C. v. Mattel, Inc.*, 552 U.S. 576 (2008), addresses the viability of federal judicial review of arbitration awards based upon nonstatutory standards, such as judicially created or privately contracted standards for review of awards. Given the FAA's limited standards for review, parties and courts began to provide for broader standards of review, such as review for "errors of law" and "manifest disregard of the law." *Hall Street* casts considerable doubt on such propositions in ruling that the FAA provides the exclusive grounds for judicial review. However, *Hall Street* did state that it "decides nothing about other possible avenues for judicial enforcement of awards." *Id.* at 590. Here, we study the procedures, statutory grounds, as well as the "other possible avenues," for judicial review of arbitration awards.

Most parties voluntarily comply with arbitration awards, and courts rarely vacate them. The legal standards to getting an arbitral award overturned are higher than for judicial decisions. Although this chapter examines instances of judicial vacatur of arbitral awards, counsel needs to advise a client that arbitration awards are nearly always confirmed. Of course, this judicial approach is much appreciated where your client prevailed in the arbitration proceeding.

Consider now what happens after an arbitral award is issued—what are a party's options to enforce, modify, or challenge an award—what process is involved, and why not just go back to the arbitrator to revisit an award that is seemingly in error? **Section B** briefly explains the doctrine of *functus officio*, which holds that once an arbitrator has issued a final award, the arbitrator has performed its office, and the arbitrator's power to act further in the case ceases. When and why are there exceptions to this rule? The remaining sections concern the role of the courts in post-award activity. **Section C** addresses procedural prerequisites to judicial review of an arbitration award, particularly in federal court. A party must consider both the statutory time frame and proper court for jurisdiction and venue in which to request judicial confirmation, vacatur, or modification of an arbitral award.

Section D explicates the central theme of this chapter: challenges to arbitration awards rarely succeed and the standard for judicial review of arbitral awards is quite limited. The Supreme Court's 1854 decision in *Burchell v. Marsh* was resurrected to demonstrate that the principle of limited judicial review of arbitration awards was well-established long before the enactment of modern arbitration statutes and before courts would enforce agreements to arbitrate disputes. Contemporary exemplars of the same theme are demonstrated in the California Supreme Court's decision in *Moncarsh v. Heily & Blaise*, as well as numerous judicial decisions not excerpted here. According to the First Circuit, "[e]ven serious error" by arbitrators will not invalidate an award and further, that "any error by the panel ... does not rise to the level necessary to justify vacatur." *Raymond James Fin. Svcs. v. Fenyk*, 780 F.3d 59 (1st Cir. 2015). This broad deference is again expressed in *Oxford Health Plans, LLC v. Sutter*, 569

U.S. 564 (2013), in which the Supreme Court stated that "[w]here an arbitrator bases a decision on the text of the parties' agreement, her construction holds, however good, bad, or ugly." Recognizing judicial deference to arbitral rulings, just how bad, ugly, or wrong must an arbitrator's award be to justify vacatur?

Section E examines the statutory grounds for vacating an arbitration award as set forth in the FAA and similar state law. The enumerated category of grounds upon which a court may vacate an arbitral award, set forth in FAA Section 10, involves serious procedural claims, such as fraud or corruption; evident partiality; misconduct in the proceedings (including evidentiary rulings); and an arbitrator exceeding her powers. Although these words leave courts some flexibility to vacate arbitration awards in egregious circumstances, they also carry a strong cautionary message — hardly ever. Whatever the meaning given to particular provisions of section 10, the bottom line is that it is far easier to get an appellate court to reverse a trial court decision than to vacate an arbitration award.

Section F examines whether private parties can contractually agree to expand the scope of judicial review of arbitration awards beyond the grounds set forth in the FAA, such as for legal error. Given the FAA's call to enforce private arbitration agreements "according to their terms" and the policies favoring parties' contractual freedom to structure their own arbitration process, should parties by contract be permitted to expand the scope for judicial review of their arbitral award? *Hall Street v. Mattel* answers in the negative. See whether you agree as you read the decision. Does this limitation also apply to judicially-created standards?

Section G delves into questions lingering in *Hall Street*'s aftermath, particularly the debate in the federal circuits and state courts on the viability of non-statutory grounds for judicial review of arbitral awards, such as the "manifest disregard of the law" doctrine and grounds not specified in the FAA. After *Hall Street*, do courts retain power to review an arbitral award using judicially created standards, such as manifest disregard of the law or violation of public policy, even if parties cannot do so? Are state courts similarly bound? Some parties attempt to achieve the result of expanded review, indirectly, through creative drafting and contractually limiting an arbitrator's powers to render legally correct decisions. In these cases, may a court review an arbitrator's legal error on the statutory grounds that the arbitrator exceeded her authority?

Petitions for judicial review of arbitral awards likely prolong the process, undo many of the efficiencies of arbitration, and simply fail, given the presumption for enforceability of awards. Section H on frivolous appeals exemplifies stern warnings by circuit courts to parties seeking to use vacatur strategically and appeal arbitration awards without justification.

Problem

Corner Avenue, owner of commercial real estate and property in Porland City, entered into a contract with Toys, Inc., which leased land for its manufacturing plant operations. The government has notified Corner Ave and Toys that they are in violation of state and federal environmental laws. Based upon this notice, Toys informed Corner Avenue that it was terminating its lease, which still had a 16-year term remaining under the contract. Corner disputed the liability for the environmental obligations and contended that Toys' operations caused the conditions. The parties agreed to arbitrate the contract and indemnification dispute. The parties' agreed-upon arbitration provision stated that a court would "vacate, modify or correct any award if the arbitrator's findings of fact were not supported by substantial evidence or where the conclusions of law were erroneous." The arbitrator issued its final award in favor of Toys. One month later, Corner filed a motion with the arbitrator requesting reversal of the award decision, arguing that the arbitrator failed to consider legal precedent in its favor. The arbitrator did nothing. Corner filed a motion to vacate the award in federal court, claiming that the arbitrator's ruling involved legal error. Applying the parties' contractual standard for review of the arbitral award for legal error, the district court determined the arbitrator's ruling was legally erroneous and vacated the award in favor of Corner. Toys seeks your advice on whether the court's vacatur ruling should be upheld.

Consider the following:

a. Did the arbitrator err in failing to reconsider its ruling in light of overlooked precedent?

b. What is the process to file a vacatur action? Suppose Corner filed the motion to vacate four months after the award?

c. Did the court have jurisdiction to hear the motion?

d. What are the arguments for upholding or reversing the court's vacatur decision?

e. Does it matter if the losing party had filed the vacatur action in state court?

B. The *Functus Officio* Doctrine

Although the major task of both judges and arbitrators is to decide disputes based on the evidence presented, the legal and structural differences between the positions of a judge and an arbitrator have important practical significance. The judge fills a public office that has a continuous existence. The arbitrator, by contrast, is appointed to hear a specific dispute and fills a temporary role. Until the arbitrator is appointed, the courts are generally the only source of interim relief (although as of 2013, major provider organizations such as AAA, JAMS, and CPR have adopted rules authorizing their appointment of an emergency arbitrator for interim relief purposes). *See* AAA R-38(a); JAMS R 2(c). Generally, once arbitrators conclude a proceeding and render an award, they have completed their office. The panel's power thereby ceases, and it lacks authority to alter the award or to reexamine the decision.

The fact that an arbitrator's authority begins with appointment and terminates with the issuance of a final opinion in a particular dispute is the basis for the common law doctrine of *functus officio*. The Supreme Court has long recognized the *functus officio* doctrine, noting in *Bayne v. Morris*, 68 U.S. 97 (1864), that "[a]rbitrators exhaust their power when they make a final determination on the matters submitted to them. They have no power after having made an award to alter it; the authority conferred on them is then at the end." The doctrine remains vital more than a century later. *See United Bhd. of Carpenters & Joiners of Am. v. Tappan Zee Constructors, LLC*, 804 F.3d 270, 277 (2d Cir. 2015) (stating that "once arbitrators have fully exercised their authority to adjudicate the issues submitted to them, their authority over those questions is ended, and the arbitrators have no further authority, absent agreement by the parties, to redetermine th[ose] issue[s]."). Major arbitration institutions have essentially codified the *functus officio* doctrine in procedural rules. For example, AAA Commercial Arbitration Rule 50 permits any party, upon notice to other parties, within 20 calendar days after transmittal of an award, to request the arbitrator to correct clerical, computational, or typographical errors in the award. But the rule states that "[t]he arbitrator is not empowered to redetermine the merits of any claim already decided...."

Under the *functus officio* doctrine, once a panel has issued a final award, the arbitrators lose the power to alter it. Once arbitral authority has ceased, only the courts can confirm, modify, or vacate the award. But exceptions to the rule exist. For example, parties can, by contract, agree to have the arbitrator continue to have authority to review the arbitration award or for appellate arbitration review. Moreover, if the award is ambiguous and "leaves doubt whether the [submitted grievance] has been fully executed," an arbitrator has the power to clarify the award. *Local 1982, Intern. Longshoremen's Assoc. v. Midwest Terminals of Toledo Intern., Inc.*, No. 16-4004, 2017 WL 2333613, at *2 (6th Cir. 2017). The *functus officio* doctrine does not prevent an arbitrator from revisiting an award that does not finally adjudicate the issue that was submitted. *Colonial Penn Ins. Co. v. Omaha Indem. Co.*, 943 F.2d 327 (3d Cir. 1991). Under the FAA, courts can independently modify or correct the award on its own motion, or return the award to the panel for modification or correction. FAA § 11.

A rather surprising retention of arbitral "continuing jurisdiction" provision was included in the arbitration award involving disgraced cyclist Lance Armstrong. A 2004 arbitration award ordered insurer SCA to pay Armstrong $6 million in prize money, which SCA had resisted paying due to suspicions of Armstrong's doping in violation of the insurance contractual terms. The 2004 award included a "continuing jurisdiction" provision empowering the arbitrators to hear any future disputes related to the award or settlement between the parties. In 2011, Armstrong was banned from cycling for an extensive scheme of doping. In 2015, SCA moved for sanctions before the same panel of arbitrators who presided in the earlier arbitration, seeking $10 million in sanctions against Armstrong due to his perjury in the arbitration. Citing the "continuing jurisdiction" provision, a 2–1 panel awarded SCA the requested amount. *See In the Arbitration Between Lance Armstrong and Tailwinds Sports Corp., and SCA Promotions, Inc., SCA Insurance Specialists Inc.*, Final Arbitration Award (Feb. 4, 2015), available at http://online.wsj.com/public/resources/documents/armstrong02162015.pdf.

C. Procedural Prerequisites to Judicial Review of Arbitration Awards

A party prevailing in arbitration may opt to seek judicial confirmation of the arbitral award so that the award has the same legal force and effect as a court judgment. *See* FAA § 13, RUAA § 23. Once a court confirms an award, the losing party may not appeal that confirmation, although a state statute may permit a motion to vacate a judgment based on an award within a specific time limit. *See, e.g.,* Cal. Rules of Ct., Rule 3.828(a) (specifying grounds). Before such confirmation, however, the dissatisfied party may petition a court to modify, correct, or vacate an arbitration award. This section explains *when* and *where* these applications must be made.

1. Statutory Timelines to Seek Confirmation, Vacatur, and Modification of Arbitral Awards

Parties may seek judicial confirmation, vacatur, and modification of arbitral awards within statutorily specified time limitations. FAA §§ 9, 10, and 11. However, a party who seeks judicial vacatur, modification, or correction of an arbitration award cannot necessarily wait for the prevailing party to request confirmation of the award. The FAA time frames for seeking vacatur and confirmation of an arbitration award are not parallel. FAA § 12 states that a motion to vacate, modify, or correct an award must be served upon the adverse party within three months after the award "is filed or delivered." Both the state uniform acts, UAA §§ 12–13 and RUAA §§ 23–24, impose similar 90-day time limits. By contrast, FAA § 9 provides that an application to confirm an award "may" be filed within one year after the award "is made." The arbitration acts enacted in specific states may provide varying deadlines. International arbitration awards governed by the New York Convention are subject to a three-year limitations period for confirmation. 9 U.S.C. § 207. *See* **Chapter 11.**

Why do you suppose the FAA provides a shorter time frame for modifying, correcting, or vacating an award, but specifies one year in which to confirm an award? In *Move v. Citigroup Global Markets, Inc.,* 840 F.3d 1152 (9th Cir. 2016), the Ninth Circuit held that the FAA is subject to equitable tolling. The Court granted a motion to vacate filed four years after the filing of an award where the party later discovered that the presiding arbitrator had lied about being a licensed attorney. For strategic matters, a prevailing party may contemplate waiting after three months has elapsed to seek confirmation of an award in order to preclude the losing party from raising defenses that would have been available had the losing party sought vacatur within the three-month period. However, a prevailing party may consider other reasons more important to proceed quickly on confirmation — e.g., risk of dissipation or removal of assets, venue flexibility (*see Cortex Byrd, infra*), and obtaining prompt execution of the arbitral award. *Cf. Karo v. Nau Country Ins. Co.,* 2017 WL 4185426 (Neb. 2017) (ruling that the periods for both confirming and vacating awards are jurisdictional, and reversing district court grant of vacatur petition filed four months after the award).

2. State or Federal Court? Jurisdiction to Review Arbitration Awards Governed by the FAA

FAA §§ 9, 10, and 11, respectively, authorize applications for confirmation, vacatur, and modification to the "United States" courts. Although federal court arbitration decisions are prominent in this book, most domestic arbitration issues are heard by state rather than federal courts. Recall from **Chapter 2** that despite its largely preemptive effects, the FAA does not provide an independent basis of federal subject matter jurisdiction.

> The FAA is something of an anomaly in the field of federal-court jurisdiction. It creates a body of federal substantive law establishing and regulating the duty to honor an agreement to arbitrate, yet it does not create any independent federal question jurisdiction ... [A]lthough enforcement of the Act is left in large part to the state courts, it nevertheless represents federal policy to be vindicated by the federal courts where otherwise appropriate.

Moses H. Cone Mem. Hospital v. Mercury Constr. Corp., 460 U.S. 1 (1983).

Federal district courts have subject matter jurisdiction over disputes involving federal questions, and between citizens of different states involving amounts in controversy currently in excess of $75,000. 28 U.S.C. §§ 1331, 1332. But when can a party seek federal court enforcement of an arbitration case under the FAA? As explained in **Chapter 2**, under *Vaden v. Discover Bank*, 556 U.S. 49 (2009), the "well pleaded complaint" rule applies in determining whether a federal district court had *federal question jurisdiction* to compel arbitration under FAA § 4 of a state law debt collection lawsuit involving a federal substantive law counterclaim. That is, federal question jurisdiction exists where initial claims alleged in the underlying arbitration are based on federal law; counterclaims based on federal law do not provide an independent basis for federal court jurisdiction. Does the *Vaden* rule equally apply to motions to *vacate* awards? As discussed in the notes in **Chapter 2**, the circuits are divided. *See e.g., Doscher v. Sea Port Grp. Secs., LLC*, 832 F.3d 372, 383 (2d Cir. 2016) (concluding that "a federal district court faced with a § 10 petition may 'look through' the petition to the underlying dispute, applying to it the ordinary rules of federal-question jurisdiction and the principles laid out by the majority in *Vaden*."); *Ortiz-Espinosa v. BBVA Sec. of P.R., Inc.*, 852 F.3d 36 (1st Cir. 2017) (extending *Dorcher* test looking through to underlying dispute to determine federal question jurisdiction over petition to vacate or modify arbitration award under FAA §§ 10–11). *Cf. Goldman v. Citigroup Global Mkts., Inc.*, 834 F.3d 242, 255 (3d Cir. 2016) (holding that "*Vaden's* 'look-through' basis for jurisdiction does not extend to § 10 motions to vacate.").

Federal court jurisdiction based on *diversity of citizenship* requires complete diversity of citizenship between the parties and an amount in controversy in excess of $75,000. 28 U.S.C. § 1332(a). *See Gyrnberg v. Kinder Morgan Energy*, 805 F.3d 901 (10th Cir. 2015) (affirming the dismissal of a petition to vacate for lack of complete diversity of citizenship because the defendant limited partnership had at least one unitholder residing in same state as movant). Is diversity of citizenship based upon the date the motion to vacate is filed or when the underlying arbitration award was filed? *Odeon Capital Group, LLC v. Ackerman*, 864 F.3d 191 (2d Cir. 2017) (ruling that diversity of citizenship, for purposes of federal jurisdiction on a motion to vacate award, is determined at the time the action is filed in court, not the date of the underlying arbitration).

The federal courts are also divided on the question of whether the *amount in controversy* for diversity jurisdiction is measured by the amount of the award or by the amount in dispute (the demand) in the underlying arbitration between the parties. The Sixth and Eleventh Circuits have followed the "award" approach, which measures the amount in controversy by the amount of the underlying arbitration award regardless of the amount sought. *See, e.g., Ford v. Hamilton Inv.*, 29 F.3d 255 (6th Cir. 1994); *Baltin v. Alaron Trading Corp.*, 128 F.3d 1466 (11th Cir. 1997). Meanwhile, the First, Fifth, Ninth, and D.C. Circuits have adopted the "demand" approach. Under the "demand" approach over the "award" approach, *Karsner v. Lothian*, 532 F.3d 876 (D.C. Cir. 2008), reasoned that the demand approach is consistent with the court's jurisdiction over a petition to compel arbitration and thus avoids the potential problem (under the award approach) that the court could compel arbitration but then lack jurisdiction to review the arbitration it ordered. *See also Pershing, LLC v. Kiebach*, 819 F.3d 179 (5th Cir. 2016) (holding that the amount in controversy for establishing diversity jurisdiction over a petition to confirm an arbitration award would be determined by the amount sought in the arbitration proceeding, not the amount actually awarded); *Bull HN Info. Sys. v. Hutson*, 229 F.3d 321 (1st Cir. 2000) (observing that the demand approach recognizes the "close connection between arbitration and subsequent enforcement proceedings" and "carr[ies] out the federal policies in favor of arbitration"); *Theis Research, Inc. v. Brown & Bain*, 400 F.3d 659 (9th Cir. 2005) (upholding federal jurisdiction over petition to vacate an arbitration award of zero dollars). Which approach is more sensible?

When judicial review of arbitral awards is sought in federal court, independent jurisdictional requirements must be satisfied. The FAA does not provide a basis for federal subject matter jurisdiction, but can apply in both state and federal court. As a result, many petitions for review of arbitration awards are routinely heard by state courts. The FAA's review provisions speak to federal courts; so consider whether state courts are bound by the FAA's stringent review provisions or perhaps more liberal interpretations of an applicable state arbitration act. The procedures and timing for seeking confirmation or vacatur of an award are also defined by the applicable arbitration code.

3. Venue

Assuming a federal district court has jurisdiction to review an arbitration award under the FAA, in which federal court may or must the case be filed—where the arbitration occurred, the award was rendered, or "any other district"? In other words, where does *venue* lie in an arbitration enforcement action?

Cortez Byrd Chips, Inc. v. Harbert Construction Co.

529 U.S. 193 (2000)

JUSTICE SOUTER delivered the opinion for a unanimous Court.

This case raises the issue whether the venue provisions of the FAA, 9 U.S.C. §§ 9–11, are restrictive, allowing a motion to confirm, vacate, or modify an arbitration award to be brought only in the district in which the award was made, or are permissive, permitting such a motion either where the award was made or in any district proper under the general venue statute. We hold the FAA provisions permissive.

Petitioner Cortez Byrd and respondent Harbert agreed that Harbert would build a wood chip mill for Cortez Byrd in Brookhaven, Mississippi. [The "chips" in which Cortez Byrd deals are wood, not potato or cow.] One of the terms was that "all claims or disputes between the Contractor and the Owner arising out of or relating to the Contract, or the breach thereof, shall be decided by arbitration in accordance with the Construction Industry Arbitration Rules of the AAA currently in effect unless the parties mutually agree otherwise." The agreement went on to provide that … the law of the place where the project was located, Mississippi, governed.

After a dispute arose, Harbert invoked the agreement by a filing with the Atlanta office of the AAA, which conducted arbitration in Birmingham, Alabama. The … arbitration panel issued an award in favor of Harbert.… Cortez Byrd filed a complaint in the United States District Court for the Southern District of Mississippi seeking to vacate or modify the arbitration award, which Harbert then sought to confirm by filing this action seven days later in the Northern District of Alabama. When Cortez Byrd moved to dismiss, transfer, or stay the Alabama action, the Alabama District Court denied the motion, concluding that venue was proper only in the Northern District of Alabama, and entering judgment for Harbert. The Court of Appeals for the Eleventh Circuit affirmed. We reverse.

The precise issue raised in the District Court was whether venue for Cortez Byrd's motion under §§ 10 and 11 was properly laid in the southern district of Mississippi, within which the contract was performed. It was clearly proper under the general venue statute, which provides, among other things, for venue in a diversity action in "a judicial district in which a substantial part of the events or omissions giving rise to the claim occurred, or a substantial part of property that is the subject of the action is situated." 28 U.S.C. § 1391(a)(2). If §§ 10 and 11 are permissive and thus supplement, but do not supplant, the general provision, Cortez Byrd's motion to vacate or modify was properly filed in Mississippi, and under principles of deference to the court of first filing, the Alabama court should have considered staying its hand. But if §§ 10 and 11 are restrictive, there was no Mississippi venue for Cortez Byrd's action, and the Northern District of Alabama correctly proceeded with the litigation to confirm. Although § 9 is not directly implicated in this action, since venue for Harbert's motion to confirm was proper in the northern district of Alabama under either a restrictive or a permissive reading of § 9, the three venue sections of the FAA are best analyzed together, owing to their contemporaneous enactment and the similarity of their pertinent language.

Enlightenment will not come merely from parsing the language, which is less clear than either party contends....

Statutory history provides a better lesson, though, which is confirmed by following out the practical consequences of Harbert's position. When the FAA was enacted in 1925, it appeared against the backdrop of a considerably more restrictive general venue statute than the one current today. At the time, the practical effect of 28 U.S.C. § 112(a) was that a civil suit could usually be brought only in the district in which the defendant resided. The statute's restrictive application was all the more pronounced due to the courts' general inhospitality to forum selection clauses, *see The Bremen v. Zapata Off-Shore Co.*, 407 U.S. 1 (1972). Hence, even if an arbitration agreement expressly permitted action to be brought in the district in which arbitration had been conducted, the agreement would probably prove to be vain. The enactment of the special venue provisions in the FAA thus had an obviously liberalizing effect, undiminished by any suggestion, textual or otherwise, that Congress meant simultaneously to foreclose a suit where the defendant resided. Such a consequence would have been as inexplicable in 1925 as it would be passing strange 75 years later. The most convenient forum for a defendant is normally the forum of residence, and it would take a very powerful reason ever to suggest that Congress would have meant to eliminate that venue for post-arbitration disputes.

The virtue of the liberalizing nonrestrictive view of the provisions for venue in the district of arbitration is confirmed by another obviously liberalizing venue provision of the Act, which in § 9 authorizes a binding agreement selecting a forum for confirming an arbitration award. Since any forum selection agreement must coexist with §§ 10 and 11, one needs to ask how they would work together if §§ 10 and 11 meant that an order vacating or modifying an arbitration award could be obtained only in the district where the award was made. The consequence would be that a proceeding to confirm the award begun in a forum previously selected by agreement of the parties (but outside the district of the arbitration) would need to be held in abeyance if the responding party objected. The objecting party would then have to return to the district of the arbitration to begin a separate proceeding to modify or vacate the arbitration award, and if the award withstood attack, the parties would move back to the previously selected forum for the confirming order originally sought.

Harbert, naturally, is far from endorsing anything of the sort and contends that a court with venue to confirm under a § 9 forum selection clause would also have venue under a later filed motion under § 10. But the contention boils down to denying the logic of Harbert's own position. The regime we have described would follow from adopting that position, and the Congress simply cannot be tagged with such a taste for the bizarre.

Nothing, indeed, would be more clearly at odds with both the FAA's statutory policy of rapid and unobstructed enforcement of arbitration agreements, or with the desired flexibility of parties in choosing a site for arbitration.

Although the location of the arbitration may well be the residence of one of the parties, or have some other connection to a contract at issue, in many cases the site will have no relation whatsoever to the parties or the dispute. The parties may be willing to arbitrate in an inconvenient forum, say, for the convenience of the arbitrators, or to get a panel with special knowledge or experience, or as part of some compromise, but they might well be less willing to pick such a location if any future court proceedings had to be held there. Flexibility to make such practical choices, then, could well be inhibited by a venue rule mandating the same inconvenient venue if someone later sought to vacate or modify the award.

A restrictive interpretation would also place §3 and §§9–11 of the FAA in needless tension, which could be resolved only by disrupting existing precedent of this Court. Section 3 provides that any court in which an action "referable to arbitration under an agreement in writing" is pending "shall on application of one of the parties stay the trial of the action until such arbitration has been had in accordance with the terms of the agreement." If an arbitration were then held outside the district of that litigation, under a restrictive reading of §§9–11 a subsequent proceeding to confirm, modify, or set aside the arbitration award could not be brought in the district of the original litigation (unless that also happened to be the chosen venue in a forum selection agreement). We have ... previously held that the court with the power to stay the action under §3 has the further power to confirm any ensuing arbitration award. *Marine Transit Corp. v. Dreyfus*, 284 U.S. 263 (1932) ("We do not conceive it to be open to question that, where the court has authority under the statute ... to make an order for arbitration, the court also has authority to confirm the award or to set it aside for irregularity, fraud, ultra vires or other defect"). Harbert ... concedes this point.... But that concession saving our precedent still fails to explain why Congress would have wanted to allow venue liberally where motions to confirm, vacate, or modify were brought as subsequent stages of actions antedating the arbitration, but would have wanted a different rule when arbitration was not preceded by a suit between the parties.

Finally, Harbert's interpretation would create anomalous results in the aftermath of arbitrations held abroad. Sections 204, 207, and 302 of the FAA together provide for liberal choice of venue for actions to confirm awards subject to the [New York and Panama Conventions]. But reading §§9–11 to restrict venue to the site of the arbitration would preclude any action under the FAA in courts of the United States to confirm, modify, or vacate awards rendered in foreign arbitrations not covered by either convention. Although such actions would not necessarily be barred for lack of jurisdiction, they would be defeated by restrictions on venue, and anomalies like that are to be avoided when they can be. True, "[t]here have been, and perhaps there still are, occasional gaps in the venue laws, [but] Congress does not in general intend to create venue gaps, which take away with one hand what Congress has given by way of jurisdictional grant with the other. Thus, in construing venue statutes it is reasonable to prefer the construction that avoids leaving such a gap." *Brunette Machine Works, Ltd. v. Kockum Industries, Inc.*, 406 U.S. 706 (1972).

Attention to practical consequences thus points away from the restrictive reading of §§ 9–11 and confirms the view that the liberalizing effect of the provisions in the day of their enactment was meant to endure through treating them as permitting, not limiting, venue choice today. . . .

4. Comments and Questions

a. *Motions to Confirm Arbitration Awards: Is One Year a Statutory Standard or Limitation?* Courts are divided on the question of whether the one-year period for confirmation is permissive or mandatory. The Fourth and Eighth Circuits have held that § 9 is permissive and does not require that a party file for confirmation within one year. *See Sverdrup Corp. v. WHC Constructors, Inc.*, 989 F.2d 148 (4th Cir. 1993); *Val-U Constr. Co. v. Rosebud Sioux Tribe*, 146 F.3d 573 (8th Cir. 1998) (allowing confirmation past one year and stating that if Congress intended otherwise, it would have stated "must" instead of "may"). The Second Circuit interpreted "may" as within the scope of the adverbial phrase: 'at any time within one year after the award is made,' " thus holding that section 9 imposes a mandatory, one-year limitations period. *See Photopaint Techs., LLC v. Smartlens Corp.*, 335 F.3d 152, 159 (2d Cir. 2003) (stating that Congress intended the remedies provided under the FAA to "streamline the process [of confirming the award] and eliminate certain defenses."). *See also Guzy v. Guzy*, 2017 WL 3032432 (W.D. Tex. 2017) (discussing the circuit split and noting that the Fifth Circuit has adopted the mandatory approach subject to equitable tolling).

The two decisions that treat the one-year provision as permissive predate *Cortez Byrd* but remain controlling precedent in those respective circuits. The court in *Photopaint* relies on *Cortez Byrd* for its mandatory reading of the one-year provision. Is this factor persuasive to you? The FAA is subject to equitable tolling. *See, e.g., Move v. Citibank*, 840 F.3d 1152 (9th Cir. 2016). In *Sure and Expedited Resolution of Disputes: The Federal Arbitration Act and the One-Year Requirement for Summary Confirmation of Arbitration Awards*, 60 Cas. W. Res. L. Rev. 889 (2010), Matthew R. Kissling argues that a mandatory limitation period, combined with equitable tolling, best accords with FAA objectives of finality and efficiency, although even under the permissive approach, prevailing parties in arbitration are unlikely to delay seeking confirmation and thereby risk collection of the award. But what is the best rule? If an award is not confirmed within one year, what remedies are available? According to *Thompson v. Lithia ND Acquisition Corp. #1*, 896 N.W.2d 230 (N.D. 2017), the FAA standards provide a nonexclusive means for judicial review to vacate or confirm awards, and parties may seek analogous remedies under state law standards. Does the doctrine of *res judicata* or claim preclusion apply to an unconfirmed award?

b. *When Is an Award "Final" for Purposes of Triggering the Statutory Timelines?* Under FAA § 12, a party seeking to challenge an arbitration award must serve a notice upon the adverse party "within three months after the award is filed or delivered." An application to confirm an award pursuant to § 9 must be made within one year of when the award "was made." The FAA does not define the terms *filed, delivered,* or *made*. In some cases, these dates may be difficult to identify and not identical if there is a time lapse between when the award is filed versus delivered. *Webster v. A.T. Kearney, Inc.*, 507 F.3d 568 (7th Cir. 2007,) stated that "*service* of a motion to vacate [rather than filing] is the act that stops the three-month statute of limitations." In identifying the date of "filing or delivery" to mark when the statutory period had begun to accrue, the court applied the AAA rules, which provide that an award is "delivered" on the date the arbitrator placed the award in the mail or by electronic service, rather than the date of receipt. *See* Am. Arb. Ass'n Com. Arb. R. & Mediation Proc. R. 49. *Cf. Sargent v. Paine Webber Jackson & Curtis, Inc.*, 882 F.2d 529, 531 (DC Cir. 1989), *cert. denied*, 494 U.S. 1028 (1990) (suggesting the date of actual or constructive receipt controls). *Fradella v. Petricca*, 183 F.3d 17 (1st Cir. 1999), held that applications to modify or clarify arbitral awards do not toll the limitations period under FAA § 12. A party who fails to file a motion to vacate within the three-month period forfeits the right to judicial review under the FAA, subject to equitable tolling. *Pfannenstiel v. Merrill Lynch, Pierce, Fenner, & Smith*, 477 F.3d 1155 (10th Cir. 2007). *See also A. Miner Contracting, Inc. v. Kepner Co.*, 696 Fed.Appx. 234 (9th Cir. 2017) (noting that "equitable tolling" would be applied "in situations where, despite all due diligence, the party invoking equitable tolling is unable to obtain vital information bearing on the existence of the claim," but ruling that the doctrine did not apply where the party could have discovered before or during the period that two partners in the arbitrator's firm represented the adversary in an unrelated divorce matter). The petition to vacate the award, filed more than three years after the award was entered, was untimely under FAA 12 and, notwithstanding, the facts did not create "reasonable impression" of evident partiality.

5. Confirmation of Award under the RUAA (2000)

RUAA § 22 provides that after a party to an arbitration proceeding receives notice of an award, a party may seek judicial confirmation of an arbitral award. The court is to issue a confirming order unless the award is changed under § 20 or vacated, modified, or corrected under §§ 23 or 24. A losing party to an arbitration has 90 days after the arbitrator gives notice of the award to file a motion to vacate under § 23(b) or to file a motion to modify or correct under § 24(a), but "[a] court need not wait 90 days before taking jurisdiction if the winning party files a motion to confirm under § 22; otherwise the losing party would have this period of 90 days in which possibly to dissipate or otherwise dispose of assets necessary to satisfy an arbitration award. If the winning party files a motion to confirm prior to 90 days after the arbitrator gives notice of the award, the losing party can either: (1) file a motion to vacate or modify at that time, or (2) file a motion to vacate or modify within the 90-day statutory period." RUAA, Comment, § 22.

6. Confirmation or Vacatur of Partial Arbitration Awards

Judicial review of an arbitration proceeding must generally await a final award— that is, a final determination on the issue similar to the "final judgment rule" necessary to appeal in civil litigation. What should a court do when the arbitrators issue a final, but only partial, award? For example, an arbitration proceeding may bifurcate liability and damages phases, or enter a ruling disposing of one claim, such as on summary judgment, while remaining claims proceed to hearing. Arbitral institution rules may allow for the issuance of partial, final awards, but does that confer jurisdiction on the courts to confirm or vacate? When does the clock start to run on confirmation or vacatur of partial awards? The usual response is to await a complete and final award in order to avoid piecemeal litigation. *See Kaiser Foundation Health Plan, Inc. v. The Superior Court of Los Angeles,* 13 Cal. App. 5th 1125 (2017) (stating that appeals from nonfinal judgments arbitration awards could result in aggrieved parties appealing "[o]rders vacating interim arbitration orders resolving discovery disputes, sustaining or overruling demurrers, granting summary adjudication on certain claims, ruling on liability but not damages in a bifurcated proceeding, and denying motions for a new arbitration hearing.").

Courts do recognize exceptions to this general rule provided the partial award "finally and definitely disposes of a separate independent claim." *Hart Surgical, Inc. v. UltraCision, Inc.,* 244 F.3d 231 (1st Cir. 2001) (permitting judicial review of partial final award on liability where agreement provided for formal bifurcation). In class arbitration cases, the AAA rules call for the arbitrator, upon appointment and as a threshold matter, to issue a "reasoned, partial final award on the construction of the arbitration clause, whether the applicable arbitration clause permits the arbitration to proceed on behalf of or against a class (the 'Clause Construction Award'). The arbitrator shall stay all proceedings following the issuance of the Clause Construction Award for a period of at least 30 days to permit any party to move a court of competent jurisdiction to confirm or to vacate the Clause Construction Award." Am. Arb. Assoc. Supplementary Rules for Class Arbitration, R. 3 (2012). Dissenting in *Stolt-Nielsen S. A. v. AnimalFeeds Int'l Corp.,* 559 U.S. 662 (2010), Justice Ginsburg argued that the arbitrators' award construing whether the parties' clause permitted class arbitration was not a final award ripe for judicial review. *See* **Chapter 10.**

Some courts have undertaken review of partial arbitration awards despite the "mutual, final, and definite award" language of § 10(a)(4), by analogizing to Rule 54(b) of the Federal Rules of Civil Procedure (permitting interlocutory review where expedient and efficient). An appeal may be taken from a district court order "confirming or denying confirmation of an award or partial award." 16 U.S.C. § 16(a)(1)(D).

D. Judicial Review of Arbitration Awards: Standard of Review

The nature of law school is to explore the outer limits of doctrine and to focus on close questions. Notwithstanding the discussion of judicial review issues in this chapter, keep in mind that such review is *extremely* limited and that courts vacate arbitration awards only infrequently. This approach is reflected not only in legal doctrine, but also in the basic attitude of judges toward challenges of arbitration awards. Even more striking, this approach has been the law in America for more than 150 years—long before the courts enforced agreements to arbitrate. *See Kulukundis Shipping Co., S/A v. Amtorg Trading Corp.*, 126 F.2d 978 (2d Cir. 1942), excerpted in Chapter 1. Apart from the absence of citations to the FAA, Justice Grier's opinion below might have been written today instead of 1855. Among the many modern decisions that might be used to illustrate the narrow scope of judicial review of arbitration awards, *Moncharsh* was selected because of the prominence of the California Supreme Court, the context of law firm arbitration, and the professional ethics issue.

Burchell v. Marsh
58 U.S. 344 (1855)

JUSTICE GRIER delivered the opinion of the court.

The appellees ... pray the court to set aside an award made between the parties, as "fraudulent and void." The bill charges that "the award was made either from improper and corrupt motives, with the design of favoring said Burchell, or in ignorance of the rights of the parties to said submission, and of the duties and powers of the arbitrators who signed the said award." The answer denies that the arbitrators acted unjustly, or with partiality or ignorance, in making their award; but avers that they acted justly, fairly, and with a due consideration of the rights of the parties....

The general principles upon which courts of equity interfere to set aside [arbitration] awards are too well settled by numerous decisions to admit of doubt. There are, it is true, some anomalous cases, which, depending on their peculiar circumstances, cannot be exactly reconciled with any general rule; but such cases can seldom be used as precedents. Arbitrators are judges chosen by the parties to decide the matters submitted to them, finally and without appeal. As a mode of settling disputes, it should receive every encouragement from courts of equity. If the award is within the submission, and contains the honest decision of the arbitrators, after a full and fair hearing of the parties, a court of equity will not set it aside for error, either in law or fact. A contrary course would be a substitution of the judgment of the chancellor in place of the judges chosen by the parties, and would make an award the commencement, not the end, of litigation. In order ... to induce the court to interfere, there must be something more than an error of judgment, such as corruption in the arbitrator, or gross mistake, either apparent on the face of the award, or to be made out by evidence; but in case of mistake, it must be made out to the satisfaction of the arbitrator, and that if it had not happened, he should have made a different award....

1. The first objection to the award in this case is that it is not within the submission. But we are of opinion this objection is without foundation.... The parties ... agreed to submit "all demands, suits, claims, causes of action, controversies, and disputes between them, to ... arbitration."

On the hearing, the arbitrators received evidence of the debts alleged to be due from Burchell to the two firms, and of the alleged oppressive and ruinous suits brought against him by one Cross, who acted as agent of the firms. The witnesses, in proving these transactions, were permitted to state certain slanderous language used by Cross in speaking to and of Burchell, charging him with dishonesty and perjury. When this testimony was offered, the complainants' counsel agreed that it might be received, subject to exceptions.

It has been argued, that because the arbitrators received evidence of the slanderous language used by Cross, that, therefore, they included in their award damages for his slanders, for which his principals would not be liable; and that, therefore, they had taken into consideration matters not contained in the submission. But the answer to this allegation is, that the record shows no admission or proof that the arbitrators allowed any damages for the slanders of Cross. Whether the complainants were liable, and how far they were justly answerable for the conduct of their agent, were questions of law and fact submitted to the arbitrators. All these questions were fully argued before them by counsel. Whether their decision on them was erroneous, does not appear. The transactions which were testified to, with regard to the suits brought against Burchell, and whether they were oppressive, wrongful, and ruinous to him, was one of the very matters submitted to the arbitrators. The words as well as the acts of Cross made part of the *res gestae*, and could not well be severed in giving a history of them. Every presumption is in favor of the validity of the award. If it had stated an account, by which it appeared that the arbitrators had made a specific allowance of damages for the slanders of Cross, it would have been annulled, to that extent at least, as beyond the submission. But it cannot be inferred that the arbitrators went beyond the submission, merely because they may have admitted illegal evidence about the subject matter of it. We are of opinion, therefore, that there is nothing on the record to show that the arbitrators, in making this award, exceeded their authority, or went beyond the limits of the submission.

2. The charges of fraud, corruption, or improper conduct in the arbitrators, as we have seen, are wholly denied by the answer, which must be assumed to be true, unless facts are admitted from which they are a necessary or legal inference. We can see nothing in the admitted facts of the case from which any such inference can be justly made. The damages allowed for the alleged oppression of Burchell, and the ruin of his business as a merchant, may seem large to some, while others may think the sum of four, or even five thousand dollars as no extravagant compensation for such injuries. It may be admitted, that, on the facts appearing on the face of the record, this court would not have assessed damages to so large an amount, nor have divided them so arbitrarily between the parties; but we cannot say that the estimate of the arbitrators is so outrageous as of itself to constitute conclusive evidence of

fraud or corruption. Damages for injuries of this sort cannot be measured by any rules, nor can the court properly impute corruption to others, because they differ with them in their estimation of a matter which depends on discretion rather than calculation. It is enough that the parties have agreed to trust the discretion and judgment of neighbors acquainted with them, and their relative standing and credit. The admission of witnesses to prove their estimate of the damages (even if it had been in the face of the objection of counsel, and not by consent) may have been an error in judgment, but it is no cause for setting aside the award; nor can the admission of illegal evidence, or taking the opinion of third persons, be alleged as a misbehavior in the arbitrators which will affect their award. If they have given their honest, incorrupt judgment on the subject matters submitted to them, after a full and fair hearing of the parties, they are bound by it; and a court of chancery have no right to annul their award because it thinks it could have made a better one.

[T]his record furnishes no evidence of corruption or misbehavior in the arbitrators, nor of "ignorance," (as charged in the bill) or of any such mistake as would justify a court of chancery in annulling it. The decree of the court below is therefore reversed, and the record remitted with directions to dismiss the bill of complaint, with costs, but without prejudice to any legal defense.

Justice Nelson dissented.

I do not agree to the judgment of the court in this case. I think the damages allowed against the complainants, by the arbitrators, are so extravagant, disproportioned, and gross, as to afford evidence of passion and prejudice, and justified the judgment of the court below, in setting aside the award. It is difficult, if not impossible, to see, upon any other ground, how between four and five thousand dollars should have been allowed against one of the firms in the submission, and but some one thousand dollars against the other, under the circumstances of the case.

Moncharsh v. Heily & Blase

832 P.2d 899 (Cal. 1992)

Lucas, Chief Justice.

For the reasons discussed below, we conclude an arbitrator's decision is not generally reviewable for errors of fact or law, whether or not such error appears on the face of the award and causes substantial injustice to the parties. There are, however, limited exceptions to this general rule, which we also discuss below.

Philip Moncharsh, an attorney, was hired by respondent Heily & Blase, a law firm. As a condition of employment as an associate attorney in the firm, Moncharsh signed an agreement containing a number of provisions governing various aspects of his employment. One provision (hereafter referred to as "paragraph X-C") [was a non-compete provision, which specified that if, after termination, a client retained Moncharsh, Heily & Blase will receive 80% of the fees actually paid.] Moncharsh terminated his employment with Heily & Blase. Five clients, whose representation by Moncharsh predated his association with Heily & Blase, chose to have Moncharsh continue to represent them. A sixth client, Ringhof, retained Moncharsh less than two weeks before he left the firm. Moncharsh continued to represent all six clients after he left the firm.

When Blase learned Moncharsh had received fees at the conclusion of these six cases, he sought a quantum meruit share of the fees as well as a percentage of the fees pursuant to paragraph X-C of the employment agreement. Blase rejected Moncharsh's offer to settle the matter for only a quantum meruit share of the fees. The parties then invoked the arbitration clause of the employment agreement and submitted the matter to an arbitrator.

The arbitrator heard two days of testimony and the matter was submitted on the briefs and exhibits. In his brief, Moncharsh argued (1) Heily & Blase was entitled to only a quantum meruit share of the fees, (2) Moncharsh and Blase had an oral agreement to treat differently the cases Moncharsh brought with him to Heily & Blase, (3) the employment agreement had terminated and was therefore inapplicable, (4) the agreement was one of adhesion and therefore unenforceable, and (5) paragraph X-C is unenforceable because it violates public policy, the Rules of Professional Conduct of the State Bar, and because it is inconsistent with *Fracasse v. Brent*, 494 P.2d 9 (Cal. 1972). In its brief, Heily & Blase contended paragraph X-C (1) is clear and unequivocal, (2) is not unconscionable, and (3) represented a reasonable attempt to avoid litigation and was thus akin to a liquidated damages provision. In addition, Heily & Blase alleged that Moncharsh solicited the six clients to remain with him, and further suggested that Moncharsh retained those six because it was probable that financial settlements would soon be forthcoming in all six matters. Heily & Blase contrasted these six matters with the other cases Moncharsh left with the firm, all of which allegedly required a significant amount of additional legal work.

The arbitrator ruled in Heily & Blase's favor, concluding that any oral side agreement between Moncharsh and Blase was never documented and that Moncharsh was thus bound by the written employee agreement. Further, the arbitrator ruled that, "except for client Ringhof, paragraph X-C is not unconscionable, and it does not violate the rules of professional conduct. At the time Mr. Moncharsh agreed to the employment contract, he was a mature, experienced attorney, with employable skills. Had he not been willing to agree to the eighty/twenty (80/20) split on termination, he could simply have refused to sign the document, negotiated something different, or if negotiations were unsuccessful, his choice was to leave his employment. The Arbitrator excludes the Ringhof client from the eighty/twenty (80/20) split because that client was obtained at the twilight of Mr. Moncharsh's relationship with Heily & Blase, and an eighty/twenty (80/20) split with respect to that client would be unconscionable." ...

The General Rule of Arbitral Finality

The arbitration clause included in the employment agreement in this case specifically states that the arbitrator's decision would be both binding and final. The parties to this action thus clearly intended the arbitrator's decision would be final. Even had there been no such expression of intent, however, it is the general rule that parties to a private arbitration impliedly agree that the arbitrator's decision will be both binding and final....

Thus, it is the general rule that, with narrow exceptions, an arbitrator's decision cannot be reviewed for errors of fact or law. In reaffirming this general rule, we recognize there is a risk that the arbitrator will make a mistake. That risk, however, is acceptable for two reasons. First, by voluntarily submitting to arbitration, the parties have agreed to bear that risk in return for a quick, inexpensive, and conclusive resolution to their dispute.... A second reason why we tolerate the risk of an erroneous decision is because the Legislature has reduced the risk to the parties of such a decision by providing for judicial review in circumstances involving serious problems with the award itself, or with the fairness of the arbitration process.

Although Moncharsh acknowledges the general rule that an arbitrator's legal, as well as factual, determinations are final and not subject to judicial review, he argues that judicial review of the arbitrator's decision is warranted on the facts of this case. In support, he claims that the fee-splitting provision of the contract that was interpreted and enforced by the arbitrator was "illegal" and violative of "public policy" as reflected in several provisions of the Rules of Professional Conduct....

We recognize that there may be some limited and exceptional circumstances justifying judicial review of an arbitrator's decision when a party claims illegality affects only a portion of the underlying contract. Such cases would include those in which granting finality to an arbitrator's decision would be inconsistent with the protection of a party's statutory rights. Without an explicit legislative expression of public policy, however, courts should be reluctant to invalidate an arbitrator's award on this ground. Absent a clear expression of illegality or public policy undermining this strong presumption in favor of private arbitration, an arbitral award should ordinarily stand immune from judicial scrutiny.

Moncharsh contends, as he did before the arbitrator, that paragraph X-C is illegal and violates public policy because, inter alia, it violates rules 2-107 [prohibiting unconscionable fees], 2-108 [prohibiting certain types of fee splitting arrangements], and 2-109 [prohibiting agreements restricting an attorney's right to practice] of the Rules of Professional Conduct of State Bar. We perceive, however, nothing in the Rules of Professional Conduct at issue in this case that suggests resolution by an arbitrator of what is essentially an ordinary fee dispute would be inappropriate or would improperly protect the public interest. Accordingly, judicial review of the arbitrator's decision is unavailable....

We conclude that an award reached by an arbitrator pursuant to a contractual agreement to arbitrate is not subject to judicial review except on the grounds set forth in sections 1286.2 (to vacate) and 1286.6 (for correction). Further, the existence of an error of law apparent on the face of the award that causes substantial injustice does not provide grounds for judicial review. Finally, the normal rule of limited judicial review may not be avoided by a claim that a provision of the contract, construed or applied by the arbitrator, is "illegal," except in rare cases when according finality to the arbitrator's decision would be incompatible with the protection of a statutory right. We conclude that Moncharsh has demonstrated no reason why the strong presumption in favor of the finality of the arbitral award should not apply here.

KENNARD, JUSTICE, concurring and dissenting.

The majority holds that when a trial court is presented with an arbitration award that is erroneous on its face and will cause substantial injustice, the court has no choice but to confirm it. Because an order confirming an arbitration award results in the entry of a judgment with the same force and effect as a judgment in a civil action, the majority's holding requires our trial courts not only to tolerate substantial injustice, but to become its active agent.

I cannot join the majority opinion. I will not agree to a decision inflicting upon this state's trial courts a duty to promote injustice by confirming arbitration awards they know to be manifestly wrong and substantially unjust. Nor can I accept the proposition, necessarily implied although never directly stated in the majority opinion, that the general policy in favor of arbitration is more important than the judiciary's solemn obligation to do justice....

Despite my disagreement with the reasoning of the majority opinion, I agree with the result it reaches. This is not a case in which error appearing on the face of an arbitration award would cause a substantial injustice. The agreement was negotiated between sophisticated parties; the disparity in bargaining power between the parties was not substantial; there is no indication of harm to the clients or other third parties; and there is no basis in the arbitrator's award for finding that the fees were wholly disproportionate to the services rendered. Therefore, the award was not substantially unjust.

1. Slim Odds of Vacatur

Studies of cases in which parties have sought vacatur of arbitral awards report that parties cite grounds of evident partiality, arbitrator misconduct, and manifest disregard, but the most oft-cited reason is "exceeding authority." L. Mills, T. Brewer, *Vacating Arbitration Awards: Study Reveals Real-World Odds of Success*, DISP. RES. J. 23 (2005), in a review of vacatur filings during a 10-month period in 2004, found that of 61 motions in federal court, only six were successful—fewer than 10 percent; in state court, 31 of 121 awards (roughly 25 percent) were vacated. Many of these were appeals from trial court decisions, which means increased cost and a serious belief in the quality of the arguments for vacatur—at least, compared to the amount of money at issue. On average, federal cases involve higher dollar amounts than state cases, so the amount at issue doesn't explain the higher percentage of state court orders vacating arbitration awards. The overall state figures disguise dramatic variations among different states. The number of vacated awards was 9 (of 25 attempts) in New York; 6 (of 27 attempts) in California; and 4 (of 12 attempts) in Connecticut. No awards were vacated in 37 states, according to the study. Apart from the large number of vacated awards from New York state courts, both in absolute and relative terms, it appears that state courts (like the federal courts) rarely vacate arbitration awards.

In a 2012 study, Mills and Brewer focused on analyzing 47 "exceeding powers" vacatur filings, reporting nine (or 20 percent) successful motions, primarily in cases in which the challenged award concerned relief to non-signatories, an arbitrator's blatant disregard of the underlying contract, or an impermissibly vague award. Lawrence R. Mills & Thomas J. Brewer, *'Exceeded Powers': Exploring Recent Trends in Cases Challenging Tribunal Authority*, 31 ALTS. TO HIGH COST LITIG. 113 (2013) (stating that almost all of the opinions caution that vacatur motions are rarely granted and note the extremely deferential standard of review of awards).

E. FAA Statutory Grounds for Review and Vacating Arbitration Awards

The FAA requires federal district courts to confirm arbitration awards as judgments where parties have so agreed, unless grounds exist to vacate, modify, or correct the award. 9 U.S.C. §§ 9, 10, 11. The court may modify or correct an award "(a) where there is an evident material miscalculation of figures on an evident material mistake in the description of any person, place, thing or property referred to in the award; (b) where the arbitrators make an award upon a matter not submitted to them unless it is a matter not affecting the merits of the decision upon the matter submitted; and (c) where the award is imperfect in form not affecting the merits of the controversy." *Id.* at § 11.

Under § 10(a) of the FAA, an arbitration award may be vacated by a federal district court "(1) where the award was procured by corruption, fraud, or undue means; (2) where there was evident partiality or corruption in the arbitrators, or either of them; (3) where the arbitrators were guilty of misconduct in refusing to postpone the hearing, upon sufficient cause shown, or in refusing to hear evidence pertinent and material to the controversy; or of any other misbehavior by which the rights of any party have been prejudiced; or (4) where the arbitrators exceeded their powers, or so imperfectly executed them that a mutual, final, and definite award upon the subject matter submitted was not made." *Id.* Prior to *Hall Street Assocs., L.L.C. v. Mattel, Inc.*, 552 U.S. 576 (2008), most federal circuits recognized that a district court could vacate an arbitration award if the award was issued in manifest disregard of the law, or where the award violated public policy or was deemed arbitrary and capricious. The viability of these nonstatutory standards is examined later in this chapter.

As demonstrated by *Burchell* and *Moncharsh*, these grounds are narrower than the standards for appellate review in a judicial case where a court reviews a lower court's legal rulings de novo and factual findings for clear error. We begin with cases involving claims for *statutory grounds* upon which a court may vacate an arbitration award under the FAA.

1. Fraud or Misconduct in the Arbitration

Where vacatur is sought on the basis of an award that was procured by fraud, corruption, or undue means, the movant must show the fraud was: (1) not discoverable by the exercise of due diligence prior to the award; (2) materially related to the issue in the arbitration; and (3) established by clear and convincing evidence. *See Renard v. Ameriprise Financial Services, Inc.*, 778 F.3d 563, 569 (7th Cir. 2015). Consider the types of conduct that could constitute fraud or undue means in an arbitration. Suppose an arbitration award was based upon perjured testimony, false documents, or withheld discovery?

Karppinen v. Karl Kiefer Machine Co.

187 F.2d 32 (2d Cir. 1951)

AUGUSTUS N. HAND, CIRCUIT JUDGE.

Eino Karppinen and John Saxman, copartners doing business as Mrs. Dixon's Products Company, moved in the district court to confirm an arbitration award which entitled them to return a machine purchased from The Karl Kiefer Machine Co. and to receive a refund of the purchase price. The award was confirmed and The Karl Kiefer Machine Co. appeals.

The underlying controversy between seller and purchaser of the machine is recited in the arbitration submission agreement and may be summarized as follows: In October 1945, appellant sold to appellees a machine for filling jams, jellies, preserves and marmalade into containers. The purchase price of $7,950 was duly paid, and the machine was delivered during February, 1948. Subsequently the purchaser claimed to be entitled to rescind because the machine was not fit for the purpose for which it was sold. The seller denied this, and asserted that in any event its guarantee was only good for thirty days after delivery, and also that any inadequacy of the machine to serve its purpose was the purchasers' own fault. In November 1949, the controversy was submitted to three arbitrators: an engineer, a businessman, and a lawyer. It was agreed that the arbitrators would inspect the machine at the buyers' premises while it was in operation in a normal commercial manner, and that the parties would abide by any award rendered pursuant to the agreement.

Upon the purchasers' motion to confirm the award granting rescission, the seller filed affidavits asking that the award be vacated. Several grounds were relied on, but the only one before us is based on an allegation that the award was induced by perjured testimony. An affidavit by the president of The Karl Kiefer Machine Co. stated that his company had contended during the arbitration proceedings that the complaints against its machine had been made in bad faith and that the buyers were seeking to rescind because they wished to buy a cheaper machine of a lower productive capacity. The affidavit further asserted that Eino Karppinen had rebutted this contention by falsely testifying before the arbitrators that his company had purchased at a higher price ($8,150) another machine with even greater capacity. In this connection it was asserted that Karppinen had produced a false copy of his purchase order for the new machine, and had thereby convinced the arbitrators of his faith and also gained their sympathy by making them believe that unless rescission were granted the purchasers would be left with two expensive machines instead of one. An accompanying affidavit by a former employee of the Hope Machine Company, which sold the second machine to Mrs. Dixon's Products Company, stated that the total price of that machine was under $7,000. This assertion was also supported by the affidavit of a person having dealings with the Hope Machine Company.

Reply affidavits were filed in support of the motion to confirm the award by Eino Karppinen, by his attorney, who was present at the arbitration proceedings, by the president of the Hope Machine Company, and by various employees of that company. These affidavits allege that Karppinen's testimony at the arbitration proceeding had no bearing on the award, that Karppinen did not testify to the price figure alleged but merely stated his belief that the Hope machine would probably cost more than the old one, and that the purchase price of the Hope machine was (apparently depending on the number of accessories) $7,620, $8,718, or $8,944.

The motion to confirm the award was heard on February 28, 1950, continued on March 1, 1950, and then adjourned to March 15, 1950. Before the last date, The Karl Kiefer Machine Co. moved for an oral examination of Karppinen, and of the president of the Hope Machine Company, and also moved for the production of all papers dealing with the sale of that machine. This motion was granted only to the extent of permitting the examination of Karppinen, during which several documents were introduced in evidence by both sides. After that examination, the arbitrators' award was confirmed, and the portion of the cross-motion demanding other oral examination and the production of papers was denied. A motion for a rehearing was also denied. The appeal is from the denial of those motions, from the decision of the court to limit the scope of Karppinen's examination, and from the entry of the judgment on the award.

The only claim that the award should be set aside is based on the appellant's contention that the buyers made false statements about the cost of the machine to be purchased from the Hope Machine Company. It is said that the buyers testified before the arbitrators that the Hope machine cost $8,150, which was $200 more than the Kiefer machine had cost, and that the alleged false statement was made to rebut any inference that the buyers were claiming rescission because the price paid for the Kiefer machine had been too high, rather than because it did not work well enough to serve its purpose.

It goes without saying that there should be great hesitation in upsetting an arbitration award. The award here must stand unless it is made abundantly clear that it was obtained through "corruption, fraud, or undue means." 9 U.S.C. § 10 (a). We will assume, as did the court below, that an arbitration award may be set aside in a case of material perjured evidence furnished the arbitrators by a prevailing party, but we do not decide the somewhat disputed question whether the word "fraud" in Section 10(a) of the FAA has a broader scope than that word has when applied so as to permit a collateral attack on a judgment rendered upon perjured testimony. We note only in passing that if perjury is "fraud" within the meaning of the statute, then, since it necessarily raises issues of credibility which have already been before the arbitrators once, the party relying on it must first show that he could not have discovered it during the arbitration, else he should have invoked it as a defense at that time. An allegation of inability to discover the alleged perjury was present in one of appellant's affidavits.

But even on the assumption that an award may be vacated for perjury as to material evidence the judgment below must be affirmed. Not only were the affidavits submitted to the district court in the proceeding to vacate the award most contradictory, but the bearing of the price of the Hope machine on the issues before the arbitrators is extremely remote. Under the terms of the submission agreement these arbitrators were to determine the fitness of the machine to do its work, were to find who was at fault if it proved unfit, and were to decide whether the thirty day limit in the guarantee had been waived. One of the arbitrators was an engineer, and all of them saw the machine in operation and evidently found that it was inadequate. The price paid by the purchasers for some other machine had no bearing on the real issues before the arbitrators and cannot reasonably be thought to have affected their decision in determining any relevant questions before them. At most it could only bear on a possible impeachment of Karppinen as to collateral matters, and he was subjected at the hearing below to an elaborate and inconclusive examination by appellant regarding the price of the Hope machine.

Nor do we think that the case required full oral testimony, if indeed it required any at all, in view of the very remote bearing of the price of the Hope machine on any issue before the arbitrators. It would be a surprising innovation if every party objecting to an arbitration award could recall all the witnesses in order to vacate the award on the basis of some evidence alleged to be untruthful which had but a remote and speculative bearing on the issues before the arbitrators. It is unnecessary for us to lay down any general rule as to when or how far oral hearings on questions of alleged perjured testimony before arbitrators should be allowed. It is enough to say that even if perjury be "fraud" within the meaning of the Arbitration Act, such hearings should only be granted with reluctance, that the price of the Hope machine had no proper relation to the issues before the arbitrators and that in any event there was sufficient investigation by the court below to show that the price paid for that machine was a trivial if not wholly irrelevant matter. We hold that in such circumstances the order confirming the award was fully justified.

a. Due Diligence, Materiality, and Nexus Requirement

Karppinen recognized that perjury at an arbitration is fraud within the meaning of the FAA, but also required that such fraud could not have been discovered prior to or during the arbitration. *See also Bonar v. Dean Witter Reynolds, Inc.*, 835 F.2d 1378 (11th Cir. 1988). In *Hakala v. Deutsche Bank AG*, 2004 U.S. Dist. LEXIS 8297 (S.D.N.Y. 2004), despite allegations that the prevailing party at the arbitration allegedly suborned perjury and procured the award by committing willful discovery violations, the court denied vacatur because the losing party failed to demonstrate that it could not have discovered the alleged fraud prior to the arbitration. Similarly, *Barahona v. Dillard's Inc.*, 376 Fed. Appx. 395 (5th Cir. 2010), reversed a district court's vacatur of an arbitration award in favor of the employer where the employee discovered the alleged fraud (withholding of email production) during the arbitration but failed to seek discovery of the extent of the fraud during the arbitration.

Clarifying when a party's alleged fraud is sufficient to vacate an arbitration award, *Odeon Capital Group, LLC v. Ackerman*, 864 F.3d 191 (2d Cir. 2017) held that for "fraud to be material within the meaning of Section 10(a)(1) of the FAA, petitioner must demonstrate a nexus between the alleged fraud and the decision made by the arbitrators, although petitioner need not demonstrate that the arbitrators would have reached a different result." The *Odeon* court determined that the employer was not able to vacate the $1.4 million award in favor of the employee based on the employee's alleged perjury, because the topic of the perjury had nothing to do with the unpaid wages claim on which he was awarded damages and the general damage to his credibility was not sufficient.

2. Evident Partiality or Arbitrator Bias

The materials from **Chapter 8.E** on Arbitrator Selection introduced arbitrator ethical standards to disclose potential or actual conflicts of interest and bias as reason for disqualification. At the post-award stage, "evident partiality" is the analogous basis to vacate an arbitration award. *Commonwealth Coatings Corp. v. Continental Casualty Co.*, 393 U.S. 145 (1968) is the leading Supreme Court decision on arbitrator impartiality. While that the arbitration involved a tripartite tribunal, in which each of the parties selects an arbitrator, *Commonwealth* examines whether the neutral arbitrator's failure to disclose his "sporadic," but "repeated and significant," business relationship with another party to the arbitration required that the arbitration award be vacated under subsection (a)(1) as being procured by undue means, as well as under subsection (a)(2) on grounds of evident partiality. Compare the respective views of Justice Black, writing for the plurality, with Justice White's concurrence on whether arbitrators should be held to the same, higher, or lesser ethical standards as public judges, and Justice Fortas's dissent that vacatur was unnecessary in this case. Is vacatur warranted based on the mere "appearance of bias" or proof of actual bias?

Commonwealth Coatings Corp. v. Continental Casualty Co.

393 U.S. 145 (1968)

JUSTICE BLACK delivered the opinion of the Court.

At issue in this case is the question whether elementary requirements of impartiality taken for granted in every judicial proceeding are suspended when the parties agree to resolve a dispute through arbitration. The petitioner, Commonwealth Coatings, a subcontractor, sued the sureties on the prime contractor's bond to recover money alleged to be due for a painting job. The contract for painting contained an agreement to arbitrate such controversies. Pursuant to this agreement petitioner appointed one arbitrator, the prime contractor appointed a second, and these two together selected the third arbitrator. This third arbitrator, the supposedly neutral member of the panel, conducted a large business in Puerto Rico, in which he served as an engineering consultant for various people in connection with building construction projects. One of his regular customers in this business was the prime contractor that petitioner sued in this case. This relationship with the prime contractor was in a sense sporadic in that the arbitrator's services were used only from time to time at irregular intervals, and there had been no dealings between them for about a year immediately preceding the arbitration. Nevertheless, the prime contractor's patronage was repeated and significant, involving fees of about $12,000 over a period of four of five years, and the relationship even went so far as to include the rendering of services on the very projects involved in this lawsuit. An arbitration was held, but the facts concerning the close business connections between the third arbitrator and the prime contractor were unknown to petitioner and were never revealed to it by this arbitrator, by the prime contractor, or by anyone else until after an award had been made. Petitioner challenged the award on this ground, among others, but the District Court refused to set aside the award. The Court of Appeals affirmed, and we granted certiorari.

In 1925 Congress enacted the FAA which sets out a comprehensive plan for arbitration of controversies coming under its terms, and both sides here assume that this Federal Act governs this case. Section 10 sets out the conditions upon which awards can be vacated. The two courts below held, however, that section 10 could not be construed in such a way as to justify vacating the award in this case. We disagree and reverse. Section 10 does authorize vacation of an award where it was 'procured by corruption, fraud, or undue means' or '[w]here there was evident partiality ... in the arbitrators.' These provisions show a desire of Congress to provide not merely for any arbitration but for an impartial one. It is true that petitioner does not charge before us that the third arbitrator was actually guilty of fraud or bias in deciding this case, and we have no reason, apart from the undisclosed business relationship, to suspect him of any improper motives. But neither this arbitrator nor the prime contractor gave to petitioner even an intimation of the close financial relations that had existed between them for a period of years.

We have no doubt that if a litigant could show that a foreman of a jury or a judge in a court of justice had, unknown to the litigant, any such relationship, the judgment would be subject to challenge. This is shown beyond doubt by *Tumey v. State of Ohio*, 273 U.S. 510 (1927), where this Court held that a conviction could not stand because a small part of the judge's income consisted of court fees collected from convicted defendants. Although in *Tumey* it appeared the amount of the judge's compensation actually depended on whether he decided for one side or the other, that is too small a distinction to allow this manifest violation of the strict morality and fairness Congress would have expected on the part of the arbitrator and the other party in this case. Nor should it be at all relevant, as the Court of Appeals apparently thought it was here, that '(t)he payments received were a very small part of (the arbitrator's) income....' For in *Tumey* the Court held that a decision should be set aside where there is 'the slightest pecuniary interest' on the part of the judge, and specifically rejected the State's contention that the compensation involved there was so small that it is not to be regarded as likely to influence improperly a judicial officer in the discharge of his duty. Since in the case of courts this is a constitutional principle, we can see no basis for refusing to find the same concept in the broad statutory language that governs arbitration proceedings and provides that an award can be set aside on the basis of 'evident partiality' or the use of 'undue means.'

It is true that arbitrators cannot sever all their ties with the business world, since they are not expected to get all their income from their work deciding cases, but we should, if anything, be even more scrupulous to safeguard the impartiality of arbitrators than judges, since the former have completely free rein to decide the law as well as the facts and are not subject to appellate review. We can perceive no way in which the effectiveness of the arbitration process will be hampered by the simple requirement that arbitrators disclose to the parties any dealings that might create an impression of possible bias.

While not controlling in this case, section 18 of the Rules of the American Arbitration Association, in effect at the time of this arbitration, is highly significant. It provided as follows:

> Section 18. Disclosure by Arbitrator of Disqualification—At the time of receiving his notice of appointment, the prospective Arbitrator is requested to disclose any circumstances likely to create a presumption of bias or which he believes might disqualify him as an impartial Arbitrator. Upon receipt of such information, the Tribunal Clerk shall immediately disclose it to the parties, who if willing to proceed under the circumstances disclosed, shall, in writing, so advise the Tribunal Clerk. If either party declines to waive the presumptive disqualification, the vacancy thus created shall be filled in accordance with the applicable provisions of this Rule.

And based on the same principle as this Arbitration Association rule is that part of the 33rd Canon of Judicial Ethics which provides:

> 33. Social Relations. (A judge) should, in pending or prospective litigation before him be particularly careful to avoid such action as may reasonably tend to awaken the suspicion that his social or business relations or friendships, constitute an element in influencing his judicial conduct.

This rule of arbitration and this canon of judicial ethics rest on the premise that any tribunal permitted by law to try cases and controversies not only must be unbiased but also must avoid even the appearance of bias. We cannot believe that it was the purpose of Congress to authorize litigants to submit their cases and controversies to arbitration boards that might reasonably be thought biased against one litigant and favorable to another. Reversed.

JUSTICE WHITE, with whom JUSTICE MARSHALL joins, concurring.

While I am glad to join my Brother BLACK's opinion in this case, I desire to make these additional remarks. The Court does not decide today that arbitrators are to be held to the standards of judicial decorum of Article III judges, or indeed of any judges. It is often because they are men of affairs, not apart from but of the marketplace, that they are effective in their adjudicatory function. This does not mean the judiciary must overlook outright chicanery in giving effect to their awards; that would be an abdication of our responsibility. But it does mean that arbitrators are not automatically disqualified by a business relationship with the parties before them if both parties are informed of the relationship in advance, or if they are unaware of the facts but the relationship is trivial. I see no reason automatically to disqualify the best informed and most capable potential arbitrators.

The arbitration process functions best when an amicable and trusting atmosphere is preserved and there is voluntary compliance with the decree, without need for judicial enforcement. This end is best served by establishing an atmosphere of frankness at the outset, through disclosure by the arbitrator of any financial transactions which he has had or is negotiating with either of the parties. In many cases the arbitrator might believe the business relationship to be so insubstantial that to make a point of revealing it would suggest he is indeed easily swayed, and perhaps a partisan of that party. But if the law requires the disclosure, no such imputation can arise. And it is far better that the relationship be disclosed at the outset, when the parties are free to reject the arbitrator or accept him with knowledge of the relationship and continuing faith in his objectivity, than to have the relationship come to light after the arbitration, when a suspicious or disgruntled party can seize on it as a pretext for invalidating the award. The judiciary should minimize its role in arbitration as judge of the arbitrator's impartiality. That role is best consigned to the parties, who are the architects of their own arbitration process, and are far better informed of the prevailing ethical standards and reputations within their business.

Of course, an arbitrator's business relationships may be diverse indeed, involving more or less remote commercial connections with great numbers of people. He cannot be expected to provide the parties with his complete and unexpurgated business biography. But it is enough for present purposes to hold, as the Court does, that where the arbitrator has a substantial interest in a firm which has done more than trivial business with a party, that fact must be disclosed. If arbitrators err on the side of disclosure, as they should, it will not be difficult for courts to identify those undisclosed relationships which are too insubstantial to warrant vacating an award.

JUSTICE FORTAS, with whom JUSTICE HARLAN and JUSTICE STEWART join, dissenting.

The facts in this case do not lend themselves to the Courts' ruling. The Court sets aside the arbitration award despite the fact that the award is unanimous and no claim is made of actual partiality, unfairness, bias, or fraud. The arbitration was held pursuant to provisions in the contracts between the parties. It is not subject to the rules of the AAA. Each party appointed an arbitrator and the third arbitrator was chosen by those two. The controversy relates to the third arbitrator.

The third arbitrator was not asked about business connections with either party. Petitioner's complaint is that he failed to volunteer information about professional services rendered by him to the other party to the contract, the most recent of which were performed over a year before the arbitration. Both courts below held, and petitioner concedes, that the third arbitrator was innocent of any actual partiality, or bias, or improper motive. There is no suggestion of concealment as distinguished from the innocent failure to volunteer information.

The third arbitrator is a leading and respected consulting engineer who has performed services for 'most of the contractors in Puerto Rico.' He was well known to petitioner's counsel and they were personal friends. Petitioner's counsel candidly admitted that if he had been told about the arbitrator's prior relationship 'I don't think I would have objected because I know Mr. Capacete [the arbitrator].'

Clearly, the District Judge's conclusion, affirmed by the Court of Appeals for the First Circuit, was correct, that 'the arbitrators conducted fair, impartial hearings; that they reached a proper determination of the issues before them, and that plaintiff's objections represent a 'situation where the losing party to an arbitration is now clutching at straws in an attempt to avoid the results of the arbitration to which it became a party.'"

The Court nevertheless orders that the arbitration award be set aside. It uses this singularly inappropriate case to announce a per se rule that in my judgment has no basis in the applicable statute or jurisprudential principles: that, regardless of the agreement between the parties, if an arbitrator has any prior business relationship with one of the parties of which he fails to inform the other party, however innocently, the arbitration award is always subject to being set aside. This is so even where the award is unanimous; where there is no suggestion that the nondisclosure indicates partiality or bias; and where it is conceded that there was in fact no irregularity, unfairness, bias, or partiality. Until the decision today, it has not been the law that an arbitrator's failure to disclose a prior business relationship with one of the parties will compel the setting aside of an arbitration award regardless of the circumstances.

I agree that failure of an arbitrator to volunteer information about business dealings with one party will, prima facie, support a claim of partiality or bias. But where there is no suggestion that the nondisclosure was calculated, and where the complaining party disclaims any imputation of partiality, bias, or misconduct, the presumption clearly is overcome....

Arbitration is essentially consensual and practical. The FAA is obviously designed to protect the integrity of the process with a minimum of insistence upon set formulae and rules. The Court applies to this process rules applicable to judges and not to a system characterized by dealing on faith and reputation for reliability. Such formalism is not contemplated by the Act nor is it warranted in a case where no claim is made of partiality, of unfairness, or of misconduct in any degree.

a. Disclosure, Provider Rules, and Evident Partiality?

Is disclosure of potential (or actual) conflicts or relationships with one of the parties enough to avoid a charge of bias or "evident partiality"? Suppose the administering institution has ruled against a party seeking arbitrator disqualification based on bias? What role does the timing of the events play in assessing partiality?

Kinkade Co. v. White

711 F.3d 719 (6th Cir. 2013)

KETHLEDGE, CIRCUIT JUDGE

In this case the coincidences all break one way. Mark Kowalsky was a purportedly neutral arbitrator in a dispute between the Kinkade Company and Nancy and David White. Nearly five years and nearly 50 hearing days into their arbitration, however, Kowalsky announced to Kinkade that its adversary, David White, and the Whites' advocate on the arbitration panel, Mayer Morganroth, had each hired Kowalsky's firm for engagements that were likely to be substantial. Kinkade objected, to no avail. A series of irregularities in the arbitration followed, all of which favored the Whites. Kowalsky eventually entered a $1.4 million award in the Whites' favor. The district court vacated the award on grounds of Kowalsky's "evident partiality." We affirm the district court.

I.

In the late 1990s, Kinkade and the Whites entered into several agreements under which the Whites agreed to be "Signature dealers" of Kinkade's artwork. The parties agreed to arbitrate any disputes between them "in accordance with the Commercial Arbitration Rules of the American Arbitration Association." Soon the parties put that clause to use: in 2002, they commenced an arbitration in which Kinkade claimed that the Whites had not paid for artwork worth hundreds of thousands of dollars, and the Whites counterclaimed that they had been fraudulently induced to enter into the dealer agreements.

Per the arbitration rules, each party was entitled to appoint one arbitrator, who would *de facto* advocate that party's position on the panel. Kinkade chose Burton Ansell as its arbitrator; the Whites chose Mayer Morganroth as theirs. Together Ansell and Morganroth chose Mark Kowalsky as the panel's neutral arbitrator, who would chair the panel and *de facto* decide the issues in the arbitration.

The arbitration itself was a model of how not to conduct one. The least of its blemishes was that it dragged on for years. In January 2006, Kinkade's counsel discovered that the Whites' counsel, Joseph Ejbeh of "the Yatooma firm" in Michigan, had been surreptitiously sending a live feed of the hearing transcripts to a hotel room miles away. There, a disgruntled former Kinkade employee, Terry Sheppard, would review the transcripts in real-time and send proposed cross-examination questions to Ejbeh via instant messages. This scheme went on for more than a year. When the panel finally confronted Ejbeh about it, he at first denied the scheme, but then admitted it "[a]fter additional inquiry by the arbitrators and an outburst of crying from the court reporter[.]" The Yatooma firm then replaced Ejbeh with Edward Fisher, but he departed after being convicted of federal tax fraud. A third Yatooma lawyer, Robert Zawideh, took his place.

Meanwhile, Kinkade sent discovery requests for "all documents" supporting the Whites' damages claim, including all of their financial records. The Whites produced virtually nothing in response, and said that "[e]xpert testimony and reports will provide additional information on the more precise calculation of damages." That turned out to be an overstatement: the Whites' expert based his damages calculations merely upon *pro formas* that the Whites had prepared prior to entering the dealer agreement, rather than upon financial records from actual operations; and the expert offered no opinion at all as to how Kinkade's conduct (as opposed to any number of other possible causes, such as the declining economy) had caused the Whites' alleged damages.

The parties thereafter submitted closing briefs and presented closing arguments on December 1, 2006. The following day, counsel for both parties stated on the record that they had received a fair opportunity to present their cases; and thus at that point, presumably, they thought their presentations were finished. Two days later, however, the panel—through a letter from Kowalsky—ordered the parties to submit further briefing "on the causation element of [the Whites'] fraud claims." Kowalsky also ordered the Whites to submit a "detailed accounting" of their damages.

Kinkade was unhappy about Kowalsky's letter because it gave the Whites another chance to fix what Kinkade thought were the most obvious weaknesses of the Whites' case—namely, their threadbare proof of causation and damages. So Kinkade objected to the letter, pointing out that Kinkade had briefed and argued both issues throughout the arbitration, whereas the Whites had largely ignored them. But the panel did not act on Kinkade's objections before the additional briefs were due, so the parties submitted them as directed.

At that point, for Kinkade, the real troubles began—for then the Whites and persons associated with them began showering Kowalsky's law firm with new business. First, on February 8, 2007, Kowalsky informed the parties that the Whites' appointed arbitrator, Morganroth (or more directly his attorneys), had hired one of Kowalsky's partners, Brad Schram, as a defense expert in a malpractice case then pending against Morganroth. Schram testified that he expected the fees for this engagement to be "substantial." Kowalsky himself signed the retention letter on behalf of Schram.

Less than eight weeks later, on April 3, 2007, Kowalsky announced that David White—one of the actual parties to the arbitration—had hired another of Kowalsky's partners, Gary Saretsky, to represent White in an unrelated NASD arbitration. Kowalsky assured the parties that he would prevent himself from obtaining any information about the NASD arbitration—which was beside the point, since the subject of that arbitration had nothing to do with the subject of this one—but Kowalsky notably did not make any "effort to separate himself from the financial benefits that would accompany the representation."

Thus, in late April 2007, Kinkade faced the following situation: Nearly five years and 50 hearing days into an arbitration already checkered by irregularities, its adversary in the arbitration and its adversary's appointed arbitrator, in the space of about eight weeks, had both retained the neutral's law firm for engagements that any litigator would have regarded as lucrative. Kinkade objected to those engagements in a letter two weeks later to the American Arbitration Association (AAA). In a response dated May 2, 2007, the AAA cryptically informed the parties that Saretsky had backed out of representing White in the NASD arbitration. Saretsky left Kowalsky's firm shortly thereafter.

Per the AAA's directions to counsel, Kowalsky himself was not copied on any of Kinkade's objections with respect to his firm's arrangements with White and Morganroth. But the Whites' attorney, Zawideh, blew that cover in a June 14 email to Kowalsky, in which he told Kowalsky that he had been "re-confirmed" as a neutral arbitrator in the case. As a result, Kinkade believed (as anyone would) that Kowalsky would surmise that one of the parties had objected to his firm's arrangements with White and Morganroth—and that the objector was Kinkade. Kinkade also believed that Kowalsky would resent the objection.

Consequently, on July 2, 2007, Kinkade filed a motion with the AAA seeking to disqualify Kowalsky outright. The motion recited in great detail the relevant facts of the arbitration, and argued that Kowalsky's disqualification was required under the AAA rules, the AAA Code of Ethics, California law (which both parties agree governs the case), the California Ethics Standards, and the ABA Model Rules.... The AAA denied Kinkade's motion. Kinkade then submitted a demand for disqualification directly to Kowalsky, which he denied.

Meanwhile, the arbitration itself began to move forward again. The Whites had neglected to include any documents or other evidence in support of the damages calculations that they had submitted pursuant to Kowalsky's direction back in December 2006—an omission normally fatal to a party that bears the burden of proof as to its claim. But Kowalsky gave the Whites a chance to remedy that omission on July 6, 2007, when he ordered them to provide backup for their damages calculations. They did so on August 9, with an 8,800-page production of financial records relating to the actual operation of the Whites' galleries. Those documents—statements, invoices, checks, ledgers for the galleries, and so on—were exactly the kinds of documents that Kinkade had requested four years earlier and that, in response, the Whites had said did not exist. (The documents also showed that the Whites had made cash payments to six fact witnesses, ranging from $5,000–$10,000.) Kinkade therefore objected to the documents' admission and moved to bar the Whites from relying upon anything but their damages expert as to causation and damages. Kowalsky denied the motion.

On May 9, 2008, the panel issued an "Interim Award." The award was conclusory, stating as to each claim merely that the proofs did or did not "support[ ] recovery[.]" The Award found that the Whites had proved five of their claims, and awarded them $567,300 in damages. The Award denied recovery on Kinkade's breach-of-contract claim for paintings that the Whites had not paid for—notwithstanding that the claim was virtually uncontested. The Award further stated that "[a]ll claims that are not expressly granted are hereby denied." Arbitrator Ansell dissented on numerous grounds, including that Kinkade had been denied a fair hearing by the panel....

On February 26, 2009—again over Ansell's dissent—the panel majority issued a Final Award. The Final Award granted the Whites $487,000 in attorneys' fees, $215,846.20 in costs, and $258,121 in prejudgment interest. The Final Award nicked the Whites $25,000 for withholding their financial records and another $75,000 for the internet-feed scheme. About Kinkade's pending objections, the Award had nothing to say. All told, the Whites' net award exceeded $1.4 million.

The next day, Kinkade filed a petition to vacate the Final Award in federal district court in Detroit ... In a 21-page opinion that canvassed the arbitration's history and the relevant law, the district court vacated the Final Award in its entirety.

This appeal followed.

II.

We review for clear error the district court's factual findings and de novo its resolution of questions of law.

The Federal Arbitration Act authorizes federal courts to vacate arbitration awards on certain specified grounds. *See* 9 U.S.C. § 10. Among those grounds is "evident partiality or corruption in the arbitrators[.]" *Id.* § 10(a)(2). That is the ground upon which the district court vacated the award here.

To establish evident partiality, the challenging party must show that "a reasonable person would have to conclude that an arbitrator was partial to one party to the arbitration." "This standard requires a showing greater than an appearance of bias, but less than actual bias"; and to meet it, a party "must establish specific facts that indicate improper motives on the part of the arbitrator."

Here, Kinkade established a convergence of undisputed facts that, considered together, show a motive for Kowalsky to favor the Whites and multiple, concrete actions in which he appeared actually to favor them. To begin with the motive: nearly five years into this arbitration, and in the space of eight weeks, the purportedly neutral arbitrator's law firm—of all the law firms that practice commercial litigation in Michigan—was hired by one party's arbitrator-advocate (Morganroth) and then again by that same party (David White) for engagements that by all appearances would be substantial.

Kowalsky's actions only added to the concern. He gave the Whites a second and then a third chance to bolster the proofs for their claims.... And Kowalsky awarded the Whites nearly $500,000 in attorneys' fees after the plain terms of the Interim Award indicated that the Whites' request for fees had been denied. These actions, when combined with the late-arbitration dealings between the Whites and Kowalsky's firm, are more than sufficient to show his evident partiality.

It is no answer to assert, as the Whites do at length in their briefs to our court, that Kowalsky fully disclosed these arrangements to the parties. Five years into an arbitration, those disclosures were little better than no disclosure at all.... "One major benefit of arbitration is that it allows parties to exercise some control over who will resolve their disputes." Disclosures at the outset of an arbitration allow a party to reject an arbitrator as ethically encumbered as Kowalsky was here; and Kinkade obviously would have rejected Kowalsky out of hand if David White and Morganroth had hired Kowalsky's firm just prior to this arbitration rather than five years in. Thus, we entirely agree with the district court that, "[w]hen the neutral arbitrator engages in or attempts to engage in mid-arbitration business relationships with non-neutral participants, it jeopardizes what is supposed to be a party structured dispute resolution process."

Then there is the dilemma that the disclosures created for Kinkade.... [as argued by counsel in his] objection to the AAA:

> [O]nce the disclosure was made the harm was done regardless of the outcome. The disclosure put our clients in the awkward position of either objecting to or appearing to approve the representation by the neutral arbitrator's firm of a party adverse to our client in another arbitration. If we object, we run the risk of offending the neutral; if we don't object, we appear to condone a clear conflict. We should never have been put in this position.

A party who pays a neutral arbitrator to prepare for, and then sit through, nearly 50 days of hearings over a five-year period, deserves better treatment than this.

The district court's judgment is affirmed.

Merit Insurance Co. v. Leatherby Insurance Co.

714 F.2d 673 (7th Cir. 1983)

POSNER, CIRCUIT JUDGE

This appeal ... requires us to decide whether the failure of one of the arbitrators to disclose a prior business relationship with a principal of one of the parties to the arbitration justified the district court ... to set aside the award. Merit Insurance Company made a contract with Leatherby Insurance Company to reinsure claims under certain insurance policies that Leatherby had issued. [Merit sought payment under the contract, a dispute arose, and arbitration ensued.]

The arbitration was conducted under the auspices of the AAA. Each party appointed one arbitrator and together the parties appointed from a list formulated by the AAA the third or "neutral" arbitrator, a Chicago lawyer named Jack Clifford. At the first meeting of the arbitration panel the panel agreed that the other two arbitrators would also be neutrals, rather than representatives of the parties that had appointed them. After an arbitration that lasted three years and produced a hearing transcript of 16,000 pages, the panel on December 1, 1980, unanimously awarded Merit $10,675,000 on its claim. Merit petitioned the district court to confirm the award; Leatherby opposed confirmation on the ground that the arbitrators had been biased, as indicated by certain evidentiary rulings in Merit's favor and by a comment the arbitrator appointed by Merit had made in the course of the proceedings. No charge of bias was leveled against Clifford specifically.

The hearing in the district court brought out the following facts. The chairman of the board of Cosmopolitan had hired Clifford late in 1960 to be head of the claims department. At the same time Stern had been promoted to executive vice-president of the company. As the vice-president in charge of the claims department Clifford reported to Stern. This relationship lasted until the beginning of 1963 when Stern left Cosmopolitan to enter private practice. Clifford left Cosmopolitan shortly afterward. Clifford and Stern both testified that they had little professional contact while at Cosmopolitan and no social contacts then or since. Clifford had been promised substantial autonomy by the chairman of the board when he took over the claims department, and Stern—who had no background in claims evaluation and was preoccupied with corporate acquisitions and other matters unrelated to Clifford's responsibilities—gave Clifford a loose rein. Their principal contact came in meetings held at intervals of several months between Stern and the department heads who reported to him. They also had occasional brief discussions over specific claims; once Clifford was asked to review the claims reserves of an insurance company that Cosmopolitan was thinking of buying; and, on orders from above, Stern once required all of his subordinates, including Clifford, to take lie-detector tests. After Clifford and Stern entered private practice they spoke to each other on the phone on one or two occasions but these contacts were of no significance, and until the arbitration the two men had not met face to face since 1963. Rotheiser, a vice-president of Merit, was also employed at Cosmopolitan during Clifford's tenure, but he was the head of a separate department and according to both his testimony and Clifford's they had no dealings with one another.

In 1975 the AAA had sent Clifford a "panel data sheet" which contained a space headed, "My prior occupational affiliations have been...." All that Clifford listed in this space (having listed private practice as his current occupation) was his job as claims manager for Firemen's Fund American Insurance Companies from 1949 to 1960. Clifford testified that he had not mentioned Cosmopolitan in part because he was not interested in doing the kind of arbitration for which his experience there would have been relevant.... Clifford filled out another panel data sheet at the AAA's request three years later, he again omitted any reference to his work at Cosmopolitan; and when the arbitration began and Clifford recognized Stern and realized that the president of Merit and the former executive vice-president of Cosmopolitan were one and the same, he had said nothing.

Leatherby argues that by failing at each of these junctures to disclose his former relationship with Stern, Clifford violated the ethical norms applicable to arbitrators, and that the only effective sanction for such a violation is to set aside the arbitration award. The panel data sheet that the AAA requires prospective arbitrators to fill out does not indicate that the information sought is for the purpose of determining whether grounds for disqualification exist, so no significance can be attached to Clifford's initial omission of his job history with Cosmopolitan. But section 18 of the

AAA's Commercial Arbitration Rules requires the neutral arbitrator to "disclose to the AAA any circumstances likely to affect his impartiality, including any bias or any financial or personal interest in the result of the arbitration or any past or present relationship with the parties or their counsel." And Canon IIA of the Code of Ethics for Arbitrators in Commercial Disputes (jointly adopted by the AAA and the ABA) requires arbitrators to disclose "any existing or past financial, business, professional, family or social relationships which are likely to affect impartiality or which might reasonably create an appearance of partiality or bias." The requirement of disclosure is a continuing one, so the fact that Clifford's failure to disclose his relationship with Cosmopolitan in his first panel data sheet was innocent could not excuse his later failure to disclose the relationship when he accepted appointment as an arbitrator of the Merit-Leatherby dispute and when he recognized Stern on the first day of the arbitration hearing.

Notwithstanding the broad language of section 18, no one supposes that either the Commercial Arbitration Rules or the Code of Ethics for Arbitrators requires disclosure of every former social or financial relationship with a party or a party's principals. The Code states that its provisions relating to disclosure "are intended to be applied realistically so that the burden of detailed disclosure does not become so great that it is impractical for persons in the business world to be arbitrators, thereby depriving the parties of the services of those who might be best informed and qualified to decide particular types of cases." ... [A]n arbitrator cannot be expected to provide the parties with his complete and unexpurgated business biography, or to disclose interests or relationships which are merely trivial.

There is a tradeoff between impartiality and expertise. The expert adjudicator is more likely than a judge or juror not only to be precommitted to a particular substantive position but to know or have heard of the parties (or if the parties are organizations, their key people). Expertise in an industry is accompanied by exposure, in ways large and small, to those engaged in it. The different weighting of impartiality and expertise in arbitration compared to adjudication is dramatically illustrated by the practice whereby each party appoints one of the arbitrators to be his representative rather than a genuine umpire. No one would dream of having a judicial panel composed of one part-time judge and two representatives of the parties, but that is the standard arbitration panel, the panel Leatherby chose—presumably because it preferred a more expert to a more impartial tribunal—when it wrote an arbitration clause into its reinsurance contract with Merit.

If Leatherby had wanted its dispute with Merit resolved by an Article III judge (to whom it had access under the diversity jurisdiction), it would not have inserted an arbitration clause in the contract, or having done so move for arbitration against Merit's wishes. Leatherby wanted something different from judicial dispute resolution. It wanted dispute resolution by experts in the insurance industry, who were bound to have greater knowledge of the parties, based on previous professional experience, than an Article III judge, or a jury. "The parties to an arbitration choose their method of dispute resolution, and can ask no more impartiality than inheres in the method they have chosen." *American Almond Products Co. v. Consolidated Pecan Sales Co.*, 144 F.2d 448 (2d Cir.1944) (L. Hand, J.).

It is no surprise, therefore, that the standards for disqualification in the Commercial Arbitration Rules and the Code of Ethics for Arbitrators are not so stringent as those in the federal statutes on judges, *see, e.g.,* Canons 2 and 3(C) of the Code of Judicial Conduct for United States Judges and the ABA's Code of Judicial Conduct. (In fact the arbitration rules and code do not contain any standards for disqualification as such, though such standards are implicit in the disclosure requirements of the AAA's Rules and the AAA-ABA Code.) We thus do not agree with Leatherby that the test for disqualification here is whether the former relationship between Stern and Clifford was "trivial" in relation to the subject matter of the arbitration. If it were trivial Clifford would not have had to disqualify himself even if he had been a judge. Interim Advisory Committee on Judicial Activities, Advisory Opinion No. 11 (Jan. 21, 1970) ("It cannot be that [law] firms are precluded from practice before judges simply because members have judges for friends.")....

The test in this case ... is whether, having due regard for the different expectations regarding impartiality that parties bring to arbitration than to litigation, the relationship between Clifford and Stern was so intimate—personally, socially, professionally, or financially—as to cast serious doubt on Clifford's impartiality. Although Stern had been Clifford's supervisor for two years and was a key witness in an arbitration where the stakes to the party of which he was the president and principal shareholder were big, their relationship had ended 14 years before, Clifford had no possible financial stake in the outcome of the arbitration, and his relationship with Stern during their period together at Cosmopolitan had been distant and impersonal. The fact that they had never socialized, either while working for the same company or afterward (though both were practicing law in Chicago all this time), indicates a lack of intimacy. And when a former employee sits in judgment on a former employer there is no presumption that he will be biased in favor of the former employer; he may well be prejudiced against him. The fact that Clifford passed his lie-detector test with flying colors might have made him grateful to Stern, or might have fanned the flames of outrage at having been subjected to such an indignity, or more likely made no difference at all because it happened so long ago. Time cools emotions, whether of gratitude or resentment.

Section 18 of the Commercial Arbitration Rules makes the AAA itself the final arbiter of disqualification once the arbitrator has been appointed, subject only (so far as relevant here) to the limited judicial review allowed by section 10 of the FAA after an arbitration award is made and judicial confirmation of it sought. On the basis of the facts reviewed above, considered in the light of the less stringent standards applicable to disqualification of arbitrators than to disqualification of judges, we doubt that the AAA would have disqualified Clifford—or that Leatherby would have wanted it to.

But even if the failure to disclose was a material violation of the ethical standards applicable to arbitration proceedings, it does not follow that the arbitration award may be nullified judicially. Although we have great respect for the Commercial Arbitration Rules and the Code of Ethics for Arbitrators, they are not the proper starting point for an inquiry into an award's validity under section 10. The arbitration rules and code do not have the force of law. If Leatherby is to get the arbitration award set aside it must bring itself within the statute and the federal rule. The statute specifies limited grounds for setting aside an arbitration award. The only one relevant here is, "Where there was evident partiality or corruption in the arbitrators, or either of them." This is strong language. It makes the grounds for setting aside an arbitrator's award because of bias narrower than the grounds for disqualification in the arbitration rules and code, not to mention the statutes and ethical codes pertaining to judges. Read literally, section 10(b) would require proof of actual bias ("evident partiality"). And not only the arbitrator appointed by Merit, as one might expect, but also the arbitrator appointed by Leatherby—a member of a distinguished Chicago law firm— gave a detailed affidavit denying absolutely and in detail that Clifford had ever evinced any partiality during the three years of the arbitration.

Although it is difficult to extract from the cases more than a mood, the mood is one of reluctance to set aside arbitration awards for failure of the arbitrator to disclose a relationship with a party.... The suggestion in *Tamari v. Bache Halsey Stuart Inc.*, 619 F.2d 1196 (7th Cir. 1980), that "appearance of bias" is a proper standard for disqualification of arbitrators is not inconsistent with anything in our present opinion; it just means that it is unnecessary to demonstrate—what is almost impossible to demonstrate—that the arbitrator had an actual bias. The standard is an objective one, but less exacting than the one governing judges....

[Leatherby] ... would be bound to submit to a new arbitration proceeding if the award were set aside. But in the old proceeding Leatherbys' own arbitrator voted against it. If we may believe that arbitrator's affidavit—and there is no reason not to—he did not regard this as a close case. According to the affidavit, both he and Merit's arbitrator pushed Merit's case harder than Clifford did. We need not decide whether Clifford was bending over backwards to avoid showing partiality toward Merit in view of his former relationship with Stern or whether, as the affidavits and his own testimony suggest, he is of a retiring disposition and had less experience in the subject matter of the arbitration than the other two arbitrators. It is enough to note that rerunning the arbitration before a different panel is unlikely to change the outcome.

We do not want to encourage the losing party to every arbitration to conduct a background investigation of each of the arbitrators in an effort to uncover evidence of a former relationship with the adversary. This would only increase the cost and undermine the finality of arbitration, contrary to the purpose of the FAA of making arbitration a swift, inexpensive, and effective substitute for judicial dispute resolution. This lawsuit is already eight years old. To uphold the district court's vacation of the arbitration award in the absence of evidence of actual or probable partiality or corruption would open a new and, we fear, an interminable chapter in the efforts of people who have chosen arbitration and been disappointed in their choice to get the courts—to which they could have turned in the first instance—... to undo the results of their preferred method of dispute resolution.

b. Comments and Questions

i. The plurality opinion in *Commonwealth* stated that an "arbitrator is required to disclose to the parties any dealings that might create an impression of bias" and suggested that arbitrators should be held to a higher standard of disclosure than judges "[s]ince the arbitrator has nearly free rein to decide the law and facts and is not subject to judicial review." 393 U.S. at 149. The dissent suggested an "actual bias" standard. Concurring only in the result, Justice White argued for a more restrained standard, noting that parties often select arbitrators because of their expertise and connections with industry.

ii. *Appearance of, Reasonable Likelihood, or Actual Bias?* The federal circuits are similarly divided as to the precise test for evident partiality. *See e.g., Scandinavian Reinsurance Co. v. St. Paul Fire & Marine Ins. Co.,* 668 F.3d 60, 78 (2d Cir. 2012) (reasonable person standard); *Positive Software Sols., Inc. v. New Century Mortg. Corp.,* 476 F.3d 278, 281 (5th Cir. 2007) (adopting a "reasonable impression of bias" standard); *Lagstein v. Certain Underwriters at Lloyd's, London,* 607 F.3d 634, 646 (9th Cir. 2010) ("To show 'evident partiality' ... [the party] either must establish specific facts indicating actual bias toward or against a party or show that [the arbitrator] failed to disclose to the parties information that creates '[a] reasonable impression of bias.'); *Trustmark Ins. Co. v. John Hancock Life Ins. Co.,* 631 F.3d 869, 874 (7th Cir. 2011) (narrow but higher than actual bias standard). *See* Seung-Woon Lee, *Arbitrator's Evident Partiality: Current U.S. Standards and Possible Solutions Based on Comparative Reviews,* 9 ARB. L. REV. 159 (2017) (analyzing cases and concluding that "[t]he Fifth Circuit approach is more practical, because failure to disclose a trivial or insubstantial relationship between an arbitrator and related parties does not result in vacatur. This therefore preserves the finality of an arbitral award and discourages the losing party from challenging the arbitral award.").

iii. Is it realistic to require arbitrators to disclose all of their personal and imputed connections with a party? Do parties in arbitration have different expectations? Judge Posner in *Leatherby* asserts that there "is a tradeoff between expertise and impartiality ... [and states that] the test ... is whether, having due regard for the different expectations regarding impartiality that parties bring to arbitration than to litigation, the relationship between [party and arbitrator] was so intimate—personally, socially, professionally, or financially—as to cast serious doubt on [arbitrator's] impartiality."

iv. *Can disclosures alone cure conflicts? In Thomas Kinkade Co. v. White,* 711 F.3d 719 (6th Cir. 2013), five years into the arbitration proceeding, the arbitrator disclosed the financial ties between his firm and the other parties and arbitrators (and the AAA refused to disqualify), as if transparency alone made him neutral. The claimant objected, but the AAA denied the request to disqualify the arbitrator. The Sixth Circuit found evident partiality, stating that the arbitrator's mid-arbitration disclosures posed a dilemma: as soon as the disclosure was made, "the harm was done" because the disclosure placed [other party] in a lose-lose situation. "If [he] object[s], [he] run[s] the risk of offending the neutral; if [he doesn't] object, [he] appear[s] to condone a clear conflict." If a conflict of interest, actual or imputed, develops well into the arbitration, is disqualification proper? In a lawyer ethics context, disclosure and withdrawal is required, Model Rule of Prof'l Conduct 1.7, but does (or should) the same outcome apply to arbitrators?

v. *Sour Grapes or Bias?* In thinking about the standards for vacating arbitration awards, understand the context in which the "evident partiality" issue usually arises. After an arbitration award, particularly a large-dollar-amount award, the angry losing party will want to have the award judicially vacated. Substantive or procedural errors by the arbitrators will only rarely provide a basis for vacating (or modifying) an award— so arbitrator bias may be the only theory available to the losing party. Because arbitrators commonly are selected for their subject-matter and industry expertise, credible conflict-of-interest arguments are easier to make against arbitrators than judges. Even when a claim of bias appears impressive, one would need to be naive or gullible not to suspect that the claimants' real concern is the award rather than the neutrality of the arbitrator(s).

vi. *Due Diligence.* In this age of technology, parties have access to more information than ever before. Following an unsuccessful arbitration, the losing party can investigate—or hire someone to investigate—public documents, social media, and other information to create a colorable claim of "evident partiality." When should such an investigation take place? In *Goldman, Sachs & Co. v. Athena Venture Partners, L.P.*, 803 F.3d 144 (3d Cir. 2015), the Third Circuit refused to vacate a FINRA award on the basis of evident partiality when the losing party brought forth evidence that an arbitrator failed to disclose the circumstances surrounding his recent disbarment. The court reasoned that the parties could have discovered this information before the arbitrators issued a final award. The Third Circuit held: "[I]f a party could have reasonably discovered that any type of malfeasance, ranging from conflicts-of-interest to non-disclosures such as those at issue here, was afoot during the hearings, it should be precluded from challenging the subsequent award on those grounds." *Id.* at 149.

vii. The UAA and RUAA also use the term "evident partiality" as a legal basis for vacating an arbitration award for improper bias. Evident partiality or bias may be found by an arbitrator's material failure to disclose a relationship with a party, or by proof of actual bias. A similar due diligence requirement applies; a party challenging an arbitrator's undisclosed relationships must demonstrate that it could not have known of or discovered the relationship "just as easily before or during the arbitration rather than after it lost the case." *Lagstein*, 607 F.3d at 646 (9th Cir. 2010) ("We decline to create a rule that encourages losing parties to challenge arbitration awards on the basis of pre-existing, publicly available background information on the arbitrator[ ] that has nothing to do with the parties to the arbitration.").

3. Misconduct in the Proceedings: Refusing to Postpone Hearing or to Hear Evidence, or Prejudicing Rights

A statutory basis for vacating an arbitration award is where the arbitrators were "[g]uilty of misconduct in refusing to postpone the hearing, upon sufficient cause shown, or in refusing to hear evidence pertinent or material to the controversy; or any other behavior by which the rights of a party have been prejudiced." FAA § 10(a)(3); *see also* RUAA § 23(a)(3). To warrant vacatur on the grounds of arbitrator misconduct, the challenged conduct must amount to a denial of fundamental fairness in the arbitration proceeding. How is that standard met, given the significant deference to arbitral powers?

a. Evidentiary Matters

Evidentiary issues arise infrequently because the exclusionary rules of evidence do not strictly apply in arbitration proceedings (unless the parties expressly provide otherwise). All probative evidence, notably including hearsay evidence, must be admitted. An arbitrator can be reversed for failing to hear material evidence, but not for hearing evidence that lacks probative value. The behavioral response of arbitrators is entirely predictable: everything is admitted into evidence, with all doubts going to the weight to be given to the evidence. The major check on a record filled with non-material or duplicative evidence is that the time of the parties and counsel has value, along with the fear of alienating a capable arbitrator.

Tempo Shain Corp. v. Bertek, Inc.

120 F.3d 16 (2d Cir. 1997)

PARKER, CIRCUIT JUDGE

Neptune Corporation ("Neptune"), an affiliate of Tempo Shain, entered into an agreement with Bertek, Inc. ("Bertek") to purchase a license agreement from Gelman Sciences ("Gelman") for a patented process to treat materials to enhance their repellency characteristics. Under the agreement, Bertek was to manufacture the treated material, which Neptune intended to sell to the apparel and footwear industries. Disagreements arose and the parties entered arbitration to resolve claims brought by Neptune against Bertek for fraudulent inducement to contract and breach of contract. Bertek counterclaimed with its own fraudulent inducement and breach of contract charges.

Bertek intended to call Wayne Pollock, former President of Bertek's Laminated Products Division, as a witness to provide what Bertek considered to be crucial testimony concerning the negotiations and dealings between the parties about which it claims only Pollock could testify. Pollock became temporarily unavailable to testify, however, after his wife was diagnosed with a recurrence of cancer. The arbitration panel was advised that Pollock remained willing to testify, but that the expected duration of his unavailability was indeterminate. Bertek urged the panel to keep the record open until Pollock could testify either in person or by deposition.

After deliberation, the panel concluded the hearings without waiting for Pollock's testimony. The arbitrators stated: "We as arbitrators have to decide does Mr. Pollock have any information that if he was here in person and you fellows are banging him with questions that some new information comes out that we haven't heard or is it going to be a rehash of what we've heard from other witnesses." The panel subsequently rendered an award in favor of Tempo Shain and Neptune, and denied Bertek's counterclaims. Appellees [sought confirmation of the award]; Bertek cross-moved to vacate the award, arguing that the arbitrators were guilty of misconduct pursuant to FAA, § 10(a)(3).... Bertek filed ... papers, which included an affidavit from Pollock stating what he would have testified to, if permitted. The district court granted the petition to confirm the arbitration award and denied the motion to vacate....

The question on appeal is whether the panel's refusal to continue the hearings to allow Pollock to testify amounts to fundamental unfairness and misconduct sufficient to vacate the arbitration award pursuant to section 10(a)(3) of the FAA. We believe that it did, and therefore vacate the courts' endorsement of the award....

The district court was correct that arbitration panel determinations are generally accorded great deference under the FAA. Judicial review of arbitration awards is necessarily narrowly limited. Undue judicial intervention would inevitably judicialize the arbitration process, thus defeating the objective of providing an alternative to judicial dispute resolution.

Courts have interpreted section 10(a)(3) to mean that except where fundamental fairness is violated, arbitration determinations will not be opened up to evidentiary review. In making evidentiary determinations, an arbitrator "need not follow all the niceties observed by the federal courts." However, although not required to hear all the evidence proffered by a party, an arbitrator "must give each of the parties to the dispute an adequate opportunity to present its evidence and argument." "Federal courts do not superintend arbitration proceedings. Our review is restricted to determining whether the procedure was fundamentally unfair."

We find that there was no reasonable basis for the arbitration panel to determine that Pollock's omitted testimony would be cumulative with regard to the fraudulent inducement claims. Said differently, the panel excluded evidence plainly "pertinent and material to the controversy." The panel did not indicate in what respects Pollock's testimony would be cumulative, but stated that there were "a number of letters in the file" and that Pollock was "speaking through the letters [he wrote], and the reports he received." These letters and reports were not specifically identified by the arbitration panel. However, after a review of the record, it appears that the letters are correspondence between Pollock and Neptune's President, Robin Delaney, which the panel dubbed the "fight letters," and the reports are certain progress and accounting reports which were the basis for many of these fight letters. These so-called fight letters and reports are not at all representative of what Pollock's testimony would likely have been in connection with the fraudulent inducement allegations. The fight letters arose from individual problems that were ongoing at the time, and did not devolve into recriminations about earlier representations. Their focus was not on the inducement to enter the contracts—rather, they were attempts to solve problems which were giving rise to disputes. As Delaney explained, the parties were trying "to keep the relationship going." The reports, like the letters, addressed discrete problems and possible courses of action. While the letters and reports might have been sufficient to represent what Pollock would have testified to in rebuttal of Neptune's breach of contract claims, which we do not decide, there is nothing to suggest that Pollock's intended testimony concerning appellees' fraudulent inducement claim and Bertek's counterclaim for fraudulent inducement was addressed by the documents admitted into evidence.

Because Bertek's alleged misrepresentations were not documented, appellees' unsupported oral testimony concerning such representations was unrebutted because Pollock, who allegedly made the representations on Bertek's behalf, was not allowed to testify, and he is the only person who could have done so. As for Bertek's counterclaim for fraudulent inducement, Bertek contends, and there was no evidence to the contrary before the arbitration panel, that Pollock was the only individual involved in the negotiation of the contract with Neptune on Bertek's behalf. Pollock was identified several times throughout the testimony as Bertek's exclusive point-man in the negotiations. Neptune's Robin Delaney admitted this in her testimony. When asked to describe who was involved in the negotiations on each side, she responded: "Mainly it was just Wayne Pollock and myself and our attorneys." ...

On the facts of this case, the panel's refusal to continue the hearings to allow Pollock to testify amounts to fundamental unfairness and misconduct sufficient to vacate the award pursuant to section 10(a)(3) of the FAA. For the reasons stated above, we vacate the district court's endorsement of the arbitration award and remand for further proceeding consistent with this opinion.

b. Comments and Questions

i. *Bertek* is a rare example of an arbitration award vacated for failure to grant a postponement to hear the evidence of an important witness. Do you have a sense of why the court of appeals vacated the arbitration award? The court tells us that Pollock was unavailable because his wife was quite sick, and that he "remained willing to testify, but that the expected duration of his unavailability was indeterminate." Neither courts nor arbitrators normally are receptive to this sort of open-ended delay. Recall that FAA § 7 empowers arbitrators with subpoena authority to summon third-party witnesses to testify before them.

ii. Why not place the burden on Bertek to get the evidence of its witness before the arbitration panel in some form — and at its expense? Does modern technology, not to mention ancient technology like the telephone, offer an array of practical solutions?

iii. *Judicial Remand to Arbitral Panel.* The *Bertek* court concluded that the Panel's failure to hear Pollock's testimony "amounted to fundamental unfairness and misconduct sufficient to vacate the award pursuant to section 10(a)(3) of the FAA." The court vacated the order confirming the arbitration award and remanded the matter to the original panel for it to consider the effect of Mr. Pollock's testimony both on the fraudulent inducement claims and the case as a whole. The FAA provides that in the event that an arbitration award is vacated, "the court may, in its discretion, direct a rehearing by the arbitrators." 9 U.S.C. § 10(b). Although not explicit in the FAA, it is within this Court's discretion to remand a matter to the same arbitration panel or a new one. Indeed, as the lower court held in *Bertek*, "a court's power to vacate an award because of an arbitrator's failure to address a crucial issue necessarily includes a lesser power to remand the case to the same arbitrator for a determination of that issue." *Tempo Shain Corp. v. Bertek, Inc.*, 1997 U.S. Dist. LEXIS 14153 (S.D.N.Y. 1997). Was the misconduct identified by the Court of Appeals of the type or order of magnitude that would require a new panel to hear the entire case again?

4. Exceeding Authority

Arbitration awards may be set aside "[w]here the arbitrators exceeded their powers, or so imperfectly executed them that a mutual, final, and definite award upon the subject matter submitted was not made." FAA § 10(a)(4). Recall that an arbitrator's power is derived from the arbitration agreement. Thus, the inquiry in determining whether an arbitrator exceeded his powers "focuses on whether the arbitrators had the power, based on the parties' submissions or the arbitration agreement, to reach a certain issue, not whether the arbitrators correctly decided the issue." *Westerbeke Corp. v. Daihatsu Motor Co.*, 304 F.3d 200 (2d Cir. 2002). As noted above, "exceeded powers" has been the most cited ground in vacatur filings. *See* Mills & Brewer, *"Exceeded Powers': Exploring Recent Trends in Cases Challenging Tribunal Authority*, 31 Alts. to High Cost Litig. 113 (2013). How might arbitrators "exceed their powers"?

Cooper v. WestEnd Capital Management, L.L.C.
832 F.3d 534 (5th Cir. 2016)

CARL E. STEWART, Chief Judge:

Plaintiff-Appellant Sean Cooper challenges the district court's orders ... confirming an award in favor of WestEnd Capital Management, L.L.C. ("WestEnd"), George Bolton Holdings, L.L.C. ("Bolton"), and Robert Ozag (together, the "WestEnd Parties"). We AFFIRM.

I.

On September 15, 2009, Bolton, Ozag, and Cooper entered into the "First Amended and Restated Operating Agreement" (the "Operating Agreement") for WestEnd as its members and managers. The Operating Agreement allows for the expulsion of a manager from WestEnd upon the unanimous consent of the other managers if the expulsion is for cause. Further, the Operating Agreement requires the parties to submit all disputes to binding arbitration.

On August 3, 2012, George Bolton informed Cooper that Ozag and Bolton had voted to expel him from WestEnd for, *inter alia*, misappropriating WestEnd's assets, breaching various fiduciary duties, and instructing WestEnd employees to impede an SEC investigation. Bolton also informed Cooper that he was banned from WestEnd's business premises under penalty of arrest.... WestEnd commenced arbitration.... JAMS ultimately appointed a retired California state court judge, Judge William Cahill (the "Arbitrator"), to serve as arbitrator.

Over the course of arbitration, Cooper [*expelled party*] discovered a relationship between George Bolton and John Bates, a JAMS arbitrator who was not involved in the WestEnd arbitration proceedings. After discovering this relationship, Cooper requested that JAMS make additional disclosures regarding whether any JAMS mediators or arbitrators had social or business connections to any of the WestEnd Parties. In response, JAMS explained that it had already made all necessary disclosures. Ultimately, the Arbitrator ruled against Cooper and in favor of the WestEnd Parties. In the final arbitration award, the Arbitrator found Cooper liable to Bolton for $346,247.28, to Ozag for $940,140.57, and to WestEnd for $130,166.64, and also awarded attorney's fees, interest, and costs.

The parties then returned to the district court, where the WestEnd Parties moved to confirm the arbitration award. Cooper opposed this motion and argued that the award should be vacated because JAMS failed to make necessary disclosures and because the Arbitrator exceeded his powers in making awards to Ozag and Bolton. The district court confirmed the award in favor of the WestEnd Parties. Cooper now appeals the district court's orders refusing to enjoin arbitration and confirming the award....

III.

The FAA reflects a national policy favoring arbitration. *See Hall St. Assocs., L.L.C. v. Mattel, Inc.*, 552 U.S. 576 (2008). "In light of the strong federal policy favoring arbitration, judicial review of an arbitration award is extraordinarily narrow." Though the district court's confirmation of an award is reviewed de novo, "the review of the underlying award is exceedingly deferential."

Under the FAA, the court "must" confirm an award unless the award is vacated under Section 10 or modified or corrected under Section 11. Section 10 provides the exclusive grounds for vacatur of an arbitration award. An award may be vacated: (1) "where the award was procured by corruption, fraud, or undue means"; (2) "where there was evident partiality or corruption in the arbitrators"; (3) "where the arbitrators were guilty of misconduct ... or of any other misbehavior by which the rights of any party have been prejudiced"; or (4) "where the arbitrators exceeded their powers, or so imperfectly executed them that a mutual, final, and definite award upon the subject matter submitted was not made." 9 U.S.C. § 10(a). The burden of proof is on the party seeking to vacate the award, and any doubts or uncertainties must be resolved in favor of upholding it....

B.

Cooper contends that the award should be vacated because JAMS and the Arbitrator failed to make certain disclosures. Under the FAA, courts may vacate an arbitration award "where there was evident partiality or corruption in the arbitrators." Evident partiality is "a stern standard." *Positive Software Sols., Inc. v. New Century Mortg. Corp.*, 476 F.3d 278 (5th Cir. 2007). "The statutory language ... seems to require upholding arbitral awards unless bias was clearly evident in the decisionmakers." Thus, for the arbitration award to be vacated, Cooper "must produce specific facts from which a reasonable person would have to conclude that the arbitrator was partial to" the WestEnd Parties. The "alleged partiality [must be] direct, definite, and capable of demonstration rather than remote, uncertain, or speculative."

Not in the case   another arbitrator

Cooper points to no specific facts that lead to the conclusion that the Arbitrator was biased in the WestEnd Parties' favor. Instead, Cooper argues that JAMS was required to make disclosures about Bates even though he was not assigned to the case. Here, the Arbitrator explicitly stated that he and Bates had never discussed this arbitration and that Bates did not know the Arbitrator was even at this hearing. In fact, there is no evidence that Bates had any relationship with the Arbitrator other than the fact that both serve as JAMS arbitrators. Most importantly, Cooper points to nothing in the record that would indicate that the Arbitrator had any prejudice against him. At best, Cooper's general allegations of partiality are "remote, uncertain, or speculative."

C.

Cooper's final argument is that the Arbitrator exceeded his powers in making the award. Section 10(a)(4) of the FAA "authorizes a federal court to set aside an arbitral award 'where the arbitrator[ ] exceeded [his] powers.'" *Oxford Health Plans LLC v. Sutter*, 133 S.Ct. 2064 (2013). "We will sustain an arbitration award as long as the arbitrator's decision 'draws its essence' from the contract—even if we disagree with the arbitrator's interpretation of the contract." *Timegate Studios, Inc. v. Southpeak Interactive, L.L.C.*, 713 F.3d 797 (5th Cir. 2013). "The question is whether the arbitrator's award was so unfounded in reason and fact, so unconnected with the wording and purpose of the [contract] as to manifest an infidelity to the obligation of an arbitrator." "[A]n arbitrator has not exceeded his powers unless he has utterly contorted the evident purpose and intent of the parties—the 'essence' of the contract. The party challenging an arbitrator's award under § 10(a)(4) "bears a heavy burden." * * *

Cooper next argues that the Arbitrator's award to Ozag requires vacatur because the claim was based solely on a 2007 agreement that was not subject to arbitration, i.e., the claim was not arbitrable. We first consider if the Arbitrator "properly determined the initial question of arbitrability, i.e., whether the claim is within the parties' agreement to arbitrate." "Preliminary issues in arbitration cases include gateway disputes, which typically require judicial determination, and procedural questions, which are to be reviewed by the arbitrator." Though "the arbitrability of disputes … is generally a gateway issue to be determined by the courts," it is instead "deferred to arbitration where the agreement espouses the parties' intent to do so."

Here, Cooper and the WestEnd Parties expressly adopted the JAMS Rules in the Operating Agreement. The JAMS Rules provide, in relevant part, that "[j]urisdictional and arbitrability disputes, including disputes over the formation, existence, validity, interpretation or scope of the agreement under which Arbitration is sought, and who are proper Parties to the Arbitration, shall be submitted to and ruled on by the Arbitrator. The Arbitrator has the authority to determine jurisdiction and arbitrability issues as a preliminary matter." "[T]he express adoption of these rules presents clear and unmistakable evidence that the parties agreed to arbitrate arbitrability." *Petrofac, Inc.*, 687 F.3d at 675 (concluding that express adoption of AAA arbitration rules showed parties' intent to arbitrate arbitrability). The Arbitrator did not exceed his powers in making this award.

An arbitration award "may not be set aside for a mere mistake of fact or law." Even assuming the Arbitrator erred in applying the statute of limitations (which is certainly not clear from the record), that "mere mistake" would not justify vacatur. *See also Oxford Health Plans*, ("It is not enough … to show that the [arbitrator] committed an error—or even a serious error." "The risk that arbitrators may construe the governing law imperfectly in the course of delivering a decision that attempts in good faith to interpret the relevant law … is a risk that every party to arbitration assumes." Such legal errors "lie far outside the category of conduct embraced by § 10(a)(4)." The judgment of the district court is AFFIRMED.

Raymond James Financial Services, Inc. v. Fenyk
780 F.3d 59 (1st Cir. 2015)

LIPEZ, Circuit Judge.

An arbitration panel awarded appellant Robert Fenyk $600,000 in back pay based on a claim that he was unlawfully terminated from his job as a stock broker because he is an alcoholic. The district court vacated the award, concluding that the arbitrators lacked authority to grant that remedy because Fenyk brought no claims under the state law the arbitrators applied. Fenyk now seeks reinstatement of the award, arguing that the district court failed to give due deference to the arbitrators' ruling.

We reverse the district court's judgment. Although the arbitration decision may have been incorrect as a matter of law, it was not beyond the scope of the panel's authority.

I.

A. Factual Background

Appellant Fenyk was associated with appellee Raymond James Financial Services ("RJFS") as a securities broker for more than seven years, first in New York City and then, beginning in October 2004, in Vermont. Fenyk managed his own small branch office in Vermont and was designated an independent contractor for RJFS under his agreement with the company. RJFS is based in Florida, and the "Independent Sales Associate Agreement" that Fenyk signed contained a provision stating that Florida law would govern disputes between the parties. Fenyk also signed RJFS's Business Ethics Policy, in which he agreed to arbitrate any conflicts "arising out of the independent contractor relationship."

In May 2009, during a routine check of Fenyk's customer communications, an RJFS reviewer noticed an email to a client, Fenyk's former domestic partner, suggesting that Fenyk had an alcohol problem. The email began with information about the client's account, but went on to note Fenyk's "slip" and his "need [for] meetings and real sobriety for a dialoug [sic] with you." The email also reported that Fenyk's "new AA friend was very hard on [him] last night."

The reviewer alerted Fenyk's RJFS supervisors in Florida to the email. On May 27, Thomas Harrington, regional director for the Northeast, and John Tholen, the assistant regional director, called Fenyk and told him they were no longer comfortable supervising him from afar and his contract would be terminated in thirty days....

Approximately two years later, in June 2011, Fenyk filed a complaint in Vermont state court alleging that he had been fired on account of his sexual orientation and his status as a recovering alcoholic, in violation of Vermont's Fair Employment Practices Act ("VFEPA"). Once alerted by RJFS of his obligation to arbitrate employment disputes, Fenyk dismissed the complaint and brought an arbitration proceeding before the Financial Industry Regulatory Authority ("FINRA"). His FINRA Statement of Claim reiterated the same two causes of action asserted in his court complaint: retaliation based on sexual orientation and disability, in violation of Vermont law. Fenyk sought $665,000 in back pay, $588,000 in front pay, and $250,000 in punitive damages, along with attorney's fees and costs....

A hearing was held before a panel of three arbitrators in January 2013. On the opening day, Fenyk asked to amend his complaint to add a claim under the Americans with Disabilities Act, 42 U.S.C. §§ 12111–12117, noting that the federal law "mirrors" the Vermont and Florida employment discrimination statutes and that, hence, there would be no prejudice to the defense. Counsel for RJFS objected to the proposed amendment as untimely, stating that she had "responded to the claims that have been proffered." She further noted that Fenyk had not, in fact, alleged discrimination per se, but had only asserted claims for retaliation. Fenyk did not at that time propose to add claims under Florida law.

The panel proceeded without deciding whether to accept Fenyk's proposed amendment and, following the four-day hearing, Fenyk again ... urged the panel, inter alia, to grant his motion to amend his Statement of Claim to add claims under federal, New York and Florida law.

B. Arbitration Ruling

In March 2013, the arbitration panel denied Fenyk's motion to amend his Statement of Claim, finding that the request was untimely and there were "no special circumstances alleged to justify such relief." At the same time, however, the panel granted what it described as a request from both parties that Florida law be applied to the proceedings.

The arbitrators announced their ruling on the merits in late April 2013, issuing only a brief statement of their conclusions. *See Zayas v. Bacardi Corp.,* 524 F.3d 65, 70 (1st Cir.2008) ("Although arbitrators frequently elect to explain their decisions in written opinions, they are under no compulsion to do so."). We reproduce here the complete "Award" section of their decision.

After considering the pleadings, the testimony and evidence presented at the hearing, and the post-hearing submissions, the Panel has decided in full and final resolution of the issues submitted for determination as follows:

1. Respondent is liable for and shall pay to Claimant compensatory damages in the amount of $600,000.00 for back pay on his claim of discrimination based on disability.

2. Respondent is liable for and shall pay to Claimant attorneys' fees in the amount of \$33,627.50 plus litigation expenses in the amount of \$2,414.53 pursuant to paragraph 22(b) of the contract between the parties and §760.11(5) of the Florida Civil Rights Act.

3. Any other relief sought under Claimant's claims of statutory discrimination [ ] is denied.

4. Any and all relief not specifically addressed herein, including punitive damages, is denied.

The panel also assessed RJFS roughly \$20,000 in arbitration fees.

C. District Court Ruling

RJFS moved in federal court to vacate the arbitration award on the ground that the arbitrators had exceeded their powers by, inter alia, awarding damages on a claim—violation of the Florida Civil Rights Act ("FCRA")—"that Fenyk never submitted to them for their review." The district court agreed with RJFS that the award was unsupportable. The court noted that the arbitration panel had determined that Florida law applied, but nonetheless had ignored Florida's one-year statute of limitations for civil rights claims "and somehow construed Florida law to find a violation of a Vermont statute—a statute which, given the governing law, was wholly inapplicable to the case." The court then concluded: "Awarding damages to a plaintiff who has pled no claims under the applicable law plainly transgressed the limits of the arbitrators' power. For this reason, the award must be vacated." This appeal by Fenyk followed.

He argues that the district court erred in construing the Florida statute of limitations to bar his claim and improperly failed to defer to the arbitrators' "good faith effort" to resolve the dispute. In response, RJFS reiterates the two primary flaws it has consistently identified in the arbitration decision: (1) the panel awarded damages despite its finding that Florida law applied and Fenyk brought no claims under Florida law; and (2) even assuming Fenyk's claims may be analyzed as alleged violations of Florida law, such claims fail as time-barred under the one-year statute of limitations for initiating a complaint under Florida's anti-discrimination law.

II.

A. Legal Principles

A district court's decision to vacate or confirm an arbitration award is subject to plenary review. However, our evaluation of an arbitrator's ruling "is extremely narrow and exceedingly deferential," and is indeed "among the narrowest known in the law,". To obtain vacatur of an arbitration award, "[i]t is not enough for [a party] to show that the panel committed an error—or even a serious error." *Stolt-Nielsen S.A. v. AnimalFeeds Int'l Corp.,* 559 U.S. 662, 671 (2010).

Rather, an arbitration ruling ordinarily is unenforceable only if it imposes the arbitrators' "own view of sound policy" instead of adhering to the agreement that governs the parties' relationship. *Stolt-Nielsen, Id.* at 672 (noting that arbitration rulings are vulnerable when the arbitrator "strays from interpretation and application of the agreement and effectively dispense[s] his own brand of industrial justice."

As we previously have noted, however, "[t]he limited scope of our review ... is not equivalent to granting limitless power to the arbitrator." The Federal Arbitration Act ("FAA") specifies a number of grounds that would support an order vacating an award, including fraud, bias, and prejudicial misbehavior. *See* 9 U.S.C. § 10(a)(1)(2)(3). Perhaps the most common basis—and the rationale invoked by the district court in this case—is "where the arbitrators exceeded their powers." *Id.* § 10(a)(4). * * *

B. Whether the Award Exceeds the Arbitrators' Authority

The district court identified two problems with the arbitration panel's decision: (1) its disregard of Florida's statute of limitations, and (2) the award of damages despite Fenyk's failure to bring any claims under Florida law—the law that everyone now agrees governs his dispute with RJFS. We consider each issue in turn.

1. Statute of Limitations

RJFS argues that Fenyk's claims, brought two years after his contract was terminated, were barred by Florida's statute of limitations for civil rights actions. The company asserts that Fenyk alleged claims under Vermont law—which has a longer limitations period—in an attempt to circumvent the Florida time-bar. That attempt necessarily fails, the company maintains, because Florida law governs the controversy.

Given the arbitration panel's determination that Florida law applies to Fenyk's claims, we agree that Florida's statute of limitations governs. That judgment does not help RJFS. At the time of the arbitration panel's decision, Florida law on the applicability of statutory limitations periods to arbitrations was evolving. Two weeks *after* the panel's April 2013 ruling in this case, the Florida Supreme Court held that a general statute of limitations provision applicable to most state law civil actions also applies to arbitration proceedings.

Given the legal uncertainty reflected in the certified question presented to the Florida Supreme Court, and the fact that even "serious error" by arbitrators will not invalidate their award, any error by the panel in refusing to dismiss Fenyk's claims as untimely does not rise to the level necessary to justify vacatur.

2. The Absence of Claims under Florida Law

The panel's award of damages based on Florida law, despite its denial of Fenyk's request to amend his Statement of Claim to include a claim under the FCRA, troubled the district court. We understand its discomfort. Yet we cannot conclude, in the particular circumstances of this case, that the arbitrators' decision to impose liability on RJFS under Florida law "willfully flouted the governing law" or otherwise exceeded the bounds of the arbitrators' authority to resolve the parties' dispute. *Stolt-Nielsen.* The reliance on Florida law would be a different matter if the pertinent statutes in Florida and Vermont materially diverged. RJFS acknowledged in its post-hearing brief, however, that the two states' anti-discrimination laws are substantially equivalent in covering disability discrimination. Moreover, not knowing how the arbitrators would treat Fenyk's inappropriate Vermont claims, the company prudently explained in its pre-hearing brief the reasons why it believed Fenyk's claims failed under both Florida and Vermont law. RJFS also noted in that filing the similarities between the two laws and their mutual reliance on federal precedents.

To the extent there are differences in the two states' laws, the arbitrators' decision to apply Florida law—the approach RJFS has demanded throughout the proceedings—protects the company from obligations at odds with those encompassed by the arbitral agreement. Although a shorter statute of limitations in Florida was a potentially crucial difference from Vermont law that favored RJFS, the panel applied the law that RJFS insisted be used and still made a determination adverse to the company. We already have explained why we may not dislodge that determination. Briefly stated, the arbitrators were empowered to resolve claims of employment discrimination against RJFS under Florida law, and that is what they did.

One might reasonably argue that the panel's decision to grant Fenyk a remedy under Florida law is incompatible with its denial of Fenyk's request to amend his arbitration complaint to include claims under the FCRA and, for that reason, was improper. In effect, the panel did what it told Fenyk it would not do: view his allegations of discrimination through the lens of Florida statutory law. Though the panel's unexplained reliance on the FCRA leaves us perplexed, and may have been erroneous, it does not render the award unsustainable. Importantly, the panel had the authority to allow the addition of Florida claims. *See* FINRA Rule 13309(b) (stating panel's authority to grant a motion to amend). As the principles governing arbitration awards recited above make clear, the question before us is not whether the arbitrators made the *correct* decision when they gave Fenyk a remedy under Florida law, but whether their decision was authorized by the parties' agreement. In the final analysis, the panel apparently decided that Fenyk's mistake in labeling his claims did not justify denying him relief. Where the arbitrators applied the substantive law that RJFS agreed would govern its conduct, that choice to apply Florida law falls within the category of judgments—even if erroneous—that we may not disturb.

III.

In opting for arbitration as its preferred mechanism for resolving employment disputes, RJFS "trade[d] the procedures and opportunity for review of the courtroom for the simplicity, informality, and expedition of arbitration." Barring exceptions inapplicable here, our limited review of arbitral decisions requires us to uphold an award, regardless of its legal or factual correctness, if it "'draw[s] its essence from the contract' that underlies the arbitration proceeding." For the reasons we have explained, the panel's ruling satisfies that standard. Accordingly, we reverse the decision of the district court and remand the case for entry of an order confirming the arbitration award.

a. Comments and Questions

i. In a claim alleging exceeding authority in a labor arbitration decision, *Major League Baseball Players Ass'n v. Garvey*, 532 U.S. 504 (2001), the Supreme Court stated that "[c]ourts are not authorized to review the arbitrator's decision on the merits despite allegations that the decision rests on factual errors or misinterprets the parties' agreement."

The Supreme Court re-emphasized this deferential standard, provided the arbitrator acts within the scope of the submission in *Oxford Health Plans v. Sutter*, 569 U.S. ___,133 S. Ct. 2064 (2013). In *Oxford*, a health insurance company sought to vacate an arbitrator's award authorizing class arbitration of a dispute regarding the company's alleged failure to make prompt and accurate reimbursement payments to physicians. Class arbitration is covered in **Chapter 10**, but note that in *Stolt-Nielsen S.A. v. AnimalFeeds International Corp.*, 559 U.S. 662 (2010), the Supreme Court had held that an arbitrator exceeded his powers in ordering class arbitration where there was no contractual basis for concluding that the parties agreed to class arbitration. In *Oxford*, the Court held that the arbitrator who ordered class arbitration based on his contractual interpretation, despite contractual silence on the issue, did not necessarily "exceed [his] powers" under FAA § 10(a)(4). *Oxford* noted that the parties agreed that the arbitrator should decide whether their contract authorized class arbitration. The Court stated:

> A party seeking relief under [§ 10(a)(4)] bears a heavy burden. It is not enough ... to show that the [arbitrator] committed an error — or even a serious error." Because the parties "bargained for the arbitrator's construction of their agreement," an arbitral decision "even arguably construing or applying the contract" must stand, regardless of a court's view of its (de)merits. Only if "the arbitrator act[s] outside the scope of his contractually delegated authority" — issuing an award that "simply reflect[s] [his] own notions of [economic] justice" rather than "draw[ing] its essence from the contract" — may a court overturn his determination. So the sole question for us is whether the arbitrator (even arguably) interpreted the parties' contract, not whether he got its meaning right or wrong. *Oxford Health*, 133 S.Ct. at 2068.

ii. Notice from *Cooper* how the "gateway" determination of arbitrability can insulate an award from an "exceeding powers" challenge. *See also Three S Del., Inc. v. DataQuick Info. Sys., Inc.*, 492 F.3d 520, 531 (4th Cir. 2007) ("In evaluating whether an arbitrator has exceeded his power, ... any doubts concerning the scope of arbitrable issues as well as any doubts concerning the scope of the arbitrators' remedial authority are to be resolved in favor of the arbitrators' authority as a matter of federal law and policy."). Only when an arbitrator "strays from interpretation and application of the agreement and effectively dispenses his own brand of industrial justice, ... an arbitration decision may be vacated ... on the ground that the arbitrator exceeded his powers." *MLB v. Garvey*, 532 at 509.

iii. Is legal error on the face of an arbitral award grounds for vacating an award? *See Broom v. Morgan Stanley DW, Inc.*, 236 P.3d 182 (Wash. 2010) (determining that an arbitrator's application of the state statute of limitations barring claims constituted legal error, and citing facial legal error as part of exceeding authority). However, the mere misconstruction of a contract or agreement is insufficient. *See Miller v. Prudential*

Bache Sec., Inc., 884 F.2d 128, 130 (4th Cir. 1989). The "sole question" for the court in evaluating whether an arbitrator exceeded his powers is "whether the arbitrator (even arguably) interpreted the parties' contract, not whether he got its meaning right or wrong." *Oxford Health Plans LLC v. Sutter*, 133 S. Ct. at 2068.

iv. In *Stark v. Sandberg, Phoenix & von Gontard, P.C.*, 381 F.3d 793 (8th Cir. 2004), the defendant's vacatur motion argued that the arbitrator exceeded his powers and acted in manifest disregard of the law in awarding punitive damages. What is the difference, if at all, between the statutory standard of exceeding powers and the non-statutory standard of manifest disregard? To many courts, manifest disregard of law is a form of "exceeding authority." "Exceeding authority" also resurfaces as a potential way to get around the restrictions announced in *Hall Street*. Consider these questions in reading **Section F**, *infra*.

F. Contract-Based Standards for Judicial Review

As businesses increasingly use arbitration to resolve high-dollar-value business disputes that involve complex factual and legal issues, many also desire to protect against arbitral awards that are based upon erroneous interpretations or applications of the facts or law, or that are just outright egregious. As a safeguard against arbitral error, some parties to arbitration contracts have included provisions that purport to limit the arbitrator's powers to rule in accordance with the law or that provide for judicial review for an arbitrator's legal error.

May the parties to an arbitration agreement provide for more expansive standards of review than those found in the FAA (or UAA)? In *Hall Street Assocs., L.L.C. v. Mattel, Inc.*, 552 U.S. 576 (2008), such question came squarely before the U.S. Supreme Court.

Hall Street Associates, L.L.C. v. Mattel, Inc.
552 U.S. 576 (2008)

JUSTICE SOUTER delivered the opinion of the Court.

The FAA provides for expedited judicial review to confirm, vacate, or modify arbitration awards. §§ 9–11. The question here is whether statutory grounds for prompt vacatur and modification may be supplemented by contract. We hold that the statutory grounds are exclusive.

This case began as a lease dispute between landlord, petitioner Hall Street and tenant, respondent Mattel. The property was used for many years as a manufacturing site, and the leases provided that the tenant would indemnify the landlord for any costs resulting from the failure of the tenant or its predecessor lessees to follow environmental laws while using the premises. Tests of the property's well water in 1998 showed high levels of trichloroethylene (TCE), the apparent residue of manufacturing discharges by Mattel's predecessors between 1951 and 1980. After the Oregon Department of Environmental Quality (DEQ) discovered even more pollutants, Mattel stopped drawing from the well and, along with one of its predecessors, signed a consent order with the DEQ providing for cleanup of the site.

After Mattel gave notice of intent to terminate the lease, Hall Street filed this suit, contesting Mattel's right to vacate on the date it gave, and claiming that the lease obliged Mattel to indemnify Hall Street for costs of cleaning up the TCE, among other things. Mattel won on the termination issue, and after an unsuccessful try at mediating the indemnification claim, the parties proposed to submit to arbitration. The District Court was amenable, and the parties drew up an arbitration agreement, which the court approved and entered as an order. The agreement provided that:

> "[t]he United States District Court for the District of Oregon may enter judgment upon any award, either by confirming the award or by vacating, modifying or correcting the award. The Court shall vacate, modify or correct any award: (i) where the arbitrator's findings of facts are not supported by substantial evidence, or (ii) where the arbitrator's conclusions of law are erroneous."

The arbitrator decided for Mattel. In particular, he held that no indemnification was due, because the lease obligation to follow all applicable federal, state, and local environmental laws did not require compliance with the testing requirements of the Oregon Drinking Water Quality Act; that Act the arbitrator characterized as dealing with human health as distinct from environmental contamination. Hall Street then filed a District Court Motion for Order Vacating Modifying And/or Correcting Arbitration Accord; on the ground that failing to treat the Oregon Act as an applicable environmental law under the terms of the lease was legal error. The District Court agreed, vacated the award, and remanded for further consideration by the arbitrator. The court expressly invoked the standard of review chosen by the parties in the arbitration agreement, which included review for legal error, and cited *LaPine Technology Corp. v. Kyocera Corp.*, 130 F.3d 884 (9th Cir. 1997), for the proposition that the FAA leaves the parties "free ... to draft a contract that sets rules for arbitration and dictates an alternative standard of review."

On remand, the arbitrator followed the District Court's ruling that the Oregon Act was an applicable environmental law and amended the decision to favor Hall Street. This time, each party sought modification, and again the District Court applied the parties' stipulated standard of review for legal error, correcting the arbitrator's calculation of interest but otherwise upholding the award. Each party then appealed to the Court of Appeals for the Ninth Circuit, where Mattel switched horses and contended that the Ninth Circuit's recent en banc action overruling *LaPine* in *Kyocera Corp. v. Prudential-Bache Trade Servs., Inc.*, 341 F.3d 987, 1000 (2003), left the arbitration agreement's provision for judicial review of legal error unenforceable. Hall Street countered that *Kyocera* (the later one) was distinguishable, and that the agreement's judicial review provision was not severable from the submission to arbitration. The Ninth Circuit reversed in favor of Mattel in holding that, "[u]nder *Kyocera* the terms of the arbitration agreement controlling the mode of judicial review are unenforceable and severable."

We granted certiorari to decide whether the grounds for vacatur and modification provided by §§ 10 and 11 of the FAA are exclusive. We agree with the Ninth Circuit that they are, but vacate and remand for consideration of independent issues....

The FAA supplies mechanisms for enforcing arbitration awards: a judicial decree confirming an award, an order vacating it, or an order modifying or correcting it. §§ 9–11. An application for any of these orders will get streamlined treatment as a motion, obviating the separate contract action that would usually be necessary to enforce or tinker with an arbitral award in court. § 6. Under the terms of § 9, a court "must" confirm an arbitration award "unless" it is vacated, modified, or corrected "as prescribed" in §§ 10 and 11. Section 10 lists grounds for vacating an award, while § 11 names those for modifying or correcting one....

Hall Street makes two main efforts to show that the grounds set out for vacating or modifying an award are not exclusive, taking the position, first, that expandable judicial review authority has been accepted as the law since *Wilko v. Swan*, 346 U.S. 427 (1953). This, however, was not what *Wilko* decided, which was that § 14 of the Securities Act of 1933 voided any agreement to arbitrate claims of violations of that Act, a holding since overruled by *Rodriguez de Quijas v. Shearson/American Express, Inc.*, 490 U.S. 477 (1989). Although it is true that the Court's discussion includes some language arguably favoring Hall Street's position, arguable is as far as it goes.

The *Wilko* Court was explaining that arbitration would undercut the Securities Act's buyer protections when it remarked (citing FAA § 10) that "[p]ower to vacate an [arbitration] award is limited," and went on to say that "the interpretations of the law by the arbitrators in contrast to manifest disregard [of the law] are not subject, in the federal courts, to judicial review for error in interpretation," Hall Street reads this statement as recognizing "manifest disregard of the law" as a further ground for vacatur on top of those listed in § 10, and some Circuits have read it the same way. Hall Street sees this supposed addition to § 10 as the camel's nose: if judges can add grounds to vacate (or modify), so can contracting parties.

But this is too much for *Wilko* to bear. Quite apart from its leap from a supposed judicial expansion by interpretation to a private expansion by contract, Hall Street overlooks the fact that the statement it relies on expressly rejects just what Hall Street asks for here, general review for an arbitrator's legal errors. Then there is the vagueness of *Wilko*'s phrasing. Maybe the term "manifest disregard" was meant to name a new ground for review, but maybe it merely referred to the § 10 grounds collectively, rather than adding to them. Or, as some courts have thought, "manifest disregard" may have been shorthand for § 10(a)(3) or § 10(a)(4), the paragraphs authorizing vacatur when the arbitrators were "guilty of misconduct" or "exceeded their powers." We, when speaking as a Court, have merely taken the *Wilko* language as we found it, without embellishment, and now that its meaning is implicated, we see no reason to accord it the significance that Hall Street urges.

Second, Hall Street says that the agreement to review for legal error ought to prevail simply because arbitration is a creature of contract, and the FAA is "motivated, first and foremost, by a congressional desire to enforce agreements into which parties ha[ve] entered." *Dean Witter Reynolds Inc. v. Byrd*, 470 U.S. 213 (1985). But, again, we think the argument comes up short. Hall Street is certainly right that the FAA lets parties tailor some, even many features of arbitration by contract, including the way arbitrators are chosen, what their qualifications should be, which issues are arbitrable, along with procedure and choice of substantive law. But to rest this case on the general policy of treating arbitration agreements as enforceable as such would be to beg the question, which is whether the FAA has textual features at odds with enforcing a contract to expand judicial review following the arbitration.

To that particular question we think the answer is yes, that the text compels a reading of the §§ 10 and 11 categories as exclusive. To begin with, even if we assumed §§ 10 and 11 could be supplemented to some extent, it would stretch basic interpretive principles to expand the stated grounds to the point of evidentiary and legal review generally. Sections 10 and 11, after all, address egregious departures from the parties' agreed-upon arbitration: "corruption," "fraud," "evident partiality," "misconduct," "misbehavior," "exceed[ing] powers," "evident material miscalculation," "evident material mistake," "award[s] upon a matter not submitted;" the only ground with any softer focus is "imperfect[ions]," and a court may correct those only if they go to "[a] matter of form not affecting the merits." Given this emphasis on extreme arbitral conduct, the old rule of *ejusdem generis* has an implicit lesson to teach here. Under that rule, when a statute sets out a series of specific items ending with a general term, that general term is confined to covering subjects comparable to the specifics it follows. Since a general term included in the text is normally so limited, then surely a statute with no textual hook for expansion cannot authorize contracting parties to supplement review for specific instances of outrageous conduct with review for just any legal error. "Fraud" and a mistake of law are not cut from the same cloth.

That aside, expanding the detailed categories would rub too much against the grain of the § 9 language, where provision for judicial confirmation carries no hint of flexibility. On application for an order confirming the arbitration award, the court "must grant" the order "unless the award is vacated, modified, or corrected as prescribed in sections 10 and 11 of this title." There is nothing malleable about "must grant," which unequivocally tells courts to grant confirmation in all cases, except when one of the "prescribed" exceptions applies. This does not sound remotely like a provision meant to tell a court what to do just in case the parties say nothing else.

Hall Street claims that § 9 supports its position, because it allows a court to confirm an award only "[i]f the parties in their agreement have agreed that a judgment of the court shall be entered upon the award made pursuant to the arbitration." Hall Street argues that this language "expresses Congress's intent that a court must enforce the agreement of the parties as to whether, and under what circumstances, a judgment shall be entered." It is a peculiar argument, converting agreement as a necessary condition for judicial enforcement into a sufficient condition for a court to bar enforcement. And the text is otherwise problematical for Hall Street: § 9 says that if the parties have agreed to judicial enforcement, the court "must grant" confirmation unless grounds for vacatur or modification exist under § 10 or § 11. The sentence nowhere predicates the court's judicial action on the parties' having agreed to specific standards; if anything, it suggests that, so long as the parties contemplated judicial enforcement, the court must undertake such enforcement under the statutory criteria. In any case, the arbitration agreement here did not specifically predicate entry of judgment on adherence to its judicial-review standard. To the extent Hall Street argues otherwise, it contests not the meaning of the FAA but the Ninth Circuit's severability analysis, upon which it did not seek certiorari. . . .

Instead of fighting the text, it makes more sense to see the three provisions, §§ 9– 11, as substantiating a national policy favoring arbitration with just the limited review needed to maintain arbitration's essential virtue of resolving disputes straightaway. Any other reading opens the door to the full-bore legal and evidentiary appeals that can render informal arbitration merely a prelude to a more cumbersome and time-consuming judicial review process, and bring arbitration theory to grief in post-arbitration process. . . .

When all these arguments based on prior legal authority are done with, Hall Street and Mattel remain at odds over what happens next. Hall Street and its *amici* say parties will flee from arbitration if expanded review is not open to them. One of Mattel's *amici* foresees flight from the courts if it is. We do not know who, if anyone, is right, and so cannot say whether the exclusivity reading of the statute is more of a threat to the popularity of arbitrators or to that of courts. But whatever the consequences of our holding, the statutory text gives us no business to expand the statutory grounds.

In holding that §§ 10 and 11 provide exclusive regimes for the review provided by the statute, we do not purport to say that they exclude more searching review based on authority outside the statute as well. The FAA is not the only way into court for parties wanting review of arbitration awards: they may contemplate enforcement under state statutory or common law, for example, where judicial review of different scope is arguable. But here we speak only to the scope of the expeditious judicial review under §§ 9, 10, and 11, deciding nothing about other possible avenues for judicial enforcement of arbitration awards.

Although one such avenue is now claimed to be revealed in the procedural history of this case, no claim to it was presented when the case arrived on our doorstep, and no reason then appeared to us for treating this as anything but an FAA case. There was never any question about meeting the FAA § 2 requirement that the leases from which the dispute arose be contracts "involving commerce." Nor is there any doubt now that the parties at least had the FAA in mind at the outset; the arbitration agreement even incorporates FAA § 7, empowering arbitrators to compel attendance of witnesses.

One unusual feature, however, prompted some of us to question whether the case should be approached another way. The arbitration agreement was entered into in the course of district-court litigation, was submitted to the District Court as a request to deviate from the standard sequence of trial procedure, and was adopted by the

District Court as an order. Hence a question raised by this Court at oral argument: should the agreement be treated as an exercise of the District Court's authority to manage its cases under Federal Rules of Civil Procedure 16? Supplemental briefing at the Court's behest joined issue on the question, and it appears that Hall Street suggested something along these lines in the Court of Appeals, which did not address the suggestion.

We are, however, in no position to address the question now, beyond noting the claim of relevant case management authority independent of the FAA. The parties' supplemental arguments on the subject in this Court implicate issues of waiver and the U.S.C. §651 *et seq.*, none of which has been considered previously in this litigation, or could be well addressed for the first time here. We express no opinion on these matters beyond leaving them open for Hall Street to press on remand. If the Court of Appeals finds they are open, the court may consider whether the District Court's authority to manage litigation independently warranted that court's order on the mode of resolving the indemnification issues remaining in this case. Although we agree with the Ninth Circuit that the FAA confines its expedited judicial review to the grounds listed in 9 U.S.C. §§ 10 and 11, we vacate the judgment and remand the case for proceedings consistent with this opinion.

1. Comments and Questions

a. Do you agree with the Court's decision? What policies might justify the Court's rejection of the parties' freedom to contract the contours of their arbitration? *See, e.g.*, Whitney R. Duesman, Hall Street Associates, L.L.C. v. Mattel, Inc.: *How the Supreme Court Balanced Arbitral Efficiency and Parties' Intent*, 83 Tul. L. Rev. 1497 (2009).

b. English law has long made provision for judicial review of arbitration awards for legal error. *See, e.g.*, Arbitration Act of 1889, 52 & 53 Vict., c. 49, sec. 7 (Eng.); and Arbitration Act, 1996, c. 23, §§ 45 (preliminary issues) and 69 (post-award appeal) (Eng.). Section 69 permits appeal by agreement of the parties or leave of the court where the arbitral decision was "obviously wrong" or raises "serious doubt" about its correctness. Parties concerned that the right to appeal may undermine arbitral finality and confidentiality may contract out of § 69. The English Arbitration Act, however, does not provide for review of questions of law, but the possibilities for review for claimed errors of law is far greater than under the FAA or the UAA. Which is the better practice?

c. The concerns about applying an "errors of law" standard of review, as provided by the parties' contract, were expressed in *New Eng. Utils. v. Hydro-Quebec*, 10 F. Supp. 2d 53 (D. Mass. 1998):

> This court would be remiss if it did not note two obvious problems with this outcome as a policy matter. First, one of the great benefits of arbitration is the efficient resolution of disputes without burdening both the courts and the parties with protracted litigation. Requiring courts to shift from a straight-

jacket review of arbitration awards ... to more searching reviews for errors of fact or law could arguably transform arbitration from a commercially useful alternative method of dispute resolution into a burdensome additional step on the march through the court system....

Second, allowing the court to expand statutory standards of judicial review implicates a prudential question, that is, what control contract should be permitted to have over the operation of the judiciary.... Though the court has not been asked to examine dead animals (except, of course, the fossil fuel) here, review of errors of Quebec law, most of which is written in French, and which the Court lacks the computer-assisted or library resources to research independently, is not far off. The issues of law here are thankfully straightforward, but it is not hard to imagine a case in which even error of law review is unrealistic, particularly where foreign law is implicated.

d. Since *Hall Street*, parties and courts continue to grapple with its implications for arbitration contracts and judicial review of arbitral awards in state, as opposed to federal, courts. The decision arguably raised more questions than it answered. Consider, for example:

1. Did *Hall Street* limit a court's power to review an arbitral award for a judicially recognized standard of manifest disregard of the law or violation of public policy?

2. Can parties achieve essentially the same result through creative drafting or by including provisions that limit an arbitrator's powers to render factually or legally correct decisions? *See* Christopher R. Drahozal, *Contracting Around RUAA: Default Rules, Mandatory Rules, and Judicial Review of Arbitral Awards*, 3 PEPP. DISP. RESOL. L.J. 419 (2003) (noting "restricted submission[s]" requiring arbitrators to follow the law).

3. Does it matter whether a dispute matter is governed by federal or state arbitration law?

4. Are state courts bound by the FAA's narrow modification and review standards and *Hall Street*'s interpretation thereof?

5. Does the FAA preempt state grounds to vacate an award that are broader than grounds enumerated in the FAA?

In short, what are the "other possible avenues" for judicial review of arbitration awards? *See* Maureen A. Weston, *The Other Avenues of* Hall Street, 14 LEWIS & CLARK L. REV. 929 (2010). *See infra*, Section F.3.

e. While recognizing, under *Hall Street*, that FAA grounds for vacatur "are exclusive" and cannot be "supplemented by contract," the Texas Supreme Court upheld an agreement for expanded review of an arbitration award under the Texas General Arbitration Act (TAA). *NAFTA Traders*, Inc. *v. Quinn*, 339 S.W.3d 84 (Tex. 2011):

We must, of course, follow *Hall Street* in applying the FAA, but in construing the TAA, we are obliged to examine *Hall Street*'s reasoning and reach our own judgment.... As a fundamental matter, Texas law recognizes and protects a broad freedom of contract.... and that [] contracts when entered into freely and voluntarily shall be held sacred and shall be enforced by Courts of justice.... the purpose of the TAA is to facilitate arbitration agreements, which have been enforceable in Texas by Constitution or statute since at least 1845. Specifically, the TAA contains no policy against parties' agreeing to limit the authority of an arbitrator to that of a judge, but rather, an express provision requiring vacatur when "arbitrators [have] exceeded their powers." Accordingly, we hold that the TAA presents no impediment to an agreement that limits the authority of an arbitrator in deciding a matter and thus allows for judicial review of an arbitration award for reversible error.

Are parties able to circumvent *Hall Street* by defining an arbitrator's powers to correctly apply the law?

G. Non-Statutory Judicial Review Standards

In *Hall Street*, the Supreme Court indicated that the enumerated grounds for vacatur in FAA § 10 are "exclusive" and may not be supplanted by private contract. Prior to *Hall Street*, courts readily recognized two nonstatutory grounds for vacating arbitration awards: "manifest disregard of the law" and "contrary to public policy." Since *Hall Street*, courts have responded differently to whether common law grounds such as manifest disregard of the law remain viable grounds for vacatur in FAA proceedings. Thus, while *Hall Street* resolved one circuit split, it paved the way for yet another. The current divide in the federal circuits as to whether manifest disregard of the law remains as an independent basis to vacate arbitration awards is analyzed in the following case.

1. Manifest Disregard of the Law

Wachovia Securities, LLC v. Brand

671 F.3d 472 (4th Cir. 2012)

DUNCAN, Circuit Judge.

Wachovia Securities, LLC ("Wachovia") appeals from the district court's refusal to vacate an arbitration award entered against it after it sued several former employees on what the arbitrators determined were frivolous claims. Wachovia argues that the arbitrators (the "Panel") violated § 10(a)(3) of the Federal Arbitration Act (the "FAA") and "manifestly disregarded" the law when they awarded $1.1 million in attorneys' fees and costs under the South Carolina Frivolous Civil Proceedings Act (the "FCPA"). For the reasons that follow, we affirm.

I.

A.

Wachovia initiated an arbitration proceeding by filing a Statement of Claim with the Financial Industry Regulatory Authority ("FINRA") against four former employees. The Former Employees, all individual financial advisors, were previously employees of A.G. Edwards & Sons, Inc. ("A.G. Edwards"), which merged with Wachovia on October 1, 2007. After the merger, the Former Employees became employees of Wachovia's Florence, South Carolina branch office. Wachovia terminated their employment on June 26, 2008. Following their termination by Wachovia, the Former Employees went to work for a competitor brokerage firm, Stifel Nicolaus & Co., Inc. ("Stifel").

In the arbitration proceeding, Wachovia alleged that the Former Employees had violated their contractual and common law obligations when they joined Stifel. Specifically, Wachovia claimed that the Former Employees conspired with Stifel to open a competitor office in Florence, South Carolina, and that they had misappropriated confidential and proprietary information in the process. Wachovia further complained that the Former Employees were soliciting current Wachovia clients and employees to join their new firm. In addition, Wachovia sought a permanent injunction, the return of records, and an award of costs and attorneys' fees associated with the arbitration.

The Former Employees' Answer described this dispute as "meritless" and an effort "to punish former employees for leaving in the wake of Wachovia's acquisition of A.G. Edwards, to intimidate and deter its current employees from making similar decisions, to prevent customers from obtaining information necessary to make an informed decision as to whether the customer wishes to do business, and to otherwise stifle legitimate competition." The Former Employees requested that the Panel award them attorneys' fees and costs incurred in defending themselves "from Wachovia's baseless and unwarranted claims." They also asserted counterclaims under the South Carolina Wage Payment Act ("Wage Act"), and the common law doctrines of unjust enrichment and conversion. They did not assert any claims under the FCPA.

The arbitration proceeded before a panel of three arbitrators in accordance with FINRA's rules ... [T]he panel asked the parties to submit accountings or proposals regarding requested attorneys' fees, forum fees, expert fees and any costs or expenses during the final two days of hearings ... Both parties' briefs contained new arguments regarding attorneys' fees. Wachovia argued, despite its own request for attorneys' fees in its Statement of Claim, that under the South Carolina Arbitration Act, neither party was entitled to attorneys' fees. The Former Employees argued for the first time that they were entitled to attorneys' fees under the FCPA.

As its name suggests, the Frivolous Civil Proceeding Act provides a mechanism for litigants to seek sanctions against attorneys who file frivolous claims. It contains a number of procedural safeguards for litigants facing sanctions. Significantly for our purposes, the statute provides for a notice period affording the accused 30 days to respond to a request for sanctions and a separate hearing on sanctions after the verdict. No such procedures were followed here.

Upon learning that the Former Employees were seeking sanctions under the FCPA, Wachovia expressed concern that the arbitrators were not affording them 30 days' response time or a post-verdict hearing on the issue of fees. Toward the end of the hearing, the chairman of the Panel asked Wachovia if "you have been given a fair opportunity to present your case in its entirety in these proceedings." Wachovia responded that it had not been given a fair opportunity with respect to "the issues raised and argued as to attorneys' fees." The Panel then asked whether additional briefing would cure the concerns. Wachovia replied:

I don't know. Because the standard and the [FCPA] from what I saw, there's notice and opportunity to be heard. So that means in other words, we need some evidence. That's why I don't think it's appropriate at the end, after our record is closed, that new issues have been injected. The statute is not referred to in the pleadings. So it's not just the element of surprise. It's a complete surprise.

After listening to Wachovia's objections to the Panel reaching any decision on the issue of attorneys' fees, the Panel stated: "The issue on attorneys' fees, I'm sure there will be something that will occur to the panel where we need to seek clarification from parties. And if that becomes necessary, be assured we will be in touch with you." The Panel subsequently asked the parties for an accounting of their November fees but did not hold any additional hearings or request additional briefing. Nor, however, did Wachovia request additional briefing.

On December 18, 2009, the Panel issued an award in which it denied all of Wachovia's claims. It awarded the Former Employees $15,080.67 in treble damages on their Wage Act claims, as well as $1,111,553.85 for attorneys' fees under the FCPA....

B.

Following arbitration, the Former Employees filed a motion to confirm the Panel's award in the District of South Carolina. Wachovia filed its own motion to vacate that portion of the Panel's award granting relief to the Former Employees.... [and] contended that the Panel exceeded its authority and manifestly disregarded the law under 9 U.S.C. § 10(a)(4) by awarding sanctions under the FCPA, for, inter alia, ignoring the FCPA's conditions precedent ... [and that the Panel "deprived Wachovia of a fundamentally fair hearing, by denying [it] the procedural safeguards guaranteed by the FCPA and by not allowing [it] to review (much less rebut) critical evidence that [the Former Employees] submitted to the Panel in support of their fee claim." The district court considered these claims in turn.

The district court began by rejecting Wachovia's argument that the arbitrators violated § 10(a)(4), which allows a district court to vacate an arbitration award "where the arbitrators exceeded their powers, or so imperfectly executed them that a mutual, final, and definite award upon the subject matter submitted was not made." 9 U.S.C. § 10(a)(4). It reasoned that arbitrators violate this provision when they decide issues not properly before them. Since the record supported the conclusion that the question of fees was properly before the Panel, the district court held that they had not violated § 10(a)(4).

The district court also disagreed with Wachovia's argument that a statute must mention arbitration in order to be applicable in arbitration. It further rejected Wachovia's claim that the language of the FCPA supported vacatur under a manifest disregard standard because the statute only applied to "courts" following a "verdict." It reasoned that Wachovia had not shown that the arbitrators understood the law as having a meaning that they chose to ignore.... Wachovia appealed.

II.

On appeal from a district court's denial of vacatur, "we review de novo the court's legal rulings." "Any factual findings made by the district court in affirming such an award are reviewed for clear error." We note that judicial review of an arbitration award in federal court "is severely circumscribed." "A court sits to 'determine only whether the arbitrator did his job—not whether he did it well, correctly, or reasonably, but simply whether he did it.'"

We turn now to Wachovia's argument that it is entitled to vacatur under a "manifest disregard" standard. Specifically, Wachovia argues that the Panel "manifestly disregarded" the law when it refused to import the FCPA's procedural requirements into the arbitration. "Manifest disregard" is, as we will explain, an old yet enigmatic ground for overturning arbitral awards. Wachovia contends the Supreme Court's 2008 decision in *Hall Street* rendered "manifest disregard" a judicial gloss on § 10(a)(3) and (4)— rather than a separate common law ground for relief—perhaps hoping that this "gloss" would help it where the text of the statute offers little relief. We do not find Wachovia's argument persuasive.

To lay a foundation for our analysis, we look first at "manifest disregard" as a basis for vacatur and our interpretation of the doctrine pre-*Hall Street*. We then consider how the Supreme Court's decisions in *Hall Street* and, more recently, *Stolt-Nielsen v. AnimalFeeds*, 130 S.Ct. 1758 (2010), have affected this analysis. Although we find that manifest disregard did survive *Hall Street* as an independent ground for vacatur, we conclude that Wachovia has not demonstrated that the arbitrators manifestly disregarded the law here.

The origins of modern manifest disregard as an independent basis for reviewing American arbitration decisions likely lie in dicta from the Supreme Court's decision in *Wilko v. Swan*, 346 U.S. 427 (1953). In *Wilko*, the Court explained that when interpreting the agreements at issue, "the interpretations of the law by the arbitrators in contrast to manifest disregard are not subject, in the federal courts, to judicial review for error in interpretation." We have read *Wilko* as endorsing manifest disregard as a common law ground for vacatur, separate and distinct from § 10's statutory grounds. Before *Hall Street*, we stated that for a court to vacate an award under the manifest disregard theory, the arbitration record must show that "'(1) the applicable legal principle is clearly defined and not subject to reasonable debate; and (2) the arbitrator[ ] refused to heed that legal principle.'" We note that under this standard, proving manifest disregard required something beyond showing that the arbitrators misconstrued the law, especially given that arbitrators are not required to explain their reasoning.

The Supreme Court's decision in *Hall Street* has been widely viewed as injecting uncertainty into the status of manifest disregard as a basis for vacatur. There, a commercial landlord and tenant had contracted for greater judicial review of any arbitral award during a dispute about the tenant's alleged failure to comply with applicable environmental laws. The Supreme Court concluded that, by permitting review for legal errors, this contract impermissibly circumvented the FAA's limited review for procedural errors. The Court rejected this approach and held that the FAA prohibited parties from contractually expanding judicial review on the theory that the grounds for vacatur in the FAA are "exclusive." This circuit has not yet interpreted manifest disregard in light of *Hall Street*, although it has acknowledged the uncertainty surrounding the "continuing viability of extra-statutory grounds for vacating arbitration awards."

We find that the Supreme Court's more recent decision in *Stolt-Nielsen* sheds further light on the operation of "manifest disregard" post-*Hall Street*. In *Stolt-Nielsen*, ... the Second Circuit [found] that although manifest disregard survived as a "judicial gloss" of the FAA after *Hall Street*, it was inapplicable because the arbitrators had not cited authority contrary to the position that they adopted.... The Supreme Court reversed the Second Circuit, finding that the arbitrators had improperly rested their decision on AnimalFeeds' public policy arguments.... The Supreme Court's reasoning in *Stolt-Nielsen* closely tracked the majority of circuits' approach to manifest disregard before *Hall Street*: it noted that there was law clearly on point, that the panel did not apply the applicable law, and that the panel acknowledged that it was departing from the applicable law. Nonetheless, the Court said,

> We do not decide whether "manifest disregard" survives our decision in *Hall Street Associates,* as an independent ground for review or as a judicial gloss on the enumerated grounds for vacatur set forth at 9 U.S.C. § 10. *AnimalFeeds* characterizes that standard as requiring a showing that the arbitrators knew of the relevant [legal] principle, appreciated that this principle controlled the outcome of the disputed issue, and nonetheless willfully flouted the governing law by refusing to apply it. Assuming, *arguendo,* that such a standard applies, we find it satisfied.

Id. at 1768 n. 3.

We read this footnote to mean that manifest disregard continues to exist either "as an independent ground for review or as a judicial gloss on the enumerated grounds for vacatur set forth at 9 U.S.C. § 10." Therefore, we decline to adopt the position of the Fifth and Eleventh Circuits that manifest disregard no longer exists....

Although we find that manifest disregard continues to exist as either an independent ground for review or as a judicial gloss, we need not decide which of the two it is because Wachovia's claim fails under both. Wachovia argues that the Panel acknowledged that it was applying the substantive provisions of the FCPA but did not follow the statute's procedural provisions when it declined to give Wachovia 30 days to respond to the request for fees or hold a separate hearing on the issue of fees. However, as discussed above, we find that the Panel was not compelled to import these procedural requirements if it found a different procedure to be better suited to the needs of the arbitration. In *Long John Silver's*, we adopted a two-part test that a party must meet in order for a reviewing court to vacate for manifest disregard: "(1) the applicable legal principle is clearly defined and not subject to reasonable debate; and (2) the arbitrator[ ] refused to heed that legal principle." We do not read *Hall Street* or *Stolt-Nielsen* as loosening the carefully circumscribed standard that we had previously articulated for manifest disregard. Whether manifest disregard is a "judicial gloss" or an independent ground for vacatur, it is not an invitation to review the merits of the underlying arbitration. Therefore, we see no reason to depart from our two-part test which has for decades guaranteed that review for manifest disregard not grow into the kind of probing merits review that would undermine the efficiency of arbitration. In this case, we find that whether the Panel erred by not applying the FCPA's procedural requirements is a question that was itself not clearly defined and was certainly subject to debate. Accordingly, we cannot hold that the arbitrators manifestly disregarded the law when they awarded Appellees $1.1 million in attorneys' fees and costs under the FCPA. Affirmed.

a. Comments and Questions

i. *Status of the Manifest Disregard Standard.* As of 2017, all of the federal circuit courts of appeal have considered the issue, reaching varied conclusions. The Fifth, Eighth, and Eleventh Circuits have concluded that *Hall Street* eliminated "manifest disregard" as an independent ground for vacatur. *See McVay v. Halliburton Energy Servs., Inc.*, 608 Fed.Appx. 222 (5th Cir. 2015); *Medicine Shoppe v. Turner*, 614 F.3d 485 (8th Cir. 2010); *Campbell's Foliage, Inc. v. Federal Crop Ins. Corp.*, 562 Fed. Appx. 828 (11th Cir. 2014).

In contrast, eight federal circuits have held that manifest disregard survives *Hall Street*, either as an independent ground for review or as a judicial "gloss" on the enumerated statutory grounds. *See Singh v. Raymond James Fin. Servs., Inc.*, 633 F. App'x 548 (2d Cir. 2015); *Wachovia Sec., LLC v. Brand*, 671 F.3d 472, 482 (4th Cir. 2012); *Coffee Beanery, Ltd. v. WW, LLC*, 300 Fed. Appx. 415, 418–19 (6th Cir. 2008), *cert. denied*, 558 U.S.819 (2009); *Renard v. Ameriprise Fin. Servs., Inc.*, 778 F.3d 563 (7th Cir. 2015); *Improv West Assocs. v. Comedy Club*, Inc., 553 F.3d 1277 (9th Cir. 2009); *Hicks v. The Cadle Co.*, 355 Fed. Appx. 186 (10th Cir. 2009) (summarizing cases), *cert. denied*, 131 S. Ct. 160 (2010); *Adviser Dealer Servs., Inc. v. Icon Advisers, Inc.*, 557 Fed. Appx. 714 (10th Cir. 2014); *Affinity Fin. Corp. v. AARP Fin., Inc.*, 468 F. App'x 4 (D.C. Cir. 2012); *Bayer CropScience AG v. Dow Agrosciences LLC*, 2017 WL 788321 (Fed. Cir. 2017).

The First and Third Circuits have expressly declined to decide the issue. *Whitehead v. Pullman Grp., LLC*, 2016 WL 279015 (3d Cir. 2016) ("[T]his Court has not yet weighed in" on whether manifest disregard is an allowable basis to vacate an award); *Raymond James Fin. Servs., Inc. v. Fenyk*, 780 F.3d 59 (1st Cir. 2015) ("[W]e have not squarely determined whether our manifest disregard case law can be reconciled with *Hall Street*.") *Cf. Ortiz-Espinosa v. BBVA Sec. of P.R., Inc.*, 852 F.3d 36, 46 (1st Cir. 2017) (stating that the doctrine remains "only as a judicial gloss.").

A summary of the circuit split on the viability of manifest disregard of the law as an independent basis for vacatur is as follows, although judicial attitudes on the doctrine indicate some shifting:

ii. *Does it Matter?* What is "manifest disregard of the law"? Is it different or subsumed within the Section 10 grounds as "exceeding powers"? Why do you suppose the

FAA 10 Statutory Grounds Exclusive	MDL & Common Law Vacatur Grounds Survive Independently or as Statutory Gloss	Status Uncertain
5th, 8th, 11th	2d, 4th, 6th, 7th, 9th, 10th, D.C., and Federal Circuits	1st, 3rd

Supreme Court has declined to clarify the issue despite the circuit split? *See Stolt-Nielsen SA v. Animal Feeds Int'l Corp.*, 559 U.S. 662 (2010) ("We do not decide whether 'manifest disregard' survives our decision in *Hall Street* as an independent ground for review or judicial gloss on the enumerated grounds for vacatur set forth [in FAA] …").

iii. The question on manifest disregard has generated significant commentary. *See* Brian Forgue, *Re-Thinking the Federal Arbitration Act § 10: Vacating "Manifest Disregard*,*"* 7 Y.B. Arb. & Mediation 255 (2015); Robert Ellis, *Imperfect Minimalism: Unanswered Questions in* Hall Street, 32 Harv. J.L. & Pub. Pol'y 1187 (2009); Jason Steed, *Appealing Arbitration Awards and the Circuit Split over "Manifest Disregard of the Law*,*"* Am. Bar. Ass'n, Litigation (May 10, 2016); *see also* Macneil et al., Federal Arbitration Law § 40.5.1.3 (1994) (taking the position that the statutory grounds for vacatur—particularly the "exceeded powers" provisions of the FAA § 10(a)(4), UAA § 12(3), and RUAA § 23(a)(4)—are sufficient to cover any situation where vacatur is appropriate).

iv. Note the question to the attorneys in *Wachovia* toward the end of the hearing where the Panel chair asked Wachovia if it had "[b]een given a fair opportunity to present your case in its entirety in these proceedings"? Arbitrators regularly ask this question of parties at the close of hearing. Why? Does this put parties in an awkward position?

b. State Arbitration Statutes and Non-Statutory Grounds for Vacatur

The split in the federal courts over the validity of the manifest disregard of the law standard has similarly ensnared state courts applying state law. Recall that the Supreme Court has held that section 2 of the FAA applies in state and federal court. Do other sections of the FAA, such as section 10, equally apply in state court? The Court has not yet addressed this question, and state courts are divided. *Compare Finn v. Ballentine Partners, LLC,* 143 A.3d 859, 866 (NH 2016) ("we conclude that §§ 9–11 of the FAA apply only to arbitration review proceedings commenced in federal courts"), *with Kilgore v. Mullenax,* 520 S.W.3d 670, 672 (Ark. 2017) (applying FAA grounds to motion to vacate in Arkansas state court).

What if the parties explicitly designate a state arbitration statute as controlling law in their arbitration agreement? In *Volt Info. Sciences v. Bd. of Trustees, Stanford Univ.,* 489 U.S. 468 (1989), the Court held that parties can contract for application of a state arbitration statute. Thus, even a federal court may be asked to apply a state arbitration statute. Although state arbitration statutes and vacatur provisions largely mirror the FAA, states can apply a different standard in which to recognize contractual agreements to expand the state statutory provisions for vacatur. In Texas, however, *Hoskins v. Hoskins,* 2016 WL 2993929 (Tex. 2016), held that an arbitrator's "manifest disregard" of the law is not a basis to vacate an arbitration award under the Texas Arbitration Act, because it is not an expressly enumerated ground for vacatur. In contrast, in *Bankers Life & Casualty Insurance Company v. CBRE, Inc.,* 830 F.3d 729 (7th Cir. 2016), the Court of Appeals vacated an arbitral award under the State of Illinois Arbitration Act (which mirrors the FAA) for "gross errors of judgment in law or a gross mistake of fact" that were "apparent upon the face of the award."

The Drafting Committee to the RUAA "[c]onsidered [but rejected] the advisability of adding two new subsections to § 23(a) sanctioning vacatur of awards that result from a 'manifest disregard of the law' or for an award that violates 'public policy.'" The RUAA does not address either the "manifest disregard" or the "public policy" standards of court review of arbitral awards. The Drafting Committee explained that this omission was intentional for two primary reasons. First, the FAA did not note either standard, and, under a ruling that FAA § 10(a) provides the exclusive grounds for vacatur, the FAA likely would preempt a state standard. The Drafters recognized that the case law on both vacatur grounds is unsettled, conflicting, and indicates further evolution in the courts. RUAA, *Commentary on the Possible Codification of the "Manifest Disregard of the Law" and the "Public Policy" Grounds for Vacatur,* § 23 (2000).

2. Public Policy

Contract law recognizes violation of public policy as a defense to enforcement of a contract. After *Hall Street,* does public policy remain a basis to vacate a commercial arbitral award? Does it matter whether state or federal public policy is at stake? Is violating public policy a more compelling reason than manifest disregard of the law to allow it as a non-statutory basis for vacatur?

Eastern Assoc. Coal Corp. v.
United Mine Workers of America

531 U.S. 57 (2000)

JUSTICE BREYER delivered the opinion of the Court.

A labor arbitrator ordered an employer to reinstate an employee truck driver who had twice tested positive for marijuana. The question before us is whether considerations of public policy require courts to refuse to enforce that arbitration award. We conclude that they do not. The courts may enforce the award. And the employer must reinstate, rather than discharge, the employee.

Eastern Coal and United Mine Workers of America (UMW), are parties to a collective bargaining agreement with arbitration provisions. The agreement specifies that, in arbitration, in order to discharge an employee, Eastern must prove it has "just cause." Otherwise the arbitrator will order the employee reinstated. The arbitrator's decision is final. James Smith worked for Eastern as a member of a road crew, a job that required him to drive heavy trucklike vehicles on public highways. As a truck driver, Smith was subject to Department of Transportation (DOT) regulations requiring random drug testing of workers engaged in "safety-sensitive" tasks.

In March 1996, Smith tested positive for marijuana. Eastern sought to discharge Smith. The union went to arbitration, and the arbitrator concluded that Smith's positive drug test did not amount to "just cause" for discharge. Instead the arbitrator ordered Smith's reinstatement, provided that Smith (1) accept a suspension of 30 days without pay, (2) participate in a substance-abuse program, and (3) undergo drug tests at the discretion of Eastern (or an approved substance-abuse professional) for the next five years.

Between April 1996 and January 1997, Smith passed four random drug tests. But in July 1997 he again tested positive for marijuana. Eastern again sought to discharge Smith. The union again went to arbitration, and the arbitrator again concluded that Smith's use of marijuana did not amount to "just cause" for discharge, in light of two mitigating circumstances. First, Smith had been a good employee for 17 years. And second, Smith had made a credible and "very personal appeal under oath … concerning a personal/family problem which caused this one time lapse in drug usage."

The arbitrator ordered Smith's reinstatement provided that Smith (1) accept a new suspension without pay, this time for slightly more than three months; (2) reimburse Eastern and the union for the costs of both arbitration proceedings; (3) continue to participate in a substance-abuse program; (4) continue to undergo random drug testing; and (5) provide Eastern with a signed, undated letter of resignation, to take effect if Smith again tested positive within the next five years. Eastern brought suit in federal court seeking to have the arbitrator's award vacated, arguing that the award contravened a public policy against the operation of dangerous machinery by workers who test positive for drugs. The District Court, while recognizing a strong regulation-based public policy against drug use by workers who perform safety-sensitive functions, held that Smith's conditional reinstatement did not violate that policy.... The Court of Appeals for the Fourth Circuit affirmed.

Eastern claims that considerations of public policy make the arbitration award un-enforceable. In considering this claim, we must assume that the collective-bargaining agreement itself calls for Smith's reinstatement.... For present purposes, the award is not distinguishable from the contractual agreement.

We must then decide whether a contractual reinstatement requirement would fall within the legal exception that makes unenforceable "a collective-bargaining agreement that is contrary to public policy." The Court has made clear that any such public policy must be "explicit," "well defined," and "dominant." It must be "ascertained by reference to the laws and legal precedents and not from general considerations of supposed public interests." And, of course, the question to be answered is not whether Smith's drug use itself violates public policy, but whether the agreement to reinstate him does so. To put the question more specifically, does a contractual agreement to reinstate Smith with specified conditions run contrary to an explicit, well-defined, and dominant public policy, as ascertained by reference to positive law and not from general considerations of supposed public interests?

Eastern initially argues that the District Court erred by asking, not whether the award is "contrary to" public policy "as ascertained by reference" to positive law, but whether the award "violates" positive law, a standard Eastern says is too narrow.... We agree, in principle, that courts' authority to invoke the public policy exception is not limited solely to instances where the arbitration award itself violates positive law. Nevertheless, the public policy exception is narrow and must satisfy the principles set forth in *W.R. Grace* and *Misco*. Moreover, in a case like the one before us, where two political branches have created a detailed regulatory regime in a specific field, courts should approach with particular caution pleas to divine further public policy in that area.

Eastern asserts that a public policy against reinstatement of workers who use drugs can be discerned from an examination of that regulatory regime, which consists of the Omnibus Transportation Employee Testing Act of 1991 and DOT's implementing regulations. The Testing Act embodies a congressional finding that "the greatest efforts must be expended to eliminate the ... use of illegal drugs, whether on or off duty, by those individuals who are involved in [certain safety-sensitive positions, including] the operation of ... trucks." ...

In Eastern's view, these provisions embody a strong public policy against drug use by transportation workers in safety-sensitive positions and in favor of random drug testing in order to detect that use. Eastern argues that reinstatement of a driver who has twice failed random drug tests would undermine that policy—to the point where a judge must set aside an employer-union agreement requiring reinstatement. Eastern's argument, however, loses much of its force when one considers further provisions of the Act that make clear that the Act's remedial aims are complex. The Act says that "rehabilitation is a critical component of any testing program," that rehabilitation "should be made available to individuals, as appropriate," and that DOT must promulgate regulations for "rehabilitation programs." The DOT regulations specifically state that a driver who has tested positive for drugs cannot return to a safety-sensitive position until (1) the driver has been evaluated by a "substance abuse professional" to determine if treatment is needed; (2) the substance-abuse professional has certified that the driver has followed any rehabilitation program prescribed; and (3) the driver has passed a return-to-duty drug test. In addition, (4) the driver must be subject to at least six random drug tests during the first year after returning to the job. Neither the Act nor the regulations forbid an employer to reinstate in a safety-sensitive position an employee who fails a random drug test once or twice. The congressional and regulatory directives require only that the above-stated prerequisites to reinstatement be met....

[T]hese expressions of positive law embody several relevant policies. As Eastern points out, these policies include Testing Act policies against drug use by employees in safety-sensitive transportation positions and in favor of drug testing. They also include a Testing Act policy favoring rehabilitation of employees who use drugs. And the relevant statutory and regulatory provisions must be read in light of background labor law policy that favors determination of disciplinary questions through arbitration when chosen as a result of labor-management negotiation.

The award before us is not contrary to these several policies, taken together. The award does not condone Smith's conduct or ignore the risk to public safety that drug use by truck drivers may pose. Rather, the award punishes Smith by suspending him for three months, thereby depriving him of nearly $9,000 in lost wages; it requires him to pay the arbitration costs of both sides; it insists upon further substance-abuse treatment and testing; and it makes clear (by requiring Smith to provide a signed letter of resignation) that one more failed test means discharge. The award violates no specific provision of any law or regulation. It is consistent with DOT rules requiring completion of substance-abuse treatment before returning to work, for it does not preclude Eastern from assigning Smith to a non-safety-sensitive position until Smith completes the prescribed treatment program. It is consistent with the Testing Act's ... driving license suspension requirements, for those requirements apply only to drivers who, unlike Smith, actually operated vehicles under the influence of drugs. The award is also consistent with the Act's rehabilitative concerns, for it requires substance-abuse treatment and testing before Smith can return to work....

We recognize that reasonable people can differ as to whether reinstatement or discharge is the more appropriate remedy here. But both employer and union have agreed to entrust this remedial decision to an arbitrator. We cannot find in the Act, the regulations, or any other law or legal precedent an "explicit," "well defined," "dominant" public policy to which the arbitrator's decision "runs contrary." We conclude that the lower courts correctly rejected Eastern's public policy claim. The judgment of the Court of Appeals is Affirmed.

JUSTICE SCALIA, with whom JUSTICE THOMAS joins, concurring in the judgment.

I concur in the Court's judgment, because I agree that no public policy prevents the reinstatement of James Smith to his position as a truck driver, so long as he complies with the arbitrator's decision, and with those requirements set out in the Department of Transportation's regulations. I do not endorse, however, the Court's statement that "[w]e agree, in principle, that courts' authority to invoke the public policy exception is not limited solely to instances where the arbitration award itself violates positive law." No case is cited to support that proposition, and none could be. There is not a single decision, since this Court washed its hands of general common-lawmaking authority, *see Erie R. Co. v. Tompkins*, 304 U.S. 64 (1938), in which we have refused to enforce on "public policy" grounds an agreement that did not violate, or provide for the violation of, some positive law.

After its dictum opening the door to flaccid public policy arguments of the sort presented by petitioner here, the Court immediately posts a giant "Do Not Enter" sign. "[T]he public policy exception," it says, "is narrow and must satisfy the principles set forth in *W.R. Grace*," which require that the applicable public policy be "explicit," "well defined," "dominant," and "ascertained by reference to the laws and legal precedents and not from general considerations of supposed public interests." *W.R. Grace & Co. v. Rubber Workers*, 461 U.S. 757 (1983). It is hard to imagine how an arbitration award could violate a public policy, identified in this fashion, without actually conflicting with positive law. If such an award could ever exist, it would surely be so rare that the benefit of preserving the courts' ability to deal with it is far outweighed by the confusion and uncertainty, and hence the obstructive litigation, that the Court's Delphic "agree[ment] in principle" will engender....

In sum, it seems to me that the game set in play by the Court's dictum endorsing "in principle" the power of federal courts to enunciate public policy is not worth the candle. Agreeing with the ... Court except insofar as this principle is concerned, I concur only in the judgment.

a. Comments and Questions

i. Does *Eastern Assoc. Coal., Corp.* square with *Hall Street*?

ii. Under *Eastern Coal*, the public policy exception to the enforcement of arbitration awards is both clearly recognized and severely circumscribed. State courts may interpret the exception differently from the federal standard, which generally provides that an arbitral award violates public policy only where it violates positive statutory law. But issues of public policy are more likely to arise in state courts that involve state public policies regarding matters such as covenants not to complete, or child custody orders. Circuit courts also have recognized violations of public policy as an independent justification for vacating an arbitration award. *See, e.g., Legacy Trading Co., Ltd. v. Hoffman*, 363 Fed. Appx. 633, 636 (10th Cir. 2010) (judicially created public policy exception provides grounds for vacatur); *Williams v. NFL*, 582 F.3d 863, 884 (8th Cir. 2009) (policy must be explicit and well-defined). However, the same question as to *Hall Street*'s impact arises with the public policy exception. *See DCR Constr., Inc. v. Delta-T Corp.*, 2009 U.S. Dist. LEXIS 122624, at *17 (M.D. Fla. Dec. 29, 2009) (following *Hall Street*, public policy is no longer a viable ground for FAA vacatur).

iii. In *Building the Civilization of Arbitration: Personal Autonomy and Vacatur After Hall Street*, 113 Penn St. L. Rev. 1103 (2009), Professor Reuben states that "[t]he public policy exception is well-grounded and well-established, and nothing in the *Hall Street* opinion evinces an intent to eliminate it. It seems likely that courts will recognize a public policy exception to the seemingly strict rule of *Hall Street*, at least for illegal arbitration awards." *See also* Alan Scott Rau, *Fear of Freedom*, 19 Am. Rev. Int'l Arb. 469, 501 (2008) (arguing that the public policy ground for vacatur must survive Hall Street because external social effects "necessarily limit every exercise of contractual autonomy, [such that] vacatur for violation of 'public policy' is a necessary fail safe, universally understood in every existing legal system as a ground ... for refusing to honor an award"). Do you agree that public policy remains a valid nonstatutory ground for vacatur? Note that international arbitration awards can be vacated on public policy grounds, *see* Chapter 11. In the labor context, arbitration awards can be vacated where the award "fails to draw its essence" from the parties' collective bargaining agreement or where enforcement would violate some explicit public policy that is "well defined and dominant, and is to be ascertained by reference to the laws and legal precedents and not from general considerations of supposed public interests." *United Paperworkers International v. Misco*, 484 U.S. 29 (1987). In the commercial context, the FAA contains only four explicit statutory grounds. What are the arguments for or against a narrow construction?

iv. *Professional Conduct Standards as Public Policy. Sands v. Menard, Inc.*, 787 N.W.2d 384 (Wis. 2010), ruled that an arbitration panel exceeded its powers when it ordered the reinstatement of an attorney where such "[w]ould clearly lead to a violation of that attorney's ethical obligations ... we could not countenance an arbitration award that ordered an individual to engage in the unauthorized practice of law, or one that ordered an attorney to use funds from the attorney's trust account in a fashion prohibited by the Rules of Professional Conduct. Similarly, we cannot countenance an award that forces an attorney to represent a client when it is clear that the complete disintegration of mutual goodwill, trust, and loyalty renders ethical representation by that attorney impossible.").

v. Potential categories of workplace public policy where disputes are likely to arise include violence, alcohol use, illegal drugs, and sexual harassment. In personal care situations, abuse of the young, elderly, mentally impaired, and incarcerated is a concern. The common feature of these situations is health and safety. *See, e.g., Newsday, Inc. v. Long Island Typographical Union*, 915 F.2d 840 (2d Cir.1990) (vacating a reinstatement award on public policy grounds when sexual harassment made the work environment too hostile); *Delta Air Lines, Inc. v. Air Line Pilots Ass'n, Int'l*, 861 F.2d 665 (11th Cir.1988) (vacating a reinstatement award on public policy grounds when the employee, a pilot, flew while intoxicated). What other areas of public policy concern should mitigate enforcement of arbitration awards beyond statutory grounds?

vi. *Public Policy and Religious Arbitration.* Should courts enforce religious arbitration awards that otherwise conflict with secular laws, where parties have otherwise contracted for application of religious law? Compare Michael Helfand, *Religious Arbitration and the New Multiculturalism: Negotiating conflicting Legal Orders*, 86 N.Y.U. L. Rev. 1231 (2011) (arguing that religious arbitral awards should be enforced even when they violate public policy), with Michael J. Brode, *The Case Against Religious Arbitration*, in Sharia Tribunals, Rabbinical Courts, and Christian Panels: Religious Panels (Oxford Univ. Press 2017).

b. Public Policy under State Law

The scope of "public policy" under state law has the potential to be considerably broader than under federal law, and not only because a state has the power to adopt public policies at substantial variance with those of the federal government or other states. State power is extremely broad with respect to matters that are most commonly the subject of arbitration—contracts, torts, and property. In addition, there seems to be far greater concern at the state than at the federal level about issues associated with the consumerization of arbitration. A few illustrations indicate the potential breadth of state law public policy as a basis for reviewing arbitration awards. Another example, mandatory disclosures by arbitrators, is considered in **Chapter 8.**

3. Options for Expanded Review

Since *Hall Street* and the uncertain status of non-statutory ground for review, parties continue to test options for expanded judicial review of arbitration awards. Two such methods are examined here.

a. Define "Excessive Powers" by Limiting Arbitral Powers to Bar Legal Error

Can parties effectively achieve the result of expanded review for legal error by contractually limiting the arbitrator's powers to require correct legal and factual rulings? The California Supreme Court in *Cable Connection, Inc. v. DirecTV, Inc.*, 190 P.3d 586, 604 (Cal. 2008), so much as advised interested parties that they could similarly get judicial review where the arbitration agreement "explicitly and unambiguously" limited the powers of the arbitrator. Although the California Supreme Court's decision in *Moncharsh* establishes that courts will not review arbitral legal error, an exception applies where an arbitration agreement limits the powers of the arbitrator.

In *Cable Connection*, the California Supreme Court ruled that "the FAA provisions governing judicial review are specific to federal courts" and that the FAA did not preempt or conflict with the California Arbitration Act (CAA) over the ability of parties to create their own contract provision for judicial review. According to the Court, "if the parties constrain the arbitrators' authority by requiring a dispute to be decided according to the rule of law, and make plain their intention that the award is reviewable for legal error, the general rule of limited review has been displaced by the parties' agreement." *Id.* at 600.

Under this interpretation, parties may still contract for expanded judicial review of arbitral awards by contracting for application of state arbitration law, at least in California (for now, few other states have adopted this view).

Even courts that apply FAA standards—whether in state or federal courts—and consider review only for the exclusive grounds set forth in the FAA must address the practice where parties seek expanded judicial review through contractual provisions that limit an arbitrator's scope of authority. Courts addressing requests for legal error review as constituting "excessive powers" under the FAA have responded differently. Some courts recognize a contractual limitation on an arbitrator's power, as opposed to contractual provisions that purport to expand a court's review standard provided by statute. Thus, a number of courts have accepted review based on party contracts that limit arbitrators from making legal errors; while other courts see this practice as a subterfuge around *Hall Street* and the exclusive statutory grounds. *Wood v. PennTex Resources, LP* determined that "[t]his reading would impermissibly circumvent *Hall Street.*" 2008 U.S. Dist. LEXIS 50071 (S.D. Tex. June 27, 2008).

The practice of contractually limiting the scope of an arbitrator's authority to issue only legally correct rulings, thus availing legal error review under the "exceeding powers" provision of the FAA, may soon be the next test of the U.S. Supreme Court's patience.

b. Opting out of the FAA and for State Arbitration Law

Another practice parties may use to exercise greater control over their arbitration agreement is by specific choice-of-law clauses that designate state arbitration law to the dispute (another option is contracting for arbitral appeal). Recall from *Volt Information Sciences, Inc. v. Board of Trustees of Leland Stanford Junior University* that "[e]ven if §§ 3 and 4 of the FAA are fully applicable in state-court proceedings, they do not prevent the application of [state law] to stay arbitration where ... the parties have agreed to arbitrate in accordance with [state] law." Thus, parties may opt to have a state arbitration statute with a different standard of review for arbitration governing their arbitration. *See* Stephen K. Huber, *State Regulation of Arbitration Proceedings: Judicial Review of Arbitration Awards by State Courts*, 10 CARDOZO J. CONFLICT RESOL. 509 (2009).

Under *Hall Street* and *Cable Connection, Inc.*, state arbitration law becomes more relevant and may govern post-arbitration challenges through an explicit choice of law provision or through procedural rules applicable in state courts. State arbitration statutes have traditionally mirrored the FAA. Does *Hall Street* invite forum shopping for state arbitration statutes where expanded review is allowed?

For additional commentary, see Christopher R. Drahozal, *Contracting Around RUAA: Default Rules, Mandatory Rules, and Judicial Review of Arbitral Awards*, 3 PEPP. DISP. RESOL. L.J. 419, 432–33 (2003) (noting "restricted submissions" requiring arbitrators to follow the law); Weston, *The Other Avenues of* Hall Street *and Prospects for Judicial Review of Arbitral Awards*, 14 LEWIS & CLARK L. REV. 929 (2010).

H. Sanctions for Frivolous Appeals

A cautionary note for those filing petitions for vacatur. *B.L. Harbert Intern., LLC v. Hercules Steel Co.*, 441 F.3d 905 (11th Cir. 2006), recognized the existence of what it called a "poor loser problem" that threatened to frustrate the purposes of the Federal Arbitration Act. The court suggested that the way to retard this trend was to award sanctions when the losing party moved to vacate an arbitration award without "any real legal basis for doing so." The court reiterated this stance, imposing sanctions against the party who sought vacatur alleging the arbitrator displayed "evident partiality" and committed misconduct in *World Business Paradise, Inc. v. SunTrust Bank*, 403 Fed. Appx. 468 (11th Cir. 2010). According to the court:

> Appellants have provided no evidence to support their claims of partiality and misconduct. They point to only the arbitration award itself as evidence, but the award on its face does not reveal any actual or potential conflict of interest or impropriety.... Appellants have failed to present any transcript of the arbitration proceedings that would allow this Court to meaningfully review the challenged rulings of the arbitrator.

> SunTrust asks this Court to impose sanctions on Appellants for assuming a "never-say-die attitude" after losing the arbitration award and "drag[ging] the dispute through the court system without an objectively reasonable belief [they] will prevail." See B.L. Harbert Intern., LLC v. Hercules Steel Co., 441 F.3d 905, 913 (11th Cir. 2006). We have warned litigants that we are "ready, willing, and able to consider imposing sanctions in appropriate cases." We have recognized that "[a]rbitration's allure is dependent upon the arbitrator being the last decision maker in all but the most unusual cases" and that when litigants pursue baseless contests of arbitration awards, "the promise of arbitration is broken." [O]ur *Hercules Steel* decision put parties on notice "that this Court is exasperated by those who attempt to salvage arbitration losses through litigation that has no sound basis in the law applicable to arbitration awards." *Id.*

I. Practice Questions

This chapter has addressed the process and legal standards involved after an arbitration award has been issued. Apply your understanding of the law as follows:

1. Advise your client on the procedures and standards for enforcing or vacating an arbitration award. What is the deadline in which to file and serve a notice to vacate an arbitration award? To confirm an award?

2. What recourse is available to the losing party in an arbitration?

3. On what grounds would you seek judicial vacatur of an arbitration award? What factors is a court likely to consider?

4. What are the relative benefits or costs of seeking review?

Chapter 10

Class Arbitration

A. Introduction

This chapter considers the relatively recent emergence of class arbitration. If a large number of individuals allege that they suffered the same monetary injury stemming from the same transaction, but the amount any one individual suffered is too small to justify incurring the expense of litigation to pursue legal claims, then those individuals might be able to join together to pursue their claim collectively in a class action procedure. Under Federal Rule of Civil Procedure 23(a), individuals may combine their claims to be heard as one case before a single trier of fact if: "(1) the class is so numerous that joinder of all members is impracticable, (2) there are questions of law or fact common to the class, (3) the claims or defenses of the representative parties are typical of the claims or defenses of the class, and (4) the representative parties will fairly and adequately protect the interests of the class."

What happens if all of those individuals entered into pre-dispute arbitration agreements with the alleged wrongdoer? The same considerations that compel individuals to combine their claims in litigation exist for those individuals who are contractually bound to resolve their disputes in arbitration. What is the impact of those agreements on the ability of individuals to sue, not only on their own behalf, but on behalf of an entire class of similarly situated individuals subject to these contracts; that is, in a class proceeding, either in court or in arbitration?

Section B of this chapter addresses threshold questions that arise in this context: did the parties agree to proceed in class arbitration? And who decides that question if the agreement is not clear? Do arbitration agreements that are silent on the issue of class proceedings bar the filing of a class action in court or in arbitration? This section will also consider what the process of class arbitration entails and how it affects absent, non-participating class members.

As class arbitrations became more accepted by courts and arbitrators, entities with greater bargaining power began to insert additional language into agreements barring parties with weaker bargaining power the right to pursue any disputes on a collective or class-wide basis in arbitration or litigation. Why is it that entities that are typically pro-arbitration with respect to bilateral claims hostile to arbitration involving a class proceeding? Plaintiffs have challenged the enforceability of these "class action waivers" in court on a variety of grounds, including unconscionability. Section C explores how the Supreme Court has resolved these challenges.

B. Did the Parties Agree to Class Arbitration?

Where arbitration contracts do not address class actions, how should silence on the matter be interpreted—to allow or prohibit class actions? And who decides: the arbitrator, who could end up arbitrating the class proceeding, or a court? The Supreme Court addressed these questions in the decisions below.

Green Tree Financial Corp. v. Bazzle

539 U.S. 444 (2003)

JUSTICE BREYER announced the judgment of the Court and delivered an opinion, in which JUSTICE SCALIA, JUSTICE SOUTER, and JUSTICE GINSBURG join.

I

In 1995, respondents Lynn and Burt Bazzle secured a home improvement loan from petitioner Green Tree. The Bazzles and Green Tree entered into a contract, governed by South Carolina law, which included the following arbitration clause:

> ARBITRATION—All disputes, claims, or controversies arising from or relating to this contract or the relationships which result from this contract ... *shall be resolved by binding arbitration by one arbitrator selected by us with consent of you.* This arbitration contract is made pursuant to a transaction in interstate commerce, and shall be governed by the Federal Arbitration Act at 9 U.S.C. section 1.... THE PARTIES VOLUNTARILY AND KNOWINGLY WAIVE ANY RIGHT THEY HAVE TO A JURY TRIAL, EITHER PURSUANT TO ARBITRATION UNDER THIS CLAUSE OR PURSUANT TO A COURT ACTION BY US (AS PROVIDED HEREIN).... The parties agree and understand that the arbitrator shall have all powers provided by the law and the contract. These powers shall include all legal and equitable remedies, including, but not limited to, money damages, declaratory relief, and injunctive relief. ([E]mphasis added, capitalization in original).

Respondents Daniel Lackey and George and Florine Buggs entered into loan contracts and security agreements for the purchase of mobile homes with Green Tree. These agreements contained arbitration clauses that were, in all relevant respects, identical to the Bazzles' arbitration clause. (Their contracts substitute the word "you" with the word "Buyer[s]" in the italicized phrase.)

At the time of the loan transactions, Green Tree apparently failed to provide these customers with a legally required form that would have told them that they had a right to name their own lawyers and insurance agents and would have provided space for them to write in those names. The two sets of customers before us now as respondents each filed separate actions in South Carolina state courts, complaining that this failure violated South Carolina law and seeking damages.

In April 1997, the Bazzles asked the court to certify their claims as a class action. Green Tree sought to stay the court proceedings and compel arbitration. On January 5, 1998, the court both (1) certified a class action and (2) entered an order compelling arbitration. Green Tree then selected an arbitrator with the Bazzles' consent. And the arbitrator, administering the proceeding as a class arbitration, eventually awarded the class $10,935,000 in statutory damages, along with attorney's fees. The trial court confirmed the award and Green Tree appealed to the South Carolina Court of Appeals claiming, among other things, that class arbitration was legally impermissible.

Lackey and the Buggses had earlier begun a similar court proceeding in which they, too, sought class certification. Green Tree moved to compel arbitration. The trial court initially denied the motion, finding the arbitration agreement unenforceable, but Green Tree pursued an interlocutory appeal and the State Court of Appeals reversed. The parties then chose an arbitrator, indeed the same arbitrator who was subsequently selected to arbitrate the Bazzles' dispute.

In December 1998, the arbitrator certified a class in arbitration. The arbitrator proceeded to hear the matter, ultimately ruled in favor of the class, and awarded the class $9,200,000 in statutory damages in addition to attorney's fees. The trial court confirmed the award. Green Tree appealed to the South Carolina Court of Appeals claiming, among other things, that class arbitration was legally impermissible.

The South Carolina Supreme Court withdrew both cases from the Court of Appeals, assumed jurisdiction, and consolidated the proceedings. That court then held that the contracts were silent in respect to class arbitration, that they consequently authorized class arbitration, and that arbitration had properly taken that form. We granted certiorari to consider whether that holding is consistent with the Federal Arbitration Act.

II

The South Carolina Supreme Court's determination that the contracts are silent in respect to class arbitration raises a preliminary question. Green Tree argued there, as it argues here, that the contracts are not silent — that they forbid class arbitration. And we must deal with that argument at the outset, for if it is right, then the South Carolina court's holding is flawed on its own terms; that court neither said nor implied that it would have authorized class arbitration had the parties' arbitration agreement forbidden it.

Whether Green Tree is right about the contracts themselves presents a disputed issue of contract interpretation. The Chief Justice believes that Green Tree is right; indeed, that Green Tree is so clearly right that we should ignore the fact that state law, not federal law, normally governs such matters, and reverse the South Carolina Supreme Court outright. The Chief Justice points out that the contracts say that disputes "shall be resolved ... by one arbitrator selected by us [Green Tree] with consent of you [Green Tree's customer]." And it finds that class arbitration is clearly inconsistent with this requirement. After all, class arbitration involves an arbitration, not simply between Green Tree and a *named customer*, but also between Green Tree and *other* (represented) customers, all taking place before the arbitrator chosen to arbitrate the initial, *named customer's* dispute.

We do not believe, however, that the contracts' language is as clear as The Chief Justice believes. The class arbitrator *was* "selected by" Green Tree "with consent of" Green Tree's customers, the named plaintiffs. And insofar as the other class members agreed to proceed in class arbitration, they consented as well.

Of course, Green Tree did *not* independently select *this* arbitrator to arbitrate its disputes with the *other* class members. But whether the contracts contain this additional requirement is a question that the literal terms of the contracts do not decide. The contracts simply say (I) "selected by us [Green Tree]." And that is literally what occurred. The contracts do not say (II) "selected by us [Green Tree] to arbitrate this dispute and no other (even identical) dispute with another customer." The question whether (I) in fact implicitly means (II) is the question at issue: Do the contracts forbid class arbitration? Given the broad authority the contracts elsewhere bestow upon the arbitrator, the answer to this question is not completely obvious.

At the same time, we cannot automatically accept the South Carolina Supreme Court's resolution of this contract-interpretation question. Under the terms of the parties' contracts, the question — whether the agreement forbids class arbitration — is for the arbitrator to decide. The parties agreed to submit to the arbitrator "[*a*]*ll* disputes, claims, or controversies arising from or relating to this contract or the relationships which result from this contract." And the dispute about what the arbitration contract in each case means (i.e., whether it forbids the use of class arbitration procedures) is a dispute "relating to this contract" and the resulting "relationships." Hence the parties seem to have agreed that an arbitrator, not a judge, would answer the relevant question. And if there is doubt about that matter — about the " 'scope of arbitrable issues' " — we should resolve that doubt "in favor of arbitration."

In certain limited circumstances, courts assume that the parties intended courts, not arbitrators, to decide a particular arbitration-related matter (in the absence of "clea[r] and unmistakabl[e]" evidence to the contrary). These limited instances typically involve matters of a kind that "contracting parties would likely have expected a court" to decide. They include certain gateway matters, such as whether the parties have a valid arbitration agreement at all or whether a concededly binding arbitration clause applies to a certain type of controversy.

The question here — whether the contracts forbid class arbitration — does not fall into this narrow exception. It concerns neither the validity of the arbitration clause nor its applicability to the underlying dispute between the parties. Unlike *First Options*, the question is not whether the parties wanted a judge or an arbitrator to decide *whether they agreed to arbitrate a matter*. Rather the relevant question here is what *kind of arbitration proceeding* the parties agreed to. That question does not concern a state statute or judicial procedures. It concerns contract interpretation and arbitration procedures. Arbitrators are well situated to answer that question. Given these considerations, along with the arbitration contracts' sweeping language concerning the scope of the questions committed to arbitration, this matter of contract interpretation should be for the arbitrator, not the courts, to decide.

III

With respect to this underlying question — whether the arbitration contracts forbid class arbitration — the parties have not yet obtained the arbitration decision that their contracts foresee. As far as concerns the *Bazzle* plaintiffs, the South Carolina Supreme Court wrote that the "trial court" issued "an order granting class certification" and the arbitrator subsequently "administered" class arbitration proceedings "without further involvement of the trial court." Green Tree adds that "the class arbitration was imposed on the parties and the arbitrator by the South Carolina trial court." Respondents now deny that this was so, but we can find no convincing record support for that denial.

As far as concerns the *Lackey* plaintiffs, what happened in arbitration is less clear. On the one hand, the *Lackey* arbitrator (the same individual who later arbitrated the *Bazzle* dispute) wrote: "*I* determined that a class action should proceed in arbitration based upon *my* careful review of the broadly drafted arbitration clause prepared by Green Tree." And respondents suggested at oral argument that the arbitrator's decision was independently made.

On the other hand, the *Lackey* arbitrator decided this question after the South Carolina trial court had determined that the identical contract in the *Bazzle* case authorized class arbitration procedures. And there is no question that the arbitrator was aware of the *Bazzle* decision, since the *Lackey* plaintiffs had argued to the arbitrator that it should impose class arbitration procedures in part because the state trial court in *Bazzle* had done so. In the court proceedings below (where Green Tree took the opposite position), the *Lackey* plaintiffs maintained that "to the extent" the arbitrator decided that the contracts permitted class procedures (in the *Lackey* case or the *Bazzle* case), "it was a reaffirmation and/or adoption of [the *Bazzle*] court's prior determination."

On balance, there is at least a strong likelihood in *Lackey* as well as in *Bazzle* that the arbitrator's decision reflected a court's interpretation of the contracts rather than an arbitrator's interpretation. That being so, we remand the case so that the arbitrator may decide the question of contract interpretation — thereby enforcing the parties' arbitration agreements according to their terms.

The judgment of the South Carolina Supreme Court is vacated, and the case is remanded for further proceedings.

JUSTICE STEVENS, concurring in the judgment and dissenting in part.

The parties agreed that South Carolina law would govern their arbitration agreement. The Supreme Court of South Carolina has held as a matter of state law that class-action arbitrations are permissible if not prohibited by the applicable arbitration agreement, and that the agreement between these parties is silent on the issue. There is nothing in the Federal Arbitration Act that precludes either of these determinations by the Supreme Court of South Carolina.

Arguably the interpretation of the parties' agreement should have been made in the first instance by the arbitrator, rather than the court. Because the decision to conduct a class-action arbitration was correct as a matter of law, and because petitioner has merely challenged the merits of that decision without claiming that it was made by the wrong decisionmaker, there is no need to remand the case to correct that possible error.

Accordingly, I would simply affirm the judgment of the Supreme Court of South Carolina. Were I to adhere to my preferred disposition of the case, however, there would be no controlling judgment of the Court. In order to avoid that outcome, and because Justice BREYER's opinion expresses a view of the case close to my own, I concur in the judgment.

CHIEF JUSTICE REHNQUIST, with whom JUSTICE O'CONNOR and JUSTICE KENNEDY join, dissenting.

The parties entered into contracts with an arbitration clause that is governed by the Federal Arbitration Act (FAA). The Supreme Court of South Carolina held that arbitration under the contracts could proceed as a class action even though the contracts do not by their terms permit class-action arbitration. The plurality now vacates that judgment and remands the case for the arbitrator to make this determination. I would reverse because this determination is one for the courts, not for the arbitrator, and the holding of the Supreme Court of South Carolina contravenes the terms of the contracts and is therefore preempted by the FAA.

The agreement to arbitrate involved here, like many such agreements, is terse. Its operative language is contained in one sentence:

> All disputes, claims, or controversies arising from or relating to this contract or the relationships which result from this contract ... shall be resolved by binding arbitration by one arbitrator selected by us with consent of you.

The decision of the arbitrator on matters agreed to be submitted to him is given considerable deference by the courts. The Supreme Court of South Carolina relied on this principle in deciding that the arbitrator in this case did not abuse his discretion in allowing a class action. But the decision of *what* to submit to the arbitrator is a matter of contractual agreement by the parties, and the interpretation of that contract is for the court, not for the arbitrator. As we stated in *First Options of Chicago, Inc. v. Kaplan*, 514 U.S. 938 (1995):

> [G]iven the principle that a party can be forced to arbitrate only those issues it specifically has agreed *to* submit to arbitration, one can understand why courts might hesitate to interpret silence or ambiguity on the 'who should decide arbitrability' point as giving the arbitrators that power, for doing so might too often force unwilling parties to arbitrate a matter they reasonably would have thought a judge, not an arbitrator, would decide.

Just as fundamental to the agreement of the parties as *what* is submitted to the arbitrator is to *whom* it is submitted. Those are the two provisions in the sentence quoted above, and it is difficult to say that one is more important than the other. I have no hesitation in saying that the choice of arbitrator is as important a component of the agreement to arbitrate as is the choice of what is to be submitted to him.

Thus, this case is controlled by *First Options*, and not by our more recent decision in *Howsam v. Dean Witter Reynolds, Inc.*, 537 U.S. 79 (2002). There, the agreement provided that any dispute "shall be determined by arbitration before any self-regulatory organization or exchange of which Dean Witter is a member." Howsam chose the National Association of Securities Dealers (NASD), and agreed to that organization's "Uniform Submission Agreement" which provided that the arbitration would be governed by NASD's "Code of Arbitration Procedure." That code, in turn, contained a limitation. This Court held that it was for the arbitrator to interpret that limitation provision:

> "[P]rocedural' questions which grow out of the dispute and bear on its final disposition' are presumptively *not* for the judge, but for an arbitrator, to decide. *John Wiley & Sons, Inc. v. Livingston*, 376 U.S. 543 (1964)] (holding that an arbitrator should decide whether the first two steps of a grievance procedure were completed, where these steps are prerequisites to arbitration). So, too, the presumption is that the arbitrator should decide 'allegation[s] of waiver, delay, or a like defense to arbitrability.

I think that the parties' agreement as to how the arbitrator should be selected is much more akin to the agreement as to what shall be arbitrated, a question for the courts under *First Options*, than it is to "allegations of waiver, delay, or like defenses to arbitrability," which are questions for the arbitrator under *Howsam*.

... [T]he interpretation of private contracts is ordinarily a question of state law, which this Court does not sit to review." But "state law may nonetheless be pre-empted to the extent that it actually conflicts with federal law — that is, to the extent that it 'stands as an obstacle to the accomplishment and execution of the full purposes and objectives of Congress.'"

The parties do not dispute that these contracts fall within the coverage of the FAA....

Under the FAA, "parties are generally free to structure their arbitration agreements as they see fit." Here, the parties saw fit to agree that any disputes arising out of the contracts "shall be resolved by binding arbitration by one arbitrator selected by us with consent of you." Each contract expressly defines "us" as petitioner, and "you" as the respondent or respondents named in that specific contract. Each contract also specifies that it governs all "disputes ... arising from ... *this* contract or the relationships which result from *this* contract." These provisions, which the plurality simply ignores, make quite clear that petitioner must select, and each buyer must agree to, a particular arbitrator for disputes between petitioner and that specific buyer.

While the observation of the Supreme Court of South Carolina that the agreement of the parties was silent as to the availability of classwide arbitration is literally true, the imposition of class-wide arbitration contravenes the just-quoted provision about the selection of an arbitrator. To be sure, the arbitrator that administered the proceedings was "selected by [petitioner] with consent of" the Bazzles, Lackey, and the Buggses. But petitioner had the contractual right to choose an arbitrator for each dispute with the other 3,734 individual class members, and this right was denied when the same arbitrator was foisted upon petitioner to resolve those claims as well. Petitioner may well have chosen different arbitrators for some or all of these other disputes; indeed, it would have been reasonable for petitioner to do so, in order to avoid concentrating all of the risk of substantial damages awards in the hands of a single arbitrator. As petitioner correctly concedes, the FAA does not prohibit parties from choosing to proceed on a classwide basis. Here, however, the parties simply did not so choose.

"Arbitration under the Act is a matter of consent, not coercion." Here, the Supreme Court of South Carolina imposed a regime that was contrary to the express agreement of the parties as to how the arbitrator would be chosen. It did not enforce the "agreemen[t] to arbitrate ... according to [its] terms." I would therefore reverse the judgment of the Supreme Court of South Carolina.

JUSTICE THOMAS, dissenting.

I continue to believe that the Federal Arbitration Act (FAA) does not apply to proceedings in state courts. For that reason, the FAA cannot be a ground for preempting a state court's interpretation of a private arbitration agreement. Accordingly, I would leave undisturbed the judgment of the Supreme Court of South Carolina.

Maureen A. Weston, *Universes Colliding:*
The Constitutional Implications of Arbitral Class Actions
47 WM. & MARY L. REV. 1711, 1737–40 (2006)

Following the *Bazzle* decision, the AAA released its Supplementary Rules concerning class arbitrations. The AAA is the first of few providers to attempt to set forth guidelines in administering arbitral class actions. The AAA has structured a modified hybrid process for administering class arbitrations, whereby the arbitrator is responsible for all aspects of the class arbitration, but parties have the option to seek judicial review of arbitral decisions regarding clause construction and class certification. The AAA policy states that it will not administer class arbitration where the underlying agreement prohibits class claims, consolidation, or joinder, unless the parties are under a court order. The AAA will administer class arbitration where the parties' agreement provides for arbitration and either expressly permits or is silent with respect to class claims. Unlike most arbitrations, which are confidential, the rules also provide for public disclosure of class arbitration hearings and filings. The AAA also maintains a case docket on its website that details key information about the case.

The AAA policy essentially sets forth a three-step process. In step one, the arbitrator makes the initial determination, in accordance with *Bazzle*, of whether the arbitration clause permits a class action and enters a "Clause Construction Award." The rules then provide for a thirty-day stay of arbitral proceedings to permit either party to seek judicial relief to confirm or vacate the Clause Construction Award. Once this time period has run without a challenge to the award, or once a challenge has been denied by the court, the arbitrator proceeds with the class action arbitration.

In step two, the arbitrator determines whether to certify the proposed class.... In this assessment, the arbitrator is to follow criteria that parallel Rule 23 of the Federal Rules of Civil Procedure for numerosity, commonality of questions of law and fact, typicality of representative claims, and adequacy of representation. The AAA rules add a requirement that the arbitrator find "each class member has entered into an agreement containing an arbitration clause which is substantially similar to that signed by the class representative(s) and each of the other class members." The arbitrator also determines whether class arbitration is manageable and maintainable by investigating whether questions of law or fact common to the class predominate over any questions facing individual members. Upon deciding whether a class can be maintained in arbitration, the arbitrator submits what is known as the "Class Determination Award." An award certifying a class arbitration must "define the class, identify the class representative(s) and counsel, and shall set forth the class claims, issues, or defenses," in addition to stating "when and how members of the class may be excluded from the class arbitration." Again, the AAA rules provide for a thirty-day stay of all proceedings following the issuance of the Class Determination Award to permit any party to seek judicial review to confirm or vacate the Class Determination Award.

After certification, the arbitrator issues a "Notice of Class Determination," which directs that class members be provided the "best notice practicable under the circumstances." This notice is required for "all members who can be identified through reasonable effort" and must describe

> (1) the nature of the action; (2) the definition of the class certified; (3) the class claims, issues, or defenses; (4) that a class member may enter an appearance through counsel if the member so desires, and that any class member may attend the hearings; (5) that the arbitrator will exclude from the class any member who requests exclusion, stating when and how members may elect to be excluded; (6) the binding effect of a class judgment on class members; (7) the identity and biographical information about the arbitrator, the class representative(s) and class counsel that have been approved by the arbitrator to represent the class; and (8) how and to whom a class member may communicate about the class arbitration, including information about the AAA Class Arbitration Docket....

Following notice, the class action arbitration proceeds to the merits stage where the arbitrator hears the evidence and arguments of both parties. The arbitrator then renders a "Final Award" on the merits that "shall be reasoned and shall define the class with specificity." The arbitrator must approve any settlement, voluntary dismissal, or compromise of arbitral class claims and conduct a hearing to determine the fairness of such disposition. The arbitrator also rules on requests for exclusion and objections to settlement. Presumably, then, all class members who have not opted out are bound by the class arbitration ruling.

The AAA does not purport to ensure that the constitutional or substantive rights of the parties involved will be upheld. Neither does it maintain that justice will be carried out. Yet, the AAA rules do reflect consideration for the implicit due process concerns of nonparticipating class members.

Stolt-Nielsen S. A. v. AnimalFeeds Int'l Corp.

559 U.S. 662 (2010)

JUSTICE ALITO delivered the opinion of the Court.

We granted certiorari in this case to decide whether imposing class arbitration on parties whose arbitration clauses are "silent" on that issue is consistent with the Federal Arbitration Act (FAA), 9 U.S.C. § 1 *et seq.*

I

[The parties in this case, Stolt-Nielsen, a shipping company, and AnimalFeeds, one of its customers, entered into a standard maritime contract which contained an arbitration clause that was silent on the issue of whether the parties can proceed as a class. In 2005, AnimalFeeds served petitioners with a demand for class arbitration. The parties entered into a supplemental agreement under which the class action would proceed under the Class Rules developed by the American Arbitration Association (AAA). As provided in the AAA Class Rules, the parties first presented arguments as to whether the arbitration clause allowed the petitioners to bring a class proceeding. After hearing the arguments, the arbitrator permitted the class procedure, but stayed the proceeding so the parties could seek judicial review.]

The District Court vacated the award, concluding that the arbitrators' decision was made in "manifest disregard" of the law insofar as the arbitrators failed to conduct a choice-of-law analysis. See *Wilko v. Swan*, 346 U.S. 427 (1953) ("[T]he interpretations of the law by the arbitrators in contrast to manifest disregard are not subject, in the federal courts, to judicial review for error in interpretation").... AnimalFeeds appealed to the Court of Appeals, which reversed. As an initial matter, the Court of Appeals held that the "manifest disregard" standard survived our decision in *Hall Street Associates v. Mattel, Inc.*, 552 U.S. 576 (2008), as a "judicial gloss" on the enumerated grounds for vacatur of arbitration awards under 9 U.S.C. § 10. Nonetheless, the Court of Appeals concluded that, because petitioners had cited no authority applying a federal maritime rule of custom and usage *against* class arbitration, the arbitrators' decision was not in manifest disregard of federal maritime law. Nor had the arbitrators manifestly disregarded New York law, the Court of Appeals continued, since nothing in New York case law established a rule against class arbitration. We granted certiorari.

II

Petitioners contend that the decision of the arbitration panel must be vacated, but in order to obtain that relief, they must clear a high hurdle. It is not enough for petitioners to show that the panel committed an error—or even a serious error. "It is only when [an] arbitrator strays from interpretation and application of the agreement and effectively 'dispense[s] his own brand of industrial justice' that his decision may be unenforceable." *Major League Baseball Players Assn. v. Garvey*, 532 U.S. 504. In that situation, an arbitration decision may be vacated under § 10(a)(4) of the FAA on the ground that the arbitrator "exceeded [his] powers," for the task of an arbitrator is to interpret and enforce a contract, not to make public policy. In this case, we must conclude that what the arbitration panel did was simply to impose its own view of sound policy regarding class arbitration.[3]

In its memorandum of law filed in the arbitration proceedings, AnimalFeeds made three arguments in support of construing the arbitration clause to permit class arbitration: [1. Class arbitration is permitted under *Bazzle*, 2) public policy is in favor of class procedures, and 3) the clause would be unenforceable as unconscionable if class arbitration is not permitted.] The arbitrators expressly rejected AnimalFeeds' first argument, and said nothing about the third. Instead, the panel appears to have rested its decision on AnimalFeeds' public policy argument [including the fact that many other arbitrators previously found that "silent" clauses permitted class actions]....

Rather than inquiring whether the FAA, maritime law, or New York law contains a "default rule" under which an arbitration clause is construed as allowing class arbitration in the absence of express consent, the panel proceeded as if it had the authority of a common-law court to develop what it viewed as the best rule to be applied in such a situation. Perceiving a post-*Bazzle* consensus among arbitrators that class arbitration is beneficial in "a wide variety of settings," the panel considered only whether there was any good reason not to follow that consensus in this case. The panel was not persuaded by "court cases denying consolidation of arbitrations," by undisputed evidence that the Vegoilvoy charter party had "never been the basis of a class action," or by expert opinion that "sophisticated, multinational commercial parties of the type that are sought to be included in the class would never intend that the arbitration clauses would permit a class arbitration." Accordingly, finding no convincing ground for departing from the post-*Bazzle* arbitral consensus, the panel held that class arbitration was permitted in this case. The conclusion is inescapable that the panel simply imposed its own conception of sound policy.

It is true that the panel opinion makes a few references to intent, but none of these shows that the panel did anything other than impose its own policy preference. The opinion states that, under *Bazzle*, "arbitrators must look to the language of the parties' agreement to ascertain the parties' intention whether they intended to permit or to preclude class action," and the panel added that "[t]his is also consistent with New York law." But the panel had no occasion to "ascertain the parties' intention"

---

3. We do not decide whether " 'manifest disregard' " survives our decision in *Hall Street*, as an independent ground for review or as a judicial gloss on the enumerated grounds for vacatur set forth at 9 U.S.C. § 10. * * *

in the present case because the parties were in complete agreement regarding their intent....

[I]nstead of identifying and applying a rule of decision derived from the FAA or either maritime or New York law, the arbitration panel imposed its own policy choice and thus exceeded its powers. As a result, under § 10(b) of the FAA, we must either "direct a rehearing by the arbitrators" or decide the question that was originally referred to the panel. Because we conclude that there can be only one possible outcome on the facts before us, we see no need to direct a rehearing by the arbitrators.

III

The arbitration panel thought that *Bazzle* "controlled" the "resolution" of the question whether the [contract] "permit[s] this arbitration to proceed on behalf of a class," but that understanding was incorrect.

...

When *Bazzle* reached this Court, no single rationale commanded a majority. The opinions of the Justices who joined the judgment—that is, the plurality opinion and Justice STEVENS' opinion—collectively addressed three separate questions. The first was which decision maker (court or arbitrator) should decide whether the contracts in question were "silent" on the issue of class arbitration. The second was what standard the appropriate decision maker should apply in determining whether a contract allows class arbitration. (For example, does the FAA entirely preclude class arbitration? Does the FAA permit class arbitration only under limited circumstances, such as when the contract expressly so provides? Or is this question left entirely to state law?) The final question was whether, under whatever standard is appropriate, class arbitration had been properly ordered in the case at hand.

The plurality opinion decided only the first question, concluding that the arbitrator and not a court should decide whether the contracts were indeed "silent" on the issue of class arbitration.... The plurality did not decide either the second or the third question noted above.

Justice STEVENS concurred in the judgment vacating and remanding because otherwise there would have been "no controlling judgment of the Court," but he did not endorse the plurality's rationale. He did not take a definitive position on the first question, stating only that "*[a]rguably* the interpretation of the parties' agreement should have been made in the first instance by the arbitrator." ... [H]is analysis bypassed the first question noted above and rested instead on his resolution of the second and third questions. Thus, *Bazzle* did not yield a majority decision on any of the three questions....

IV

... [A] party may not be compelled under the FAA to submit to class arbitration unless there is a contractual basis for concluding that the party *agreed* to do so. In this case, however, the arbitration panel imposed class arbitration even though the parties concurred that they had reached "no agreement" on that issue. The critical point, in the view of the arbitration panel, was that petitioners did not "establish that the parties to the charter agreements intended to *preclude* class arbitration." Even though the parties are sophisticated business entities, even though there is no tradition of class arbitration under maritime law, and even though AnimalFeeds does not dispute that it is customary for the shipper to choose the charter party that is used for a particular shipment, the panel regarded the agreement's silence on the question of class arbitration as dispositive. The panel's conclusion is fundamentally at war with the foundational FAA principle that arbitration is a matter of consent.

In certain contexts, it is appropriate to presume that parties that enter into an arbitration agreement implicitly authorize the arbitrator to adopt such procedures as are necessary to give effect to the parties' agreement.... An implicit agreement to authorize class-action arbitration, however, is not a term that the arbitrator may infer solely from the fact of the parties' agreement to arbitrate. This is so because class-action arbitration changes the nature of arbitration to such a degree that it cannot be presumed the parties consented to it by simply agreeing to submit their disputes to an arbitrator. In bilateral arbitration, parties forgo the procedural rigor and appellate review of the courts in order to realize the benefits of private dispute resolution: lower costs, greater efficiency and speed, and the ability to choose expert adjudicators to resolve specialized disputes. But the relative benefits of class-action arbitration are much less assured, giving reason to doubt the parties' mutual consent to resolve disputes through class-wide arbitration.

Consider just some of the fundamental changes brought about by the shift from bilateral arbitration to class-action arbitration. An arbitrator chosen according to an agreed-upon procedure no longer resolves a single dispute between the parties to a single agreement, but instead resolves many disputes between hundreds or perhaps even thousands of parties. Under the Class Rules, "the presumption of privacy and confidentiality" that applies in many bilateral arbitrations "shall not apply in class arbitrations," thus potentially frustrating the parties' assumptions when they agreed to arbitrate. The arbitrator's award no longer purports to bind just the parties to a single arbitration agreement, but adjudicates the rights of absent parties as well. And the commercial stakes of class-action arbitration are comparable to those of class-action litigation, even though the scope of judicial review is much more limited. We think that the differences between bilateral and class-action arbitration are too great for arbitrators to presume, consistent with their limited powers under the FAA, that the parties' mere silence on the issue of class-action arbitration constitutes consent to resolve their disputes in class proceedings.

The dissent minimizes these crucial differences by characterizing the question before the arbitrators as being merely what "procedural mode" was available to present AnimalFeeds' claims. If the question were that simple, there would be no need to consider the parties' intent with respect to class arbitration. See *Howsam* [537 U.S.] at 84 (committing "procedural questions" presumptively to the arbitrator's discretion (internal quotation marks omitted)). But the FAA requires more. Contrary to the dissent, but consistent with our precedents emphasizing the consensual basis of arbitration, we see the question as being whether the parties *agreed to authorize* class arbitration. Here, where the parties stipulated that there was "no agreement" on this question, it follows that the parties cannot be compelled to submit their dispute to class arbitration.

V

For these reasons, the judgment of the Court of Appeals is reversed, and the case is remanded for further proceedings consistent with this opinion. *It is so ordered.*

JUSTICE GINSBURG, with whom JUSTICE STEVENS and JUSTICE BREYER join, dissenting.

When an arbitration clause is silent on the question, may arbitration proceed on behalf of a class? The Court prematurely takes up that important question and, indulging in *de novo* review, overturns the ruling of experienced arbitrators.

The Court errs in addressing an issue not ripe for judicial review. Compounding that error, the Court substitutes its judgment for that of the decisionmakers chosen by the parties. I would dismiss the petition as improvidently granted. Were I to reach the merits, I would adhere to the strict limitations the FAA places on judicial review of arbitral awards. Accordingly, I would affirm the judgment of the Second Circuit, which rejected petitioners' plea for vacation of the arbitrators' decision....

II

I consider, first, the fitness of the arbitrators' clause-construction award for judicial review. The arbitrators decided the issue, in accord with the parties' supplemental agreement, "as a threshold matter." Their decision that the charter-party arbitration clause permitted class arbitration was abstract and highly interlocutory....

The Court does not persuasively justify judicial intervention so early in the game or convincingly reconcile its adjudication with the firm final-judgment rule prevailing in the federal court system. *See, e.g.,* 28 U.S.C. § 1257 (providing for petitions for certiorari from "[f]inal judgments or decrees" of state courts); § 1291 (providing for Court of Appeals review of district court "final decisions"); *Catlin v. United States,* 324 U.S. 229 (1945) (describing "final decision" generally as "one which ends the litigation on the merits and leaves nothing for the court to do but execute the judgment").

We have equated to "final decisions" a slim set of "collateral orders" that share these characteristics: They "are conclusive, [they] resolve important questions separate from the merits, and [they] are effectively unreviewable on appeal from the final judgment in the underlying action."... Congress, of course, can provide exceptions to the "final-decision" rule.... Did Congress provide for immediate review of the preliminary ruling in question here?

Section 16 of the FAA, governing appellate review of district court arbitration orders, lists as an appealable disposition a district court decision "confirming or denying confirmation of an award or partial award." Notably, the arbitrators in the matter at hand labeled their decision "Partial Final Clause Construction Award." It cannot be true, however, that parties or arbitrators can gain instant review by slicing off a preliminary decision or a procedural order and declaring its resolution a "partial award."

. . .

While lower court opinions are thus divided, this much is plain: No decision of this Court, until today, has ever approved immediate judicial review of an arbitrator's decision as preliminary as the "partial award" made in this case.

III

Even if Stolt-Nielsen had a plea ripe for judicial review, the Court should reject it on the merits....

The controlling FAA prescription authorizes a court to vacate an arbitration panel's decision "only in very unusual circumstances." The four grounds for vacatur codified in § 10(a) restate the longstanding rule that, "[i]f [an arbitration] award is within the submission, and contains the honest decision of the arbitrators, after a full and fair hearing of the parties, a court ... will not set [the award] aside for error, either in law or fact." *Burchell v. Marsh*, 58 U.S. 344 (1855).

The sole § 10 ground Stolt-Nielsen invokes for vacating the arbitrators' decision is § 10(a)(4). The question under that provision is "whether the arbitrators had the power, based on the parties' submissions or the arbitration agreement, to reach a certain issue, not whether the arbitrators correctly decided that issue." The parties' supplemental agreement, referring the class-arbitration issue to an arbitration panel, undoubtedly empowered the arbitrators to render their clause-construction decision. That scarcely debatable point should resolve this case.

The Court's characterization of the arbitration panel's decision as resting on "policy," not law, is hardly fair comment, for "policy" is not so much as mentioned in the arbitrators' award. Instead, the panel tied its conclusion that the arbitration clause permitted class arbitration to New York law, federal maritime law, and decisions made by other panels pursuant to Rule 3 of the American Arbitration Association's Supplementary Rules for Class Arbitrations.

. . .

The question properly before the Court is not whether the arbitrators' ruling was erroneous, but whether the arbitrators "exceeded their powers." § 10(a)(4). The arbitrators decided a threshold issue, explicitly committed to them, about the procedural mode available for presentation of AnimalFeeds' antitrust claims. That the arbitrators endeavored to perform their assigned task honestly is not contested. "Courts ... do not sit to hear claims of factual or legal error by an arbitrator as an appellate court does in reviewing decisions of lower courts." The arbitrators here not merely "arguably," but certainly, "constru[ed] ... the contract" with fidelity to their commission. This Court, therefore, may not disturb the arbitrators' judgment, even if convinced that "serious error" infected the panel's award.

. . .

IV

For arbitrators to consider whether a claim should proceed on a class basis, the Court apparently demands contractual language one can read as affirmatively authorizing class arbitration. See *ante* ("[A] party may not be compelled under the FAA to submit to class arbitration unless there is a contractual basis for concluding that the party *agreed* to do so."). The breadth of the arbitration clause, and the absence of any provision waiving or banning class proceedings, will not do.

The Court ties the requirement of affirmative authorization to "the basic precept that arbitration 'is a matter of consent, not coercion.'" Parties may "specify *with whom* they choose to arbitrate," the Court observes, just as they may "limit the issues they choose to arbitrate." But arbitrators, in delineating an appropriate class, need not, and should not, disregard such contractual constraints. In this case, for example, AnimalFeeds proposes to pursue, on behalf of a class, only "claims … arising out of any [charter party agreement] … *that provides for arbitration*." Should the arbitrators certify the proposed class, they would adjudicate only the rights of persons "with whom" Stolt-Nielsen agreed to arbitrate, and only "issues" subject to arbitration.

The Court also links its affirmative-authorization requirement to the parties' right to stipulate rules under which arbitration may proceed. The question, however, is the proper default rule when there is no stipulation. Arbitration provisions, this Court has noted, are a species of forum-selection clauses. Suppose the parties had chosen a New York *judicial forum* for resolution of "any dispute" involving a contract for ocean carriage of goods. There is little question that the designated court, state or federal, would have authority to conduct claims like AnimalFeeds' on a class basis. Why should the class-action prospect vanish when the "any dispute" clause is contained in an arbitration agreement? If the Court is right that arbitrators ordinarily are not equipped to manage class proceedings, then the claimant should retain its right to proceed in that format in court.

When adjudication is costly and individual claims are no more than modest in size, class proceedings may be "the thing," *i.e.*, without them, potential claimants will have little, if any, incentive to seek vindication of their rights. *Amchem Products v. Windsor*, 521 U.S. 591 (1997); *Carnegie v. Household Int'l*, 376 F.3d 656 (C.A.7 2004) ("The *realistic* alternative to a class action is not 17 million individual suits, but zero individual suits, as only a lunatic or a fanatic sues for $30."). Mindful that disallowance of class proceedings severely shrinks the dimensions of the case or controversy a claimant can mount, I note some stopping points in the Court's decision.

First, the Court does not insist on express consent to class arbitration. Class arbitration may be ordered if "there is a contractual basis for concluding that the part[ies] *agreed*" "to submit to class arbitration." Second, by observing that "the parties [here] are sophisticated business entities," and "that it is customary for the shipper to choose the charter party that is used for a particular shipment," the Court apparently spares from its affirmative-authorization requirement contracts of adhesion presented on a take-it-or-leave-it basis. While these qualifications limit the scope of the Court's decision, I remain persuaded that the arbitrators' judgment should not have been disturbed.

. . .

For the foregoing reasons, I would dismiss the petition for want of a controversy ripe for judicial review. Were I to reach the merits, I would affirm the Second Circuit's judgment confirming the arbitrators' clause-construction decision.

1. Comments and Questions

a. As Professor Weston notes, in direct response to the Supreme Court's decision in *Bazzle*, the AAA promulgated its Supplementary Rules for Class Arbitration to set forth guidelines for the administration of class arbitrations. These rules incorporate many of the standards under Rule 23 of the Federal Rules of Civil Procedure and appear to provide for substantial interaction between courts and the arbitrator. The full text of the rules can be accessed on the AAA website at https://www.adr.org/active-rules.

What are some of the differences between class actions and class arbitration? What procedural difficulties do you anticipate in class arbitration? If you were an absentee class member, what would your concerns be? If you were a defendant in a class arbitration, what would your concerns be?

b. The AAA class arbitration rules also provide a 30-day stay in which to afford parties the option to seek judicial confirmation or vacatur of the panel's "partial, final awards" on "Clause Construction," and "Class Determination." In *Stolt-Nielsen*, Justice Ginsburg contended that judicial review of the "clause construction" award was not ripe for review and should have awaited final judgment. *Stolt-Nielsen*, 559 U.S. at 691 (Ginsburg, J., dissenting) ("It cannot be true, however, that parties or arbitrators can gain instant review by slicing off a preliminary decision or a procedural order and declaring its resolution a " 'partial award.' "). Can the AAA rules dictate to courts when they should review a partial award?

c. After *Bazzle* and *Stolt-Nielsen*, what is the Court's position on whether the availability of class arbitration is a question for a court or an arbitrator? The plurality in *Bazzle* suggested that it is a question of procedural arbitrability, but the five-member majority in *Stolt-Nielsen* (Justices Alito, Kennedy, Scalia, Thomas, and Roberts) appears to shun the "procedure" rationale in *Bazzle*. Instead, the *Stolt-Nielsen* majority emphasized the consensual foundation of arbitration:

> [T]he differences between bilateral and class-action arbitration are too great for arbitrators to presume, consistent with their limited powers under the FAA, that the parties' mere silence on the issue of class-action arbitration constitutes consent to resolve their disputes in class proceeding.

After *Stolt-Nielsen*, what is left of *Bazzle*?

d. After *Stolt-Nielsen*, can a court ever conclude that the parties intended to arbitrate on a class basis if their arbitration clause is silent with respect to class arbitration? In *Oxford Health Plans, LLC v. Sutter*, 569 U.S. 564 (2013), a dispute between Oxford, a health insurance company, and Sutter, a physician provider in its network, Oxford moved to vacate the arbitrator's decision that the parties' arbitration agreement authorized class arbitration. The district court denied the motion; the Third Circuit affirmed. Oxford sought review in the Supreme Court.

Justice Kagan, writing for a unanimous Court, held that an arbitrator who orders class arbitration based on his interpretation of the parties' contract that was silent on the issue does not necessarily "exceed [his] powers" under FAA § 10(a)(4). In *Oxford*, unlike in *Stolt-Nielsen* where the parties had stipulated that the parties' arbitration agreement did not address class arbitration, the parties disagreed as to how to interpret the contract, and agreed to allow the arbitrator to decide the issue. And the *Oxford* arbitrator concluded that "on its face, the arbitration clause ... expresses the parties' intent that class arbitration can be maintained." *Id.* at 2067. The Court wrote:

> Oxford chose arbitration, and it must now live with that choice. Oxford agreed with Sutter that an arbitrator should determine what their contract meant, including whether its terms approved class arbitration. The arbitrator did what the parties requested: He provided an interpretation of the contract resolving that disputed issue. His interpretation went against Oxford, maybe mistakenly so. But still, Oxford does not get to rerun the matter in a court. Under § 10(a)(4), the question for a judge is not whether the arbitrator construed the parties' contract correctly, but whether he construed it at all. Because he did, and therefore did not 'exceed his powers,' we cannot give Oxford the relief it wants.

Id. at 2071.

In light of *Oxford Health Plans*, under what circumstances can an arbitrator conclude that an arbitration agreement authorizes class arbitration?

Does interpreting silence as a ban on, or lack of consent to, class arbitration allow the drafting party to "[e]ffectively prevent class actions against it without having to say it was doing so in the agreement"? *Stolt-Nielsen*, 559 U.S. at 678 (citing South Carolina Supreme Court).

C. Express Contractual Bans on Class Actions

Can the "stroke of a pen" via an express ban on class actions be used to eviscerate class action recourse altogether? Until recently, courts were divided on the validity of class action waivers in arbitration agreements and whether such bans may be voided under state unconscionability doctrine (or require "enforcement as written" under

§ 2 of the Federal Arbitration Act). In two recent cases, however, the Supreme Court rejected challenges (on two different grounds) to class action waivers.

AT&T Mobility LLC v. Concepcion
563 U.S. 333 (2011)

[A different excerpt of *AT&T Mobility*, a 5–4 decision, is reproduced in Chapter 2, *supra*, on the topic of FAA preemption. The Supreme Court ruled that the FAA preempted California's unconscionability doctrine that conditioned the enforcement of an arbitration agreement upon the availability of class-wide arbitration. Justice Scalia, writing for the majority, addressed class arbitration:]

Although we have had little occasion to examine classwide arbitration, our decision in *Stolt-Nielsen* is instructive. In that case we held that an arbitration panel exceeded its power under § 10(a)(4) of the FAA by imposing class procedures based on policy judgments rather than the arbitration agreement itself or some background principle of contract law that would affect its interpretation. We then held that the agreement at issue, which was silent on the question of class procedures, could not be interpreted to allow them because the "changes brought about by the shift from bilateral arbitration to class-action arbitration" are "fundamental." This is obvious as a structural matter: Classwide arbitration includes absent parties, necessitating additional and different procedures and involving higher stakes. Confidentiality becomes more difficult. And while it is theoretically possible to select an arbitrator with some expertise relevant to the class-certification question, arbitrators are not generally knowledgeable in the often-dominant procedural aspects of certification, such as the protection of absent parties. The conclusion follows that class arbitration, to the extent it is manufactured by *Discover Bank* rather than consensual, is inconsistent with the FAA.

First, the switch from bilateral to class arbitration sacrifices the principal advantage of arbitration—its informality—and makes the process slower, more costly, and more likely to generate procedural morass than final judgment. "In bilateral arbitration, parties forgo the procedural rigor and appellate review of the courts in order to realize the benefits of private dispute resolution: lower costs, greater efficiency and speed, and the ability to choose expert adjudicators to resolve specialized disputes." But before an arbitrator may decide the merits of a claim in classwide procedures, he must first decide, for example, whether the class itself may be certified, whether the named parties are sufficiently representative and typical, and how discovery for the class should be conducted. A cursory comparison of bilateral and class arbitration illustrates the difference. According to the American Arbitration Association (AAA), the average consumer arbitration between January and August 2007 resulted in a disposition on the merits in six months, four months if the arbitration was conducted by documents only. As of September 2009, the AAA had opened 283 class arbitrations. Of those, 121 remained active, and 162 had been settled, withdrawn, or dismissed. Not a single one, however, had resulted in a final award on the merits. For those cases that were no longer active, the median time from filing to settlement, withdrawal, or dismissal—not judgment on the merits—was 583 days, and the mean was 630 days.

Second, class arbitration *requires* procedural formality. The AAA's rules governing class arbitrations mimic the Federal Rules of Civil Procedure for class litigation. And while parties can alter those procedures by contract, an alternative is not obvious. If procedures are too informal, absent class members would not be bound by the arbitration. For a class-action money judgment to bind absentees in litigation, class representatives must at all times adequately represent absent class members, and absent members must be afforded notice, an opportunity to be heard, and a right to opt out of the class. At least this amount of process would presumably be required for absent parties to be bound by the results of arbitration.

We find it unlikely that in passing the FAA Congress meant to leave the disposition of these procedural requirements to an arbitrator. Indeed, class arbitration was not even envisioned by Congress when it passed the FAA in 1925; as the California Supreme Court admitted in *Discover Bank,* class arbitration is a "relatively recent development." And it is at the very least odd to think that an arbitrator would be entrusted with ensuring that third parties' due process rights are satisfied.

Third, class arbitration greatly increases risks to defendants. Informal procedures do of course have a cost: The absence of multilayered review makes it more likely that errors will go uncorrected. Defendants are willing to accept the costs of these errors in arbitration, since their impact is limited to the size of individual disputes, and presumably outweighed by savings from avoiding the courts. But when damages allegedly owed to tens of thousands of potential claimants are aggregated and decided at once, the risk of an error will often become unacceptable. Faced with even a small chance of a devastating loss, defendants will be pressured into settling questionable claims. Other courts have noted the risk of "in terrorem" settlements that class actions entail, and class arbitration would be no different.

Arbitration is poorly suited to the higher stakes of class litigation.... We find it hard to believe that defendants would bet the company with no effective means of review, and even harder to believe that Congress would have intended to allow state courts to force such a decision.

American Express Co. v. Italian Colors Restaurant

570 U.S. Ct. 228 (2013)

[In *Italian Colors,* another 5–4 decision authored by Justice Scalia and excerpted in Chapter 4, *supra,* the Court "consider[ed] whether a contractual waiver of class arbitration is enforceable under the Federal Arbitration Act when the plaintiff's cost of individually arbitrating a federal statutory claim exceeds the potential recovery." The Court upheld a class action waiver in merchants' agreements with American Express, rejecting the merchants' argument that enforcing the class action waiver would prevent them from vindicating their rights under federal antitrust laws. The majority wrote:]

... the fact that it is not worth the expense involved in *proving* a statutory remedy does not constitute the elimination of the *right to pursue* that remedy. The class-action waiver merely limits arbitration to the two contracting parties. It no more eliminates those parties' right to pursue their statutory remedy than did federal law before its adoption of the class action for legal relief in 1938. Or, to put it differently, the individual suit that was considered adequate to assure "effective vindication" of a federal right before adoption of class-action procedures did not suddenly become "ineffective vindication" upon their adoption.

* * *

Truth to tell, our decision in *AT&T Mobility* all but resolves this case. There we invalidated a law conditioning enforcement of arbitration on the availability of class procedure because that law "interfere[d] with fundamental attributes of arbitration." "[T]he switch from bilateral to class arbitration," we said, "sacrifices the principal advantage of arbitration—its informality—and makes the process slower, more costly, and more likely to generate procedural morass than final judgment." We specifically rejected the argument that class arbitration was necessary to prosecute claims "that might otherwise slip through the legal system."

The regime established by the Court of Appeals' decision would require—before a plaintiff can be held to contractually agreed bilateral arbitration—that a federal court determine (and the parties litigate) the legal requirements for success on the merits claim-by-claim and theory-by-theory, the evidence necessary to meet those requirements, the cost of developing that evidence, and the damages that would be recovered in the event of success. Such a preliminary litigating hurdle would undoubtedly destroy the prospect of speedy resolution that arbitration in general and bilateral arbitration in particular was meant to secure. The FAA does not sanction such a judicially created superstructure.

The judgment of the Court of Appeals is reversed.

[In the dissenting opinion, Justice Kagan wrote:]

Here is the nutshell version of this case, unfortunately obscured in the Court's decision. The owner of a small restaurant (Italian Colors) thinks that American Express (Amex) has used its monopoly power to force merchants to accept a form contract violating the antitrust laws. The restaurateur wants to challenge the allegedly unlawful provision (imposing a tying arrangement), but the same contract's arbitration clause prevents him from doing so. That term imposes a variety of procedural bars that would make pursuit of the antitrust claim a fool's errand. So if the arbitration clause is enforceable, Amex has insulated itself from antitrust liability—even if it has in fact violated the law. The monopolist gets to use its monopoly power to insist on a contract effectively depriving its victims of all legal recourse.

And here is the nutshell version of today's opinion, admirably flaunted rather than camouflaged: Too darn bad.

1. Comments and Questions

a. What is the Supreme Court's current view on class arbitration as a form of arbitration? What are some of the Court's concerns with class arbitration? Of course, because class actions did not exist at the time of the passage of the FAA, the FAA does not mention class arbitration. Do you agree with Justice Scalia's statement in *AT&T Mobility* that class arbitration "is inconsistent with the FAA"? For a thoughtful analysis of this question, see S.I. Strong, *Does Class Arbitration "Change the Nature" of Arbitration? Stolt-Nielsen, AT&T, and A Return to First Principles*, 17 HARV. NEGOT. L. REV. 201, 205 (2012).

b. Justice Scalia's majority opinion in *AT&T Mobility* also rejected the dissent's concern that class proceedings are necessary to protect against small-value claims falling through the cracks of the legal system, reasoning that "[s]tates cannot require a procedure that is inconsistent with the FAA, even if it is desirable for unrelated reasons." Do you agree?

Many arbitration scholars sharply criticized the decision as anti-consumer, claim suppressing, and at odds with the fundamental right to have a dispute heard in a courtroom. *See, e.g.,* Jean R. Sternlight, *Tsunami: AT&T Mobility LLC v. Concepcion Impedes Access to Justice*, 90 OR. L. REV. 703 (2012); David S. Schwartz, *Claim-Suppressing Arbitration: The New Rules*, 87 IND. L.J. 239, 240 (2012).

c. Are Justice Kagan's concerns—expressed "in a nutshell" in the dissent in *Italian Colors*—justified? Do you think class action waivers combined with arbitration clauses suppress claims? After *AT&T Mobility* and *Italian Colors,* what avenue of relief is available for parties with nominal individual but significant collective claims?

d. *Class Action Waivers in Labor Contracts.* The National Labor Relations Board (NLRB) relied upon federal labor law in invalidating a class action waiver in *In re D.R. Horton, Inc.*, 357 N.L.R.B. No. 184, at *16–17 (Jan. 3, 2012). The three-member panel, ruled that class action waivers in employment agreements violate the National Labor Relations Act (NLRA), which guarantees employees the "right to engage in concerted action for mutual aid or protection." *D.R. Horton v. Nat'l Labor Relations Bd*, 737 F.3d 344 (5th Cir. 2013) (overruling NLRB's decision that the right to collective action under the NLRA invalidates the class action waiver but agreeing that the employer's arbitration clause impermissibly suggested that the employee waived all rights to report unfair labor practices to the Board).

Since *D.R. Horton,* federal circuits have split on the effect of the NLRA on class waivers. The Second, Fifth, and Eighth Circuits have upheld waivers over NLRB objections. *See Sutherland v. Ernst & Young, Inc.*, 726 F.3d 290 (2nd Cir. 2013); *Murphy Oil USA, Inc. v. NLRB*, 808 F.3d 1013 (5th Cir. 2015); *Cellular Sales of Missouri v. NLRB* (8th Cir. 2016). By contrast, the Sixth, Seventh and Ninth Circuits have held that class waiver bans violate the NLRA. *See National Labor Relations Board v. Alternative Entertainment, Inc.*, 858 F.3d 392 (6th Cir. 2017); *Epic Systems Corp. v. Lewis*, 823 F.3d 1147 (7th Cir. 2016), *cert. granted*, 137 S. Ct. 809 (2017); *Ernst & Young LLP v. Morris*, 834 F.3d 975 (9th Cir. 2016).

The consolidated appeal in *Epic Systems v. Lewis*, pitting the NLRA against the FAA on the viability of class waivers in employment arbitration agreements, was argued before the U.S. Supreme Court in October 2017. The issue before the court is: "Whether an agreement that requires an employer and an employee to resolve employment-related disputes through individual arbitration, and waive class and collective proceedings, is enforceable under the Federal Arbitration Act, notwithstanding the provisions of the National Labor Relations Act." As of the time this book went to press, the Supreme Court had not yet released its decision.

e. *Regulatory Bans on Class Action Waivers.* The Financial Industry Regulatory Authority (FINRA), a self-regulatory organization that regulates the securities industry under supervision of the Securities and Exchange Commission, has long banned broker-dealers from including class action waivers in their agreements with customers. *See* FINRA R. 2268; FINRA R. 12204. When broker-dealer Charles Schwab & Co. inserted a class action waiver into its customer agreement that contained a pre-dispute arbitration clause, FINRA brought an enforcement action against Schwab alleging the class action waiver violated FINRA's rules. Ultimately, Schwab settled the action, but not before FINRA's Board of Governors, in an administrative ruling, held that the FINRA rule barring class action waivers constituted a "contrary Congressional command" sufficient to override the FAA's mandate. *See Dep't of Enforcement v. Charles Schwab & Co.*, Disc. No. 2011029760201, 2014 WL 1665738 (FINRA Bd. of Gov. Apr. 24, 2014); *see also* Barbara Black and Jill Gross, *Investor Protection Meets the Federal Arbitration Act*, 1 STAN. J. COMPLEX. LITIG. 1 (2012) (arguing that FINRA's ban on class action waivers in customer agreements constitutes a "contrary Congressional command" sufficient to overcome the FAA). However, courts have held that these FINRA rules — which were enacted to protect investors — do not ban class action waivers in broker-dealers' agreements with their *employees*. *See Credit Suisse Sec. (USA) LLC v. Tracy*, 812 F.3d 249 (2d Cir. 2016).

Modeled, in part, on FINRA's ban, in July 2017 the Consumer Financial Protection Bureau (CFPB) exercised its regulatory authority and issued a rule barring class action waivers in consumer financial services agreements. *See* Bureau of Consumer Financial Protection, *Arbitration Agreements*, 82 Fed. Reg. 33210 (July 19, 2017). The CFPB rule was supposed to be effective September 2017 and apply to agreements entered into on or after March 19, 2018. However, the business community challenged the rule as unconstitutional and arbitrary, and Congress struck it down in October 2017.

f. For additional commentary on class arbitration, *see* Maureen A. Weston, *The Death of Class Arbitration After* Concepcion?, 60 KAN L. REV. 767 (2012); S.I. Strong, *Enforcing Class Arbitration in the International Sphere: Due Process and Public Policy Concerns*, 30 U. PA. J. INT'L L. 1 (2008); Kristen M. Blankley, *Class Actions Behind Closed Doors? How Consumer Claims Can (and Should) Be Resolved by Class-Action Arbitration*, 20 OHIO ST. J. ON DISP. RESOL. 451, 451–52 (2005).

D. Problems

1. You represent Betty Smith, who purchased and downloaded on her tablet a new, user-friendly app developed by EasyReader, Inc., that allowed her to read books that she purchased online. When Smith downloaded the app, she agreed to a contract labeled "Terms and Conditions," including a generic, broad pre-dispute arbitration clause, which requires that all disputes arising under or relating to the contract be submitted to arbitration. As it turns out, the app had a virus, which, upon download, infected her tablet. She had to replace the tablet. Your research determines that Smith's situation is not unique, as thousands of other users suffered the same damage when they downloaded the app. Although the individual claim amounts are small (less than $1,000 each), in the aggregate, hundreds of thousands of dollars are at stake. Thus, you decide to file a claim against EasyReader as a class action. Consider the following:

   a. The arbitration contract is *silent* with respect to class proceedings. May the case proceed as a class action in arbitration?

   b. Who decides that question—a court or an arbitrator?

   c. Alternatively, suppose the contract contains an express ban on class actions and requires "any dispute between the parties to be brought in an individual capacity in arbitration." Can Smith proceed with her class action? What is EasyReader's likely response?

2. West Fargo Bank (WFB) is one of the nation's largest banks, and it has operations in every state in the United States. WFB uses arbitration agreements in all of its consumer contracts, including in its deposit accounts and credit card accounts. WFB has three clauses at issue here:

> You and we agree that any Covered Disputes between or among you and us, regardless of when it arose, will, upon demand by either you or us, be resolved by the arbitration process described in Section (d) below. **You understand and agree that you and we are each waiving the right to a jury trial or a trial before a judge in a public court.**

And:

> A dispute is any unresolved disagreement between or among you and us. Disputes include:

- Claims based on broken promises or contracts.
- Torts (injuries caused by negligent or intentional conduct) or other wrongful actions.
- Statutory, common law, and equitable claims.
- Any disagreement about the meaning of this Arbitration Provision.
- Whether a disagreement is a "dispute" subject to binding arbitration as provided for in this Arbitration Provision.

And:

> Neither you nor we will be entitled to:
>
> • Join, consolidate or combine Covered Disputes by or against others in any arbitration; or
>
> • To include in any arbitration any Covered Dispute as a representative or member of a class.

Gloria Chavez came to your office in tears. She recently learned from the news that WFB employees opened up millions of fraudulent bank accounts in actual customers' names, and then WFB charged the customers excessive fees on the duplicative accounts. She checked her credit report and realized that she was a victim of this scheme. Although her actual damages are low—only $75—she feels victimized and wants you to file a class action lawsuit against WFB.

You decide to file a putative class action lawsuit against WFB in federal court. You expect that the WFB would like the case arbitrated.

    a. What types of procedural actions do you expect WFB to take with respect to arbitration?

    b. What types of substantive arguments do you expect WFB to make with respect to arbitration?

    c. How will you respond to both the actions and the arguments? How would you expect the court to resolve these issues?

    d. How will you counsel your client on the likelihood of litigating these claims?

Chapter 11

Complex Arbitration Procedures Involving Multiple Parties and Forums

A. Introduction

The prototype arbitration illustrated and discussed in many of the prior chapters involved only two parties, who at some point had at least arguably agreed to arbitrate their dispute. The parties may have disagreed about what forum—arbitration or court—should be used for resolving their dispute, or even who should decide that question, but their dispute was adjudicated in a single forum.

Many disputes are dyadic, with only two primary interests at stake, even when multiple parties are involved. For example, a dissatisfied former employee sues her former employer, her manager, a human resources manager, and perhaps members of the board of directors. In the securities industry, a customer may have a dispute with his financial advisor, the brokerage firm employing the advisor, and perhaps direct supervisors of the advisor and compliance officers of the brokerage. In these situations, it makes sense to consider the disputes as involving two "sides," even if the individual parties do not have identical interests for all purposes.

This chapter considers three situations in which additional levels of complexity arise in arbitration. These situations include disputes brought in multiple forums, claims by non-signatories to arbitration agreements, and the preclusive effect of arbitration awards in related proceedings. **Section B** begins by considering situations in which an arbitration agreement does not cover all of the disputes between the parties. In the leading case of *Dean Witter Reynolds v. Byrd*, the Supreme Court ruled that the agreement of the parties as to what issues are to be arbitrated versus tried in court trumps efficiency considerations. If the consequence is that some issues in dispute between two parties get heard by a court and some by an arbitrator, so be it. The costs of the separate, multiple proceedings approach, however, can be substantial. *See Quackenbush v. Allstate Ins. Co.*, 121 F.3d 1372 (9th Cir. 1997).

Section C examines the situation when a non-signatory to an arbitration agreement seeks either to compel a signatory to an arbitration agreement to arbitrate a dispute with that non-signatory or to intervene in an arbitration between the parties to the arbitration agreement but in which the non-signatory has interests at stake. The rules and underlying policies surrounding non-signatories usually vary depending on whether the non-signatory wants to be part of the arbitration or is resisting another party's attempt to include it in arbitration. Courts rely heavily on both arbitration law and traditional contract law dealing with third parties in ruling on these issues.

Finally, **Section D** deals with the effect of an earlier proceeding on a later proceeding—i.e. claim preclusion (res judicata) and issue preclusion (collateral estoppel). The basic question is whether, and to what extent, results or doctrine are different because either the former decision or the later proceeding is in arbitration.

Problem

NextGen, Inc., is a three-year-old biotech firm based in California. NextGen was incorporated to develop and market a new solvent for use in the manufacturing industry. In its first year of existence, NextGen received an "angel" investment from Chris Bonfire, a wealthy individual from California who has no background in solvents but is interested in new and promising businesses. Prior to investing $2.5 million in exchange for a two percent equity position in NextGen and a seat on NextGen's Board of Directors, the owners and principals of NextGen provided Bonfire with an extensive presentation detailing the scientific background of, and progress on, the solvent, and its potential market share. The contract between NextGen and Bonfire does not contain an arbitration agreement.

In NextGen's second year of existence, it received additional funding from TechInvestors, Inc., a company that routinely invests in early funding for small startups. NextGen made a technical presentation to TechInvestors that was nearly identical to the presentation it made to Bonfire. Ultimately, TechInvestors invested $10 million in exchange for a 30 percent equity position in NextGen and a seat on NextGen's Board of Directors. The investment paperwork between NextGen and TechInvestors includes an arbitration agreement.

Over the course of the next year, TechInvestors and Bonfire began to suspect that NextGen's technology was not nearly as advanced as it was advertised to these investors. The reports that they received at the Board of Directors' meetings did not seem to align with the marketing materials that they had previously reviewed. Bonfire and TechInvestors both want to bring claims against NextGen for fraud. When confronted with the allegations, NextGen stated that it would seek to arbitrate any claims relating to the investments.

Assume that TechInvestors concedes to the jurisdiction of the arbitral tribunal. Must Bonfire arbitrate, too? Even if not required to arbitrate, why might Bonfire consider arbitration at this point? If TechInvestors arbitrates and Bonfire litigates, which proceeding would you expect to end first? How might that affect the other proceeding? For a similar situation, *see Bouriez v. Carnegie Mellon University*, 430 Fed. Appx 182 (3d Cir. 2011).

B. Divided Disputes and Multiple Forums

Dean Witter Reynolds, Inc. v. Byrd

470 U.S. 213 (1985)

JUSTICE MARSHALL delivered the opinion of the Court. JUSTICE WHITE, concurring.

The question presented is whether, when a complaint raises both federal securities claims and pendent state claims, a Federal District Court may deny a motion to compel arbitration of the state-law claims despite the parties' agreement to arbitrate their disputes ...

I.

In 1981, A. Lamar Byrd sold his dental practice and invested $160,000 in securities through Dean Witter Reynolds Inc., a securities broker-dealer. The value of the account declined by more than $100,000 between September 1981 and March 1982. Byrd filed a complaint against Dean Witter in the United States District Court California, alleging violations the Securities Exchange Act of 1934, and of various state law provisions. Federal jurisdiction over the state law claims was based on diversity of citizenship and the principle of pendent jurisdiction. In the complaint, Byrd alleged that an agent of Dean Witter had traded in his account without his prior consent, that the number of transactions executed on behalf of the account was excessive, that misrepresentations were made by an agent of Dean Witter as to the status of the account, and that the agent acted with Dean Witter's knowledge, participation, and ratification.

When Byrd invested his funds with Dean Witter in 1981, he signed a Customer's Agreement providing that "[a]ny controversy between you and the undersigned arising out of or relating to this contract or the breach thereof, shall be settled by arbitration." Dean Witter accordingly filed a motion for an order severing the pendent state claims, compelling their arbitration, and staying arbitration of those claims pending resolution of the federal court action. It argued that the Federal Arbitration Act, which provides that arbitration agreements "shall be valid, irrevocable, and enforceable, save upon such grounds as exist at law or in equity for the revocation of any contract," required that the District Court compel arbitration of the state-law claims. The Act authorizes parties to an arbitration agreement to petition a federal district court for an order compelling arbitration of any issue referable to arbitration under the agreement. Because Dean Witter assumed that the federal securities claim was not subject to the arbitration provision of the contract and could be resolved only in the federal forum, it did not seek to compel arbitration of that claim. The District Court denied in its entirety the motion to sever and compel arbitration of the pendent state claims, and on an interlocutory appeal the Court of Appeals for the Ninth Circuit affirmed.

II.

Confronted with the issue [of] whether to compel arbitration of pendent state law claims when the federal court will in any event assert jurisdiction over a federal-law claim, the Federal Courts of Appeals have adopted two different approaches. Along with the Ninth Circuit in this case, the Fifth and Eleventh Circuits have relied on the "doctrine of intertwining." When arbitrable and nonarbitrable claims arise out of the same transaction, and are sufficiently intertwined factually and legally, the district court, under this view, may in its discretion deny arbitration as to the arbitrable claims and try all the claims together in federal court. These courts acknowledge the strong federal policy in favor of enforcing arbitration agreements but offer two reasons why the district courts nevertheless should decline to compel arbitration in this situation. First, they assert that such a result is necessary to preserve what they consider to be the court's exclusive jurisdiction over the federal securities claim; otherwise, they suggest, arbitration of an "intertwined" state claim might precede the federal proceeding and the fact finding done by the arbitrator might thereby bind the federal court through collateral estoppel. The second reason they cite is efficiency; by declining to compel arbitration, the court avoids bifurcated proceedings and perhaps redundant efforts to litigate the same factual questions twice.

In contrast, the Sixth, Seventh, and Eighth Circuits have held that the Arbitration Act divests the district courts of any discretion regarding arbitration in cases containing both arbitrable and nonarbitrable claims, and instead requires that the courts compel arbitration of arbitrable claims, when asked to do so. These courts conclude that the Act, both through its plain meaning and the strong federal policy it reflects, requires courts to enforce the bargain of the parties to arbitrate, and "not substitute [its] own views of economy and efficiency" for those of Congress.

We agree with these latter courts that the Arbitration Act requires district courts to compel arbitration of pendent arbitrable claims when one of the parties files a motion to compel, even where the result would be the possibly inefficient maintenance of separate proceedings in different forums. Accordingly, we reverse the decision not to compel arbitration.

III.

... By its terms, the Act leaves no place for the exercise of discretion by a district court, but instead mandates that district courts shall direct the parties to proceed to arbitration on issues as to which an arbitration agreement has been signed. Thus, insofar as the language of the Act guides our disposition of this case, we would conclude that agreements to arbitrate must be enforced, absent a ground for revocation of the contractual agreement.

It is suggested, however, that the Act does not expressly address whether the same mandate—to enforce arbitration agreements—holds true where, as here, such a course would result in bifurcated proceedings if the arbitration agreement is enforced. Because the Act's drafters did not explicitly consider the prospect of bifurcated proceedings, we are told, the clear language of the Act might be misleading. Thus, courts that have adopted the view of the Ninth Circuit in this case have argued that the Act's goal of speedy and efficient decision making is thwarted by bifurcated proceedings, and that, given the absence of clear direction on this point, the intent of Congress in passing the Act controls and compels a refusal to compel arbitration....

The legislative history of the Act establishes that the purpose behind its passage was to ensure judicial enforcement of privately made agreements to arbitrate. We therefore reject the suggestion that the overriding goal of the Arbitration Act was to promote the expeditious resolution of claims. The Act, after all, does not mandate the arbitration of all claims, but merely the enforcement — upon the motion of one of the parties — of privately negotiated arbitration agreements....

[P]assage of the Act was motivated, first and foremost, by a congressional desire to enforce agreements into which parties had entered, and we must not overlook this principal objective when construing the statute, or allow the fortuitous impact of the Act on efficient dispute resolution to overshadow the underlying motivation....

IV.

It is also suggested, however, and some Courts of Appeals have held, that district courts should decide arbitrable pendent claims when a nonarbitrable federal claim is before them, because otherwise the findings in the arbitration proceeding might have collateral estoppel effect in a subsequent federal proceeding. This preclusive effect is believed to pose a threat to the federal interest in resolution of securities claims, and to warrant a refusal to compel arbitration. Other courts have held that the claims should be separately resolved, but that this preclusive effect warrants a stay of arbitration proceedings pending resolution of the federal securities claim. In this case, Dean Witter also asked the District Court to stay the arbitration proceedings pending resolution of the federal claim, and we suspect it did so in response to such holdings.

... We conclude that neither a stay of proceedings, nor joined proceedings, is necessary to protect the federal interest in the federal-court proceeding, and that the formulation of collateral estoppel rules affords adequate protection to that interest.

Initially, it is far from certain that arbitration proceedings will have any preclusive effect on the litigation of nonarbitrable federal claims ... The full-faith-and-credit statute requires that federal courts give the same preclusive effect to a State's judicial proceedings as would the courts of the State rendering the judgment, and since arbitration is not a judicial proceeding, we held that the statute does not apply to arbitration awards. The same analysis inevitably would apply to any unappealed state arbitration proceedings. We also declined, in *McDonald*, to fashion a federal common-law rule of preclusion, in part on the ground that arbitration cannot provide an adequate substitute for a judicial proceeding in protecting the federal statutory and constitutional rights that § 1983 is designed to safeguard. *McDonald v. West Branch*, 466 U.S. 284 (1984). We therefore recognized that arbitration proceedings will not necessarily have a preclusive effect on subsequent federal-court proceedings.

Significantly, *McDonald* also establishes that courts may directly and effectively protect federal interests by determining the preclusive effect to be given to an arbitration proceeding. Since preclusion doctrine comfortably plays this role, it follows that neither a stay of the arbitration proceedings, nor a refusal to compel arbitration of state claims, is *required* in order to assure that a precedent arbitration does not impede a subsequent federal court action. The Courts of Appeals that have assumed collateral estoppel effect must be given to arbitration proceedings have therefore sought to accomplish indirectly that which they erroneously assumed they could not do directly....

1. Comments and Questions

a. *Byrd* holds that the FAA requires district courts to compel arbitration of arbitrable claims, even if they are "intertwined" with non-arbitrable claims and so "the result would be the possibly inefficient maintenance of separate proceedings in different forums." *See also Moses H. Cone Mem'l Hosp. v. Mercury Constr. Corp.*, 460 U.S. 1 (1983) (arbitration should proceed even though one party was also a plaintiff in a related lawsuit against a third party not subject to arbitration; stating "the relevant federal law ... requires piecemeal resolution when necessary to give effect to an arbitration agreement"). What tools of statutory interpretation did the Court use to determine that the FAA dictates this result? Do you agree?

b. Is the teaching of *Byrd* that enforcement of a contract completely trumps efficiency considerations? Courts will stay arbitration only where there is a question regarding the scope or validity of the arbitration agreement. The FAA provides for a stay of judicial proceedings where the issue is referable to arbitration as well as an immediate appeal of any order granting an injunction against arbitration. *See* FAA §§ 3 & 16, respectively. When a case involves both arbitral and nonarbitral claims, a court has discretion to stay the litigation of the nonarbitral claims until after the arbitration. The FAA does not address whether a court has the authority to stay arbitration pending resolution of litigated issues. Does the silence of the FAA on the matter of duplicate proceedings require the result reached by the Supreme Court in *Byrd*?

c. Although decided more than 30 years ago, the *Byrd* case remains good law. In a recent case from the Second Circuit, the court stated:

> The claim splitting doctrine does not bar arbitration of claims or defenses that the parties have agreed to arbitrate, while litigating overlapping claims or defenses that the parties have not agreed to arbitrate. LG cites no case applying the claim splitting doctrine—which is typically confined to "situations where the second suit is duplicative of another federal court suit,"— in the arbitration context. To the contrary, the Supreme Court has explained that the Federal Arbitration Act "requires piecemeal resolution when necessary to give effect to an arbitration agreement." *Dean Witter Reynolds, Inc. v. Byrd*, 470 U.S. 213, 221 (1985). In such circumstances, a court must "compel arbitration of pendent arbitrable claims..., even where the result would be the possibly inefficient maintenance of separate proceedings in different forums." Because the parties agreed to arbitrate the interpretation of the PLA, but did not agree to arbitrate the entirety of future infringement claims, the district court was correct to compel arbitration of the PLA defense, while allowing the underlying suit to proceed in federal court pending

resolution of that arbitrable issue. To the extent LG protests arbitrating a defense that might apply to certain of its allegedly infringing products but not others, that "splitting" likewise is not barred by the doctrine. "When a dispute consists of several claims, the court must determine on an issue-by-issue basis whether a party bears a duty to arbitrate," compelling arbitration of arbitrable claims, and permitting litigation of non-arbitrable claims.

LG Electronics v. Wi-Lan USA, 623 Fed. Appx. 568 (2nd Cir. 2015). Has anything changed in the last 30 years in arbitration or litigation practice that might require the Supreme Court to revisit the *Byrd* rule, such as the increased use of arbitration in consumer and employment contracts?

d. California has sought to address the inefficiency problem in at least a limited way. The California Arbitration Act provides:

> If the court determines that there are other issues between the petitioner and the respondent which are not subject to arbitration and which are the subject of a pending action or special proceeding between the petitioner and the respondent and that a determination of such issues may make the arbitration unnecessary, the court may delay its order to arbitrate until the determination of such other issues or until such earlier time as the court specifies. If the court determines that a party to the arbitration is also a party to litigation in a pending court action or special proceeding with a third party as set forth under subdivision (c) herein, the court (1) may refuse to enforce the arbitration agreement and may order intervention or joinder of all parties in a single action or special proceeding; (2) may order intervention or joinder as to all or only certain issues; (3) may order arbitration among the parties who have agreed to arbitration and stay the pending court action or special proceeding pending the outcome of the arbitration proceeding; or (4) may stay arbitration pending the outcome of the court action or special proceeding.

Cal. Civ. Proc. Code § 1281.2(c). In what ways is the California Arbitration Act an insufficient answer to the efficiency problem? How could the FAA and UAA provide a better approach to the efficiency problem? Can the courts effectively and inexpensively implement your system? Which policy matters more—efficiency or ordering of procedures? Do you think that this California statute is preempted by the FAA? Recall also from *Volt Information Sciences v. Board of Trustees*, 489 U.S. 468 (1989), that parties can elect in their agreement to be governed by a specific set of state arbitration laws and opt out of the FAA. *See id.* at 476; *see also* Alan Scott Rau, *Contracting Out of the Arbitration Act*, 8 Am. Rev. Int'l Arb. 225 (1997). Thus, contractual choice of forum, as well as choice of law, provisions are enforceable.

C. Third-Party Issues—Allowing and Requiring Non-Signatories to Arbitrate under Another Party's Agreement

As a general matter, only parties to a contract have rights and duties thereunder. The same general rule is true in arbitration. Accordingly, parties who are not signatories to contracts with an arbitration clause usually do not have to arbitrate claims arising out of that contract. The *First Options* case discussed in Chapter 3 is an example of this general rule. *First Options v. Kaplan*, 514 U.S. 938 (1995). On the other hand, non-parties to contracts may either be liable under those contracts or be able to take advantage of those contracts.

Under general contract law, a non-party may be bound to an arbitration agreement or take advantage of another's arbitration agreement under contract and agency law principles, such as (1) agency; (2) estoppel; (3) alter ego/veil piercing; (4) incorporation by reference (guarantors and sureties); (5) assumption or implied conduct, (6) successor in interest or sublessee, and (7) third-party beneficiary. For a thorough explanation of these theories, see Michael H. Bagot, Jr. & Dana A. Henderson, *Not Party, Not Bound? Not Necessarily: Binding Third Parties to Maritime Arbitration*, 26 Tul. Mar. L.J. 413, 435–58 (2002).

The question of whether a non-signatory agreed to submit the dispute to arbitration is a "question of arbitrability" and therefore subject to judicial determination. *See Howsam v. Dean Witter Reynolds, Inc.*, 537 U.S. 79 (2002). The absence of a contractual relationship may be raised by a party to avoid arbitration. For example, in typical financing situations, an obligation to pay money may be sold to a third party. Financing parties may be complete strangers to the underlying contract or may be closely related to the seller, as exemplified by home mortgages, auto, or consumer financing arrangements.

Does a litigant who is not a signatory to an arbitration agreement have standing to request a stay of litigation under section 16(a)(1)(A) of the FAA or to seek interlocutory review from a denial of a motion to stay litigation pending arbitration? Is interlocutory review available? Does availability of the non-signatory litigant to request the stay depend on the applicable state contract law? Consider the next case.

Arthur Andersen LLP v. Carlisle

129 S. Ct. 1896 (2009)

Justice Scalia delivered the opinion of the Court.

Section 3 of the FAA entitles litigants in federal court to a stay of any action that is "referable to arbitration under an agreement in writing." Section 16(a)(1)(A), in turn, allows an appeal from "an order ... refusing a stay of any action under section 3." We address in this case whether appellate courts have jurisdiction under § 16(a) to review denials of stays requested by litigants who were not parties to the relevant arbitration agreement, and whether § 3 can ever mandate a stay in such circumstances. We hold that the Sixth Circuit had jurisdiction to review the denial of petitioners' request for a § 3 stay and that a litigant who was not a party to the relevant arbitration agreement may invoke § 3 if the relevant state contract law allows him to enforce the agreement.

Respondents Carlisle, Bushman, and Strassel set out to minimize their taxes from the 1999 sale of their construction-equipment company. Arthur Andersen LLP, a firm that had long served as their company's accountant, auditor, and tax adviser, introduced them to Bricolage Capital, LLC, which in turn referred them for legal advice to Curtis, Mallet-Prevost, Colt & Mosle, LLP. According to respondents, these advisers recommended a "leveraged option strategy" tax shelter designed to create illusory losses through foreign-currency-exchange options. As a part of the scheme, respondents invested in various stock warrants through newly created limited liability corporations (LLCs), which are also respondents in this case. The respondent LLCs entered into investment-management agreements with Bricolage, specifying that "[a]ny controversy arising out of or relating to this Agreement or the breach thereof, shall be settled by arbitration conducted in New York, New York, in accordance with the Commercial Arbitration Rules of the AAA.

As with all that seems too good to be true, a controversy did indeed arise. The warrants respondents purchased turned out to be almost entirely worthless, and the Internal Revenue Service (IRS) determined in August 2000 that the "leveraged option strategy" scheme was an illegal tax shelter. The IRS initially offered conditional amnesty to taxpayers who had used such arrangements, but petitioners failed to inform respondents of that option. Respondents ultimately entered into a settlement program in which they paid the IRS all taxes, penalties, and interest owed.

Respondents filed this diversity suit in the Eastern District of Kentucky against Bricolage, Arthur Andersen and others (all except Bricolage and its employees hereinafter referred to as petitioners), alleging fraud, civil conspiracy, malpractice, breach of fiduciary duty, and negligence. Petitioners moved to stay the action, invoking § 3 of the FAA and arguing that the principles of equitable estoppel demanded that respondents arbitrate their claims under their investment agreements with Bricolage. The District Court denied the motions. (Bricolage also moved for a stay under § 3, but it filed for bankruptcy while its motion was pending, and the Court denied the motion as moot.) Petitioners filed an interlocutory appeal, which the Court of Appeals for the Sixth Circuit dismissed for want of jurisdiction. We granted certiorari.

Ordinarily, courts of appeals have jurisdiction only over "final decisions" of district courts. 28 U.S.C. § 1291. The FAA, however, makes an exception to that finality requirement, providing that "an appeal may be taken from … an order … refusing a stay of any action under section 3 of this title." § 16(a)(1)(A). By that provision's clear and unambiguous terms, any litigant who asks for a stay under § 3 is entitled to an immediate appeal from denial of that motion — regardless of whether the litigant is in fact eligible for a stay. Because each petitioner in this case explicitly asked for a stay pursuant to § 3, the Sixth Circuit had jurisdiction to review the District Court's denial.

The courts that have declined jurisdiction over § 3 appeals of the sort at issue here have done so by conflating the jurisdictional question with the merits of the appeal. They reason that because stay motions premised on equitable estoppel seek to expand (rather than simply vindicate) agreements, they are not cognizable under §§ 3 and 4, and therefore the relevant motions are not actually "under" those provisions. The dissent makes this step explicit, by reading the appellate jurisdictional provision of § 16 as "calling for a look-through" to the substantive provisions of § 3. Jurisdiction over the appeal, however, "must be determined by focusing upon the category of order appealed from, rather than upon the strength of the grounds for reversing the order." The jurisdictional statute here unambiguously makes the underlying merits irrelevant, for even utter frivolousness of the underlying request for a § 3 stay cannot turn a denial into something other than "an order … refusing a stay of any action under section 3." 9 U.S.C. § 16(a).

Respondents argue that this reading of § 16(a) will produce a long parade of horrible, enmeshing courts in fact-intensive jurisdictional inquiries and permitting frivolous interlocutory appeals. Even if these objections could surmount the plain language of the statute, we would not be persuaded. Determination of whether § 3 was invoked in a denied stay request is immeasurably more simple and less fact bound than the threshold determination respondents would replace it with: whether the litigant was a party to the contract (an especially difficult question when the written agreement is not signed). It is more appropriate to grapple with that merits question after the court has accepted jurisdiction over the case. Second, there are ways of minimizing the impact of abusive appeals. Appellate courts can streamline the disposition of meritless claims and even authorize the district court's retention of jurisdiction when an appeal is certified as frivolous. And, of course, those inclined to file dilatory appeals must be given pause by courts' authority to "award just damages and single or double costs to the appellee" whenever an appeal is "frivolous." Fed. Rule App. Proc. 38.

Even if the Court of Appeals were correct that it had no jurisdiction over meritless appeals, its ground for finding this appeal meritless was in error. We take the trouble to address that alternative ground, since if the Court of Appeals is correct on the merits point we will have awarded petitioners a remarkably hollow victory. We consider, therefore, the Sixth Circuit's underlying determination that those who are not parties to a written arbitration agreement are categorically ineligible for relief. * * *

Respondents do not contest that the term "parties" in § 3 refers to parties to the litigation rather than parties to the contract. The adjacent provision, which explicitly refers to the "subject matter of a suit arising out of the controversy between the parties," 9 U.S.C. § 4, unambiguously refers to adversaries in the action, and "identical words and phrases within the same statute should normally be given the same meaning." Even without benefit of that canon, we would not be disposed to believe that the statute allows a party to the contract who is not a party to the litigation to apply for a stay of the proceeding.

Section 2 explicitly retains an external body of law governing revocation (such grounds "as exist at law or in equity"). And we think § 3 adds no substantive restriction to § 2's enforceability mandate. "[S]tate law," therefore, is applicable to determine which contracts are binding under § 2 and enforceable under § 3 "*if* that law arose to govern issues concerning the validity, revocability, and enforceability of contracts generally." Because traditional principles of state law allow a contract to be enforced by or against nonparties to the contract through assumption, piercing the corporate veil, alter ego, incorporation by reference, third-party beneficiary theories, waiver and estoppel, the Sixth Circuit's holding that nonparties to a contract are categorically barred from § 3 relief was error.

Respondents argue that, as a matter of federal law, claims to arbitration by non-parties are not "referable to arbitration *under* an agreement in writing," because they "seek to bind a signatory to an arbitral obligation *beyond* that signatory's strictly con-tractual obligation to arbitrate," Perhaps that would be true if § 3 mandated stays only for disputes between parties to a written arbitration agreement. But that is not what the statute says. It says that stays are required if the claims are "referable to arbitration under an agreement in writing." If a written arbitration provision is made enforceable against (or for the benefit of) a third party under state contract law, the statute's terms are fulfilled. We thus reject the dissent's contention that contract law's long-standing endorsement of third-party enforcement is "a weak premise for inferring an intent to allow third parties to obtain a § 3 stay." It seems to us not weak at all, in light of the terms of the statute. There is no doubt that, where state law permits it, a third-party claim is "referable to arbitration under an agreement in writing." It is not our role to conform an unambiguous statute to what we think "Congress probably intended."

Respondents' final fallback consists of reliance upon dicta in our opinions, such as the statement that "arbitration … is a way to resolve those disputes—but only those disputes—that the parties have agreed to submit to arbitration," and the statement that "[i]t goes without saying that a contract cannot bind a nonparty." The former state-ment pertained to *issues* parties agreed to arbitrate, and the latter referred to an entity (the Equal Employment Opportunity Commission) which obviously had no third-party obligations under the contract in question. Neither these nor any of our other cases have presented for decision the question whether arbitration agreements that are otherwise enforceable by (or against) third parties trigger protection under the FAA.

Respondents may be correct in saying that courts' application of equitable estoppel to impose an arbitration agreement upon strangers to the contract has been "somewhat loose." But we need not decide here whether the relevant state contract law recognizes equitable estoppel as a ground for enforcing contracts against third parties, what standard it would apply, and whether petitioners would be entitled to relief under it. These questions have not been briefed before us and can be addressed on remand. It suffices to say that no federal law bars the State from allowing petitioners to enforce the arbitration agreement against respondents and that § 3 would require a stay in this case if it did.

JUSTICE SOUTER, with whom THE CHIEF JUSTICE and JUSTICE STEVENS join, dissenting.

Section 16 of the FAA authorizes an interlocutory appeal from the denial of a motion under § 3 to stay a district court action pending arbitration. The question is whether it opens the door to such an appeal at the behest of one who has not signed a written arbitration agreement. Based on the longstanding congressional policy limiting interlocutory appeals, I think the better reading of the statutory provisions disallows such an appeal, and I therefore respectfully dissent.

The Court says that any litigant who asks for and is denied a § 3 stay is entitled to an immediate appeal. The majority's assumption is that "under section 3" is merely a labeling requirement, without substantive import, but this fails to read § 16 in light of the "firm congressional policy against interlocutory or piecemeal appeals.

The right of appeal is a creature of statute, and Congress has granted the Federal Courts of Appeals jurisdiction to review "final decisions," 28 U.S.C. § 1291. Congress has, however, recognized the need of exceptions for interlocutory orders in certain types of proceedings where the damage of error unreviewed before the judgment is definitive and complete has been deemed greater than the disruption caused by intermediate appeal. Section 16 functions as one such exception, but departures from the dominant rule in federal appellate practice are extraordinary interruptions to the normal process of litigation and ought to be limited carefully.

An obvious way to limit the scope of such an extraordinary interruption would be to read the § 16 requirement that the stay have been denied "under section 3" as calling for a look-through to the provisions of § 3, and to read § 3 itself as offering a stay only to signatories of an arbitration agreement. It is perfectly true that in general a third-party beneficiary can enforce a contract, but this is a weak premise for inferring an intent to allow third parties to obtain a § 3 stay and take a § 16 appeal. While it is hornbook contract law that third parties may enforce contracts for their benefit as a matter of course, interlocutory appeals are a matter of limited grace. Because it would therefore seem strange to assume that Congress meant to grant the right to appeal a § 3 stay denial to anyone as peripheral to the core agreement as a nonsignatory, it follows that Congress probably intended to limit those able to seek a § 3 stay.

Asking whether a § 3 movant is a signatory provides a bright-line rule with predictable results to aid courts in determining jurisdiction over § 16 interlocutory appeals. And that rule has the further virtue of mitigating the risk of intentional delay by savvy parties who seek to frustrate litigation by gaming the system. Why not move for a § 3 stay? If granted, arbitration will be mandated, and if denied, a lengthy appeal may wear down the opponent. The majority contends, that "there are ways of minimizing the impact of abusive appeals." Yes, but the sanctions suggested apply to the frivolous, not to the far-fetched; and as the majority's opinion concludes, such an attenuated claim of equitable estoppel as petitioners raise here falls well short of the sanctionable. Because petitioners were not parties to the written arbitration agreement, I would hold they could not move to stay the District Court proceedings under § 3, with the consequence that the Court of Appeals would have no jurisdiction under § 16 to entertain their appeal.

1. Comments and Questions

a. Regarding the right to immediate appeal under § 16, the majority stated: "By that provision's clear and unambiguous terms, any litigant who asks for a stay under § 3 is entitled to an immediate appeal from denial of that motion—regardless of whether the litigant is in fact eligible for a stay." By contrast, the dissent responds: "Because it would therefore seem strange to assume that Congress meant to grant the right to appeal a § 3 stay denial to anyone as peripheral to the core agreement as a nonsignatory, it follows that Congress probably intended to limit those able to seek a § 3 stay." Which is the better argument?

b. You may recall from **Chapter 2** that the Supreme Court in the 2010 *Vaden* decision employed a look-through philosophy to determine jurisdiction under § 4 of the FAA. Should the 2009 *Carlisle* decision be revisited in light of the adoption of the look-through doctrine for some purposes in *Vaden*?

c. The dissenting Justices in *Carlisle* were Souter, Roberts, and Stevens—not the usual triumvirate. While a judge on the District of Columbia Court of Appeals, Roberts served on a panel that ruled against a third-party appeal in a case materially identical to *Anderson*—and he wrote the opinion. *See DSMC Inc. v. Convera Corp.*, 349 F.3d 679 (D.C. Cir. 2003). Roberts was not required to recuse himself because the case being reviewed by the Supreme Court was not one that he had previously decided. Roberts was noticeably silent during the oral argument in *Carlisle* while Justice Souter was an active participant. The *Carlisle* decision provides powerful ammunition for those who would argue that the Chief Justice of the Supreme Court is *primus inter pares* (i.e., first among equals), but no more.

d. The U.S. Chamber of Commerce filed an interesting amicus brief in *Carlisle*. *See Amicus Brief of the U.S. Chamber of Commerce*, 2008 WL 5417431. (Neither the majority nor the dissenting opinion mentioned the Chamber's brief.) As a long-time supporter of arbitration, it was no surprise that the Chamber supported the pro-review (Anderson) side of the case, but its usual rationale for favoring arbitration does not obviously lead to that result. The Chamber's standard argument for arbitration was based on efficiency (faster and cheaper), coupled with freedom of contract to choose arbitration over a judicial forum. Allowing appeals from adverse district court decisions at the behest of non-parties to an arbitration agreement does not promote efficient disposition of disputes, and arguably is contrary to the freedom of contract approach.

The Chamber's brief noted this difficulty, but argued that businesses had "settled expectations" of being able to enforce arbitration agreements entered into by others, based on conventional contract and agency principles. This argument has considerable merit in claims by successors in interest and family members. Here, however, Carlisle had separate contracts with Anderson, Bricolage, and Curtis. Thus, it is difficult to seriously suggest that permitting Anderson and Curtis to rely on the arbitration provision in Carlisle's contract with Bricolage to enjoin litigation promotes freedom of contract. Anderson and Curtis, both sophisticated business entities, consciously decided not to provide for arbitration in their respective contracts with Carlisle. Furthermore, there was no arbitration proceeding between Bricolage and Carlisle for Anderson and Curtis to join and, had there been such a proceeding, neither Anderson nor Curtis would be entitled to join it. At most, Anderson could obtain a stay of litigation until arbitration was completed, in the event that Bricolage exercised its power to require arbitration. The special circumstance of the Bricolage bankruptcy filing further clouds the picture. It is quite clear that what Anderson and Curtis desired was delay rather than efficient dispute resolution.

e. The obvious solution to the inefficiency associated with multiple proceedings is to get all the parties into a single forum. Apart from efficiency, an excluded party may fear that a decision in one proceeding will have an adverse effect on its interests, and therefore may wish to intervene in the arbitration to protect those interests. Is this a viable option in arbitration? Recall that this question also arose in the Problem involving Chris Bonfire and NextGen.

Belnap, M.D. v. Iasis Healthcare
844 F.3d 1272 (2d Cir. 2017)

HOLMES, CIRCUIT JUDGE.

Dr. Belnap is a general surgeon. In 2009, he joined the staff of the Salt Lake City hospital, SLRMC. Dr. Belnap was appointed Surgical Director of [the Salt Lake Regional Medical Center's ("SLRMC")] intensive-care unit. As an SLRMC staff member, Dr. Belnap's relationship with the hospital is governed by the SLRMC Bylaws. In addition to governing the treatment and care of patients, the Bylaws provide rules for investigating a physician, implementing a suspension, and guaranteeing due process through fair hearing procedures. The Bylaws do not contain an arbitration provision.

On February 1, 2012, Dr. Belnap entered into an Agreement with SLRMC. It related to the development of a "Hepatic Surgical department devoted to a[n] Abdominal Treatment Program," called the "Center." Specifically, the Agreement engaged Dr. Belnap's "management and consulting services" to develop and operate the Center. [The Agreement created an independent contractor relationship for Dr. Belnap.] ...

[SLMRC suspended Dr. Belnap's medical privileges based on allegations of sexual harassment. Those allegations were later dismissed, and SLMRC reinstated his privileges. During the suspension, SLRMC reported the suspension to a national medical reporting agency and allegedly did not adequately correct the record after the suspension was lifted. In addition, SLMRC renewed Dr. Belnap's privileges for only three months, rather than the customary two years.

Dr. Belnap filed suit in the District of Utah against SLMRC, SLMRC's parent company (Iasis), four physicians, a SLMRC Risk Manager, and Does 1–10. The Complaint asserts seven causes of action, including, inter alia, conspiracy regarding competition, breach of contract, defamation, and intentional infliction of emotional distress.

Defendants moved to stay the litigation based on the Agreement. The district court granted in part and denied in part the motion. Because Dr. Belnap and SLRMC have an arbitration agreement with a delegation clause, the court ordered those two parties to arbitrate any arbitrability issues. As to the other defendants, the court found that none of those parties were signatories to an arbitration agreement with Dr. Belnap, and none could compel Dr. Belnap to arbitrate under the Agreement.]

* * *

Next, we address the arbitrability of the claims against the Defendants that did *not* sign the Agreement, the "non-SLRMC" or "nonsignatory" defendants. These Defendants are: (1) SLRMC's alleged parent company, "Iasis"; (2) four physician[s]; (3) an SLRMC Risk Manager; and (4) Does 1–10. To determine whether these Defendants can compel Dr. Belnap to arbitrate based on the arbitration provision of the Agreement — an agreement that they never signed — we look to Utah law. Below, we conclude that the Defendants have not asserted a theory under Utah law under which the nonsignatory Defendants can compel Dr. Belnap to arbitrate his claims against them. Thus, we conclude that the district court correctly denied the motion to compel with respect to all of Dr. Belnap's claims against all of the nonsignatory Defendants.

The district court dealt with the nonsignatory Defendants on a claim-by-claim basis. First, it concluded that the first cause of action fell within the scope of the Agreement; however, it summarily stated that only signatories to the Agreement could compel Dr. Belnap to arbitrate that claim. Then, the court concluded that the remaining six causes of action fell outside the scope of the Agreement, and thus, no Defendant could compel Dr. Belnap to arbitrate those claims.

The nonsignatory Defendants now argue that the district court erred when it refused to compel Dr. Belnap to arbitrate any of his claims against them. Although they did not sign the Agreement, they argue that as principals and agents of SLRMC, they too are entitled to the protection of the Agreement's arbitration provision. More specifically, they argue that "Utah law recognizes at least five theories under which a nonsignatory to an arbitration agreement may be bound." They argue, first, that Iasis (i.e., SLRMC's alleged parent company) can invoke a parent-subsidiary estoppel theory. And they argue, second, that the individual Defendants can invoke the theory of agency because they "have been named in this lawsuit based solely on their conduct as ... representatives of SLRMC ... acting pursuant to SLRMC's Bylaws...."

In response, Dr. Belnap argues that he "did not agree to arbitrate disputes regarding the ... Agreement with anyone other than SLRMC by specifically limiting arbitration to 'any dispute *between them*,' i.e. between the parties to the contract." Dr. Belnap acknowledges that "there are five exceptions" to the general rule that "only parties to a contract may enforce the rights and obligations created by the contract," but he argues that the estoppel and agency exceptions that the nonsignatory Defendants rely on do not apply here. He explains that estoppel only applies "when the non-signatory seeks to benefit from some portions of the contract but avoid the arbitration provisions," or "when the non-signatory sues the signatory on the agreement after receiving 'direct benefits' but seeks to avoid arbitration"—and he contends that neither of these circumstances applies to Iasis. And Dr. Belnap further argues that the individual Defendants cannot invoke an agency theory because "the Complaint alleges that the individual Defendants acted on behalf of themselves," and because, regardless, "[a]n agency relationship with a principal to a contract does not give the agent the authority to enforce a contractual term *for the agent's own benefit*."

The Utah Supreme Court has held that "as a general rule, only parties to the contract may enforce the rights and obligations created by the contract." However, that court has stated that "under certain circumstances, a nonsignatory to an arbitration agreement can enforce or be bound by an agreement between other parties." Specifically, "five theories for binding a nonsignatory to an arbitrate on agreement have been recognized: (1) incorporation by reference; (2) assumption; (3) agency; (4) veil-piercing/alter-ego; and (5) estoppel." We conclude that the nonsignatory Defendants cannot compel Dr. Belnap to arbitrate under the two theories that they advance here—i.e., estoppel and agency.

First, we conclude that Iasis has failed to demonstrate that, under Utah law, it may estop Dr. Belnap from avoiding arbitration because it is SLRMC's parent company.

The Utah Supreme Court has recognized three circumstances in which nonsignatory estoppel applies. Only one conceivably is relevant here; it applies when a nonsignatory defendant employs estoppel against a signatory plaintiff, instead of the obverse, where a signatory defendant seeks to estop a nonsignatory plaintiff." More specifically, the one theory that is conceivably implicated by these facts is the "variety of nonsignatory estoppel [that is] enforced *by a nonsignatory* when the signatory plaintiff sues a nonsignatory defendant on the contract but seeks to avoid the contract-mandated arbitration by relying on the fact that the defendant is a nonsignatory." Critically, however, Defendants do *not* seek relief under that theory of nonsignatory estoppel. Instead, they argue that yet a *fourth* theory applies—parent-subsidiary nonsignatory estoppel.

Whether Utah law would recognize such a theory is an unsettled question. Significantly, when an appeal presents an unsettled question of state law, we must ordinarily "attempt to predict how [the] highest court would interpret [the issue]."

As noted, the Utah Supreme Court has recognized three *specific* varieties of nonsignatory estoppel, none of which include the parent-subsidiary theory that Defendants urge us to consider here. Absent a strong showing to the contrary, we are disinclined to predict that the Utah Supreme Court would recognize another variety; "it is not our place to expand Utah state law beyond the bounds set by the Utah Supreme Court." And Defendants fail to make such a strong showing. Accordingly, we predict that the Utah Supreme Court would not expand the doctrine of nonsignatory estoppel beyond the three varieties that it has explicitly defined to embrace a theory of parent-subsidiary nonsignatory estoppel.

Defendants' showing for the parent-subsidiary theory is especially weak because it has no footing in Utah law. Defendants allege only that the theory was recognized by the federal district court in *Nueterra*, 835 F.Supp.2d at 1161–63. In *Nueterra*, the United States District Court for the District of Utah held that, even though a parent company plaintiff had not signed an arbitration agreement with the defendants, it nevertheless had to arbitrate its claims against the defendants because the defendants had signed the arbitration agreement at issue with *the parent plaintiff's subsidiary*. The court reasoned that the nonsignatory parent's relationship with its "wholly owned subsidiary" was "close" and that its claims were "intertwined" with the contract containing the arbitration agreement. As to the latter point, the court observed in particular that the nonsignatory parent had sued the signatory defendants based on the contract and that the nonsignatory parent's claims were predicated on its subsidiary's "success in enforcing its rights under the [contract containing the arbitration agreement]." The court consequently concluded that the nonsignatory parent had "manifested an intent to be bound by the [contract]"—and, thus, by its arbitration agreement.

Defendants claim that *Nueterra* shows that Utah law recognizes a parent-subsidiary theory of nonsignatory estoppel, apparently distinct from the three theories of nonsignatory estoppel that the Utah Supreme Court recognized in *Ellsworth*. We disagree. At the outset, we state the obvious: *Nueterra*—a federal trial court decision—is not binding on us, irrespective of its view of Utah law. In addition, *Nueterra* does not clearly rest its relevant holding on decisions of Utah appellate courts. Specifically, in articulating its parent-subsidiary theory of nonsignatory estoppel, the *Nueterra* court does not rely on decisions of the Utah Supreme Court, or any other Utah appellate court for that matter. Rather, it places its principal reliance on a solitary federal district court decision. *I-Link Inc. v. Red Cube Int'l AG*, 2001 WL 741315 (D. Utah Feb. 5, 2001). And that case does not even rely on Utah law.

In *I-Link Inc.*, the federal district court turned exclusively to federal decisions from our sister circuits in concluding that the nonsignatory defendant—a "wholly-owned subsidiary" of the codefendant signatory parent,—had a "sufficiently close" relationship with its parent, and the claims against the subsidiary were "sufficiently intertwined with" the contract containing the arbitration agreement, which the signatory parent had executed, that the signatory *plaintiff* also should be compelled to arbitrate *with* the nonsignatory subsidiary defendant, along with the codefendant signatory parent. But, notably, *I-Link* does not even suggest that it is announcing or applying Utah law. Accordingly, *Nueterra*'s reliance on *I-Link* does not ground that decision's parent-subsidiary holding in Utah law.

Thus, we conclude that Defendants—who have placed their reliance on *Nueterra*—have not persuasively demonstrated that Utah law recognizes a parent-subsidiary theory of nonsignatory estoppel. More specifically, for the reasons explicated *supra*, we predict that the Utah Supreme Court would not adopt such a parent-subsidiary theory. Accordingly, because that is the only estoppel theory that they have advanced here, Defendants' estoppel argument necessarily fails.

Next, we conclude that the individual Defendants have failed to demonstrate that under Utah law, they may require Dr. Belnap to arbitrate with them, as SLRMC's agents. Dr. Belnap does not dispute that the individual Defendants are agents of SLRMC. Instead, he disputes whether Utah law allows nonsignatory agents to enforce contracts *for their own benefit*, as undisputedly would be the case here. Dr. Belnap relies on the Utah Supreme Court's express statement that "an agency relationship with a principal to a contract does not give the agent the authority to enforce a contractual term *for the agent's own benefit*." Defendants respond that the Utah Supreme Court announced an exception to the general rule stated in *Fericks* in its subsequent case.

In *Fericks*, prospective real estate buyers appealed from the dismissal of their claims against the sellers' agents, as well as the award of attorney's fees to those agents. After reversing the dismissal of the plaintiffs' claims, the Utah Supreme Court addressed the attorney-fee issue to provide guidance to the district court. With respect to the attorney-fee issue, the defendants argued that as agents of the sellers, they were entitled to enforce an attorney-fee provision in the purchase contract that the sellers had signed. The plaintiffs countered that because the agents were not parties to the contract, they could not recover fees under that provision. The Utah Supreme Court held that the defendants were not entitled to attorney's fees—even though they were agents of the signatory sellers—because "an agency relationship with a principal to a contract does not give the agent the authority to enforce a contractual term for the agent's own benefit."

Two years after handing down *Fericks*, the Utah Supreme Court again applied nonsignatory agency theory in *Ellsworth*. In *Ellsworth*, a construction company filed an arbitration demand against Mr. Ellsworth and his ex-wife for claims involving a contract that only she had signed. The Utah Supreme Court held that agency theory did not bind Mr. Ellsworth to the arbitration clause in the contract because there was no evidence of an agency relationship between Mr. Ellsworth and his ex-wife.

We conclude that *Ellsworth* left unscathed *Fericks*'s express statement that "an agency relationship with a principal to a contract does not give the agent the authority to enforce a contractual term for the agent's own benefit." *Ellsworth* and *Fericks* dealt with fundamentally different issues and do not conflict. In *Ellsworth*, the alleged agent—the nonsignatory defendant Mr. Ellsworth—never attempted to enforce contractual terms for his own benefit. Instead, the signatory plaintiff did, and so the (alleged) agent sought to *avoid* the enforcement of contractual terms against himself. As a result, the Utah Supreme Court never addressed in *Ellsworth* whether an agent can enforce a contractual term for the agent's own benefit; indeed, the *Ellsworth* opinion did not even mention *Fericks*. Thus, we remain bound by *Fericks*'s express statement that an agent acting for its own benefit cannot enforce such a term. As applied here, because Defendants do not dispute that they seek to enforce the Agreement's arbitration provision for their own benefit, we conclude that they cannot compel Dr. Belnap to arbitrate.

In sum, neither the estoppel nor the agency exception permits the nonsignatory Defendants to compel Dr. Belnap to arbitrate based on the arbitration provision in the Agreement they never signed. We therefore conclude that the district court correctly denied the motion to compel arbitration with respect to all of the claims against all of the non-SLRMC defendants.

2. Comments and Questions

a. Dr. Belnap clearly signed an arbitration agreement, at least with respect to SLRMC. Do you think that the test for determining if a non-party is bound to an arbitration agreement should be the same or different if the non-party is (1) the non-signatory trying to enforce against the signatory, or (2) the signatory trying to enforce against the non-signatory? Or should both situations be treated exactly the same? For instance, imagine if Dr. Belnap wanted to arbitrate all of his claims against all of the parties so that they are all in a single forum. Dr. Belnap could make the argument that the parent company is bound by the arbitration agreement of the subsidiary and the individuals are bound as agents. Is this argument more or less compelling than the argument made in the case?

b. The *Belnap* case is hardly an anomaly in the courts. As arbitration has become more common in resolving disputes, multiparty disputes increasingly involve these types of complex questions. Of particular interest to lawyers may be the Third Circuit's decision in *Sanford v. Bracewell & Guiliani*, 618 Fed. App'x 114 (3d Cir. 2015). In that case, Mr. Sanford had an attorney/client engagement letter with the Bracewell firm, and Mrs. Sanford never signed it. The Sanfords jointly sued the law firm, seeking $12 million in damages. The lower court ordered Mr. Sanford to arbitrate, but not Mrs. Sanford, because she did not sign the arbitration agreement. Ultimately, the Third Circuit ordered both Sanfords to arbitrate. The Third Circuit agreed that Mr. Sanford should arbitrate under the agreement. As to Mrs. Sanford, the court found that she was trying to take advantage of the contract and sue for damages and, therefore, was also bound by the arbitration agreement under an estoppel theory.

c. For other recent cases on the issue—some allowing arbitration of third-party claims and some not, see *Muecke Co. v. CVS Caremark, Corp.*, 615 Fed. Appx. 837 (5th Cir. 2015) (compelling arbitration against non-signatories under an estoppel theory); *Crawford Prof'l Drugs, Inc. v. CVS Caremark, Corp.*, 748 F.3d 249 (5th Cir. 2014) (same); *Pershing, L.L.C. v. Bevis*, 606 Fed. App'x 754 (5th Cir. 2015) (finding the test for estoppel not met and affirming district court's decision that non-signatories could not arbitrate their investment dispute through FINRA); *Dr. Robert L. Meinders DC, Ltd. v. UnitedHealthcare, Inc.*, 800 F.3d 853 (7th Cir. 2015) (remanding case to allow parties to develop an argument over whether a wholly owned subsidiary assumed a contract containing an arbitration agreement between the parties); *Andermann v. Sprint Spectrum*, 785 F.3d 1157 (7th Cir. 2015) (holding that telecommunications company Sprint assumed the consumer contract at issue, including the arbitration agreement, and requiring parties to arbitrate under the contract); and *Hanover Ins. Co. v. Atlantis Drywall & Framing LLC*, 611 Fed. Appx. 585 (11th Cir. 2015) (affirming denial of motion to compel arbitration between a signatory and non-signatory in a construction contract because the signatory could not show that the non-signatory was a third-party beneficiary under the contract). For recent commentary on the issue, see Clayton A. Morton & Tyler G. Doyle, *Equitable Estoppel in the Context of Claims for Tortious Interference with Contractual Relations: Has the Texas Supreme Court Gone Too Far?*, 57 S. Tex. L. Rev. 249 (2016) (discussing equitable estoppel theory of binding non-signatories to arbitration agreements); Dwayne Williams, *Binding Nonsignatories to Arbitration Agreements*, 25 Franchise L.J. 175 (Spring 2006) (proving an overview of the different theories).

D. Preclusion: Res Judicata and Collateral Estoppel

As you likely learned in your Civil Procedure classes, court judgments have preclusive effect, preventing unhappy parties from re-litigating a claim over and over until they receive a favorable judgment — only to have that newly unhappy party try to re-litigate, too. Should arbitration awards be treated the same way? Should the doctrines of *res judicata* (claim preclusion) and *collateral estoppel* (issue preclusion) apply to arbitration awards in a second arbitration or litigation? Finality is one of the policies underlying the preclusion doctrines. Arbitration is also a process governed by principles of finality. Does the fact that finality is an important policy consideration for both arbitration and preclusion sway your thoughts on the applicability of preclusion to arbitral awards?

The Restatement (Second) of Judgments § 84(a) provides that, unless certain exceptions apply, "a valid final award by arbitration has the same effects under the rules of res judicata, subject to the same exceptions and qualifications, as a judgment of a court." The exceptions apply, *inter alia*, when other law would permit re-litigation of the claim, when the procedure does not meet certain minimum procedural standards, or when the arbitration agreement limits the preclusive effect of any future award. The general test for preclusion is: "When an issue of fact or law is actually litigated and determined by a valid and final judgment, and the determination is essential to the judgment, the determination is conclusive in a subsequent action between the parties, whether on the same or a different claim." Restatement (Second) of Judgments § 27. Individual jurisdictions may have slightly different versions of this test, and many jurisdictions divide the test into different elements.

The cases that follow explore the use of collateral estoppel in subsequent court and arbitration proceedings.

Catroppa v. Carlton

998 A.2d 643 (Pa. Super. Ct. 2010)

BENDER, JUDGE:

This case arises out of an automobile accident that occurred on September 10, 2004, when the vehicle operated by the Defendant, Amanda Carlton[,] struck the rear of the Plaintiff's [Yvonne Catroppa's] vehicle causing personal injuries. The common denominator in this case is that State Farm Insurance Company insured the Defendant ... for liability coverage with a $50,000 third party policy limit and also the Plaintiff, Yvonne Catroppa, for underinsure[ed] motorist coverage with a $50,000 policy limit.

On September 26, 2007, Robert E. Kunselman, President Judge, granted the Plaintiff's Motion for Stay [] pending the Arbitration of the [UIM] claim. On June 16, 2008, a [UIM] arbitration hearing was conducted[.] On July 31, 2008, a unanimous award was entered for a total damage amount of $100,000 to the Plaintiff ... with a deduction for the third party policy limit of the Defendant ... of $50,000. The award for the Plaintiff was therefore a net of $50,000. On September 22, 2008, Plaintiff filed a Motion for Summary Judgment on the issue of damages on the basis of the doctrine of collateral estoppel since State Farm Mutual Insurance was not only involved in the third party action but also provided [UIM] coverage to the Plaintiff.... The response filed by State Farm admits that it provides both of these coverages but denies that the Defendant ... had any contractual relationship with the Plaintiff in the [UIM] arbitration; that the Defendant was not in privity and the Defendant did not have a fair and full opportunity to litigate the issue of damages.... [The trial court found that collateral estoppel applied and that the arbitrators had established damages at $100,000. Appellant appealed the estoppel ruling.]

In the instant case, Appellee relied on the prior decision of the arbitrators where they determined that her damages were $100,000. As stated above, the proceeding before the arbitrators was for Appellee's UIM claim against State Farm. Appellant was not a party to that proceeding, nor could she have been, as she had no interest in the matter. This is so because she was not a party to the insurance contract at issue, and the purpose of the proceeding was to determine the amount that State Farm was to pay Appellee on her UIM claim, which had no pecuniary ramifications for Appellant. Nonetheless, Appellee claimed that since the arbitrators decided Appellee's damages in this proceeding, and since State Farm insured Appellant in a liability policy (which was not at issue in the UIM proceeding), Appellant was estopped from disputing the amount of damages determined by the arbitrators. The trial court agreed, and since the parties stipulated to liability, it granted Appellee's motion for summary judgment.

The court's ruling on the motion for summary judgment was based on the doctrine of the collateral estoppel. Collateral estoppel applies if (1) the issue decided in the prior case is identical to one presented in the later case; (2) there was a final judgment on the merits; (3) the party against whom the plea is asserted was a party or in privity with a party in the prior case; (4) the party or person privy to the party against whom the doctrine is asserted had a full and fair opportunity to litigate the issue in the prior proceeding and (5) the determination in the prior proceeding was essential to the judgment. Collateral estoppel is also referred to as issue preclusion. It is a broader concept than res judicata and operates to prevent a question of law or issue of fact which has once been litigated and fully determined in a court of competent jurisdiction from being relitigated in a subsequent suit.

Assuming *arguendo* that four of the five prongs are met, we conclude that as a matter of law, the third prong was unsatisfied, as there was no privity between Appellant and State Farm in the UIM proceeding. The third prong requires that the party against whom the plea is asserted, which in this case is Appellant, was a party in the prior case or was in privity with a party in the prior case. Clearly, Appellant was not a party to the proceeding in which the arbitrators determined whether Appellee was entitled to UIM coverage under the UIM portion of Appellee's insurance policy with State Farm. Thus, the only way that collateral estoppel could apply would be if Appellant was in privity with State Farm....

While an insurer is in privity with its insured regarding matters implicating the insurance policy that establishes this relationship, this privity does not extend to matters arising from other insurance contracts between the insurer and third parties. That is the case we have here. Appellant had no interest whatsoever in the arbitration proceeding for Appellee's UIM claim against State Farm. Indeed, even had Appellant desired to intervene in this proceeding, this Court is unaware of any precedent that would grant her such a right.

This point becomes clear when one considers that privity requires "such an identification of interest of one person with another as to represent the same legal right." Ostensibly, the matter proceeded to arbitration on Appellee's UIM claim because she and State Farm disagreed as to the amount of damages recoverable under her UIM coverage. In this proceeding, State Farm had a contractual duty to Appellee to determine the actual amount of her damages as she was its insured. Yet as a practical business matter, State Farm's interest at the UIM proceeding was to pay as small an amount as possible on Appellee's UIM claim. Thus, since Appellant's liability coverage was for $50,000, State Farm would have sought to minimize any award of damages beyond this amount. While this interest coincided with Appellant's subsequent interest in the underlying litigation to minimize Appellee's damages, this coincidence of interest between State Farm and Appellant at the arbitration proceeding only extended to the limit of coverage under State Farm's policies, $100,000 ($50,000 on Appellee's UIM claim and $50,000 on Appellant's liability claim). To demonstrate that there was not a substantial identification of interests between State Farm and Appellant at the arbitration proceeding, one need only consider whose interests would have been harmed had the arbitrators determined that Appellee's damages were in excess of the limits of both State Farm policies. As the Amicus Brief of the Pennsylvania Defense Institute argues, if the damages had exceeded $100,000, it would have been Appellant that suffered, not State Farm.

Thus, had there been a determination of damages of $120,000, under the theory of collateral estoppel espoused by Appellee here, Appellee could have precluded Appellant from disputing that her damages were less than $120,000 in the instant action. After receiving the limits of the State Farm policies, Appellee could have sought payment of the additional $20,000 of damages from Appellant personally. This demonstrates that there was a divergence of interests for State Farm and Appellant at the UIM proceeding because State Farm had no interest if the damages exceeded $100,000, while Appellant had an interest in ensuring that the damages did not exceed this amount.

It is for this reason that we decline to hold that Appellant and State Farm were in privity at the arbitration proceeding. Accordingly, we conclude that the trial court erred in determining that Appellant was collaterally estopped from claiming that the amount of damages was less than the amount established at the arbitration proceeding. Appellant was not a party to the UIM claim, or the policy from which it arose, and she had no other legal interest that would have permitted her to intervene in the matter. Accordingly, she cannot be bound by a determination from a proceeding to which she was not a party.

Judgment reversed. Case remanded for further proceedings consistent with this Opinion. Jurisdiction relinquished.

Manganella v. Evanston Ins. Co.
700 F.3d 585 (1st Cir. 2012)

STAHL, CIRCUIT JUDGE.

[This insurance coverage dispute arises from the allegations of sexual harassment brought by Donna Burgess, a human resources employee, against Luciano Manganella, the former president of Jasmine Company. The allegations of harassment were also relevant in an arbitration regarding money due under a stock purchase agreement, which included a penalty against Burgess for a "Major Employment Breach."]

The arbitration panel held ten days of hearings and received extensive written and oral argumentation. The panel issued its ruling in April 2007, finding that Manganella had "sexually propositioned several women employees and inappropriately touched and propositioned one of these employees." The panel explained: "We find, despite his protestations to the contrary, that [Manganella] was well acquainted with the Company's policy on sexual harassment and other acts of inappropriate conduct. We find thus that he did not comply with the policy and that his refusal was willful." ... The arbitration award was confirmed by a federal court in August 2007.

Burgess filed a charge of discrimination ... with the Massachusetts Commission Against Discrimination ("MCAD"). The MCAD charge alleged that, "[t]hroughout her employment with Jasmine[ ], Manganella subjected Ms. Burgess to nearly constant physical and verbal sexual harassment" ... [Manganella notified his insurance company of the claim, but the insurer ("Evanston") denied coverage.] Manganella filed this action against Evanston in July 2009, seeking a ruling that Evanston was required under the Policy to defend and indemnify him against Burgess's MCAD charge.... After discovery, Manganella and Evanston cross-moved for summary judgment.... The court found that the arbitration panel's determination that Manganella had harassed his employees (including Burgess) ... also established that, for purposes of [this case], Manganella acted "with wanton, willful, reckless or intentional disregard of" the Massachusetts sexual harassment law underlying Burgess's MCAD charge. The district court thus held that the doctrine of issue preclusion barred Manganella from relitigating that question, and granted summary judgment for Evanston. Manganella now appeals that ruling.

II. Analysis

The crux of this appeal is whether the district court properly applied the doctrine of issue preclusion to bar Manganella from litigating whether the Policy's Disregard Exclusion applies to the conduct alleged in Burgess's MCAD charge.... Issue preclusion (also called collateral estoppel) "prevents a party from relitigating issues that have been previously adjudicated." The doctrine applies to issues of fact as well as those of law, and can apply where the subsequent proceeding involves a cause of action different from the first. Under modern preclusion doctrine, "the central question is 'whether a party has had a full and fair opportunity for judicial resolution of the same issue.'"

Generally, final arbitral awards are afforded the same preclusive effects as are prior court judgments. As we have noted, however, "there may be particular difficulties" in applying preclusion principles to an arbitral award, especially where the reasoning behind the award is unexplained. Thus, "it has been suggested that courts have discretion as to whether issue preclusion is appropriate" in the arbitration context. Here, though, "[w]e need not consider that suggestion, as we find it clear that the outcome we reach is consistent with the traditional requirements."

Under those traditional requirements, issue preclusion may be applied to bar relitigation of an issue decided in an earlier action where: (1) the issues raised in the two actions are the same; (2) the issue was actually litigated in the earlier action; (3) the issue was determined by a valid and binding final judgment; and (4) the determination of the issue was necessary to that judgment. Here, Manganella argues that two of these predicates are missing: identity of the issues and necessity to the judgment. We begin with identity of the issues.

... The identity of the issues need not be absolute; rather, it is enough that the issues are in substance identical. Further, the issue need not have been the ultimate issue decided by the arbitration; issue preclusion can extend to necessary intermediate findings, even where those findings are not explicit....

Manganella argues that the arbitrators were simply never called upon to decide whether he acted in disregard of state law. He claims that [the company's] Code of Conduct is broader and stricter than state sexual harassment law; the Code, he says, reaches not only sexual harassment serious enough to violate the law, but also less serious harassment, as well as behavior that would embarrass the company or constitute a failure of leadership. Thus, Manganella argues, the arbitrators did not, in the process of deciding whether he violated the Code, decide anything about the relationship between his conduct and state law.

We think that Manganella overstates the differences.... [B]oth the state law and the Code reach "sexual advances," "requests for sexual favors," and other "verbal" or "physical" "conduct of a sexual nature." To be sure, the law does impose a severity requirement absent from the Code ... But this requirement does not, as Manganella suggests, mean that a single incident cannot constitute unlawful sexual harassment. In fact, the Supreme Judicial Court has declined to require sexual harassment claims to be based on any particular number of incidents. Thus, the fact that the arbitrators did not expressly find that Manganella had propositioned any particular employee more than once does not mean that his conduct could not have run afoul of the law.

None of this is to say that we see no distinction between the standard imposed by the Code and that created by the law. Rather, the point is that the two standards are similar enough that we are unable to discern a meaningful difference, on the facts of this case, between acting in willful violation of the former (which the arbitrators found Manganella to have done) and acting with wanton disregard of the latter (which triggers the Disregard Exclusion). Because of this similarity, sexually harassing conduct committed in willful violation of the Code, by a person familiar with the law, would, on these facts, show a wanton or reckless disregard for whether that conduct was lawful....

III. Conclusion

For the foregoing reasons, we *affirm.*

Citigroup, Inc. v. Abu Dhabi Investment Authority
776 F.3d 126 (2d Cir. 2015)

HALL, CIRCUIT JUDGE.

The facts are straightforward. Citigroup, Inc. and the Abu Dhabi Investment Authority ("ADIA") were parties to an Investment Agreement under which ADIA invested billions of dollars in Citigroup. The Agreement contained an arbitration clause providing that "any dispute that arises out of or relates to the [Agreement], or the breach thereof, ... will be decided through arbitration administered by the American Arbitration Association." In 2009, ADIA commenced arbitration proceedings pursuant to this clause, alleging that Citigroup had diluted the value of its investment by issuing preferred shares to other investors. It asserted claims of fraud, securities fraud, negligent misrepresentation, breach of fiduciary duty, breach of contract, and breach of the implied covenant of good faith and fair dealing. The arbitrators rejected ADIA's claims and returned an award in favor of Citigroup after a lengthy and hard-fought proceeding that included extensive discovery and a multi-day hearing. Citigroup moved in the United States District Court for the Southern District of New York for entry of an order confirming the award. The district court granted Citigroup's motion, rejecting ADIA's arguments that the award should be vacated on the grounds that the arbitrators' choice-of-law ruling and two evidentiary rulings were made in manifest disregard of the law and prevented ADIA from presenting its case. ADIA appealed, and this Court affirmed, holding that the arbitrators did not act in manifest disregard of the law or exceed their authority.

In August 2013, while the district court's confirmation judgment remained pending before this Court on appeal, ADIA served Citigroup with a new notice of arbitration pursuant to the Investment Agreement, again asserting claims of breach of contract and breach of the implied covenant of good faith and fair dealing. Shortly thereafter, Citigroup instituted this action pursuant to the Declaratory Judgment Act, the All Writs Act, the Federal Arbitration Act ("FAA"), and the district court's "inherent authority to protect its proceedings and judgments." By way of relief, Citigroup sought to enjoin the second arbitration on the ground that ADIA's new claims were barred by the doctrine of claim preclusion, or *res judicata,* because they were or could have been raised in the first arbitration. Citigroup maintained that the second arbitration constituted an "assault" on the district court's March 2013 judgment confirming the first award, and that applying the All Writs Act to enjoin the second arbitration was necessary to protect the integrity of that judgment. ADIA moved to dismiss Citigroup's complaint and to compel arbitration.

The district court granted ADIA's motions. After first flagging the strong federal policy favoring arbitration, the district court then pointed to our decision in *National Union Fire Insurance Co. of Pittsburgh, PA v. Belco Petroleum Corp.* ("*Belco*"), 88 F.3d 129 (2d Cir.1996), in which we held that the preclusive effect of a prior arbitration that had been confirmed by a state court was to be decided by the arbitrators, not the court. Given our holding in *Belco,* other similar decisions, and the parties' "broad arbitration clause" governing "any dispute that arises out of the" Investment Agreement, the district court held that Citigroup's preclusion defense was properly resolved in arbitration.

Regarding Citigroup's request to enjoin the second arbitration pursuant to the All Writs Act, the district court first observed that our decision in *In re American Express Financial Advisors Securities Litigation,* 672 F.3d 113 (2d Cir.2011), "allow[ed] the possibility that, in certain circumstances, the All Writs Act could permit a court to enjoin an arbitration." The court noted, however, that we had previously sanctioned the use of the Act to enjoin arbitration only when the arbitration threatened to undermine a longstanding federal consent judgment that encompassed extensive equitable relief. Citigroup's case, by contrast, presented only "garden-variety res judicata concerns" because there was "no separate, ongoing proceeding at risk of being undermined" by the second arbitration. Accepting the argument that application of the All Writs Act was necessary in the circumstances of Citigroup's case, the district court reasoned, would "swallow the *Belco* rule" because it "would apply to virtually any instance where a second arbitration is purportedly precluded by a federal court judgment confirming the first arbitration award." *Id.* Accordingly, the court held that there was "no basis for an extraordinary remedy to issue under the All Writs Act." Citigroup timely appealed the resulting judgment.

Here, it is undisputed that two sophisticated parties voluntarily contracted to arbitrate "any dispute" arising from or relating to their Investment Agreement. As provided for under the FAA, the district court's March 2013 judgment merely confirmed the result of the parties' earlier arbitration through a limited procedure that did not require consideration of the merits of the underlying claims. The sole issue in this appeal is whether the district court erred when it refused to enjoin the second arbitration pursuant to the All Writs Act based on what Citigroup asserts is the claim-preclusive effect of the March 2013 judgment and instead compelled the parties to arbitrate ADIA's second set of claims.

The resolution of this issue implicates competing considerations. On the one hand, the FAA expresses "a national policy favoring arbitration when the parties contract for that mode of dispute resolution." The FAA's framework, moreover, authorizes the federal courts to conduct only a limited review of discrete issues before compelling arbitration, leaving the resolution of all other disputes to the arbitrators. Set against these considerations, on the other hand, is the weighty practical concern for the integrity of federal judgments that could arise if parties felt free to relitigate in arbitration proceedings claims previously resolved by a federal court. In recognition of this concern, several of our sister circuits have held that the All Writs Act, which empowers the federal courts to "issue all writs necessary or appropriate in aid of their respective jurisdictions," permits district courts to enjoin arbitrations that threaten to undermine federal judgments. Borrowing language from the Third Circuit, we have characterized these competing considerations as presenting "'a high order challenge.'" We now must decide the proper balance that should be struck between them in this case.

In addition to manifesting a policy strongly favoring arbitration when contracted for by parties to a dispute, the FAA establishes a "body of federal substantive law of arbitrability[ ] applicable to any arbitration agreement within coverage of the Act," and also "supplies ... a procedural framework applicable in federal courts." Under this framework, most disputes between parties to a binding arbitration agreement are "arbitrable," meaning that they are to be decided by the arbitrators, not the courts. See Howsam, 537 U.S. at 83–84, 123 S.Ct. 588. There is one exception to this general rule: unless the parties "unmistakably" provide otherwise, courts are to decide "question[s] of arbitrability." Such questions include disputes "about whether the parties are bound by a given arbitration clause" or "disagreement[s] about whether an arbitration clause in a concededly binding contract applies to a particular type of controversy." All other "questions which grow out of the dispute and bear on its final disposition are presumptively *not* for the judge, but for an arbitrator, to decide." "[A]ny doubts concerning the scope of arbitrable issues should be resolved in favor of arbitration, whether the problem at hand is the construction of the contract language itself or an allegation of waiver, delay, or a like defense to arbitrability."

The All Writs Act is a "residual source of authority to issue writs that are not otherwise covered by statute." Thus, while the Act authorizes a federal court to issue commands that are "necessary or appropriate to effectuate or prevent the frustration of orders it has previously issued in its exercise of jurisdiction otherwise obtained." We review *de novo* a district court's interpretation of the All Writs Act, but will overturn its decision to grant or deny an injunction under the Act only upon identifying an abuse of discretion.

In *American Express,* we considered an injunction that barred investors from arbitrating claims against a financial services company that the investors had previously released in a federal class action settlement over which the district court retained jurisdiction. Explaining that the FAA did not "explicitly confer on the judiciary the authority to ... enjoin a private arbitration," we nonetheless concluded that the injunction was proper in that case because the company, by entering into the settlement agreement, had effectively withdrawn its consent to arbitrate the released claims and the district court had retained "exclusive" jurisdiction to implement the terms of that settlement agreement. In so holding, we "pause[d] to note" that some of our sister circuits had authorized the use of the All Writs Act to enjoin arbitrations in similar circumstances to prevent the relitigation of federal judgments. We found it unnecessary to consider whether we agreed with that practice given our conclusion that the district court's authority to enter the injunction flowed from its retention of jurisdiction over the settlement agreement. We thus left unanswered the question of "whether the dictates of the All Writs Act might, in another case without the type of jurisdictional retention present [in *American Express*], give a district court the authority to enjoin arbitration to prevent re-litigation." *Id.* (internal quotation marks omitted).

In this case the district court did not retain jurisdiction over the March 2013 judgment, much less in a manner comparable to the court's retention of jurisdiction over the settlement agreement in *American Express.* Citigroup contends that because *American Express* left unresolved whether the All Writs Act permits courts to enjoin an arbitration in the absence of such "jurisdictional retention," Judge Castel erred when he concluded, in Citigroup's words, that the court "lacked the power to prevent ADIA from frustrating the [c]ourt's final judgment" by bringing new claims that were or could have been raised in the parties' first arbitration. We disagree with that assertion. The FAA's policy favoring arbitration and our precedents interpreting that policy indicate that it is the arbitrators, not the federal courts, who ordinarily should determine the claim-preclusive effect of a federal judgment that confirms an arbitration award. Citigroup, moreover, has failed to demonstrate that the circumstances of this case justify use of the federal courts' authority codified in the All Writs Act to obtain a different result.

We reason from our prior decisions interpreting the FAA that the determination of the claim-preclusive effect of a prior federal judgment confirming an arbitration award is to be left to the arbitrators. In *Belco,* we held that the claim-preclusive effect of a prior arbitration award confirmed by a state court judgment was an issue for the arbitrators to decide rather than the federal court. In so holding, we reasoned that claim preclusion was not a question of arbitrability because it, like other affirmative defenses such as time limits and laches, was a legal defense to the opposing party's claims and, as such, was "itself a component of the dispute on the merits." Several months later, we held in *United States Fire Ins. Co. v. National Gypsum Co.* ("*National Gypsum*") that the arbitrators, not the court, were also to decide whether the doctrine of issue preclusion, or collateral estoppel, barred a party from arbitrating certain issues that had previously been resolved in litigation resulting in a federal judgment. Noting that *Belco* involved the preclusive effect of a prior arbitration, we concluded in *National Gypsum* that its reasoning was nonetheless equally applicable to the "issue-preclusive effect of a prior judgment" because issue preclusion is also an affirmative defense that is "part of the dispute on the merits."

Given our holdings in *Belco* and *National Gypsum* that arbitrators are to resolve the claim-preclusive effect of an arbitration award confirmed by a state court and the issue-preclusive effect of a federal judgment, it is a simple intuitive step to conclude that arbitrators should also decide the claim-preclusive effect of a federal judgment confirming an arbitral award. This is especially so because Citigroup has not challenged the validity of the arbitration clause at issue in this case and that clause, like the one in *Belco,* is sufficiently broad to cover any dispute over whether ADIA's current claims were or could have been raised during the first arbitration. And even if we harbored some doubt as to whether the claim-preclusion dispute in this case is arbitrable, we would resolve that doubt in favor of arbitration.

Citigroup argues that this case warrants a different result because it, unlike *Belco,* involves the claim-preclusive effect of a prior *federal* judgment. In support, Citigroup points to the various decisions we cited in *American Express* in which other courts have sanctioned the use of the All Writs Act to enjoin arbitrations that threaten federal judgments. There is, however, one significant difference between the precedent established in the cases to which Citigroup cites and the circumstances here. The relevant judgments given preclusive effect via the All Writs Act in those cases followed from federal judicial proceedings addressing the merits of the underlying claims. Thus, in the cases on which Citigroup relies, the main justification given for resorting to the All Writs Act is that the district court that resolved the merits of a case is in the best position to protect its judgment because it is the most familiar with what it considered and decided in the proceedings leading to that judgment.

We need not, and do not, consider whether we agree with this justification because it is simply absent from this case. Citigroup seeks to preclude a second arbitration based on the district court's March 2013 confirmation judgment because it fears that the second arbitration will give ADIA an opportunity to relitigate the same underlying substantive claims that were or could have been raised in the parties' first arbitration. The district court's March 2013 judgment, however, simply confirmed the arbitration award, which ordinarily is "a summary proceeding that merely makes what is already a final arbitration award a judgment of the court." Indeed, in confirming the award, the district court did not review the merits of any of ADIA's substantive claims or the context in which those claims arose. Instead, it considered only whether the arbitration panel's evidentiary rulings and application of New York choice-of-law principles violated the FAA. Thus, even assuming, as we stated in *American Express,* that there "might" be circumstances under which the All Writs Act authorizes district courts to enjoin arbitration to prevent relitigation of their prior judgments, this case does not present them.

One additional consideration supports our conclusion. Were we to agree with Citigroup that the preclusive effect of federal confirmation judgments should be decided by the courts, we would effectively create in this Circuit a hierarchy of judgments confirming arbitration awards: the claim-preclusive effect of confirmation judgments issued by state courts would, pursuant to *Belco,* always be decided by the arbitrators, while the claim-preclusive effect of federal confirmation judgments may be decided by the federal courts pursuant to their authority under the All Writs Act. This seems an anomalous result, especially because we are required to afford state-court judgments full faith and credit, and are obliged to accord recognition to the preclusive effect of state court judgments. Citigroup has not explained why it is an appropriate use of the All Writs Act's "extraordinary remedies" to treat state and federal confirmation judgments differently. The better rule, we think, is to treat them the same and, in line with *Belco* and *National Gypsum,* permit the arbitrators to determine the preclusive effect of both ...

For the foregoing reasons, we affirm the judgment of the district court.

Shell Oil Co. v. CO₂ Committee, Inc.

589 F.3d 1105 (10th Cir. 2009)

TACHA, CIRCUIT JUDGE.

The sole issue presented in this appeal is whether the applicability of a res judicata defense based on a prior arbitration order should be resolved by (1) the arbitration panel that issued the prior order, or (2) a new arbitration panel chosen pursuant to the selection process outlined in the parties' arbitration agreement. Because we conclude that the arbitration agreement provides that applicability of the defense must be determined by a new arbitration panel, we REVERSE the order of the district court.

CO_2 Committee was created in 2001 to monitor and enforce future-relief provisions of a class action settlement agreement between its members and the plaintiffs. The agreement contains a binding arbitration section which refers all future disputes arising from or relating to the agreement to arbitration. Additionally, the binding arbitration section contains a panel selection provision that prescribes the manner in which the Committee and the plaintiffs select members of the arbitration panels that will resolve their future disputes: each party chooses one panel member and the parties' chosen members then jointly choose the third member.

In 2006, the Committee brought an arbitration complaint in which it alleged that the plaintiffs' accounting practices violated the agreement. The parties selected an arbitration panel pursuant to the panel selection provision, and that panel ("the original panel") determined that the plaintiffs had not violated the agreement. A federal district court then confirmed the original panel's order and entered judgment in favor of the plaintiffs on June 21, 2007.

In October 2007, the Committee filed a second arbitration complaint against the plaintiffs. This complaint also challenged the plaintiffs' accounting practices. Contending that the complaint raised issues that were decided or could have been decided by the original panel in the prior arbitration proceeding, the plaintiffs filed suit against the Committee in federal district court seeking a declaration that the second arbitration complaint was barred by res judicata and an injunction prohibiting the Committee from further pursuing the second arbitration complaint.

Before the district court resolved the plaintiffs' suit, it approved a stipulation agreement between the parties that stayed the second arbitration proceeding and provided in part:

> All of the parties' respective rights and obligations concerning the New Arbitration Proceeding shall be tolled until the resolution of this matter by the District Court In the event that the court dismisses the complaint or rules that any portion of the arbitration proceeding may go forward, Plaintiffs shall have ten (10) days following their receipt of such ruling in which to submit a response to [the Committee's] complaint in the *New Arbitration Proceeding*, to identify any additional matters to be arbitrated, and *to designate Plaintiffs' party-appointed arbitrator.* Plaintiffs reserve the right to appeal any such ruling by the District Court, and to seek a stay from the District Court or any appellate court of *the New Arbitration Proceeding* until such appeal is final (emphasis added).

The Committee moved to dismiss the plaintiffs' complaint, arguing that the res judicata effect of a prior arbitration order is an arbitrable issue that should be decided in arbitration, not in court. The district court agreed and granted the Committee's motion to dismiss. In its written order the court directed the parties to "proceed with arbitration in accordance with their arbitration Agreement."

Thereafter, the plaintiffs filed a motion with the original panel requesting a determination that the Committee's second arbitration complaint was barred by res judicata. The Committee, however, refused to submit the res judicata issue to the original panel and threatened to sue its members if they attempted to take any action in that regard. The plaintiffs then filed a response to the Committee's second arbitration complaint in which they objected to the formation of a new panel, argued that the second arbitration complaint was barred, and conditionally designated their arbitrator for the new panel.

The plaintiffs also filed a motion in district court seeking clarification of the court's May 16 order. Specifically, the plaintiffs asked the district court to clarify whether it had intended to refer the res judicata issue to the original panel or to a new arbitration panel. The district court issued another written order clarifying that the res judicata issue must be resolved by the original panel. The district court reasoned that the original panel was already familiar with the complex facts of the case and was in the best position to determine the scope of its prior order. Indeed, the district court found that the formation of a new panel would vitiate the primary purposes of arbitration—the cost-effective and expeditious resolution of disputes. Finally, the court ruled that if the original panel determined the second arbitration complaint was not barred, the merits of the second arbitration complaint should be decided by a new panel selected pursuant to the panel selection provision. The Committee now timely appeals from the order referring the res judicata issue to the original panel....

The FAA expressly favors the selection of arbitrators by parties rather than courts. FAA § 5. provides in relevant part, "if in the agreement provision be made for a method of naming or appointing an arbitrator or arbitrators ... such method shall be followed." Indeed, Congress has articulated only three instances in which a court may designate arbitrators: (1) if the arbitration agreement does not provide a method for selecting arbitrators; (2) if the arbitration agreement provides a method for selecting arbitrators but any party to the agreement has failed to follow that method; or (3) if there is "a lapse in the naming of an arbitrator or arbitrators." *Id.*

In this case, the panel selection provision, which follows in the same section, provides:

> Within ten (10) days after notice by one party to the other of its demand for arbitration, which demand shall also set forth the matter or matters to be submitted and the name of its arbitrator, the other party shall name its arbitrator, identify any additional matter(s) to be submitted, and so notify the demanding party. Within ten (10) days thereafter the two arbitrators shall select a third arbitrator.

The agreement unambiguously reflects the parties' intent that "*any and all* disputes, disagreements, and claims" arising out of the class settlement agreement are arbitrable. Such broad and expansive language clearly encompasses not only the merits of a substantive arbitration complaint but also the applicability of various defenses to such a complaint. Indeed, the parties agree to arbitrate not only "claims" but also "any and all disputes" arising from the class settlement agreement, and the panel selection clause reinforces this provision by permitting the party served with an arbitration demand to identify additional matters—which necessarily includes the applicability of potential defenses—it wishes the panel to determine.

We disagree, however, with the district court's interpretation of the arbitration provisions as providing for a prior panel to resolve, after the fact, a dispute regarding the res judicata effect of its prior order on a newly submitted arbitration complaint. The arbitration provisions state that each time a party files a new arbitration complaint, the parties shall select panel members in the manner prescribed by the panel selection provision. The fact that one party contends that the arbitration complaint must be dismissed for raising the same issues already resolved by a prior arbitration proceeding has no bearing on the panel selection process in this particular agreement. The agreement is clear: a new panel is convened each time a party demands arbitration on an arbitrable issue, and there is no provision for a panel's appointment beyond the resolution of a particular complaint.

The district court correctly determined that the res judicata effect of the original panel's order is an arbitrable issue that should not be decided by a court. That issue, however, arises as a defense to the Committee's second arbitration complaint, and the panel selection provision requires the formation of a new panel for each new arbitration complaint. Therefore, by referring the res judicata issue to the original panel, the district court effectively designated the arbitrators for that issue in direct contravention of the panel selection provision. Notwithstanding the potential efficiency benefits of having the original panel determine the precise scope of its own prior order, the district court's authority to designate arbitrators was limited by § 5 and the parties' panel selection provision. Accordingly, the district court erroneously interpreted the class settlement agreement and exceeded its limited role under the circumstances when it referred the res judicata issue to the original panel.

1. Comments and Questions

a. These cases demonstrate the variety of situations in which preclusion issues may apply. Federal and state courts deal with these issues, as well as judges and arbitrators.

b. When is res judicata an issue for the arbitrator to decide, and when should a court decide it? The Second Circuit's *Citigroup* case is essentially an arbitrability case, as is the Tenth Circuit's *Shell Oil* case. Do those cases provide any overarching guidance on the arbitrability issue?

c. As you may recall from Civil Procedure, preclusion can be invoked both defensively by a defendant or offensively by a plaintiff to prevent re-litigation of certain claims and issues. In addition, preclusion may be invoked when a mutuality of the parties exists (i.e., the parties are the same as the previous action) or in situations involving non-mutuality (one party from the previous action and one new party). In these cases, was the collateral estoppel offensive or defensive? Mutual or non-mutual?

d. Do you think that arbitration meets the litigation requirement of estoppel generally? Does pursuing a claim in arbitration have the same procedural protections as in litigation? Do any due process concerns exist?

Chapter 12

The U.S. Law of International Arbitration

A. Introduction

Arbitration is an established method of dispute resolution in international business and foreign direct investment. Its sustained and growing popularity reflects, perhaps in equal measure, a desire on the parts of international businesses to avoid foreign courts, the utility of having a process that can be adapted to address differences in legal culture (sometimes called the common law-civil law divide), and the attractiveness of an adjudicative system that produces globally enforceable results. The focus of this Chapter is the United States law of International Arbitration. The emphasis is on international arbitration proceedings that take place in the United States and on international arbitration agreements and awards that, while executed and rendered outside the United States, are brought before U.S. courts for recognition and enforcement.

Law schools commonly teach a separate course devoted entirely to International Arbitration. This chapter offers simply an introduction to this vast subject, presenting the U.S. perspective, not out of parochialism but due to limitation of time and space. **Section B** provides background about the Convention on the Recognition of Foreign Arbitral Awards (the New York Convention) and its promulgation in the United States. **Section C** considers the law relating to disputes that are subject to international arbitration. **Section D** examines the availability of interim relief in international disputes, including anti-suit injunctions and asset attachment orders. These issues are particularly difficult in the international arbitration context because of the strong policy for keeping courts out of the arbitration process—at least until the post-award stage. **Section E** addresses the recognition and enforcement of international arbitral awards in the United States. In **Section F**, we revisit selected arbitration topics previously considered in the domestic context and consider their application in the international context.

1. Volume of International Arbitration Proceedings

International arbitration has been a growth industry in recent decades, and this trend is all but certain to continue. Filings with the International Centre for Dispute Resolution (ICDR), the international arm of the AAA founded in 1996, exceeded 700 cases in 2008, and 1,063 in 2015, with amounts of claims and counterclaims exceeding $8.2 billion. The greatest number of case filings involved construction, franchise, hospitality/travel, insurance, technology, energy banking, finance, shipping, and commodities matters. In 2016, a near-record 1,000 arbitration cases were filed with the International Chamber of Commerce (ICC) based in France (involving 3,099 parties from 137 countries). The London Court of International Arbitration (LCIA) also reported a robust caseload for 2016, with an increasing diversity of cases and parties from Europe, Russia, Africa, and the United States. While the absolute numbers are smaller, the percentage increases in administered arbitrations are even greater for regional administering institutions such as those serving Geneva, Hong Kong, Singapore, and Vienna. With the stunning growth of the Chinese economy, the case load of the China International Economic and Trade Arbitration Commission (CIETAC) is sure to grow. *Ad hoc* international arbitration (that is, non-administered arbitration) has seen similar growth, although precise data are unavailable. For sources and additional data, see Gary B. Born, *Arbitration and the Freedom to Associate*, 38 GA. J. INT'L & COMP. L. 7, 8–10 (2009). These numbers are limited to arbitrations involving parties from different countries. They do not include the large number of arbitration proceedings in the United States between two American parties that may qualify as international because the underlying transaction has a relation with one or more foreign States.

Even taking into account all international arbitration proceedings, the absolute numbers pale in comparison to the number of domestic arbitrations in the U.S. However, the value at issue in international claims far exceeds that in domestic proceedings. In addition, the greater costs associated with international arbitration raises the settlement threshold so that claims that would be arbitrated in the domestic setting often will be settled in the international context. High-stakes disputes are the rule, not the exception, in international arbitration. *See* 9 U.S.C. § 202.

2. The Importance of Treaties

Treaties play an essential role in making international arbitration function well and account for its continued popularity. The most important of these treaties is the 1958 Convention on the Recognition and Enforcement of Foreign Arbitral Awards ("New York Convention"), to which at least 156 countries have acceded. There is widespread agreement that the New York Convention works, and works well. As noted by Professor Silberman, "[o]ne can only marvel at the success of the New York Convention over its fifty-year span.... Even though one can identify particular flaws, the Convention has proved a success in providing a basic framework that has ensured the enforcement of arbitration agreements and arbitration awards for the international commercial community." Linda Silberman, *The New York Convention After Fifty Years: Some Reflections on the Role of National Law*, 38 GA. J. INT'L & COMP. L. 25, 26 (2009).

Despite the overwhelming prominence of the New York Convention, U.S. courts from time to time must also consider the 1975 Inter-American Convention on International Commercial Arbitration (the "Panama Convention"), a substantially parallel treaty that has facilitated arbitration in Latin American and been adopted by 17 South or Central American countries, as well as the United States and Mexico. *See* Albert J. van den Berg, *The New York Convention 1958 and Panama Convention 1975: Redundancy or Compatibility?*, 5 ARB. INT'L 214 (1989). Both the New York and Panama Conventions obligate signatory nation states (countries) to enforce written agreements to arbitrate and to recognize and enforce arbitral awards that qualify for Convention treatment, subject to important exceptions. The U.S. codification of these Conventions is set forth in Chapters 2 and 3, respectively, of the Federal Arbitration Act (FAA). *See* **Appendix I.**

A third Convention of importance is the 1965 Convention on the Settlement of Investment Disputes between States and Nationals of Other States ("ICSID Convention"). Ratified by 153 contracting States, ICSID establishes the International Centre for the Settlement of Investment Disputes (ICSID), an administering institution and member of the World Bank Group, and sets forth a regime for the arbitration of disputes between contracting nation states and foreign investors. The Centre's jurisdiction is limited to administering only proceedings that relate to a direct foreign investment and involve a Member State or a State-related agency or instrumentality as a party. It is not available to administer arbitrations concerning international business-to-business disputes. Overwhelmingly, ICSID arbitrations involve claims brought by a putative investor alleging breaches by a State of its investment treaty obligations. Commonly, for example, the claimant-investor alleges that it received unfair treatment from the State, in contravention of an investment treaty's "fair and equitable treatment" provision. *See* Antonio R. Parra, THE HISTORY OF ISCID (Oxford University Press 2012); Smutny et al., *Enforcement of ICSID Convention Arbitral Awards in U.S. Courts*, 43 PEPP. L. REV. 649 (2016).

Although beyond the scope of this Chapter, ICSID Convention arbitration is noteworthy because of the large monetary stakes typically in controversy, the explosive manner in which its docket has been enlarged over the last two decades (the docket now involves several hundred cases), and the wide adherence the Convention enjoys (rivaling that of the New York Convention). ICSID proceedings are also relatively transparent compared to arbitral proceedings of ordinary commercial disputes. Many dozens of ICSID awards are available for study. The ICSID regime is also distinctive because of its autonomy from domestic legal systems. National courts are not empowered, for example, to review ICSID Convention awards, but must enforce them without considering the kinds of defenses permitted when the award is governed by the New York or Panama Conventions. Note also that the Convention for the Pacific Settlement of International Disputes, with 121 contracting States, established the Permanent Court of Arbitration (PCA), located in The Hague, as an inter-governmental organization that administers arbitration involving nations. Again, the study of international commercial arbitration is vast, and this Chapter focuses only on the U.S. law of international arbitration, as codified in Chapters 2 and 3 of the FAA.

3. Administering Institutions and Procedural Rules

Reference has already been made to administering institutions, such as the ICC, ICDR, LCIA, and CIETAC. While many dozens of entities—including scores of regional chambers of commerce—stand ready to supervise commercial arbitration, the better known (and most trusted) such institutions serving international business probably number fewer than two dozen. Institutions are not interchangeable; each has specific traits and policies, and the fees they charge are but one basis of comparison. Each institution in turn has promulgated one or more sets of procedural rules designed to supply a framework for the arbitrations they supervise. When, as often happens, the parties designate an institution in a pre-dispute arbitration clause, they are delegating to that institution important functions and incorporating by reference that institution's arbitration rules and internal policies.

In many jurisdictions, including the United States, it is not necessary to enlist the services of an institution. An ad hoc (non-administered) arbitration can produce an award that is equally enforceable under the New York Convention. To assist in the conduct of such arbitrations, organizations such as the United Nations Commission on International Trade Law (UNCITRAL), whose mandate is "to further the progressive harmonization and unification of the law of international trade," and certain other entities have produced rule texts for use in non-administered arbitrations. *See* **Appendix 3.**

4. Enforcement of Written Agreements to Arbitrate

The United States' adoption of the New York Convention is implemented through Chapter 2. 9 U.S.C. § 201 (providing that "The Convention on the Recognition and Enforcement of Foreign Arbitral Awards of June 10, 1958, shall be enforced in United States courts in accordance with this chapter"). Accordingly, references to the Convention's obligations are incorporated and part of U.S. law.

Article II of the New York Convention provides for the enforcement of written agreements to arbitrate and requires that

1. Each Contracting State shall recognize an agreement in writing under which the parties undertake to submit to arbitration all or any differences which have arisen or which may arise between them in respect of a defined legal relationship, whether contractual or not, concerning a subject matter capable of settlement by arbitration.

2. The term "agreement in writing" shall include an arbitral clause in a contract or an arbitration agreement, signed by the parties or contained in an exchange of letters or telegrams.

In addition to a written agreement to arbitrate, the jurisdictional prerequisites are that the agreement provides for arbitration in the territory of a signatory of the Convention; the agreement arises out of a legal relationship, whether contractual or not, that is considered commercial; and a party to the agreement is not a U.S. citizen, or that the commercial relationship has some reasonable relation with one or more foreign states. The range of matters being "capable of being settled by arbitration" is interpreted broadly. *See Mitsubishi Motors v. Soler Chrysler-Plymouth*, 473 U.S. 614 (1985), *infra*. However, contracting States may disallow arbitration of certain disputes such as criminal, family law, child custody, bankruptcy or patent law matters on grounds of public policy. *See* Margaret L. Moses, INTERNATIONAL COMMERCIAL ARBITRATION 35 (Cambridge Press, 3d ed. 2016).

Upon finding that parties have agreed to arbitrate, courts are required to refer the matter to arbitration "[u]nless it finds that the said agreement is null and void, inoperative, or incapable of being performed." Article II(3). This exception to the obligation to enforce arbitration agreements contemplates that certain contract law and similar defenses (e.g., fraud, duress, misrepresentation, undue influence, waiver, or lack of capacity, claim preclusion, statute of limitations) might be raised by the party resisting arbitration. *See Bautista v. Star Cruises*, 369 F.3d 1289 (11th Cir 2005). U.S. courts, like leading authorities, have assumed generally that the "unless" clause "should be construed narrowly." See Albert J. Van Den Berg, THE NEW YORK ARBITRATION CONVENTION OF 1958, at 155 (1981).

In most jurisdictions outside of the United States, the obligation to refer the parties to arbitration is fulfilled by the court disallowing a lawsuit that is brought in contravention of an agreement to arbitrate (accomplished in U.S. courts by the court issuing a stay or dismissal). United States courts, however, are also authorized under the New York and Panama Conventions, as implemented through the FAA, to "compel" arbitration; the latter power is manifest in affirmative court orders to one or more parties to go to arbitration, and is a distinctive feature of U.S. law. 9 U.S.C. § 206.

The doctrines of competence-competence (*kompetenz-kompetenz* in German), or the authority of arbitrators to determine their own jurisdiction, and separability are central to international arbitration. These topics were considered at length in the domestic context, and the same principles apply to arbitral agreements with international facets. Taken together, the effect of these doctrines as applied by U.S. courts is to allocate authority to arbitrators and to limit the role of courts. Courts outside the United States may approach the two doctrines in a fashion similar to their American counterparts, although important differences can often be detected. What can be taken for granted amidst the variation is that, in jurisdictions based on a modern law of arbitration such as that promoted by the UNCITRAL Model Law on Commercial Arbitration (in place in more than 100 jurisdictions) and in the United States: (1) an arbitration clause will for some purposes be treated by courts as an agreement separate from the contract in which it is embedded (separability); and (2) an arbitral tribunal will itself be entitled to rule on attacks on its jurisdiction, without the question first being referred to a national court (competence-competence). UNCITRAL is the United Nations Commission on International Trade Law, whose mandate is "to further the progressive harmonization and unification of the law of international trade." *See* **Appendix 3**.

The subtle but related question of how conclusive an arbitral tribunal's rulings on its own jurisdiction are before a court subsequently seized of the question gives rise to some interesting comparisons. *See* John J. Barceló III, *Who Decides the Arbitrators' Jurisdiction? Separability and Competence-Competence in Transnational Perspective*, 36 Vand. J. Transnat'l L. 1115, 1116 (2003) (discussing American, English, French, and German law); *see also* William W. Park, *The Arbitrability Dicta in* First Options v. Kaplan: *What Sort of Kompetenz-Komeptenz Has Crossed the Atlantic?*, 12 Arb. Int'l 137 (1996).

5. Significance of the Seat of the Arbitrations

In common understanding, each international arbitration is anchored in a specific national legal system, dictated by the "seat" (typically a city) that has been designated for that arbitration. Parties are encouraged by best practices to designate the seat (known also as the "situs" or "place") in their pre-dispute arbitration clause. If they fail to do so, one will be stipulated by the institution or the arbitral tribunal (depending on the applicable institutional or ad hoc rules). The importance of the seat is reflected in both the governing law of arbitration and the powers of certain courts that result from the designation. Thus, when an issue requires resolution by resort to the governing law of arbitration, it will be to the arbitration law of the seat that reference is made.

Equally, in modern arbitration doctrine, it is assumed that awards are rendered at the seat of arbitration, which in turn gives them a national affiliation for purposes of the New York and Panama Conventions. The place of rendition is critical because many States have ratified the New York Convention subject to "reciprocity" (satisfied when the award is rendered in another Convention State). Relatedly, the courts of the seat have exclusive power to set aside (vacate, annul) awards rendered there. Thus, ordinarily, a U.S. court could not vacate an award rendered in London, England, any more than an English court could set aside an award rendered in New York. A U.S. court might express this by saying a given court has, or does not have, "primary" jurisdiction (as opposed to "secondary" jurisdiction). We return to this basic tenet in Section 3.a, below.

Courts are authorized under the New York and Panama Conventions to consider defenses to recognition and enforcement of a foreign award, but a decision by them that a defense has been established does not work an annulment of the award. These permitted grounds for refusing recognition and enforcement are explored in detail in several of the cases excerpted below. *See* **Section E,** *infra*.

In the United States, actions to enforce New York and Panama Convention awards benefit from federal question jurisdiction. Do U.S. courts also need personal jurisdiction over foreign parties? When is an arbitration award "foreign" or non-domestic to trigger application of the Conventions, as opposed to domestic arbitration under FAA Section 1? A particular wrinkle in the standard analysis arises in U.S. courts because the United States has expressed its willingness to apply the New York Convention to certain awards rendered in the United States. These questions and others are addressed in the following sections.

B. The New York Convention:
Background and Adoption in the United States

The New York Convention was promulgated in 1958, after proceedings in which the United States was an active participant. However, the U.S. did not accede to the Convention until 1970. The adoption process involved two related steps: accession to the Convention, and implementing legislation, 9 U.S.C. §§ 201–208. The full text of both the New York Convention and FAA Chapters implementing it are found in Appendix I. The two decisions that follow provide useful background on the need for the Convention, and the differing views about its scope.

Cooper v. Ateliers de la Motobecane, S.A.
442 N.E.2d 1239 (N.Y. 1982)

COOKE, CHIEF JUDGE.

The United Nations Convention on the Recognition and Enforcement of Foreign Arbitral Awards (UN Convention) was drafted to minimize the uncertainty of enforcing arbitration agreements and to avoid the vagaries of foreign law for international traders. This policy would be defeated by allowing a party, contrary to contract, to bring multiple suits and to obtain an order of attachment before arbitration....

Arbitration is preferred over litigation by the business world as a process that combines finality of decision with speed, low expense, and flexibility in the selection of principles and mercantile customs to be used in solving a problem.... The desirability of arbitration is enhanced in the context of international trade, where the complexity of litigation is often compounded by lack of familiarity with foreign procedures and law. Thus, resolving disputes through arbitration allows all parties to avoid unknown risks inherent in resorting to a foreign justice system.

The prevalent problem in international contracts containing arbitration clauses has been in enforcing the agreement to arbitrate. The old antagonism to arbitration is shared by many countries, so that there is often uncertainty whether a contracting party may be compelled to arbitrate or whether an arbitrator's award may be enforced....

It was against this background that the UN Convention was drafted in New York in 1958. Generally, the UN Convention eased the difficulty in enforcing international arbitration agreements by minimizing uncertainties and shifting the burden of proof to the party opposing enforcement. The question whether an arbitral award is "foreign," a matter unclear in some civil law countries, is answered by adopting a territorial definition of domesticity. When an action is brought in court and a party asserts the arbitration agreement, the court shall refer the parties to arbitration, unless it finds that the said agreement is null and void, inoperative or incapable of being performed. Moreover, foreign arbitration awards are to be enforced on the same terms as domestic awards. [T]he UN Convention requires the party opposing enforcement to prove the award's invalidity, and it limits the grounds for objection. Moreover, if enforcement is opposed, the proponent of the award may request that the other party be ordered to give suitable security. This gives the courts a tool to discourage attempts to avoid arbitration awards which attempts are made merely as obstructionist tactics.

Bergesen v. Joseph Muller Corp.

710 F.2d 928 (2d Cir. 1983)

CARDAMONE, CIRCUIT JUDGE:

The question before us on this appeal is whether the New York Convention is applicable to an award arising from an arbitration held in New York between two foreign entities. The facts are undisputed and may be briefly stated. Bergesen, a Norwegian shipowner, and Joseph Muller, a Swiss company, entered into three charter parties. Each charter party [called for arbitration in New York. A dispute led to arbitration and a written award in favor of Bergeson.] Bergesen then sought enforcement of its award in Switzerland where Muller was based. For over two years Muller successfully resisted enforcement. Shortly before the expiration of the three-year limitations period provided in 9 U.S.C. § 207, Bergesen filed a petition in the Southern District of New York to confirm the arbitration award....

On appeal, Muller contends that the Convention does not cover enforcement of the arbitration award made in the United States because it was neither territorially a "foreign" award nor an award "not considered as domestic" within the meaning of the Convention. Muller also claims that the reservations adopted by the United States in its accession to the Convention narrowed the scope of its application so as to exclude enforcement of this award in United States courts, and that the statute implementing the treaty was not intended to cover awards rendered within the United States.... We turn first to the Convention's history.

A proposed draft of the 1958 Convention which was to govern the enforcement of foreign arbitral awards stated that it was to apply to arbitration awards rendered in a country other than the state where enforcement was sought. This proposal was controversial because the delegates were divided on whether it defined adequately what constituted a foreign award. On one side were ranged the countries of western Europe accustomed to civil law concepts; on the other side were the eastern European states and the common law nations. For example, several countries, including France, Italy and West Germany, objected to the proposal on the ground that a territorial criterion was not adequate to establish whether an award was foreign or domestic. These nations believed that the nationality of the parties, the subject of the dispute and the rules of arbitral procedure were factors to be taken into account in determining whether an award was foreign. In both France and West Germany, for example, the nationality of an award was determined by the law governing the procedure. Thus, an award rendered in London under German law was considered domestic when enforcement was attempted in Germany, and an award rendered in Paris under foreign law was considered foreign when enforcement was sought in France.

As an alternative to the territorial concept, eight European nations proposed that the Convention "apply to the recognition and enforcement of arbitral awards other than those considered as domestic in the country in which they are relied upon." Eight other countries, including the United States, objected to this proposal, arguing that common law nations would not understand the distinction between foreign and domestic awards. These latter countries urged the delegates to adopt only the territorial criterion.

A working party composed of representatives from ten states to which the matter was referred recommended that both criteria be included. Thus, the Convention was to apply to awards made in a country other than the state where enforcement was sought as well as to awards not considered domestic in that state. The members of the Working Party representing the western European group agreed to this recommendation, provided that each nation would be allowed to exclude certain categories of awards rendered abroad. At the conclusion of the conference this exclusion was omitted, so that the text originally proposed by the Working Party was adopted as Article I of the Convention. A commentator noted that the Working Party's intent was to find a compromise formula which would restrict the territorial concept. The final action taken by the Convention appears to have had the opposite result, i.e., except as provided in paragraph 3, the first paragraph of Article I means that the Convention applies to all arbitral awards rendered in a country other than the state of enforcement, whether or not such awards may be regarded as domestic in that state; "*it also applies to all awards not considered as domestic in the state of enforcement, whether or not any of such awards may have been rendered in the territory of that state.*" *Id.* at 293–94 (emphasis supplied).

To assure accession to the Convention by a substantial number of nations, two reservations were included. They are set forth in Article I(3). The first provides that any nation "may on the basis of reciprocity declare that it will apply the Convention" only to those awards made in the territory of another contracting state. The second states that the Convention will apply only to differences arising out of legal relationships "considered as commercial under the national law" of the state declaring such a reservation. These reservations were included as a necessary recognition of the variety and diversity of the interests represented at the conference.

With this background in mind, we turn to Muller's contentions regarding the scope of the Convention.... The territorial concept expressed in the first sentence of Article I(1) presents little difficulty. Muller correctly urges that since the arbitral award in this case was made in New York and enforcement was sought in the United States, the award does not meet the territorial criterion. Simply put, it is not a foreign award as defined in Article I(1) because it was not rendered outside the nation where enforcement is sought.

Muller next contends that the award may not be considered a foreign award within the purview of the second sentence of Article I(1) because it fails to qualify as an award "not considered as domestic." Muller claims that the purpose of the "not considered as domestic" test was to provide for the enforcement of what it terms "stateless awards," i.e., those rendered in the territory where enforcement is sought but considered unenforceable because of some foreign component. This argument is unpersuasive since some countries favoring the provision desired it so as to preclude the enforcement of certain awards rendered abroad, not to enhance enforcement of awards rendered domestically.

Additionally, Muller urges a narrow reading of the Convention contrary to its intended purpose. The Convention did not define nondomestic awards. The definition appears to have been left out deliberately in order to cover as wide a variety of eligible awards as possible, while permitting the enforcing authority to supply its own definition of "nondomestic" in conformity with its own national law. Omitting the definition made it easier for those states championing the territorial concept to ratify the Convention while at the same time making the Convention more palatable in those states which espoused the view that the nationality of the award was to be determined by the law governing the arbitral procedure. We adopt the view that awards "not considered as domestic" denotes awards which are subject to the Convention not because made abroad, but because made within the legal framework of another country, e.g., pronounced in accordance with foreign law or involving parties domiciled or having their principal place of business outside the enforcing jurisdiction. We prefer this broader construction because it is more in line with the intended purpose of the treaty, which was entered into to encourage the recognition and enforcement of international arbitration awards, *see Scherk v. Alberto Culver Co.*, 417 U.S. 506 (1974). Applying that purpose to this case involving two foreign entities leads to the conclusion that this award is not domestic.

Muller also urges us to interpret the Convention narrowly based on the fact that the 1970 accession by the United States to the Convention adopted both reservations of Article I(3). The fact that the United States acceded to the Convention with a declaration of reservations provides little reason for us to construe the accession in narrow terms. Had the United States acceded to the Convention without these two reservations, the scope of the Convention doubtless would have had wider impact. Nonetheless, the treaty language should be interpreted broadly to effectuate its recognition and enforcement purposes. *See Scherk*, 417 U.S. at 520 n. 15 (the Convention's goal was "to encourage the recognition and enforcement of commercial arbitration agreements in international contracts"); cf. *Parsons & Whittemore Overseas Co. v. Societe Generale de L'Industrie du Papier (Rakta)*, 508 F.2d 969, 974 (2d Cir.1974) (defenses to enforcement of foreign awards under the Convention are narrowly construed)....

Additional support for the view that awards rendered in the United States may qualify for enforcement under the Convention is found in the remaining sections of the implementing statute. Section 203 of the statute provides jurisdiction for disputes involving two aliens. Section 204 supplies venue for such an action and section 206 states that "[a] court having jurisdiction under this chapter may direct that arbitration be held ... at any place therein provided for, *whether that place is within or without the United States*" (emphasis supplied). It would be anomalous to hold that a district court could direct two aliens to arbitration within the United States under the statute, but that it could not enforce the resulting award under legislation which, in large part, was enacted for just that purpose.

Muller's further contention that it could not have been the aim of Congress to apply the Convention to this transaction because it would remove too broad a class of awards from enforcement under the FAA, is unpersuasive. That this particular award might also have been enforced under the FAA is not significant. There is no reason to assume that Congress did not intend to provide overlapping coverage between the Convention and the FAA. Similarly, Muller's argument that Bergesen only sought enforcement under the terms of the Convention because it has a longer statute of limitations than other laws under which Bergesen could have sued is irrelevant. Since the statutes overlap in this case Bergesen has more than one remedy available and may choose the most advantageous.

1. Comments and Questions

a. Is an arbitration involving non-U.S. parties (corporate or individual) from different countries that is rendered in the U.S. and sought to be enforced in U.S. courts a "foreign" arbitral award under the New York Convention? Does *Bergeson* provide guidance on standards to determine whether an arbitral award is foreign or domestic? *Bergeson* notes that the U.S. acceded to the Convention with two reservations, namely "reciprocity" and "commercial." How do such reservations impact the analysis?

b. The leading American article about the New York Convention process is Leonard V. Quigley, *Accession by the United States to the United Nations Convention on the Recognition and Enforcement of Foreign Arbitral Awards*, 70 YALE L.J. 1049 (1961). Other commonly cited international arbitration texts, in addition to the ICA Restatement, are Gary B. Born, INTERNATIONAL COMMERCIAL ARBITRATION (2d ed. 2015); Alan Redfern & Martin Hunter, LAW AND PRACTICE OF INTERNATIONAL ARBITRATION (6th ed. 2015); and William W. Park, ARBITRATION OF INTERNATIONAL BUSINESS DISPUTES (2d ed. 2012).

c. *Secondary Sources of Guidance*—ALI Restatement of the U.S. Law of International Commercial Arbitration. In 2008, the American Law Institute (ALI) began work on a Restatement project devoted to International Commercial Arbitration under U.S. Law (ICA Restatement). The ICA Restatement consists of five chapters, arranged as follows: *Chapter 1*—Definitions and Federal Preemption of State Law; *Chapter 2*—Enforcement of the Arbitration Agreement; *Chapter 3*—The Judicial Role in Connection with the Arbitral Proceeding; *Chapter 4*—Post-Award Relief; and *Chapter 5*—Investor-State Arbitration.

The ICA Restatement has proven to be influential and, increasingly, U.S. courts rely on its various provisions. In addition, because the ICA Restatement contains more than three dozen definitions, it has begun to promote a uniform vocabulary for international arbitration. Those definitions, in turn, are essential to fully understanding the Restatement's five chapters and international commercial arbitration law and practice.

C. Arbitrability Issues in International Arbitration

Chapter 3 addressed the law on arbitrability in the domestic arbitration context. Recall the basic allocation of authority, absent delegation otherwise, that courts decide the substantive "gateway" questions of whether the parties agreed to arbitrate, and whether the dispute is subject to arbitration. All other matters are within the province of the arbitrator. Does this same approach apply in international arbitration? Does the obligation to arbitrate disputes in a foreign tribunal include claims involving U.S. statutory law? Who decides whether the parties agreed to arbitrate?

Mitsubishi Motors Corp. v. Soler Chrysler-Plymouth, Inc.
473 U.S. 614 (1985)

JUSTICE BLACKMUN delivered the opinion of the Court.

The principal question presented by these cases is the arbitrability, pursuant to the FAA and the New York Convention, of claims arising under the Sherman Act, 15 U.S.C. § 1 *et seq.*, and encompassed within a valid arbitration clause in an agreement embodying an international commercial transaction.

Mitsubishi Motors is the product of a joint venture between Chrysler International, S.A. (CISA), a Swiss corporation registered in Geneva and wholly owned by Chrysler Corporation, and Mitsubishi Heavy Industries, Inc., a Japanese corporation. The aim of the joint venture was the distribution through Chrysler dealers outside the continental United States of vehicles manufactured by Mitsubishi and bearing Chrysler and Mitsubishi trademarks. Soler is a Puerto Rico corporation.

Soler entered into a Distributor Agreement with CISA which provided for the sale by Soler of Mitsubishi-manufactured vehicles within a designated area, including metropolitan San Juan. On the same date, CISA, Soler, and Mitsubishi entered into a Sales Agreement which, referring to the Distributor Agreement, provided for the direct sale of Mitsubishi products to Soler and governed the terms and conditions of such sales. [The agreement called for arbitration of disputes in Japan under the rules and regulations of the Japan Commercial Arbitration Association.]

Initially, Soler did a brisk business in Mitsubishi-manufactured vehicles. As a result of its strong performance, its minimum sales volume, specified by Mitsubishi and CISA, and agreed to by Soler, for the 1981 model year was substantially increased. In early 1981, however, the new-car market slackened. Soler ran into serious difficulties in meeting the expected sales volume, and by the spring of 1981 it felt itself compelled to request that Mitsubishi delay or cancel shipment of several orders. Attempts to work out these difficulties failed. Mitsubishi brought an action under the FAA and the Convention, pursuant to 9 U.S.C. §§ 4 and 201, to compel arbitration. Shortly thereafter, Mitsubishi filed a request for arbitration before the Japan Commercial Arbitration Association....

At the outset, we address the contention raised in Soler's cross-petition that ... as a matter of law a court may not construe an arbitration agreement to encompass claims arising out of statutes designed to protect a class to which the party resisting arbitration belongs unless that party has expressly agreed to arbitrate those claims. Soler reasons that, because it falls within the class for whose benefit the federal and local antitrust laws and dealers' Acts were passed, but the arbitration clause at issue does not mention these statutes or statutes in general, the clause cannot be read to contemplate arbitration of these statutory claims. We do not agree, for we find no warrant in the FAA for implying in every contract within its ken a presumption against arbitration of statutory claims....

Soler's concern for statutorily protected classes provides no reason to color the lens through which the arbitration clause is read. By agreeing to arbitrate a statutory claim, a party does not forgo the substantive rights afforded by the statute; it only submits to their resolution in an arbitral, rather than a judicial, forum. It trades the procedures and opportunity for review of the courtroom for the simplicity, informality, and expedition of arbitration. We must assume that if Congress intended the substantive protection afforded by a given statute to include protection against waiver of the right to a judicial forum, that intention will be deducible from text or legislative history. Nothing prevents a party from excluding statutory claims from the scope of an agreement to arbitrate.

We now turn to consider whether Soler's antitrust claims are nonarbitrable even though it has agreed to arbitrate them. In holding that they are not, the Court of Appeals followed the decision of the Second Circuit in *American Safety Equipment Corp. v. J.P. Maguire & Co.*, 391 F.2d 821 (1968). Notwithstanding the absence of any explicit support for such an exception in either the Sherman Act or the FAA, the Second Circuit there reasoned that "the pervasive public interest in enforcement of the antitrust laws, and the nature of the claims that arise in such cases, combine to make antitrust claims inappropriate for arbitration." We find it unnecessary to assess the legitimacy of the *American Safety* doctrine as applied to agreements to arbitrate arising from domestic transactions. As in *Scherk v. Alberto-Culver Co.*, 417 U.S. 506 (1974), we conclude that concerns of international comity, respect for the capacities of foreign and transnational tribunals, and sensitivity to the need of the international commercial system for predictability in the resolution of disputes require that we enforce the parties' agreement, even assuming that a contrary result would be forthcoming in a domestic context....

Scherk establish a strong presumption in favor of enforcement of freely negotiated contractual choice-of-forum provisions. Here, as in *Scherk*, that presumption is reinforced by the emphatic federal policy in favor of arbitral dispute resolution. And at least since this Nation's accession in 1970 to the New York Convention, and the implementation of the Convention in the same year by amendment of the FAA, that federal policy applies with special force in the field of international commerce. Thus, we must weigh the concerns of *American Safety* against a strong belief in the efficacy of arbitral procedures for the resolution of international commercial disputes and an equal commitment to the enforcement of freely negotiated choice-of-forum clauses....

The mere appearance of an antitrust dispute does not alone warrant invalidation of the selected forum on the undemonstrated assumption that the arbitration clause is tainted. A party resisting arbitration of course may attack directly the validity of the agreement to arbitrate. See *Prima Paint Corp. v. Flood & Conklin Mfg. Co.*, 388 U.S. 395 (1967). Moreover, the party may attempt to make a showing that would warrant setting aside the forum-selection clause — that the agreement was affected by fraud, undue influence, or overweening bargaining power; that enforcement would be unreasonable and unjust; or that proceedings in the contractual forum will be so gravely difficult and inconvenient that the resisting party will for all practical purposes be deprived of his day in court. But absent such a showing — and none was attempted here — there is no basis for assuming the forum inadequate or its selection unfair.

For similar reasons, we also reject the proposition that an arbitration panel will pose too great a danger of innate hostility to the constraints on business conduct that antitrust law imposes. International arbitrators frequently are drawn from the legal as well as the business community; where the dispute has an important legal component, the parties and the arbitral body with whose assistance they have agreed to settle their dispute can be expected to select arbitrators accordingly We decline to indulge the presumption that the parties and arbitral body conducting a proceeding will be unable or unwilling to retain competent, conscientious, and impartial arbitrators. We are advised by Mitsubishi and *amicus* ICC, without contradiction by Soler, that the arbitration panel selected to hear the parties' claims here is composed of three Japanese lawyers, one a former law school dean, another a former judge, and the third a practicing attorney with American legal training who has written on Japanese antitrust law.

We are left, then, with the core of the *American Safety* doctrine — the fundamental importance to American democratic capitalism of the regime of the antitrust laws. Without doubt, the private cause of action plays a central role in enforcing this regime. A claim under the antitrust laws is not merely a private matter. The Sherman Act is designed to promote the national interest in a competitive economy; thus, the plaintiff asserting his rights under the Act has been likened to a private attorney-general who protects the public interest. The treble-damages provision wielded by the private litigant is a chief tool in the antitrust enforcement scheme, posing a crucial deterrent to potential violators. The importance of the private damages remedy, however, does not compel the conclusion that it may not be sought outside an American court....

There is no reason to assume at the outset of the dispute that international arbitration will not provide an adequate mechanism. To be sure, the international arbitral tribunal owes no prior allegiance to the legal norms of particular states; hence, it has no direct obligation to vindicate their statutory dictates. The tribunal, however, is bound to effectuate the intentions of the parties. Where the parties have agreed that the arbitral body is to decide a defined set of claims which includes, as in these cases, those arising from the application of American antitrust law, the tribunal therefore should be bound to decide that dispute in accord with the national law giving rise to the claim. And so long as the prospective litigant effectively may vindicate its statutory cause of action in the arbitral forum, the statute will continue to serve both its remedial and deterrent function.

The Sales Agreement includes a choice-of-law clause which reads: "This Agreement is made in, and will be governed by and construed in all respects according to the laws of the Swiss Confederation as if entirely performed therein." The United States [as *amicus*] raises the possibility that the arbitral panel will read this provision not simply to govern interpretation of the contract terms, but wholly to displace American law even where it otherwise would apply. The ICC opines that it is "conceivable, although we believe it unlikely, that the arbitrators could consider Soler's affirmative claim of anticompetitive conduct by CISA and Mitsubishi to fall within the purview of this choice-of-law provision, with the result that it would be decided under Swiss law rather than the U.S. Sherman Act." At oral argument, however, counsel for Mitsubishi conceded that American law applied to the antitrust claims and represented that the claims had been submitted to the arbitration panel in Japan on that basis.

We therefore have no occasion to speculate on this matter at this stage in the proceedings, when Mitsubishi seeks to enforce the agreement to arbitrate, not to enforce an award. Nor need we consider now the effect of an arbitral tribunal's failure to take cognizance of the statutory cause of action on the claimant's capacity to reinitiate suit in federal court. We merely note that in the event the choice-of-forum and choice-of-law clauses operated in tandem as a prospective waiver of a party's right to pursue statutory remedies for antitrust violations, we would have little hesitation in condemning the agreement as against public policy.

Having permitted the arbitration to go forward, the national courts of the United States will have the opportunity at the award-enforcement stage to ensure that the legitimate interest in the enforcement of the antitrust laws has been addressed. The Convention reserves to each signatory country the right to refuse enforcement of an award where the "recognition or enforcement of the award would be contrary to the public policy of that country." Art. V(2)(b). While the efficacy of the arbitral process requires that substantive review at the award-enforcement stage remain minimal, it would not require intrusive inquiry to ascertain that the tribunal took cognizance of the antitrust claims and actually decided them. (The rules of the Japan Commercial Arbitration Association provide for the taking of a "summary record" of each hearing, … and for a statement of reasons for the award unless the parties agree otherwise.)

As international trade has expanded in recent decades, so too has the use of international arbitration to resolve disputes arising in the course of that trade. The controversies that international arbitral institutions are called upon to resolve have increased in diversity as well as in complexity. Yet the potential of these tribunals for efficient disposition of legal disagreements arising from commercial relations has not yet been tested. If they are to take a central place in the international legal order, national courts will need to "shake off the old judicial hostility to arbitration," *Kulukundis Shipping Co. v. Amtorg Trading Corp.*, 126 F.2d 978 (2d Cir.1942), and also their customary and understandable unwillingness to cede jurisdiction of a claim arising under domestic law to a foreign or transnational tribunal. To this extent it will be necessary for national courts to subordinate domestic notions of arbitrability to the international policy favoring commercial arbitration....

The utility of the Convention in promoting the process of international commercial arbitration depends upon the willingness of national courts to let go of matters they normally would think of as their own. Doubtless, Congress may specify categories of claims it wishes to reserve for decision by our own courts without contravening this Nation's obligations under the Convention. But we decline to subvert the spirit of the United States' accession to the Convention by recognizing subject-matter exceptions where Congress has not expressly directed the courts to do so. Accordingly, we "require this representative of the American business community to honor its bargain," *Alberto-Culver Co. v. Scherk*, 484 F.2d 611 (7th Cir. 1973) (Stevens, J., dissenting), by holding this agreement to arbitrate enforceable in accord with the explicit provisions of the FAA. It is so ordered.

1. Comments and Questions

a. In his prior capacity as a judge on the Seventh Circuit Court of Appeals, Justice Stevens dissented in the *Scherk* case; the Supreme Court opinion "upheld" the Stevens dissent and agreed that U.S. securities claims were arbitrable in an international arbitration. Justice Stevens wrote the dissenting opinion in *Mitsubishi* — which is why the majority opinion closed by quoting the earlier Stevens opinion that favored international arbitration.

b. Stevens offered the following policy rationale for dissenting in *Mitsubishi*, 473 U.S. at 665:

In my opinion, the elected representatives of the American people would not have us dispatch an American citizen to a foreign land in search of an uncertain remedy for the violation of a public right that is protected by the Sherman Act. This is especially so when there has been no genuine bargaining over the terms of the submission, and the arbitration remedy provided has not even the most elementary guarantees of fair process. Consideration of a fully developed record by a jury, instructed in the law by a federal judge, and subject to appellate review, is a surer guide to the competitive character of a commercial practice than the practically unreviewable judgment of a private arbitrator.

c. One might think that Justice Stevens would be concerned that foreign arbitrators would not give due consideration to American antitrust law. However, his worry was quite the opposite: "The greatest risk, of course, is that the arbitrator will condemn business practices under the antitrust laws that are efficient in a free competitive market." Absent a record of the proceedings, "a reviewing district court would not be able to undo the damage wrought." *Id.* at 657.

d. Is the potential judicial review of the eventual arbitral award envisioned by the majority opinion likely to occur, or is Stevens right that the outcome will be practically unreviewable? Note that an American court would come into contact with the Japanese award only if it was presented for enforcement in the United States. And, even then, under the New York Convention there would be allowed no review on the merits nor easy-to-predict violation of U.S. public policy to justify non-recognition or non-enforcement.

BG Group PLC v. Republic of Argentina
134 S. Ct. 1198 (2014)

Justice BREYER delivered the opinion of the Court.

Article 8 of an investment treaty between the United Kingdom and Argentina contains a dispute-resolution provision, applicable to disputes between one of those nations and an investor from the other. See Agreement for the Promotion and Protection of Investments, Art. 8(2), Dec. 11, 1990, 1765 U.N.T.S. 38 (hereinafter Treaty). The provision authorizes either party to submit a dispute "to the decision of the competent tribunal of the Contracting Party in whose territory the investment was made," *i.e.,* a local court. Art. 8(1). And it provides for arbitration

> (i) where, after a period of eighteen months has elapsed from the moment when the dispute was submitted to the competent tribunal..., the said tribunal has not given its final decision; [or]

> (ii) where the final decision of the aforementioned tribunal has been made but the Parties are still in dispute. Art. 8(2)(a).

The Treaty also entitles the parties to agree to proceed directly to arbitration. Art. 8(2)(b).

This case concerns the Treaty's arbitration clause, and specifically the local court litigation requirement set forth in Article 8(2)(a). The question before us is whether a court of the United States, in reviewing an arbitration award made under the Treaty, should interpret and apply the local litigation requirement *de novo,* or with the deference that courts ordinarily owe arbitration decisions. That is to say, who—court or arbitrator—bears primary responsibility for interpreting and applying the local litigation requirement to an underlying controversy? In our view, the matter is for the arbitrators, and courts must review their determinations with deference.

I.

A

In the early 1990's, the petitioner, BG Group plc, a British firm, belonged to a consortium that bought a majority interest in an Argentine entity called MetroGAS. MetroGAS was a gas distribution company created by Argentine law in 1992, as a result of the government's privatization of its state-owned gas utility. Argentina distributed the utility's assets to new, private companies, one of which was MetroGAS. It awarded MetroGAS a 35-year exclusive license to distribute natural gas in Buenos Aires, and it submitted a controlling interest in the company to international public tender. BG Group's consortium was the successful bidder.

At about the same time, Argentina enacted statutes providing that its regulators would calculate gas "tariffs" in U.S. dollars, and that those tariffs would be set at levels sufficient to assure gas distribution firms, such as MetroGAS, a reasonable return.

In 2001 and 2002, Argentina, faced with an economic crisis, enacted new laws. Those laws changed the basis for calculating gas tariffs from dollars to pesos, at a rate of one peso per dollar. The exchange rate at the time was roughly three pesos to the dollar. The result was that MetroGAS' profits were quickly transformed into losses. BG Group believed that these changes (and several others) violated the Treaty; Argentina believed the contrary.

B

In 2003, BG Group, invoking Article 8 of the Treaty, sought arbitration. The parties appointed arbitrators; they agreed to site the arbitration in Washington, D.C.; and between 2004 and 2006, the arbitrators decided motions, received evidence, and conducted hearings. BG Group essentially claimed that Argentina's new laws and regulatory practices violated provisions in the Treaty forbidding the "expropriation" of investments and requiring that each nation give "fair and equitable treatment" to investors from the other. Argentina denied these claims, while also arguing that the arbitration tribunal lacked "jurisdiction" to hear the dispute. According to Argentina, the arbitrators lacked jurisdiction because: (1) BG Group was not a Treaty-protected "investor"; (2) BG Group's interest in MetroGAS was not a Treaty-protected "investment"; and (3) BG Group initiated arbitration without first litigating its claims in Argentina's courts, despite Article 8's requirement. In Argentina's view, "failure by BG to bring its grievance to Argentine courts for 18 months renders its claims in this arbitration inadmissible."

In late December 2007, the arbitration panel reached a final decision. It began by determining that it had "jurisdiction" to consider the merits of the dispute. In support of that determination, the tribunal concluded that BG Group was an "investor," that its interest in MetroGAS amounted to a Treaty-protected "investment," and that Argentina's own conduct had waived, or excused, BG Group's failure to comply with Article 8's local litigation requirement.... Argentina had established a "renegotiation process" for public service contracts, such as its contract with MetroGAS, to alleviate the negative impact of the new economic measures. But Argentina had simultaneously barred from participation in that "process" firms that were litigating against Argentina in court or in arbitration. These measures, while not making litigation in Argentina's courts literally impossible, nonetheless "hindered" recourse "to the domestic judiciary" to the point where the Treaty implicitly excused compliance with the local litigation requirement. Requiring a private party in such circumstances to seek relief in Argentina's courts for 18 months, the panel concluded, would lead to "absurd and unreasonable result[s]."

On the merits, the arbitration panel agreed with Argentina that it had not "expropriate[d]" BG Group's investment, but also found that Argentina had denied BG Group "fair and equitable treatment." It awarded BG Group $185 million in damages.

C

In March 2008, both sides filed petitions for review in the District Court for the District of Columbia. BG Group sought to confirm the award under the New York Convention and the Federal Arbitration Act (providing that a party may apply "for recognition and enforcement" of an arbitral award subject to the Convention); 9 U.S.C. §§ 204, 207 (providing that a party may move "for an order confirming [an arbitral] award" in a federal court of the "place designated in the agreement as the place of arbitration if such place is within the United States"). Argentina sought to vacate the award in part on the ground that the arbitrators lacked jurisdiction. See § 10(a)(4) (a federal court may vacate an arbitral award "where the arbitrators exceeded their powers").

The District Court denied Argentina's claims and confirmed the award. But the Court of Appeals for the District of Columbia Circuit reversed. In the appeals court's view, the interpretation and application of Article 8's local litigation requirement was a matter for courts to decide *de novo*, *i.e.*, without deference to the views of the arbitrators. The Court of Appeals then went on to hold that the circumstances did not excuse BG Group's failure to comply with the requirement. Rather, BG Group must "commence a lawsuit in Argentina's courts and wait eighteen months before filing for arbitration." Because BG Group had not done so, the arbitrators lacked authority to decide the dispute. And the appeals court ordered the award vacated.

BG Group filed a petition for certiorari. Given the importance of the matter for international commercial arbitration, we granted the petition. *See, e.g.*, K. Vandevelde, *Bilateral Investment Treaties: History, Policy & Interpretation* 430–432 (2010) (explaining that dispute-resolution mechanisms allowing for arbitration are a "critical element" of modern day bilateral investment treaties); C. Dugan, D. Wallace, N. Rubins, & B. Sabahi, Investor-State Arbitration 51–52, 117–120 (2008) (referring to the large number of investment treaties that provide for arbitration, and explaining that some also impose prearbitration requirements such as waiting periods, amicable negotiations, or exhaustion of local remedies).

II

As we have said, the question before us is who—court or arbitrator—bears primary responsibility for interpreting and applying Article 8's local court litigation provision. Put in terms of standards of judicial review, should a United States court review the arbitrators' interpretation and application of the provision *de novo*, or with the deference that courts ordinarily show arbitral decisions on matters the parties have committed to arbitration? Compare, *e.g.*, *First Options of Chicago, Inc. v. Kaplan*, 514 U.S. 938 (1995) (example where a "court makes up its mind about [an issue] independently" because the parties did not agree it should be arbitrated), with *Oxford Health Plans LLC v. Sutter*, 569 U.S. 564, (2013) (example where a court defers to arbitrators because the parties " 'bargained for' " arbitral resolution of the question).

In answering the question, we shall initially treat the document before us as if it were an ordinary contract between private parties. Were that so, we conclude, the matter would be for the arbitrators. We then ask whether the fact that the document in question is a treaty makes a critical difference. We conclude that it does not.

III

Where ordinary contracts are at issue, it is up to the parties to determine whether a particular matter is primarily for arbitrators or for courts to decide. If the contract is silent on the matter of who primarily is to decide "threshold" questions about arbitration, courts determine the parties' intent with the help of presumptions.

On the one hand, courts presume that the parties intend courts, not arbitrators, to decide what we have called disputes about "arbitrability." These include questions such as "whether the parties are bound by a given arbitration clause," or "whether an arbitration clause in a concededly binding contract applies to a particular type of controversy." *Howsam v. Dean Witter Reynolds, Inc.*, 537 U.S. 79 (2002); accord, *Granite Rock Co. v. Teamsters*, 561 U.S. 287 (2010) (disputes over "formation of the parties' arbitration agreement" and "its enforceability or applicability to the dispute" at issue are "matters ... the court must resolve"). See *AT & T Technologies, Inc. v. Communications Workers*, 475 U.S. 643 (1986) ("Unless the parties clearly and unmistakably provide otherwise, the question of whether the parties agreed to arbitrate is to be decided by the court, not the arbitrator").

On the other hand, courts presume that the parties intend arbitrators, not courts, to decide disputes about the meaning and application of particular procedural preconditions for the use of arbitration. *See Howsam* (courts assume parties "normally expect a forum-based decisionmaker to decide forum-specific *procedural* gateway matters"). These procedural matters include claims of "waiver, delay, or a like defense to arbitrability." And they include the satisfaction of " 'prerequisites such as time limits, notice, laches, estoppel, and other conditions precedent to an obligation to arbitrate.' " *Howsam* (quoting the Revised Uniform Arbitration Act of 2000 §6, Comment 2, 7 U.L.A. 13 (Supp. 2002)). *See also* §6(c) ("An arbitrator shall decide whether a condition precedent to arbitrability has been fulfilled").

The provision before us is of the latter, procedural, variety. The text and structure of the provision make clear that it operates as a procedural condition precedent to arbitration. It says that a dispute "shall be submitted to international arbitration" if "one of the Parties so requests," as long as "a period of eighteen months has elapsed" since the dispute was "submitted" to a local tribunal and the tribunal "has not given its final decision." Art. 8(2). It determines *when* the contractual duty to arbitrate arises, not *whether* there is a contractual duty to arbitrate at all. Neither does this language or other language in Article 8 give substantive weight to the local court's determinations on the matters at issue between the parties. To the contrary, Article 8 provides that *only* the "arbitration decision shall be final and binding on both Parties." Art. 8(4). The litigation provision is consequently a purely procedural requirement — a claims-processing rule that governs when the arbitration may begin, but not whether it may occur or what its substantive outcome will be on the issues in dispute. Moreover, the local litigation requirement is highly analogous to procedural provisions that both this Court and others have found are for arbitrators, not courts, primarily to interpret and to apply.... we can find nothing in Article 8 or elsewhere in the Treaty that might overcome the ordinary assumption. It nowhere demonstrates a contrary intent as to the delegation of decisional authority between judges and arbitrators. Thus, were the document an ordinary contract, it would call for arbitrators primarily to interpret and to apply the local litigation provision.

IV

A

We now relax our ordinary contract assumption and ask whether the fact that the document before us is a treaty makes a critical difference to our analysis. The Solicitor General argues that it should. He says that the local litigation provision may be "a condition on the State's consent to enter into an arbitration agreement." He adds that courts should "review de novo the arbitral tribunal's resolution of objections based on an investor's non-compliance" with such a condition. And he recommends that we remand this case to the Court of Appeals to determine whether the court-exhaustion provision is such a condition.

We do not accept the Solicitor General's view as applied to the treaty before us. As a general matter, a treaty is a contract, though between nations. Its interpretation normally is, like a contract's interpretation, a matter of determining the parties' intent. *Air France v. Saks*, 470 U.S. 392 (1985) (courts must give "the specific words of the treaty a meaning consistent with the shared expectations of the contracting parties"); *Sullivan v. Kidd*, 254 U.S. 433 (1921) ("[T]reaties are to be interpreted upon the principles which govern the interpretation of contracts in writing between individuals, and are to be executed in the utmost good faith, with a view to making effective the purposes of the high contracting parties"). And where, as here, a federal court is asked to interpret that intent pursuant to a motion to vacate or confirm an award made in the United States under the FAA, it should normally apply the presumptions supplied by American law. See New York Convention, Art. V(1)(e) (award may be "set aside or suspended by a competent authority of the country in which, or under the law of which, that award was made"); Vandevelde, *Bilateral Investment Treaties* (arbitral awards pursuant to treaties are "subject to review under the arbitration law of the state where the arbitration takes place"); Dugan, *Investor-State Arbitration*, at 636 ("[T]he national courts and the law of the legal situs of arbitration control a losing party's attempt to set aside [an] award").

... And we apply our ordinary presumption that the interpretation and application of procedural provisions such as the provision before us are primarily for the arbitrators.

B

[A] requirement that a party exhaust its remedies in a country's domestic courts before seeking to arbitrate may seem particularly important to a country offering protections to foreign investors.... As discussed, the text and structure of the litigation requirement set forth in Article 8 make clear that it is a procedural condition precedent to arbitration—a sequential step that a party must follow before giving notice of arbitration. The Treaty nowhere says that the provision is to operate as a substantive condition on the formation of the arbitration contract, or that it is a matter of such elevated importance that it is to be decided by courts. International arbitrators are likely more familiar than are judges with the expectations of foreign investors and recipient nations regarding the operation of the provision. *See Howsam* (comparative institutional expertise a factor in determining parties' likely intent). And the Treaty itself authorizes the use of international arbitration associations, the rules of which provide that arbitrators shall have the authority to interpret provisions of this kind. Art. 8(3) (providing that the parties may refer a dispute to the International Centre for the Settlement of Investment Disputes (ICSID) or to arbitrators appointed pursuant to the arbitration rules of the United Nations Commission on International Trade Law (UNCITRAL)); accord, UNCITRAL Arbitration Rules, Art. 23(1) (rev. 2010 ed.) ("[A]rbitral tribunal shall have the power to rule on its own jurisdiction"); ICSID Convention, Regulations and Rules, Art. 41(1) (2006 ed.) ("Tribunal shall be the judge of its own competence").

The upshot is that our ordinary presumption applies and it is not overcome. The interpretation and application of the local litigation provision is primarily for the arbitrators. Reviewing courts cannot review their decision *de novo*. Rather, they must do so with considerable deference....

In sum, we agree with the dissent that a sovereign's consent to arbitration is important. We also agree that sovereigns can condition their consent to arbitrate by writing various terms into their bilateral investment treaties. But that is not the issue. The question is whether the parties intended to give courts or arbitrators primary authority to interpret and apply a threshold provision in an arbitration contract—when the contract is silent as to the delegation of authority. We have already explained why we believe that where, as here, the provision resembles a claims-processing requirement and is not a requirement that affects the arbitration contract's validity or scope, we presume that the parties (even if they are sovereigns) intended to give that authority to the arbitrators....

Consequently, we conclude that the arbitrators' jurisdictional determinations are lawful. The judgment of the Court of Appeals to the contrary is reversed.

Justice SOTOMAYOR, concurring in part.

I agree with the Court that the local litigation requirement at issue in this case is a procedural precondition to arbitration (which the arbitrators are to interpret), not a condition on Argentina's consent to arbitrate (which a court would review *de novo*). Importantly, in reaching this conclusion, the Court acknowledges that "the treaty before us does *not* state that the local litigation requirement is a 'condition of consent' to arbitration." ...

Consent is especially salient in the context of a bilateral investment treaty, where the treaty is not an already agreed-upon arbitration provision between known parties, but rather a nation state's standing offer to arbitrate with an amorphous class of private investors. In this setting, a nation-state might reasonably wish to condition its consent to arbitrate with a previously unspecified investor counterparty on the investor's compliance with a requirement that might be deemed "purely procedural" in the ordinary commercial context. Moreover, as THE CHIEF JUSTICE notes, "[i]t is no trifling matter" for a sovereign nation to "subject itself to international arbitration" proceedings, so we should "not presume that any country ... takes that step lightly." (dissenting opinion).... Accordingly, if the local litigation requirement at issue here were labeled a condition on the treaty parties' "consent" to arbitrate, that would in my view change the analysis as to whether the parties intended the requirement to be interpreted by a court or an arbitrator. As it is, however, all parties agree that the local litigation requirement is not so denominated.... In light of these many indicators that Argentina and the United Kingdom did not intend the local litigation requirement to be a condition on their consent to arbitrate, and on the understanding that the Court does not pass on the weight courts should attach to a treaty's use of the term "consent," I concur in the Court's opinion.

Chief Justice ROBERTS, with whom Justice KENNEDY joins, dissenting.

The Court begins by deciding a different case, "initially treat[ing] the document before us as if it were an ordinary contract between private parties." The "document before us," of course, is nothing of the sort. It is instead a treaty between two sovereign nations: the United Kingdom and Argentina. No investor is a party to the agreement. Having elided this rather important fact for much of its analysis, the majority finally "relax[es] [its] ordinary contract assumption and ask[s] whether the fact that the document before us is a treaty makes a critical difference to [its] analysis." It should come as no surprise that, after starting down the wrong road, the majority ends up at the wrong place.

I would start with the document that *is* before us and take it on its own terms. That document is a bilateral investment treaty between the United Kingdom and Argentina, in which Argentina agreed to take steps to encourage U.K. investors to invest within its borders (and the United Kingdom agreed to do the same with respect to Argentine investors). The Treaty does indeed contain a completed agreement for arbitration—between the signatory countries. The Treaty also includes, in Article 8, certain provisions for resolving any disputes that might arise between a signatory country and an investor, who is not a party to the agreement.

One such provision—completely ignored by the Court in its analysis—specifies that disputes may be resolved by arbitration when the host country and an investor "have so agreed." No one doubts that, as is the normal rule, whether there was such an agreement is for a court, not an arbitrator, to decide.

When there is no express agreement between the host country and an investor, they must form an agreement in another way, before an obligation to arbitrate arises. The Treaty by itself cannot constitute an agreement to arbitrate with an investor. How could it? No investor is a party to that Treaty. Something else must happen to *create* an agreement where there was none before. Article 8(2)(a) makes clear what that something is: An investor must submit his dispute to the courts of the host country. After 18 months, or an unsatisfactory decision, the investor may then request arbitration.

Submitting the dispute to the courts is thus a condition to the formation of an agreement, not simply a matter of performing an existing agreement. Article 8(2)(a) constitutes in effect a unilateral *offer* to arbitrate, which an investor may accept by complying with its terms. To be sure, the local litigation requirement might not be absolute. In particular, an investor might argue that it was an implicit aspect of the unilateral offer that he be afforded a reasonable opportunity to submit his dispute to the local courts. Even then, however, the question would remain whether the investor has managed to form an arbitration agreement with the host country pursuant to Article 8(2)(a). That question under Article 8(2)(a) is—like the same question under Article 8(2)(b)—for a court, not an arbitrator, to decide. I respectfully dissent from the Court's contrary conclusion.

By incorporating the local litigation provision in Article 8(1), paragraph 8(2)(a) establishes that provision as a term of Argentina's unilateral offer to arbitrate. To accept Argentina's offer, an investor must therefore first litigate its dispute in Argentina's courts—either to a "final decision" or for 18 months, whichever comes first. Unless the investor does so (or, perhaps, establishes a valid excuse for failing to do so), it has not accepted the terms of Argentina's offer to arbitrate, and thus has not formed an arbitration agreement with Argentina.

Although the majority suggests that the local litigation requirement would not be a "condition of consent" even if the Treaty explicitly called it one, the Court's holding is limited to treaties that contain no such clear statement. . . . BG Group concedes that other terms of Article 8(1) constitute conditions on Argentina's consent to arbitrate, even though they are not expressly labeled as such. See Tr. of Oral Arg. 57 ("You have to be a U.K. investor, you have to have a treaty claim, you have to be suing another party to the treaty. And if those aren't true, *then there is no arbitration agreement*.") The Court does not explain why the *only other term*—the litigation requirement—should be viewed differently.

. . . The majority seems to regard the local litigation requirement as a condition precedent to *performance* of the contract, rather than a condition precedent to *formation* of the contract. But that cannot be. Prior to the fulfillment of the local litigation requirement, there was no contract between Argentina *and BG Group* to be performed. The Treaty is not such an agreement, since BG Group is of course not a party to the Treaty. Neither the majority nor BG Group contends that the agreement is under Article 8(2)(b), the provision that applies "where the Contracting Party and the investor of the other Contracting Party have so agreed." An arbitration agreement must be *formed*, and Article 8(2)(a) spells out how an investor may do that: by submitting the dispute to local courts for 18 months or until a decision is rendered. . . .

The nature of the obligations a sovereign incurs in agreeing to arbitrate with a private party confirms that the local litigation requirement is a condition on a signatory country's consent to arbitrate, and not merely a condition on performance of a pre-existing arbitration agreement. There are good reasons for any sovereign to condition its consent to arbitrate disputes on investors' first litigating their claims in the country's own courts for a specified period. It is no trifling matter for a sovereign nation to subject itself to suit by private parties; we do not presume that any country—including our own—takes that step lightly. Cf. *United States v. Bormes*, 568 U.S. ___ (2012) (Congress must "unequivocally express[ ]" its intent to waive the sovereign immunity of the United States). But even where a sovereign nation has subjected itself to suit in its own courts, it is quite another thing for it to subject itself to international arbitration. Indeed, "[g]ranting a private party the right to bring an action against a sovereign state in an international tribunal regarding an investment dispute is a revolutionary innovation" whose "uniqueness and power should not be over-looked." That is so because of both the procedure and substance of investor-state arbitration.

Procedurally, paragraph (3) of Article 8 designates the Arbitration Rules of the United Nations Commission on International Trade Law (UNCITRAL) as the default rules governing the arbitration. Those rules authorize the Secretary-General of the Permanent Court of Arbitration at The Hague to designate an "appointing authority" who—absent agreement by the parties—can select the sole arbitrator (or, in the case of a three-member tribunal, the presiding arbitrator, where the arbitrators nominated by each of the parties cannot agree on a presiding arbitrator). UNCITRAL Arbitration Rules, Arts. 6, 8–9. The arbitrators, in turn, select the site of the arbitration (again, absent an agreement by the parties) and enjoy broad discretion in conducting the proceedings.

Substantively, by acquiescing to arbitration, a state permits private adjudicators to review its public policies and effectively annul the authoritative acts of its legislature, executive, and judiciary. Consider the dispute that gave rise to this case: Before the arbitral tribunal, BG Group challenged multiple sovereign acts of the Argentine Government taken after the Argentine economy collapsed in 2001—in particular, Emergency Law 25,561, which converted dollar-denominated tariffs into peso-denominated tariffs at a rate of one Argentine peso to one U.S. dollar; Resolution 308/02 and Decree 1090/02, which established a renegotiation process for public service contracts; and Decree 214/02, which stayed for 180 days injunctions and the execution of final judgments in lawsuits challenging the effects of the Emergency Law. Indeed, in awarding damages to BG Group, the tribunal held that the first three of these enactments violated Article 2 of the Treaty.

Perhaps they did, but that is not the issue. Under Article 8, a Contracting Party grants to private adjudicators not necessarily of its own choosing, who can meet literally anywhere in the world, a power it typically reserves to its own courts, if it grants it at all: the power to sit in judgment on its sovereign acts. Given these stakes, one would expect the United Kingdom and Argentina to have taken particular care in specifying the limited circumstances in which foreign investors can trigger the Treaty's arbitration process. And that is precisely what they did in Article 8(2)(a), requiring investors to afford a country's own courts an initial opportunity to review the country's enactments and assess the country's compliance with its international obligations.

Contrast this with Article 9, which provides for arbitration between the signatory countries of disputes under the Treaty without any preconditions. Argentina and the United Kingdom considered arbitration with particular foreign investors to be different in kind and to require special limitations on its use.

The majority regards the local litigation requirement as toothless simply because the Treaty does not require an arbitrator to "give substantive weight to the local court's determinations on the matters at issue between the parties," but instead provides that "[t]he arbitration decision shall be final and binding on both Parties," Art. 8(4), 1765 U.N.T.S. 38. While it is true that an arbitrator need not defer to an Argentine court's judgment in an investor dispute, that does not deprive the litigation requirement of practical import. Most significant, the Treaty provides that an "arbitral tribunal shall decide the dispute in accordance with ... the laws of the Contracting Party involved in the dispute." Art. 8(4). I doubt that a tribunal would give no weight to an Argentine court's authoritative construction of Argentine law, rendered in the same dispute, just because it might not be formally bound to adopt that interpretation....

None of this should be interpreted as defending Argentina's history when it comes to international investment. That history may prompt doubt that requiring an investor to resort to that country's courts in the first instance will be of any use. But that is not the question. Argentina and the United Kingdom reached agreement on the term at issue. The question can therefore be rephrased as whether it makes sense for either Contracting Party to insist on resort to its courts before being compelled to arbitrate anywhere in the world before arbitrators not of its choosing. The foregoing reasons may seem more compelling when viewed apart from the particular episode before us.

Given that the Treaty's local litigation requirement is a condition on consent to arbitrate, it follows that whether an investor has complied with that requirement is a question a court must decide *de novo*, rather than an issue for the arbitrator to decide subject only to the most deferential judicial review. The logic is simple: Because an arbitrator's authority depends on the consent of the parties, the arbitrator should not as a rule be able to decide for himself whether the parties have in fact consented. Where the consent of the parties is in question, "reference of the gateway dispute to the court avoids the risk of forcing parties to arbitrate a matter that they may well not have agreed to arbitrate." ...

Indeed, the question in this case—whether BG Group accepted the terms of Argentina's offer to arbitrate—presents an issue of contract formation, which is the starkest form of the question whether the parties have agreed to arbitrate.... Here ... the question is whether the arbitration clause in the Treaty between the United Kingdom and Argentina gives rise to an arbitration agreement between Argentina *and BG Group* at all....

The majority never even starts down this path. Instead, it preempts the whole inquiry by concluding that the local litigation requirement is the kind of "procedural precondition" that parties typically expect an arbitrator to enforce. But as explained, the local litigation requirement does not resemble the requirements we have previously deemed presumptively procedural. It does not merely regulate the timing of arbitration. Nor does it send the parties to non-judicial forms of dispute resolution.

More importantly, all of the cases cited by the majority as examples of procedural provisions involve commercial contracts between two private parties. None of them—not a single one—involves an agreement between sovereigns or an agreement to which the person seeking to compel arbitration is not even a party. The Treaty, of course, is both of those things.... The key point, which the majority never addresses, is that there is no completed agreement whatsoever between Argentina and BG Group. An agreement must be formed, and whether that has happened is—as it is in the private commercial contract context—an issue for a court to decide....

I respectfully dissent.

2. Notes and Comments

a. The Majority in *BG* applies ordinary contract principles in interpreting the arbitration provision in the Treaty between the United Kingdom and Argentina. Justice Roberts, in dissent, says that the Treaty is "nothing of the sort. It is instead a treaty between two sovereign nations ... No investor is a party to the agreement." How does that difference in perspective affect the ultimate questions of arbitrability and consent?

b. Consider the rather incredible power that a private international arbitral tribunal has, such as in *BG*, where the panel awarded BG Group $185 million in damages against the Argentinian government. Why would a nation-state agree to cede its significant sovereign immunity protections to arbitration? As the arbitration itself was conducted in Washington, D.C. (the seat), and enforcement and challenge of the award were before the U.S. courts, what application does U.S. law have to this arbitration involving a foreign private company and a foreign government?

D. Interim Relief Related to International Litigation and Arbitration

In certain circumstances, courts and arbitrators are authorized to grant interim measures in aid of an arbitration. **Chapter 6.D.** addressed preliminary, interim, and emergency relief from courts and arbitrators in the context of a domestic arbitration. There are many circumstances in which a party to an arbitration agreement, or to an ongoing arbitration, might seek provisional injunctive relief from a court instead of from an arbitral tribunal. Perhaps the tribunal has not yet been constituted; or, perhaps the entity that is to be the target of the court order is not a party to the arbitration, so that the authority of the arbitral tribunal is in doubt. Perhaps the request is sought to make more meaningful the court's earlier order sending the parties to arbitration (such as when one party ignores the order and prosecutes an action in another judicial or arbitral forum).

Whatever the factual backdrop to the request for the court's assistance, the relief sought is discretionary; how the court exercises that discretion will of course depend on myriad considerations. In the international context, consider how a court senses the dictates of "comity," as reflecting both respect for other nations and their legal systems, and a recognition that whatever approach is taken in one country can be reciprocated in another ("reciprocity").

1. Anti-Suit (and Anti-Anti-Suit) Injunctions

The focus here is on measures by U.S. courts that enjoin a disputant from pursuing a dispute in a foreign court in order to enforce an international arbitration agreement. Sometimes these orders are sought as a means of fortifying normal enforcement of an agreement to arbitrate the dispute in question; other times, the parties' agreement to limit themselves to a particular judicial forum is being protected. Even though the kinds of injunctions sought would be addressed to one or more private litigants, rather than to foreign courts or arbitral tribunals, principles of international comity often have a bearing on the court's approach. As seen below, the question is: how do concerns of "comity" influence a decision to dismiss a case?

Goss Int'l Corp. v.
Man Roland Druckmaschinen Aktiengesellschaft
491 F.3d 355, 359–61 (8th Cir. 2007)

RILEY, CIRCUIT JUDGE.

The propriety of issuing a foreign antisuit injunction is a matter of first impression for our circuit. Other circuits having decided the issue agree that federal courts have the power to enjoin persons subject to their jurisdiction from prosecuting foreign suits. The circuits are split, however, on the level of deference afforded to international comity in determining whether a foreign antisuit injunction should issue. The First, Second, Third, Sixth, and District of Columbia Circuits have adopted the "conservative approach," under which a foreign antisuit injunction will issue only if the movant demonstrates (1) an action in a foreign jurisdiction would prevent United States jurisdiction or threaten a vital United States policy, and (2) the domestic interests outweigh concerns of international comity. In contrast, the Fifth and Ninth Circuits follow the "liberal approach," which places only modest emphasis on international comity and approves the issuance of an antisuit injunction when necessary to prevent duplicative and vexatious foreign litigation and to avoid inconsistent judgments. The Seventh Circuit has indicated its agreement with the liberal approach.

Under either the conservative or liberal approach, courts are required to balance domestic judicial interests against concerns of international comity.

We agree with the observations of the First Circuit that the conservative approach (1) "recognizes the rebuttable presumption against issuing international antisuit injunctions," (2) "is more respectful of principles of international comity," (3) "compels an inquiring court to balance competing policy considerations," and (4) acknowledges that issuing an international antisuit injunction is a step that should "be taken only with care and great restraint" and with the recognition that international comity is a fundamental principle deserving of substantial deference." *Quaak v. Klynveld Peat Marwick Goerdeler Bedrijfsrevisoren*, 361 F.3d 11 (1st Cir. 2004). Likewise, we agree with the Sixth Circuit's observation that the liberal approach "conveys the message, intended or not, that the issuing court has so little confidence in the foreign court's ability to adjudicate a given dispute fairly and efficiently that it is unwilling even to allow the possibility." *Gau Shan Co. v. Bankers Trust Co.*, 956 F.2d 1349 (6th Cir.1992).

Although comity eludes a precise definition, its importance in our globalized economy cannot be overstated. *Compare Hilton v. Guyot*, 159 U.S. 113 (1895) (defining comity as "the recognition which one nation allows within its territory to the legislative, executive or judicial acts of another nation"), *with Turner Entm't Co. v. Degeto Film GmbH*, 25 F.3d 1512 (11th Cir.1994) (noting commentators have defined comity using terms such as, "courtesy, politeness, convenience or goodwill between sovereigns, a moral necessity, expediency, reciprocity or consideration of high international politics concerned with maintaining amicable and workable relationships between nations.") Indeed, the world economic interdependence has highlighted the importance of comity, as international commerce depends to a large extent on the ability of merchants to predict the likely consequences of their conduct in overseas markets. We also note, the Congress and the President possess greater experience with, knowledge of, and expertise in international trade and economics than does the Judiciary. The two other branches, not the Judiciary, bear the constitutional duties related to foreign affairs. For these reasons, we join the majority of our sister circuits and adopt the conservative approach in determining whether a foreign antisuit injunction should issue.

a. Comments and Questions

i. The anti-suit debate, both in the United States and elsewhere, has generated considerable comment. *See* Mohammed Zaheeruddin, *The Remedy of Provisional or Interim Measures in International Commercial Arbitration and Conditions for Grant of Such Measures*, 4 INT'L J. ARTS & COMM. 8 (2015); Ali et al., *Anti-Suit Injunctions in Support of International Arbitration in the United States and the United Kingdom*, 11 INT'L ARB. L. REV. 12 (2008); Julian D.M. Lew, *Does Nation Court Involvement Undermine the International Arbitration Process?*, 24 AM. U. INT'L L. REV. 489 (2009) (author's answer: "it depends").

ii. *Anti-Suit Injunctions in Aid of Arbitration.* The ICA Restatement proposes a three-pronged test. Section 2-28 provides that "A court may enjoin a party to an international arbitration agreement from proceeding with pending or prospective litigation before another court to the extent that: (a) the agreement is enforceable ... (b) the party being enjoined is bound by the agreement ... (c) claims in the other litigation are within the scope of the agreement." Restatement of the Law (Third), THE U.S. LAW OF INTERNATIONAL COMMERCIAL ARBITRATION, (Draft No. 4, 2015).

2. May Arbitrators Issue Anti-Suit Orders?

While earlier discussion focused on the issuance of anti-suit injunctions by courts, consider whether an arbitrator has authority to issue an anti-suit injunction. Although immediate enforcement would require resort to a court, the issuance of such an injunction would provide a basis for the imposition of subsequent sanctions by the arbitral panel. For an argument that such action is appropriate, *see* Alejandro Leáñez, *The Future of Anti-Suit Injunctions: The Power of the Arbitral Tribunal to Issue Anti-Suit Injunctions*, 14 VINDOBONA J. INT'L COM. L. & ARB. 33 (2010). The author concludes that "the power to issue anti-suit injunctions by arbitrators is part of their power to take all the necessary measures to protect the international effectiveness of the future award."

Central to the argument for arbitral authority to issue anti-suit injunctions is the competence-competence principle of international arbitration, under which the arbitral tribunal makes the initial determination of its own jurisdiction. An anti-suit order may be necessary to ensure the proper course of the proceeding, as determined by the arbitral tribunal, and to "ensure the effectiveness of the upcoming award." The author does end with a caution: the arbitrators must "guarantee that these measures do not violate a party's fundamental right to seek relief before national courts. Therefore, the conditions for granting interim measures must be strictly satisfied. The relevant measure must be urgent and aimed at preventing irreparable harm, or necessary to facilitate the enforcement of the upcoming award." *Id.* This language is sufficiently general to provide arbitrators with as much latitude as they need to meet exigent circumstances.

3. Anti-Arbitration Injunctions

U.S. courts are highly supportive of arbitration in general, and this policy preference is even stronger in the international sphere. Accordingly, anti-arbitration injunctions are rarely issued. For an exception in the context of complex financial and securities transactions, see *Citigroup Global Markets, Inc. v. VCG Special Opportunities Master Fund, Ltd.*, 598 F.3d 30 (2d Cir. 2010).

The 2015 Draft ICA Restatement (3d) § 2-29 proposes that "A court may enjoin a party to an international arbitration agreement from proceeding with an arbitration to the extent that: (a) the party seeking the injunction establishes a defense to the enforcement of the agreement … ; (b) issuance of an injunction is appropriate after consideration of the following: (1) the seat of the arbitration; (2) whether circumstances exist that raise substantial and justifiable doubt about the integrity of the arbitration proceeding; and (3) other principles applied by the forum court in determining whether to grant injunctive relief."

4. Pre-Award Asset Attachment Orders by Courts: United States and England

Problem

Your U.S. client has a contract-based claim against a firm based in another country. The agreement calls for arbitration of all disputes arising out of or relating to the dealings between the parties. Your client is quite concerned about dissipation or hiding of assets between now and when the arbitral panel issues its favorable ruling. Can you obtain from a court a preliminary injunction to protect access to assets needed to pay the expected award?

Grupo Mexicano de Desarrollo, S.A. v. Alliance Bond Fund, Inc.

527 U.S. 308 (1999)

JUSTICE SCALIA delivered the opinion of the Court.

This case presents the question whether, in an action for money damages, a United States District Court has the power to issue a preliminary injunction preventing the defendant from transferring assets in which no lien or equitable interest is claimed. [The district court and the court of appeals said yes; the Supreme Court said no.] ...

As further support for the proposition that the relief accorded here was unknown to traditional equity practice, it is instructive that the English Court of Chancery, from which the First Congress borrowed in conferring equitable powers on the federal courts, did not provide an injunctive remedy such as this until 1975. In that year, the Court of Appeal decided *Mareva Compania Naviera S.A. v. International Bulkcarriers S.A.*, 2 Lloyd's Rep. 509. The *Mareva* injunction has now been confirmed by statute. See Supreme Court Act of 1981, §37, 11 Halsbury's Statutes 966, 1001. (Apparently the first "*Mareva*" injunction was actually issued in *Nippon Yusen Kaisha v. Karageorgis*, [1975] 2 Lloyd's Rep. 137 (C. A.), in which Lord Denning recognized the prior practice of not granting such injunctions, but stated that "the time has come when we should revise our practice." For whatever reason, *Mareva* has gotten the credit (or blame), and we follow the tradition of leaving *Nippon Yusen* in the shadows.)

Commentators have emphasized that the adoption of *Mareva* injunctions was a dramatic departure from prior practice. See Wasserman, Equity Renewed: Preliminary Injunctions to Secure Potential Money Judgments, 67 Wash. L.Rev. 257, 337 (1992) (stating that *Mareva* "revolutionized English practice"). The *Mareva* injunction has been recognized as a powerful tool for general creditors; indeed, it has been called the "nuclear weapon of the law." R. Ough & W. Flenley, *The Mareva Injunction and Anton Piller Order: Practice and Precedents* xi (2d ed. 1993).

The parties debate whether *Mareva* was based on statutory authority or on inherent equitable power. Regardless of the answer to this question, it is indisputable that the English courts of equity did not actually *exercise* this power until 1975, and that federal courts in this country have traditionally applied the principle that courts of equity will not, as a general matter, interfere with the debtor's disposition of his property at the instance of a nonjudgment creditor. We think it incompatible with our traditionally cautious approach to equitable powers, which leaves any substantial expansion of past practice to Congress, to decree the elimination of this significant protection for debtors.... As one treatise writer explained:

> A rule of procedure which allowed any prowling creditor, before his claim was definitely established by judgment, and without reference to the character of his demand, to file a bill to discover assets, or to impeach transfers, or interfere with the business affairs of the alleged debtor, would manifestly be susceptible of the grossest abuse. A more powerful weapon of oppression could not be placed at the disposal of unscrupulous litigants.

Wait, *Fraudulent Conveyances* § 73. The requirement that the creditor obtain a prior judgment is a fundamental protection in debtor-creditor law-rendered all the more important in our federal system by the debtor's right to a jury trial on the legal claim. There are other factors which likewise give us pause: The remedy sought here could render Federal Rule of Civil Procedure 64, which authorizes use of state prejudgment remedies, a virtual irrelevance. Why go through the trouble of complying with local attachment and garnishment statutes when this all-purpose prejudgment injunction is available? More importantly, by adding, through judicial fiat, a new and powerful weapon to the creditor's arsenal, the new rule could radically alter the balance between debtor's and creditor's rights which has been developed over centuries through many laws — including those relating to bankruptcy, fraudulent conveyances, and preferences.

It is significant that, in England, use of the *Mareva* injunction has expanded rapidly. Since 1975, the English courts have awarded *Mareva* injunctions to freeze assets in an ever-increasing set of circumstances both within and beyond the commercial setting to an ever-expanding number of plaintiffs. As early as 1984, one observer stated: "there are now a steady flow of such applications to our Courts which have been estimated to exceed one per month." Shenton, *Attachments and Interim Court Remedies in Support of Arbitration*, 1984 Int'l Bus. Law. 101.

We do not decide which side has the better of these arguments. Even when sitting as a court in equity, we have no authority to craft a "nuclear weapon" of the law like the one advocated here. The debate concerning this formidable power over debtors should be conducted and resolved where such issues belong in our democracy: in the Congress.

a. Comments and Questions

i. *Freezing and Protecting Assets Pending Arbitration*. Pre-award attachment of assets dramatically changes the leverage of disputing parties, with the defendant then having a far greater incentive to settle. Even if the total number of settlements did not increase, plaintiffs surely will achieve more favorable settlements than if pretrial attachment were unavailable. When should a court issue a pre-award injunction preventing a party from disposing of assets pending a foreign arbitration? Does a foreign party have access to U.S. courts to seek a pre-award attachment against a U.S. party? Would a foreign court entertain such a pre-award attachment request from a U.S. party? What standards apply?

ii. With large amounts of money at stake, and talk of nuclear options, *Grupo Mexicano* and *Maraeva* have generated considerable discussion in the law reviews. *See, e.g.*, Panagiota Kelali, *Provisional Relief in Transnational Litigation in the Internet Era: What Is in the US Best Interest?*, 24 J. MARSHALL J. COMPUTER & INFO. L. 263 (2006); Jeffrey L. Wilson, *Three if by Equity: Mareva Orders & the New British Invasion*, 19 ST. JOHN'S J. LEGAL COMMENT. 673 (2005); David Capper, *The Need for Mareva Injunctions Reconsidered*, 73 FORDHAM L. REV. 2161 (2005).

iii. *Grupo Mexicano* leaves untouched the availability of state-law attachment. New York recently amended its Civil Procedure law, CPLR 7502(C), to permit pre-judgment asset freezes. The local arbitration community was instrumental in the enactment of this provision. Although there is no federal law basis for ordering asset freezes, federal courts sometimes rely on state court procedures to do so.

E. Recognition and Enforcement of International Arbitral Awards in the United States

1. Grounds for Denying Recognition of an Arbitration Award

Section 207 of the FAA states that "[t]he court *shall* confirm the award unless it finds one of the grounds for refusal or deferral of recognition or enforcement of the award specified in the said Convention." 9 U.S.C. § 207. New York Convention Art V(2) provides that "Recognition and enforcement of an arbitral award may also be refused if the competent authority in the country where recognition and enforcement is sought finds that: (a) The subject matter of the difference is not capable of settlement by arbitration under the law of that country; or (b) The recognition or enforcement of the award would be contrary to the public policy of that country." Consider how courts interpret the scope of this exception.

Parsons & Whittemore Overseas Co., Inc. v. Societe Generale de L'Industrie du Papier (RAKTA)
508 F.2d 969 (2d Cir. 1984)

Parsons & Whittemore Overseas (Overseas), an American corporation, appeals from the entry of summary judgment on the counter-claim by Societe Generale de L'Industrie du Papier (RAKTA), an Egyptian corporation, to confirm a foreign arbitral award holding Overseas liable to RAKTA for breach of contract. Jurisdiction is based on 9 U.S.C. 203, which empowers federal district courts to hear cases to recognize and enforce foreign arbitral awards, and 9 U.S.C. 205, which authorizes the removal of such cases from state courts, as was accomplished in this instance. We affirm the district court's confirmation of the foreign award.... Since it has been established that RAKTA can fully satisfy the award out of a supersedeas bond posted by Overseas, we need not and do not rule on RAKTA's ... letter of credit claim.

In November 1962, Overseas consented by written agreement with RAKTA to construct, start up and, for one year, manage and supervise a paperboard mill in Alexandria, Egypt. The Agency for International Development (AID), a branch of the United States State Department, would finance the project by supplying RAKTA with funds with which to purchase letters of credit in Overseas' favor. Among the contract's terms was an arbitration clause, which provided a means to settle differences arising in the course of performance, and a *force majeure* clause, which excused delay in performance due to causes beyond Overseas' reasonable capacity to control.

Work proceeded as planned until May, 1967. Then, with the Arab-Israeli Six Day War on the horizon, recurrent expressions of Egyptian hostility to Americans—nationals of the principal ally of the Israeli enemy—caused the majority of the Overseas work crew to leave Egypt. On June 6, the Egyptian government broke diplomatic ties with the United States and ordered all Americans expelled from Egypt except those who would apply and qualify for a special visa. Having abandoned the project for the present with the construction phase near completion, Overseas notified RAKTA that it regarded this postponement as excused by the *force majeure* clause. RAKTA disagreed and sought damages for breach of contract. Overseas refused to settle and RAKTA, already at work on completing the performance promised by Overseas, invoked the arbitration clause. Overseas responded by calling into play the clause's option to bring a dispute directly to a three-man arbitral board governed by the rules of the International Chamber of Commerce....

The tribunal ... recognized Overseas' *force majeure* defense as good only during the period from May 28 to June 30, 1967. In so limiting Overseas' defense, the arbitration court emphasized that Overseas had made no more than a perfunctory effort to secure special visas and that AID's notification that it was withdrawing financial backing did not justify Overseas' unilateral decision to abandon the project. Overseas was held liable to RAKTA for $312,000 in damages for breach of contract and $30,000 for RAKTA's costs; additionally, the arbitrators' compensation was set at $49,000, with Overseas responsible for three-fourths of the sum....

Overseas' defenses, all rejected by the district court, form the principal issues for review on this appeal. Four of these defenses are derived from the express language of the applicable New York Convention, and a fifth is arguably implicit in the Convention. These include: enforcement of the award would violate the public policy of the United States, the award represents an arbitration of matters not appropriately decided by arbitration; the tribunal denied Overseas an adequate opportunity to present its case; the award is predicated upon a resolution of issues outside the scope of contractual agreement to submit to arbitration; and the award is in manifest disregard of law.

The New York Convention superseded the Geneva Convention of 1927. The 1958 Convention's basic thrust was to liberalize procedures for enforcing foreign arbitral awards: While the Geneva Convention placed the burden of proof on the party seeking enforcement of a foreign arbitral award and did not circumscribe the range of available defenses to those enumerated in the convention, the 1958 Convention clearly shifted the burden of proof to the party defending against enforcement and limited his defenses to seven set forth in Article ... Under 9 U.S.C. 208, the existing FAA applies to the enforcement of foreign awards except to the extent to which the latter may conflict with the Convention.

A. Public Policy

Article V(2)(b) of the Convention allows the court in which enforcement of a foreign arbitral award is sought to refuse enforcement, on the defendant's motion or sua sponte, if "enforcement of the award would be contrary to the public policy of (the forum) country." The legislative history of the provision offers no certain guidelines to its construction. Its precursors in the Geneva Convention and the 1958 Convention's ad hoc committee draft extended the public policy exception to, respectively, awards contrary to "principles of the law" and awards violative of "fundamental principles of the law."

The general pro-enforcement bias informing the Convention and explaining its supersession of the Geneva Convention points toward a narrow reading of the public policy defense. An expansive construction of this defense would vitiate the Convention's basic effort to remove preexisting obstacles to enforcement. Additionally, considerations of reciprocity—considerations given express recognition in the Convention itself—counsel courts to invoke the public policy defense with caution lest foreign courts frequently accept it as a defense to enforcement of arbitral awards rendered in the United States. (In a system based upon reciprocity any tendency to take an overly narrow view of foreign arbitral awards will be balanced by a desire to obtain the widest acceptance of America's awards among the courts of other signatory states, which also have the public policy loophole available to them.)

We conclude, therefore, that the Convention's public policy defense should be construed narrowly. Enforcement of foreign arbitral awards may be denied on this basis only where enforcement would violate the forum state's most basic notions of morality and justice. Under this view of the public policy provision in the Convention, Overseas' public policy defense may easily be dismissed. Overseas argues that various actions by United States officials subsequent to the severance of American-Egyptian relations—most particularly, AID's withdrawal of financial support for the Overseas-RAKTA contract—required Overseas, as a loyal American citizen, to abandon the project. Enforcement of an award predicated on the feasibility of Overseas' returning to work in defiance of these expressions of national policy would therefore allegedly contravene United States public policy. In equating "national" policy with United States "public" policy, the appellant quite plainly misses the mark. To read the public policy defense as a parochial device protective of national political interests would seriously undermine the Convention's utility. This provision was not meant to enshrine the vagaries of international politics under the rubric of "public policy." Rather, a circumscribed public policy doctrine was contemplated by the Convention's framers and every indication is that the United States, in acceding to the Convention, meant to subscribe to this supranational emphasis.

To deny enforcement of this award largely because of the United States' falling out with Egypt in recent years would mean converting a defense intended to be of narrow scope into a major loophole in the Convention's mechanism for enforcement. We have little hesitation, therefore, in disallowing Overseas' proposed public policy defense.

B. Non-Arbitrability

Article V(2)(a) authorizes a court to deny enforcement, on a defendant's or its own motion, of a foreign arbitral award when "the subject matter of the difference is not capable of settlement by arbitration under the law of that (the forum) country." ... It may well be that the special considerations and policies underlying a truly international agreement, call for a narrower view of non-arbitrability in the international than the domestic context. *Cf. Scherk v. Alberto-Culver Co.*, 417 U.S. 506, 515 (1974) (enforcement of international but not domestic agreement to arbitrate claim based on alleged Securities Act violations).

Resolution of Overseas' non-arbitrability argument, however, does not require us to reach such difficult distinctions between domestic and foreign awards. For Overseas' argument—that United States foreign policy issues can hardly be placed at the mercy of foreign arbitrators who are charged with the execution of no public trust and whose loyalties are to foreign interests—plainly fails to raise so substantial an issue of arbitrability. The mere fact that an issue of national interest may incidentally figure into the resolution of a breach of contract claim does not make the dispute not arbitrable. Furthermore, even were the test for non-arbitrability of an ad hoc nature, Overseas' situation would almost certainly not meet the standard, for Overseas grossly exaggerates the magnitude of the national interest involved in the resolution of its particular claim. Simply because acts of the United States are somehow implicated in a case one cannot conclude that the United States is vitally interested in its outcome. The court below was correct in denying relief to Overseas under the Convention's non-arbitrability defense to enforcement of foreign arbitral awards. There is no special national interest in judicial, rather than arbitral, resolution of the breach of contract claim underlying the award in this case.

C. Inadequate Opportunity to Present Defense

Under Article V(1)(b) of the Convention, enforcement of a foreign arbitral award may be denied if the defendant can prove that he was "not given proper notice ... or was otherwise unable to present his case." This provision essentially sanctions the application of the forum state's standards of due process. Overseas seeks relief under this provision for the arbitration court's refusal to delay proceedings in order to accommodate the speaking schedule of one of Overseas' witnesses, David Nes, the United States Charge d'Affairs in Egypt at the time of the Six Day War. This attempt to state a due process claim fails for several reasons. First, inability to produce one's witnesses before an arbitral tribunal is a risk inherent in an agreement to submit to arbitration. By agreeing to submit disputes to arbitration, a party relinquishes his courtroom rights—including that to subpoena witnesses—in favor of arbitration with all of its well known advantages and drawbacks. Secondly, the logistical problems of scheduling hearing dates convenient to parties, counsel and arbitrators scattered about the globe argues against deviating from an initially mutually agreeable time plan unless a scheduling change is truly unavoidable. In this instance, Overseas' allegedly key witness was kept from attending the hearing due to a prior commitment to lecture at an American university—hardly the type of obstacle to his presence which would require the arbitral tribunal to postpone the hearing as a matter of fundamental fairness to Overseas. Finally, the tribunal did have before it an affidavit by Mr. Nes in which he furnished, by his own account, "a good deal of the information to which I would have testified." Moreover, had Mr. Nes wished to furnish all the information to which he would have testified, there is every reason to believe that the arbitration tribunal would have considered that as well.

D. Arbitration in Excess of Jurisdiction

Under Article V(1)(c), one defending against enforcement of an arbitral award may prevail by proving that: "The award deals with a difference not contemplated by or not falling within the terms of the submission to arbitration, or it contains decisions on matters beyond the scope of the submission to arbitration...." This provision tracks in more detailed form section 10(d) of the FAA, which authorizes vacating an award "where the arbitrators exceeded their powers." Both provisions basically allow a party to attack an award predicated upon arbitration of a subject matter not within the agreement to submit to arbitration. This defense to enforcement of a foreign award should be construed narrowly. Once again a narrow construction would comport with the enforcement-facilitating thrust of the Convention. In addition, the case law under the similar provision of the FAA strongly supports a strict reading. In making this defense, Overseas must therefore overcome a powerful presumption that the arbitral body acted within its powers....

Although the Convention recognizes that an award may not be enforced where predicated on a subject matter outside the arbitrator's jurisdiction, it does not sanction second-guessing the arbitrator's construction of the parties' agreement. The appellant's attempt to invoke this defense, however, calls upon the court to ignore this limitation on its decision-making powers and usurp the arbitrator's role. The district court took a proper view of its own jurisdiction in refusing to grant relief on this ground.

E. Award in Manifest Disregard of Law

Both the legislative history of Article V, and the statute enacted to implement the United States' accession to the Convention are strong authority for treating as exclusive the bases set forth in the Convention for vacating an award. On the other hand, the FAA has been read to include an implied defense to enforcement where the award is in manifest disregard of the law. *Wilko v. Swan*, 346 U.S. 427 (1953). This case does not require us to decide whether this defense stemming from dictum in *Wilko* obtains in the international arbitration context. For even assuming that the manifest disregard defense applies under the Convention, we would have no difficulty rejecting the appellant's contention that such manifest disregard is in evidence here. Overseas in effect asks this court to read this defense as a license to review the record of arbitral proceedings for errors of fact or law—a role which we have emphatically declined to assume in the past and reject once again. Extensive judicial review frustrates the basic purpose of arbitration, which is to dispose of disputes quickly and avoid the expense and delay of extended court proceedings.

a. Comments and Questions

i. *Parsons & Whittemore* continues to be cited for its explication of the grounds for confirmation or denial of an arbitration award. Unlike the FAA, the New York Convention does not make provision for vacating an arbitration award, but does provide a limited basis to refuse enforcement of the award.

ii. Although in the domestic context (**Chapter 9**), the status of manifest disregard as a defense to confirmation of an arbitral award is in doubt, the grounds set forth in the Conventions for denying recognition or enforcement of an arbitral award are considered exclusive, and courts may not rely on grounds not stated in the applicable Convention to refuse recognition or enforcement. *See* ICA Restatement, Tentative Draft No. 2, § 4-11 (Grounds for Post-Award Relief—Generally) (April 16, 2012), cmt. c (Convention grounds exclusive; no error of law ground available).

iii. "Interestingly, with respect to the substantive defenses to enforcement, where national law is given a prominent role, such as arbitrability (Article V(2)(a)) and public policy (Article V(2)(b)), national courts have not been parochial in using national law applicable under these Articles, and national courts have acknowledged the need to take account of international and not merely domestic norms. Accordingly, these Convention exceptions for national law have not created great disharmony where one might have thought they would." Linda Silberman, *The New York Convention After Fifty Years: Some Reflections on the Role of National Law*, 38 GA. J. INT'L & COMP. L. 25, 26–27 (2009).

2. Jurisdictional Requirements for U.S. Courts to Enforce Arbitration Awards

Must a U.S. court establish personal or *in rem* jurisdiction in order to enforce a foreign arbitration award involving two non-U.S. parties? Is lack of personal jurisdiction a defense during a proceeding to recognize or enforce a foreign arbitral award? Reminisce on Civil Procedure in reading the following cases.

Frontera Resources Azerbaijan Corp. v. State Oil Co. of the Azerbaijan Republic

582 F.3d 393 (2d Cir. 2009)

JOHN M. WALKER, JR., CIRCUIT JUDGE:

Frontera appeals from the dismissal of its petition to enforce a Swedish arbitration award against State Oil Corporation of the Azerbaijan Republic ("SOCAR"). The district court granted SOCAR's motion to dismiss for want of personal jurisdiction. We conclude that SOCAR is not entitled to the Due Process Clause's jurisdictional protections if it is an agent of the Azerbaijani state. Accordingly, we vacate and remand for the district court to reconsider its analysis.

Frontera and SOCAR are two companies in the oil industry. Frontera is based in the Cayman Islands, and SOCAR is based in and owned by the Republic of Azerbaijan ("Azerbaijan"). The parties entered into a written agreement under which Frontera developed and managed oil deposits in Azerbaijan and delivered oil to SOCAR. A dispute arose over SOCAR's refusal to pay for some of this oil, and in response, Frontera allegedly sought to sell oil that was supposed to be sold to SOCAR to parties outside of Azerbaijan instead. After instructing local customs authorities to block Frontera's oil exports, SOCAR seized the oil.

Subsequently, the bank that had financed Frontera's involvement in Azerbaijan foreclosed on its loan, forcing Frontera to assign its rights in the project to the bank. The bank settled its claims with SOCAR; Frontera, however, continued to seek payment for both previously delivered and seized oil. Based on its settlement with the bank, SOCAR denied liability to Frontera. [Arbitration ensued.] After a hearing on the merits with full participation by both parties, a Swedish arbitral tribunal awarded Frontera approximately $1.24 million plus interest.

Frontera filed a petition to confirm the award pursuant to Article II(2) of the New York Convention. The district court dismissed the petition for lack of personal jurisdiction, on the basis that SOCAR had insufficient contacts with the United States to meet the Due Process Clause's requirements for the assertion of personal jurisdiction. The district court also declined to find quasi in rem jurisdiction over SOCAR, because Frontera had not identified SOCAR assets within the court's jurisdiction. The district court denied jurisdictional discovery and dismissed Frontera's petition. This appeal followed.

Generally, personal jurisdiction has both statutory and constitutional components. A court must have a statutory basis for asserting jurisdiction over a defendant, and the Due Process Clause typically also demands that the defendant, if "not present within the territory of the forum, ... have certain minimum contacts with it such that the maintenance of the suit does not offend traditional notions of fair play and substantial justice." *Int'l Shoe Co. v. Washington*, 326 U.S. 310, 316 (1945). The parties do not challenge the district court's reliance on the Foreign Sovereign Immunities Act ("FSIA"), 28 U.S.C. § 1608(a), as the statutory basis for jurisdiction over SOCAR. *See Argentine Republic v. Amerada Hess Shipping Corp.*, 488 U.S. 428 (1989) (stating that the FSIA "provides the sole basis for obtaining jurisdiction over a foreign state in federal court"). This appeal instead is focused on the Due Process Clause's place in the district court's analysis.

Frontera contends (1) that a court does not need personal jurisdiction over a party in order to confirm a foreign arbitral award against that party, and (2) that ... Due Process Clause's protections should not apply to foreign states or their instrumentalities. Frontera also challenges the district court's denial of jurisdictional discovery. We address each argument in turn.

A. The Need for Jurisdiction

Frontera argues that a district court does not need personal jurisdiction over a respondent to confirm a foreign arbitral award against that party. Yet, Frontera contends, the district court's dismissal of its petition "necessarily rested upon an assumption" that personal jurisdiction over SOCAR was indispensable. We read the district court's decision differently. Although the district court considered whether it could assert personal jurisdiction over SOCAR, it did not make that question dispositive. Instead, after finding SOCAR's contacts with the United States insufficient to establish personal jurisdiction, the district court examined whether it had jurisdiction over any of SOCAR's assets, because in the absence of minimum contacts, quasi in rem jurisdiction may be exercised to attach property to collect a debt. Thus, by suggesting that the district court required personal jurisdiction, Frontera misunderstands the framework of the court's analysis. And to the extent that Frontera's challenge is to the district court's requirement of *either* personal or quasi in rem jurisdiction, it is without merit.

We have previously avoided deciding whether personal or quasi in rem jurisdiction is required to confirm foreign arbitral awards pursuant to the New York Convention. *See Dardana Ltd. v. A.O. Yuganskneftegaz*, 317 F.3d 202 (2d Cir. 2003). However, the numerous other courts to have addressed the issue have each required personal or quasi in rem jurisdiction. *See, e.g., Telcordia Tech Inc. v. Telkom SA Ltd.*, 458 F.3d 172 (3d Cir. 2006); *Glencore Grain Rotterdam B.V. v. Shivnath Rai Harnarain Co.*, 284 F.3d 1114 (9th Cir. 2002); *Base Metal Trading, Ltd. v. OJSC "Novokuznetsky Aluminum Factory,"* 283 F.3d 208 (4th Cir. 2002).

Frontera contends that none of these courts addressed the precise argument it advances here: that there is no "positive statutory or treaty basis" for such a jurisdictional requirement. (This position is not as novel as Frontera suggests. The Ninth Circuit rejected an identical argument in *Glencore Grain*.) The statute that implements the New York Convention requires a court to confirm an award "unless it finds one of the grounds for refusal or deferral of recognition or enforcement of the award specified in the said Convention." 9 U.S.C. §207. Article V of the New York Convention provides the exclusive grounds for refusing confirmation, and specifies seven grounds for refusing to enforce an arbitral award, none of which include a lack of jurisdiction over the respondent or the respondent's property. Frontera accordingly argues that we cannot impose a jurisdictional requirement if the Convention does not already have one. We disagree.

Unlike state courts, which are courts of general jurisdiction, federal courts are courts of limited jurisdiction which thus require a specific grant of jurisdiction. The validity of an order of a federal court depends upon that court's having jurisdiction over both the subject matter and the parties. While the requirement of subject matter jurisdiction functions as a restriction on federal power, the need for personal jurisdiction is fundamental to the court's power to exercise control over the parties. Some basis must be shown, whether arising from the respondent's residence, his conduct, his consent, the location of his property or otherwise, to justify his being subject to the court's power.

Because of the primacy of jurisdiction, "jurisdictional questions ordinarily must precede merits determinations in dispositional order." *Sinochem Int'l Co. v. Malay. Int'l Shipping Corp.*, 549 U.S. 422 (2007). The Article V defenses ... pertain to *substantive* matters rather than to procedure. Article V's exclusivity limits the ways in which one can challenge a request for confirmation, but it does nothing to alter the fundamental requirement of jurisdiction over the party against whom enforcement is being sought. We therefore hold that the district court did not err by treating jurisdiction over either SOCAR or SOCAR's property as a prerequisite to the enforcement of Frontera's petition. The district court may, however, have given the Constitution's Due Process Clause an unwarranted place in its analysis, which we discuss next.

B. SOCAR's Rights under the Due Process Clause

The district court recognized that our precedent *Texas Trading & Milling Corp. v. Federal Republic of Nigeria*, 647 F.2d 300 (2d Cir.1981), compelled it to hold that SOCAR possessed rights under the Due Process Clause, thus requiring that jurisdiction over SOCAR meet the minimum contacts requirements of *International Shoe*. The district court, however, questioned *Texas Trading's* soundness. These doubts were well-founded.

The Due Process Clause famously states that "no *person* shall be ... deprived of life, liberty or property without due process of law." U.S. Const. amend. V (emphasis added). In *Texas Trading*, we held that a foreign state was a "person" within the meaning of the Due Process Clause, and that a court asserting personal jurisdiction over a foreign state must — in addition to complying with the FSIA — therefore engage in a due process scrutiny of the court's power to exercise its authority over the state. Subsequently, we applied *Texas Trading* not only to foreign states but also to their agencies and instrumentalities.

Since *Texas Trading*, however, the case law has marched in a different direction. In *Republic of Argentina v. Weltover, Inc.*, 504 U.S. 607 (1992), the Supreme Court assumed, without deciding, that a foreign state is a "person" for purposes of the Due Process Clause," but then cited *South Carolina v. Katzenbach*, 383 U.S. 301 (1966), which held that States of the Union are not persons for purposes of the Due Process Clause. *Weltover* did not require deciding the issue because Argentina's contacts satisfied the due process requirements, but the Court's implication was plain: If the "States of the Union" have no rights under the Due Process Clause, why should foreign states? In the instant case, ... only the Due Process Clause prevented the district court from asserting personal jurisdiction over SOCAR.

In *Price v. Socialist People's Libyan Arab Jamahiriya*, 294 F.3d 82 (D.C. Cir. 2002), the D.C. Circuit reasoned that because the word "person" in the context of the Due Process Clause of the Fifth Amendment cannot, by any reasonable mode of interpretation, be expanded to encompass the States of the Union, absent some compelling reason to treat foreign sovereigns more favorably than "States of the Union," it would make no sense to view foreign states as "persons" under the Due Process Clause," The *Price* court found no such reason, and we find that case's analysis persuasive. If the States, as sovereigns that are part of the Union, cannot avail themselves of the fundamental safeguards of the Due Process Clause, we do not see why foreign states, as sovereigns wholly outside the Union, should be in a more favored position. This is particularly so when the Supreme Court has never suggested that foreign nations enjoy rights derived from the Constitution, and when courts have instead relied on principles of comity and international law to protect foreign governments in the American legal system.

SOCAR argues otherwise by defending not *Texas Trading's* reasoning but its significance as precedent. And, to be sure, our court's decisions are binding until overruled by us sitting *en banc* or by the Supreme Court, neither of which has happened to *Texas Trading*. "We do, however, recognize an exception to this general rule where there has been an intervening Supreme Court decision that casts doubt on our controlling precedent." *Gelman v. Ashcroft*, 372 F.3d 495 (2d Cir.2004). Although *Weltover* arguably casts sufficient doubt on *Texas Trading* to justify its overruling by this panel, we have nonetheless circulated this opinion to all active members of our court, and none has objected to our departure from *Texas Trading*. *See United States v. Parkes*, 497 F.3d 220 (2d Cir.2007) (describing our "mini-en banc" process). Accordingly, to the extent that *Texas Trading* conflicts with our holding today that foreign states are not "persons" entitled to rights under the Due Process Clause, it is overruled.

Simply overruling *Texas Trading*, however, and holding that a sovereign state does not enjoy due process protections does not decide the precise question in this case, because SOCAR is not a sovereign state, but rather an instrumentality or agency of one. Frontera contends that, because the FSIA treats foreign states and their agencies and instrumentalities identically, citing 28 U.S.C. § 1603(a), we should treat SOCAR just as we would treat Azerbaijan for constitutional purposes. The simple fact that SOCAR is deemed a foreign state as a *statutory* matter, however, does not answer the *constitutional* question of SOCAR's due process rights. SOCAR may indeed lack due process rights like a foreign state, but similar statutory treatment will not be the reason.

However, if the Azerbaijani government "exerted sufficient control over" SOCAR "to make it an agent of the State, then there is no reason to extend to [SOCAR] a constitutional right that is denied to the sovereign itself." Although "government instrumentalities established as juridical entities distinct and independent from their sovereign should normally be treated as such," this presumption can be overcome if the state so "extensively controls" the instrumentality "that a relationship of principal and agent is created," or if "adhering blindly to the corporate form ... would cause ...

injustice." *First Nat'l City Bank v. Banco Para El Comercio Exterior de Cuba* ("*Bancec*"), 462 U.S. 611 (1983); *see also Zappia Middle E. Constr. Co. v. Emirate of Abu Dhabi*, 215 F.3d 247 (2d Cir.2000) ("While the presumption of separateness is a strong one, it may be overcome if a corporate entity is so extensively controlled by the sovereign that the latter is effectively the agent of the former, or if recognizing the corporate entity as independent would work a fraud or injustice."). Although *Banco* asked when a state instrumentality can be treated like its state for the attribution of liability, we think, as the D.C. Circuit did in *TMR Energy*, that *Bancec's* analytic framework is also applicable when the question is whether the instrumentality should have due process rights to which the state is not entitled. Accordingly, if SOCAR is an agent of the Azerbaijani state, as recognized in *Bancec* and subsequent cases, then, like Azerbaijan, SOCAR lacks due process rights.

The district court did not decide whether SOCAR is an agent of the state because *Texas Trading* rendered the question unnecessary and, unsurprisingly, there was scant briefing on the issue.... Accordingly, we remand so that the district court can determine, in light of *Texas Trading's* demise and *Bancec's* new relevance to this context, (1) whether SOCAR is an agent of Azerbaijan, and if not, (2) whether SOCAR is entitled to the protections of the Due Process Clause.

Frontera also argues that the district court erred by rejecting its request for limited discovery of SOCAR's contacts with the United States. This issue is relevant only if the Due Process Clause protects SOCAR, which is for the district court to determine on remand.... Assuming for the moment that SOCAR has the jurisdictional protections of the Due Process Clause, to establish jurisdiction Frontera must show that SOCAR had "continuous and systematic general business contacts" with the United States, a highly fact-sensitive "contextual inquiry" with no one factor having "talismanic significance." The district court is free to consider further discovery requests in light of the questions it must decide on remand.

Finally, SOCAR asks us to affirm the district court's dismissal on the alternate basis of *forum non conveniens*. Having dismissed for want of jurisdiction, the district court expressly declined to address this argument. Following our settled practice of allowing district courts to address arguments in the first instance, we express no view on SOCAR's *forum non conveniens* argument, which it is free to raise again on remand.

Glencore Grain Rotterdam B.V. v. Shivnath Rai Harnarain Co.
284 F.3d 1114 (9th Cir. 2002)

TROTT, CIRCUIT JUDGE.

Glencore Grain filed an application under the New York Convention for an order confirming its arbitration award against Shivnath Rai. We hold that the Convention does not eliminate the due process requirement that a federal court have jurisdiction over a defendant's person or property in a suit to confirm a previously issued arbitration award. Because Glencore Grain fails (1) to identify any property owned by

Shivnath Rai in the forum, or (2) to allege facts that support a finding of personal jurisdiction, we affirm the district court's dismissal of the complaint....

In the absence of personal jurisdiction, Glencore Grain can avoid dismissal of its suit only by showing that the court could base its jurisdiction on property owned by Shivnath Rai and located in the forum.... Considerable authority supports Glencore Grain's position that it can enforce the award against Shivnath Rai's property in the forum even if that property has no relationship to the underlying controversy between the parties. In *Shaffer v. Heitner*, 433 U.S. 186 (1977), the Supreme Court endorsed the position urged by Glencore Grain. Nevertheless, the *sine qua non* of basing jurisdiction on a defendant's assets in the forum is the identification of some asset. Glencore Grain fails to identify any property owned by Shivnath Rai in the forum against which Glencore Grain could attempt to enforce its award.

3. Award Annulled in the Country Where the Award Was Made

TermoRio S.A. v. Electranta S.P.
487 F.3d 928 (D.C. Cir. 2007)

EDWARDS, SENIOR CIRCUIT JUDGE.

Appellant TermoRio and appellee Electranta. a state-owned public utility, entered into a Power Purchase Agreement pursuant to which TermoRio agreed to generate energy and Electranta agreed to buy it. When appellee allegedly failed to meet its obligations under the Agreement, the parties submitted their dispute to an arbitration Tribunal in Colombia in accordance with their Agreement. The Tribunal issued an award in excess of $60 million in favor of TermoRio. Shortly after the Tribunal issued its award, Electranta filed an "extraordinary writ" in a Colombia court seeking to overturn the award. In due course, the Consejo de Estado ("Council of State"), Colombia's highest administrative court, nullified the arbitration award on the ground that the arbitration clause contained in the parties' Agreement violated Colombian law.

Following the judgment by the Consejo de Estado, TermoRio and co-appellant LeaseCo, an investor in TermoRio, filed suit in the District Court against Electranta and the Republic of Colombia seeking enforcement of the Tribunal's arbitration award. Appellants contended that enforcement of the award is required under the FAA, 9 U.S.C. § 201 which implements the New York Convention. The District Court dismissed LeaseCo as a party for want of standing, dismissed appellants' enforcement action for failure to state a claim upon which relief could be granted, and, in the alternative, dismissed appellants' action on the ground of forum non conveniens. We affirm....

The arbitration award was made in Colombia and the Consejo de Estado was a competent authority in that country to set aside the award as contrary to the law of Colombia. Because there is nothing in the record here indicating that the proceedings before the Consejo de Estado were tainted or that the judgment of that court is other than authentic, the District Court was, as it held, obliged to respect it. *See Baker Marine (Nigeria) Ltd. v. Chevron (Nigeria) Ltd.,* 191 F.3d 194 (2d Cir.1999). Because the arbitration award was lawfully nullified by the country in which the award was made, appellants have no cause of action in the United States to seek enforcement of the award under the FAA or the New York Convention....

Because it is clear and undisputed that TermoRio has standing to bring this lawsuit, we need not address the standing of LeaseCo. In addition, because we hold that the District Court properly dismissed appellants' enforcement action under Article V(1)(e) of the New York Convention, we find it unnecessary to determine whether the case might have been dismissed on the ground of *forum non conveniens....* The only issue of consequence before this court is whether the District Court erred in dismissing appellants' claim to enforce the disputed arbitration award.

The United States has ratified and codified two Conventions that allow courts in one country to enforce arbitral awards rendered in other signatory countries: the Panama Convention and the New York Convention. Colombia is a signatory to both of these Conventions. The New York Convention provides that signatory nations are to recognize and enforce arbitral awards rendered in other nations. However, enforcement of awards "may be refused" if, *inter alia,* they were set aside by a competent authority in the country in which the award was made. *See* Art. V(1)(e). Appellants maintain that the Panama Convention applies to this dispute because a majority of the parties to the arbitration agreement are citizens of states that have ratified the Panama Convention. *See* 9 U.S.C. §305(1). However, codification of the Panama Convention incorporates by reference the relevant provisions of the New York Convention, *see* 9 U.S.C. §302, making discussion of the Panama Convention unnecessary.... We therefore resolve this matter with reference to and using the language of the New York Convention.

Under the Convention, the critical element is the place of the award: if that place is in the territory of a party to the Convention, all other Convention states are required to recognize and enforce the award, regardless of the citizenship or domicile of the parties to the arbitration. The Convention provides a carefully crafted framework for the enforcement of international arbitral awards; only a court in a country with primary jurisdiction over an arbitral award may annul that award.

A secondary Contracting State normally may not enforce an arbitration award that has been lawfully set aside by a "competent authority" in the primary Contracting State. Art. V(1)(e). Because the Consejo de Estado is undisputedly a "competent authority" in Colombia (the primary State), and because there is nothing in the record here indicating that the proceedings before the Consejo de Estado were tainted or that the judgment of that court is other than authentic, ... appellants have no cause of action under the FAA or the New York Convention to enforce the award in a Contracting State outside of Colombia.

In reaching this conclusion, we generally subscribe to the reasoning of the Second Circuit in *Baker Marine,* 191 F.3d 194. In that case, Baker Marine, a barge company, executed a services contract with Danos, a shipping concern. The contract contained a clause requiring the parties to arbitrate disputes or controversies arising under their agreement. Following such a dispute, the parties submitted to arbitration before panels of arbitrators in Lagos, Nigeria. The panels awarded Baker Marine damages, but the award was subsequently set aside by a Nigerian court. Baker Marine then sought enforcement of the award in the United States.... The trial court refused to recognize the award, citing Article V(1)(e) of the New York Convention, as well as principles of comity. On appeal, Baker Marine argued that the trial court erred in refusing to enforce the award, because it had been set aside by the Nigerian court on grounds that would have been invalid under U.S. law if presented in an American court. The appellate court rejected this argument, noting that the parties contracted in Nigeria that their disputes would be arbitrated under the laws of Nigeria. The court also remarked on the undesirable consequences that would likely follow from adoption of Baker Marine's argument:

> As a practical matter, mechanical application of domestic arbitral law to foreign awards under the Convention would seriously undermine finality and regularly produce conflicting judgments. If a party whose arbitration award has been vacated at the site of the award can automatically obtain enforcement of the awards under the domestic laws of other nations, a losing party will have every reason to pursue its adversary with enforcement actions from country to country until a court is found, if any, which grants the enforcement.

The same principles and concerns govern here, where appellants seek to enforce an arbitration award that has been vacated by Colombia's Consejo de Estado. For us to endorse what appellants seek would seriously undermine a principal precept of the New York Convention: an arbitration award does not exist to be enforced in other Contracting States if it has been lawfully "set aside" by a competent authority in the State in which the award was made. This principle controls the disposition of this case.

Appellants argue that courts in the United States have discretion under the Convention to enforce an award despite annulment in another country, because Article V(1)(e) merely says that "recognition and enforcement *may* be refused" if the award has been set aside by a competent authority in the primary state. More particularly, appellants contend that "a state is not required to give effect to foreign judicial proceedings grounded on policies which do violence to its own fundamental interests." Appellants' characterizations of the applicable law are ... misguided.

Appellants concede that *Baker Marine* is not incorrect in its holding that "it is insufficient to enforce an award solely because a foreign court's grounds for nullifying the award would not be recognized under domestic United States law." Rather, appellants allege that the District Court should have exercised its discretion to enforce the award in this case, because "the Council of State's decision was contrary to both domestic Colombian and international law; recognition of that decision would frustrate clearly expressed international and United States policy; and the process leading to the nullification decision demonstrated the Colombian government's determination to deny Plaintiffs fair process."

In advancing their claims, appellants rely heavily on *In re Chromalloy Aeroservices*, 939 F.Supp. 907 (D.D.C. 1996). In that case, the District Court addressed an arbitration agreement between the Egyptian Air Force and an American firm in which the parties provided that the losing party would not seek review of the arbitration award. While the American company's petition for enforcement of its award was pending before the District Court, Egypt filed an appeal with the Egyptian Court of Appeal to nullify the award. The District Court refused to recognize the decision of the Egyptian court to nullify the award, finding that to do so would violate clear United States public policy in favor of arbitration and would reward Egypt's breach of the express contractual agreement not to take any appeal from the arbitration award. We need not decide whether the holding in *Chromalloy* is correct, because the present case is plainly distinguishable from *Chromalloy* where an express contract provision was violated by pursuing an appeal to vacate the award. Here, Electranta preserved its objection that the panel was not proper or authorized by law, promptly raised it in the Colombian courts, and received a definitive ruling by the highest court on this question of law."

Furthermore, appellants are simply mistaken in suggesting that the Convention policy in favor of enforcement of arbitration awards effectively swallows the command of Article V(1)(e). A judgment whether to recognize or enforce an award that has not been set aside in the State in which it was made is quite different from a judgment whether to disregard the action of a court of competent authority in another State. The Convention specifically contemplates that the state in which, or under the law of which, the award is made, will be free to set aside or modify an award in accordance with its domestic arbitral law and its full panoply of express and implied grounds for relief. This means that a primary State necessarily may set aside an award on grounds that are not consistent with the laws and policies of a secondary Contracting State. The Convention does not endorse a regime in which secondary States (in determining whether to enforce an award) routinely second-guess the judgment of a court in a primary State, when the court in the primary State has lawfully acted pursuant to "competent authority" to "set aside" an arbitration award made in its country. Appellants go much too far in suggesting that a court in a secondary State is free as it sees fit to ignore the judgment of a court of competent authority in a primary State vacating an arbitration award. It takes much more than a mere assertion that the judgment of the primary State "offends the public policy" of the secondary State to overcome a defense raised under Article V(1)(e)....

In applying Article V(1)(e) of the New York Convention, we must be very careful in weighing notions of "public policy" in determining whether to credit the judgment of a court in the primary State vacating an arbitration award. The test of public policy cannot be simply whether the courts of a secondary State would set aside an arbitration award if the award had been made and enforcement had been sought within its jurisdiction.... The Convention contemplates that different Contracting States may have different grounds for setting aside arbitration awards. Therefore, it is unsurprising that the courts have carefully limited the occasions when a foreign judgment is ignored on grounds of public policy.

A judgment is unenforceable as against public policy to the extent that it is "repugnant to fundamental notions of what is decent and just in the State where enforcement is sought." The standard is high, and infrequently met. Only in clear-cut cases ought it to avail defendant. In the classic formulation, a judgment that "tends clearly" to undermine the public interest, the public confidence in the administration of the law, or security for individual rights of personal liberty or of private property is against public policy.

Article V(2)(b) of the Convention, unlike Article V(1)(e), incorporates an express public policy exception. It is noteworthy that in construing this provision the courts have been very careful not to stretch the compass of "public policy." … The public policy defense is to be construed narrowly to be applied only where enforcement would violate the forum state's most basic notions of morality and justice. Given that Article V(1)(e) contains no exception for public policy, it would be strange indeed to recognize such an implicit limitation in Article V(1)(e) that is broader than the express limitation in Article V(2)(b).

Accepting that there is a narrow public policy gloss on Article V(1)(e) of the Convention and that a foreign judgment is unenforceable as against public policy to the extent that it is "repugnant to fundamental notions of what is decent and just in the United States," appellants' claims still fail. Appellants have neither alleged nor provided any evidence to suggest that the parties' proceedings before Colombia's Consejo de Estado or the judgment of that court violated any basic notions of justice to which we subscribe. Appellants contend that the Consejo de Estado's ruling conflicts with Colombia's obligation under the New York Convention, but that bare allegation surely provides no basis for us to ignore Article V(1)(e) on grounds of public policy.… The Consejo de Estado, Colombia's highest administrative court, is the final expositor of Colombian law, and we are in no position to pronounce the decision of that court wrong.

Corporación Mexicana de Mantenimiento Integral v. Pemex-Exploración y Producción

832 F.3d 92 (2d Cir. 2016)

Petitioner-appellee Corporación Mexicana De Mantenimiento Integral, S. De R.L. De C.V. ("COMMISA") contracted with respondent-appellant Pemex-Exploración Y Producción ("PEP"), a state-owned enterprise, to build oil platforms in the Gulf of Mexico. The contracts provided that arbitration would be the exclusive mechanism for dispute resolution. When the parties' relationship disintegrated, each side accused the other of breach. COMMISA initiated arbitration proceedings, prevailed, and in 2009 obtained an award of approximately $300 million.

COMMISA then petitioned the United States District Court for the Southern District of New York (Hellerstein, J.) ("Southern District") for confirmation of the award, which was done. PEP appealed the district court's judgment to this Court ("First Appeal") and simultaneously attacked the arbitral award in the Mexican courts. The Eleventh Collegiate Court in Mexico set aside the arbitral award on the ground that PEP, as an entity deemed part of the Mexican government, could not be forced to arbitrate. Armed with that decision, PEP moved in this Court to vacate the Southern District's judgment and remand the First Appeal in light of the Eleventh Collegiate Court's decision. We granted that motion. On remand, the Southern District conducted an evidentiary hearing, adhered to its previous ruling, issued a new judgment confirming the arbitral award, and thus set the stage for the present appeal.

We hold that the Southern District properly exercised its discretion in confirming the award because giving effect to the subsequent nullification of the award in Mexico would run counter to United States public policy and would (in the operative phrasing) be "repugnant to fundamental notions of what is decent and just" in this country. We further conclude that PEP's personal jurisdiction and venue objections are without merit. Finally, we hold that the Southern District did not exceed its authority by including in its judgment $106 million attributed to performance bonds that PEP collected. The judgment is affirmed. * * *

Two developments in Mexican law transpired while arbitration proceedings were ongoing. In December 2007, the Mexican Congress changed the available forum for claims that (like COMMISA's) raise issues related to public contracts, and vested exclusive jurisdiction for such disputes in the Tax and Administrative Court. Not incidentally, the switch curtailed the applicable statute of limitations: previously, ten years for suits in the Mexican District Courts; afterward, for suits in the Tax and Administrative Court, 45 days.

Second, in May 2009, the Mexican Congress enacted Section 98 of the Law of Public Works and Related Services ("Section 98"), which ended arbitration for certain claims (such as those by COMMISA):

> An arbitration agreement may be executed regarding the disputes arising between the parties related to the construction of contractual clauses or related to issues arising from the performance of the contracts ... The administrative rescission, early termination of the contracts and such cases as the Regulation of this Law may determine may not be subject to arbitration proceedings.

J.A. at 3758.

Promptly after the issuance of the Preliminary Award in November 2006—and before the enactment of Section 98—PEP asked the arbitration tribunal to reconsider its Preliminary Award and—for the first time—contended that administrative rescission was categorically exempt from arbitration as an act of authority on behalf of the Mexican government. The tribunal rejected this argument in its December 2009 Final Award, and, in a voluminous decision, found that PEP breached the contracts and awarded COMMISA approximately $300 million in damages.

COMMISA raced to confirm the award in the Southern District, which ruled in COMMISA's favor in August 2010. PEP appealed that judgment to this Court in the

First Appeal and simultaneously challenged the arbitral award in Mexico by filing its own *amparo* action, which eventually made its way to the Eleventh Collegiate Court, the analog of the United States Court of Appeals for the District of Columbia Circuit. In September 2011, the Eleventh Collegiate Court held that PEP's rescission was not arbitrable and ordered that the award be annulled; its analysis repeatedly referenced the newly-enacted Section 98....

DISCUSSION

In reviewing a district court's confirmation of an arbitral award, we ordinarily review legal issues de novo and findings of fact for clear error ... because the Southern District's holding necessarily encompassed its decision to deny comity to a foreign judgment, the standard of review is modified: "[w]e review a district court's decision to extend or deny comity to a foreign proceeding for abuse of discretion." Accordingly, we review the Southern District's denial of comity for abuse of discretion, and we review underlying conclusions of law *de novo* and the underlying findings of fact for clear error.... As to the remaining issues on appeal, we review the Southern District's conclusions of law *de novo* and findings of fact for clear error....

III

The domestic enforcement of foreign arbitral awards is governed by two international Conventions: the Inter-American Convention on International Commercial Arbitration ("Panama Convention") and the Convention on the Recognition and Enforcement of Foreign Arbitral Awards ("New York Convention"). There is no substantive difference between the two: both evince a "pro-enforcement bias." *Yusuf Ahmed Alghanim & Sons v. Toys "R" Us, Inc.*, 126 F.3d 15 (2d Cir. 1997). The Federal Arbitration Act ("FAA") expressly incorporates the terms of the Panama Convention. *See* 9 U.S.C. § 301.

Article V of the Panama Convention sets out — and limits — the discretion of courts in enforcing foreign arbitral awards: "The recognition and execution of the decision *may* be refused, at the request of the party against which it is made, only if such party is able to prove to the competent authority of the State in which recognition and execution are requested" one of seven defenses. Panama Convention art. V(1). "Article V provides the exclusive grounds for refusing confirmation under the Convention, [and] one of those exclusive grounds is where '[t]he award ... has been [annulled] or suspended by a competent authority of the country in which, or under the law of which, that award was made.'" *See* 9 U.S.C. § 207 ("The court shall confirm the award unless it finds one of the grounds for refusal or deferral of recognition or enforcement of the award specified in the said Convention."). In sum, a district court *must* enforce an arbitral award rendered abroad unless a litigant satisfies one of the seven enumerated defenses; if one of the defenses is established, the district court *may* choose to refuse recognition of the award.

At first look, the plain text of the Panama Convention seems to contemplate the unfettered discretion of a district court to enforce an arbitral award annulled in the awarding jurisdiction. However, discretion is constrained by the prudential concern of international comity, which remains vital notwithstanding that it is not expressly codified in the Panama Convention. *See Pravin Banker Assocs., Ltd. v. Banco Popular Del Peru*, 109 F.3d 850 (2d Cir. 1997) ("Although courts in this country have long recognized the principles of international comity and have advocated them in order to promote cooperation and reciprocity with foreign lands, comity remains a rule of 'practice, convenience, and expediency,' rather than of law." *In re Maxwell Comm'n Corp. plc*, 93 F.3d 1036 (2d Cir. 1996) ("When construing a statute, the doctrine of international comity is best understood as a guide where the issues to be resolved are entangled in international relations.").

Accordingly, "a final judgment obtained through sound procedures in a foreign country is generally conclusive … *unless* … enforcement of the judgment would offend the public policy of the state in which enforcement is sought." "A judgment is unenforceable as against public policy to the extent that it is 'repugnant to fundamental notions of what is decent and just in the State where enforcement is sought.'" *See also Fed. Treasury Enter. Sojuzplodoimport v. Spirits Int'l B.V.*, 809 F.3d 737 (2d Cir. 2016) ("Nevertheless, 'courts will not extend comity to foreign proceedings when doing so would be contrary to the policies or prejudicial to the interests of the United States.'").

The public policy exception does not swallow the rule: "[t]he standard is high, and infrequently met"; "a judgment that 'tends clearly' to undermine the public interest, the public confidence in the administration of the law, or security for individual rights of personal liberty or of private property is against public policy." The exception accommodates uneasily two competing (and equally important) principles: [i] "the goals of comity and res judicata that underlie the doctrine of recognition and enforcement of foreign judgments" and [ii] "fairness to litigants."

Precedent is sparse; but the few cases that are factually analogous have endorsed this approach. *See Baker Marine (Nig.) Ltd. v. Chevron (Nig.) Ltd.*, 191 F.3d 194 (2d Cir. 1999) ("Recognition of the Nigerian [annulment of the arbitral award] in this case does not conflict with United States public policy."); *see also TermoRio S.A. E.S.P. v. Electranta S.P.*, 487 F.3d 928 (D.C. Cir. 2007) ("*Baker Marine* is consistent with the view that when a competent foreign court has nullified a foreign arbitration award, United States courts should not go behind that decision absent extraordinary circumstances not present in this case…. Therefore, it is unsurprising that the courts have carefully limited the occasions when a foreign judgment is ignored on grounds of public policy. A judgment is unenforceable as against public policy to the extent that it is 'repugnant to fundamental notions of what is decent and just in the State where enforcement is sought.'").

Consequently, although the Panama Convention affords discretion in enforcing a foreign arbitral award that has been annulled in the awarding jurisdiction, and thereby advances the Convention's pro-enforcement aim, the exercise of that discretion here is appropriate only to vindicate "fundamental notions of what is decent and just" in the United States….

IV

Applying this standard, we conclude that the Southern District did not abuse its discretion in confirming the arbitral award notwithstanding invalidation of the award in the Mexican courts. The high hurdle of the public policy exception is surmounted here by four powerful considerations: (1) the vindication of contractual undertakings....; (2) the repugnancy of retroactive legislation that disrupts contractual expectations; (3) the need to ensure legal claims find a forum; and (4) the prohibition against government expropriation without compensation ...

a. Comments and Questions

i. Suppose the *TermoRio* and *Pemex* decisions both made their way to the U.S. Supreme Court. What results, and why?

ii. The Second Circuit in *Pemex* introduced its decision by observing "[t]he truly unusual procedural history of this case requires us to reconcile two settled principles that militate in favor of opposite results: a district court's discretion to confirm an arbitral award, and the comity owed to a foreign court's ruling on the validity of an arbitral award rendered in that country[.]" In turn, it closed its opinion by concluding:

> Any court should act with trepidation and reluctance in enforcing an arbitral award that has been declared a nullity by the courts having jurisdiction over the forum in which the award was rendered. However, we do not think that the Southern District second-guessed the Eleventh Collegiate Court, which appears only to have been implementing the law of Mexico. Rather, the Southern District exercised discretion, as allowed by treaty, to assess whether the nullification of the award offends basic standards of justice in the United States. We hold that in the rare circumstances of this case, the Southern District did not abuse its discretion by confirming the arbitral award at issue because to do otherwise would undermine public confidence in laws and diminish rights of personal liberty and property ... Taken together, these circumstances validate the exercise of discretion and justify affirmance.

To what extent does the Second Circuit's approach in *Pemex* depart from the D.C. Circuit's methodology in *TermoRio*? Can the two decisions be reconciled? One was decided under the New York Convention and the other under the Panama Convention, but that was not the critical difference. The *TermoRio* decision has been the subject of some criticism. *See, e.g.*, 2 Gary B. Born, INTERNATIONAL COMMERCIAL ARBITRATION 2685–87 (2d ed. 2014).

iii. For its part, the ICA Restatement posits that an award falling under either convention may be enforced despite having been annulled at the seat if the judgment setting the award aside "is not entitled to recognition under principles governing the recognition of judgments in the court where such relief is sought, or in other appropriate circumstances." Tentative Draft No. 2, §4-16 (Award Set Aside or Subject to Set-Aside Proceedings) (April 16, 2012). To what extent does either *TermoRio* or *Pemex* present "other appropriate circumstances"?

iv. The recognition of an arbitration award by a U.S. court after the award has been denied recognition by the courts in the nation that is the seat of the arbitration is not cost-free for U.S. businesses and U.S. foreign policy. To begin with, U.S. courts do this only rarely, but those few instances are enough to generate considerable litigation. For multimillion-dollar awards, even a five or ten percent chance of success is a sound economic proposition. And behavioral economics, as well as professional experience, suggest that a firm deprived of the fruits of a large arbitration award will be unduly optimistic about its chances of success—and counsel is unlikely to vigorously argue otherwise.

vi. The French position is that arbitration awards are international in character, and not anchored to a single nation. Accordingly, French courts will determine whether to recognize a foreign arbitral award rather than being bound by the annulment of the award at the place of the arbitration. Consider an arbitration in London. The award favors buyer, but is annulled by an English court as contrary to law. The second award favors seller. The French courts confirm the first award, and reject the second as precluded by recognition of the first award. That, in simplified form, is the much-discussed *Putrabali* proceeding. *See* Richard Hulbert, *When the Theory Doesn't Fit the Facts—A Further Comment on Putrabali*, 25 ARB. INT'L 157 (2009). Courts in England and most other countries will recognize the second rather than the first award. This is what occurred in *Hilmarton*, where a Swiss award set aside by a Swiss court was recognized by a French court, while the second award was given effect in England. *Omnium de Traitement et de Valorisation S.A., Ltd.*, [1999] 2 Lloyd's Rep. 222 (Q.B.) (Eng.).

vii. The opposite of the French position is that other nations should be bound by a final judicial determination at the place of the arbitration. There are also some in-between positions. For an excellent discussion of these issues, see Linda Silberman, *The New York Convention After Fifty Years: Some Reflections on the Role of National Law*, 38 GA. J. INT'L & COMP. L. 25 (2009).

F. Revisiting Select Arbitration Topics — With an International Twist

In this section we revisit several arbitration topics that were previously examined in the domestic context. These topics are interesting and important precisely because of the (at least arguable) difference in treatment between domestic and international disputes.

1. Opt-In Judicial Review of International Arbitration Awards

a. The Law in Other Nations

The arbitration statute in most nations does not include an express provision regarding opt-in review of awards. The most common position on expanded review in national legislation is silence. Canada provides an example. *See* Barry Leon & Laila Karimi, *The Canadian Position: Can Parties to an Arbitration Agreement Vary the Statutory Scope of Judicial Review of the Award?*, 14 ILSA J. INT'L & COMP. L. 451

(2008). Nations that permit parties to expand the scope of review include the United Kingdom, Arbitration Act, 1996, c. 23 §69; and Singapore, Arbitration Act, 2002, c. 10, §49 (Sing.). France is prominent among the nations that reject expanded review. Paris Court of Appeal, Oct. 24, 1968, J.C.P. 1969, II, 15738.

Discussion of this legislation and much more is found in Mark D. Wasco, *When Less is More: The International Split over Expanded Judicial Review in Arbitration*, 62 RUTGERS L. REV. 599 (2010) (addresses four scenarios where differences in national laws could easily cause difficulties, and undermine consistency in international arbitration); *see also* Margaret Moses, *Can Parties Tell Courts What to Do? Expanded Judicial Review of Arbitral Awards*, 52 U. KAN. L. REV. 429 (2004) (issues with enforcing international arbitral awards).

b. An International Arbitration Appeals Tribunal?

Even where parties are not authorized to expand the scope of judicial review, they are permitted to contract for use of a private review tribunal. This approach is best suited for high-value disputes, a common feature of international arbitration proceedings. William H. Knull III & Noah D. Rubins, *Betting the Farm on International Arbitration: Is It Time to Offer an Appeal Option?*, 11 AM. REV. INT'L ARB. 531 (2000), provides an extended discussion of such an appeal mechanism.

2. Employment Arbitration

Rogers v. Royal Caribbean Cruise Line
547 F.3d 1148 (9th Cir. 2008)

WILLIAM A. FLETCHER, CIRCUIT JUDGE:

Section 1 of the FAA includes a special carve-out for "contracts of employment of seamen." For purposes of our analysis, we refer to this language in Section 1 as the "exemption clause." ... We must decide whether the exemption clause in Section 1 of the FAA applies to arbitration agreements that would, in the absence of the exemption clause, be covered by the Convention Act. We hold that it does not.

The Convention Act applies to arbitration agreements arising out of legal relationships that are "considered as commercial." 9 U.S.C. §202. The Convention Act states that such agreements include, but are not limited to, agreements described in Section 2 of the FAA. Section 2 describes provisions in contracts "evidencing a transaction involving commerce to settle by arbitration a controversy thereafter arising out of such contract." The Supreme Court has concluded that contracts "evidencing a transaction involving ... commerce" include employment contracts.

The exemption clause in Section 1 is neither part of the definition of commerce in Section 1, nor a limitation on which relationships are "considered as commercial" pursuant to Section 2. Rather, it operates as an exemption. In other words, the exemption clause does not state that transportation workers are *not* engaged in commerce or that their employment contracts are not "considered as commercial." Instead, it states that *even though* such workers are engaged in commerce and *even though* their employment contracts are considered as commercial, the FAA does not apply to them.

Because the exemption clause does not affect the definition of "commerce" or the statutory description of which relationships are "considered as commercial," the exemption is not incorporated into the Convention Act by virtue of Section 202. The only limitation placed on the scope of the Convention Act, other than the language of the Convention itself, is the limitation in Section 202 that "an arbitration agreement ... arising out of a legal relationship ... which is considered as commercial, including a transaction, contract, or agreement described in section 2 of this title, falls under the convention." The employment contracts of seafarers arise out of legal relationships which are considered as commercial, and therefore ... fall under the Convention.

The exemption clause is also not incorporated into the Convention Act by Section 208. That section incorporates the provisions of the FAA unless they are "in conflict with" either the Convention Act or the Convention. The only mechanism the Convention provides for limiting applicability of the Convention is the opportunity for Contracting States to declare that the Convention applies "only to differences arising out of legal relationships ... which are considered as commercial under the national law of the State making such declaration." Art. I(3). Congress' declaration to that effect, as codified in Section 202 of the Convention Act, did not include the exemption clause. The Convention Act does not allow the exemption clause to operate as an additional limitation, over and above Section 202, on the applicability of the Convention. Nor, indeed, does the exemption clause purport to be such an additional limitation, for it does not narrow the definition of "commercial." Rather, as emphasized above, the exemption clause specifies that the FAA does not apply to contracts within the scope of the clause even though such contracts are commercial.

Thomas v. Carnival Corp.
573 F.3d 1113 (11th Cir. 2009)

[Philippine national] Puliyurumpil Mathew Thomas appeals the district court's Order granting Carnival's Motion to Compel Arbitration and denying his Motion to Remand this case to state court. Thomas originally brought suit against Carnival, his former employer, for ... failure to pay wages under the Seaman's Wage Act. Relying on the arbitration clause of its most recent Seafarer's Agreement with Thomas in conjunction with the New York Convention, Carnival filed to remove the suit to federal court and have the district court compel the parties to arbitrate. The district court granted these motions. Thomas appeals this decision.

Thomas notes that the Convention provides that courts need not enforce an arbitration clause when to do so would be contrary to the public policy of that country, arguing that forcing him to arbitrate in a forum that would apply non-U.S. law constitutes a prospective waiver of his U.S. statutory rights and thus ... violates U.S. public policy.... The Seaman's Wage Act provides that seamen are entitled to the balance of their wages by the earlier of twenty-four hours after the cargo has been discharged or four days after the seaman himself has been discharged. 46 U.S.C. § 10313(f).... We must consider Thomas's affirmative defense under the Convention that the enforcement of the Arbitration Clause should be precluded as a violation of public policy.

Article V of the Convention provides specific affirmative defenses to a suit that seeks a court to compel arbitration including the following: "if the competent authority in the country where recognition and enforcement is sought finds that ... recognition or enforcement of the award would be contrary to the public policy of that country." Article V(2)(b). Thomas argues that the Arbitration Clause, which forces him to resolve any disputes in an arbitral forum that must apply non-U.S. law, effectuates a waiver of his U.S. statutory rights in violation of public policy and, therefore, should not be enforced. Both parties rely on the two Supreme Court cases that discuss the concerns expressed in this particular affirmative defense under the Convention.

In *Mitsubishi Motors Corp. v. Soler Chrysler-Plymouth, Inc.*, 473 U.S. 614 (1985).... the court found that enforcing the arbitration agreement in the international context would not violate U.S. public policy because the parties had agreed that American law would, in fact, be applied to the antitrust claims in the Japanese arbitration proceedings. The Court specifically noted that counsel for Mitsubishi conceded at oral argument that American law would apply to the antitrust claims and represented that the claims had been submitted to the arbitration panel in Japan on that basis. Thus, U.S. statutory rights, while not being heard by a federal judge, were nonetheless not being ignored or violated but specifically protected. The Court did, however, note that if "the choice-of-forum and choice-of-law clauses operated in tandem as a prospective waiver of a party's right to pursue statutory remedies, ... we would have little hesitation in condemning the agreement as against public policy." The agreement's choice of an arbitrable forum, by itself, is not a cause for concern. As the Supreme Court said, statutory rights can be vindicated in arbitration as well as in court. The important question, however, is choice of law: What law will apply in that arbitral forum? ... The Agreement *explicitly states* that Panamanian law will apply.

The Supreme Court revisited the question of whether an international arbitration clause could violate U.S. public policy in *Vimar Seguros y Reaseguros v. M/V Sky Reefer*, 515 U.S. 528 (1995), which involved a dispute between a New York fruit distributor and a Japanese carrier.... The Carrier moved to compel arbitration in Japan pursuant to the arbitration clause in the bill of lading. The Distributor argued that the arbitration clause was unenforceable under the FAA because to compel arbitration would violate U.S. public policy. Specifically, it claimed that the foreign arbitrators would apply the Japanese enactment of the Hague Rules, which would significantly lessen the Carrier's liability in violation of "the central guarantee" of COGSA. The Court held: Whatever the merits of petitioner's comparative reading of COGSA and its Japanese counterpart, its claim is premature. At this interlocutory stage *it is not established what law the arbitrators will apply to petitioner's claims* or that petitioner will receive diminished protection as a result. The Supreme Court reaffirmed *Vimar's* emphasis on the procedural posture of the arbitration dispute in *PacifiCare Health Systems v. Book*, 538 U.S. 401 (2003), when it upheld arbitration of a claim because, as in *Vimar*, it was "mere speculation that an arbitrator might interpret these ambiguous agreements in a manner that casts their enforceability into doubt."

The Court, then, has held that arbitration clauses should be upheld if it is evident that either U.S. law definitely will be applied or if, there is a possibility that it might apply *and* there will be later review. The arbitration clauses that provided the bases for these holdings are in direct contradistinction to the Arbitration Clause in the present case, which specifies ex ante that *only* foreign law would apply in arbitration. There is no uncertainty as to the governing law in these proposed arbitral proceedings—only Panamanian law will be applied....

There is no dispute that the IMAGINATION's flag of convenience is Panamanian nor that Thomas's Seaman's Wage Act claim is a U.S. statutory remedy. Thus, under the terms of the Arbitration Clause, Thomas must arbitrate in the Philippines (choice-of-forum) under the law of Panama (choice-of-law). As the arbitrator is bound to effectuate the intent of the parties irrespective of any public policy considerations, these arbitration requirements have "operated in tandem" to completely bar Thomas from relying on any U.S. statutorily-created causes of action. This inability to bring a Seaman's Wage Act claim certainly qualifies as a "prospective waiver" of rights, including one of a private litigant's "chief tools" of statutory enforcement—the Act's treble-damages wage penalty provision for late payments. *See, e.g., Mitsubishi*, 473 U.S. at 635 ("The treble-damages provision wielded by the private litigant is a chief tool in the antitrust enforcement scheme, posing a crucial deterrent to potential violators.").

Moreover, there is no assurance of an "opportunity for review" of Thomas's Seaman's Wage Act claim. Although we are at an interlocutory stage, the possibility of any later opportunity presupposes that arbitration will produce *some* award which the plaintiff can seek to enforce. But, in accordance with our holdings above, in this case Thomas would only be arbitrating a single issue—the Seaman's Wage Act claim, one derived solely from a U.S. statutory scheme. If, applying Panamanian law, Thomas receives no award in the arbitral forum—a distinct possibility given the U.S. based nature of his claim—he will have nothing to enforce in U.S. courts, which will be deprived of any later opportunity to review. Despite our general deference to arbitration agreements in an era of international trade expansion, the possibility of such a result would counsel against being deferential in this circumstance, as it is exactly the sort that the Supreme Court has described as a "prospective waiver of parties' rights to pursue statutory remedies" without the assurance of a "subsequent opportunity for review." The Court explicitly stated that in such situations it "would have little hesitation in condemning the agreement as against public policy." *Id.* For the reasons expressed, we find the Arbitration Clause requiring arbitration in the Philippines under Panamanian law null and void as it relates to Thomas's Seaman's Wage Act Claim.

a. Comments and Questions

i. The purpose of protecting foreign seamen under the Seaman's Wage Act is to promote American employment. If foreign workers were not covered, there would be an additional incentive to hire foreign rather than American seamen.

ii. The *Rogers* approach regarding the application of the New York Convention to seamen followed other courts. *See Bautista v. Star Cruises*, 396 F.3d 1289 (11th Cir. 2005); *Francisco v. Stolt Achievement MT*, 293 F.3d 270 (5th Cir. 2002).

iii. What result in the *Thomas* case if *certiorari* was granted by the Supreme Court?

3. Unconscionability — Arbitration Fees

Kam-Ko Bio-Pharm Trading Co. Ltd-Australasia v. Mayne Pharma (USA) Inc.

560 F.3d 935 (9th Cir. 2009)

Milan D. Smith, Jr., Circuit Judge:

Kam-Ko successfully sued Mayne in district court to compel arbitration before the ICC. A short time later, however, Kam-Ko filed a new lawsuit in district court seeking a declaration that the ICC's $220,000 advance arbitration fee was so high as to be substantively unconscionable under the FAA and Washington law. The district court rejected Kam-Ko's argument.... In this purely commercial context, we hold that Kam-Ko has failed to meet its burden of showing that the costs of the ICC arbitration are so excessive as to be substantively unconscionable. Nor do we find that Kam-Ko was entitled to a jury trial or an evidentiary hearing, or that the district court failed properly to consider sworn testimony regarding Kam-Ko's alleged financial hardship.

Kam-Ko is a Washington company that assisted other companies in securing distribution deals in the Pacific Rim for anti-cancer drugs produced by NaPro. Kam-Ko provided its services to help Mayne's alleged predecessor-in-interest obtain a distribution deal with NaPro in exchange for an agreement (Royalty Agreement) that required an up-front payment of $50,000 and a seventeen-year royalty equal to 5% of the bulk price paid to to NaPro. During contract negotiations, Kam–Ko proposed a process for dispute resolution, and its draft language was included, unaltered, as paragraph six of the Royalty Agreement: Disputes. Any disputes will be settled by binding arbitration under an outside committee of three attorneys acceptable to both parties, under terms of International Chamber of Commerce arbitration guidelines, in Vancouver, B.C., Canada, should such dispute not be resolved within 30 days between the parties. The losing party will pay the cost of such arbitration.

In December 2003, Mayne informed Kam-Ko that the Royalty Agreement was terminated because Mayne had purchased NaPro and believed this acquisition relieved Mayne of any obligations to continue making payments. Kam-Ko replied that the purchase did not relieve Mayne of its obligation to pay.... Kam-Ko filed a request for arbitration with the ICC in July 2005. Upon submission of the request, the ICC required Kam-Ko to pay a $2500 non-refundable deposit. The ICC then required a provisional advance from Kam-Ko of $45,000 with credit for the previously paid $2500. After some delay, Kam-Ko's principals personally loaned the company the money to pay the balance due. The ICC confirmed the parties' choices of one arbitrator each, appointed a third arbitrator to act as chairman of the tribunal, and set the advance costs at $220,000 to be split by Kam-Ko and Mayne, with credit to Kam-Ko for the amount it had previously paid.

Kam-Ko objected to the $220,000 amount as "confiscatory and punitive," and as "wholly unforeseeable to the parties." Mayne also objected to the amount, saying it "appears excessive and is unduly burdensome to both parties." Neither party submitted further payment to the ICC. Under the ICC rules, for the arbitration to proceed, Kam-Ko, as the claimant, was required to pay the entire amount due, or some form of security in lieu of cash, if Mayne did not pay. After a number of extensions of payment deadlines, the ICC deemed the arbitration withdrawn. The ICC fixed the costs already incurred in the arbitration at $40,053, deducted that amount from Kam-Ko's payments of $45,000, and refunded $4947 to Kam-Ko.

The district court denied Kam-Ko's declaratory judgment motion, finding that "the arbitration clause is not void for substantive unconscionability." The district court also granted Mayne's request for a stay and directed the parties to proceed to arbitration within sixty days. When the parties failed to proceed to arbitration as directed, the district court entered a stipulated order dismissing Kam-Ko's declaratory judgment action with prejudice. Kam-Ko timely appealed....

Kam-Ko first argues that the costs required by the ICC render the arbitration clause in the Royalty Agreement substantively unconscionable.... Because Kam-Ko filed its complaint in Washington and the Royalty Agreement contains no superseding choice-of-law provision, Washington law applies.... Under Washington law, substantive unconscionability alone can support a finding of unconscionability. Additionally, in a commercial context, the relevant clause must be substantively unconscionable at the time of contracting.

The record establishes that (1) Kam-Ko itself proposed paragraph six of the Royalty Agreement; (2) Kam-Ko effectively controlled the amount of arbitration expenses and fees by the sum it chose to claim in dispute and by the number of arbitrators it requested; and (3) the ICC rules Kam-Ko had in its possession before it sought to compel arbitration clearly indicated that arbitration expenses and fees might be as high as $286,088. Moreover, (4) Kam-Ko has failed to provide any evidence regarding what other arbitration fora would charge to conduct the arbitration it sought or the administrative expenses that the ICC would actually incur in arbitrating the matter; and (5) it is well known that "in international commercial arbitrations, the fees of the arbitral tribunal can be considerable." John Y. Gotanda, *Setting Arbitration Fees: An International Survey*, 33 Vand. J. Transnat'l L. 779 (2000) (noting, for example, that "a dispute involving $100 million and a panel of three arbitrators appointed under the Rules of the ICC could result in arbitrators' fees totaling $780,000"). Kam-Ko's claim exceeds $2.5 million, thereby dwarfing its $110,000 share of the advance fee sought by the ICC. In light of these facts, we fail to see how the requested $220,000 arbitration fee can fairly be characterized as one-sided, shocking to the conscience," or monstrously harsh.

Kam-Ko cites only one commercial case, *In re Arbitration Between Teleserve Sys., Inc. & MCI Telecommc'ns Corp.*, 230 A.D.2d 585 (N.Y.App.Div.1997), in support of its substantive unconscionability argument. *Teleserve* has no precedential authority in our court and, even if it did, is readily distinguishable from the facts in this case. In *Teleserve*, the court held that an arbitration fee of $204,000 was substantively unconscionable under both federal and state law. The arbitration agreement provided that all disputes arising out of a commercial contract involving telecommunications required arbitration pursuant to the rules of the AAA The court concluded that the "filing fee is patently excessive and bears no reasonable relation to the arbitration forum's administrative expenses in processing the claim. A filing fee of $204,000 far exceeds fees typically charged by neutral arbitration forums."

Importantly, however, the parties in *Teleserve* had originally reached an agreement in which the arbitration fee was merely the flat fee of $4000 required by the AAA. MCI then "unilaterally" drafted a new, superceding set of agreements—which incorporated an independent "MCI Tariff"—setting "a filing fee of $4,000 plus .5% of the amount claimed. Petitioner was thus required to pay a filing fee of $204,000 based on its claim of $40 million in compensatory damages. Here, by contrast, the filing fee was not increased many times over that required by the arbitral forum by a separate "tariff" that grossly favored the party that proposed the arbitration clause. Rather, the ICC based its fees only upon the table of costs in the ICC rules to which Kam-Ko expressly agreed when it submitted its request for arbitration and set the sum in dispute at $2,527,000 or more. Kam-Ko has failed to meet its burden of showing that the arbitration clause in the Royalty Agreement is substantively unconscionable....

Finally, Kam-Ko contends that the district court erred by disregarding the declaration that Kam-Ko submitted regarding the company's alleged lack of assets and inability to pay the $220,000 arbitration fee. That assertion is factually incorrect. The district court explicitly noted in its order that "Kam-Ko represents to the Court that if the arbitration clause is enforced, it will be unable to proceed due to its inability to pay the arbitration fee," and then cited the declaration in support of that proposition. As noted above, in a purely commercial transaction, the fact an unfortunate result occurs *after* the contracting process does not render an otherwise standard limitation of remedies clause substantively unconscionable. Thus, the fact that Kam-Ko—a mere shell company that distributed many millions of dollars directly to its stakeholders—claims it is "unable to pay" many years after it proposed and agreed to the arbitration clause, does not create a genuine issue of material fact.

a. Comments and Questions

i. *Kam-Ko* offers a reminder that international arbitration has high costs when measured in absolute numbers, but not when compared to the amount in dispute.

ii. The Gotanda article cited by the *Kam-Ko* court is still valuable, although the specific cost figures have no doubt increased in many if not most instances.

iii. Unconscionability claims by merchants virtually always are rejected by courts. Any commercial client who wants to make an unconscionability claim must be informed in the clearest terms that doing so is a waste of money, and may undermine the force of stronger claims. If the client still insists on making such a claim, it might be prudent to obtain a written instruction to that effect. Is state law unconscionability a viable defense to enforcement of an international commercial arbitration agreement?

4. Non-Neutral Neutrals: Biased Party-Appointed Arbitrators

In **Chapter 8** we saw that the AAA/ABA Code of Ethics for Arbitrators in Commercial Disputes (2004) in Canon X authorized the use of non-neutral, party-appointed arbitrators. The use of such arbitrators — now called Canon X arbitrators — is well established in America, despite repeatedly expressed concerns about this approach. Outside the United States, the concept of an overtly non-neutral party-appointed arbitrator is not accepted — even shocking. The European view is that party-appointed arbitrators must be neutrals in the same way as other arbitrators, even if the neutrality is not complete. This approach led Professor Rau to observe: "When the continental jurist writes that a party appointed arbitrator must be impartial — but can be impartial 'in his own fashion' — the echo of Cole Porter is undoubtedly inadvertent." Alan Scott Rau, *Integrity in Private Judging*, 38 S. Tex. L. Rev. 485, 508 (1997). Even bearing this *caveat* in mind, however, a norm that prohibits bias is different from a norm that permits bias — even if the no-bias norm may be imperfectly achieved.

Appendix I

Statutes, Uniform Laws, Arbitration Procedural Rules, Conventions, Institutional Provider References

A. Federal Arbitration Act

Chapter One, General Provisions

(9 U.S.C. §§ 1–16)

§ 1. "Maritime transactions" and "commerce" defined; exceptions to operation of title

"Maritime transactions," as herein defined, means charter parties, bills of lading of water carriers, agreements relating to wharfage, supplies furnished vessels or repairs to vessels, collisions, or any other matters in foreign commerce which, if the subject of controversy, would be embraced within admiralty jurisdiction; "commerce", as herein defined, means commerce among the several States or with foreign nations, or in any Territory of the United States or in the District of Columbia, or between any such Territory and another, or between any such Territory and any State or foreign nation, or between the District of Columbia and any State or Territory or foreign nation, but nothing herein contained shall apply to contracts of employment of seamen, railroad employees, or any other class of workers engaged in foreign or interstate commerce.

§ 2. Validity, irrevocability, and enforcement of agreements to arbitrate

A written provision in any maritime transaction or a contract evidencing a transaction involving commerce to settle by arbitration a controversy thereafter arising out of such contract or transaction, or the refusal to perform the whole or any part thereof, or an agreement in writing to submit to arbitration an existing controversy arising out of such a contract, transaction, or refusal, shall be valid, irrevocable, and enforceable, save upon such grounds as exist at law or in equity for the revocation of any contract.

§ 3. Stay of proceedings where issue therein referable to arbitration

If any suit or proceeding be brought in any of the courts of the United States upon any issue referable to arbitration under an agreement in writing for such arbitration, the court in which such suit is pending, upon being satisfied that the issue involved in such suit or proceeding is referable to arbitration under such an agreement, shall on application of one of the parties stay the trial of the action until such arbitration has been had in accordance with the terms of the agreement, providing the applicant for the stay is not in default in proceeding with such arbitration.

§ 4. Failure to arbitrate under agreement; petition to United States court having jurisdiction for order to compel arbitration; notice and service thereof; hearing and determination

A party aggrieved by the alleged failure, neglect, or refusal of another to arbitrate under a written agreement for arbitration may petition any United States district court which, save for such agreement, would have jurisdiction under Title 28, in a civil action or in admiralty of the subject matter of a suit arising out of the controversy between the parties, for an order directing that such arbitration proceed in the manner provided for in such agreement. Five days' notice in writing of such application shall be served upon the party in default. Service thereof shall be made in the manner provided by the Federal Rules of Civil Procedure. The court shall hear the parties, and upon being satisfied that the making of the agreement for arbitration or the failure to comply therewith is not in issue, the court shall make an order directing the parties to proceed to arbitration in accordance with the terms of the agreement. The hearing and proceedings, under such agreement, shall be within the district in which the petition for an order directing such arbitration is filed. If the making of the arbitration agreement or the failure, neglect, or refusal to perform the same be in issue, the court shall proceed summarily to the trial thereof. If no jury trial be demanded by the party alleged to be in default, or if the matter in dispute is within admiralty jurisdiction, the court shall hear and determine such issue. Where such an issue is raised, the party alleged to be in default may, except in cases of admiralty, on or before the return day of the notice of application, demand a jury trial of such issue, and upon such demand the court shall make an order referring the issue or issues to a jury in the manner provided by the Federal Rules of Civil Procedure, or may specially call a jury for that purpose. If the jury find that no agreement in writing for arbitration was made or that there is no default in proceeding thereunder, the proceeding shall be dismissed. If the jury find that an agreement for arbitration was made in writing and that there is a default in proceeding thereunder, the court shall make an order summarily directing the parties to proceed with the arbitration in accordance with the terms thereof.

§ 5. Appointment of arbitrators or umpire

If in the agreement provision be made for a method of naming or appointing an arbitrator or arbitrators or an umpire, such method shall be followed; but if no method be provided therein, or if a method be provided and any party thereto shall fail to avail himself of such method, or if for any other reason there shall be a lapse in the naming of an arbitrator or arbitrators or umpire, or in filling a vacancy, then upon the application of either party to the controversy the court shall designate and appoint an arbitrator or arbitrators or umpire, as the case may require, who shall act under the said agreement with the same force and effect as if he or they had been specifically named therein; and unless otherwise provided in the agreement the arbitration shall be by a single arbitrator.

§ 6. Application heard as motion

Any application to the court hereunder shall be made and heard in the manner provided by law for the making and hearing of motions, except as otherwise herein expressly provided.

§ 7. Witnesses before arbitrators; fees; compelling attendance

The arbitrators selected either as prescribed in this title or otherwise, or a majority of them, may summon in writing any person to attend before them or any of them as a witness and in a proper case to bring with him or them any book, record, document, or paper which may be deemed material as evidence in the case. The fees for such attendance shall be the same as the fees of witnesses before masters of the United States courts. Said summons shall issue in the name of the arbitrator or arbitrators, or a majority of them, and shall be signed by the arbitrators, or a majority of them, and shall be directed to the said person and shall be served in the same manner as subpoenas to appear and testify before the court; if any person or persons so summoned to testify shall refuse or neglect to obey said summons, upon petition the United States district court for the district in which such arbitrators, or a majority of them, are sitting may compel the attendance of such person or persons before said arbitrator or arbitrators, or punish said person or persons for contempt in the same manner provided by law for securing the attendance of witnesses or their punishment for neglect or refusal to attend in the courts of the United States.

§ 8. Proceedings begun by libel in admiralty and seizure of vessel or property

If the basis of jurisdiction be a cause of action otherwise justiciable in admiralty, then, notwithstanding anything herein to the contrary, the party claiming to be aggrieved may begin his proceeding hereunder by libel and seizure of the vessel or other property of the other party according to the usual course of admiralty proceedings, and the court shall then have jurisdiction to direct the parties to proceed with the arbitration and shall retain jurisdiction to enter its decree upon the award.

§ 9. Award of arbitrators; confirmation; jurisdiction; procedure

If the parties in their agreement have agreed that a judgment of the court shall be entered upon the award made pursuant to the arbitration, and shall specify the court, then at any time within one year after the award is made any party to the arbitration may apply to the court so specified for an order confirming the award, and thereupon the court must grant such an order unless the award is vacated, modified, or corrected as prescribed in sections 10 and 11 of this title. If no court is specified in the agreement of the parties, then such application may be made to the United States court in and for the district within which such award was made. Notice of the application shall be served upon the adverse party, and thereupon the court shall have jurisdiction of such party as though he had appeared generally in the proceeding. If the adverse party is a resident of the district within which the award was made, such service shall be made upon the adverse party or his attorney as prescribed by law for service of notice of motion in an action in the same court. If the adverse party shall be a non-resident, then the notice of the application shall be served by the marshal of any district within which the adverse party may be found in like manner as other process of the court.

§ 10. Same; vacation; grounds; rehearing

(a) In any of the following cases the United States court in and for the district wherein the award was made may make an order vacating the award upon the application of any party to the arbitration—

   (1) where the award was procured by corruption, fraud, or undue means;

   (2) where there was evident partiality or corruption in the arbitrators, or either of them;

   (3) where the arbitrators were guilty of misconduct in refusing to postpone the hearing, upon sufficient cause shown, or in refusing to hear evidence pertinent and material to the controversy; or of any other misbehavior by which the rights of any party have been prejudiced; or

   (4) where the arbitrators exceeded their powers, or so imperfectly executed them that a mutual, final, and definite award upon the subject matter submitted was not made.

(b) If an award is vacated and the time within which the agreement required the award to be made has not expired, the court may, in its discretion, direct a rehearing by the arbitrators.

(c) The United States district court for the district wherein an award was made that was issued pursuant to section 580 of title 5 may make an order vacating the award upon the application of a person, other than a party to the arbitration, who is adversely affected or aggrieved by the award, if the use of arbitration or the award is clearly inconsistent with the factors set forth in section 572 of title 5.

§ 11. Same; modification or correction; grounds; order

In either of the following cases the United States court in and for the district wherein the award was made may make an order modifying or correcting the award upon the application of any party to the arbitration—

(a) Where there was an evident material miscalculation of figures or an evident material mistake in the description of any person, thing, or property referred to in the award.

(b) Where the arbitrators have awarded upon a matter not submitted to them, unless it is a matter not affecting the merits of the decision upon the matter submitted.

(c) Where the award is imperfect in matter of form not affecting the merits of the controversy.

The order may modify and correct the award, so as to effect the intent thereof and promote justice between the parties.

§ 12. Notice of motions to vacate or modify; service; stay of proceedings

Notice of a motion to vacate, modify, or correct an award must be served upon the adverse party or his attorney within three months after the award is filed or delivered. If the adverse party is a resident of the district within which the award was made, such service shall be made upon the adverse party or his attorney as prescribed by law for service of notice of motion in an action in the same court. If the adverse party shall be a nonresident then the notice of the application shall be served by the marshal of any district within which the adverse party may be found in like manner as other process of the court. For the purposes of the motion any judge who might make an order to stay the proceedings in an action brought in the same court may make an order, to be served with the notice of motion, staying the proceedings of the adverse party to enforce the award.

§ 13. Papers filed with order on motions; judgment; docketing; force and effect; enforcement

The party moving for an order confirming, modifying, or correcting an award shall, at the time such order is filed with the clerk for the entry of judgment thereon, also file the following papers with the clerk:

(a) The agreement; the selection or appointment, if any, of an additional arbitrator or umpire; and each written extension of the time, if any, within which to make the award.

(b) The award.

(c) Each notice, affidavit, or other paper used upon an application to confirm, modify, or correct the award, and a copy of each order of the court upon such an application.

The judgment shall be docketed as if it was rendered in an action. The judgment so entered shall have the same force and effect, in all respects, as, and be subject to all the provisions of law relating to, a judgment in an action; and it may be enforced as if it had been rendered in an action in the court in which it is entered.

§ 14. Contracts not affected

This title shall not apply to contracts made prior to January 1, 1926.

§ 15. Inapplicability of the Act of State doctrine

Enforcement of arbitral agreements, confirmation of arbitral awards, and execution upon judgments based on orders confirming such awards shall not be refused on the basis of the Act of State doctrine.

§ 16. Appeals

(a) An appeal may be taken from—

    (1) an order—

        (A) refusing a stay of any action under section 3 of this title,

        (B) denying a petition under section 4 of this title to order arbitration to proceed,

        (C) denying an application under section 206 of this title to compel arbitration,

(D) confirming or denying confirmation of an award or partial award, or

(E) modifying, correcting, or vacating an award;

(2) an interlocutory order granting, continuing, or modifying an injunction against an arbitration that is subject to this title; or

(3) a final decision with respect to an arbitration that is subject to this title.

(b) Except as otherwise provided in section 1292(b) of title 28, an appeal may not be taken from an interlocutory order

(1) granting a stay of any action under section 3 of this title;

(2) directing arbitration to proceed under section 4 of this title;

(3) compelling arbitration under section 206 of this title; or

(4) refusing to enjoin an arbitration that is subject to this title.

Federal Arbitration Act, Chapter 2, Convention on the Recognition and Enforcement of Foreign Awards

9 U.S. C. §§ 201–208

§ 201. Enforcement of Convention

The Convention on the Recognition and Enforcement of Foreign Arbitral Awards of June 10, 1958, shall be enforced in United States courts in accordance with this chapter.

§ 202. Agreement or award falling under the Convention

An arbitration agreement or arbitral award arising out of a legal relationship, whether contractual or not, which is considered as commercial, including a transaction, contract, or agreement described in section 2 of this title, falls under the Convention. An agreement or award arising out of such a relationship which is entirely between citizens of the United States shall be deemed not to fall under the Convention unless that relationship involves property located abroad, envisages performance or enforcement abroad, or has some other reasonable relation with one or more foreign states. For the purpose of this section a corporation is a citizen of the United States if it is incorporated or has its principal place of business in the United States.

§ 203. Jurisdiction; amount in controversy

An action or proceeding falling under the Convention shall be deemed to arise under the laws and treaties of the United States. The district courts of the United States (including the courts enumerated in section 460 of title 28) shall have original jurisdiction over such an action or proceeding, regardless of the amount in controversy.

§ 204. Venue

An action or proceeding over which the district courts have jurisdiction pursuant to section 203 of this title may be brought in any such court in which save for the arbitration agreement an action or proceeding with respect to the controversy between the parties could be brought, or in such court for the district and division which embraces the place designated in the agreement as the place of arbitration if such place is within the United States.

§ 205. Removal of Cases From State Courts

Where the subject matter of an action or proceeding pending in a State court relates to an arbitration agreement or award falling under the Convention, the defendant or the defendants may, at any time before the trial thereof, remove such action or proceeding to the district court of the United States for the district and division embracing the place where the action or proceeding is pending. The procedure for removal of causes otherwise provided by law shall apply, except that the ground for removal provided in this section need not appear on the face of the complaint but may be shown in the petition for removal. For the purposes of Chapter 1 of this title any action or proceeding removed under this section shall be deemed to have been brought in the district court to which it is removed.

§ 206. Order to compel arbitration; appointment of arbitrators

A court having jurisdiction under this chapter may direct that arbitration be held in accordance with the agreement at any place therein provided for, whether that place is within or without the United States. Such court may also appoint arbitrators in accordance with the provisions of the agreement.

§ 207. Award of arbitrators; confirmation; jurisdiction; proceeding

Within three years after an arbitral award falling under the Convention is made, any party to the arbitration may apply to any court having jurisdiction under this chapter for an order confirming the award as against any other party to the arbitration. The court shall confirm the award unless it finds one of the grounds for refusal or deferral of recognition or enforcement of the award specified in the said Convention.

§ 208. Chapter 1; residual application

Chapter 1 applies to actions and proceedings brought under this chapter to the extent that chapter is not in conflict with this chapter or the Convention as ratified by the United States.

FAA, Chapter 3, Inter-American Convention on International Commercial Arbitration (Panama Convention)
9 U.S.C. §§ 301–307

§ 301. Enforcement of Convention

The Inter-American Convention on International Commercial Arbitration of January 30, 1975, shall be enforced in United States courts in accordance with this chapter.

§ 302. Incorporation by reference

Sections 202, 203, 204, 205, and 207 of this title shall apply to this chapter as if specifically set forth herein, except that for the purposes of this chapter "the Convention" shall mean the Inter-American Convention.

§ 303. Order to compel arbitration; appointment of arbitrators; locale

(a) A court having jurisdiction under this chapter may direct that arbitration be held in accordance with the agreement at any place therein provided for, whether that place is within or without the United States. The court may also appoint arbitrators in accordance with the provisions of the agreement.

(b) In the event the agreement does not make provision for the place of arbitration or the appointment of arbitrators, the court shall direct that the arbitration shall be held and the arbitrators be appointed in accordance with Article 3 of the Inter-American Convention.

§ 304. Recognition and enforcement of foreign arbitral decisions and awards; reciprocity

Arbitral decisions or awards made in the territory of a foreign State shall, on the basis of reciprocity, be recognized and enforced under this chapter only if that State has ratified or acceded to the Inter-American Convention.

§ 305. Relationship between the Inter-American Convention and the Convention on the Recognition and Enforcement of Foreign Arbitral Awards of June 10, 1958

When the requirements for application of both the Inter-American Convention and the Convention on the Recognition and Enforcement of Foreign Arbitral Awards of June 10, 1958, are met, determination as to which Convention applies shall, unless otherwise expressly agreed, be made as follows:

> (1) If a majority of the parties to the arbitration agreement are citizens of a State or States that have ratified or acceded to the Inter-American Convention and are member States of the Organization of American States, the Inter-American Convention shall apply.

> (2) In all other cases the Convention on the Recognition and Enforcement of Foreign Arbitral Awards of June 10, 1958, shall apply.

§ 306. Applicable rules of Inter-American Commercial Arbitration Commission

(a) For the purposes of this chapter the rules of procedure of the Inter-American Commercial Arbitration Commission referred to in Article 3 of the Inter-American Convention shall, subject to subsection (b) of this section, be those rules as promulgated by the Commission on July 1, 1988.

(b) In the event the rules of procedure of the Inter-American Commercial Arbitration Commission are modified or amended in accordance with the procedures for amendment of the rules of that Commission, the Secretary of State, by regulation in accordance with section 553 of title 5, consistent with the aims and purposes of this Convention, may prescribe that such modifications or amendments shall be effective for purposes of this chapter.

§ 307. Chapter 1; residual application

Chapter 1 applies to actions and proceedings brought under this chapter to the extent Chapter 1 is not in conflict with this Chapter or the Inter-American Convention as ratified by the United States.

United Nations Convention on the Recognition and Enforcement of Foreign Arbitral Awards

(New York, 10 June 1958)

Article I

1. This Convention shall apply to the recognition and enforcement of arbitral awards made in the territory of a State other than the State where the recognition and enforcement of such awards are sought, and arising out of differences between persons, whether physical or legal. It shall also apply to arbitral awards not considered as domestic awards in the State where their recognition and enforcement are sought.

2. The term "arbitral awards" shall include not only awards made by arbitrators appointed for each case but also those made by permanent arbitral bodies to which the parties have submitted.

3. When signing, ratifying or acceding to this Convention, or notifying extension under article X hereof, any State may on the basis of reciprocity declare that it will apply the Convention to the recognition and enforcement of awards made only in the territory of another Contracting State. It may also declare that it will apply the Convention only to differences arising out of legal relationships, whether contractual or not, which are considered as commercial under the national law of the State making such declaration.

Article II

1. Each Contracting State shall recognize an agreement in writing under which the parties undertake to submit to arbitration all or any differences which have arisen or which may arise between them in respect of a defined legal relationship, whether contractual or not, concerning a subject matter capable of settlement by arbitration.

2. The term "agreement in writing" shall include an arbitral clause in a contract or an arbitration agreement, signed by the parties or contained in an exchange of letters or telegrams.

3. The court of a Contracting State, when seized of an action in a matter in respect of which the parties have made an agreement within the meaning of this article, shall, at the request of one of the parties, refer the parties to arbitration, unless it finds that the said agreement is null and void, inoperative or incapable of being performed.

Article III

Each Contracting State shall recognize arbitral awards as binding and enforce them in accordance with the rules of procedure of the territory where the award is relied upon, under the conditions laid down in the following articles. There shall not be imposed substantially more onerous conditions or higher fees or charges on the recognition or enforcement of arbitral awards to which this Convention applies than are imposed on the recognition or enforcement of domestic arbitral awards.

Article IV

1. To obtain the recognition and enforcement mentioned in the preceding article, the party applying for recognition and enforcement shall, at the time of the application, supply:

(a) The duly authenticated original award or a duly certified copy thereof;

(b) The original agreement referred to in article II or a duly certified copy thereof.

2. If the said award or agreement is not made in an official language of the country in which the award is relied upon, the party applying for recognition and enforcement of the award shall produce a translation of these documents into such language. The translation shall be certified by an official or sworn translator or by a diplomatic or consular agent.

Article V

1. Recognition and enforcement of the award may be refused, at the request of the party against whom it is invoked, only if that party furnishes to the competent authority where the recognition and enforcement is sought, proof that:

(a) The parties to the agreement referred to in article II were, under the law applicable to them, under some incapacity, or the said agreement is not valid under the law to which the parties have subjected it or, failing any indication thereon, under the law of the country where the award was made; or

(b) The party against whom the award is invoked was not given proper notice of the appointment of the arbitrator or of the arbitration proceedings or was otherwise unable to present his case; or

(c) The award deals with a difference not contemplated by or not falling within the terms of the submission to arbitration, or it contains decisions on matters beyond the scope of the submission to arbitration, provided that, if the decisions on matters submitted to arbitration can be separated from those not so submitted, that part of the award which contains decisions on matters submitted to arbitration may be recognized and enforced; or

(d) The composition of the arbitral authority or the arbitral procedure was not in accordance with the agreement of the parties, or, failing such agreement, was not in accordance with the law of the country where the arbitration took place; or

(e) The award has not yet become binding on the parties, or has been set aside or suspended by a competent authority of the country in which, or under the law of which, that award was made.

2. Recognition and enforcement of an arbitral award may also be refused if the competent authority in the country where recognition and enforcement is sought finds that:

(a) The subject matter of the difference is not capable of settlement by arbitration under the law of that country; or

(b) The recognition or enforcement of the award would be contrary to the public policy of that country.

Article VI

If an application for the setting aside or suspension of the award has been made to a competent authority referred to in article V (1) (e), the authority before which the award is sought to be relied upon may, if it considers it proper, adjourn the decision on the enforcement of the award and may also, on the application of the party claiming enforcement of the award, order the other party to give suitable security.

Article VII

1. The provisions of the present Convention shall not affect the validity of multilateral or bilateral agreements concerning the recognition and enforcement of arbitral awards entered into by the Contracting States nor deprive any interested party of any right he may have to avail himself of an arbitral award in the manner and to the extent allowed by the law or the treaties of the country where such award is sought to be relied upon.

2. The Geneva Protocol on Arbitration Clauses of 1923 and the Geneva Convention on the Execution of Foreign Arbitral Awards of 1927 shall cease to have effect between Contracting States on their becoming bound and to the extent that they become bound, by this Convention.

Article VIII

1. This Convention shall be open until 31 December 1958 for signature on behalf of any Member of the United Nations and also on behalf of any other State which is or hereafter becomes a member of any specialized agency of the United Nations, or which is or hereafter becomes a party to the Statute of the International Court of Justice, or any other State to which an invitation has been addressed by the General Assembly of the United Nations.

2. This Convention shall be ratified and the instrument of ratification shall be deposited with the Secretary-General of the United Nations.

Article IX

1. This Convention shall be open for accession to all States referred to in article VIII.

2. Accession shall be effected by the deposit of an instrument of accession with the Secretary-General of the United Nations.

Article X

1. Any State may, at the time of signature, ratification or accession, declare that this Convention shall extend to all or any of the territories for the international relations of which it is responsible. Such a declaration shall take effect when the Convention enters into force for the State concerned.

2. At any time thereafter any such extension shall be made by notification addressed to the Secretary-General of the United Nations and shall take effect as from the ninetieth day after the day of receipt by the Secretary-General of the United Nations of this notification, or as from the date of entry into force of the Convention for the State concerned, whichever is the later.

3. With respect to those territories to which this Convention is not extended at the time of signature, ratification or accession, each State concerned shall consider the possibility of taking the necessary steps in order to extend the application of this Convention to such territories, subject, where necessary for constitutional reasons, to the consent of the Governments of such territories.

Article XI

In the case of a federal or non-unitary State, the following provisions shall apply:

(a) With respect to those articles of this Convention that come within the legislative jurisdiction of the federal authority, the obligations of the federal Government shall to this extent be the same as those of Contracting States which are not federal States;

(b) With respect to those articles of this Convention that come within the legislative jurisdiction of constituent states or provinces which are not, under the constitutional system of the federation, bound to take legislative action, the federal Government shall bring such articles with a favourable recommendation to the notice of the appropriate authorities of constituent states or provinces at the earliest possible moment;

(c) A federal State Party to this Convention shall, at the request of any other Contracting State transmitted through the Secretary-General of the United Nations, supply a statement of the law and practice of the federation and its constituent units in regard to any particular provision of this Convention, showing the extent to which effect has been given to that provision by legislative or other action.

Article XII

1. This Convention shall come into force on the ninetieth day following the date of deposit of the third instrument of ratification or accession.

2. For each State ratifying or acceding to this Convention after the deposit of the third instrument of ratification or accession, this Convention shall enter into force on the ninetieth day after deposit by such State of its instrument of ratification or accession.

Article XIII

1. Any Contracting State may denounce this Convention by a written notification to the Secretary-General of the United Nations. Denunciation shall take effect one year after the date of receipt of the notification by the Secretary-General.

2. Any State which has made a declaration or notification under article X may, at any time thereafter, by notification to the Secretary-General of the United Nations, declare that this Convention shall cease to extend to the territory concerned one year after the date of the receipt of the notification by the Secretary-General.

3. This Convention shall continue to be applicable to arbitral awards in respect of which recognition and enforcement proceedings have been instituted before the denunciation takes effect.

Article XIV

A Contracting State shall not be entitled to avail itself of the present Convention against other Contracting States except to the extent that it is itself bound to apply the Convention.

Article XV

The Secretary-General of the United Nations shall notify the States contemplated in article VIII of the following:

(a) Signatures and ratifications in accordance with article VIII;

(b) Accessions in accordance with article IX;

(c) Declarations and notifications under articles I, X and XI;

(d) The date upon which this Convention enters into force in accordance with article XII;

(e) Denunciations and notifications in accordance with article XIII.

Article XVI

1. This Convention, of which the Chinese, English, French, Russian and Spanish texts shall be equally authentic, shall be deposited in the archives of the United Nations.

2. The Secretary-General of the United Nations shall transmit a certified copy of this Convention to the States contemplated in article VIII.

B. Uniform Arbitration Act (1955)

§ 1. Validity of Arbitration Agreement

A written agreement to submit any existing controversy to arbitration or a provision in a written contract to submit to arbitration any controversy thereafter arising between the parties is valid, enforceable and irrevocable, save upon such grounds as exist at law or in equity for the revocation of any contract. This act also applies to arbitration agreements between employers and employees or between their respective representatives [unless otherwise provided in the agreement].

§ 2. Proceedings to Compel or Stay Arbitration

(a)On application of a party showing an agreement described in Section 1, and the opposing party's refusal to arbitrate, the Court shall order the parties to proceed with arbitration, but if the opposing party denies the existence of the agreement to arbitrate, the Court shall proceed summarily to the determination of the issue so raised and shall order arbitration if found for the moving party, otherwise, the application shall be denied.

(b) On application, the court may stay an arbitration proceeding commenced or threatened on a showing that there is no agreement to arbitrage. Such an issue, when in substantial and bona fide dispute, shall be forthwith and summarily tried and the stay ordered if found for the opposing party. If found for the opposing party, the court shall order the parties to proceed to arbitration.

(c) If an issue referable to arbitration under the alleged agreement is involved in an action or proceeding pending in a court having jurisdiction to hear applications under subdivision (a) of this Section, the application may be made in any court of competent jurisdiction.

(d) Any action or proceeding involving an issue subject to arbitration shall be stayed if an order for arbitration or an application therefor has been made under this section or, if the issue is severable, the stay may be with respect thereto only. When the application is made in such action or proceeding, the order for arbitration shall include such stay.

(e) An order for arbitration shall not be refused on the ground that the claim in issue lacks merit or bona fides or because any fault or grounds for the claim sought to be arbitrated have not been shown.

§ 3. Appointment of Arbitrators by Court

If the arbitration agreement provides a method of appointment of arbitrators, this method shall be followed. In the absence thereof, or if the agreed method fails or for any reason cannot be followed, or when an arbitration appointed fails or is unable to act and his successor has not been duly appointed, the court on application of a party shall appoint one or more arbitrators. An arbitration so appointed has all the powers of one specifically named in the agreement.

§ 4. Majority Action by Arbitrators

The powers of the arbitrators may be exercised by a majority unless otherwise provided by the agreement or by this act.

§ 5. Hearing

Unless otherwise provided by the agreement:

(a) The arbitrators shall appoint a time and place for the hearing and cause notification to the parties to be served personally or by registered mail not less than five days before the hearing. Appearance at the hearing waives such notice. The arbitrators may adjourn the hearing from time to time as necessary and, on request of a party and for good cause, or upon their own motion may postpone the hearing to a time not later than the date fixed by the agreement for making the award unless the parties consent to a later date. The arbitrators may hear and determine the controversy upon the evidence produced notwithstanding the failure of a party duly notified to appear. The court on application may direct the arbitrators to proceed promptly with the hearing and determination of the controversy.

(b) The parties are entitled to be heard, to present evidence material to the controversy and to cross-examine witnesses appearing at the hearing.

(c) The hearing shall be conducted by all the arbitrators but a majority may determine any question and render a final award. If, during the course of the hearing, an arbitrator for any reason ceases to act, the remaining arbitrator or arbitrators appointed to act as neutrals may continue with the hearing and determination of the controversy.

§6. Representation by Attorney

A party has the right to be represented by an attorney at any proceeding or hearing under this act. A waiver thereof prior to the proceeding or hearing is ineffective.

§7. Witnesses, Subpoenas, Depositions

(a) The arbitrators may issue (cause to be issued) subpoenas for the attendance of witnesses and for the production of books, records, documents and other evidence, and shall have the power to administer oaths. Subpoenas so issued shall be served, and upon application to the Court by a party or the arbitrators, enforced, in the manner provided by law for the service and enforcement of subpoenas in a civil action.

(b) On application of a party and for use as evidence, the arbitrators may permit a deposition to be taken, in the manner and upon the terms designated by the arbitrators, of a witness who cannot be subpoenaed or is unable to attend the hearing.

(c) All provisions of law compelling a person under subpoena to testify are applicable.

(d) Fees for attendance as a witness shall be the same as for a witness in the … Court.

§8. Award

(a) The award shall be in writing and signed by the arbitrators joining in the award. The arbitrators shall deliver a copy to each party personally or by registered mail, or as provided in the agreement.

(b) An award shall be made within the time fixed therefor by the agreement or, if not so fixed, within such time as the court orders on application of a party. The parties may extend the time in writing either before or after the expiration thereof. A party waives the objection that an award was not made within the time required unless he notifies the arbitrators of his objection prior to the delivery of the award to him.

§9. Change of Award by Arbitrators

On application of a party or, if an application to the Court is pending under Sections 11, 12 or 13, on submission to the arbitrators by the Court under such conditions as the Court may order, the arbitrators may modify or correct the award upon the grounds stated in paragraphs (1) and (3) or subdivision (a) of Section 13, or for the purpose of clarifying the award. The application shall be made within twenty days after delivery of the award to the applicant. Written notice thereof shall be given forthwith to the opposing party, stating he must serve his objections thereto, if any, within ten days from the notice. The award so modified or corrected is subject to the provisions of Sections 11, 12 and 13.

§10. Fees and Expenses of Arbitration

Unless otherwise provided in the agreement to arbitrate, the arbitrators' expenses and fees, together with other expenses, not including counsel fees, incurred in the conduct of the arbitration, shall be paid as provided in the award.

§ 11. Confirmation of an Award

Upon application of a party, the Court shall confirm an award, unless within the time limits hereinafter imposed grounds are urged for vacating or modifying or correcting the award, in which case the Court shall proceed as provided in Sections 12 and 13.

§ 12. Vacating an Award

(a) Upon application of a party, the Court shall vacate an award where:

(1) The award was procured by corruption, fraud or other undue means;

(2) There was evident partiality by an arbitrator appointed as a neutral or corruption in any of the arbitrators or misconduct prejudicing the right of any party;

(3) The arbitrators exceeded their powers;

(4) The arbitrators refused to postpone the hearing upon sufficient cause being shown therefor or refused to hear evidence material to the controversy or otherwise so conducted the hearing, contrary to the provision of Section 5, as to prejudice substantially the rights of a party; or

(5) There was no arbitration agreement and the issue was not adversely determined in proceedings under Section 2 and the party did not participate in the arbitration hearing without raising the objection; but the fact that the relief was such that it could not or would not be granted by a court of law or equity is not ground for vacating or refusing to confirm the award.

(b) An application under this Section shall be made within ninety days after delivery of a copy of the award to the applicant, except that, if predicted upon corruption, fraud or other undue means, it shall be made within ninety days after such grounds are known or should have been known.

(c) In vacating the award on grounds other that stated in clause (5) of Subsection (a) the court may order a rehearing before new arbitrators chosen as provided in the agreement, or in the absence thereof, by the court in accordance with Section 3, or if the award is vacated on grounds set forth in clauses (3) and (4) of Subsection (a) the court may order a rehearing before the arbitrators who made the award or their successors appointed in accordance with Section 3. The time within which the agreement requires the award to be made is applicable to the rehearing and commences from the date of the order.

(d) If the application to vacate is denied and no motion to modify or correct the award is pending, the court shall confirm the award.

§ 13. Modification or Correction Award

(a) Upon application made within ninety days after delivery of a copy of the award to the applicant, the court shall modify or correct the award where:

(1) There was an evident miscalculation of figures or an evident mistake in the description of any person, thing or property referred to in the award;

(2) The arbitrators have awarded upon a matter not submitted to them and the award may be corrected without affecting the merits of the decision upon the issues submitted; or

(3) The award is imperfect in a matter of form, not affecting the merits of the controversy.

(b) if the application is granted, the court shall modify and correct the award so as to effect its intent and shall confirm the award as so modified and corrected. Otherwise, the court shall confirm the award as made.

(c) An application to modify or correct an award may be joined in the alternative with an application to vacate the award.

§ 14. Judgment or Decree on Award

Upon the granting of an order confirming, modifying or correcting an award, judgment or decree shall be entered in conformity therewith and be enforced as any other judgment or decree. Costs of the application and of the proceedings subsequent thereto, and disbursements may be awarded by the court.

§ 15. Judgment Roll, Docketing

(a) On entry of judgment or decree, the clerk shall prepare the judgment roll consisting, to the extent filed, of:

(1) The agreement and each written extension of the time within which to make the award;

(2) The award;

(3) A copy of the order confirming, modifying or correcting the award; and

(4) A copy of the judgment or decree.

(b) The judgment or decree may be docketed as if rendered in an action.

§ 16. Applications to Court

Except as otherwise provided, an application to the Court under this act shall be by motion and shall be heard in the manner and upon the notice provided by law or rule of court for the making and hearing of motions. Unless the parties have agreed otherwise, notice of an initial application for an order shall be served in the manner provided by law for the service of a summons in an action.

§ 17. Court, Jurisdiction

The term "Court" means any Court of competent jurisdiction of this State. The making of an agreement described in Section 1 providing for arbitration in this State confers jurisdiction on the Court to enforce the agreement under this Act and to enter judgment on an award thereunder.

§ 18. Venue

An initial application shall be made to the Court of the [county] in which the agreement provides the arbitration hearing shall be held or, if the hearing has been held, in the county in which it was held. Otherwise the application shall be made in the [county] where the adverse party resides or has a place of business or, if he has not residence or place of business in this State, to the Court of any [county]. All subsequent applications shall be made to the Court hearing the initial application unless the Court otherwise directs.

§ 19. Appeals

(a) An appeal may be taken from:

   (1) An order denying an application to compel arbitration made under Section 2;

   (2) An order granting an application to stay arbitration made under Section 2(b);

   (3) An order confirming or denying confirmation of an award;

   (4) An order modifying or correcting an award;

   (5) An order vacating an award without directing a rehearing, or;

   (6) A judgment or decree entered pursuant to the provisions of this act.

(b) The appeal shall be taken in the manner and to the same extent as from orders or judgments in a civil action.

§ 20. Act Not Retroactive

This act applies only to agreements made subsequent to the taking effect of this act.

§ 21. Uniformity of Interpretation

This act shall be so constructed as to effectuate its general purpose to make uniform the law of those states which enact it.

§ 22. Constitutionality

If any provision of this act or the application thereof to any person or circumstance is held invalid, the invalidity shall not affect other provisions or applications of the act which can be given effect without the invalid provision or application, and to this end the provisions of this act are severable.

§ 23. Short Title

This act may be cited as the Uniform Arbitration Act.

§ 24. Repeal

All acts or parts of acts which are inconsistent with the provisions of this act are hereby repealed.

§ 25. Time of Taking Effect

This act shall take effect [insert date].

C. Revised Uniform Arbitration Act (2000)

§ 1. Definitions.

(1) "Arbitration organization" means an association, agency, board, commission, or other entity that is neutral and initiates, sponsors, or administers an arbitration proceeding or is involved in the appointment of an arbitrator.

(2) "Arbitrator" means an individual appointed to render an award, alone or with others, in a controversy that is subject to an agreement to arbitrate.

(3) "Court" means [a court of competent jurisdiction in this State].

(4) "Knowledge" means actual knowledge.

(5) "Person" means an individual, corporation, business trust, estate, trust, partnership, limited liability company, association, joint venture, government; governmental subdivision, agency, or instrumentality; public corporation; or any other legal or commercial entity.

(6) "Record" means information that is inscribed on a tangible medium or that is stored in an electronic or other medium and is retrievable in perceivable form.

§ 2. NOTICE.

(a) Except as otherwise provided in this [Act], a person gives notice to another person by taking action that is reasonably necessary to inform the other person in ordinary course, whether or not the other person acquires knowledge of the notice.

(b) A person has notice if the person has knowledge of the notice or has received notice.

(c) A person receives notice when it comes to the person's attention or the notice is delivered at the person's place of residence or place of business, or at another location held out by the person as a place of delivery of such communications.

§ 3. WHEN [ACT] APPLIES.

(a) This [Act] governs an agreement to arbitrate made on or after [the effective date].

(b) This [Act] governs an agreement to arbitrate made before [the effective date of this [Act]] if all the parties to the agreement or to the arbitration proceeding so agree in a record.

(c) On or after [a delayed date], this [Act] governs an agreement to arbitrate whenever made.

§ 4. EFFECT OF AGREEMENT TO ARBITRATE; NONWAIVABLE PROVISIONS.

(a) Except as otherwise provided in subsections (b) and (c), a party to an agreement to arbitrate or to an arbitration proceeding may waive or, the parties may vary the effect of, the requirements of this [Act] to the extent permitted by law.

(b) Before a controversy arises that is subject to an agreement to arbitrate, a party to the agreement may not:

(1) waive or agree to vary the effect of the requirements of Section 5(a), 6(a), 8, 17(a), 17(b), 26, or 28;(2) agree to unreasonably restrict the right under Section 9 to notice of the initiation of an arbitration proceeding;(3) agree to unreasonably restrict the right under Section 12 to disclosure of any facts by a neutral arbitrator; or(4) waive the right under Section 16 of a party to an agreement to arbitrate to be represented by a lawyer at any proceeding or hearing under this [Act], but an employer and a labor organization may waive the right to representation by a lawyer in a labor arbitration.

(c) A party to an agreement to arbitrate or arbitration proceeding may not waive, or the parties may not vary the effect of, the requirements of this section or Section 3(a) or (c), 7, 14, 18, 20(d) or (e), 22, 23, 24, 25(a) or (b), 29, 30, 31, or 32.

§ 5. [APPLICATION] FOR JUDICIAL RELIEF.

(a) Except as otherwise provided in Section 28, an [application] for judicial relief under this [Act] must be made by [motion] to the court and heard in the manner provided by law or rule of court for making and hearing [motions].

(b) Unless a civil action involving the agreement to arbitrate is pending, notice of an initial [motion] to the court under this [Act] must be served in the manner provided by law for the service of a summons in a civil action. Otherwise, notice of the motion must be given in the manner provided by law or rule of court for serving [motions] in pending cases.

§ 6. VALIDITY OF AGREEMENT TO ARBITRATE.

(a) An agreement contained in a record to submit to arbitration any existing or subsequent controversy arising between the parties to the agreement is valid, enforceable, and irrevocable except upon a ground that exists at law or in equity for the revocation of a contract.

(b) The court shall decide whether an agreement to arbitrate exists or a controversy is subject to an agreement to arbitrate.

(c) An arbitrator shall decide whether a condition precedent to arbitrability has been fulfilled and whether a contract containing a valid agreement to arbitrate is enforceable.

(d) If a party to a judicial proceeding challenges the existence of, or claims that a controversy is not subject to, an agreement to arbitrate, the arbitration proceeding may continue pending final resolution of the issue by the court, unless the court otherwise orders.

§ 7. [MOTION] TO COMPEL OR STAY ARBITRATION.

(a) On [motion] of a person showing an agreement to arbitrate and alleging another person's refusal to arbitrate pursuant to the agreement:

   (1) if the refusing party does not appear or does not oppose the [motion], the court shall order the parties to arbitrate; and

   (2) if the refusing party opposes the [motion], the court shall proceed summarily to decide the issue and order the parties to arbitrate unless it finds that there is no enforceable agreement to arbitrate.

(b) On [motion] of a person alleging that an arbitration proceeding has been initiated or threatened but that there is no agreement to arbitrate, the court shall proceed summarily to decide the issue. If the court finds that there is an enforceable agreement to arbitrate, it shall order the parties to arbitrate.

(c) If the court finds that there is no enforceable agreement, it may not pursuant to subsection (a) or (b) order the parties to arbitrate.

(d) The court may not refuse to order arbitration because the claim subject to arbitration lacks merit or grounds for the claim have not been established.

(e) If a proceeding involving a claim referable to arbitration under an alleged agreement to arbitrate is pending in court, a [motion] under this section must be made in that court. Otherwise a [motion] under this section may be made in any court as provided in Section 27.

(f) If a party makes a [motion] to the court to order arbitration, the court on just terms shall stay any judicial proceeding that involves a claim alleged to be subject to the arbitration until the court renders a final decision under this section.

(g) If the court orders arbitration, the court on just terms shall stay any judicial proceeding that involves a claim subject to the arbitration. If a claim subject to the arbitration is severable, the court may limit the stay to that claim.

§ 8. PROVISIONAL REMEDIES.

(a) Before an arbitrator is appointed and is authorized and able to act, the court, upon [motion] of a party to an arbitration proceeding and for good cause shown, may enter an order for provisional remedies to protect the effectiveness of the arbitration proceeding to the same extent and under the same conditions as if the controversy were the subject of a civil action.

(b) After an arbitrator is appointed and is authorized and able to act:

(1) the arbitrator may issue such orders for provisional remedies, including interim awards, as the arbitrator finds necessary to protect the effectiveness of the arbitration proceeding and to promote the fair and expeditious resolution of the controversy, to the same extent and under the same conditions as if the controversy were the subject of a civil action and

(2) a party to an arbitration proceeding may move the court for a provisional remedy only if the matter is urgent and the arbitrator is not able to act timely or the arbitrator cannot provide an adequate remedy.

(c) A party does not waive a right of arbitration by making a [motion] under subsection (a) or (b).

§ 9. INITIATION OF ARBITRATION.

(a) A person initiates an arbitration proceeding by giving notice in a record to the other parties to the agreement to arbitrate in the agreed manner between the parties or, in the absence of agreement, by certified or registered mail, return receipt requested and obtained, or by service as authorized for the commencement of a civil action. The notice must describe the nature of the controversy and the remedy sought.

(b) Unless a person objects for lack or insufficiency of notice under Section 15(c) not later than the beginning of the arbitration hearing, the person by appearing at the hearing waives any objection to lack of or insufficiency of notice.

§ 10. CONSOLIDATION OF SEPARATE ARBITRATION PROCEEDINGS.

(a) Except as otherwise provided in subsection (c), upon [motion] of a party to an agreement to arbitrate or to an arbitration proceeding, the court may order consolidation of separate arbitration proceedings as to all or some of the claims if:

(1) there are separate agreements to arbitrate or separate arbitration proceedings between the same persons or one of them is a party to a separate agreement to arbitrate or a separate arbitration proceeding with a third person;

(2) the claims subject to the agreements to arbitrate arise in substantial part from the same transaction or series of related transactions;

(3) the existence of a common issue of law or fact creates the possibility of conflicting decisions in the separate arbitration proceedings; and

(4) prejudice resulting from a failure to consolidate is not outweighed by the risk of undue delay or prejudice to the rights of or hardship to parties opposing consolidation.

(b) The court may order consolidation of separate arbitration proceedings as to some claims and allow other claims to be resolved in separate arbitration proceedings.

(c) The court may not order consolidation of the claims of a party to an agreement to arbitrate if the agreement prohibits consolidation.

§ 11. APPOINTMENT OF ARBITRATOR; SERVICE AS A NEUTRAL ARBITRATOR.

(a) If the parties to an agreement to arbitrate agree on a method for appointing an arbitrator, that method must be followed, unless the method fails. If the parties have not agreed on a method, the agreed method fails, or an arbitrator appointed fails or is unable to act and a successor has not been appointed, the court, on [motion] of a party to the arbitration proceeding, shall appoint the arbitrator. An arbitrator so appointed has all the powers of an arbitrator designated in the agreement to arbitrate or appointed pursuant to the agreed method.

(b) An individual who has a known, direct, and material interest in the outcome of the arbitration proceeding or a known, existing, and substantial relationship with a party may not serve as an arbitrator required by an agreement to be neutral.

§ 12. DISCLOSURE BY ARBITRATOR.

(a) Before accepting appointment, an individual who is requested to serve as an arbitrator, after making a reasonable inquiry, shall disclose to all parties to the agreement to arbitrate and arbitration proceeding and to any other arbitrators any known facts that a reasonable person would consider likely to affect the impartiality of the arbitrator in the arbitration proceeding, including:

(1) a financial or personal interest in the outcome of the arbitration proceeding; and

(2) an existing or past relationship with any of the parties to the agreement to arbitrate or the arbitration proceeding, their counsel or representatives, a witness, or another arbitrators.

(b) An arbitrator has a continuing obligation to disclose to all parties to the agreement to arbitrate and arbitration proceeding and to any other arbitrators any facts that the arbitrator learns after accepting appointment which a reasonable person would consider likely to affect the impartiality of the arbitrator.

(c) If an arbitrator discloses a fact required by subsection (a) or (b) to be disclosed and a party timely objects to the appointment or continued service of the arbitrator based upon the fact disclosed, the objection may be a ground under Section 23(a)(2) for vacating an award made by the arbitrator.

(d) If the arbitrator did not disclose a fact as required by subsection (a) or (b), upon timely objection by a party, the court under Section 23(a)(2) may vacate an award.

(e) An arbitrator appointed as a neutral arbitrator who does not disclose a known, direct, and material interest in the outcome of the arbitration proceeding or a known, existing, and substantial relationship with a party is presumed to act with evident partiality under Section 23(a)(2).

(f) If the parties to an arbitration proceeding agree to the procedures of an arbitration organization or any other procedures for challenges to arbitrators before an award is made, substantial compliance with those procedures is a condition precedent to a [motion] to vacate an award on that ground under Section 23(a)(2).

§ 13. ACTION BY MAJORITY.

If there is more than one arbitrator, the powers of an arbitrator must be exercised by a majority of the arbitrators, but all of them shall conduct the hearing under Section 15(c).

§ 14. IMMUNITY OF ARBITRATOR; COMPETENCY TO TESTIFY; ATTORNEY'S FEES AND COSTS.

(a) An arbitrator or an arbitration organization acting in that capacity is immune from civil liability to the same extent as a judge of a court of this State acting in a judicial capacity.

(b) The immunity afforded by this section supplements any immunity under other law.

(c) The failure of an arbitrator to make a disclosure required by Section 12 does not cause any loss of immunity under this section.

(d) In a judicial, administrative, or similar proceeding, an arbitrator or representative of an arbitration organization is not competent to testify, and may not be required to produce records as to any statement, conduct, decision, or ruling occurring during the arbitration proceeding, to the same extent as a judge of a court of this State acting in a judicial capacity. This subsection does not apply:

(1) to the extent necessary to determine the claim of an arbitrator, arbitration organization, or representative of the arbitration organization against a party to the arbitration proceeding; or

(2) to a hearing on a [motion] to vacate an award under Section 23(a)(1) or (2) if the [movant] establishes prima facie that a ground for vacating the award exists.

(e) If a person commences a civil action against an arbitrator, arbitration organization, or representative of an arbitration organization arising from the services of the arbitrator, organization, or representative or if a person seeks to compel an arbitrator or a representative of an arbitration organization to testify or produce records in violation of subsection (d), and the court decides that the arbitrator, arbitration organization, or representative of an arbitration organization is immune from civil liability or that the arbitrator or representative of the organization is not competent to testify, the court shall award to the arbitrator, organization, or representative reasonable attorney's fees and other reasonable expenses of litigation.

§ 15. ARBITRATION PROCESS.

(a) An arbitrator may conduct an arbitration in such manner as the arbitrator considers appropriate for a fair and expeditious disposition of the proceeding. The authority conferred upon the arbitrator includes the power to hold conferences with the parties to the arbitration proceeding before the hearing and, among other matters, determine the admissibility, relevance, materiality and weight of any evidence.

(b) An arbitrator may decide a request for summary disposition of a claim or particular issue:

(1) if all interested parties agree; or

(2) upon request of one party to the arbitration proceeding if that party gives notice to all other parties to the proceeding, and the other parties have a reasonable opportunity to respond.

(c) If an arbitrator orders a hearing, the arbitrator shall set a time and place and give notice of the hearing not less than five days before the hearing begins. Unless a party to the arbitration proceeding makes an objection to lack or insufficiency of notice not later than the beginning of the hearing, the party's appearance at the hearing waives the objection. Upon request of a party to the arbitration proceeding and for good cause shown, or upon the arbitrator's own initiative, the arbitrator may adjourn the hearing from time to time as necessary but may not postpone the hearing to a time later than that fixed by the agreement to arbitrate for making the award unless the parties to the arbitration proceeding consent to a later date. The arbitrator may hear and decide the controversy upon the evidence produced although a party who was duly notified of the arbitration proceeding did not appear. The court, on request, may direct the arbitrator to conduct the hearing promptly and render a timely decision.

(d) At a hearing under subsection (c), a party to the arbitration proceeding has a right to be heard, to present evidence material to the controversy, and to cross-examine witnesses appearing at the hearing.

(e) If an arbitrator ceases or is unable to act during the arbitration proceeding, a replacement arbitrator must be appointed in accordance with Section 11 to continue the proceeding and to resolve the controversy.

§ 16. REPRESENTATION BY LAWYER.

A party to an arbitration proceeding may be represented by a lawyer.

§ 17. WITNESSES; SUBPOENAS; DEPOSITIONS; DISCOVERY.

(a) An arbitrator may issue a subpoena for the attendance of a witness and for the production of records and other evidence at any hearing and may administer oaths. A subpoena must be served in the manner for service of subpoenas in a civil action and, upon [motion] to the court by a party to the arbitration proceeding or the arbitrator, enforced in the manner for enforcement of subpoenas in a civil action.

(b) In order to make the proceedings fair, expeditious, and cost effective, upon request of a party to or a witness in an arbitration proceeding, an arbitrator may permit a deposition of any witness to be taken for use as evidence at the hearing, including a witness who cannot be subpoenaed for or is unable to attend a hearing. The arbitrator shall determine the conditions under which the deposition is taken.

(c) An arbitrator may permit such discovery as the arbitrator decides is appropriate in the circumstances, taking into account the needs of the parties to the arbitration proceeding and other affected persons and the desirability of making the proceeding fair, expeditious, and cost effective.

(d) If an arbitrator permits discovery under subsection (c), the arbitrator may order a party to the arbitration proceeding to comply with the arbitrator's discovery-related orders, issue subpoenas for the attendance of a witness and for the production of records and other evidence at a discovery proceeding, and take action against a non-complying party to the extent a court could if the controversy were the subject of a civil action in this State.

(e) An arbitrator may issue a protective order to prevent the disclosure of privileged information, confidential information, trade secrets, and other information protected from disclosure to the extent a court could if the controversy were the subject of a civil action in this State.

(f) All laws compelling a person under subpoena to testify and all fees for attending a judicial proceeding, a deposition, or a discovery proceeding as a witness apply to an arbitration proceeding as if the controversy were the subject of a civil action in this State.

(g) The court may enforce a subpoena or discovery-related order for the attendance of a witness within this State and for the production of records and other evidence issued by an arbitrator in connection with an arbitration proceeding in another State upon conditions determined by the court so as to make the arbitration proceeding fair, expeditious, and cost effective. A subpoena or discovery related order issued by an arbitrator in another State must be served in the manner provided by law for service of subpoenas in a civil action in this State and, upon [motion] to the court by a party to the arbitration proceeding or the arbitrator, enforced in the manner provided by law for enforcement of subpoenas in a civil action in this State.

§ 18. JUDICIAL ENFORCEMENT OF PREAWARD RULING BY ARBITRATOR.

If an arbitrator makes a preaward ruling in favor of a party to the arbitration proceeding, the party may request the arbitrator to incorporate the ruling into an award under Section 19. A prevailing party may make a [motion] to the court for an expedited order to confirm the award under Section 22, in which case the court shall summarily decide the [motion]. The court shall issue an order to confirm the award unless the court vacates, modifies, or corrects the award under Section 23 or 24.

§ 19. AWARD.

(a) An arbitrator shall make a record of an award. The record must be signed or otherwise authenticated by any arbitrator who concurs with the award. The arbitrator or the arbitration organization shall give notice of the award, including a copy of the award, to each party to the arbitration proceeding.

(b) An award must be made within the time specified by the agreement to arbitrate or, if not specified therein, within the time ordered by the court. The court may extend or the parties to the arbitration proceeding may agree in a record to extend the time. The court or the parties may do so within or after the time specified or ordered. A party waives any objection that an award was not timely made unless the party gives notice of the objection to the arbitrator before receiving notice of the award.

§ 20. CHANGE OF AWARD BY ARBITRATOR.

(a) On [motion] to an arbitrator by a party to an arbitration proceeding, the arbitrator may modify or correct an award:

   (1) upon a ground stated in Section 24(a)(1) or (3);

   (2) because the arbitrator has not made a final and definite award upon a claim submitted by the parties to the arbitration proceeding; or

   (3) to clarify the award.

(b) A [motion] under subsection (a) must be made and notice given to all parties within 20 days after the movant receives notice of the award.

(c) A party to the arbitration proceeding must give notice of any objection to the [motion] within 10 days after receipt of the notice.

(d) If a [motion] to the court is pending under Section 22, 23, or 24, the court may submit the claim to the arbitrator to consider whether to modify or correct the award:

   (1) upon a ground stated in Section 24(a)(1) or (3);

   (2) because the arbitrator has not made a final and definite award upon a claim submitted by the parties to the arbitration proceeding; or

   (3) to clarify the award.

(e) An award modified or corrected pursuant to this section is subject to Sections 19(a), 22, 23, and 24.

§ 21. REMEDIES; FEES AND EXPENSES OF ARBITRATION PROCEEDING.

(a) An arbitrator may award punitive damages or other exemplary relief if such an award is authorized by law in a civil action involving the same claim and the evidence produced at the hearing justifies the award under the legal standards otherwise applicable to the claim.

(b) An arbitrator may award reasonable attorney's fees and other reasonable expenses of arbitration if such an award is authorized by law in a civil action involving the same claim or by the agreement of the parties to the arbitration proceeding.

(c) As to all remedies other than those authorized by subsections (a) and (b), an arbitrator may order such remedies as the arbitrator considers just and appropriate under the circumstances of the arbitration proceeding. The fact that such a remedy could not or would not be granted by the court is not a ground for refusing to confirm an award under Section 22 or for vacating an award under Section 23.

(d) An arbitrator's expenses and fees, together with other expenses, must be paid as provided in the award.

(e) If an arbitrator awards punitive damages or other exemplary relief under subsection (a), the arbitrator shall specify in the award the basis in fact justifying and the basis in law authorizing the award and state separately the amount of the punitive damages or other exemplary relief.

§ 22. CONFIRMATION OF AWARD.

After a party to an arbitration proceeding receives notice of an award, the party may make a [motion] to the court for an order confirming the award at which time the court shall issue a confirming order unless the award is modified or corrected pursuant to Section 20 or 24 or is vacated pursuant to Section 23.

§ 23. VACATING AWARD.

(a) Upon [motion] to the court by a party to an arbitration proceeding, the court shall vacate an award made in the arbitration proceeding if:

(1) the award was procured by corruption, fraud, or other undue means;

(2) there was:

(A) evident partiality by an arbitrator appointed as a neutral arbitrator;

(B) corruption by an arbitrator; or

(C) misconduct by an arbitrator prejudicing the rights of a party to the arbitration proceeding;

(3) an arbitrator refused to postpone the hearing upon showing of sufficient cause for postponement, refused to consider evidence material to the controversy, or otherwise conducted the hearing contrary to Section 15, so as to prejudice substantially the rights of a party to the arbitration proceeding;

(4) an arbitrator exceeded the arbitrator's powers;

(5) there was no agreement to arbitrate, unless the person participated in the arbitration proceeding without raising the objection under Section 15(c) not later than the beginning of the arbitration hearing; or

(6) the arbitration was conducted without proper notice of the initiation of an arbitration as required in Section 9 so as to prejudice substantially the rights of a party to the arbitration proceeding.

(b) A [motion] under this section must be filed within 90 days after the [movant] receives notice of the award pursuant to Section 19 or within 90 days after the [movant] receives notice of a modified or corrected award pursuant to Section 20, unless the [movant] alleges that the award was procured by corruption, fraud, or other undue means, in which case the [motion] must be made within 90 days after the ground is known or by the exercise of reasonable care would have been known by the [movant].

(c) If the court vacates an award on a ground other than that set forth in subsection (a)(5), it may order a rehearing. If the award is vacated on a ground stated in subsection (a)(1) or (2), the rehearing must be before a new arbitrator. If the award is vacated on a ground stated in subsection (a)(3), (4), or (6), the rehearing may be before the arbitrator who made the award or the arbitrator's successor. The arbitrator must render the decision in the rehearing within the same time as that provided in Section 19(b) for an award.

(d) If the court denies a [motion] to vacate an award, it shall confirm the award unless a [motion] to modify or correct the award is pending.

§ 24. MODIFICATION OR CORRECTION OF AWARD.

(a) Upon [motion] made within 90 days after the [movant] receives notice of the award pursuant to Section 19 or within 90 days after the [movant] receives notice of a modified or corrected award pursuant to Section 20, the court shall modify or correct the award if:

   (1) there was an evident mathematical miscalculation or an evident mistake in the description of a person, thing, or property referred to in the award;

   (2) the arbitrator has made an award on a claim not submitted to the arbitrator and the award may be corrected without affecting the merits of the decision upon the claims submitted; or

   (3) the award is imperfect in a matter of form not affecting the merits of the decision on the claims submitted.

(b) If a [motion] made under subsection (a) is granted, the court shall modify or correct and confirm the award as modified or corrected. Otherwise, unless a motion to vacate is pending, the court shall confirm the award.

(c) A [motion] to modify or correct an award pursuant to this section may be joined with a [motion] to vacate the award.

§ 25. JUDGMENT ON AWARD; ATTORNEY'S FEES AND LITIGATION EXPENSES.

(a) Upon granting an order confirming, vacating without directing a rehearing, modifying, or correcting an award, the court shall enter a judgment in conformity therewith. The judgment may be recorded, docketed, and enforced as any other judgment in a civil action.

(b) A court may allow reasonable costs of the [motion] and subsequent judicial proceedings.

(c) On [application] of a prevailing party to a contested judicial proceeding under Section 22, 23, or 24, the court may add reasonable attorney's fees and other reasonable expenses of litigation incurred in a judicial proceeding after the award is made to a judgment confirming, vacating without directing a rehearing, modifying, or correcting an award.

§ 26. JURISDICTION.

(a) A court of this State having jurisdiction over the controversy and the parties may enforce an agreement to arbitrate.

(b) An agreement to arbitrate providing for arbitration in this State confers exclusive jurisdiction on the court to enter judgment on an award under this [Act].

§ 27. VENUE.

A [motion] pursuant to Section 5 must be made in the court of the [county] in which the agreement to arbitrate specifies the arbitration hearing is to be held or, if the hearing has been held, in the court of the [county] in which it was held. Otherwise, the [motion] may be made in the court of any [county] in which an adverse party resides or has a place of business or, if no adverse party has a residence or place of business in this State, in the court of any [county] in this State. All subsequent [motions] must be made in the court hearing the initial [motion] unless the court otherwise directs.

§ 28. APPEALS.

(a) An appeal may be taken from:

    (1) an order denying a [motion] to compel arbitration;

    (2) an order granting a [motion] to stay arbitration;

    (3) an order confirming or denying confirmation of an award;

    (4) an order modifying or correcting an award;

    (5) an order vacating an award without directing a rehearing; or

    (6) a final judgment entered pursuant to this [Act].

(b) An appeal under this section must be taken as from an order or a judgment in a civil action.

§ 29. UNIFORMITY OF APPLICATION AND CONSTRUCTION.

In applying and construing this uniform act, consideration must be given to the need to promote uniformity of the law with respect to its subject matter among States that enact it.

§ 30. RELATIONSHIP TO ELECTRONIC SIGNATURES IN GLOBAL AND NATIONAL COMMERCE ACT.

The provisions of this Act governing the legal effect, validity, and enforceability of electronic records or electronic signatures, and of contracts performed with the use of such records or signatures conform to the requirements of Section 102 of the Electronic Signatures in Global and National Commerce Act.

§ 31. EFFECTIVE DATE.

This [Act] takes effect on [effective date].

§ 32. REPEAL.

Effective on [delayed date should be the same as that in Section 3(c)], the [Uniform Arbitration Act] is repealed.

§ 33. SAVINGS CLAUSE.

This [Act] does not affect an action or proceeding commenced or right accrued before this [Act] takes effect. Subject to Section 3 of this [Act], an arbitration agreement made before the effective date of this [Act] is governed by the [Uniform Arbitration Act].

D. American Arbitration Association, Commercial Arbitration Rules (effective Oct. 1, 2013)

The following lists the Topic and associated Rule of the AAA, Commercial Arbitration Rules. The complete Rules are available online at adr.org/commercial.

R-1. Agreement of Parties

R-2. AAA and Delegation of Duties

R-3. National Roster of Arbitrators

R-4. Filing Requirements

R-5. Answers and Counterclaims

R-6. Changes of Claim

R-7. Jurisdiction

R-8. Interpretation and Application of Rules

R-9. Mediation

R-10. Administrative Conference

R-11. Fixing of Locale

R-12. Appointment from National Roster

R-13. Direct Appointment by a Party

R-14. Appointment of Chairperson by Party-Appointed Arbitrators or Parties

R-15. Nationality of Arbitrator

R-16. Number of Arbitrators

R-17. Disclosure

R-18. Disqualification of Arbitrator

R-19. Communication with Arbitrator

R-20. Vacancies

R-21. Preliminary Hearing

R-22. Pre-Hearing Exchange and Production of Information

R-56. Deposits

R-57. Remedies for Nonpayment

R-58. Sanctions

E. Website References: Conventions and Arbitration Institutional Providers

1. American Arbitration Association (AAA), https://www.adr.org/

2. CPR International Institute for Conflict Prevention and Resolution, https://www.cpradr.org/

3. JAMS ADR, https://www.jamsadr.com/

4. Financial Industry Regulation Authority (FINRA), https://www.finra.org/

5. ABA Code of Ethics for Arbitrators in Commercial Disputes, https://www.americanbar.org/groups/dispute_resolution/resources/Ethics/Code_Ethics_Com_Arb_Ann.html

6. The London Court of International Arbitration ("LCIA"), http://www.lcia.org/

7. International Centre for Dispute Resolution (ICDR) — AAA, https://www.icdr.org/icdr/faces/home

8. International Chamber of Commerce (ICC) International Court of Arbitration (Paris), https://iccwbo.org/dispute-resolution-services/arbitration/icc-international-court-arbitration/

9. China International Economic and Trade Arbitration Commission, http://www.cietac.org/?l=en

10. UNCITRAL Model Law on Commercial Arbitration http://www.uncitral.org/uncitral/en/uncitral_texts/arbitration/1985Model_arbitration.html

11. Court of Arbitration for Sport (CAS), Procedural Rules, http://www.tas-cas.org/en/arbitration/code-procedural-rules.html

12. United Nations Convention on the Recognition and Enforcement of Foreign Arbitral Awards (New York, 10th June 1958), http://www.newyorkconvention.org/

13. 1965 Convention on the Settlement of Investment Disputes between States and Nationals of other States (ICSID Convention), https://icsid.worldbank.org/en/Pages/icsiddocs/ICSID-Convention-Arbitration-Rules.aspx

14. American Law Institute (ALI), Restatement of the U.S. Law of International Commercial Arbitration (2015), https://www.ali.org/projects/show/international-commercial-arbitration/

15. American Bar Association, Arbitration Competition for Law Students, https://abaforlawstudents.com/events/law-student-competitions/practical-skills-competitions/arbitration-competition/

Appendix II

Arbitration Case File^{©*}

New Dover Arbitration Board,
In the Matter of the Arbitration between:
Del Pearson, Claimant v. Newton Care Homes, LLC

Case Overview

This is an arbitration of a dispute between Del Pearson and Newton Care Homes, LLC (referred to by the witnesses as either "Newton Care" or "NCH"), a for-profit limited liability corporation that operates care homes for disabled adults. Both parties are fictional and have no relation to any existing individuals or organizations of the same name. Until September of 20XX[-1], Del Pearson worked as an associate director for NCH. On September 25 of that year, NCH terminated Pearson's employment. Pearson has filed this arbitration claim seeking damages for wrongful termination and alleging that the termination was in retaliation for Pearson's decision to report violations of New Dover state statutes to the New Dover Department of Human Services.

Legal Background

This case takes place in the fictional jurisdiction of fifty-first state, New Dover. New Dover is a common law jurisdiction.

Case File: The Case File consists of the following materials:

A. Del Pearson Demand for Arbitration.

B. Newton Care Homes' Arbitration Response.

C. Summary of the deposition testimony of Del Pearson, Claimant.

D. Summary of the deposition testimony of Morgan Kestrel, an employee of Respondent.

E. Affidavit of Lee Benson, who will testify for Pearson.

F. Affidavit of Lynn Watkins, who will testify for Newton Care Homes.

G. A document from NCH personnel files entitled "Agreement to Arbitrate," signed by Del Pearson.

H. E-mails from Morgan Kestrel and Del Pearson.

I. A letter and enclosure from Del Pearson to the New Dover Department of Human Services.

J. A letter from Matthew Johnson of the Department of Human Services to Newton Care Homes.

K. A short memorandum of law summarizing the holdings in the leading New Dover cases relevant to the arbitration.

No other documentary evidence, testimony, or information is available.

Supplemental Instructions

1. The arbitration will be conducted as an *ad hoc* arbitration, meaning that no particular arbitral institution rules govern the arbitration. Rather parties are to follow generally acceptable arbitration practices and the following procedures:

2. Presentation of Evidence and Law

- Both parties shall present relevant and material evidence and oral and written arguments to allow the arbitrator to understand and determine the dispute.

- Counsel must confine presentations to the facts and legal issues contained in or supported by the case file, including reasonable inferences and arguments. Counsel is permitted to present demonstrative evidence based on the information in the case file. Counsel may not add claims or defenses not asserted in the case file and may not enhance their position by presenting evidence or arguments about other facts or legal issues. Counsel may ask the Arbitrators to take arbitral notice of uncontroverted facts.

- Witnesses shall testify under an oath administrated by the Panel Chair.

- All documents, statements, discovery responses, depositions, diagrams, photographs, signatures, and other materials included as part of the case file are deemed to be originals and authentic. All documents, records, and other materials that were sent to or by a witness are deemed to have been received or sent by that witness.

- The Arbitrator or Panel Chair will determine what evidence shall be considered and will give such evidence appropriate weight. The Arbitrators may refer to, but shall not be bound by, the Federal Rules of Evidence.

- Either party may object to evidence offered by the opposing party. The Arbitrator or Panel Chair shall make final determinations on admissibility, keeping in mind that this is not a civil trial in state or federal court and that the parties desire a fair and timely resolution.

- The memorandum of law represents law in New Dover. The memorandum is not intended to limit legal research on or a presentation of national trends in the relevant area of law. It is the obligation of counsel for the parties to educate the arbitrators as to the governing law. The legal memorandum is not "evidence" and may not be provided to the arbitrators. Rather, counsel can orally communicate/argue the law to the panel during closings based on that memorandum.

3. The names for the witnesses are gender neutral and all witnesses may be portrayed by any gender. Any references in the case file to the gender of the witnesses are unintentional and should be ignored.

4. Although New Dover Arbitration Board Procedural Rules do not expressly authorize depositions, the Rules do confer upon the arbitrator(s) the power "to manage any necessary exchange of information among the parties with a view to achieving an efficient and economical resolution of the dispute, while at the same time promoting equality of treatment and opportunity to fairly present its claims and defenses." *See, e.g.*, Am. Arb. Ass'n Commercial Arbitration R-22(a). Pursuant to this Rule, the arbitration panel has authorized pre-hearing depositions in this case; the parties have stipulated to one per side as well as to permit the advance submission of affidavits of two non-party witnesses.

5. The arbitration should last approximately two hours, with one hour designated to each side for its presentation (opening, two direct examinations, two cross-examinations, and summation). Additional time may be added if the arbitrators ask questions of counsel and the witnesses.

6. Within the time limit prescribed by the forum, arbitrators shall deliberate and decide the dispute. The panel must decide each claim for relief, including counterclaims, if any, and allocate all forum fees by a percentage attributable to each party. The arbitrators will issue a written Award by circulating it to all counsel. Arbitrators may choose to include an explanation in the Award but are not required to do so.

7. Any questions regarding procedures or the arbitration hearing shall be directed to the forum's Staff Attorney. Do not attempt to contact the arbitrators or the Director of Arbitration directly. No ex parte communications with the arbitrators are permitted at any time.

New Dover Arbitration Board

Name, address, and phone number for

Claimant: DEMAND FOR ARBITRATION

Del Pearson
1992 Lincoln Avenue   Filing Date: *March 18, 20XX*
Landonville, New Dover 11442

200.867-5309

Name, address, and phone number for

Respondent: Record Number: *20XX-012345*

Newton Care Homes, LLC
401 First Avenue, Suite 4000
Landonville, New Dover 11101

200.765.6300

RESPONDENT: A demand for arbitration has been filed with the New Dover Arbitration Board. Respondent has 30 days to file an answering statement or counter claim.

Claimant states:

1. Del Pearson and Newton Care Homes, LLC ("NCH"), a for-profit limited liability corporation, agree to arbitrate this dispute by neutral binding arbitration.

2. From January of 20XX[-6], to [the last Friday of] September, 20XX[-1], I was employed by NCH. From April of 20XX[-2], through [the last Friday of] September, 20XX[-1], I held the position of associate director of NCH's Valley View care facility. The Valley View facility provides day training and habilitation services to disabled adults. As part of my job duties, I supervised direct care staff and was one of the persons responsible for the management of the facility, including ensuring the facility was in compliance with all relevant New Dover statutes and regulations.

3. During June of 20XX[-1], and continuing through August of 20XX[-1], the Valley View facility was, from time to time, out of compliance with New Dover statutes setting forth required staffing ratios for facilities providing adult day training and habilitation services, such as Valley View. These instances of noncompliance were the result of a reduction in staff over which I had no control.

4. From June of 20XX[-1], until September of 20XX[-1], I reported my concern about these instances of noncompliance to the chief program director, Morgan Kestrel, my direct supervisor. On [the first Tuesday following Labor Day, 20XX[-1]], I submitted a written report to Morgan Kestrel which set out in detail eight instances of noncompliance during August of 20XX[-1]. Neither Morgan Kestrel nor anyone else at NCH took steps necessary to correct future occurrences of instances of noncompliance. I had a good faith belief that the instances of noncompliance had jeopardized

the safety and welfare of clients at Valley View, and I had a good faith belief that future instances of noncompliance would occur, continuing to jeopardize the clients' safety and welfare.

5. On [the first Wednesday following Labor Day,] 20XX[-1], I sent a letter to the New Dover Department of Human Services reporting my good faith belief that NCH had violated the New Dover statutes mandating staffing ratios at Valley View.

6. On [the first Friday following Labor Day], 20XX[-1], NCH terminated my employment because I had made this good faith report.

7. As a direct cause of the termination of my employment, I have suffered damages due to a loss of wages of over $25,000 to the date of this Statement, and emotional distress. Pursuant to New Dover Code § 122.93, I am entitled to recover these damages, as well as reasonable attorneys' fees and costs. Because I was terminated for making a good faith report of the violation of a statute protecting the health and well-being of the general public, I am entitled by law to treble damages.
Claimant's Oath of Authenticity:

I, Del Pearson, assert, under penalty of perjury, that the facts supporting this Demand for Arbitration, the supporting documents, and the arbitration agreement are accurate and correct.

Claimant's Signature:
/s/ Del Pearson   Date: 03/18/20XX

New Dover Arbitration Board

Respondent(s):   **ANSWERING STATEMENT**

Newton Care Homes, LLC
401 First Avenue, Suite 4000
Landonville, New Dover 11101

200.765.6300

Initial Claimant(s):

Del Pearson   Record Number: 20XX-012345
1992 Lincoln Avenue   *(As it appears on Initial Claim)*
Landonville, New Dover 11442

200.867-5309

Respondent states:

1. Newton Care Homes, LLC ("NCH") is a for-profit business which operates multiple facilities providing adult day training and habilitation services to disabled adults. From 20XX[-6] through [the last Friday of] September, 20XX[-1], NCH employed Del Pearson ("Pearson"). From April of 20XX[-2] through [the last Friday of Sep-

tember], 20XX[-1], Pearson held a position as one of two associate directors at NCH-Valley View.

2. During 20XX[-1], NCH made a decision to eliminate one of the two associate director positions at NCH-Valley View. NCH informed Pearson of this decision on [the first Tuesday following Labor Day of September, 20XX[-1]], and made known to Pearson the availability of a similar position at another facility owned and operated by NCH. Pearson declined to consider transfer to the other facility.

3. Subsequently, NCH eliminated the position of associate director held by Pearson. Pearson's communication to the Department of Human Services on or about [the first Wednesday following Labor Day of September, 20XX[-1]], was not a factor in the decisions NCH made regarding the elimination of Pearson's associate director positions at NCH-Valley View.

4. The Department of Human Services investigated Pearson's complaint and, on November 19, 20XX[-1], issued a "No Further Action Required" report.

Respondent's Oath of Authenticity:

I, Morgan Kestrel, Chief Program Director for Newton Care Homes, LLC, assert, under penalty of perjury, that the facts supporting this Answering Statement are accurate and correct.

Respondent's Signature:
s/ *Morgan Kestrel*   Date: 04/16/20XX

In the Arbitration between:
Pearson v. Newton Care Homes, LLC

A. Deposition Summary—Del Peterson, Claimant

The following is a summary of the deposition testimony of Del Pearson. The deposition was taken on June 7, 20XX, in the offices of the lawyers for Newton Care Homes.

For five years, from January of 20XX[-6] until [the last Friday of] September, 20XX[-1], I worked for Newton Care Homes. My last position at Newton Care was serving as one of the associate directors at the Valley View day facility, where I earned a final annual salary of $54,500. I really enjoyed working for Newton Care because here in Landonville, they have always had a great reputation. I was truly upset when I was fired from my job last September.

I was born in Landonville and graduated from Landonville Central High School. I've always known that I wanted to do work helping care for others. When I was in grade school, my grandmother moved in with us when she got too sick to stay in her own apartment. I spent a lot of my time helping my mom take care of her. My friends thought I was crazy, but even then I knew that was the work I wanted to devote my life to. After my grandma died, I volunteered time in a senior care home and eventually got a part-time paying job there while I was in high school. I worked full-time there for several years after I graduated from high school, while I got my Associate of Arts degree at Landonville Community College. Once I had my A.A. degree, I was able to look for a better job. I thought I was really lucky to get a job working as a Personal Care Attendant ("PCA") for Newton Care. The pay and benefits were a lot better, and I felt like I was working for an extremely professional organization.

While I was working as a PCA at Newton Care, I finished my college degree in health care administration in the evenings through a program at New Dover University. Things seemed to be going really well for me at Newton Care. I got regular raises and promotions. In 20XX[-2], I was named as associate director at Newton Care's Valley View facility (NCH-Valley View). NCH Valley View is a day facility for minimally disabled adults, serving over fifty clients. I became a salaried employee for the first time in my life. I remember signing the Agreement to Arbitrate when I took the position as associate director. Valley View was a great place to work. We provided day training and living services for minimally disabled adults. Each day, the clients would come to the facility from their group homes and do crafts, light occupational work, and eat their meals. I really liked working with the clients. All of them could walk and communicate basic needs, though some needed individual attention and minimal physical assistance when it was time to eat or use the toilet.

In some ways, becoming an associate director wasn't that great. Don't get me wrong—there were parts of the job that I really liked. I think I was pretty good managing staff and I particularly liked training new employees. I didn't like working with off-site management from the corporate office, however. That wasn't something I'd ever had to do before, and I was surprised at the attitude of most of the corporate management. None of them seemed to have any genuine sense of care or concern for the residents, and most of them were really two-faced in the way they talked about the front-line staff. When staff were in the same room for a facility meeting or something like that, the corporate types were fine. Once the meeting was over and the staff were all out of the room, most of the managers from corporate talked about staff like they were nothing more than the hired help. That was a real eye-opener for me because, when I was working as staff, I'd always bought into the Newton Care motto: "We are all valued members of the same team. It takes all of us to do the job." I guess I might have been a little naïve.

While the corporate attitude bothered me, I still liked my job. My then executive director, Nina Juarez, was great to work with and, all in all, I didn't have a whole lot of contact with corporate. That started to change in the summer of 20XX[-1]. In April of 20XX[-1], after over twenty-five years with Newton Care, Nina retired. Once she left, things at NCH-Valley View started to change very quickly. First of all, corporate didn't bring anyone in to replace Nina! Instead of getting a new executive director, Lynn Watkins—the other associate director at Valley View—and I began reporting directly to Morgan Kestrel, the chief program director at corporate. Lynn and I both started as associate directors about the same time, though I've been with Newton Care quite a bit longer. Anyway, we both had a lot less supervisory experience than Nina, so neither of us thought we were in line for the job as executive director for Valley View. We both were really surprised that corporate wasn't going to replace Nina.

The second thing that happened that summer really should have been a warning sign to me that things were going to go from bad to worse. In May, Grace Munya, one of the newer members of the care staff, gave notice that she'd be going on maternity leave sometime in June. I told Morgan that we'd need to hire someone to start in the summer and asked if Lynn and I should start the process to hire a replacement. Morgan told me that corporate would be taking care of that. That kind of made sense to me because hiring was something that Nina always did, but Nina had always made sure that a good cross-section of the staff met any possible new employee before the hire. When I asked about the process for hiring, Morgan said, "I told you that we'd be handling this. You do your job. We'll do ours." I was a little angry to be talked to like that, but I figured it was typical corporate behavior. I told Lynn that we didn't need to do anything about hiring and waited to hear from Morgan.

Staff coverage was something that was really important to me, because I'd worked in situations where homes skimped on staff. One of the things that had always made me proud to work at Newton Care is that it seemed we didn't do that. That was a point Nina Juarez had always stressed when she first trained me. Nina had always told both Lynn and me that we needed to be very careful about staffing ratios. The ratios are critical when clients are gathered together working on crafts, doing occupational therapy, or at meal times. In fact, New Dover Department of Human Services regulations require that facilities provide a minimum of one staff member for every eight clients. So Nina had trained both of us to make sure that when clients were together in any group setting, we always had at least one staff person for every eight clients.

I know Nina had us read the Department of Human Services regulations, but what I remember best is her telling us, "It's not just the law, it's a matter of client safety." To me, this was a life and death matter and that's not an exaggeration. At Valley View, during the day, residents were divided into four rooms with between twelve and fourteen clients in each room. Especially at lunch time, it was critical to have at least two staff in each room. There's simply no way that a single staff person can give adequate attention to a room at mealtime—someone could choke to death! That's why we always tried to have at least two staff assigned to each room, plus one extra "floating" staff member available. The floating staff member would be available to cover for any staff member who was on break or could come into a room, particularly at lunch, if a client needed extra help. For example, if a client needed to use the toilet at lunch, one of the staff assigned to the room would take the client and the floating staff member would come into the room to help out so there would be two staff in the room.

Anyway, that's one of the reasons Morgan's attitude offended me. To me, it seemed like having adequate staff was my job. Well, to make a long story short, I waited and waited and never did hear anything from Morgan about the new hire to replace Grace while she was out. During our regular June check-in conference call, I asked Morgan when we'd be able to interview candidates for the staff opening. Morgan told me—and I remember this exactly—that "there were no present plans to fill that position." I couldn't believe it! I told Morgan that it was essential that we fill the position because there was no other way during the summer that we'd be able to staff our rooms adequately. Morgan seemed unimpressed and unconcerned, so I repeated the point. "Morgan," I emphasized, "if we don't hire staff, we're not going to be able to meet the state required staffing ratios." I wasn't exactly sure if that was true, but it was the best way I could think of to stress how critical the situation was becoming. I was pretty sure Morgan didn't have a clue whether we'd be in violation of the state law or not, so I thought saying this would end matters. The answer I got blew me away. All Morgan said was, "you'll just have to do the best job you can." And then Morgan hung up on me.

I was furious! But when I talked to Lynn after Morgan hung up on us, Lynn didn't seem to think it was that big of deal. I just couldn't believe that Lynn was going to let Morgan get away with shorting us on staff. I was upset enough that I called Lee Benson. Lee was the executive director of the first Newton Care facility I worked at right after high school. Ever since then, Lee has been a real mentor to me. It was Lee who encouraged me to finish my Associate of Arts degree and then go on and get my Bachelor's degree. Lee recommended me for the associate director position at NCH-Valley View. Especially since Nina had retired, when I'd run into problems that I thought I couldn't handle, I'd go to Lee for advice. Talking to Lee about this issue helped calm me down. We hadn't lost the staff position—at least not yet—and so far the problems that I was worried about hadn't happened. On the other hand, talking to Lee also confirmed what I'd been thinking—Newton Care was letting money concerns get in the way of client care and client safety. I knew I'd really need to be on my guard with Morgan because there was certainly no way that I was going to let that happen at Valley View.

Through the rest of June and the first part of July, things seemed to be going along pretty well, even though Grace left in the middle of June and we didn't get to hire anyone to replace her. To cope with being a person short, Lynn and I both spent some time working in the rooms, floating through the rooms during lunch to make sure we had everything covered adequately. I have to admit that Lynn's help that summer really made a big difference. Lynn wasn't very supportive after Morgan told me that Grace was not being replaced during her maternity leave. But once Grace was gone, Lynn really pitched in. Between the two of us, we did a good job. For the first time ever, I felt like Lynn and I were a good team. In a lot of ways, I felt like the two of us had figured out a way to do more with less.

Well, the problem with doing more with less is that pretty soon management expects you to do everything with nothing. During the first week of each month, Lynn and I usually had a conference call with Morgan to go over whatever issues were bothering corporate that month. On the first Monday of August, Lynn and I sat down in the office at about 9:00 a.m. to listen to Morgan go through that month's agenda. Near the end of the call, Morgan suddenly said something about a staff level study that NCH had just finished. "As you know," Morgan said, "we've been analyzing staff levels at all our facilities the past three months and we think we can all be a bit more efficient." I'd been around long enough to know that we were about to get some bad news, so I jumped in. "Morgan," I said, "I have absolutely no idea what you're talking about. Nobody told me anything about any sort of study of staffing levels. We're short at least one position here and are just barely holding on until Grace can come back from her maternity leave." That's when Morgan told us that not only was Grace not coming back to Valley View, but we were going to lose another staff position.

At that point, I pretty much lost it. I know I raised my voice and I guess I may have sworn, but I wanted Morgan to understand just how crazy it would be to take another person off the staff at Valley View. Morgan didn't really say anything, but it became pretty obvious to me that corporate had decided money was more important than client safety. I wanted to keep pushing the issue, but I could see that I'd climbed out on the limb on my own. Lynn took Morgan's news without putting up a fight. In the end, Morgan told me I "needed to voice my concerns in a more professional manner," and the call ended. I went back to work, but not before I had told Lynn that it was idiotic to let corporate walk all over us like that.

I knew I hadn't reacted to the news "professionally," but I was mad. Later that day, I called Lee Benson and asked if we could sit down and talk after work. That evening, I drove over to the Happy Clam, a bar not too far from where Lee worked and met Lee for a couple of drinks. We talked a lot about how much Newton Care had changed and how out of touch corporate seemed. Lee was plenty concerned about the direction Newton Care was moving in and agreed with me that the staff cuts at Valley View were a terrible idea. Lee seemed less persuaded that there would be a problem with the state-required staffing ratios, but he gave me a good suggestion. "If you're worried about that—if you really think this is an issue—keep good track of what's going on in the rooms," Lee said. After a couple of hours of talking, I came away thinking that the only way I was going to be able to change things would be to convince Morgan that further staff cuts would create problems for Newton Care with the Department of Human Services. And, at Lee's suggestion, the next day I called Morgan to apologize.

Through the rest of August, I tried to keep close track of every time we were short of staff in any of the four rooms. Each time we ended up short, I made a note of the date, room, and length of time we were out of compliance with the state standards. All in all, there weren't as many days with problems as I thought there would be. Even when Paul Evans, one of our best direct care staff, left to start school, we were still able to manage to cover all four rooms most of the time. Still, there were a number of times during the month when we simply didn't have enough bodies at work to adequately cover all four rooms, so we ended up out of compliance. To my way of thinking, that meant we were operating in violation of state law. I thought it would make the most sense to go back to Morgan at the end of the month with proof that we needed to add staff to make sure that didn't happen. I planned to do exactly that during the September conference call Lynn and I would have with Morgan.

On the Friday right before the Labor Day weekend, Morgan called and left a message that Lynn and I should meet in person with Morgan at the corporate offices at 4:30 p.m. on the following Tuesday. This seemed a little strange, but it wasn't the first time that Morgan had changed a schedule at the last minute. At the end of work on [the first Tuesday after Labor Day], I headed over to the corporate offices. While I wasn't happy to have to take time to drive downtown, it was going to be my first visit to Newton Care's headquarters. I did think it might be good to meet with Morgan face-to-face. I thought I might be able to do a better job convincing Morgan that we needed to add staff if we were both sitting in the same room. Looking back, that seems pretty naïve. I had no idea what I was in for.

I don't think Lynn and I had been sitting in the conference room where we had the meeting for more than thirty seconds when Morgan walked in, sat down, and told us that one of us was going to lose our job. Of course, that's not the way it was put to us. I think Morgan said something like, "NCH has decided to make an important change to our management structure. We're moving in the direction of having just one associate director at each facility, so I will need to reassign one of you to NCH-Harmon Plaza." My jaw must have dropped a foot. Losing another person at Valley View would make it impossible to stay in compliance with the state ratios. Plus, from a more personal point of view, Harmon Plaza was on the other side of the city and would have added at least an hour to my commute each day. "Morgan," I said, "this plan is crazy. We're short staffed at Valley View now." I handed Morgan my report. "Just look at this. We've been under the state staffing ratios on and off all through August. The only reason the problem hasn't been worse is because Lynn and I have been floating rooms to try to keep us in compliance. If you get rid of one of us, the problem is going to get worse and someone's going to get hurt!" Morgan didn't seem to care, and Lynn didn't say a word. I could see the handwriting on the wall. Even though I'd been at Valley View much longer, there was no chance that Morgan was going to move Lynn. Morgan was going to send me to Harmon Plaza. I know I shouldn't have done it, but I stood up to walk out of the meeting. When Morgan yelled at me to stop, I turned around and said, "There is absolutely no way I am placing my clients in danger and agreeing to move to Harmon Plaza. Someday, you're going to end up sorry that you didn't take these staffing problems more seriously."

The next day, [the first Wednesday after Labor Day], I was way too upset to go into work. I called in sick and then I called Lee Benson. I explained what had happened. Lee was as shocked and angry as I was. I told Lee that I couldn't see standards at Valley View compromised like this. I explained that Morgan had completely ignored the information I put together about the staff ratio problems and said that I felt like I had to do something about that. Lee tried to put things into perspective, but it seemed to me there was no way to put repeated violations of state law in a good light. I remember Lee finally said, "Look, if you truly believe that your clients aren't being served, if you believe clients are at risk, you need to do something more."

I decided to do something more. I mailed a letter to the Department of Human Services with the information I'd put together about the Valley View violations of the state staffing ratios. That wasn't something that was easy to do, but I felt I had no choice. We were out of compliance with the state laws and things were going to get worse. The person who should have fixed things, Morgan, wasn't doing anything and, in fact, was going to make matters worse. I decided that our clients had to come first, so I wrote the letter, walked to the corner, and dropped it in the mailbox. When I got back home, I checked my work e-mail and found the e-mail Morgan had sent to me and sent an answer.

The next day, when I went into work, I told Lynn that I had sent the letter to the Department of Human Services. Lynn didn't actually seem that surprised. I thought Lynn would probably go straight to Morgan with the news, but I decided I really didn't have anything to lose. Things seemed kind of hectic all morning long, and it wasn't until that afternoon that I finally had a chance to check my e-mail and see Morgan's response. It seemed to me that it was only a matter of time before Morgan sent me packing, so I just decided not to answer.

The [Friday after Labor Day], I got notice that I was being fired — or, as Morgan put it, my "position was being eliminated." I guess I could have taken the next two weeks off and been paid anyway, but I chose to come in and do my part up until the bitter end. My last day at Valley View and at Newton Care was [the last Friday of September.] The staff and clients had a small goodbye party for me that afternoon.

There's no doubt in my mind that Morgan fired me because of the letter to the Department. I'm not sorry I sent the letter, though. Morgan got rid of me, but she hired a new "assistant" director to help Lynn and try to see that Valley View stays in compliance with the staffing ratios. Looking back, Morgan's decision to fire me seems kind of stupid now. The Department found there had been violations of the law, but then ignored everything that had happened, so Newton Care didn't get fined or anything.

Things haven't worked out so well for me, however. I haven't been able to find a job anywhere near as good as my job at Valley View. When I've interviewed with other care facilities, everyone seems to have heard what happened at my old job. All this has really taken a toll on my finances and on my mental state. I've been unemployed for almost nine months and my mental state is so bad that I have had to seek medical treatment. This is the first time in my life that I have needed to see a doctor for depression. My doctor, whom I have been seeing for six months, told me that my depression is the result of what happened to me at work. I can't believe that Newton Care has gotten away with this.

In the Arbitration between:
Pearson v. Newton Care Homes, LLC

B. Deposition Summary — Morgan Kestrel

The following is a summary of the deposition testimony of Morgan Kestrel. The deposition was taken on June 9, 20XX, in the offices of the lawyers for Del Pearson.

I am the chief program director for Newton Care Homes, LLC (NCH), a for-profit company that owns and operates residential care facilities serving disabled adults. NCH has several different facilities, all located in the greater Landonville area. Until [the last Friday of September, 20XX[-1]], Del Pearson worked as an associate director at our NCH-Valley View facility, which is one of our smaller day facilities.

I have worked for NCH for nearly three years as the chief program director. Among the duties of the chief program director is to ensure financial stability of the organization. I received my undergraduate degree and M.B.A. from New Dover University, and I have spent my career working in the health care industry. Prior to coming to NCH, I worked for about five years with Bellamy Care Services, a nationwide chain of care homes for the elderly. I came to NCH because I thought I'd have a better chance for advancement and because I wanted to work for an organization that had a reputation for providing excellent care for its clients. Working at NCH can be a challenge, particularly if you are working in our central administrative offices, as I do. NCH-Downtown, our central administrative office, is responsible for overseeing every facet of NCH's operations at all of our facilities. We have to make sure that each of our facilities provides a level of care that comports with our reputation for excellence, but we also have to recognize that NCH is a business. If we don't operate at a profit, we will have no choice but to close our doors and no one would benefit if that happened.

I would be the first to admit that there can be, at times, a tension between the business side of our operations and our mission to provide the best possible care to our clients. In large part, my job involves brokering that tension. From time to time, I need to remind the staff in our care facilities—and particularly the directors of our care facilities—that NCH is a business. I know there is a lot of whispering behind my back about what "corporate" is doing and what "corporate" is demanding. That's fine. I can live with that. I can also live with the fact that I may not be the most popular person with our facility directors. In the past couple of years, we've had to make some tough decisions as an organization. That has placed extra demands on our care staff and I fully expect to bear the brunt of their resentment. At the end of the day, however, I also expect everyone to do their jobs. As long as that happens, everything can work out just fine.

In 20XX[-1], NCH realized that it needed to overhaul its administrative structure. At virtually every one of our facilities, we were top-heavy with management. I don't want to single out NCH-Valley View unfairly, but it is a perfect example of the situation we were facing. NCH-Valley View is a relatively small facility serving fifty-plus clients yet, at the time, it had a long-time executive director, as well as two associate directors! We decided that we needed to phase out several director positions across our system. Fortunately, many executive directors were nearing the end stages of their careers. We believed that rather than eliminating superfluous associate positions, it would be more cost-effective to winnow the ranks of the executive directors. We would centralize as many of the executive director job functions as we could, and then use existing associate directors to fill the gaps at the individual facilities. This was not an easy decision, and we went into this with our eyes open. Doing this would mean that many people—including me—would have to work smarter and probably have to work harder. We felt that in the existing health care economy we had no other good choice.

This, of course, is exactly what happened at NCH-Valley View. A long-term executive director, Nina Juarez, was retiring in April of 20XX[-1], and we had two experienced associate directors at the facility. Lynn Watkins was a highly-trained employee who had actually begun her career with NCH in our central administrative office. In fact, for a time, Lynn had worked directly for me. Lynn had been an associate director at NCH-Valley View since March of 20XX[-03]. Del Pearson had worked as NCH direct service staff for several years, and Nina had, somewhat surprisingly in my view, promoted Del to associate director in April of 20XX[-2]. In addition to two associate directors, NCH-Valley View also had relatively little turnover of its rather sizable direct care staff. I believed that there was no better facility than NCH-Valley View to begin revamping our management structure. Over time, I suspected that it would be possible to maintain one associate director position at NCH-Valley View and transfer Del or possibly Lynn to a similar position at one of our other facilities.

When we made the change in management structure at NCH-Valley View, I expected to have trouble with Del. Prior to Nina's retirement, I had only a few opportunities to meet or work with Del, but those experiences had not been good. I had not expected matters to improve once Nina retired, but I had hoped that, with Lynn's help, Del could be brought around. Put simply, Del had a bad attitude about central administration. I've worked with NCH long enough to recognize that management and staff in our care facilities often believe that those of us in central administration don't really understand what is going on "out in the real world." I can live with skepticism, I can live with distrust. Del took it a step farther. In my opinion, Del was openly disdainful of virtually everything that anyone in central administration said or did.

That disdain came through loud and clear during a regular monthly phone check-in I had with Lynn and Del in June of 20XX[-1]. I remember quite clearly the telephone conversation that Del and I had that June about a possible staff vacancy at Valley View due to a parenting leave. At a May planning meeting a couple of weeks earlier, Del had mentioned in passing that one of the Valley View staff would probably be going on maternity leave in a month or so. Del started to complain about how time-consuming the interview process would be to find a replacement. We had a full agenda for the meeting that day, and I didn't want the others to have to sit and listen to another litany of Del's complaints, so I curtailed the discussion and told Del that corporate would take whatever steps were necessary to handle the situation when it arose. I thought the matter was closed, but at the monthly phone check-in with Lynn and Del in June, Del again complained that we still had not provided additional staff for NCH-Valley View. I very patiently explained that we were in the process of reassessing staff levels for all of our care facilities and I did not believe that there was a need for additional staff at Valley View at the present. As I recall, my exact words were, "Based on our system-wide review, we have no plans to add staff at Valley View at present."

For some reason, Del apparently found my response unsatisfactory. Del then tried to tell me that without replacement coverage for the staff member on leave, it would be "impossible" for the facility to remain in compliance with the state-required staffing ratios. Del then started to lecture me about the state ratios, as if I were not already completely familiar with the state laws. After I'd listened to as much as I could tolerate, I told Del I was completely familiar with the legal requirements for operating care facilities and, in my judgment, the staffing levels at NCH-Valley View were more than adequate both to ensure client safety and comply with all relevant statutes and regulations. When Del interrupted, I said simply, "My job is to help administer NCH as best I can. It is your job to operate NCH-Valley View with the resources we give you as best you can. Do your job." And then I ended the conference call. I regret being less patient with Del than I should have been, I suppose.

Part of my reaction stemmed from the fact that this wasn't the first time that I'd had a facility supervisor attempt to use the state staffing ratios to challenge a decision about efficient operation of one of our facilities. The reality is that the staffing ratios are just one of a number of factors our licensing authority, the New Dover Department of Human Services, examines. The ratios are important, but they are by no means the only test of whether a facility is operating within established parameters for client safety. To be frank, at a facility like NCH-Valley View, which serves clients who need far less close supervision or hand-over-hand assistance, the DHS is far less likely to insist on scrupulous adherence to the state ratios.

While the June conversation was not pleasant, it did alert me to the fact that there would be some resistance to plans for further staff reductions at NCH-Valley View. In July, after a great deal of work involving assessment of staff levels at all of our facilities and after consultation with a broad array of decision-makers in our central administration, I had determined that NCH had several facilities that were not operating at an optimal staff level. NCH-Valley View was at the top of my list for changes. I believed that it would be possible to eliminate two direct care staff positions, as well as scale back facility administration to a single associate director. I felt it would be wisest to implement the changes at NCH-Valley View in three stages. The first stage, which I planned for August, was reduction of the first direct care staff position. Because I believed it ought to be possible to accomplish that step through normal attrition, I thought it would be the easiest place to begin. I knew, of course, that Del would be resistant.

Looking back, I should have anticipated just how entrenched Del had become on this issue. I hadn't heard any additional whining about the reduced staff level during July, however, so I suppose I was less on my guard than I should have been. When I raised the issue at the August phone check-in, Del's response astonished me. First, Del denied having ever heard anything about the ongoing review of staffing levels. That was just nonsense! Not only had we discussed the reassessment in June, we had talked about it in the context of staffing levels at NCH-Valley View. I emphasized that both Del and Lynn had been well aware of the reassessment and the net result was, at this stage, a reduction of one direct care staff position. At this point, Del lost all reason and began shouting and swearing. There was nothing to do but to let Del vent, and vent Del did. At some point, I think, Del must have realized how pointless this kind of response was. Del stopped and neither Lynn nor I said anything. After a moment of silence, I said, "Del, you need to collect yourself and then voice these concerns in a professional manner." I told Lynn and Del that I did not believe further discussion would be useful at this time and suggested we end the conference call and revisit this matter at a later time if there were still concerns.

I called Lynn about an hour later. Lynn had spent time in central administration and had a better grip on the business side of administration. Lynn and I had a very frank conversation. Though quick to agree that Del had responded inappropriately, Lynn also voiced concerns about the staff reduction. I spent more time than I thought necessary going back over the basis for the decision, but by the end of our discussion, I felt Lynn had a better grasp on the need to move forward. I didn't feel it would be fair to anyone to talk about the second stage of implementation—reduction in the number of associate directors at NCH-Valley View—so I did not discuss these issues with Lynn. I did, however, make sure that Lynn understood that the staff assessment had encompassed supervisory personnel, as well as direct care staff. I thought I would hear back from Del later that day, but I did not. I do not know if Lynn informed Del of our conversation after the phone check-in.

While I didn't get a call from Del, the next day I did get a call from Lee Benson, the executive director of NCH-Riverside Park. With well over thirty years at the company, Lee is something of an institution at NCH. Lee's facility serves adult clients in need of total supervision and Lee runs the facility with an iron hand. It may be an iron hand in a velvet glove, but it is an iron hand nonetheless. Lee was very respectful—Lee is always very respectful—and came to the point quickly. "Morgan," Lee said, "I'm calling to ask for a favor for a manager who still has a lot to learn, but also has a lot to give." (That was classic Lee.) "I know Del feels badly about what happened, but I also know that you want your associate directors to speak their minds freely when they believe they are dealing with issues of client safety. All I'm asking is that you take into account the motives that prompted Del's reaction to the reduction in staff. Del was speaking out of a concern for client welfare and the welfare of Newton Care. I hope you can find it in your heart to remember that. I'm sure you'll be hearing from Del soon." When I asked Lee if concerns about the staffing decisions had prompted this call, Lee told me no: "I know you're making tough decisions and I'm confident that you're making them with a healthy consideration for client safety." Just as Lee had said, I did get a call from Del offering what I thought was a pretty half-hearted apology.

By the end of August, things had been quiet enough at NCH-Valley View that I thought it made sense to move to stage two of our staffing plan: reduction of the number of associate directors. Let me say at the outset that it was never my plan to terminate either Lynn or Del. I had my issues with Del, to be sure, but I truly believed that the reduction could be accomplished via transfer of either one of them to NCH-Harmon Plaza, one of our smaller day facilities. The associate director at NCH-Harmon Plaza was planning on leaving at the end of October and it seemed like the best available option for Lynn or Del. Thinking about what had happened during the August phone check-in, I did think it would be best to meet with Del and Lynn in person. We would normally have been scheduled to do our regular phone check-in during the first non-holiday week of the month, but I decided there was no reason to wait that long. Shortly before Labor Day, I called NCH-Valley View and left a message asking Lynn and Del to meet with me at NCH-Downtown, our central administrative offices, at 4:30 on the Tuesday after Labor Day, 20XX[-1].

On Tuesday, when Lynn and Del arrived, we all sat down to talk in the large conference room on the nineteenth floor, right next to my office. I felt there was no reason to beat around the bush, so I opened the meeting by explaining that our staffing assessment had included supervisory personnel, as well as direct care staff. I told Lynn and Del that NCH had made a corporate decision to begin moving to a new model of administration for our care facilities and that, across time, we wanted to have a single associate director at each site. I said I thought the two of them were both sufficiently capable and experienced that we felt NCH-Valley View was the site best-suited to begin implementation of this plan. I emphasized that no one was going to lose their job, and I specifically mentioned the opportunity at NCH-Harmon Plaza.

It turns out that it was foolish of me to hope that an in-person meeting would help contain Del's reaction to this news. Del stood up and started shouting that I was crazy and that there was no way NCH-Valley View could be run with fewer people. And then Del pushed a piece of paper with a list of dates across the table and demanded I look at it. I picked up the paper and glanced at it, but Del just kept shouting. Del seemed to think that this "report" showed that NCH-Valley View had been out of compliance with the state staffing ratios. While I tried to read through the paper, Del just kept ranting. "You're not going to get rid of me," Del shouted, "and if you try, this company is going to get hurt!" I told Del to sit down and calm down, but it was a lost cause. Del started to move to the door of the conference room and I felt I had to do something. I remember saying forcefully, "Sit down, we're not done here," but Del wasn't listening anymore. Walking through the door, Del turned and said, "There is no way I'm going to sit by and watch my clients put in danger! There is no way I'm driving all the way over to Harmon Plaza everyday! I'm going to make you sorry you didn't take me seriously!" And then Del walked out.

I remember turning to Lynn and making some sort of weak joke. I think I said, "Well, that went well." In any event, I didn't really think there was much point in continuing. I said that the decision to move to the single director model was firm and told Lynn I'd be happy to answer any questions. Lynn looked down and said quietly, "I don't have questions, but I do want you know that I want to stay at Valley View and I'll do whatever I can to make the new policy work." I thanked Lynn and the meeting ended.

The next day, I decided I needed to communicate with Del. I opted for e-mail though that is something we are trying to move away from in NCH corporate culture. I suppose I should have tried to call Del, but I felt I could be more measured in an e-mail. I sent the e-mail, but didn't get a reply until much later in the afternoon. I later learned that Del had not been at work that day, but I didn't know that at the time. It seemed to me that Del was completely unwilling to entertain any possibility of transferring to another facility, but I felt I needed to double-check, so I sent a follow up e-mail later on that day after I'd gone home.

I didn't hear back from Del all the next day, but I did get a call from Lynn. Lynn told me that Del had sent the "report" from our meeting to the DHS and reported NCH for being out of compliance with the state staffing ratios! I have to confess that, when I learned what Del had done, I was very surprised and very angry. During the time I'd worked with Del, I'd witnessed undisciplined behavior, unprofessional behavior, and even irrational behavior. I'd never seen Del act in a way that was so disloyal to NCH, however. As angry as I was, I did not allow Del's actions with the DHS to influence my own decision about how to move forward with supervisory staffing at NCH-Valley View. In many ways, of course, it wasn't a decision I made; it was a decision that Del made. Once Del refused to even consider a transfer to NCH-Harmon Plaza, I had no other choice. I kept Lynn at NCH-Valley View, and, after reviewing matters with HR, decided to let Del go.

I thought seriously about terminating Del for insubordination. As I saw it, Del had refused a work assignment. In light of the outburst at the meeting in my office and the unprofessional behavior during the August conference call, termination was a very real option, and I discussed that option with HR. In the end, however, it seemed fairer and less complicated to simply state that Del's position at NCH had been eliminated, so that's what I did. I sent the September 11 letter to Del via courier. Del was a long-time NCH employee so, even though it galled me to do it, at HR's advice I gave Del two weeks' severance pay through [the last Friday of September]. To my amazement, Del chose to work up until the very last day.

Of course, on [second Tuesday after Labor Day], I contacted DHS myself to discuss the letter Del sent. I offered to meet with Matt Jacobson, the DHS inspector assigned to the matter and someone I'd worked with before. Lynn and I already had reviewed the NCH-Valley View records and, somewhat to my surprise, Lynn confirmed that the information in Del's "report" was essentially correct, even though the conclusions in Del's letter seemed wildly inaccurate. I met with Matt and Lynn at NCH-Valley View around October 20. I told Matt we didn't want to waste his time with factual disputes. I explained that the letter and accompanying information had been sent by a disgruntled former employee whose position had been eliminated and who had refused a transfer. Nonetheless, I assured Matt that NCH took these issues very seriously and we had decided to hire an assistant director to work with our associate director, thus ensuring we had adequate staff for the facility. Lynn essentially confirmed what I had said, Matt asked a few follow up questions, and the meeting ended. A few weeks later, we received the "No Further Action" letter from the DHS, dated November 19, 20XX[-1]. I considered the matter closed.

I am very sorry Del has chosen to prolong matters with this arbitration. I can honestly say that Del's letter to the DHS had absolutely nothing to do with the decision to eliminate Del's position. While I am sorry Del has been unable find new employment in our industry, I am not surprised. It is a very competitive market these days. I can say that Del's inability to find a job has nothing to do with anything NCH had done or said since Del's departure. I have personally handled every inquiry about Del from other care providers, and I have confined my comments to a statement confirming Del's dates of employment and a simple statement that the position Del had with NCH was eliminated.

In the Arbitration between:
Pearson v. Newton Care Homes, LLC

C. Affidavit of Lee Benson

Lee Benson testifies that the following statements are true under penalty of perjury:

1. My name is Lee Benson. I am the executive director for Newton Care Homes' Riverside Park Day Home in Landonville. I have been the executive director at that facility for nearly twenty years, and worked for Newton Care in a variety of other capacities for fifteen years prior to that. I have a Bachelor of Arts degree from New Dover University, as well as a Masters in Social Work. My career has been long and rewarding, but will soon be ending. I plan to retire next year.

2. NCH-Riverside Park Day Home provides day training for disabled adults. Our clients arrive at our facility in the morning, participate in a variety of activities during the day, and then return to their residential care homes at the end of the day. Most of our clients are not ambulatory, and many of our clients need total care and monitoring or "hand-over-hand" physical guidance to eat their meals or use the toilet. Some of our clients display frequent dysfunctional behaviors or are self-injurious. According to state law, many of our clients require a staff ratio of one to four. In other words, there must be one direct service staff member on duty for every four of our clients.

3. I have known and worked with Del Pearson for many years. One of the great pleasures of my job is encouraging young people who work with me to take a chance on themselves. When I first started in this profession, I had no thought of ever becoming a shift supervisor, much less an executive director. If I hadn't had people watching over me and encouraging me every step of the way, I could never have done what I've done. I believe that it's my responsibility to do the same for young people I work with. Del is one of those people. When we first met, Del was a diamond in the rough just waiting for some polishing. I encouraged Del to get a good education and I encouraged Del to apply for promotions, but Del did the work necessary to earn those degrees and get those promotions. I am deeply saddened that Del's career at Newton Care ended the way it did, but I have faith that Del is going to go on to do great things in life.

4. I first talked to Del about some of the problems at NCH-Valley View in June of 20XX[-1]. Del called me and was quite upset. According to Del, Morgan Kestrel had indicated that a staff vacancy at Valley View was not going to be filled. Del was next to certain that this meant Valley View wouldn't have adequate staff to meet state standards, and Del seemed pretty fired up about this. Valley View serves clients who are not as severely disabled as our clients here at Riverside Park. In addition, whether it's written into the state law or not, the reality is that the Department of Human Services is much more concerned about close compliance with the state ratios at facilities where

clients need more direct care, such as Riverside Park. Del tends to see the world in black and white, however, and I'm not sure how much of this sank in. I did emphasize to Del that, while the problems that a staff reduction could cause might well be serious, there had not yet been a staff reduction. Del remained concerned that budgetary concerns at our central corporate offices were driving decisions about care in our facilities like Valley View, and I told Del that I shared those concerns.

5. Morgan's part in this matter was one of the reasons I shared those concerns. You see, Morgan was a relative newcomer to our company and, like many of our newer administrators, too keenly focused on finding efficiencies in account books. What has set Newton Care apart, what has distinguished Newton Care here in New Dover, is our deep and abiding concern with care. I knew that Morgan had been one of the principal administrators supporting the decision to abandon our commitment to having strong, experienced executive directors at each of our care facilities. That commitment has been part of our heritage at Newton Care and, I believe, a vital part of the reason that facilities like the one I direct, Riverside Park, have been able to thrive. When my good friend Nina Juarez retired, I was deeply saddened to learn that her position at Valley View would not be filled. I suspected that Morgan would continue to trim staff at Valley View and I was worried about Del. There was a time here at Newton Care that a young person like Del would have been treasured because of a devotion to care. There was a time here when that kind of devotion would have been seen as yielding its own sort of efficiency. I'm afraid that day has come and gone, however. I was quite certain that Morgan did not treasure Del.

6. Sadly, as it turned out, I was right. In early August of that year, Del called me, quite upset. Del told me that during the monthly "phone check-in," Morgan had talked about some sort of analysis of staffing levels at all the Newton Care facilities, and then announced there would be another staff cut at Valley View. Del was very agitated, but I came to understand that a direct care staff member who'd left on maternity leave in June had not been replaced while on leave. Now, according to Del, there would be a further cut in the near future. Del wanted to talk to me and suggested we meet at the Happy Clam, a nearby bar, that evening. Though I long ago stopped drinking, I agreed to meet Del that evening. I was worried about Del and I was worried about what this "analysis of staffing levels" meant for the rest of Newton Care.

7. That evening, the news I heard at the Happy Clam was all bad. Del was still very angry and complained bitterly that losing another staff position at Valley View would mean it was impossible to comply with the required state staffing ratios. I suspected the situation was not quite as dire as Del made it seem. I was certain, however, that an additional reduction in staff would make adequate staffing at Valley View quite challenging, especially in light of Nina's departure in April. Del complained, quite bitterly, about how "corporate" decisions were jeopardizing Newton Care's reputation as a top-flight care institution. I told Del I sympathized, to be sure, and that I thought that our administration had made several recent decisions that gave too little attention to client care. After a period of time, the conversation turned in a more productive direction. Del and I talked through different ways that the upcoming challenge could

be met, such as sharing floating duties with the other associate director, careful rationing of staff vacation, judicious use of overtime, and the like. I also emphasized to Del how important it was to document problems that occurred. It is one thing to say that staff cuts will make it hard to comply with the state ratios. It is far more effective to be able to point out, chapter and verse, particular problems that have actually arisen. I want to emphasize that, though Del was clearly angry with Morgan, the whole time we talked Del was motivated by a genuine concern for the clients at Valley View and a desire to do what was best for Newton Care. As the evening wound down, I made one final point to Del. Based on my acquaintance with Del and Del's own description of the conversation with Morgan, I suspected that Del owed Morgan an apology. I strongly encouraged Del to call Morgan and apologize for acting in a fashion that was not respectful.

8. The next day, I decided to call Morgan myself. I'm sure some might have felt this was meddling in matters that did not concern me, but, truth be told, I was concerned about Del. I also was concerned that the friction between Del and Morgan might lead to problems at Valley View that would undermine the real work we do here at Newton Care. And so, because I know Del and because I am fortunate enough to enjoy the confidence of Newton Care's more senior executives and board members, I decided to call Morgan and see if I could help move this matter to a resolution more fruitful for Newton Care. After all, a gentle tongue can be a tree of life.

9. Knowing Morgan values a straightforward approach, I came to the point quickly. I told Morgan I was calling on Del's behalf, but I wanted to be sure that Morgan knew I understood Del had been in the wrong. I explained that, while Del might have a lot to learn, I also felt that Del had an important contribution to make to Newton Care. I emphasized how important I felt it was to have staff and associates who would speak freely to me, but acknowledged that I too often felt frustration when I thought my considered decisions were being second-guessed. I told Morgan that I knew that, though the two of us had very different roles in the company, I was confident that both of us wanted what was best for our clients. I asked Morgan to keep in mind that it was this same motivation that had prompted Del. Morgan seemed receptive to what I said, but I remained concerned that this was a situation that could very quickly get much thornier. That was one reason I felt it was important to use this opportunity to find out just a bit more about the "analysis of staffing levels" Morgan had apparently made. Not surprisingly, Morgan was somewhat closed-mouth about this. I did learn, however, that Morgan's plans encompassed more than the direct care staff at Valley View. Morgan had also given thought to "optimal supervisory structures" for Valley View and the other Newton Care facilities that had lost executive directors. I closed the conversation by thanking Morgan for taking the time to talk and then I assured Morgan that Del would call to apologize. And after we hung up, I called Del to make sure that apology would be made.

10. Looking back at what happened in August and early September, I believe that my words to Del led to a very unfortunate misunderstanding and for that, I am heartily sorry. I next heard from Del on the morning of [the Wednesday following

Labor Day.] Del called from home in a terrible state. Apparently, during a meeting with Morgan the day before, Morgan had surprised both Del and Lynn Watkins with an announcement that, moving forward, there would be only one associate director assigned to work at Valley View. Del responded by giving Morgan documentation of all the times in the past month that, according to Del, Valley View had been out of compliance with the state staffing ratios. It was easy to imagine Morgan's reaction and Del's response, and as Del described the rest of the abbreviated meeting, my heart sank. I wish I had had more time to talk to Del that morning, but unfortunately I was overwhelmed with work. To me, the first and most important issue we needed to talk through was what Del planned to do next. Del insisted, however, on giving me a detailed account of each of example of noncompliance documented in the "report." Listening to Del, some of the situations sounded relatively minor, but two gave me some concern. I tried to bring Del back to first principles and asked if any of the Valley View clients had been injured during the times Del believed rooms were short-staffed. Del told me no, but insisted that clients had been exposed to unnecessary risk. Strictly speaking, Del was right. Del pressed the point and asked, "It can't be right to do nothing when clients are being put at risk, can it?" I answered, "No, if we believe our clients are not receiving adequate care, if we believe that our clients are at risk, we cannot sit by idly. We must do something more." By that time, I was already late for a critical meeting and I told Del I had to go. I asked Del to call me later that afternoon, but unfortunately, Del chose a different path.

11. I learned the next day that Del had mailed the "report" of alleged violations of the staffing ratios to the New Dover Department of Health and Safety. I wish Del had chosen a different way to raise these concerns, but I can understand Del's decision. Del had already made a report to his/her direct supervisor, to no avail. Morgan is the chief program director for Newton Care and would normally be the person charged with internal investigation of a complained violation such as this. It might have been wiser for Del to contact Morgan's superior, our Chief Officer of Operations, but I doubt Del had ever had any contact with the COO. In light of the circumstances, Del's decision seems reasonable to me.

12. Since Del's termination, I have reviewed the letter and report sent to the Department of Human Services. I have many years of experience working with the state staffing ratios and many years of experience dealing with the New Dover Department of Human Services. It is my opinion that, assuming the factual information in the report is accurate, the incidents described do constitute violations of the state staffing ratios. However, several of the instances of noncompliance described in the report are relatively minor infractions. I have to admit that, even at Riverside Park, where the need for close supervision of our clients is much greater, from time to time, we have had similar instances of noncompliance. It is virtually impossible to avoid these sorts of violations. On the other hand, the report details two occurrences that seem far more serious to me. Both incidents involve protracted periods during a mealtime

when, in my opinion, the rooms in question were inadequately staffed, clients were at risk, and Valley View was out of compliance with the state ratios. I take every precaution to prevent this sort of situation at Riverside Park and cannot remember a similar situation occurring at my facility while I was executive director.

13. It is also my opinion that Del, or for that matter, anyone else working at Newton Care, would have regarded a transfer from Valley View to Harmon Plaza as a demotion. Our Harmon Plaza facility is much smaller, inconveniently located, and generally considered a much less desirable place to work. That being said, there is no doubt in my mind that Del's decision to report the instances of noncompliance to the Department of Human Services was motivated by a good faith belief that Valley View clients had been exposed to unnecessary risk. Throughout my relationship with Del and during all our conversations, Del always seemed sincerely concerned with client welfare and never seemed motivated by a desire to harm Newton Care.

Dated: October 19, 20XX
Further affiant sayeth not,
Lee Benson

In the Arbitration between:
Pearson v. Newton Care Homes, LLC

D. Affidavit — Lynn Watkins

Lynn Watkins testifies that the following statements are true under penalty of perjury:

1. My name is Lynn Watkins. I currently am employed as the associate director of NCH-Valley View, a day facility providing care to moderately disabled adults. I have worked for NCH ever since my graduation from New Dover University. I received a B.A. from the University in May 20XX[-7], with a major in health care administration. I started work for NCH in our central corporate office in Landonville the fall after graduation. For the first three years I was with NCH, I worked as an assistant program director, and for the last year of those three, Morgan Kestrel was my direct supervisor. I didn't mind working in the corporate office, NCH-Downtown, but I was much more interested in working in a care facility. I was very happy to be transferred out of corporate in the fall of 20XX[-4], and happier still when, in March of 20XX[-3], I was promoted to associate director at the Valley View facility.

2. One of the best things about being at Valley View was working with Nina Juarez, the executive director. Nina was a wonderful person and a fabulous teacher. She did a very good job making sure I had exposure to every facet of administration of a care facility: she had me help with the budget; she allowed me to supervise staff and help solve personnel problems; she asked me to sit in on planning sessions with corporate staff; she invited me to meetings with state inspectors from the Department of Human Services. I think I learned more about Newton Care in one year working for Nina than I did in three years working at the corporate office.

3. On the other hand, one of the worst things about being at Valley View was working with Del Pearson, the other associate director. There's no question that Del did a great job working with clients and had a real knack for motivating direct care staff, but Del never seemed that interested in the nuts and bolts of administration. A lot of the time, I felt I had to do my work and Del's. If there was a schedule to be planned, I planned it. If there was a report to be filed, I filed it. To top it off, Del spent a lot of time talking about how things used to be at NCH and complaining about the way NCH had changed in the last several years. Del was deeply antagonistic toward co-workers from the NCH corporate office. That may be one of the reasons Del didn't like me. Whatever the reason, we didn't get along. When I expressed my resentment to Nina, I was surprised that she was so supportive of Del. She told me, "if you keep your eyes open, you'll learn just as much from Del as you do from me."

4. Nina announced her retirement at the beginning of 20XX[-1]. I was very sorry that she was going to be leaving, but reasonably sure that meant I'd have an opportunity to become executive director. I was more than a little disappointed when Morgan informed us that Newton Care was changing its facility management model and did not plan to replace Nina. Instead, Del and I would stay on as associate directors and report directly to Morgan. Though I was disappointed, I wasn't that surprised. I had worked at corporate and I knew that Morgan was feeling pressure from the top management to cut personnel costs at the facility level. In the time I'd been at Newton Care, more and more of the administrative work of the company had been centralized and done at the corporate office. The corporate office had grown, but the company hadn't really made any cuts to administrative staff in the care facilities. Morgan's plan didn't seem unreasonable to me. Del had a different opinion, of course. Del was enraged by the news and saw it as some kind of conspiracy of "corporate" against Valley View. That kind of thinking was typical for Del.

5. Del's reaction to Grace Munya's maternity leave was another good example of that "us/them" mentality. Grace was direct care staff, and had planned on going out on leave in June. At a May planning meeting for supervisory staff from all the NCH care facilities, Del brought up Grace's leave out of the blue and asked Morgan what was going to happen. Del's question didn't really have anything to do with what we were discussing and when Del pressed the point, Morgan kind of blew off the question and told Del not to worry about it. A few weeks later, at our monthly "phone check-in" (a phone conference Morgan had with Del and me the first Monday of every month), Del asked when we were going to get a replacement for Grace. When Morgan said corporate hadn't decided if we needed a replacement, Del tried to play the staffing ratio card. I knew that wouldn't work. When I was working at the central offices, facility directors always said they needed additional staff to stay in compliance with state requirements. Morgan wasn't buying it and when Del kept pressing the point, Morgan got impatient and finally hung up. Del was really angry. I made a stab at trying to calm things down, but Del was certain we'd end up in trouble with DHS. I wasn't worried because I thought we'd probably get some temporary help,

which is what usually happened when these issues came up while I was working at NCH-Downtown.

6. My prediction was wrong. We didn't actually get any help at all from the time Grace left on maternity leave in the middle of June. All through the last half of June and July, Del and I had to share "floating" duties. We were more or less "on call" to help out in any room if a staff member had to leave the room to take a client to the toilet, for example, or if a staff member had to leave early. In a lot of ways, those six weeks changed my perspective about Del. Del complained about a lot of things, but never about helping out with clients. If it hadn't been for the two of us, we would have been short-staffed in one or more of the rooms several times during June and July.

7. In August, at the regular phone check in, Morgan told us things were going to get worse. I wasn't really surprised, because in June Morgan had told us that NCH was "engaged in staff level reassessment," and from my experience at NCH-Downtown, I knew that could only mean there were going to be more staff cuts. Del, on the other hand, apparently didn't remember hearing Morgan tell us about the reassessment. When Morgan told us we were going to lose another staff position, Del went ballistic. Del started in by saying that if it hadn't been for the extra time and effort the two of us had put in across the last six weeks, we would never have been able to stay in compliance with the state ratios. I know I rolled my eyes when Del said that—not because Del was wrong, but because I knew that Morgan would just stop listening. Morgan may have stopped listening, but Del didn't stop talking. Del's voice got louder and louder, and Del's language got more and more intense, but the point stayed pretty much the same: we didn't have enough staff to cover the four rooms now and what Morgan was doing would make things go from bad to impossible. Eventually, Del stopped and Morgan jumped in and said, "Del, you need to get control of yourself. I'm not listening to any concern that isn't voiced in a professional manner." Morgan said until that happened there was no point in continuing discussion and hung up.

8. After the call, Del took a walk around the facility and I went back to the office. I was pretty amazed at what had happened. I don't believe I'd ever heard a co-worker swear at a supervisor. I was pretty sure if it had been me doing the swearing, I would have been suspended or even terminated. I doubted that would happen to Del, however, because Del traveled under the care and protection of Lee Benson. It's hard to explain the influence Lee has at Newton Care. Part of it is explained by the fact that Lee is the executive director of Newton Care's largest and most profitable facility and the company's most senior employee, and part of it is explained by the fact that senior management and the chair of the board all put great stock in anything Lee told them. One of the things you learned right away when you worked at NCH-Downtown is that if Lee called to ask for something, you paid attention. You could be assured that Lee wouldn't make a request that wasn't reasonable, but you could also be assured that if you said no, eventually someone higher up in the company would say yes.

9. About an hour after the phone check-in had ended, Morgan called me. I assured Morgan that I agreed Del had spoken inappropriately, but I had to tell Morgan that

I thought additional staff cuts were a very bad idea. I didn't say anything about staffing ratios, because I knew that wouldn't carry much weight, but I did emphasize that I didn't see how we'd be able to keep coverage in all four rooms at an adequate level without giving staff a lot more overtime. Overtime, which is paid out at either time-and-a-half or double-time depending on seniority, is of course something I knew Morgan would want to avoid. Morgan and I went back and forth for quite a while and I started to get a little angry. It was all I could do to keep from saying that the real problem was that Del was right and Morgan knew it. In the end, Morgan convinced me that if Del and I continued to help out by floating into rooms as needed, and if we carefully planned vacation time so that it did not overlap, we could manage another cut in direct care staff. Morgan also made sure that I understood that NCH was also reassessing supervisory staffing levels, which made me think twice about pressing any harder. I never told Del about this phone conversation. I should have, and I still feel guilty about that.

10. All through August, Del and I scrambled to make sure we had adequate staff in each of the rooms and didn't make too much use of overtime. Paul Evans, one of our best direct care staff, quit to go back to school about a week into August and wasn't replaced. It took some doing, but Del and I made things work even after Paul left. Before Labor Day, Morgan called and asked Del and me to come to NCH-Downtown on September 8, at 4:30 for what Morgan said would be the September check-in. Del didn't know what was coming, but I had a pretty good idea. I thought about saying something beforehand and then decided not to ruin Del's Labor Day weekend. On [the first Tuesday after Labor Day], I kept meaning to talk with Del before our face-to-face with Morgan, but I never did. I'm not sure, looking back, that it would have helped.

11. On [the first Tuesday after Labor Day], near the end of the day, Del and I drove separately to NCH's central administrative offices downtown. We walked into the nineteenth floor conference room right by Morgan's office. I'd been in the conference room a thousand times, I suppose, but I don't think Del had ever been there. When Morgan walked in, Del was looking out the window at the downtown skyline. Morgan started the meeting without even waiting for Del to sit down. Morgan said that after doing the staffing reassessment, NCH had decided to move to a single-director model for each of its facilities, and that, because Del and I were both experienced directors, NCH had decided to begin implementing the new model at Valley View. Morgan explained that neither of us would be demoted but, instead, one of us would be offered a transfer sometime soon to a position as sole associate director for another facility, such as NCH-Harmon Plaza. You could have heard a pin drop. Finally, Del looked straight at Morgan and said, "This is crazy! We don't have enough staff at Valley View now to keep in compliance with the state ratios!" And then Del reached into a folder and pulled out a sheet of paper and shoved it at Morgan, saying, "This is a record of every time we've been out of compliance during the last month, and there would be

more dates on this list if it wasn't for the work Lynn and I have been doing." Morgan picked up the paper, but didn't say anything. Del shouted, "What you're doing is going to make this problem worse and someone is going to get hurt!" Del headed toward the door and now it was Morgan yelling, "Sit down!" Del only stopped long enough to turn and say, "I'm not letting you put my clients in danger and I'm not letting you move me to Harmon Plaza. I'm going to make you sorry you didn't take this problem more seriously!" And then Del stormed out.

12. After Del left the meeting, not much happened. Morgan made some dumb joke, and I didn't really know what to do. I did know I didn't want to transfer to Harmon Plaza. Not only is that facility way out in the northern suburbs, but in the NCH hierarchy, Harmon Plaza would be a huge step down from Valley View. It's the smallest and least prestigious facility the company has. I looked at Morgan and said, "I'd like to continue as associate director at Valley View. You know I'll do what I can to make the new policy work." I suppose that was a betrayal of Del, but I felt Del had betrayed me. The two of us worked hard to keep the rooms at Valley View adequately staffed and keep our clients well-cared for. Del shouldn't have turned around and made some sort of "report" to our supervisor without at least talking to me.

13. The biggest betrayal was still to come. Del called in sick the next day, but fortunately we weren't missing any other staff so that wasn't much of a problem. I next saw Del on [the first Friday after Labor Day]. In the middle of the morning, while we were talking about staffing issues the next week, Del told me about sending the report and letter to the Department of Human Services telling them about our problems in August. I was stunned speechless. I couldn't believe someone I'd worked with would do that to me. As soon as Del was out of the room, I picked up the phone to report to Morgan about what Del had done. Morgan was of course furious and said Del was an "idiot to cause this kind of trouble over nothing." I didn't say much more, but I suspected I'd be the person staying on as associate director at Valley View. Later that day, Morgan called and confirmed that. I told Morgan I was happy to continue as the associate director. I also said that I thought we'd need some staff help to fill in if Del was no longer going to be here. The next day, we all learned that Del had been fired, or as Morgan put, "the position Del held with NCH has been eliminated." Del chose to work the next two weeks, which surprised me, but I was glad to have the help.

14. I met with Morgan in the middle of September to prepare for the DHS investigation. I looked over Del's "report" and our staff records and the list of "incidents" all seemed correct to me. They also all seemed very minor, with only one or two exceptions—the sort of temporary lapses that happen every so often each week. When the DHS investigator came to Valley View on October 20, I sat in on the meeting with Morgan, but I didn't say much at all. Of course, by that time, Morgan had let me hire the new assistant director—Grace, back from her maternity leave. About a

month later, Morgan called and told me that DHS had decided the matter was closed and no further action needed to be taken. I wasn't surprised, but I was relieved.

Dated: October 22, 20XX
Further affiant sayeth not,
Lynn Watkins

E. Newton Care Homes, LLC

AGREEMENT TO ARBITRATE

The undersigned employee, DEL PEARSON, and Newton Care Homes, LLC, enter into this agreement in connection with the undersigned employee's acceptance of a position of employment as ASSOCIATE DIRECTOR, NCH-VALLEY VIEW. Newton Care Homes, LLC, and the undersigned employee agree that any claim or dispute between us arising out of the undersigned's employment at Newton Care Homes, LLC, shall be resolved by neutral binding arbitration by the New Dover Arbitration Board. This arbitration agreement is made pursuant to a transaction involving interstate commerce, and shall be governed by and interpreted under the Federal Arbitration Act (FAA), 9 U.S.C. Sections 1–16*. Any award of the arbitrators may be entered as a judgment in any court having jurisdiction. In the event a court having jurisdiction finds any portion of this agreement unenforceable, that portion shall not be effective and the remainder of the agreement shall remain effective.

NEWTON CARE HOMES, LLC

Signature	*_/s/ Morgan Kestrel*	Date: *04/06/20XX[-6]*
Name/Title	*Morgan Kestrel, Chief Program Director*	

EMPLOYEE

Signature	*_/s/ Del Pearson*	Date: *04/04/20XX[-6]*
Name	*Del Pearson*	

F. Emails

The following e-mails were recovered from the computer system at Newton Care Homes, LLC, and produced in chronological order in connection with the present arbitration.

From: morgan.kestrel@nch.org
Sent: [First Wednesday after Labor Day 20XX[-1]]   12:36 p.m.
To: del.pearson@nch.org
Subject: Meeting Yesterday

Del:

I am very concerned about your conduct during the meeting yesterday. At this point, I believe you are unwilling to change your position concerning the matters we discussed and the opportunity at Harmon Plaza. I will not take any further action until you have confirmed that.

Morgan

From: del.pearson@nch.org
Sent: [First Wednesday after Labor Day 20XX[-1]]   4:18 p.m.
To: morgan.kestrel@nch.org
Subject: RE: Meeting Yesterday

Morgan: you made it very clear you are not going to do anything about the serious concerns I have so I have done what I had to do. I do not think there is more that can be done. I still cannot believe that you have so little concern for our clients, but I have said all I can say about that and it has not done any good at all.

Del

From: morgan.kestrel@nch.org
Sent: [First Wednesday after Labor Day 20XX[-1]]   8:58 p.m.
To: del.pearson@nch.org
Subject: RE: Meeting Yesterday

Del:

I am not certain I understand. You know that my concern for NCH clients is every bit as great as your own. I need your answer about Harmon, but after your behavior at the meeting I can make no promises. Please let me know immediately.

Morgan

G.

September 9, 20XX[-1]

Department of Human Services
Adult Care Facilities Division
181 Constitution Avenue
Landonville, New Dover 11101

RE: Newton Care Homes-Valley View Adult Day Home

Violations of State Staffing Ratios

To the Divisional Investigator:

I am writing about a serious problem at Newton Care's Valley View facility. I am one of the associate directors at Valley View and I have already brought this problem to the attention of my supervisor, Morgan Kestrel, who works at NCH-Downtown. Unfortunately, no one at corporate is willing to do anything.

Because of staffing cuts here at Valley View, we no longer have enough direct care staff to stay in compliance with state law staffing ratios. This has been going on all year, but the problem got worse in August and that is why I am writing you. I am enclosing a detailed report I made of each time we were out of compliance during August, leaving only one direct care staff in a room of 12 to 14 clients. There may have been more times, but these are the ones I know about. If the other associate director and I hadn't done as much as we did, there would have been more. The times that are listed are all times when we were short staff and both of us associate directors needed to be in other rooms, so no one else could help. The initials that are listed are the missing staff, but I don't want them to get in trouble. It wasn't their fault.

Fortunately, none of our clients suffered any maltreatment or injury. We were lucky. I know if your Department does not do something, the problem will not be fixed and we might not be so lucky next month.

Please look into this problem right away.

Sincerely,

Del Pearson
1992 Lincoln Ave.
Landonville 11442

H.

VALLEY VIEW
AUGUST DATES NOT IN COMPLIANCE

DATE	ROOM	TIME	REASON
8/7	C	9:27–9:38 am	MJ late from break
8/10	A	3:45–3:55 pm	DD with client in toilet
8/11	D	11:25–11:55 am	Lunch! RT out sick Lynn in A for DD I was in C for MJ until I could cover
8/13	D	8:00–8:18 am	CC late, missed bus
8/18	C	11:05–11:39 am	Lunch! MJ out sick Lynn in A for DD I was in D backing up CC
8/19	A	3:55–4:02 pm	DD helping client
8/19	D	4:01–4:10 pm	RT left early for doctor
8/26	C	7:56–8:09 am	MJ helping client in parking lot

I.

STATE OF NEW DOVER

DEPARTMENT OF HUMAN SERVICES

Adult Care Division

November 19, 20XX[-1]

Newton Care Homes, LLC
Landonville, New Dover 11101

   ATTN: Morgan Kestrel, Chief Program Director

RE: NCH-Valley View: Report of sec. 294D.16(a) Ratio Violation

On [the First Monday after Labor Day, 20XX[-1]], our office received a credible report of multiple violations of required staffing ratios set forth in sec. 294D.16. The undersigned spoke in person to Chief Program Director Morgan Kestrel on September 15 and made site visit on October 20, 20XX[-1], meeting with Program Director Kestrel and Valley View Associate Director Lynn Watkins.

FINDINGS

NCH-Valley View personnel confirmed factual substance of report re: eight instances of non-compliance. On all occasions, between twelve and fourteen adult clients rated for an eight-to-one ratio were in a facility room under care and supervision of one direct care staff member. Period of time facility was out of compliance ranged from 7 to 34 minutes per occurrence. No client injured. No other evidence of maltreatment.

CONCLUSIONS

Six of violations (8/7, 8/10, 8/13, 8/19a, 8/19b, 8/26) were de minimis. Though compliance with statutory ratios is mandatory, transitory nature of infractions does not warrant sanction. Two violations (8/11, 8/18) were for more substantial periods of time during service of meals. Facility cooperated with investigation and has taken appropriate corrective action, addition of staff resources, to prevent future like occurrences.

NO FURTHER ACTION RECOMMENDED

Matthew C. Jacobson
Senior Divisional Investigator

J. Legal Memorandum

The New Dover Whistleblower Act

New Dover is an employment-at-will state. An employer may fire an employee for any reason at all or for no reason at all, so long as the employer's actions do not violate another law or breach a contract. Other than the signed Agreement to Arbitrate, Del Pearson did not have a contract of employment with Newton Care Homes, LLC.

In 2002, the New Dover legislature passed a law prohibiting an employer from terminating or otherwise disciplining an employee because that employee had reported a violation of state law to the government (the New Dover Whistleblower Act). The statute creates a civil cause of action for a violation and sec. 122.93 reads in pertinent part:

> Subd. 1. Prohibited Action. An employer shall not discharge or otherwise take action adverse to the employee's terms and conditions of employment because the employee has in good faith reported a violation of any state law or administrative rule to any government entity or law enforcement official …

> Subd. 3. Civil Cause of Action. An employee aggrieved by a violation of subd. 1 herein may bring civil suit against the employer for all damages, compensatory or otherwise, that the employee has suffered as a direct cause of that violation, as well as attorneys' fees and costs.

> Subd. 4. Treble Damages. An employee who has been aggrieved by a violation of subd. 1 herein is entitled to treble the damages awarded in any civil suit brought pursuant to subd. 3 herein if that employee, in good faith, reports a violation of a statute meant to protect the health and well-being of the general public.

Only two New Dover decisions have dealt with actions under the statute that may be relevant to this dispute. In *Xiong v. University of New Dover*, (N.Dov. 20XX[-7]), the New Dover Supreme Court held that an employee need *not* prove that the employer's sole motivation for termination or adverse action was the reporting of the alleged violation. Instead, the court reasoned, the employee must show that the making of the report "was a significant factor" in the employer's decision to terminate or take other employment action adverse to the employee. *Id.* In *Farnsworth v. MCD Enterprises, Inc.*, (N.Dov. Ct. of App. 20XX[-1]), the New Dover Court of Appeals affirmed a case that, following a bench trial, had resulted in a judgment for the defendant. The court ruled that the evidence was sufficient to support the trial court's finding that the employee had been "principally motivated by animus toward her supervisor." Having reached that ruling, the court of appeals found it unnecessary to address the other question on appeal: whether an employee's good faith report of a violation was protected under the New Dover Whistleblower Act, if that belief was mistaken and no actual violation had occurred.

The New Dover Statute Governing Staffing Ratios

All parties agree that New Dover statute sec. 294D.16(a), was applicable to New Dover's Valley View facility during the times in question. That statute sets forth a variety of staffing ratios that apply to facilities that offer "adult day training and habilitation services," which includes all of the Newton Care facilities relevant to this arbitration. The provision of the statute relevant to Valley View reads, in pertinent part:

> Subd. 1. Persons requiring staff ratio of one to eight. A person is assigned a staff ratio requirement of one to eight if that person, on a daily basis, requires verbal prompts or spot checks and minimal to no physical assistance to complete three of the following activities: use of the toilet; communication of basic needs; eating of meals; or ambulation.

All parties agree that this definition is applicable to all the Valley View clients for the dates in question.

Appendix III

United States Supreme Court Commercial Arbitration Decisions[1]

	Name/Date	Subject(s)	Summary
1.	Wilko v. Swan, 346 US 427 (1953)	Arbitrability of Statutory Claims	
2.	Prima Paint Corp. v. Flood & Conklin Mfg. Co., 388 U.S. 395 (1967)	Separability Doctrine	
3.	Commonwealth Coatings Corp. v. Continental Casualty Co., 393 U.S. 145 (1968)	Arbitrator Neutrality	
4.	Alexander v. Gardner-Denver, Co., 415 U.S. 36 (1974)	Application of external law in arbitration. Title VII	
5.	Scherk v. Albert-Culver Co, 417 U.S. 506 (1974)	Arbitrability of statutory claims; international	
6.	Barrentine v. Arkansas-Best Freight System, Inc., 450 U.S. 728 (1981)	Application of external law in arbitration. Limited by *Gilmer*.	
7.	Moses H. Cone v. Mercury Const. Corp., 460 U.S. 1 (1983)	Presumption of Arbitrability	
8.	Southland Corporation v. Keating, 465 U.S 1 (1984)	Preemption	
9.	Mitsubishi Motors Corp. v. Soler Chrysler-Plymouth, Inc., 473 U.S. 614 (1985).	Arbitrability	
10.	Dean Witter Reynolds, Inc. v. Byrd, 470 U.S 213 (1985)	Arbitrable and nonarbitrable claims	

1. For use with Weston, Blankley, Gross & Huber, Arbitration: Law, Policy, & Practice. Copyright © 2018 Carolina Academic Press.

	Name/Date	Subject(s)	Summary
11.	AT&T Technologies v. Communication Workers Am., 475 U.S. 643 (1986)	Arbitrability	
12.	Shearson/American Express, Inc. v. McMahan, 482 U.S. 220 (1987)	Arbitrability	
13.	Perry v. Thomas, 482 U.S. 483 (1987)	Preemption.	
14.	United Paperworkers v. Misco, 484 U.S. 29 (1987)	Judicial Review.	
15.	Rodriguez de Quijas v. Shearson/American Express, Inc. 490 U.S. 477 (1989)		
16.	Volt Information Sciences, Inc. v. Stanford, 489 U.S. 468 (1989)	Preemption.	
17.	Gilmer v. Interstate/ Johnson Lane Corp, 500 U.S. 20 (1991)	Application of external law in arbitration. Limits *Gardner-Denver, Barrentine, McDonald*.	
18.	Mastrobuono v. Shearson Lehman Hutton, Inc., 514 U.S. 62 (1995)	Punitive Damages	
19.	Allied Bruce Terminix Co. v Dobson, 513 U.S. 265 (1995)	Preemption	
20.	First Options of Chicago v. Kaplan, 514 U.S. 538 (1995)	Arbitrability	
21.	Doctor's Assoc., Inc. v. Casarotto, 517 U.S. 681 (1996)	Preemption	
22.	Wright v. Universal Maritime, 525 U.S. 70 (1998)	Arbitration and Collective Bargaining	
23.	Cortez Byrd v. Harbert Construction Company, 529 U.S. 193 (2000)	Venue for action to confirm, vacate, or modify.	
24.	Eastern Assoc. Coal v. United Mine Workers of America, 531 U.S. 57 (2000)	Judicial review	

	Name/Date	Subject(s)	Summary
25.	Green Tree v. Randolph, 531 U.S. 79 (2000)	Finality; Appeal Attorney fees and costs	
26.	C & L Ent. Inc v. Potawatomi Indian Tribe, 532 U.S. 411 (2001)	Arbitration and sovereign immunity	
27.	Circuit City v. Adams, 532 U.S. 105 (2001)	Application of FAA to employment contracts. FAA § 1 exemption.	
28.	Major League Baseball Players Association v. Garvey, 532 U.S. 504 (2001)	Judicial review of arbitration awards.	
29.	EEOC v. Waffle House, Inc. 534 U.S. 279 (2002)	Arbitration as the Exclusive Forum	
30.	Howsam v. Dean Witter Reynolds, 537 U.S. 79 (2002)	Arbitrability Deferral to arbitrator	
31.	Green Tree Financial Corp. v. Bazzle, 539 U.S. 444 (2003)	Class action silence	
32.	Pacificare Health Systems, Inc. v. Book, 538 U.S. 401 (2003)	Punitive damages	
33.	Citizens Bank v. Alafabco, Inc., 539 U.S. 52 (2003)	Interstate Commerce under FAA	
34.	Hall Street Associates, L.L.C. v. Mattel, Inc., 552 U.S. 576 (2008)	FAA § 10 Vacatur	
35.	Preston v. Ferrer, 552 U.S. 346, 359 (2008)	Preemption	
36.	Vaden v. Discover Bank, 556 U.S. 49 (2009)	Federal Court Jurisdiction	
37.	Arthur Anderson LLP v. Carlisle, 556 U.S. 624 (2009)	Litigation Stay and Appeal under FAA	
38.	Rent-A-Center, W., Inc. v. Jackson, 561 U.S. 63 (2010)	Arbitration Agreements	
39.	Granite Rock v. Int'l Teamsters, 561 US 287 (2010)	Arbitrability	

	Name/Date	Subject(s)	Summary
40.	Stolt-Nielsen SA v. Animal Feeds Int'l Corp., 559 U.S. 662 (2010)	Class Arbitration	
41.	KPMG LLP v. Cocci, 132 S.Ct. 23 (2011)	Arbitrability	
42.	AT&T Mobility v. Concepcion, 563 U.S. 333 (2011)	Preemption	
43.	CompuCredit Corp. v. Greenwood, 565 U.S. 95 (2012)	FAA & CROA	
44.	Marmet Health Care Center, Inc. v. Brown, 565 U.S. 530 (2012)	Preemption	
45.	Nitro-Lift Technologies, LLC v. Howard, 568 U.S. 17 (2012)	Arbitrability Preemption	
46.	Oxford Health Plans, LLC v. Sutter, 569 U.S. 564 (2013)	Arbitrability Judicial Review	
47.	American Exp. Co. v. Italian Colors Restaurant, 570 U.S. 228 (2013)	Vindication of Rights	
48.	DirecTV, Inc. v. Imburgia, 577 U.S. ___, 136 S.Ct. 463 (2015)	Preemption	
49.	BG Group PLC v. Republic of Argentina, ___ U.S. ___, 134 S.Ct. 1198 (2014)	Arbitrability; Int'l Deference to arbitrator	
50.	Kindred Nursing Centers LLP v. Clark, 581 U.S. ___, 137 S.Ct. 1421 (2017)	Preemption	
51.	Epic Systems, Corp. v. Lewis, 823 F.3d 1147 (7th Cir. 2016), *cert. granted,* 137 S.Ct. 809 (Jan. 2017)	NLRA (collective action) v. FAA (express waivers)	Oral Argument October 2, 2017.

Index